Creating Writers

Through 6-Trait Writing Assessment and Instruction

FOURTH EDITION

Vicki Spandel

Director and Lead Trainer at Write Traits

With a Foreword by Cindy Marten

PEARSON
A and B

Boston ■ New York ■ San Francisco

Mexico City ■ Montreal ■ Toronto ■ London ■ Madrid ■ Munich ■ Paris

Hong Kong ■ Singapore ■ Tokyo ■ Cape Town ■ Sydney

SENIOR SERIES EDITOR: *Aurora Martínez Ramos*
EDITORIAL ASSISTANT: *Erin Beatty*
SENIOR EDITORIAL-PRODUCTION ADMINISTRATOR: *Karen Mason*
EDITORIAL-PRODUCTION SERVICE: *Modern Graphics, Inc.*
ELECTRONIC COMPOSITION: *Modern Graphics, Inc.*
COMPOSITION AND PREPRESS BUYER: *Linda Cox*
MANUFACTURING BUYER: *Andrew Turso*
COVER ADMINISTRATOR: *Linda Knowles*
COVER DESIGNER: *Susan Paradise*

For related titles and support materials, visit our online catalog at
www.ablongman.com

Between the time Web site information is gathered and then published, it is not unusual for some sites to have closed. Also, the transcription of URLs can result in unintended typographical errors. The publisher would appreciate notification where these errors occur so that they may be corrected in subsequent editions.

LIBRARY OF CONGRESS CATALOGING-IN-PUBLICATION DATA

Spandel, Vicki.
    Creating writers : through 6-traits writing assessment and instruction / Vicki Spandel.—4th ed.
        p. cm.
    Includes bibliographical references (p.) and index.
    ISBN 0-205-41032-4
    1. English language—Rhetoric—Study and teaching. 2. English language—Composition and exercises—Study and teaching. 3. Report writing—Study and teaching. 4. English language—Ability testing. 5. College prose—Evaluation. 6. School prose—Evaluation. I. Title.

PE1404.S69 2005
808′.042′071—dc22

                                                                            2004044485

Printed in the United States of America

10   9   8   7   6   5   4   3   VH-E   09   08   07   06   05

Contents

5 Adding Flavor: Voice, Word Choice, and Sentence Fluency   91

6 Framing the Picture: Conventions and Presentation   120

12 Exploring the World of Beginning Writers   310

13 Communicating with Students: Comments, Conferences, Peer Review, Grades, and Bringing Parents In   345

14 Believing   368

Appendices   374

Foreword

It is only with the heart that one can see rightly; what is essential is invisible to the eye.
—Antoine de Saint-Exupéry, *The Little Prince,* 1943

To the untrained eye, writing is writing, mere marks on a page. How do we look at writing with our hearts and see what is invisible to the eye? When we use the power of the six traits, we are able to make the invisible visible. Vicki Spandel teaches us to read a child's writing with our red pens tucked safely away and our hearts wide open for the messages and the stories. I've always loved teaching writing workshops and giving students time to write. I just never knew for sure if I was effective. Were my students really becoming good writers? How could I tell?

This fourth edition of *Creating Writers* comes to us at a time when measurement and accountability play the starring roles in education across the nation. We are mandated to evaluate and measure our students, and the stakes are high. Multiple measures, standardized tests, norm-referenced, criterion-referenced, leading indicators, lagging indicators, performance assessment, summative, normative, formative, inventories, rubrics, and standards—the list of measurement-related terms is endless. The standards movement shouts to educators that we must measure; our nation's educational system is counting on seeing the results. Vicki has been writing about assessments since long before the testing craze began. She knows better than anyone I've ever met that assessment must come from within first. Many outsiders want to know how our students are measuring up. Politicians and taxpayers have a right to check on the academic achievement of our students. Taxpayers want to see the return on their investment. So they look to tests for information. But theirs are not the tests that drive our teaching or give helpful feedback to our students. With assessment too often used as a measuring stick, not a teaching tool, it's a gift to find an assessment model that actually makes a direct, noticeable, and positive impact on the ways in which we interact with our students about their writing.

Assessment that keeps our eyes on the children and on the message in their writing distinguishes teaching from testing. When we teach children to be their own assessors, we see returns that soar well beyond the once-a-year high-stakes test that tells us very little about our individual students. Vicki knew this a long time ago. In this edition of *Creating Writers*, we can look to Chapter 14 to get to the heart of the matter. Vicki's deep belief that compassion is a huge part of what is missing from today's landscape of assessment allows us to stay centered and realize that assessment is more about discovery than judgment.

Too often we look at writing through one lens or filter; we are looking for mistakes rather than messages. When we look at a piece of writing using a "right/wrong," "good/bad" lens, we are trapping our students in an "either/or" paradigm that is limiting. In *Creating Writers*, Vicki shows us exactly how to look at writing with our hearts *and* minds. She shows us how to take a child's writing in our hands and find the heart of the message inside the marks on the page. We should all seek to be as fluent as Vicki in spotting great writing. She has honed this skill through years and years of listening and paying attention to children, and she knows when a piece of writing sings. Notice that I didn't say through "years and years of teaching the traits." It really doesn't matter how well you teach the traits if you fail to teach the child!

We can probably agree that good writing is so much more than the visible marks on a page. Sure, spelling, grammar, punctuation, and spacing matter. But if it is in fact more than that, what else is it that makes writing good? Vicki was wise enough to systematically ask this very question in pursuit of improving the revision part of writing workshops. In her work with a team of teachers, she asked, "What makes writing work?" We don't buy books at the bookstore just because all the words are spelled right and the grammar is textbook perfect. We buy books that speak to us. But what makes that happen? When we unlock the answer to "What makes writing work?" we are able to help our students become real writers who communicate for real purposes and with real audiences.

For years as a writing workshop teacher I looked at writing with novice eyes. I knew how to edit a piece of student writing. But when it came to revising, really *teaching* revision, I was as lost as my students. I think I could tell if a piece of writing wasn't good, but I couldn't explain it very well, nor could I teach how to improve a piece. After reading Vicki's first edition of *Creating Writers*, I realized that for too long I had been looking only at the surface structures of writing, such as grammar, spelling, and punctuation. If good writing is more than these surface structures, then what else is it? It's not enough to be editors standing ready to correct student writing. What I found in the traits was a way to look at writing qualitatively and analytically through multiple lenses. I've learned to see the hidden structures of writing. I've learned to teach children to find their voice and their ideas. I've learned to teach revision instead of assigning it. Thanks to Vicki's deep understanding of the writing process, we share a common vision that can guide the revision of our writing.

Teaching writing is hard work. Assessing writing is even more difficult. There are so many quick-fix answers knocking on our classroom doors offering the foolproof method. We need to remind ourselves that there are no shortcuts in creating writers. I know that the six-trait model has sometimes been misused and distorted. I've seen it separated from the writing process. I've seen it used almost as a gimmick or a trick or even as a district writing curriculum.

Such misuses take us far from the original intent. Think of the traits as a shared vision for good writing. The most powerful and yet elusive trait is voice. It's the trait that matters most, yet it's the hardest for teachers (who don't understand the writing process) to learn.

Vicki has dedicated this book to Donald Graves. It is because of his influence that the six-trait model came into being in its present form. Don's work shows us over and over that the most important trait is *voice*. The heart of writing workshop begins to beat when we learn to listen to our students and find the voice in their writing. You will hear students' voices speaking clearly and passionately throughout his book, and you will gain the language you need to respond effectively. In this book, Vicki shares the tools writers need to better assess their own writing. Thanks to her endless work, supportive words, and rich examples of student writing, we are able to handle the complexities of teaching and assessing writing in ways that create strong writers who write with purpose and voice.

Cindy Marten
Vice-Principal, Central Elementary School
San Diego City Schools
Author of Word Crafting: Teaching Spelling
Grades K–6
San Diego
February 2004

Preface

A teacher stopped me in the coffee line at a workshop recently. "I told my students I was going to be working with the woman who helped develop the six traits," she said to me, "and one little guy asked, 'My God, how old *is* she? You told us the traits had been around as long as writing itself!'" Well, let me clarify that I have not been working with the traits for quite as long as writing has been on earth. However, I *have* been working with them for nearly twenty years. And everything I have learned about the teaching and assessing of writing in those twenty years I wish to share with you.

This book is for teachers—current and future. If you are using the book as part of a class or study group, you will find that it is set up specifically to meet your needs, with numerous discussion questions and activities that complement each chapter and extend your learning.

This is a book about writing and about teaching writing by using what we learn from being writers ourselves. It is a book founded on the belief that what we can assess, we can revise, and so our revision skills are strengthened when we learn to assess writing not for the purpose of putting grades or scores on it—but for the purpose of understanding how writing works. Stronger revision skills mean very good news for most writing teachers, who find revision the most difficult part of the writing process to teach or coach. Clear criteria that define proficient writing performance spell out the kinds of things writers do when they revise. And so when you become familiar with those criteria, you are not only prepared to assess writing with greater skill, ease, and consistency than ever before, but you are also prepared to teach it with a confidence and insight you never thought possible. Authors often use the preface to promise the moon, of course, but I truly think that when you come to the closing chapter of this book, you will feel that these claims are not only realistic, but actually modest.

This is not to say that you will (or should) abandon any good writing practices that are part of your current course work or curriculum—such things as use of writing process or writer's workshop, conferences with students, student response groups, teaming, or one-on-one instruction. Nothing about the six traits requires you to give up *any* sound instructional strategy. On the contrary, the traits will fully support, complement, and *enhance* the best of your own curriculum.

This is so because the traits themselves are not a quick fix, gimmick—*or* curriculum unto themselves. They are a *vision*—a way of seeing and talking about writing that helps us to understand better what makes it work. The six traits are an inherent part of writing—all writing. And so "trait language" is nothing more than the language writers use to talk about their work. How very different writing instruction—and assessment—can be when teachers of writing and their students share a common vocabulary that allows them to think, speak, and plan like writers. Working with six-traits rubrics (or scoring guides) teaches students (and all of us) to assess for the purpose of answering questions like these: What reaches readers? What doesn't? How do you prewrite, draft, and revise to solve common writing problems?

We often think of assessment as grading or scoring. This is only a tiny corner of the assessment world. If you have ever looked at a butterfly or flower under a magnifying glass and known the excitement of seeing things you did not know were there, you understand what true assessment is all about: *Discovery*. We can learn to look at writing with this same intense curiosity and desire for understanding.

This fourth edition—which, by the way, marks the twentieth anniversary of the six-trait model—includes several features that teachers (and student writers) should find useful. All rubrics (scoring guides) have been updated, and there are both five- and six-point versions for creative writing (narratives, personal essays, and memoirs) and for informational writing (research or technical pieces, persuasive essays, and business letters). In addition, all rubrics are presented in both teacher and student versions. Reviewers (who are nearly always much more helpful than you think the first time you read their reviews) asked for formatting changes, and I have tried to accommodate their wishes, making the information as accessible as possible. In this edition I also introduce the traits one by one so that readers who are new to the model can gain confidence first scoring papers for foundational traits (ideas and organization), then adding flavor (with voice, word choice, and sentence fluency), and finally putting on the finishing touches with conventions (and presentation). The book includes numerous new papers, along with a number of old favorites. As before, the papers represent many genres, grade levels, and degrees of proficiency—and as always, *every* paper has important lessons to teach us. By the time you finish scoring and discussing them all, you will know a very great deal about writing, about assessment, and about what to teach student writers that will be genuinely helpful.

Writing process has always been the foundation for trait-based instruction, but this fourth edition makes the connection more clear and explicit, a feature that should be of particular assistance to any teachers who have not enjoyed extensive instruction in writing process. All the lesson ideas included in this book (and there are many) are designed to fit a process-based curriculum. As I emphasize throughout the book, the six traits support writing process at every step and provide a critical understanding of writing that is invaluable during the steps of revision, editing, sharing, and publishing.

It's helpful, I think, to see how other teachers do it. Previous editions have taken readers into classrooms, but this time we have a chance to visit additional classrooms and to learn a number of innovative teaching ideas from some of the most creative and effective teachers I have been privileged to work with and learn from. As you will discover, each teacher's approach is slightly different. There is no one way.

Because of the recent release of *Creating Young Writers* (2004), a complementary text intended for K–3, I have not greatly expanded the chapter on primary writing. However, this text does now include the writing continuums from that companion book.

The six-trait model shared here has proven its worth in hundreds of writing assessments and thousands of classrooms across the country. It has been incorporated into writing standards in numerous states and is the creative force behind many state-level writing assessments. It can be used with virtually any form of prose writing (and to a limited extent, with poetry). Like a good rail fence, it provides enough structure that you can lean on it; it will (if you like) give you guidance on what to teach when. But its structure is open, not restrictive, and will not require you to sacrifice your personal style.

Every chapter is written to meet the needs of the classroom teacher who says, "I want to do this—show me how." Do you want your student writers to taste success—success you can see and measure? This is your book.

ACKNOWLEDGMENTS

Countless people have contributed to the development of this book. First and foremost, I wish to acknowledge how much I—indeed, all teachers—owe to the tens of thousands of student writers who, through their writings, have taught *all* of us so much. Without their voices, this book could not exist. Not just the best of the writing, but all the writing has contributed to our understanding of what makes writing work.

Every effort has been made to contact every student writer whose work appears in this book. We have not knowingly included any work without the writer's or artist's explicit written permission. If any work inadvertently has been included without such permission, we will gladly remedy that oversight with the next publication.

Special thanks to the following students for their willingness to share insights, invaluable student perspective, and in many case the samples of work that are the heart and soul of this text: Amanda Anderson, Jacob Barker, Aaron Bartels, Eric Breisch, Emily Brown, Kallie Ciechomski, Jocelyn Coats, Sarah Coligan, Richard Croft, Stacy Croft, Brian Dales, Veronica D'Aprile, Katie Ehly, Sarah Evans, Christina Figueroa, Corinne Fish, Aaron Fogarty, Maggie Foti, Natalie Elizabeth

Frasier, Bradley Friedman, José Garcia, Sammy Geiger, Ashley Gibson, Scott Goldstein, Greg Gorraiz, Charlie Goulder, Sydney Ham, Amanda Hancock, Rachel Hargis, Stephanie Harris, Leah Hauser, Christopher Henningsen, Nicole Henningsen, Jessica Hemmerly, Kristen Hess, Kirsten Heydel-Knorr, Andrew Hicks, Andrew Holding, Kendall Irvin, Kevin Karetsky, Katie Kellerstrass, Kirsta Kellin, Andrew Koster, Kelsea Larson, Reilly Leith, Merideth Marland, Carl Matthes, Kira McConnell, Kean McDermott, Katie Miller, Jeff Montgomery, Noah Myers, Ellie Oligmueller, Megan Oxton, Maggie Parker, Jessica Pauley, Stephen Paur, Logan Perlstein, Bill Price, Enedina Ramos, Kirsten Ray, Mason Reed, Rhonda Reilly, Brian Richards, Kevin Ross, Rocky Ross, Lauren Rothrock, Maegan Rowley, Anne Marie Ruckdeschel, Chelsey Santino, Abigail Sayre, Conner Scott, Madison Sessums, Ellie Simas, Cody Simon, Brett Smith, Kaitlin Snyder, Michael Spandel, Nikki Spandel, Ryan Sterner, Jovana Stewart, Nicholas Tatalias, Angela Tate, Curtis Wackerle, Mackenzie Wadas, Cynthia Watkins, Randy Wainwright, Lincoln Weiss, Sara Wertman, Jack Wolf, Becca Zoller, and Gail Robinson's fourth grade class. (Thanks also to any student whose name I have inadvertently failed to include.) Your contribution to learning is incalculable, and I am honored to share your writing. I hope that you will continue to share your writing. Also, thank you to those writers whose work we did not have the space to include. I am most grateful for your response to my request for student writing. We simply ran out of room.

I am particularly indebted to Ronda Woodruff, a member of the original Analytical Writing Assessment Model Committee and a former fourth and sixth grade teacher at West Tualatin View Elementary School in Beaverton (where the trait model originated). Ronda, my mentor, invited me into her classroom and taught me what I was so eager to know: *How to teach writing in a way that works.* Because she believed that student writers could achieve anything, Ronda lit the fire that gave other teachers the courage and inspiration to share the traits with their students. Now, in 2004, it's hard to recall a time when trait-based instruction wasn't a routine part of classroom practice. But Ronda was the first to make it so. She was an original and is irreplaceable. Her spirit lives in every page of this book.

Special thanks to the following remarkably talented teachers who offered extended opportunities to work with their students and teach lessons and/or who provided ideas, materials, or suggestions that greatly enriched the classroom perspective of the book: Jeff Anderson, Faith Arsanis, Mary Ann Beggs, Jim Burke, Penny Clare, Roseann Comfort, Andrea Dabbs, Darle Fearl, Sammie Garnett, Kathy Hawkins, Lenore Hay, Jeff Hicks, Karen Verti Hungate, Billie Lamkin, Judy Mazur, Paula Miller, Arlene Moore, Beth Olshansky, Wendy Pruiett, Lynn Radcliffe, Jeanne Richards, Lynne Shapiro, Sally Shorr, Ellen Tatalias, Jennifer Wallace, Fred Wolff, and Robert Young—as well as *all* the remarkable teacher-trainers who have come together to form Write Traits, our teacher in-service group. What a team you make.

My deepest thanks to those persons who have been my personal teachers: to the phenomenally talented Lois Burdett, who taught me to "take the lid off" because there are no limits to what children of any age or ability can accomplish; to Cindy Martin, who knows that genius is hollow without compassion and whose wise interpretation of the traits enhanced dramatically my own understanding of writing process; to the inimitable Barry Lane, the finest teacher of revision skills I have yet to encounter and unquestionably the wittiest (who always seems to make me laugh just when I need it most and who always writes the very book I'd love to use just before I need to use it—now, *that's* timing); to my dear friend and mentor Donna Flood, who has supported this project in a thousand ways through her own teaching and writing and who continues to share her vast knowledge and wisdom, sensitivity toward students, and gentle humor with fortunate teachers and students everywhere; to Tommy Thomason and Sneed B. Collard, my writer–teacher friends who do not just talk writing but who *do* it; to Richard Stiggins, the guru of classroom and performance assessment (okay, fly fishing, too), who inspired the very first edition of this text and who has taught me much more about quality assessment than I could fit into one book (and a few things about fishing, too); and to my many talented and wonderful Great Source friends, including (just to name a few), Shannon Murphy, Ed Kennedy, Lisa Bingen, Sue Paro, and Al Bursma. A very special thanks to Phil LaLeike, also of Great Source, who is my friend and hero and who moved mountains to chart a new course for my life. What a gift.

My continued appreciation to those who started the ball rolling so long ago. In particular, thanks to the generous and brilliant Carol Meyer, former assessment and evaluation specialist for the Beaverton, Oregon school district, and to those 17 teachers from Beaverton—the Analytical Writing Assessment Model Committee—who started it all. Thanks for making history and for letting me be there. Thank you from my heart, Phil.

No book comes together without a lot of behind-the-scenes effort. I wish to thank my editor, notably Aurora Martínez and her assistant, Erin Beatty, for believing in and supporting this project and providing much needed expertise. Special thanks to Kathryn McCormick, for coordinating production of the photographs that grace this book; to Nikki Henningsen, whose dazzling skill at the keyboard made the formatting of rubrics look easy; and to Ann Marland, my wonderful associate and friend, who helped keep me sane and even volunteered to stay all night at the office. Thanks to the student reviewer who said of the third edition, "This book is easy to understand but hard to read." That's the best single critique, bar none, I have ever received. I owe you.

My sincere thanks to the reviewers of this edition: Carol P. Harrell, Kennesaw State University; Jane Jackson, Centerville Elementary School; Judy Mazur, third-grade teacher, Buena Vista Elementary School; Cindy Marten, Literacy Coordinator, Poway SD; and Dennis O'Connor, University of Northern Iowa.

Somewhere in Montana lives the woman who in many ways is more responsible for this book than anyone else. Her name is Margery Stricker Durham, and she taught me to write. I took seven classes from her (both graduate and undergraduate), and she never covered the same ground twice. On the first day of class she walked into the room (all 90 pounds of her), pulled off her wild raccoon hat to reveal equally wild hair beneath, and wrote her name on the board: S-T-R-I-C-K-E-R. "My name is Stricker," she said. "If you're late, don't bother coming. If you don't do the work, don't waste my time." I loved her immediately. I was only late once (and came anyway)—and I did the work. And I found what I had been looking for all my life without knowing it: a teacher who waited for my writing, read every word, and wrote back. She taught us to analyze literature and life, to connect points of history, to value reflection, and to see all great books, paintings, architecture, music, and other expressions of the human spirit as an interconnected record of intelligent thought. She taught us to think. It is the finest, most unselfish gift we give one another, for a piece of ourselves goes with it. This gift is the reason that teachers are so loved. Margery, I wish you all the best. I think of you each day and always will.

For Don Graves . . .
who has taught us to trust the voice within.

1 Creating a Vision

The best change occurs slowly and comes from teachers themselves. It takes longer but it lasts.

—Donald H. Graves
Testing Is Not Teaching, 2000, p.52

Good assessment always begins with a vision of success.

—Rick Stiggins
President, Assessment Training Institute

I wish we could change the world by creating powerful writers for forever instead of just indifferent writers for school.

—Mem Fox
Radical Reflections, 1993, p. 22

*S*ix-trait writing is not a curriculum. It is not a program. It is a *vision*—a way of looking at writing that takes teachers and students (all writers) right inside the process to where the action is. The six-trait model, in simplest terms, is an answer to the question all writers must ask: *What makes writing work?* Answering this question takes us far along the path to teaching writing effectively and, in addition, makes the teaching of writing easier.

Easier is good. No teacher anywhere these days is saying, "I don't know what it is with this skimpy curriculum. I simply *cannot* fill the days." Teachers are treading water faster than ever, and the tide continues to rise. While trait-based assessment and instruction cannot make classes smaller or testing go away, it can ease writing teachers' stress by showing them how to help students

✔ Take charge of their own writing process.
✔ Understand the difference between strong and weak writing—and use that knowledge to write stronger drafts.
✔ Revise and edit their own writing because they can "read" it and because they know what to do to make it better.

All this sounds a little like magic, but really, it's logic. The key has been right before us the whole time; we had only to unlock the door. The key is language—*writers'* language that opens the door to revision.

Consider for a moment the power of language to influence thinking. What medical intern can diagnose or treat patients without knowing such terms as *hypoglycemia, myotonia,* and *toxemia?* Would we place much faith in an investment advisor who could not readily address such items as *market risk, return on equity,* and *price-to-earnings ratio?* Writers, similarly, must know about *development, detail, clarity, leads and conclusions, transitions, conventions,* and *voice*—and must use these terms with ease in discussing their own and others' work. I am not talking about a superficial vocabulary-list-of-the-week approach here but an in-depth understanding of how to write, how to revise, and how to assess. We begin with assessment and build a bridge to writing instruction so powerful that it can change the way students write, read, and think—forever. In this book I will show you how.

WHO INVENTED THE SIX TRAITS?

No one. Though the number of persons who take credit for having "invented" or "developed" the six traits seems to grow geometrically each year, the truth is that the traits themselves are not *anyone's* invention. Like stars or far-off planets awaiting discovery, the traits have been around as long as writing itself and are an inherent part of what makes writing work. What *is* new (within the last few decades) is a written description of what the traits *look like* at different levels of performance. In other words, a *rubric,* or *scoring guide,* if you prefer that term.

The original six-trait rubric for assessing and teaching writing came *from teachers.* It was developed in 1984 by the Analytical Writing Assessment Committee, a group of seventeen teachers from the Beaverton, Oregon, school district with whom I was privileged to work. Since its inception, the six-trait model has been revised nearly twenty times and currently exists in both five- and six-point versions for teachers and students. The six traits themselves have since been woven into the fabric of numerous state assessments and standards. They include

Ideas—The heart of it all, the writer's main message and the details, evidence, or anecdotes that support or expand that message.

Organization—The internal structure (skeleton, if you will) of a piece that gives support and direction to the ideas.

Voice—Verbal fingerprints. A mix of individuality, confidence, engagement with the topic, and reader rapport—that something that keeps readers reading.

Word choice—A knack for selecting the *just right* word or phrase to make meaning clear and to bring images or thoughts to life.

Sentence fluency—Rhythm and flow, the music and poetry of language, and the way text plays to the ear.

Conventions—The writer's skill in using an editor's tools (punctuation, spelling, grammar, capitalization, and layout) to clarify and enhance meaning.

Paul Diederich: The Inspiration

Beaverton's innovative research design was based largely on work done by Paul Diederich (as documented in *Measuring Growth in English,* 1974) in the 1960s. Deiderich had been curious to know whether people could agree on what makes writing work and whether they could come up with language to describe what they found. His research method was ingenious in its simplicity. He assembled a group of fifty or so writers, editors, attorneys, business executives, and English, natural science, and social science teachers and asked them to read numerous student essays and rank them into three groups: effective, somewhat effective (about halfway home), and problematic. Then—this is the interesting part—they were asked to record their reasons for ranking the papers as they had. In the process, they discovered something rather striking: In most cases they were influenced by nearly identical qualities (traits) in the writing. Here (listed here in order of apparent influence) are the traits Diederich's team identified:

- ✔ Ideas
- ✔ Mechanics (usage, sentence structure, punctuation, and spelling)
- ✔ Organization and analysis
- ✔ Wording and phrasing
- ✔ Flavor (voice, tone, style, and personal qualities)

Ideas and organizational structure were slightly weighted in later ratings because these were perceived to be the most significant of the traits identified. Mechanics was subdivided into (1) usage and sentence structure, (2) punctuation and use of capitals, abbreviations, and numbers, (3) spelling, and finally, (4) general neatness.

Confirmation from Purves and Murray

Over the years, Diederich's method of ranking and systematically recording the thinking behind the ranking has been replicated by other researchers, including Alan Purves (1992) in his work on international writing assessment. In the international writing study directed by Purves, raters identified these *significant* traits:

- ✔ Content
- ✔ Organization
- ✔ Style and tone (what we call voice, word choice, and sentence fluency)
- ✔ Surface features (essentially conventions, but also including neatness)
- ✔ Personal response of the reader (essentially, response to the quality we call voice)

In 1982, Donald Murray (pp. 66–67) identified these six traits—also closely aligned with those in this book:

- ✔ Meaning
- ✔ Authority
- ✔ Voice
- ✔ Development
- ✔ Design
- ✔ Clarity

Meaning and clarity equate with the trait of ideas, design with organization, voice and authority with voice. "It is my belief," Murray claimed at that time, "that these qualities are the same for poetry and fiction as well as non-fiction."

Beaverton: The First Six-Trait Rubric

Inspired by Diederich's research design, the seventeen-member Analytical Assessment Model Committee set about replicating it. Carol Meyer (then director of evaluation and assessment for the district) and I were privileged to direct and work with this team. We spent weeks reading student papers at every grade level from 3 through 12, sorting them into high, middle, and beginning levels and documenting our reasons for ranking them as we did. Eventually, we arranged our documentation along a continuum of writing performance, and the result was a draft of what would eventually become the six-trait assessment model (see Figure 1.1 for an in-process copy of an early draft).

Shortly thereafter, Portland Public Schools conducted a similar study—in which I also participated. Minus any collaboration with Beaverton, Portland came up with virtually identical traits, their list also closely matching that of Deiderich. Since Portland had no knowledge of Beaverton's work or Deiderich's, this similarity demonstrated to us all that teachers do in fact share common values about what is important in writing. True enough, the language may be slightly different list to list (*voice* versus *flavor, tone,* or *style; internal structure* or *design* versus *organization; surface features* versus *conventions* or *mechanics*). Yet the concepts underlying these terms are remarkably consistent.

The six-trait model is now used in virtually every state by one or more districts—and in some states, such as Alaska, Arizona, California, Colorado, Hawaii, Kansas, Montana, Nebraska, Nevada, Oregon, Texas, Washington, and Wisconsin, the model (as of this writing) is very closely aligned to statewide testing or state standards. (See Appendix 1 for correlations between the six traits and selected state standards of writing.) The model also has spread throughout the world so that many teachers from South America to Africa and the Far East are now using some version of six-trait writing. Its is largely due to two things: First, it simply reflects the heart and soul of what good writing is about, with definitions expressed in clear, easy-to-understand language from which teachers can teach. Second, it has a kind of déjà vu feel to it, echoing good teaching practice that process-based writing teachers have been using for years. Indeed, six-trait writing would never have enjoyed such widespread success had it been only a model for assessment. It has far-reaching implications for writing instruction. In this sense, the six traits are writing teachers' gift to themselves.

ASSESSING TO LEARN: THE BRIDGE TO REVISION

Isn't assessment an odd place from which to begin writing instruction? Actually, no. It's the very *best* place, once we understand what assessment is.

When we think *assessment,* we usually think *grading* or *testing.* This is a very limited view. Assessment is looking within. It is the door through which

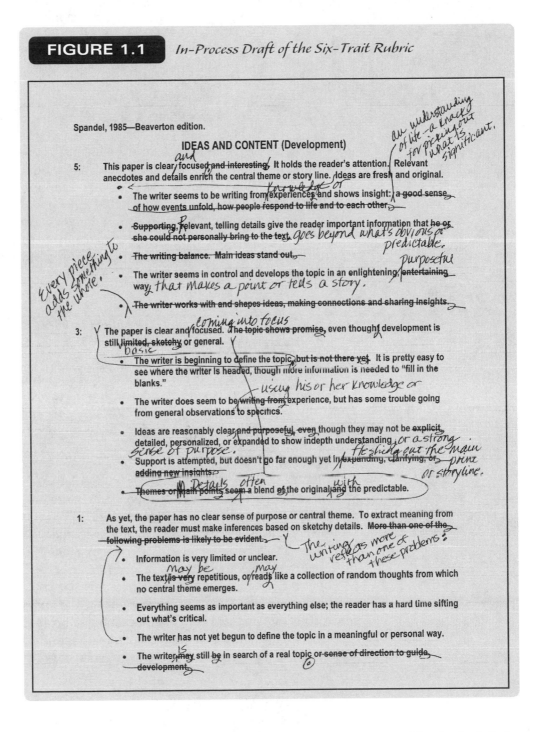

FIGURE 1.1 *In-Process Draft of the Six-Trait Rubric*

we must pass to gain understanding of any content area, writing included. As Lucy Calkins so eloquently points out in her revised edition of *The Art of Teaching Writing* (1994), we assess *to learn:* "If . . . children can't talk easily about texts, they will have a hard time being critical readers of their own or anyone else's writing" (p. 326). They will also have a difficult time revising. You cannot repair a car until you know specifically what is not working. You cannot rework writing unless you can hear the problems within the text.

Looking deep within is essential not only to students' understanding of their own writing but also to the very act of writing itself. "We teach [students] how to read books," Donald Graves (1994, p. xvi) points out, "but not how to read their own writing. Unless we show children how to read their own writing, their work will not improve." This, in a nutshell, then, is our vision of success: students who can read their own writing and who know what to do to make it stronger. The very core of this book rests on one foundational belief: *What you can assess, you can revise.*

To help student writers reach this level of assessment, we (as teachers) must first teach ourselves what good writing is. We must know how to recognize it—not just the mistakes, but the moments of voice, detail, wonder, and magic—and we must have a language for talking about it. (This is what Chapters 3 through 6 are all about.) Then we make students partners in the assessment process. Partners. Not targets. Not victims. Not just recipients of our grades or comments. But fully active *participants* who speak writers' language, have their own rubrics (written in student-friendly terms) and learn alongside us how to think critically about writing.

TEN REASONS TO MAKE SIX-TRAIT WRITING PART OF THE VISION

First, let me say that it is virtually impossible to teach writing *without* incorporating the six traits in some form. You certainly can do so without referring to these concepts as *traits* or without using rubrics, but terminology and rubrics are only tools; they do not define what you teach.

Look again at the list of traits and ask yourself, "Could I seriously teach writing without emphasizing the importance of good ideas and organization? Without worrying about the words my students use or how they construct sentences or whether their text is conventionally correct? Without stressing the importance of audience?" Of course not. If you are currently teaching writing using a process-based approach, you are already teaching the traits—in some form. So this book is not a blueprint for making your teaching more complicated by adding a whole new layer of instruction. On the contrary, it will help you streamline and organize the best of what you already do—and give you a language for talking to students about their work.

Having said that, there are at least ten important reasons to include six-trait writing in your instructional program—to make it part of your vision of success:

1. The model provides consistent language for talking about writing.
2. Using a rubric you believe in keeps your assessment consistent and honest.
3. The six traits can help make both writing and revising manageable for students by breaking it into small steps.
4. The traits support and strengthen writing process.
5. Trait-based instruction makes revision and editing purposeful.
6. Partnership in writing assessment empowers students.
7. Learning to assess with confidence and skill increases student motivation while promoting thinking skills.
8. Six-trait instruction links reading and writing by encouraging students to read like writers—and write like readers.

9. Six-trait writing is *real*.
10. Working with well-written rubrics can save you time in assessing student work.

Let me expand, very briefly, on each of these.

1. Consistent Language

Do you recall as a student wondering what on earth it was the teacher wanted? It seemed that each school year brought with it the challenge of finding the magic button to push. My third grade teacher liked l-o-n-g pieces of writing, regardless of what we actually wrote, so we filled pages, whether we had something to say or not. Length for its own sake was her "vision of success." My fourth grade teacher did not care a whit about length; penmanship was the target to hit. Mine was good, so I sailed through that year effortlessly (and mindlessly), while my friend Gary spent hours inscribing, "I will write neatly" (a promise he never fulfilled). In fifth grade, the teacher wouldn't allow anyone but herself to touch her desk; she valued neatness and organization above all things. My penmanship had improved, and I had the straightest margins in town. It was a whiz-bang year. Then, in sixth grade, the roof caved in; that was the year we had to *think*. None of us had seen this lightning bolt coming, so we were unprepared. We floundered. And that, of course, was only the beginning. Each successive year brought its own challenges and revelations about what teachers "really wanted": research, citations, expanded ideas, condensed ideas, three paragraphs, five paragraphs, ten pages with documentation, details, quotations, objectivity, analysis. More. Less. Everything. How much more successful we would all have been had we had writing rubrics *from the first*, language to carry us along, buoy us up, and give us a clear vision of where we needed to go instead of an endless succession of mysteries to solve.

2. Consistent, Honest Assessment

Have you ever come to the bottom of a thick stack of papers you are reviewing/grading, and thought to yourself, "I really *should* start over—I would assess those early papers *sooooo* differently now"? If you have had this experience, or if you have wondered whether you assess differently class to class, day to day, or in some way that conflicts totally with what a colleague is doing, then you know the value of consistency and how hard it is to achieve. Now think how confusing it is to a student to receive a grade of A in one class on a paper dashed off in a hurry and a C+ from another instructor for a sincere effort. Rubrics help because they give us a reference point, a safe harbor to which we (and our students) can return. And if our thinking or what we value changes over time, we can revise our rubrics to reflect that new thinking.

3. Manageable Steps

One of my favorite writing stories comes from author/teacher Anne Lamott, who tells of her older brother, just ten at the time of the story, who was struggling to complete a research report on birds that he had had three months to write. The boy was close to tears, surrounded by papers and books, overcome by the daunting task ahead. Anne's father put a reassuring arm around her brother and said, "Bird by bird, buddy. Just take it bird by bird" (Lamott, 1995, p. 19). In this anecdote, Lamott perfectly captures how overwhelming writing can feel (to say nothing of the teaching of writing). Because the six traits define writing, they allow us to take it "bird by bird." So one day perhaps you teach a lesson on leads, and on another day you show students how to come up with a good title or use transitional phrases effectively. No one wants to take on a pyramid, but you can put one stone into place, can't you?

4. Support for Writing Process

Do you believe in process or use a writers' workshop approach in your classroom? Do you give your students time to write, revise, and edit? Model writing for them? Read to them? Confer with them and encourage response groups? Good. You will not need to give up *any* of these tried and true instructional strategies, nor should you. Each and every one will be strengthened by your use and your students' use of writers' vocabulary—six-trait language. Trait-based instruction *enhances* a process-based approach to writing instruction; *it does not replace it.*

Imagine yourself modeling in front of your class and being able to say (and have your students understand), "Here, let me show you some ways I have found to write an effective conclusion." Imagine your students meeting in a response group and making comments such as, "I really heard your voice in the second part of the paper" or "That dialogue was *so* authentic—I know someone who talks just like that." Such comments make us feel good as teachers because we know our students are *getting* it; but even better, specific comments are actually useful to the student writers to whom they are directed. A shared vocabulary turns us all into writing teachers and coaches and enriches our understanding of how writing works.

5. Purposeful Revision and Editing

FIGURE 1.2

Two-Way Picture

Look carefully at Figure 1.2. What do you see? Perhaps you see a tall, elegant vase. But if you look at the picture another way, you'll see two women looking at each other. A good writing rubric should be just like that. Look at it one way, and it's a tool for assessment. Look at it another, and it becomes a guide to revision—adding detail, focusing on one main message, rewriting a lead or conclusion, or adjusting voice or wording to meet the needs of an audience: These *are* the things writers do when they revise. This is why, when students use a scoring guide to assess their own and others' writing, they also learn the secrets of good revision and editing.

6. Empowering Students

When we make students partners in the assessment process, they learn to assess their own work as a natural part of revision. This makes them much less dependent on us to give them a specific blueprint for revision:

"You need to cut this first paragraph. . . . I'd add more detail here. . . . You might think about changing the structure of this sentence." Writing is mostly problem solving, after all. You cannot get better at it, therefore, if someone else is always solving the problems for you. In classes where the traits are taught as part of a process-based approach, students use rubrics to guide the way they view their own and others' writing; talk about writing as a group, focusing on strengths and problems; and use literature as models of what to do or not do. They take charge of their own writing process and learn to be independent problem solvers.

> Many of my teacher education students, after twelve years at school, come to me helpless and fearful as writers, detesting it in the main, believing that they can't write because they have nothing to say because they haven't cared about saying anything because it hasn't mattered because there's been no real investment for so long.
>
> **—Mem Fox**
> *Radical Reflections*, 1993, p. 21

7. Promoting Student Motivation—and Encouraging Thinking Skills

Research by Paulette Wasserstein (1995) shows that students learn best when they are challenged, actively engaged, and asked to be self-reflective: "Hard work does not turn students away, but busywork destroys them" (p. 43). With six-trait assessment, students become part of a writing community in which their opinions about the quality of writing are frequently, actively sought. It's emotionally draining and dis-empowering to be on the other end of the critique *all* the time. It feels good, by contrast, to have your opinion valued. It teaches you to think, and it makes you feel that your presence in the classroom has purpose.

What about motivation? Many students simply do not like to write, are afraid to write, or feel that they have nothing important to say. Perhaps engagement is too much to hope for—or is it?

In their analysis of this question, Richard Strong and his colleagues (Strong, Silver, and Robinson, 1995, p. 10) suggest that three factors are essential to student motivation:

- ✔ *We must clearly articulate the criteria for success and provide clear, immediate and constructive feedback.*

- ✔ *We must show students that the skills they need to be successful are within their grasp by clearly and systematically modeling those skills.*

- ✔ *We must help students see success as a valuable aspect of their personalities.*

We do all three with six-trait assessment. Rubrics define success in student-friendly language. The immediate feedback is there if students are taught to understand the criteria within the rubric and use those criteria to assess their own work. Modeling (second bullet) is key. You are modeling writing success every time you write or read with students, share your own writing, or share and discuss writing samples that show what to do—or not do. Finally, in order for success to become part of you (third bullet), you must experience it. Many of our students have *never* experienced the joy of that moment when you hear your own voice or see how much your writing has touched someone. All the assessment and monitoring in the world will not do as much for those students as one genuinely appreciative voice saying, "I *loved* that. Please write more." Among the true

> Writing begins with listening. Don't we all, as writers, want to be listened to?
>
> **—Arlene Moore**
> *K–1 teacher,*
> *Mt. Vernon, Washington*

> *Teachers should focus on students' strengths rather than on deficiencies.*
>
> **—Kathleen Strickland and James Strickland**
> *Reflections on Assessment,* 1998, p. 25

> *Every student ought to have the equivalent of a baseball card—many different kinds of abilities measured and a brief narrative report—if we are seriously interested in accurately documenting and improving complex performance.*
>
> **—Grant Wiggins**
> *"Creating Tests Worth Taking,"* 1993, p. 33

advantages of the six-trait model is that it offers *every* student multiple opportunities for success.

Consider fourth grader Rocky. In his first few years of school, he rarely wrote more than a line or two. Negative comments and multiple corrections taught Rocky an important lesson: Keep it short. Get in and get out; that way, they can't hurt you too much.

When he had an opportunity to serve as an assistant to Harry, the school custodian, it was an enormous boost to Rocky's spirit. In addition, Rocky encountered a teacher who could see beyond his conventional problems and who encouraged him to express his voice on paper. Not surprisingly, he chose the topic most important to him at the time: his friend Harry (see Figure 1.3).

Rocky's paper contains a number of conventional errors. His teacher, however, chose to focus on other features: "Your ideas are so clear in this piece. I can tell from your paper what a special friend Harry is. And your voice in this last paragraph really shines."

That night Rocky went home and told his mother, "I can write."

8. Linking Reading and Writing

In her brilliantly insightful book, *What You Know by Heart* (2002), Katie Wood Ray points out that "Every single text we encounter represents a whole chunk of curriculum, a whole set of things to know about writing" (p. 92). When we teach our students to read not just for meaning but also to discover clues about the writer's craft, we make every reading venture a lesson in how to write. The same things that help Gary Paulsen or Sandra Cisneros put voice into their writing work for student writers too. Professional writers do not inhabit a dif-

---

FIGURE 1.3
Rocky's Paper on Harry

Harry is the one that made me stop fighting help me focos and do my work.

Ever sense I've been friends with Harry I've got all A & B on my reportcards. He's brought me to his camp, brought me fishing, let me sleep over his house I think hes the best friend a kid could have.

He brought me to eat at a resteront in Wiscasset. He bouht me an carereokey isn't that so nice. Harry and I play the gutar together my gutar is alatrek his I have know idea. Harry plays like the greatest singer there is. I help Harry at lunch time he let's me help him dump trays.

The day Harry and I stop being friends is the day I die, and that's along time from now.

from Rocky

Grade 4

> *Feedback has been shown to improve learning when it gives each pupil specific guidance on strengths and weaknesses, preferably without any overall marks.*
>
> **—Paul Black and Dylan Wiliam**
> "Inside the Black Box: Raising Standards Through Classroom Assessment," 1998, p. 140

> *Every book you pick up has its own lesson or lessons, and quite often the bad books have more to teach than the good ones.*
>
> **—Stephen King**
> On Writing, 2000, p. 145

ferent universe or use secret skills unavailable to our students. They too must consider which details to include or omit, how to begin and end, and how to make sentences sing. Their text has much to teach—if we read like writers. We also must write like readers, not just *thinking* of the audience out there but literally putting ourselves in their place and asking ourselves as we write, "Does this make sense? Is it interesting?" Questioning our text keeps us focused and makes our voices strong and true.

9. Six-Trait Writing Is Real

Knowledge of the six traits has impact on student performance because *all* writers (not just those in K through 12) need strong, clear ideas, good organization, and compelling voice to make writing successful. By *successful*, I do not mean writing that receives a high grade (although that is one way of measuring success during school years). I am talking about a larger measure of success—holding the attention of an audience, getting published, getting someone to buy what you have published, and most important of all, reaching or moving someone.

When we teach six-trait writing to students, we offer them a vision of writing proficiency that will serve them all their lives in any writing context. This book isn't *just* about success in grade school or high school or college—or improving scores on state tests. It is about students becoming strong and confident writers in any context for any purpose.

The College Board's National Commission on Writing issued a report in 2003 (*The Neglected "R": The Need for a Writing Revolution*) that cites several critical writing skills students need to work successfully in a twenty-first-century environment. Among them are "first-rate organization" (p. 16), ability to generate "convincing and elaborate" text, the use of "rich, evocative and compelling language" (p. 17), knowledge of "mechanics of grammar and punctuation" and a "'voice' and . . . feel for the audience" (p. 20). Do these traits sound familiar? We should not be surprised. The six traits are, after all, the very foundation of good writing—not a tack-on to good writing but the essence of writing itself.

This same report points out that many Americans "would not be able to hold their positions if they were not excellent writers" (p. 10). But this is only the beginning. "At its best," the report continues, "writing has helped transform the world. Revolutions have been started by it. Oppression has been toppled by it. And it has enlightened the human condition. American life has been richer because people like Rachel Carson, Cesar Chavez, Thomas Jefferson, and Martin Luther King, Jr., have given voice to the aspirations of the nation and its people. And it has become fuller because writers like James Baldwin, William Faulkner, Toni Morrison, and Edith Wharton have explored the range of human misery and joy" (p. 10).

Our student writers will soon add their voices to the mix. What sorts of things will they write about in the twenty-first century? Turn on an upscale television that will be obsolete almost faster than you can order and install it, and capture a cross-section of today's world, from surgical makeovers to global changes in weather. From war games to games of war. The traditional—and the dazzlingly innovative. With each year, we view our solar system and indeed our whole universe differently. It may collapse in on itself, we're told, or stretch indefinitely—or do both in an endless cycle. New moons and planets appear. Everyone it seems has a Web site. Cell phones do everything but experience life for us. Through DNA research we track the genetic history of the human adventure and the sometimes revealing tales of our everyday lives. We capture criminals and learn to clone sheep. We discover life forms we didn't know existed within the depths of our oceans and shrinking rain forests.

What will make us care about these things? What will help us to understand them, recall them, or connect them to our own lives? Writing, of course. In their capacity as writers, our students will document these discoveries and thousands of others through film and television scripts, essays, textbooks, travel brochures, voter pamphlets, greeting cards, cartoons, letters and journals, poems, legal briefs, medical reports, advertisements, picture books, novels, editorials, song lyrics, and countless other forms. Someone will probably write a play satirizing overdependence on e-mail or a song about reality television. Only a few of our students will compete for the Pulitzer Prize. Like it or not, however, we will all, through most of our working lives, be writing to inform; to record; to define and explain concepts; to condense, summarize, and interpret data; to teach; to persuade, prompt, amuse, or inspire; and generally, to make sense of the world. And because, as Mem Fox (1993, p. 38) tells us, "No one writes for no one to read," knowing how to touch a reader's soul can only help us to do it better.

10. Trait Rubrics: A Time Saver

Wait just a minute, now. Rubrics as *time savers?* Surely, you're saying to yourself (feeling somewhat protective of those few precious moments not already eaten up by lesson planning and preparing for the state test), a teacher cannot *save* time by assessing students' writing performance on *six traits.* You'd have to read a paper six times to make that work, wouldn't you? No, actually. One thorough, attentive reading will do. Internalizing the traits and *teaching them to students* is the secret, though.

Paul Diederich (1974) demonstrated the practical value of good criteria (and the use of rubrics) when he and some colleagues analyzed how long teachers were spending grading student essays. Results of his study showed that teachers who marked student essays line by line spent, on average, a remarkable *eight minutes per essay.* This means that a teacher with 130 students (a much smaller class load than many have these days) could spend nearly eighteen hours per assignment *just responding to students' work.* (As a teacher, you might wish to have this figure handy the next time someone asks, "Why don't teachers assign more writing?") But here's the interesting part: When teachers abandoned their old ways of grading, stopped functioning as editors for their students, used consistent criteria that were *familiar to student writers,* and kept their comments to a minimum (brief marginal notes on what the student had done well plus one short suggestion), that time dropped to just two minutes per paper—*one-fourth the time they had been spending.*

Rubrics save time because they act as a kind of shorthand between you and the student. You don't need to say everything; the rubric says some things for you. Then you can add a personal comment that gives your students what they hunger for most: Your own words about how the writing touched you.

BUILDING A PERSONAL VISION

A vision of success in writing is not just about the writing product, of course. It must reflect classroom culture and the whole way in which writing is taught—along with what is valued and the way in which we respond to student writers. You must build this vision for yourself. Let me suggest, though, some elements that I feel are critical, and as you go through the book, continue to reflect on the role traits might play in shaping *your* personal vision. In my vision, successful writing would have these qualities:

✔ Clarity, focus, insight, and meaning
✔ Attention to carefully selected details
✔ An effective organizational design that showcases meaning
✔ Authenticity, passion, and voice—the capacity to move an audience
✔ Words that open doors or paint pictures in a reader's mind
✔ The kind of fluency that supports expressive, interpretive reading
✔ Sufficient control over standard writing conventions to enhance meaning and voice

If *writing process* is working as it should, students would

✔ Write frequently.
✔ Identify and write on topics of personal importance in their own lives.
✔ Write in many forms for different audiences and purposes.
✔ Understand the value of research in all forms of writing, including personal narrative and fiction.
✔ Assess and discuss the work of others and apply the lessons learned to their own writing.
✔ Explore the world of literature and, in doing so, learn additional valuable lessons about writing.
✔ Serve as writing coaches for one another (and for the teacher).
✔ Form an interpretive community of learners.
✔ Feel at home with the writing process, shaping it to suit their needs and using personal strategies for prewriting, drafting, revising, and editing.
✔ Assess their own work for the purpose of strengthening revision and editing.
✔ Have the option to keep personal portfolios as a means of preserving and honoring written work and charting growth.
✔ Have the option to publish written work but view audience response and personal satisfaction (not publication) as the ultimate goals of writing.
✔ Know and apply strategies for performing well in a large-scale writing assessment—a genre unto itself.
✔ Read like writers—and write like readers.

✔ Know the value of their work without outside intervention.
✔ Take risks.
✔ Love to write.

In the chapters that follow, we will explore ways of making this vision a reality.

CHAPTER 1 IN A NUTSHELL

● Six-trait writing is not a curriculum but a vision—a way of thinking about writing.

● Students who can "read" their own writing stand a better chance of revising effectively: *What you can assess, you can revise.*

● The six traits are not an invention but an inherent part of what makes writing work.

● The original six-trait rubric was developed *by* teachers *for* teachers.

● The six-trait rubric (or any good rubric) is not just a tool for assessment but a guide to thoughtful, effective revision.

● Assessment provides an important link to instruction because it takes us inside a process or concept, such as writing.

● We assess to understand, and once we understand, we can write and revise with purpose.

● To be effective teachers of writing, we must first teach *ourselves* what good writing is, and then we are better equipped to teach our students.

● There are (at least) ten reasons to make six-trait writing part of your personal vision for writing success: It provides—a language for talking about writing, consistency in assessment, a way of making revision and editing manageable, support for writing process, a guide to purposeful revision and editing, empowerment for students, increased motivation and thinking skills, a way of linking reading and writing, a foundation for real-world writing, and a way of saving assessment time.

● A personal vision of success in writing helps students to understand expectations—and thus increases their chances of success.

● Such a vision must incorporate attention to both process and product.

EXTENSIONS

1. How many of your *own* writing teachers created a clear vision of success? In what ways did their visions influence your behavior as a writer or teacher? Describe this in a journal, or use it as a basis for discussion with colleagues.

2. Take time to write out your vision of success in writing. Do it as a list, an essay, or a poem. Back it with examples of student work, your own work, or quotations from favorite authors. Share it with a classmate or colleague.

3. With students or colleagues, compile a list of all the writing you do over the course of a week (or month). For how many purposes did you write? How many different forms did the writing take? Use your dis-

coveries as a base for discussing the importance of writing in the twenty-first century. How does this information influence your vision of success for the classroom?

4. How do you think your students (if you are now teaching) would rate your individual vision of success? How would you rate it yourself?

_____ Very clear. Students know precisely what is expected.

_____ Somewhat clear. Students have a general idea what I want.

_____ Unclear. Students are guessing what is expected of them.

WHY I WRITE

I write because I am a visual learner. Seeing something in text makes me learn it. I also write because I like to read. I can go back to something I wrote months or even years ago and have a great time reading what I wrote myself!

—Sammy Geiger, student writer

LOOKING AHEAD

Chapter 2 provides a thorough discussion of elements that affect the quality of writing assessment, including rubrics, prompts, general approach, validity and reliability, bias, and numerous other relevant issues. It is revealing to consider six-trait assessment and instruction in light of these issues. However, if you are eager to begin working with the traits, Chapter 3 provides a brief introduction to get you started; Chapters 4 through 6 take you trait by trait through the model with practice papers specifically selected to enhance your understanding.

2 Creating Assessment to Match the Vision

*G*ood assessment does not just happen. It takes planning. Tests are not inherently good, nor is assessment inherently beneficial or even helpful. When we judge the quality of our writing assessment, here are eight keys to success that we should be measuring our assessments against all the time (Spandel, 2001, Stiggins, 2001).

KEYS TO QUALITY ASSESSMENT
Key 1—Making the Target Visible

Good assessment is never about entrapment of students (or teachers, for that matter). It's about giving students an opportunity to show what they can do. As my friend and colleague Rick Stiggins is fond of saying, "Students can hit any target that holds still for them." When we define our expectations (as in a rubric), we dramatically increase the chances that students will perform better just by virtue of the fact that we have made clear what it is we want; we have held the target still.

Of course, as teachers of writing, we must know what the target is, and our expectations must be consistent with skills that will make a twenty-first-century writer successful: communicating an idea clearly, reading the needs of the audience, and so on. A written rubric captures our thinking on paper, making it not only visible but also consistent across time and across performances. The indicators of success that make up the "strong" performance level of a good rubric are like the bull's-eye of the target. Students who are taught to use rubrics in assessing their own work can "read" their writing, as Donald Graves has suggested they must, and they don't need us to take aim for them; they can hit the bull's-eye all on their own.

Key 2—Constructing Rubrics with Thought and Care

Rubrics begin with traits: qualities or characteristics. The traits of good ice skating may be balance, grace, athletic agility, and so on. The traits of a good restaurant may be ambiance, quality of the food, cleanliness, and service. Criteria are the language we use to define those traits at various levels of performance.

Take the trait of ideas. Ideas consist of *the main point, thesis, storyline, or message, together with all the details (anecdotes, facts, examples) that support or enrich that main message.* At a beginning level, criteria defining the trait of *ideas* might look like this:

✔ The central message is not yet clear—or there is no central message yet.
✔ Details are missing or based on general knowledge.
✔ Important questions remain unanswered.
✔ The writing lacks focus and may consist of a list of unrelated factlets.

At a proficient or strong level, the criteria defining *ideas* might look like this:

✔ The central message is clear enough to state in one sentence.
✔ Details expand the message and increase the reader's understanding.
✔ Helpful, thorough information responds to the reader's key questions.
✔ The writing is focused and thoroughly explores the main idea(s).

Notice that in the preceding example the beginning-level criteria point out problems with the writing but do not point fingers at the writer; e.g., "The main idea is weak" or "Details are poor." Wording is critical because the language we use teaches students to think about themselves and about their work. Grant Wiggins (1992) reminds us that to the extent possible, "scoring criteria should rely on descriptive language, not on evaluative and/or comparative language such as 'excellent' or 'fair'" (p. 30). Such words are impossible to define rater to rater and promote inconsistencies in scoring. Wiggins also encourages us to focus on "the most salient characteristics" of performance at each level—those things, in other

> I always did well on essay questions. Just put everything you know on there, maybe you'll hit it. And then you'd get the paper back from the teacher, and she's just written one word across the entire page, "vague." I thought "vague" was kind of a vague thing to say. I'd write underneath it, "unclear," send it back.
>
> **—Jerry Seinfeld**
> *Sein Language*, 1993, p. 164

> A student who remains dependent on the teacher's grades for evaluation is defectively taught in a simple, functional sense. He cannot, strictly speaking, do what he was supposed to do because he cannot do it alone; without help, he cannot tell whether he did it right.
>
> **—Peter Elbow**
> *Embracing Contraries*, 1986, p. 167

> *We must speak to our students with an honesty tempered by compassion. Our words will literally define the ways they perceive themselves as writers.*
>
> **—Ralph Fletcher**
> *What a Writer Needs,*
> 1993, p. 19

words, that would truly cause us to score a performance higher or lower. He also suggests linking criteria to "wider-world" expectations. In other words, we need to ask, Does what we are teaching and emphasizing lead to successful performance in a broader educational sense—out there in the competitive real world?

Once we are convinced that the criteria we have come up with are significant and that they are worded in a clear and constructive fashion, we arrange them along a continuum like that in Figure 2.1. This helps us and our students to understand what ideas look like as they grow. Multiple traits can be arranged in chart format, traits along the horizontal axis and numbers along the vertical axis. This format matches the rubrics in this book.

A good rubric is enhanced by examples that show the trait in action, as in this excerpt from Roald Dahl's classic *Matilda:*

> When she marched—Miss Trunchbull never walked, she always marched like a stormtrooper with long strides and arms aswinging—when she marched along a corridor you could actually hear her snorting as she went, and if a group of children happened to be in her path, she ploughed right on through them like a tank, with small people bouncing off her to left and right [1988, p. 67].

When we hear Miss Trunchbull snorting and visualize her tanklike body ploughing through a group of children, we have a much better sense of what good detail is about.

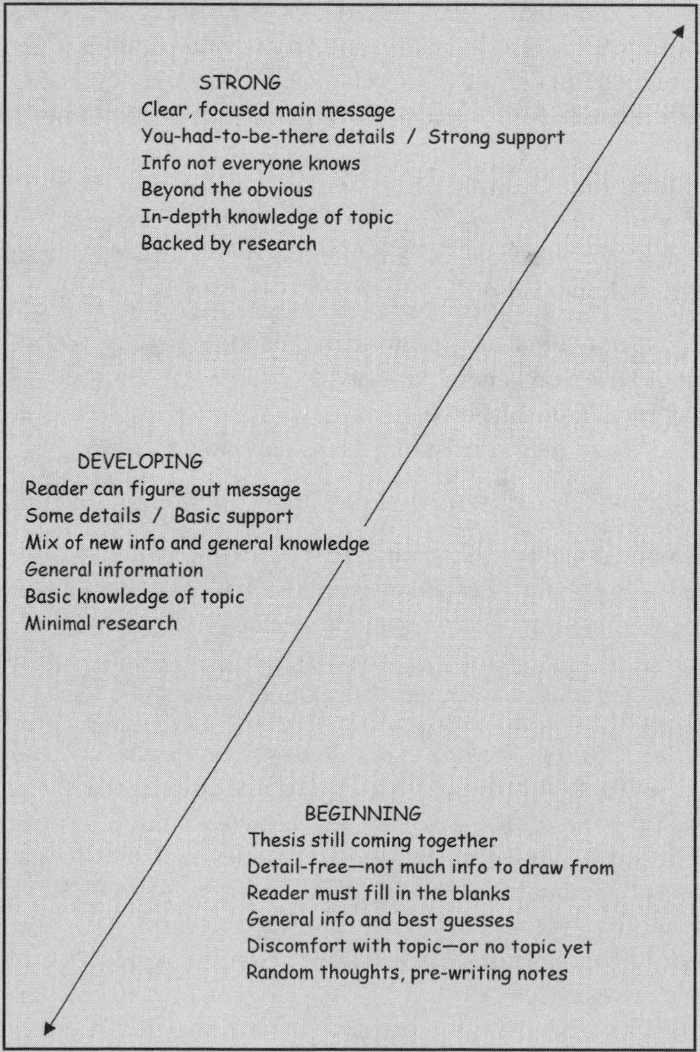

■ *Beware of "Armchair Criteria"*

Too many rubrics consist of "armchair criteria" hastily scribbled down without validation through actual examples. This method of criteria development is dangerous because what is in our imaginations may or may not reflect real-life performance. If we want to know what's important in public speaking, for instance, we should listen to speakers and watch their behavior. To assess writing well, we must look at examples of text and assess our own responses—and we must expect a few surprises.

We may start out believing that correctness is what we'd most like to see in a strong piece of writing; then we look carefully at the examples that move us most. When I curl up to read E. Annie Proulx's *Close Range* (1999), I cannot really say I do not care about the punctuation and spelling. Of course I do.

FIGURE 2.1 *Continuum for the Trait of Ideas*

STRONG
Clear, focused main message
You-had-to-be-there details / Strong support
Info not everyone knows
Beyond the obvious
In-depth knowledge of topic
Backed by research

DEVELOPING
Reader can figure out message
Some details / Basic support
Mix of new info and general knowledge
General information
Basic knowledge of topic
Minimal research

BEGINNING
Thesis still coming together
Detail-free—not much info to draw from
Reader must fill in the blanks
General info and best guesses
Discomfort with topic—or no topic yet
Random thoughts, pre-writing notes

Still, I don't put the book down and say to myself, "Wow. Now *that* was exciting use of commas." But you can believe I am closely tuned in when Proulx writes, "In the long unfurling of his life, from tight-wound kid hustler in a wool suit riding the train out of Cheyenne to geriatric limper in this spooled-out year, Mero had kicked down thoughts of the place where he began, a so-called ranch on strange ground at the south hinge of the Big Horns" (p. 19). I read this compelling line over and over, thinking what a fine choice *unfurling* is and how well the contrast of *tight-wound kid* and *geriatric limper* works or how often I feel that I am living in a *spooled-out year* myself. My response tells me that a good rubric should include features such as word choice and voice. We read to learn about life and about ourselves, and so only writing that teaches and touches us can ultimately be successful.

■ *How Will You Recognize Good Criteria When You See Them?*

Here are a few guidelines to help you. Good criteria

- ✔ *Are clearly written*—easy to understand, explicit, and complemented by samples of strong and weak performance.
- ✔ *Focus on significant aspects* of performance (organization), not on trivia (size of margins).
- ✔ *Create clear distinctions* among performance levels so that raters have little difficulty agreeing on scores.
- ✔ *Thoroughly cover what is important* to quality performance; they do not pass over vital qualities (such as voice) just because they're difficult to define.
- ✔ *Use positive language*, even to describe beginning performance levels, thereby teaching students to think about themselves and their work in positive terms.
- ✔ *Are easy to teach from* because they are written in student-friendly language.
- ✔ *Are generalizable across tasks* so that it is not necessary to invent brand-new criteria for every new assignment.
- ✔ *Are forever changing* as we refine our thinking.

Key 3—Assessing What Is Important, Not What's Easy to Measure

We should be careful what we commend or encourage. I often think of my friend and colleague Barry Lane (author of *After THE END* and *The Reviser's Toolbox*), whose high school teacher commented on one piece of his writing, "It's nice to read typewritten work." Yes, it is. But it's even more rewarding to read work that reflects thinking. The obvious and easy thing to assess is not always what we value most. It is critical to distinguish between the two because what we assess is what we'll get.

In *Reflections on Assessment*, Kathleen and James Strickland caution that "Many rubrics we use are invalid because we don't score what's important in the real-world application of the content being assessed. Instead we design rubrics to assess what's easiest to describe rather than what really matters" (1998, p. 81).

> *The scoring criteria should be authentic, with points awarded or taken off for essential successes and errors, not for what is easy to count or observe.*
>
> **—Grant Wiggins**
> *"Creating Tests Worth Taking,"*
> 1992, p. 27

As teachers of writing, we usually mean well. We start out on a noble mission in pursuit of content, voice, fluency, or organization (and even go so far as to tell students that this is what we will be looking for), but we get bushwhacked by a pet peeve and wind up basing the grade on neatness, choice of topic, use of a pen rather than a pencil, perceived effort, length, or how closely the writer follows the assignment. One teacher actually gave an F to a third grade student who had written a clever, original fairy tale—in purple ink; the teacher did not consider this color appropriate for a serious writing assignment. We might counter that giving a low grade for such a superficial reason is not appropriate in serious assessment.

Key 4—Matching the Assessment Approach to the Task

Complex tasks usually cannot be measured well with simple approaches—e.g., true-false questions. Most large-scale writing assessment done today involves *direct assessment*, a form of performance assessment that requires students to actually write. *Indirect assessment* is, as its name implies, is a somewhat more roundabout way of getting at *writing-related skills*, through fill-in or multiple-choice questions, such as that shown in Figure 2.2. Such questions measure foundational skills, such as knowledge of grammar or punctuation, but knowing rules of grammar and punctuation will not make you a good writer—any more than memorizing recipes will make you a good cook. Nevertheless, indirect assessment was popular for many years largely because such tests were easy to construct and to score.

What's most interesting about indirect assessment these days is that its inherent emphasis on conventions continues to influence the way many *direct* tests of writing are assessed. It is far easier to write multiple-choice test items about grammar and punctuation than about concepts such as voice and organization. Thus indirect assessments of writing have traditionally tended to favor conventions, and this favoritism is still felt in the way some rubrics are constructed and some direct tests of writing are scored. A student whose conventions are weak may score lower on other traits than a comparable writer whose conventions are close to flawless. For that matter, strong conventions have saved many a banal, content-free paper from the relatively lower scores it should have earned in other traits. Conventions are, of course, much easier to see than underlying qualities such as fluency or design.

FIGURE 2.2 *Sample Multiple-Choice Question*

Which of the following is not a complete sentence?

1. As of February 1, his projection seemed accurate.

2. How accurate could that February 1 projection be?

3. Accurate: That was the word for the February 1 projection.

4. An accurate projection, no doubt, as of February 1.*

5. All of the above are complete sentences.

■ Forms of Direct Assessment

Assessors have searched for years for some formulaic method of assessing writing that would eliminate pain, time, and expense. Some methods have included such things as counting numbers of words per sentence (think how high legal contracts would score on this one) or favoring complex sentence structure over simple (William Faulkner and Norman Mailer would easily outdistance Ernest Hemingway here). Unfortunately for those who favor the quick approach, no one as yet has been able to pinpoint any definitive relationship between writing quality and something so superficial as words per sentence or numbers of interlinked independent clauses (Huot, 1990).

All widely accepted methods of direct writing assessment demand careful reading and attention to qualities that reflect thinking, e.g., idea development and organization of information. Of the three most widely accepted scoring methods for direct assessment, *analytical scoring* (of which the six-trait model is one example) has become the most popular because, most assessors agree, it provides the richest information for the time invested. To best appreciate the advantages of this approach, it is worth looking at it in comparison with two other scoring methods: *holistic* and *primary trait*.

Holistic scoring is based on the premise that the whole is more than the sum of its parts and that the most valid assessment of writing will consider how all components—ideas, mechanics, voice, and so forth—work in harmony to achieve an overall effect. Most often a holistic approach is based on explicit criteria, in which case it is termed *focused holistic scoring*. See Figure 2.3 for an example of a focused holistic scoring scale. When raters assign scores by matching students' papers to exemplars (also known as *anchor papers*), samples that typify performance at various score points, the process is called *general impression scoring*.

Holistic scoring is an efficient method of selecting students who are likely candidates for special help in writing or who show potential for being successful in a more challenging writing course. Because each paper receives only one score, however, holistic assessment has limited effectiveness in diagnosing writing skills (and therefore limited value in the classroom). Since papers are not usually weak or strong across all writing traits, raters must make the best match they can. One paper that receives a score of 3 on a 6-point rating scale may have powerful voice but so-so conventions, whereas another may receive a 3 because, although fluent and mechanically sound, it lacks detail. Because so many different interpretations are possible, holistic scores are often frustrating to both students and teachers, who wonder what the scores actually mean. Holistic scoring is most useful when a quick, overall assessment fits the bill.

Primary-trait scoring is based on the premise that all writing is done for an audience and that successful writing will have the desired effect on the audience, mainly due to the impact of the primary, or most important, trait within the piece. The primary trait varies with audience and purpose.

Let's say a writer is putting together a set of directions on assembling a bicycle that will be included with the bicycle components shipped to customers. Of course, it is important to write clearly, to use terms correctly, and to have sound mechanics, but perhaps the most critical trait of all is to organize the steps correctly, to tell the customer exactly how to begin and precisely what to do next and after that. We can say, then, that in this case organization is the primary trait.

Primary-trait assessment has never really caught on in large-scale state or district writing assessments because many educators feel that it is too limited in scope to provide all the feedback they want about their students' writing. On

FIGURE 2.3   *Focused Holistic Scale*

6
Clear, focused main idea enriched with telling, unusual details
Inviting lead, satisfying conclusion, compelling organization
Irresistible voice that asks to be shared
Vivid, memorable, precise words—each carries its own weight
Clear, fluent sentences that make expressive reading easy
No further editing needed prior to publication

5
Clear, focused main idea with striking details
Strong lead and conclusion, structure that guides the reader
Individual, confident voice speaks to readers
Accurate, well-chosen words that make meaning clear
Clear, fluent sentences that make expressive reading possible
Light touch-ups will prepare document for publication

4
Clear main idea—noteworthy details
Functional lead, conclusion, structure
Moments of strong voice that speak to readers
Functional, clear language that carries general message
Clear sentences that can be read without difficulty
A good once-over will prepare document for publication

3
Main idea can be inferred—broad, general details
Organization formulaic—or requires re-reading
Voice often fades—a moment that connects with readers
Functional language mixes with vague, tired words
Problems with sentence repetition, choppiness
Thorough editing needed before publication

2
Reader must guess at emerging main idea—few details
Minimal structure—or formula that smothers ideas
Distant voice—writing to get it done
Vague or general language that does not convey message
Problems with sentence repetition, choppiness, awkward structure
Line by line editing needed before publication

1
No main idea yet—a collection of thoughts
Structure random
Unidentifiable voice—writer not "at home" in the piece
Word choice confusing, general, vague
Hard to tell where sentences begin or end
Word by word editing needed before publication

the other hand, it can be useful at the classroom level for teachers who wish to focus on a particular skill. For instance, if a teacher is helping students learn to write good business letters, a primary-trait approach can encourage them to pay particular attention to the right business tone or appropriate format.

Because of its strong, natural link to revision, *analytical assessment* has virtually swept the popularity polls over the past 10 years, becoming far and away the most preferred form of direct writing assessment at classroom, district, and state levels. Like its holistic counterpart, analytical scoring acknowledges the underlying premise that in writing the whole is more than the sum of its parts, but it adds that if we are to teach students to write, we must take writing apart—temporarily—in order to focus on one skill at a time (remember—"bird by bird").

In order for analytical scoring to work well, all traits must be significant; e.g., use of voice appropriate to purpose and audience would seem important to most readers; placement of a title in the center of a page, less so. A good scale has *horizontal integrity*. That is, traits are distinct enough from one another that we do not wind up scoring the same thing twice. For example, we would just be duplicating efforts (and assessing unfairly) if we scored *ideas*, *content*, and *meaning* as separate traits because all cover basically the same thing. In addition, all traits must reunite to form a cohesive whole, a full definition of quality writing. We must not leave out anything important; nor must we make any one trait overly dominant.

A good scale also has *vertical integrity*. In other words, the "distance" from a 1 to 2 is the same as from a 2 to a 3 and so on. Definitions must reflect this difference. Vertical integrity also demands that any factor (leads or transitions) considered at one level must be considered at *all* levels. A scale that provides rich, thorough definitions at the level of proficiency but scant definitions at other levels lacks vertical integrity (see Figure 2.4).

Key 5—Considering Multiple Samples

> Since single assessments are unlikely to be able to show the range of a student's abilities—and cannot conceivably measure growth—a writing assessment, ideally, should rest on several pieces of writing, written for different audiences and on different occasions. Writing assessment is a genuine challenge.
>
> —**The National Commission on Writing**
> *The Neglected "R,"* 2003, p. 21

Hoping one writing sample will "tell all" is risky. Reviewing multiple samples collected over time (and across forms of writing) gives us a more accurate picture of student proficiency and helps to minimize bias. Such an approach is particularly important in high-stakes decisions such as graduation, entrance into college, and so on.

The value of this multisample approach is confirmed by Alan Purves' (1992) ten-year study of primary and secondary writing within fourteen international school systems, including those in the United States, England, Finland, Wales, Italy, Chile, Nigeria, New Zealand, and others. Among this study's many intriguing findings is this conclusion: "To make any assessment of students' [overall] writing ability, one at least needs multiple samples across the domain" (p. 112). Most of us would agree without thinking twice, but the "one sample tells all" approach is used widely at district and state levels, where funding is scarce and time short. This is unfortunate because significant decisions affecting both teachers and students are often based on this scant, limited information.

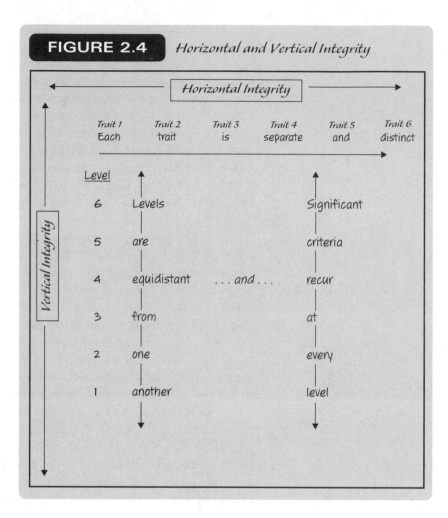

FIGURE 2.4   *Horizontal and Vertical Integrity*

Horizontal Integrity

Trait 1	Trait 2	Trait 3	Trait 4	Trait 5	Trait 6
Each	trait	is	separate	and	distinct

Vertical Integrity

Level			
6	Levels		Significant
5	are		criteria
4	equidistant	. . . and . . .	recur
3	from		at
2	one		every
1	another		level

At the classroom level, we know instinctively that we need as much information as possible, yet the reality of huge class loads makes us ask, "What's reasonable?" Few teachers (especially those with class load totals of 150 students or more) can hope to assess dozens of samples of writing per year per student. On the other hand, though, a teacher who assessed only one or two samples per year could not possibly count on such a small snapshot to tell him or her definitively whether Mike's writing was strong in voice or whether Emilè could organize information well. Somewhere between these hypothetical extremes lies a realistic and valid compromise—a representative sample of all possibilities small enough to manage yet large enough to yield strong inferences about how well students write.

Because each classroom is different, we may never come up with a magic formula to tell us precisely how many samples we need for grading purposes. Yet there are guidelines to help us. First, the number of samples we can grade should not restrict how much students write. Not every piece of writing needs to be assessed. Students may keep files of drafts from which they select only a few to revise and hand in for formal assessment. Such assessment may occur only about once every one to two weeks. This plan will easily result in four to six samples per grading pe-

> *Careful research shows us what common sense tells us is obvious: no matter how trustworthily we may evaluate any sample of a student's writing, we lose all that trustworthiness if we go on to infer from just that one sample the student's actual skill in writing.*
>
> **—Peter Elbow**
> *Embracing Contraries,*
> 1986, p. 37

riod, a good minimum (a small body of work) on which to base defensible conclusions about student performance. Teachers who are able to do more (especially if students are writing in more than one genre), of course, will receive a proportionately more thorough picture of students' writing skills. Smaller assignments mean less to assess, and so minimizing assignment length in favor of more opportunities to write seems a good strategy if we wish students to receive as much feedback as possible. (See Chapter 13 for a more thorough discussion of grading.)

Let's not forget too that students who are skilled self-assessors are assessing and reflecting on their own work all the time. They self-assess as they plan, read their work, and revise until it becomes as natural as breathing. This self-assessment, in which the student goes inside the writing and thinks her way out, is the most important assessment by far, for it is the student (with guidance from the teacher) who has the power to change her writing and the way in which she writes. No matter how much data we scramble to collect, until the student knows what to do, assessment from without has no impact.

> *Current approaches to evaluation have it backwards. At the moment, the most important evaluator is some person out of town who knows nothing of the teaching situation. In fact, the student, who is closest to the work . . . ought to be and is the most important evaluator.*
>
> **—Donald H. Graves**
> *Testing Is Not Teaching,*
> 2002, p. 28

Key 6—Minimizing Bias

Bias involves basing a writing assessment score or grade on some factor unrelated to actual writing performance, e.g., length of the document, handwriting (for pieces that are not word processed), previous performance, choice of topic, and so on. In large-scale writing assessment, raters (who may be teachers, writers, editors, college students, or trained professionals) may fail to use criteria, misinterpret those criteria, place too much emphasis on one factor while disregarding others, or ignore criteria altogether in favor of some personal basis for making a judgment; e.g., "This student wrote a science fiction piece, and I just don't like science fiction." Not surprisingly, many of these same factors influence teacher grading at the classroom level. (See Chapter 3 for a list of common pet peeves and other causes of bias among raters or classroom teachers.) In order to minimize bias, whether in the classroom or in a large-scale testing situation, we need to

- ✔ Be aware of common causes of bias.
- ✔ Train raters (and ourselves) to watch for and avoid bias by comparing our criteria and our ratings regularly with those of other teachers.
- ✔ Be sure the writing assessment (including the wording of prompts) is fairly designed to give all participants an equal chance for success.
- ✔ Ensure that criteria are designed to measure the kind of writing students are asked to produce.

■ *Isn't Bias Just Another Word for Subjectivity?*

In a word, no. *Subjectivity* refers to the application—not the misapplication—of human judgment. Whether a test is *subjective* or *objective* has nothing to do with fairness or bias; it has to do with when human judgment is applied.

In direct writing assessment, judgments are made *during scoring;* such assessment is therefore known as *subjective.* In multiple-choice tests, human judgment is applied *during test construction* but not during scoring. In designing a multiple-choice test, someone must determine which content to include, which questions are significant enough to bother asking in the first place, how those questions will be worded, and which possible answers are plausible enough to look correct yet not so plausible as to *be* correct. These are all subjective judgments. Because multiple-choice (or fill-in or true-false) tests frequently are scored by machine, however, no human judgment is applied *during scoring.*

This common misperception about objectivity is important because it causes some assessors as well as the general public to place undue faith in "scientific" testing approaches, such as multiple-choice tests, when in truth, such methods are incredibly ill-suited to the measure of writing proficiency. By extension, some people may also place undue faith in grammar and usage drills, sentence diagramming, memorization of formulas, vocabulary lists, spelling tests, and other shortcuts to the *teaching* of writing. Research cited in the National Commission on Writing's report, *The Neglected "R"* (2003), notes that "Writing extends far beyond mastering grammar and punctuation. The ability to diagram a sentence does not make a good writer. There are many students capable of identifying every part of speech who are barely able to produce a piece of prose" (p. 13). Writing as thinking demands creative instruction and assessment by thoughtful readers, not machines.

■ *A Little Subjectivity = Brain at Work*

We must also be cautious about taking the position that subjectivity is somehow inherently wrong or that it invalidates the assessment process. There's nothing wrong with subjectivity if it's applied with consistency and intelligence. After all, lots of things in this world—films, books, restaurants, and performers in the Olympics—are rated subjectively; but we trust those ratings when they are given based upon relevant, consistent criteria and by persons with the training, insight, and experience to make ratings meaningful.

Key 7—Ensuring That Assessments Are Both Reliable and Valid

Consistency, sometimes called *reliability*, depends on the specificity of the scoring criteria and the quality of rater training. When the criteria are highly refined and very explicit, and when the raters are very thoroughly trained and feel confident in applying those criteria (so confident that they could score a paper without even looking at the criteria, but they look anyway), the likelihood of their scoring consistently increases dramatically. This is important not only in large-scale assessment but also in the classroom.

A good assessment of writing is also said to have *validity*, the closest possible connection with the knowledge or skills we wish to assess. Four kinds of validity are possible (and you should consider them all as you use the six-trait model I present in this text):

Predictive validity—the extent to which performance on a writing assessment
    will be a good predictor of performance in a related context (e.g., in a more
    advanced writing course or job that requires writing).

Concurrent validity—the extent to which performance on one writing assessment will be a good predictor of performance on another similar assessment. (Would a student who did well on your state's writing assessment likely receive high scores on in-class assessments?)

Construct validity—the extent to which the assessment measures skills and abilities truly essential to writing competence. (Will the student who clearly presents a complex concept in an organized fashion receive a high score? Will she receive that score even if her topic sentence is implicit, i.e., embedded in the text, not stated outright? Will her scores be unfairly influenced by tangential concerns such as margins or overall neatness?)

Face validity—the extent to which the assessment measures skills and abilities that teachers of writing (and employers who require writing) deem important.

Direct writing assessment has a potentially high degree of validity because students are really writing. It is also important, though, that we provide time for students to think, plan, and revise; otherwise, we are measuring hasty drafting, not reflective writing.

Key 8—Making Parents Part of the Process

Research is crystal clear: Schools that do well insist that their students write every day and that teachers provide regular and timely feedback with the support of parents.

—National Commission on Writing

The Neglected "R," 2003, p. 28

Although it is inherently more (not less) demanding, a six-trait, criterion-based assessment model can look suspiciously (and ironically) lenient to parents haunted by memories of the good old days when sentences were stretched on racks and the red ink flowed. Too often parents have not had the opportunity—or the invitation—to question what was truly being assessed in those classrooms of long ago or to question whether writing instruction covers (or should cover) clear thinking and organizational skills.

As teachers, we can show parents how six-trait assessment works by sharing rubrics and by inviting them into our classrooms to observe and work with student writers using writers' language. We can even ask them to write and to identify the strengths and weaknesses, trait by trait, within their own writing—an enlightening experience for anyone. And we can request their support in being coaches for their children. (See Chapter 13 for further suggestions on bringing parents into the world of trait-based writing.)

MAKING ASSESSMENT SUPPORT INSTRUCTION (NOT VICE VERSA)

We often expect assessment, especially large-scale assessment, to magically improve performance, when the reality is that only instruction can do that. If assessment alone were the key, we would need only to weigh ourselves daily to lose weight. Would that it were so. If you think this sounds silly, ask yourself what it is we do when our student writers do not perform as we feel they should. We assess more often, make our standards more rigorous, and heighten our expectations. Well, then, perhaps if we weighed ourselves *hourly* . . .

Assessment serves us best when we use it to support, not direct, instruction. We must use results responsibly, as indicators. A writing assessment is one indicator of writing proficiency, as your temperature at any given moment is one indicator of your general health. We don't, if we are wise, rely on one indicator to tell us *everything*. Assessment *can* support instruction if we teach students to be self-assessors; use assessment results not to rank students, schools, or teachers but to pinpoint specific writing problems that we can address together; and finally, identify the lessons learned through classroom and large-scale assessment to make each stronger.

LARGE-SCALE AND CLASSROOM ASSESSMENT: LESSONS LEARNED FROM TWO PERSPECTIVES

As teachers, we sometimes tend to think of classroom assessment as friendly and comfortable and of large-scale assessment as threatening and intimidating—mostly because it is sometimes wielded as a weapon to judge teacher performance. The truth is, though, that while both large-scale assessment and classroom assessment have limitations, each has important lessons to offer the other.

LARGE-SCALE WRITING ASSESSMENT: HOW IT LOOKS

In large-scale assessment, students usually write on one prompt (or a choice of two) that is preselected and often cannot be explained fully by the teacher during the assessment because such explaining is considered unfair coaching. (Isn't this interesting? Picture a hospital administrator saying with a straight face, "I can't explain the appropriate surgical procedures once the operation begins. You will need to figure those out as best you can. And please do not consult a medical textbook or talk to other doctors while you are operating.")

Students must complete their work in a prescribed time frame, as little as 25 minutes total or as much as two or three 45-minute periods. (A few forward-thinking states and districts allow as much time as the student reasonably requires.) Once students turn in their work, their papers are read and scored by two trained raters (often but not always teachers) working separately.

Many large-scale assessments do not parallel at all a process-based approach to teaching writing; students have little or no choice of topic, no opportunity to explore a topic outside their own heads, limited time to compose their thoughts mentally or on paper, and minimal time to revise or edit.

■ *On the Positive Side*

For all the furor and anxiety it produces though, large-scale assessment performs several good writing deeds. First, it keeps writing in the public eye, reminding everyone of its importance in education. Second, it encourages the development and use of sound scoring criteria, which make the assessment of writing more valid and consistent. And third, it offers teachers who may work for years in one building or at one grade level an opportunity to gain a broader perspective—seeing several hundred samples of student writing from throughout a state or district is very different from seeing only the writing of your own students. Often they say, "This is the most valuable in-service experience I have had as a teacher of writing" and "I will never see assessment, or my own students' writing, in the same way again."

Few people outside the teaching profession can realize how isolated a teacher often feels. Opportunities for teacher-to-teacher sharing are more rare than most people might think, and many teachers are troubled by a persistent, sometimes daunting perception that much of what we do as teachers—including assessment and grading—we must do alone. Large-scale assessment has taught us the infinite value of an interpretive community—people who openly create, shape, discuss, and live by criteria that influence their thinking and their performance, whether in writing or in any academic area. This idea, transported to the classroom, has power that can scarcely be measured.

Large-scale assessment does one more thing, too, and this (excepting the promotion of criteria) is perhaps the primary contribution that this form of writing assessment has made to the world of writing instruction in the past 10 years: It raises expectations about student performance.

■ *How Well Do Students Write?*

For many students, getting one coherent sentence on paper is a victory—a big one. There are also students, however (a few appear in this book), who write with power and grace, who move us to laughter—or tears. They write better than many of us did at the same age. This does not make for good press, though, so you won't see headlines that read "Student Writers Startle Teacher Raters with Their Eloquence." Make no mistake, I am not saying that many student writers do not struggle. What I am suggesting is that we will not know the extent of the problem definitively until we have created writing assessments that allow self-selected prompts and that effectively measure serious skills, such as marshaling ideas, and stop obsessing over such trivial matters as whether students stay "on topic."

Several years ago I came across a newspaper article entitled, "Most Students Stumble on Writing Exam" (*The Oregonian*, September 29, 1999). The article began by stating that "only one in four U.S. students is able to write reports, narratives and persuasive pieces at a proficient level, according to the U.S. Department of Education." This "proficient level" is not defined in the article, but we are told that the results are based on two writing samples, with 25 minutes of writing time allowed for each. We are also given one of the prompts:

> Imagine this situation! A noise outside awakens you one night. You look out the window and see a spaceship. The door of the spaceship opens, and out walks a space creature. What does the space creature look like? What do you do? Write a story about what happens next [National Assessment of Educational Progress].

Do you see anything wrong with this picture—this so-called test of writing proficiency? The 25-minute time limit says clearly to students: "Writing is a quick activity that requires little thinking or reflection. If you cannot do it quickly, you are not proficient. Revision is not important; if it were, we would have provided time for it."

This prompt, I suggest, would make almost any thinking person "stumble." Written for eighth graders, it does not take into account what might interest or intrigue them, nor is it written at their level. Notice the short, simple sentences; it's almost a parody of a basal reader: *Open, spaceship, open. Walk, space creature, walk.* Further, it begins with a highly unlikely premise: a space ship landing outside someone's window. Come on.

The 2002 prompts are not an improvement: "You wake up one morning, and there are clouds on your breakfast plate." Maybe it's a foggy day. If I cannot write to this prompt, there's a so-called alternative: "You look out the window and see stars littering the streets." Last time we looked, weren't stars rather large—and *hot?* In any case, students are further instructed to write a story called "The Very Unusual Day." They are given 25 minutes. "Faced with that task," the article (*USA Today*, July 11–13, 2003) continues, "fewer than one in five fourth-graders could write a respectable story." Really? So—given a wholly implausible premise completely outside the range of human experience, nine-year-olds could not concoct fanciful, coherent stories sufficiently riveting to engage an adult audience? Imagine that. This article ("Most Students Unable to Write Respectably") concludes with some thoughtful remarks by Gerald Bracey of George Mason University, Fairfax, VA. Bracey is said to be critical of the way writing tests are scored: ". . . by $7-an-hour temps who spend, at most, 30 seconds on an essay." This statistic is enough to depress Mary Poppins. Forget for a moment the simple truth that *writing teachers* should be scoring writing tests. Let me help you with the math. If that 30-second estimate is correct, these "raters" are scoring roughly 120 essays an hour. At $7 an hour, that's about 6 cents per essay to discover what any teacher of writing could have told them: 25 minutes is an insufficient amount of time to rescue prompts that force students into a mental clash with common sense.

Let's be fair. For all I know, students to whom imaginative writing comes easily loved these prompts. I suspect that for others, though, they seemed either dull or just plain bewildering. Either way, here is what really disturbs me: How many of those who read the headline (and feel a moment of concern that students' "proficiency" is apparently slipping) will take time to sit down and write for 25 minutes on one of those prompts? Do it right now. I dare you. And now for something truly imaginative—and a lot scarier than invasions by clouds or stars. Imagine that a high school diploma, a commendation, entrance to college, or your professional future hangs on a stranger's 30-second assessment of what you have just written. Can you live with it?

We should be careful—much more careful than we now are—about the conclusions we draw based on tests of "writing proficiency." Let's ask what we're *really* measuring and how we're doing it. What *these* prompts really measure is my ability to string together enough coherent sentences in 25 short minutes to appear far more engaged in this writing task than I really am. This kind of game playing is not an appropriate response from an educated person, and we should stop encouraging it, even if it does earn points on an assessment.

> *I've often wondered who in our national, state, or local government keeps an eye on the type of learner we are trying to develop in our public schools. Until we can begin to agree on what basics make up this ideal learner, it will be difficult to consider the best assessment approaches to tell us if our schools are succeeding.*
>
> **—Donald H. Graves**
> *Testing Is Not Teaching,*
> 2002, p. 23

LESSONS LEARNED FROM LARGE-SCALE ASSESSMENT
Lesson 1: Prompts Count!

Because the identity of prompt writers is hard to discover (I think there is a Prompt Writers Protection Program), they often live to write another day. In all fairness to prompt writers everywhere (I have been one myself and have written my share of losers), let me say at the outset that writing good prompts is very hard. On a scale of 1 to 10, measuring difficulty and tendency to promote frustration, writing a dictionary is a 4, whereas prompt writing is roughly an 8. This is one of many reasons we should (1) provide students with choices across topic and mode and (2) whenever possible allow students to write on self-selected topics. In addition, though, we should scrutinize prompts (in the classroom and out) to be sure that they open doors for students instead of locking them.

■ *A Few Good Prompts*

Ugly rumors to the contrary, there actually *are* a few reasonably good prompts out there that allow most students to show off their writing skills. Don't get too excited; the list, in my experience, is *very* short. Further, I don't claim that any prompt on this list will cause students to say, "Hurry—a pen!" But for what it's worth, here are some of my favorites. Notice that each of these *functional* prompts allows students to use personal knowledge and experience and to take a basic idea in numerous directions:

1. Think of something you own that means a lot to you and that was not purchased in a store. Explain why it is important to you *or* write a story connected to this object.
2. Can very young and very old people be friends? Use your experience to write a convincing paper that answers this question for your reader.
3. Think of a place so important and special to you that you would like to return to it many times. Describe it so clearly that a reader can see, hear, and feel what it is like to be there.
4. Think of a story (funny, sad, frightening, or embarrassing) that you might still enjoy telling to friends when you are older. Write your story as if it were going to be published in a magazine.
5. Think of a teacher (friend/family member) you will never forget. Tell one story that comes to mind when you think about what makes this person unforgettable.
6. Some people feel that video games, television, and other electronic media have decreased our ability as human beings to concentrate and learn new things. Do you agree—or not? Write a convincing paper based on your experiences and observations.
7. Imagine that you are a historian living 200 years in the future. You are writing a description of life on planet Earth in the year 200_. Think carefully about what you will say because your writing might be published in a future textbook for fifth graders.
8. What is it like to be in your place in your family—youngest child, oldest child, middle child, twin, only child, or whatever? Write a persuasive essay that defends your position as the best, worst, or just okay.
9. What if you could spend one day with any person, real or fictional, from the past or present? Who would you choose and why? Write a hypothetical interview you might have with this person.

Following are a few favorites from my friend and colleague Barry Lane (1993, p. 56), who often favors a single-word or phrase approach to prompts:

1. Lost
2. Running away

3. Home

4. No longer a child

5. Funny now—not then

6. Unbelievable

7. The other side

8. The one thing

9. The key

One of my favorite prompts was a simple picture of an old leather suitcase, circa 1940, that looked like something Humphrey Bogart might have carried into an exotic hotel. For a picture, students can create a description, story, mystery, essay, or whatever. Good prompts always yield variety in the responses.

For countless additional ideas, I recommend Marjorie Frank's delightful book, *If You're Trying to Teach Kids How to Write . . . you've gotta have this book* (1995).

■ *Bad Prompt Alert*

Of course, there's the dark side. Just because a prompt is on someone's list is no sign that you should use it. Here are some prompts to avoid at all costs:

1. Describe your favorite dinner. Be specific. (We should have said, "Limit your description to the entrée. Do not use the words *fluffy, crispy,* or *tender.*")

2. Should you or should you not eat junk food? Write a letter to a friend explaining your position and convincing your friend to agree with you. (Who needs more lectures on the wonders of broccoli? Breathes there a man with soul so dead who never to himself has said, "Sometimes you just *gotta* have a doughnut"?)

3. What are the qualities required to be a good president? (It takes *leadership.* End of paper. See? It wasn't as complicated as we thought.)

4. Think of a time when weather affected your life. Tell what happened. (Think of a time when weather *didn't* affect your life. Now *that* might have had possibilities.)

5. Explain how to make a decision. (We should have asked, "Explain how to write a good prompt. All reasonable suggestions will be welcome.")

■ *Tips for Effective Prompts*

Writing good prompts is a challenge. Here are a few rules of the road to keep in mind:

1. Consider the grade level and experience of the student writers. The topic should be reasonably familiar (they won't have time or opportunity for research) but also *interesting.* If you aren't sure, ask students. Not all are enchanted by clouds on their plates.

2. Do *not* give students any prompt that you would not like to write on yourself. The revenge factor is built in (you will have to read the results).

3. Avoid any prompt that is likely to elicit 5000 responses that sound like clones of one another (e.g., "What does it take to be a good student?").

4. Avoid controversial issues that are likely to trigger rater bias (e.g., "Should professional female golfers be allowed to compete with men?")

5. Think about wording. Avoid prompts that can be answered with a simple yes or no (e.g., "Should the driving age in our state be lowered to 14?")

6. Avoid wordy prompts packed with "helpful hints:" e.g., "Write about a time you will always remember. It could be a happy or sad time. It could even be a funny or embarrassing or exciting experience. It could be a time long ago or something that happened recently. Put in as many sensory details as you can—sights, sounds, smells, and feelings—to help your reader experience this special time with you." Oops—time's up, and we've only read the prompt! Even from the speedy writers, expect a worksheet-like response in which all questions are methodically answered as if the student were under hypnosis.

7. Ask yourself whether you care if students write a narrative, an informational piece, or a persuasive essay. If you do, then wording of the prompt is a *big* issue. Key words can help direct students to the form you want:
   ✔ *Narrative:* Tell the story. Tell about time when.
   ✔ *Informational:* Explain. Give directions for. Provide an analysis of.
   ✔ *Persuasive:* Write an argument. Convince. Take a position on.
   ✔ *Descriptive:* Describe. Give details about. Help your reader picture.

8. Whenever possible, allow students to *select their own topics*; their ability to do so then becomes part of what you assess.

Lesson 2: "Off Topic" Is Often "Off Base"

Many papers in district or state assessments (way too many) judged as "off topic" are in reality highly individual, even ingenious responses to a vague or uninspiring topic. Prompts are not holy writ. They are invitations to write, nothing more. Often students who wander "off topic" are penalized for thinking in an original manner, the very thing our instruction seeks (or should seek) to promote. In reality, these writers are finding their way *into* their own personal topics, "prompted" by a word, an association, or a recollection. It's ironic to impose our topics on students and then complain when the responses lack individuality, imagination, or voice. It's like saying that someone else fails to wear your clothing with flair.

> *Current approaches to assessing writing usually provide a single prompt. . . . A far more demanding yet fairer approach, for both students and teachers, is to have students write on a topic that interests them and on which they have already prepared their ideas by reading and turning possibilities over in their minds.*
>
> **—Donald H. Graves**
> *Testing Is Not Teaching,*
> 2002, p. 46

Lesson 3: We Must Be Very, Very Good Assessors

Most writing teachers are fair spellers and can recognize a comma splice at 10 paces, and so the old world of assessment, with its emphasis on conventions, felt safe. Now the National Commission on Writing (2003, p. 16) tells us that we need students who can create "precise, engaging, coherent prose." Our state standards and our rubrics typically echo such lofty goals, and this is a good thing. But keep in mind that when we raise the bar for our students, we raise it for ourselves as assessors, too. We must know the precise from the imprecise, the engaging from the voiceless, the coherent from the disorganized. Do we? We must not ask of our students what we are not prepared to assess with consistency and perception. A well-planned assessment is a contract. It pledges, "If you present clear and expansive ideas, I will understand; if you organize information effectively, I will follow; if you write with voice, I will hear you."

Lesson 4: Students Need Test-Taking Strategies

Students must know how to *use* their time as writers. We must teach them to scan the landscape so that they have some idea of how long a writing task will take. We must teach multiple forms of prewriting so that if they do not have an opportunity to talk or read, they can use webbing or listing. We must also teach them to read and respond to prompts quickly. See Figure 2.5 for 12 writing tips that can be helpful in a formal, large-scale testing situation.

In the absence of such strategies, students resort to survival-skill writing. They repeat the language of the prompt or ramble endlessly to fill the page. This is understandable. If I am drowning, I do not care how graceful my Australian crawl looks. Students keep their heads above water by filling pages with repetition and generalities. I recall a paper from a state assessment some years ago in which a third grader attempted the comparison of two animals; he chose a dog and cat. He had little to say on this topic (a position for which I have boundless sympathy), and so, to fill the space, he found a hundred different ways to say that when the pets were good, they were good. In fact, they were very good. They were good because they liked to be good, and they liked it when they were good. They probably wanted to be good, and they were good when they wanted to be. And so on. We could simply dismiss this paper with a low score on ideas, or we could recognize what is really going on. This little writer has retreated to survival mode; we pushed him there with our prompt and our oversized writing booklet. The appropriate response to such a paper is not a score at all (the paper is not ready for that) but a lesson in strategy: "I see that you filled the whole booklet! Wow. That's a lot—but I want to let you in on a secret. Sometimes you don't *have* to fill the *whole* booklet. You can just write a note about what you think. What if a dog and cat had an argument about which one made a better pet? What do you think they would say? Why don't you write me a note about that?" I might then do the same. Later, we can compare notes and also have a chat about other (potentially more interesting) things we might write notes about. The lesson? Condense. Focus. And don't ever let a booklet boss you around.

CLASSROOM ASSESSMENT: HOW DOES IT LOOK?

In the classroom, the world of writing and assessment usually looks quite different from what we see at the district or state level. Given a process-based curriculum (in which students choose topics, prewrite, draft, share, revise and edit, and go public with the writing) and a teacher with a strong commitment to writing instruction (someone who writes with students; models prewriting, revision, and editing; and reads aloud often), student writers have both time and opportunity on their side. They are not mentally bludgeoned by topics that feel restrictive or hard to decipher, nor are they held to deadlines no writer (even a professional) could hope to meet. If something is unclear about the prompt, the teacher can explain it, abandon the prompt altogether, or best of all, invite students to choose topics they know well and feel strongly about. Students can use resources of all kinds—dictionaries, handbooks, spell-

FIGURE 2.5 *Twelve Tips for Succeeding on Writing Tests*

1. Read the prompt carefully. Figure out the main *focus* (what the prompt writers want you to talk about) and the best *form* (story, argument, or informational essay).

2. Take a minute or two to plan your writing, even if time is short. Consider how you will begin and end. Have a clear main message you can express in one sentence, and state it to yourself, silently or aloud.

3. Mentally or on scratch paper construct a *rough and simple* outline you will follow in a flexible way; e.q., for a persuasive piece—(1) a lead that includes an enlightening summary of the issue or controversy, (2) a summary of what many people (with opposing views) believe, (3) a clear statement of what you believe (the thesis), (4) opposing arguments with your rebuttals, supporting arguments backed by evidence, (5) a closing paragraph that leads readers right to the inevitable, sane conclusion.

4. In a persuasive or informational piece, state your main idea outright. Don't make a tired reader guess. Make sure that everything in your piece relates to that main idea. Don't wander from the path even if you have something interesting to say. Save that kind of writing for when you get published.

5. Spend time on your lead and conclusion. That's where the reader is likely to pay closest attention.

6. Do not try to tell everything. Choose three to five key events in a story, three to five informational "moments" in an essay or argument—no more.

7. If your writing includes characters, have them speak, and make what they say important and memorable.

8. If your writing includes a setting, include sensory details not everyone would notice—sounds or smells.

9. Don't rely on adjectives and adverbs. Think of them as salt and pepper, using only what you need. Let verbs carry the weight of the writing.

10. Tell the truth. When it comes to putting voice in writing, there is no substitute for saying just what you mean.

11. In your conclusion, don't summarize or review old ground. Cite something significant (perhaps unexpected) you gained from your experience or observations.

12. Think carefully about your title and write it *last*. It will look as if your paper flowed right out of the title when just the opposite is true.

checker—as any real-world writer would do without a thought. Some may keep portfolios that showcase their work and track growth.

Assessment is more personal, managed by someone who knows the student. In a classroom where a written rubric forms the basis for assigning grades, students can actively participate in the assessment process, reviewing their own work before any grade is assigned and revising it as needed. Portfolio assessment may play a much greater role than is usually true at a state level. As of this writing, the Kentucky state assessment offers a notable exception to this rule (Hillocks, 2002, pp. 163ff.), coming much closer to what we see in the classroom. As part of their state test, Kentucky students respond to an on-demand writing prompt but also compile a portfolio over a period of months, even years. Hillocks calls it "an opportunity for students to show their best work developed over a series of drafts, replete with feedback, revision, editing, and time to think carefully." He adds that this is "writing as real writers do it" (p. 163). Indeed! This is also large-scale writing assessment taking one important lesson from the classroom. There are others.

LESSONS LEARNED FROM CLASSROOM ASSESSMENT

Lesson 1: Writing Process Must Be Learned

Writing process is magical—*if* students make use of it. They cannot do so automatically, and simply providing time to write (or revise and edit) is not sufficient. We must show them what prewriting, drafting, revision, sharing, and editing are all about—not by talking about them but by being writers ourselves. They must see us do it. They must also see our own "before" and "after" samples so that they know what is possible in revision, and our rubrics must reflect the kinds of changes they *see* before to after.

Lesson 2: Choosing a Topic Is Not Just a Privilege— It's an Art

We want our students to have choices. The truth is, though, that many student writers do not know how to go about choosing their own topics because someone else has frequently done this part for them. We must model for them what it means to sift through your life as an archaeologist sifts through sand and pick what should be recorded on paper. It's not that simple. Try it. Grab a piece of scratch paper right now and jot down five possible topics you could write on. And if you can do this, do it at your very next opportunity *while your students are watching*—on the overhead, perhaps. If you cannot, at least you've gained some appreciation for what students face in finding good topics, and so you can begin—right now— to learn together.

> *Teachers should write so they understand the process of writing from within.*
>
> **—Donald M. Murray**
> *A Writer Teaches Writing,*
> 2004, p. 74

Lesson 3: We Need to Model Revision, Too

Did you see any of your teachers write? I did not. So naturally, I did not see them revise either. If you did, you were lucky.

> *When [a student] writes, she is on the inside looking out; later, as she rereads her work, she is on the outside again, wondering whether the page properly reflects her feelings and her ideas.*
>
> **—Donald H. Graves**
> *Testing Is Not Teaching,*
> 2002, p. 59

Many students breeze through prewriting and drafting; then they hit a brick wall. In the absence of any models or guidelines, they often settle for neatening up the piece, making it longer, or using a spell-checker. Time is not the whole answer either. Time to revise is of minimal help to the student who does not know how to narrow and define a topic, craft a good lead, play with phrasing, "hear" the conclusion, or fine-tune voice.

The good news is that teaching revision is so much easier with sound writing criteria that it is almost like cheating. When students can assess the work of others, they are only one small step away from assessing their own work. And from self-assessment comes the foundation for revision—the most difficult step in the writing process to teach.

Lesson 4: Best Writing Is Produced under Best Conditions

Teachers often say, when they receive their students' writing samples back from large-scale assessment, "These samples do not reflect my students' best writing." They are right. If we wish to see what students can do as writers, we must give them time to gather information, talk, think, and revisit their writing over a period of time.

Lesson 5: The "Hurry Up and Write" Approach = More Stress, Less Quality

> *We need to avoid assessment environments steeped in mystery and illusion, intimidation and vulnerability, stress and anxiety. . . . Maximum anxiety does not lead to maximum learning.*
>
> **—Richard J. Stiggins**
> *Student-Involved Classroom Assessment,* 2001, p. 3

Most people drive from 5 to 10 miles (or more) over the speed limit and grow impatient with those who observe it. We love *fast* food, *instant* messaging, *speed* dialing, and *rapid* transit. Our reverence for speed has an unfortunate impact on assessment. It creates stress, for one thing. Writing is not by nature a speedy activity but a reflective one. Until we recognize this, our large-scale measurements cannot dip beneath the superficial. In addition, stress potentially reduces quality. Some students freeze under pressure and write nothing. Others resort to formulaic writing because it's quick and easy to produce—and also voiceless and tedious to read. In the end, because formulaic writing requires no synthesis of ideas or creative organization, it results in a *lowering* of standards for quality writing—just the opposite of what we wanted.

Lesson 6: We Must Create Assessments That More Closely Match What Is Demanded of Real Writers

> *Currently, we are testing what we value, quick thinking. But what about long thinking? . . . Can we identify and encourage the children who can formulate a question, find the information, design an evaluation, and know whether they have answered their original question?*
>
> **—Donald H. Graves**
> *Testing Is Not Teaching,*
> 2002, p. 34

Instead of throwing topics at students like darts, we need to ask them what information they'd like to share and in what form they'd like to share it (e.g., report, children's book, interview for a journal). Instead of assessing rough drafts stu-

> *Teachers are buried in an avalanche of expectations: standards, testing, and expanded curricula. The expectations come from every level of government and administration as well as from parents and the community. They are rarely part of a long-term plan carefully developed in conjunction with the teachers.*
>
> **—Donald H. Graves**
> *Testing Is Not Teaching,*
> 2002, p. 50

dents have dashed off in minutes, let's gather and hold them for a time, discuss and model revision, and then return the drafts to students for refining and polishing. Let's give students realistic time frames. State legislatures may set limits on the number of hours that can be devoted to testing, thereby slicing time for revision and editing (Hillocks, 2002, p. 114). How contrary to real-world writing can you get? How many students would be hugging Harry Potter books if J. K. Rowlings' editor gave her one week per edition or demanded to print the first draft? We already know how many things students cannot do when confronted with assessment hurdles. Aren't we just the least bit curious to know what they *can* do if we set it up right?

Lesson 7: Teachers Themselves Should Lead Us

Who better? With guidance from successful professional writers, teachers can set up a writing assessment that reflects writing process, that engages students, and that measures skills we care about, such as formulating and answering significant questions through writing. Remember, the six traits did not come from any agency, research organization, or testing firm. They came from teachers. They came from *you*. When classroom teachers guide how writing assessments are administered and scored, students will not lie awake the night prior to a writing assessment, cry when they stare at a sheet of blank paper, or glaze over in bewilderment when they cannot figure out what a poorly worded prompt is asking of them. Instead, they will walk into any assessment situation, any time, any place, with the confidence that only comes from knowing that you write well enough to meet head on any assessment they can throw at you.

CHAPTER 2 IN A NUTSHELL

- Good assessment does not just happen; it requires thoughtful planning.
- Important keys to quality writing assessment include these:

  - ✔ Making the target visible
  - ✔ Constructing rubrics with care
  - ✔ Assessing what is important
  - ✔ Matching the assessment approach to the task
  - ✔ Reviewing multiple samples before drawing conclusions
  - ✔ Minimizing bias
  - ✔ Ensuring reliability and validity
  - ✔ Inviting parents to help support our instruction

- Assessment measures student proficiency; it does not change performance in and of itself. Only instruction can do that.

- Both classroom and large-scale writing assessment have some inherent problems, yet both have lessons to teach about how assessment works best.
- From large-scale assessment we learn that prompts count. The concept of "off topic" is often misapplied to writing that reflects a process of discovery. We must be very good assessors if we ask students to meet complex standards. Students need test-taking strategies.
- From classroom assessment we learn that writing process must be learned. Choosing a topic is not just a privilege—it's an art. If students are to engage in true revision, we must show them how. *Best* writing is produced under best conditions. The "hurry up and write" approach yields more stress and less quality. We must create assessments that more closely match what is demanded of real writers. And teachers themselves should lead us in this endeavor.

EXTENSIONS

1. In his eloquent book, *Testing Is Not Teaching* (2002), Donald Graves presents an alternative writing assessment plan (p. 46) in which students would have from May to September to explore personally important topics, concurrently developing a list of six or seven on which they felt qualified to write. In May, the teacher would select two items from the list, on which the student would write in a genre specified by the teacher. Compare this approach to the on-demand writing assessment most states and districts currently use. What advantages does it offer? How might it better meet a classroom teacher's vision of success? How would our view of assessment need to change to support Graves' plan?

2. Do you think of large-scale and classroom assessment as more adversarial or more mutually supportive? Write a journal entry on how each can best support the other.

3. This chapter makes a case for teachers being the driving force for shaping writing assessment in the twenty-first century. If you agree, make a list of ways in which teachers can help to bring this about.

4. List explicit writing skills today's students will need once they enter the workforce. How can our assessment support the teaching of these skills?

5. Review the eight keys to successful assessment that appear in this chapter. How many apply to your classroom, school, or district? What (very specific) changes might you make if you could?

6. Does your state currently assess writing? Using the keys to success, create a short evaluation of your state's assessment methods. How closely does it align with your vision of good writing? Discuss this with colleagues and/or write a letter to your state legislature sharing your thoughts or suggestions.

7. As a class or study group, practice writing some prompts that might be used in a district writing assessment. Analyze your list. Which ones seem strongest? Why?

8. Choose one of the prompts from the national assessment of educational progress (see pages 29–30). Try responding to it within a restricted time frame of 25 minutes or so. What conclusions can you draw from this experience?

9. On a scale of 1 to 10, how would you rate the quality of your own classroom assessment in writing from a student's or teacher's perspective?

10. Select any rubric that does not appear in this book. With a partner or group, check the rubric for horizontal and vertical integrity, referring to Figure 2.4.

WHY I WRITE

Most of all, I write to soar. To soar through the clouds of imagination, dreams and possibilities. To soar on the words of hope. I am an eagle, catching the air and rising up to greatness.

—Maegan Rowley, student writer

LOOKING AHEAD

In Chapter 3 we will look at all six traits with an introductory scoring activity that will prepare you for trait-by-trait assessment in Chapters 4, 5, and 6.

3 Coming Face to Face with the Six Traits

*T*he six traits are basically a summary of what teachers value (or look for) in writing. Therefore, whether you are introducing the traits to students, colleagues, or parents, it helps to begin with this foundational question: *What makes writing work?* A few years ago, I asked this question of fifth graders who had no previous experience with trait-based instruction. In Figure 3.1 you will see the responses I received. Notice the overwhelming emphasis on conventions—on *getting it right*. Where does this come from? Perhaps a misperception that these are the things most teachers value (some do, it's true, but not all). Or perhaps these students had been praised (by teachers *and* parents) for correct spelling, strong punctuation—even neatness. Such things are important but are not the qualities that engage readers. Have you ever in your life said to someone, "You *must* read this book. *Killer* margins"?

We need to help students think like readers by sharing text that moves them. This is what I did, reading to the fifth graders from Gary Paulsen, Louis Sachar, Mem Fox, Sandra Cisneros, and other

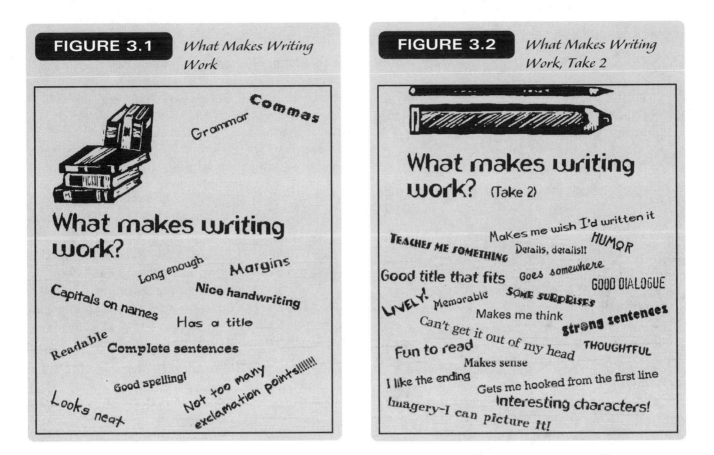

FIGURE 3.1 *What Makes Writing Work*

FIGURE 3.2 *What Makes Writing Work, Take 2*

writers with great margins (just kidding). Their concept of what makes writing work evolved within a very short time, and the initial result is what you see in Figure 3.2—comments from the same students three weeks later.

BUILDING A COMMUNITY OF WRITERS

Students need to see that they are part of a larger community of readers and writers, that what speaks to them from the page is also what speaks to teachers, and further, that what defines quality in professional writing also defines quality in student writing. There are no classes of writing. There is just writing.

Once students were happy with their list of things that make writing work, I asked if they would like to compare their thoughts with a list of things *teachers* valued. They were very eager. When I passed out six-trait rubrics written in student-friendly language (see Chapter 8 for copies), their response was, "These are the same things we said." Absolutely. Our sense of community had begun.

Responding to Writing

You cannot simply have someone talk to you about writing features such as *ideas* or *voice*. You need physical samples to fix in your mind what these concepts are about, and it helps to begin with a contrast. I like to use "The Redwoods" (a paper written by one of my own students) and "Mouse Alert," written by a middle school student I coached.

FIGURE 3.3   *The Redwoods*

Last year, we went on a vacation and we had a wonderful time. The weather was sunny and warm and there was lots to do, so we were never bored.

My parents visited friends and took pictures for their friends back home. My brother and I swam and also hiked in the woods. When we got tired of that, we just ate and had a wonderful time.

It was exciting and fun to be together as a family and to do things together. I love my family, and this is a time that I will remember for a long time. I hope we will go back again next year for more fun and an even better time than we had this year.

You could use these same papers (Figures 3.3 and 3.4) when introducing the six traits to students or to adults (colleagues, parents). Begin by copying the papers onto overhead transparencies and then (1) *reading each aloud*, (2) asking respondents to discuss each paper with a partner, and finally, (3) discussing the paper with the whole group.

Reading aloud is important. We are very visual in our response to writing, and hearing a piece causes us to assess with our ears—not just our eyes. When you read, project as much voice as the piece will allow, helping readers to interpret the writer's intended message. Don't worry that you will put in voice what isn't there. Trust me: In the end, even the finest of actors can only make a script so good.

What are *your* personal reactions to "The Redwoods" (Figure 3.3)? If you are like most readers/listeners (including that group of fifth graders), your responses probably match some of these:

✔ Boring—it put me right to sleep.
✔ Flat, empty.
✔ Safe.
✔ She was writing just to get it done.
✔ Conventions are pretty good—but otherwise. . . .
✔ It doesn't *say* anything.
✔ The organization isn't too bad.
✔ *What* Redwoods? The title doesn't go with the paper.
✔ She (he?) seems like a nice kid—I *want* to like it.
✔ It's not *that* bad for third or fourth grade—I assume that's what it is, right?

I often do *not* share the grade level of this writer until after people have had a chance to respond to the paper because it is fun to guess. Actually, the writer is an eleventh grader (this is her first piece of writing for the year). Knowing the grade level leads to some intriguing discussions about assumptions we often make as we read (including the sex and age of the writer) and why we make them. Once they know the grade level, teachers often say, "Well, for *eleventh* grade I expected more, you know? If you'd told me it was third grade, I would have felt different." But would they really? Would *you?* I agree that the conventions would be excellent if this were a third grade paper. The sentence fluency wouldn't be bad either, for it's controlled and correct, if not musical. But would it *say* more? Or could we say, "Well, for grade three, this is a powerhouse in voice." Hardly. When the voice is missing, it is just missing.

Still, as one teacher pointed out, "Look, she's in eleventh grade, and she wants to go vacationing with her family. I'd like to give her a couple points for that." Me, too. There's a likable tone to this piece that makes me want to say, "Come out of hiding. I know you have more to share." One lesson of "The Redwoods" is that sometimes there is a story buried beneath the story that we get.

I have taught college students and first graders in the same day. I can see the same qualities emerging in their work. I see detail. I see voice. I see various forms of organization.

—Barry Lane
"Quality in Writing," 1996, p. 4

Now for the contrast. I chose the paper "Mouse Alert" (Figure 3.4) as a companion to "The Redwoods" because the topic is essentially the same (family vacation), making the two papers easy to compare.

Does this sound more like the real-life vacations you recall? In place of the "wonderful time" of "The Redwoods," we learn immediately that "Nothing went the way it was supposed to." We are immediately intrigued. It is comforting to

FIGURE 3.4　*Mouse Alert*

As soon as school was out, we left on vacation. Nothing went the way it was supposed to. Dad backed into a tree on the way out of the driveway, pushing the bike rack through the rear window and nearly scaring my sister to death. She was cranky the rest of the trip. We had to take our other car, which is smaller and you can't hook the bike rack up to it. Now my sister and me were crowded together so much she kept complaining about me breathing on her and taking up all her air and foot room. Plus now Dad knew a big bill would be waiting for him when we got home. It put everyone in a lovely trip starting mood.

We were supposed to go to Yellowstone Park. Well, actually, we did but just barely. I think we hold the world's record for shortest time spent in the park. This was all due to my mother's new attitude toward animals. The night before Yellowstone we stayed in a cabin on the edge of the park. It had a lot of mice, but most of them had the good sense to stay hidden in the walls. One poor furry guy had a death wish and showed himself. The whole family went into action. My father got a broom, which looked like an oversized weapon for a mouse. My mother hugged her pink flanel nightgown around her knees, jumped up on a wood chair and started shrieking "Kill him! Kill him!" Her eyes were as big as her fists. I had never seen her quite so blood thirsty. My sister spent the whole time dancing on the bed crying her eyes out and yelling, "Don't kill it Dad! Don't kill it!" It was up to Dad and me to trap it. We got it in a pickle jar and took it down to the lake and let it go. It seemed really happy to get away from us. I thought I knew how it felt.

The next day we raced through Yellowstone and then headed home. My Mother said she had enough of animals. For weeks afterwards, this was the big story she told everyone who asked about our vacation. You'd have thought the whole point of our trip was to go on a mouse hunt. Dad said all the money we saved by not staying at Yellowstone could go to pay for the broken car window, so for him the trip worked out perfect. As for me, I'm still planning to get back to Yellowstone one day. I want to see something bigger than a mouse.

know that someone else deals with bickering siblings, poked-out windows, and mice in the walls. This writer has learned an important secret: Vacations on which all goes wrong may be miserable to live through, but they are often the stuff of good writing. Teachers' comments on "Mouse Alert" typically include these:

- ✔ I can just *see* it. I feel like I'm *in* that car. (Actually, I was once.)
- ✔ I love the line "Her eyes were as big as her fists."
- ✔ He's having a good time. (Most readers assume that the writer is male.)
- ✔ I know these people.
- ✔ Lively!
- ✔ I sympathize with Mom—I hate mice, too. "Eyes as big as fists"—*love* that.
- ✔ I like the pickle jar. I can see it, and I even smell the pickles.
- ✔ This writer is a storyteller. Erma Bombeck move over.
- ✔ Great images—love Dad backing into the tree and Mom in the nightgown.
- ✔ Lots of voice. Who *is* this kid? Can I get him next year?
- ✔ It comes full circle—great organization.
- ✔ You get every point of view in this story—even the mouse's!

Students love this paper, too. Details and voice shine. True, there are minor problems with conventions, many more than in "The Redwoods," but the text is also more complex. Moreover, we tend to be forgiving of conventional errors when we are having a good time. If the writer of "The Redwoods" made this many errors, we might not be so forgiving.

WHAT TEACHERS VALUE IN WRITING

We have seen how teachers responded to "The Redwoods" and to "Mouse Alert." Take additional teacher comments, based on responses to *many* pieces of writing, group them together by theme (trait), and Figure 3.5 is the result.

Most likely you recognize many things that *you* value on this list. Understand, though: A list, however complete, is not yet a rubric. Why not? Because it does not yet define performance at multiple levels. Put these same qualities along a performance continuum beginning level (1) to strong or proficient (5 or 6), and you have a rubric.

In this book I present four rubrics or scoring guides. The two in this chapter (see Figure 3.6 for the five-point scale and Figure 3.7 for the six-point scale) cover virtually *any* type of prose writing—narrative, expository/informational, persuasive, descriptive, and so on. The two in Chapter 11 (a five-point scale and a six-point scale) are designed specifically for use with research-based technical or professional business writing. Those rubrics take a slightly different focus, looking at such issues as thoughtful research and citation of sources, organizing for instructional effectiveness, appropriate voice for a professional audience, effective use of content-specific terminology, and so on. My suggestion is to work with one of the rubrics in this chapter *first* (five- or six-point, depending on your preference) and to use the other only if you need it. If you are not teaching research writing or technical writing, don't worry about it. Ah, but—which to choose? five- or six-point?

FIGURE 3.5   *What Teachers Value in Writing*

Ideas

It's clear—makes sense

Writer narrows topic to manageable size

Steady focus on one main message—or several key messages

Information teaches me something, holds my interest

A fresh, original perspective

Important, telling details that go beyond common knowledge

Absence of "filler" (unneeded information)

Organization

Seizes my attention with an inviting lead

Starts somewhere and goes somewhere, builds to something

Provides connections—section to section, detail to detail, beginning to end

Well paced, spending time where it matters

Like a good road map, easy to follow

Doesn't just stop—has a sense of resolution or completion

Doesn't end with "Then I woke up, and it was all a dream"

Doesn't end with a redundant, banal, or preachy summary: "Now you know the three reasons why we must all join in the war on drugs"

Voice

Sounds like a person wrote it, not a committee

Writer seems engaged, involved with topic

Sounds like *this* particular writer

Brings topic to life

Speaks to me—shows writer to reader connection

Individual—sounds like this writer and no other

Makes me respond—I laugh, smile, cry, wince, get the chills

Shows energy, life, spontaneity, confidence

Word Choice

Memorable moments—"just right" words

Words and phrases I wish I'd thought of myself

Creates word pictures

Wording is accurate, precise, and enlightening

Every word or phrase crystal clear

Strong verbs

Simple language used well

Repeats words only as necessary—or for effect

Uses language to inform or entertain—not to impress

Sentence Fluency

Easy to read aloud

Inviting, easy-on-the-ear rhythm, cadence

Carefully crafted sentences

Variety in sentence length, structure

Concise, straightforward structure in business/informational writing

Fragments used only for effect

Authentic dialogue—sounds like real people speaking

Consistency in tense (present, past, future)

Conventions and Layout

Looks clean, edited, polished—free of distracting errors

Reader does not need to do any mental editing

Conventions help reader process text

Conventions support meaning and voice

Design and presentation (as needed) draw reader's eye to key points

Avoids distracting overload of multiple fonts, hard-to-read graphics

Makes use of graphics, as appropriate, to enhance text

FIGURE 3.6   *Teachers' Five-Point Writing Guide*

TEACHER 5-POINT WRITING GUIDE

IDEAS & DEVELOPMENT

5   *The writing is clear, focused, and well-developed, with many important, intriguing details.*
- The writer is selective, avoiding trivia, and choosing details that keep readers reading.
- Details work together to clarify and expand the main.
- The writer's knowledge, experience, insight or perspective lend the piece authenticity.
- The amount of detail is just right—not skimpy, not overwhelming.

3   *The writer has made a solid beginning. It is easy to see where the piece is headed, though more expansion or clearer focus would be helpful.*
- Global information provides the big picture, making the reader long for more specifics.
- Intriguing details blend with common knowledge or generalities.
- Occasionally, the writer draws from personal knowledge/ experience.
- Occasionally, filler eats up space—or detail is too sketchy.

1   *Sketchy, loosely focused information forces the reader to make inferences. Readers may notice these problems:*
- The main message is undefined or unclear; the writing is a jumble of factlets.
- Generalities dominate; the writer does not continually fill in the blanks.
- The writing fills space, but lacks substance; the writer does not seem to have enough information from which to draw.
- Everything seems as important as everything else. What is the main message?

ORGANIZATION

5   *The order, presentation, and structure of the piece are compelling and guide the reader purposefully through the text.*
- The entire piece has a strong sense of direction and balance. Key ideas stand out.
- The structure effectively showcases ideas without dominating them.
- An inviting lead pulls the reader in; a satisfying conclusion provides a sense of closure.
- Details fit just where they are placed.
- Transitions are smooth, helpful, and natural.
- Pacing is effective; the writer knows when to linger and when to move along.

3   *The order allows the reader to move through the text without undue confusion.*
- Information is reasonably ordered; key ideas can be identified.
- The structure may be so formulaic it takes attention from ideas.
- A lead and conclusion are present, though one or both may need work.
- The reader may feel an urge to re-order or delete some information.
- Transitions are often present, but not always smoothly embedded in text.
- Pacing *usually* works with the text; sometimes the reader wishes to speed ahead or slow down to reflect.

1   *Ideas, events, or details seem loosely strung together, creating confusion. Readers may notice these problems:*
- The writing lacks a strong sense of direction and balance. Structure is missing—or so formulaic it overpowers ideas.
- No real lead sets things up; no conclusion brings the piece to closure.
- Order feels random or forced.
- Missing or unclear transitions force the reader to build bridges.
- Pacing and organization do not work in harmony.

FIGURE 3.6 *continued*

TEACHER 5-POINT WRITING GUIDE

VOICE

5 *The writer's passion for the topic drives the writing, making the text lively, expressive, and engaging.*
- The tone and flavor of the piece are well-suited to topic, purpose, and audience.
- The writing bears the clear imprint of *this* writer.
- The writer seems to know the audience and to care about their interests and informational needs.
- Narrative text is moving and honest; informational text is lively and engaging.
- This is a piece readers want to share aloud.

3 *The writing communicates in a sincere, functional manner. It has lively moments but is not passionate overall.*
- The tone and flavor of the piece are generally acceptable for topic, purpose, and audience.
- The writer has not quite found his/her voice but is experimenting.
- On occasion, the writer seems to reach out to the audience.
- Voice (in any genre) comes and goes; moments reflect enthusiasm, liveliness, spirit, individuality.
- Readers may wish to share brief passages aloud.

1 *The writer seems distanced from the audience, topic, or both. Readers may notice these problems:*
- The voice does not suit the topic, purpose, or audience.
- This writer's individual spirit is hiding behind an "anybody" voice.
- The reader has difficulty paying attention; the writer is not working to make this topic come alive for an audience.
- There is no person "at home" in the words. The reader has difficulty finding moments of liveliness or individuality.
- The writing is not yet "asking" to be shared aloud.

WORD CHOICE

5 *Precise, vivid, natural language enhances the message and paints a clear picture in the reader's mind.*
- The writer's meaning is clear throughout the piece.
- Phrasing is original—even memorable—yet the language is never overdone.
- Lively verbs lend the writing energy and power.
- Modifiers are effective and not overworked. Clichés, tired words, and jargon are avoided.
- The writer repeats words only for effect and does not overdo it.
- Striking words or phrases linger in the reader's memory.

3 *The language communicates in a routine, workable manner; it gets the job done.*
- Most words are used correctly and adequately convey the general message.
- A memorable phrase here and there leaves the reader hungry for more. *Some* passages may be overwritten.
- A strong verb or two . . . keep them coming!
- The writer may rely too heavily on modifiers—or clichés, overworked phrases, jargon. (Put the thesaurus away.)
- Some words are repeated, but it doesn't hurt the message.
- Promising words/phrases catch readers' attention.

1 *The writer struggles with a limited vocabulary, OR uses words that do not speak to the audience. Readers may notice these problems:*
- Words may be used incorrectly (*The bus impelled into the motel*).
- Vague words and phrases (*She was nice . . . The budget had impact . . .*) convey only broad, imprecise messages.
- Modifier overload—verb deficit.
- Inflated language makes text hard to penetrate.
- Repetition becomes a distraction.
- Word choice makes the message hard to grasp.

FIGURE 3.6 *continued*

TEACHER 5-POINT WRITING GUIDE

SENTENCE FLUENCY

5 *Easy flow and sentence sense make text a delight to read aloud.*
- Sentences are well-crafted, with a strong, varied structure that invites expressive oral reading.
- Striking variety in structure and length gives writing texture and interest.
- Purposeful sentence beginnings show how ideas connect.
- The writing has cadence, as if the writer hears the beat in his/her head.
- Fragments, if used, add style and punch; dialogue, if used, is natural and effective.

3 *The text hums along with a steady beat. It is fairly readable.*
- Most sentences are easy to read aloud with practice.
- Text shows some variety in sentence structure/length.
- Some sentences show purposeful beginnings (*After a while, As it turned out, On the other hand*).
- Graceful, natural phrasing intermingles with mechanical structure.
- Fragments are not always effective; dialogue does not always echo real speech.

1 *A fair interpretive reading of this text takes practice. Readers may notice these problems:*
- Irregular or unusual word patterns impair readability; it may be hard to tell where sentences begin and end.
- Repetitive patterns or choppy sentences are common.
- Endless connecting phrases (*and then, so then, because*) create long, gangly "sentences" that leave readers breathless.
- The beat feels jarring and irregular; the reader must often re-read for meaning
- Fragments seem accidental; dialogue sounds stiff/forced

CONVENTIONS

5 *The writer shows excellent control over a wide range of age-appropriate conventions, and uses them accurately—sometimes creatively—to enhance meaning.*
- Errors are so few and minor a reader could skip right over them unless searching for them.
- The text appears clean, edited, polished. It's easy to process.
- Only light touch-ups are needed before publication.
- Conventions enhance the message and voice.
- As appropriate, the writer uses layout to showcase the message.

3 *The writer shows reasonable control over widely used, grade-appropriate conventions.*
- Errors are noticeable, but the writer also handles many conventions well.
- Text is lightly edited; a little "mental editing" is needed.
- Moderate line-by-line editing is needed for publication.
- Conventional problems do not obscure the message.
- Layout is adequate.

1 *The writer demonstrates limited control even over widely used conventions. Readers notice these problems:*
- Errors are frequent and/or serious enough to be distracting, even to "forgiving" readers.
- Text does not appear edited. The reader must frequently pause, mentally edit, or re-read.
- Extensive, word-by-word editing is needed for publication.
- Conventions may obscure the message.
- Layout misdirects reader's attention or is otherwise distracting.

WAR OF THE RUBRICS

> *Many years ago, psychologists found that there is a limit to what we can hold in short-term memory and the number of criteria we can use in making absolute judgments. George A. Miller (1956) called it "the magic number 7, plus or minus 2."*
>
> **—George Hillocks, Jr.**
> *The Testing Trap: How State Writing Assessments Control Learning,* 2002, p. 6

Across the country, states and teachers are using five- *and* six-point scales (even four-point in some cases). You may be wondering what difference this makes, and curiously enough, it does not make as much as you might think. The reason for this is that virtually all scales are *conceptually* three-level scales. Each reflects a range of proficiency from beginning (lowest scores) through developing (middle scores) to strong (highest scores).

No matter how many numerical points we may put along our performance continuum, it does not change this basic concept. If we want a six-point scale, for example, we simply define the beginning-level scores as 1s and 2s, developing scores as 3s and 4s, and strong performance scores as 5s and 6s. We could even put 100 points along our continuum if we seriously believed we could distinguish between, say, a 72 and a 73.

Of course, it is ridiculous to suggest anything even approaching such precision. You'll know when you've pushed the limits. If you cannot tell a 7 from an 8 (and cannot find a sample 7 or a sample 8 to show what you mean), your points are no longer meaningful. Let's consider some advantages and limitations of various scales.

■ *Four-Point*

The four-point scale is concise and provides definitions of performance at all four levels: 4 is proficient, 3 is midlevel tending up, 2 midlevel tending down, and 1 signifies beginning performance. Although its simplicity makes it popular for large-scale assessment, I am not a fan of the four-point scale for classroom purposes. Having a limited number of descriptors can oversimplify qualitative differences in performance, and further, such a compressed scale does not allow much room for growth. The smaller the scale, clearly, the more a student writer must improve to move up even one point. Also, in my experience, many readers are reluctant to assign scores at the top of a scale ("No room left to improve") or the bottom ("No one is *that* low, surely"). As a result, most papers scored on a four-point scale receive scores of 2 or 3, turning the scale effectively into a two-point rubric—*almost made it* (3) versus *problematic but redeemable* (2). In any assessment, it is critical to use *the full scale*—or to revise it if you feel uncomfortable with that. If you find that you are almost never assigning top or bottom scores, perhaps the top as you have defined it *is* out of reach, realistically; perhaps the lower end *is* abysmal—and not (as it should be) merely an indicator of beginning performance. Given these limitations, I have chosen to focus on five- and six-point scales in this book.

■ *Five-Point*

Because performance on the five-point scale is defined in writing at only three of the five levels, the language at those levels is rich and detailed, making it extremely easy to understand what we mean by beginning, developing, and proficient within each trait. Review the five-point rubric (see Figure 3.6), and you will see at once that this is so. This detail within the descriptors makes the five-point easy to internalize for both teachers and students. This is the scale's big advantage.

Critics have two problems with the five-point scale. First, performance is not defined for the scores of 4 and 2. Personally, I do not find this troubling. The 4 and 2 are compromise scores—which will exist no matter *how* many points we put on the scale. Define the 4 in writing, and someone is sure to say, "Well, *this* paper is a 4 ½, actually—I just can't quite give it a 5." No matter how much we fine-tune, someone always wants to relegate some performances to the land of in-between.

The second criticism is that the five-point scale has a built-in midpoint "dumping ground" (score of 3)—the score we assign a performance when we are tired or have difficulty balancing out the strengths and problems in our minds. This does happen, but the problem is not as extensive as some critics would suggest. Many pieces truly *are* a balance of strengths and problems. A score of 3 is not always a cop-out; it's often real. The notion that expanding the scoring scale will reduce the number of 3s is the height of irony. The problem lies with the *writing*—not with the scale. On a six-point scale, developing samples will receive scores of 3 or 4; on a five-point scale, they will receive 3s; on our hypothetical 100-point scale, they would receive 49s, 50s, or 51s. We can pretend that these scores are different, but in reality, their interpretive meaning is the same. The only real way to change the scores is to improve our writing instruction so that our students are stronger writers in the first place. Nevertheless, if you simply must know whether the performance tends—however slightly—either up or down, an even-numbered scale is for you.

■ *Six-Point*

The six-point scale (see Figure 3.7) was developed to serve two purposes. First, it breaks out the midpoint score to a 3-4 split. A score of 3 is a midlevel score leaning down. A score of 4 is a midlevel score leaning up. I call the six-point scale the "Leaping the River" model because as you cross from 3 to 4, it's like leaping into the "land of proficiency." Remember jumping a creek as a child? Maybe you just made it, pulling yourself up by a tree branch—that's a 4, a "just barely." Or maybe your feet found no purchase, and you slipped down the muddy bank and into the water—that's a 3, "not quite."

Second, this scale provides a "place" (score of 6) to put those performances that not only meet but in many respects exceed usual expectations for grade level, performances that are striking, memorable, and worthy of sharing for instructional purposes.

The six-point scale offers two other distinct advantages: (1) it defines performance at all six levels, which many teacher/raters like (even if the descriptors are a bit more compressed), and (2) it is expansive enough to capture even relatively modest growth in writing skills. It is far easier to go from a 3 to a 4 on the six-point scale than on the four-point, and for purposes of tracking growth at the classroom level, this offers a distinct advantage.

I suggest keeping both five- and six-point scales accessible as you score papers. The five-point scale may help you to develop a more expansive understanding of each trait; the six-point scale will likely make scoring easier and faster.

FIGURE 3.7 *Teachers' Six-Point Writing Guide*

TEACHER 6-POINT WRITING GUIDE

IDEAS

6
- ☐ Clear, focused, compelling—holds reader's attention
- ☐ Striking insight, impressive knowledge of topic
- ☐ Takes reader on a journey of understanding
- ☐ Clear main idea and significant, intriguing details

5
- ☐ Clear and focused
- ☐ Reflects in-depth knowledge of topic
- ☐ Authentic, convincing info from experience/research
- ☐ Clear main idea well supported by details

4
- ☐ Clear and focused more often than not
- ☐ Writer knows topic well enough to write in broad terms
- ☐ Some new info, some common knowledge
- ☐ Main idea can be easily inferred, quality details outweigh generalities

3
- ☐ Clear, focused moments overshadowed by undeveloped, rambling text
- ☐ Writer needs greater knowledge of topic—gaps apparent
- ☐ Mostly common knowledge and best guesses
- ☐ Generalities dominate, writer has a weak grip on the main idea

2
- ☐ Writer lacks clear vision—still defining topic; key question
- ☐ Writer struggles with insufficient knowledge—writing is strained
- ☐ Broad unsupported observations, invented details
- ☐ Filler dominates—main idea wanders in and out of focus

1
- ☐ Very foggy—no "land in sight" yet
- ☐ Main idea never emerges due to writer's lack of knowledge
- ☐ Hastily assembled notes, random thoughts
- ☐ Bits of info wander in search of a main idea

ORGANIZATION

6
- ☐ Thoughtful structure guides reader through text like a bright beacon.
- ☐ Provocative opening—enlightening conclusion
- ☐ Smooth, well-crafted transitions give whole piece cohesion
- ☐ Structure enhances reader's understanding/enjoyment of the piece

5
- ☐ Purposeful organization draws attention to key ideas
- ☐ Strong lead—conclusion that provides closure
- ☐ Thoughtful transitions clearly connect ideas
- ☐ Structure helps reader track/process ideas

4
- ☐ Organization works in harmony with ideas
- ☐ Functional lead and conclusion
- ☐ Helpful transitions often suggest connections
- ☐ Structure helpful, but often predictable

3
- ☐ Reader must be attentive—organization loose, or out of synch with ideas
- ☐ Lead and/or conclusion need work
- ☐ Transitions sometimes missing or formulaic
- ☐ Structure relies too much on formula—or necessitates re-reading

2
- ☐ Hard to follow, even with effort—a faint light in the distance
- ☐ Lead and/or conclusion missing or formulaic, minimally helpful
- ☐ Transitions often unclear or missing
- ☐ Significant re-organization needed—reader often baffled

1
- ☐ Lights out—path is dark.
- ☐ Stars right in (no lead)—just stops (no conclusion)
- ☐ Transitions missing—perhaps points *aren't* connected
- ☐ Disjointed collection of details/thoughts—no structure

FIGURE 3.7 *continued*

TEACHER 6-POINT WRITING GUIDE

VOICE

6
- As individual as fingerprints
- *Begs* to be read aloud—reader can't wait to share it
- Uses voice as tool to enhance meaning
- Passionate, vibrant, electric, compelling

5
- Original—definitely distinctive
- A good "read aloud" candidate
- Voice appealing and well-suited to topic/audience
- Spontaneous, lively, expressive, enthusiastic

4
- Sparks of individuality
- Reader might share a line or two
- Voice fades at times—acceptable for topic/audience
- Pleasant, sincere, emerging, earnest

3
- Voice emerges sporadically—not strong or distinctive
- A "share-aloud" moment
- Voice often distant, not always directed to audience
- Quiet, subdued, restrained, inconsistent

2
- Writer seems to be in hiding
- A *hint* of voice—text not ready for sharing
- Voice faint—OR, not right for audience, purpose
- Distant, encyclopedic—OR inappropriately informal

1
- No sense of person behind words—is anyone *home?*
- Reader feels no invitation to share text aloud
- No apparent engagement with topic, concern for audience
- Voice . . . just . . . missing . . .

WORD CHOICE

6
- Everyday language used in original ways
- You want to read it more than once—quotable
- Every word carries its own weight
- Powerful, stunning verbs, unique phrasing
- Words invoke sensory impressions, create vivid images

5
- Natural language used well
- Engaging—when you start reading, you cannot stop
- Concise, clear
- Strong verbs, striking phrasing
- Words appeal to senses, create clear images

4
- Functional, clear language used correctly
- Easy to understand, some eye-catching phrases
- Vague words (*fun, nice*) or wordiness—meaning still clear, though
- Some strong verbs—modifiers may be overworked
- Strong moments outweigh clichés, over-written text

3
- Generally clear but imprecise language—"first thoughts"
- Now and then, a "gem" amidst the agates
- Vague words or wordiness water down the message
- Overused modifiers/weak verbs outnumber strong moments
- Reader may encounter clichés, or overwritten text (writing to impress)

2
- Overworked language, words used incorrectly, or thesaurus overload
- Have to search hard for "gems"
- Word choice and wordiness *cloud* the message, leave reader confused
- Adjective avalanche—where are the *verbs?*
- Reader must work hard even for general meaning

1
- Words chosen at random—something to fill the page
- Apparent struggle to get words on paper
- Message buried
- Language not functional
- Words do not speak to reader

FIGURE 3.7 *continued*

TEACHER 6-POINT WRITING GUIDE

SENTENCE FLUENCY

6
- ☐ Easy to read with inflection that brings out voice
- ☐ Dances along like a lively script
- ☐ Stunning variety in style, length
- ☐ Fragments effective, dialogue authentic/dramatic/performable

5
- ☐ Can be read with expression
- ☐ Easy going rhythm, flow, cadence
- ☐ Significant variety in style, length
- ☐ Fragments add emphasis, dialogue authentic

4
- ☐ Natural phrasing—easy to read
- ☐ Rhythmic flow dominates—a few awkward moments
- ☐ Some variety in style, length
- ☐ Fragments not a problem, dialogue natural

3
- ☐ Mechanical but readable
- ☐ Gangly, tangly, never-ending or chop-chop-choppy text common
- ☐ Repetitive beginnings, little variety in length
- ☐ Fragments (if used) do not work, dialogue (if used) a little stiff

2
- ☐ You can read it if you're patient—*and* you rehearse
- ☐ Many run-ons, choppy sentences, non-sentences, or other problems
- ☐ Minimal variety in style, length
- ☐ Fragments (if used) are oversights, dialogue hard to perform

1
- ☐ Hard to read, even with effort
- ☐ Missing words, awkward moments, irregular structure
- ☐ Hard to judge variety—hard to tell where sentences begin
- ☐ Fragments (if used) impair readability, dialogue hard to read

CONVENTIONS

6
- ☐ Only the pickiest editors will spot errors
- ☐ Thoroughly edited—conventions enhance meaning, voice
- ☐ Complexity of text showcases wide range of conventions
- ☐ Enticing layout (*optional*)
- ☐ Virtually ready to publish

5
- ☐ Minor errors that are easily overlooked
- ☐ Edited—conventions support meaning, voice
- ☐ Sufficient complexity reflects skill in numerous conventions
- ☐ Pleasing layout (*optional*)
- ☐ Ready to publish with light touch-ups

4
- ☐ Noticeable errors—message still clear
- ☐ Edited for general readability
- ☐ Shows control over basics (e.g., cap's, end punctuation)
- ☐ Acceptable layout (*optional*)
- ☐ Good once-over needed prior to publication

3
- ☐ Noticeable, distracting errors—may slow reading, affect message
- ☐ Erratic editing—many things missed
- ☐ Problems even with basic conventions
- ☐ More attention to layout needed (*optional*)
- ☐ Thorough, careful editing needed prior to publication

2
- ☐ Frequent, distracting errors get in way of message
- ☐ Minimal editing—if any
- ☐ Numerous errors even on basics
- ☐ Limited attention to layout (*optional*)
- ☐ Line-by-line editing needed prior to publication

1
- ☐ Serious, frequent errors make reading a real effort
- ☐ Lack of editing leaves even patient readers struggling
- ☐ Errors on basics obscure meaning, put up road blocks
- ☐ No apparent attention to layout (*optional*)
- ☐ Word-by-word editing needed prior to publication

Throughout this book I will share suggested scores based on both scales, but precise scores are much less important than your overall sense of whether a paper is at a beginning (1–2), developing (3–4), or strong (5–6) level and *why*. When you teach the traits to students, you likely will find that they love to score papers and to compare their scores with those of other students, but keep your eye always on what is most important: (1) conversation about writing, (2) a growing sense of shared values that creates a community of writers, and (3) your students' growing repertoire of lessons learned based on the papers you read and share.

GETTING READY TO SCORE PAPERS

Our earlier assessment of "The Redwoods" and "Mouse Alert" focused on general personal responses. This time we'll put scores on the papers using the five- or six-point rubrics (your choice—I will give you scores on both).

Print out both papers and the rubrics so that you can see them easily and write on them. Then score both "The Redwoods" and "Mouse Alert" on *all six traits*. Don't worry about getting the "right answer." Ask yourself whether each paper is *strong* or *in need of revision* on a particular trait, *then* zero in on the specific score that seems most appropriate. This practice will acquaint you with all the traits and make the focused scoring of each individual trait in Chapters 4, 5, and 6 much easier. If possible, work with a partner so that you can discuss each paper throughout your practice. Commit your scores to paper *before* looking at the suggested scores that follow.

If you are working with a group, you can record your scores on a hard copy or overhead of the scoring grid master in Figure 3.8. Simply write, in the appropriate box, the number of people who give a paper each possible score, e.g., how many 6s in ideas, how many 5s, how many 4s, and so on.

Keeping a record of scores gives you a good basis for discussion. If your personal scores differ markedly and repeatedly from those of others in your group and from those suggested in this book, it is quite possible you are either (1) not sufficiently familiar with the scoring guide to use it consistently or (2) influenced by elements other than the traits of writing (such as topic choice). I'll touch on causes of rater bias in a minute. For now, let's consider recommended scores for these two introductory papers. Suggested scores on the five-point rubric appear first, followed by those for the six-point rubric. This general format is used throughout this book. *Be sure you score both papers before going on.*

SUGGESTED SCORES AND COMMENTS
"The Redwoods" (Grade 11, Narrative)

Ideas: 2, 3 (a 2 on the five-point scale and 3 on the six-point scale)

Organization: 3, 4

Voice: 1, 2

Word choice: 2, 3

Sentence fluency: 3, 4

Conventions: 4, 4

FIGURE 3.8 *Scoring Grid Master*

Scoring Sheet
6-Point Scale*

	Ideas	Organization	Voice	Word Choice	Sentence Fluency	Conventions
6						
5						
4						
3						
2						
1						

* Can be used with 5-Point scale also.

■ *Lessons Learned from This Paper*

✔ Conventions alone will not carry the day.
✔ Don't be afraid to let the "buried" story out!
✔ Voice dies without details.
✔ Tell the truth.

■ *Comments*

This paper is classic in its total restraint. It's safe and impersonal. The writer is barely here. It communicates, but only on the most general level. There's a moment—just a *moment*—of voice: "I love my family, and this is a time I will remember for a long time." It's as if the writer wants to move in for a chat but can't quite bring herself to do it. The language is masterfully vague, and there is a significant lack of involvement in the topic. What about this "wonderful time"? *How* was it wonderful? What is the brother really like? Comical? Pesky? Rude? What happened on this trip to delight, surprise, annoy, or captivate this writer? Imagine making a film of this paper: *Redwoods, the Movie. Could* you? Not without fleshing out ideas and characters. It's a "greeting card" essay—bright and cheery, nothing too deep. Conventions are clean but extremely simple for eleventh grade (hence the slightly lower scores on that trait).

"Mouse Alert" (Grade 7, Narrative)

Ideas: 5, 6

Organization: 5, 6

Voice: 5, 6

Word choice: 4, 4

Sentence fluency: 5, 5

Conventions: 3, 4

■ Lessons Learned from This Paper

✔ Writing "small" (focusing on the mouse incident) works better than telling everything (Imagine "My Trip to Yellowstone").

✔ Readers do not expect (or want) your family to be perfect; real people are more interesting.

✔ Sensory details put the reader at the scene.

■ Comments

This story is deliciously crammed with tiny acts of everyday heroism. Nothing much goes right, but everything from Dad backing into the tree to the mouse hunt, the big release, and the race through Yellowstone is extraordinarily visual (you *could* make a movie of this, with Chevy Chase or Steve Martin as Dad) and a tribute to the pitfalls of planning. These people are extremely human—unlike the people in "The Redwoods." They argue. They worry over money, mice, and who gets enough air in the car. We can picture Mom in her nightgown and smell the aroma of the pickle jar. Readers are often sorry this piece is so short, and that is about the best compliment you can give a writer. Conventions need work, yes, but we tend to forgive these problems because we're enjoying the ride, and this writer will find a professional editor one day.

MAKING YOUR SCORING CONSISTENT

Before extending our scoring practice trait by trait (in Chapters 4, 5, and 6), let me offer some tips to make your assessment even more consistent and efficient.

1. Remember—There Is No "Right" Score

All the student papers in this book have been scored by experienced teachers/raters. Their suggested scores *should not be considered the "correct"*

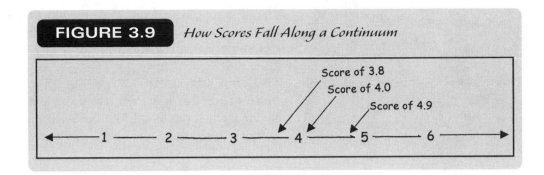

FIGURE 3.9   *How Scores Fall Along a Continuum*

Score of 3.8
Score of 4.0
Score of 4.9

1 ——— 2 ——— 3 ——— 4 ——→ 5 ——— 6

scores. There is no such thing. They are *suggestions* and cannot be more. The goal is to come up with a *defensible* score, one based on thorough reading of the paper and analysis of the rubric—never on personal bias or casual observation.

If you disagree by one point on a given score, you can still consider that agreement. On a continuum, remember, a high 3, let's say, and a low 4 would actually be quite close (see Figure 3.9).

2. Refer to the Scoring Guide Often

Once you have chosen a scoring guide (five- or six-point), read it through thoroughly, like a recipe that you don't know well yet; don't skim. Print out a copy so that you can write on it and highlight phrases that speak to you. Make it your own. Don't try to memorize it, though. You'll be surprised how quickly it will feel as comfortable and familiar to you as your name and address. (*Tip:* Score one paper a day for 30 days, recording scores for all six traits each time, and you'll find that at the end of that time, you are both fast and consistent.)

3. Find the Balance

Scoring with a rubric is a balancing act: strengths versus problems. Where does the paper fall? Ask this question first: Do strengths outweigh problems, or vice versa? Then you'll have a good notion of just where to place a paper along the continuum.

4. Score Each Trait Separately

Just because a paper is a 6 in ideas, that's not a guarantee that it will be a 6 in voice—or conventions. Individual scores create a kind of performance profile richer than any single score. Further, a student may receive very different "profiles" on different pieces of writing, and this can be a good way to show growth over time, in a portfolio, for example.

5. Remember That a Score of 1 Indicates Beginning Performance, Not Failure

Notice that the language, even at beginning levels of performance (scores of 1), is fairly positive. It identifies problems clearly but avoids accusatory phrases such as "poor performance." When you give a score of 1, you are saying to the student, in effect, "You have made a beginning. You put something on paper, and you get a point for that. Now we'll build from there."

Descriptors such as *excellent* or *poor* indicate a fundamental misunderstanding of how writing works. It does not start out "bad" and suddenly become "good." It begins as a seed and grows to reveal the writer's thinking.

6. Remember That a Score of 5 or 6 Represents Strength and Proficiency, Not Perfection

If you feel that a performance is strong, let your score show that. Papers that receive 5s and 6s are not all alike. Some are hilarious, and some are profoundly moving or well-researched. If you feel that a paper has strength, go for the gusto; don't wait for that mythical "better" paper that still waits round the bend. You can give another 5 or 6 tomorrow.

7. Take Your Time

Beginning raters worry about time, and so often rush through the paper and spend time going through the rubric, agonizing over whether to give a 2 or 3. Don't do this. Spend your time *reading the paper.* Get inside the writer's thinking. Pay attention to details. Notice how it begins and ends. When you turn to the rubric, the "right" score will jump out at you.

8. Consider Grade Level, But Don't Make It the Factor

Do consider grade level as you score, but be careful not to overweight it. Voice is still voice, whether it appears in the work of an 8-year-old or of someone 16 or 42. Some expectations do change slightly, yes. For instance, more knowledge of conventions is expected of a middle or high school student than of an elementary student. We also expect a more highly developed vocabulary. A given quality—say, voice—remains constant across grade levels. What changes, with experience and sophistication, is the writer's control over that quality. An eleventh grader may have consistently strong voice throughout a piece of writing, for example; a second grader may lack that consistency and control but still have spontaneous moments when her voice rivals that of any other writer.

9. Don't Overweight Mode Either

Do *not* worry about mode (narrative, expository, etc.) for now. The six-trait scale you are using will work equally well with most prose samples (poetry is a little different), and part of my reason for including a variety is to demonstrate that. An exception is more formal research writing or technical writing. (See Chapter 11 for informational rubrics and papers.)

10. Respect Your Own Individuality

You should look for patterns in the way you respond to student writing (*I'm always high on voice; I'm always a point lower on conventions*), and take steps to make your responses as consistent and reflective of the true quality within students' work as possible.

Do not expect to agree with our recommendations on *every single score*, however. As readers, we are individuals after all, and we respond differently to *all* writing, not just student writing. Not everyone loves *Lonesome Dove* or *Seabiscuit*. Some readers find Hawthorne tedious and Joyce convoluted or wish that Melville would come to the point. If we cannot agree on popular literature and classics, it stands to reason that we will see and hear some differences in students' work. Never mind. Your goal should be understanding the traits (knowing what you're looking for). Over time, given sufficient discussion and an open-minded approach by everyone, you will find yourself agreeing with colleagues on *most* pieces of work *most* of the time. More important, you'll know the six traits well enough to teach them.

11. Watch Out for Rater Bias

Many little things can get in the way of scoring fairly or appropriately. Here are a few pitfalls to watch out for, whether in large-scale assessment or in the classroom. Did any of these affect your scoring of "The Redwoods" or "Mouse Alert"?

■ The Positive–Negative Leniency Error

This technical-sounding term means a tendency to be too hard (or too easy) on everyone as a matter of principle. We've all known the teacher who cannot bear to give anything but an A—or the one who is holding As in reserve for that special student he or she hopes to meet one day. Good scoring shouldn't be about the rater's attitude or philosophy of life.

■ The Trait Error

This is a tendency to lend too much weight to one trait (e.g., conventions) while ignoring others. Research cited by Brian Huot (1990) shows that readers do not always know what trait they are responding to as they read; they may *think* they are scoring organization, for example, when in fact it is the voice of the piece or the conventions to which they are reacting.

■ Appearance

We may find ourselves irritated by messy or tiny handwriting, especially when we're tired. But poor handwriting, while often annoying, is not the same thing as weak voice, unsupported ideas, or faulty conventions and should not influence trait-based scores. Similarly, neat, word-processed copy, while more attractive than

> In the past 30 years, researchers and theorists have come to know that teaching writing entails teaching thinking.
>
> **—George Hillocks, Jr.**
> *The Testing Trap: How State Writing Assessments Control Learning*, 2002, p. 6

scribbles and cross-outs, should not rescue weak, unsupported ideas. Writing is thinking on paper and should be scored accordingly, cosmetics aside.

■ *Length*

Is longer better? We might like to think so. This is another one of those traits that is easy to assess because it's easy to see. In fact, though, many students who write well for one or two pages have enormous difficulty sustaining the flow. They just run out of juice. Furthermore, ability to condense is often a virtue; it may give voice just the boot it needs.

■ *Fatigue*

This is an occupational hazard for teachers. The trick is to pace yourself so that you are not scoring dozens of papers in a row without at least a stretch break. It makes more difference than you might think.

■ *Personal Preferences*

So you love football? Hate cats? Vice versa? These little quirks and preferences can and do get in the way of fair scoring. In large-scale assessment, you can ask another rater to score the paper. In the classroom, you usually do not have that option, but you can occasionally ask for a second opinion, just to be sure that you are not overreacting.

■ *Preconceptions*

Preconceived notions about the writer can trip us up as well. Researcher and writer Paul Diederich (1974) discovered that raters actually scored the very same essays higher when told they had been written by honors English students. We might ask ourselves, *How often do similar expectations influence our assessments within the classroom?*

■ *Repetition Factor*

You can grow weary of crashing waves, roaring surf, or screeching gulls after 500 papers or so. An open topic—"Memorable Place" versus "My Trip to the Beach"—encourages more individuality by giving writers room to breathe. But what if it's too late, and both you and your students are already victims of a troublesome prompt? Don't despair. Reward those writers who manage to personalize the topic. Later, consider the suffocating nature of the prompt as you interpret scores. In the classroom, of course, you can abandon the assignment and start fresh.

■ *Skimming*

Some readers think that they can tell after the first few lines whether a paper will be strong or not. Rarely is this true. A strong lead may disintegrate into generalities; a slow start may explode into a burst of inspiration on page two. To score fairly, read the whole thing.

■ *Self-Scoring*

Are you a perceptive reader? If so, be careful that you score the work of the writer and not your own talent in deciphering the hidden message.

■ *Sympathy Score*

It is possible to write about, say, the death of a pet in a way that is touching and heart-wrenching or in a way that is factual and fairly emotion-free. We cannot expect students to know the difference unless we respond honestly. Assessment is response to the writing, not the event itself. If you feel uncomfortable with that, it may be that a given piece is too personal to make assessment appropriate; offer your heartfelt response without grades or numbers.

■ *Vulgar Language*

How do you respond to vulgar language in student writing? To profanity? To extreme violence? Some people have a very ho-hum attitude; others are readily offended. This is not a question others can really resolve for you; it's too personal, and responses are too varied.

My position usually has been this: If the language works in context and is not used simply to distract or shock the reader, I assess the work as I would any piece of literature. Profanity is part of the landscape in a narrative on war; it may seem jolting, cumbersome, or self-conscious in a persuasive essay on school locker searches. The question (for me) is not really about violence or profanity per se but about whether the writing works and whether the language is appropriate for the context and intended audience.

> The plot may be filled with blood and guts, but it's fine writing that keeps the audience rapt: it's exquisitely constructed sentences; it's carefully honed cadences; it's the marvelous satisfaction of the sensual rhythm of perfect prose.
>
> **—Mem Fox**
> *Radical Reflections*, 1993, p. 54

Pet Peeves

Everyone has a pet peeve. Some of us have many. The trick is to know what they are so that they will not trap you into assessing unfairly. Do you recognize any of your own in this teacher-generated list?

✔ *Big, loopy writing*
✔ *Teeny-tiny writing*
✔ Writing that fills the whole page, leaving no margins
✔ Commas or periods outside quotation marks
✔ Shifting tenses without reason and then going back again
✔ Writing in all capital letters
✔ Mixing *it's* and *its*
✔ Mixing *their, there,* and *they're* when we've just finished a unit on it
✔ Mixing *are, hour,* and *our*—They don't even *sound* alike, do they?
✔ *Goes* for *said,* as in *So he goes, "Let's dance." And I go, "Yeah, cool."*
✔ Endless connectives: *and, but then, but, because, so now, and so* . . .
✔ The words *ugh, yuck, awesome, neat, rad, dude, guy, great, hot, humongous, in the zone,* and *cool* (I use it myself but still hate it in print)
✔ Missing words—Didn't the writer notice?

✔ Writing just to fill the page with no substance, no heart, and no reader either if I had a choice

✔ Empty words used to snow the reader: *"She was obliterated by her compassion for nostalgic memories"*

✔ *The end* (as if I would look for more)

✔ Backhand that tips so far it looks tired

✔ Writing that is too light (*Burn* all no. 3 pencils!)

✔ The phrase *"You know what I mean"*—I can't tell if it's more annoying when I do know or when I don't

✔ The cop-out ending: *"Then I woke up, and it was all a dream"*

✔ *A lot*—If you can have "alot," what's wrong with "alittle"?

✔ *Alright*—It just looks "alwrong"

✔ Adjectives that are clichés: *fluffy* clouds, *clear, blue* skies

✔ A total absence of paragraphs

✔ No punctuation at all—like taking down the traffic signs

✔ Repeating a word or phrase every few lines

✔ The phrase *"between you and I"*

✔ *"Me and him"* or *"Her and me"* as the subject of a sentence

✔ Exclamation points after every breathless line!!!!

Keep a list of your own pet peeves. Share it openly with your students. It can teach us all a little about the way we respond to writing. Then use your awareness of good scoring practice to extend your skill with the papers in Chapters 4, 5, and 6.

CHAPTER 3 IN A NUTSHELL

● The question "What makes writing work?" underlies the search for the six traits and is a good place to begin teaching them.

● Contrast (as seen in "The Redwoods" and "Mouse Alert") is important in teaching writing and provokes discussion of those qualities that define strong writing.

● Ask your students what makes writing work, and they are likely to come up with the same qualities as teachers; then they "own" the traits, too.

● While four-, five-, and six-point scales all offer certain advantages, this book encourages use of a five- or six-point scale in the classroom, where it is important to show growth.

● Many factors, including the length of a paper or the topic, can trigger bias. Knowing what causes bias minimizes its effects.

● Teaching yourself the traits *first* paves the way for you to teach them to students through scoring, discussion, and focused lessons.

 ## EXTENSIONS

1. Ask yourself or your group the question, "What makes writing work?" How do your responses compare with the list of things teachers value in writing (Figure 3.5)?

2. In *Embracing Contraries*, Peter Elbow (1986) describes research conducted by Alan Purves (1992), in which it is shown that readers make more accurate and reliable judgments about the features of student writing if, while making them, they're also asked to

give a quick account of "their subjective responses or feelings" (p. 230). Giving voice to a personal response, Elbow hypothesizes, may allow a reader-rater to be more "objective" in scoring or grading. Do you agree? Why would this be true? Write a journal entry about this.

3. Make an individual or group list of your own pet peeves. Compare it with the list in this chapter.

4. Expand your scoring skills by assessing writing not

generated by students. You might look at a company's annual report, a driver's manual, a textbook, a how-to manual for assembling or using any product, an advertisement, a public relations letter or brochure, a complaint letter, a lease agreement—or any other writing that's part of your life. Compare your scores with those of students or colleagues.

5. Be daring. Create a piece of your own writing to assess with your group—anonymously. (It needs to be word-processed, clearly.) Ask the group to comment on the two strongest traits and to share one recommendation for revision. See if their assessment matches yours.

6. If you are currently teaching, assess a paper by one of your students on all six traits using both five- and six-point scales. Compare the scores and the difficulty of using each. Which scale do you prefer? Why?

WHY I WRITE

I write because I like hearing the river of words flow like the ocean, so smooth and graceful. I like to read it over and over until the words ask me to stop.

Ryan Sterner, student writer

LOOKING AHEAD

Now that you are acquainted with all six traits, we can take a deeper look at each of them, beginning with the foundational traits: ideas and organization. In Chapter 4 we'll practice scoring more papers for these two key traits. Chapter 5 looks at voice, word choice, and sentence fluency, and Chapter 6 looks at conventions and presentation.

4 Building a Foundation
Ideas and Organization

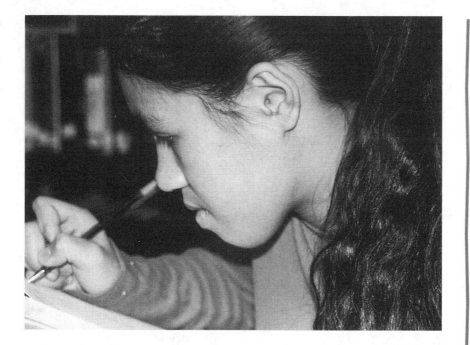

This cannot be stated bluntly
enough: The writer must have
something to say.
                              —Ralph Fletcher
                  What a Writer Needs, 1993, p. 151

An effective piece of writing says
one dominant thing. As Kurt
Vonnegut, Jr., says, "Don't put
anything in a story that does not
advance the action." The same thing
can be said for argument, memo,
technical writing or poetry. Every
element in the text supports and
advances the main point. Planning
starts with the search for that
dominant meaning.
                              —Donald M. Murray
                  A Writer Teaches Writing, 2004, p. 18

The order in which traits are presented in this book is deliberate—and important. I suggest that you teach them in order because one builds on another. Ideas and organization are foundational. The need to write, the itch to write, begins with a story to tell, a point to make, an argument to put forth, a descriptive picture to paint—ideas that shift and change and grow with the act of writing. That act, the writing process, is driven and shaped by questions: "Where do I begin? What do I say first—and next, and after that? How do I bring it all to resolution?" These are the questions of organization. Of course, organization is flexible and grows to accommodate the ideas. As Donald Murray (2004, p. 18) says, "The writer does not arrive at the final destination before taking the trip," so while it helps to imagine what that destination might be, unanticipated side excursions often enrich the journey. So we begin here with the foundation. This chapter has two purposes:

1. To give you a chance to teach the traits of ideas and organization to yourself first by assessing, discussing, and reflecting on student work.

2. To discover papers that you can share with your students as you teach them these same traits.

IDEAS: THE HEART OF IT ALL
Focus for Assessing and Teaching Ideas

✔ Discovering a personally important topic
✔ Making the message clear and interesting to a reader
✔ Staying focused
✔ Expanding and clarifying the idea with significant details
✔ Tossing out what does not matter (the deadwood)

It is helpful to know the focus of instruction for each trait because this will determine in part which papers you select for scoring or to use as models in your classroom. We'll begin with two pieces selected especially for practice scoring in ideas. Then we'll look at two papers selected for practice scoring in organization. This trait-by-trait approach is very useful when you introduce the traits to students.

Note that although this practice is focused, the papers selected for inclusion in this chapter are scored for all six traits. This is important because I want you to keep the bigger picture in your mind as we go, even though I will introduce one trait at a time (just as you will when you teach the six traits to your students). In addition, remember that in teaching, you can use papers to teach more than one trait. For example, a paper I have selected for ideas may seem just right to you for voice, word choice, or whatever, so you may wish to refer to these scores down the road.

PRACTICE PAPERS
What To Do

✔ Be sure that you have a printed copy of the scoring guide in front of you.
✔ Have a copy of the scoring grid (Figure 3.8) if you are working with a group.
✔ Make copies of papers if you wish to write on them.
✔ Make overheads of the papers if you wish to share them aloud.
✔ Read each paper aloud prior to scoring.
✔ Score papers using a five- or six-point rubric.
✔ Discuss your scores and the reasons for them with a partner or group.
✔ Check your scores against the suggested scores provided in this book.
✔ Consider the "Lessons Learned" for each paper.

Tips on Scoring Papers for the Trait of Ideas

A good writer never tells everything but seeks those details that put us right at the scene. The writing becomes real, and we are absorbed into it effortlessly. Consider this passage from Walter Dean Myers' book *Slam* (1996), in which the main character describes the sounds of the city:

GETTING A MINDSET

Ideas are the heart of the writer's message—which may take any of several forms—story, argument, informational summary, and so on. All other traits *take their cue* from this foundational trait and work in harmony to ensure that the message from writer to reader is clear and intriguing.

> When it's late night you hear the sound of car doors and people talking and boom boxes spilling out the latest tunes. When it rains the tires hiss on the street and when there's a real rain with the wind blowing sometimes you can hear it against the tin sign over Billy's bicycle shop. If there's a fight you hear the voices rising and catching each other up. The sound of broken glass can cut through other noises, even if it's just a bottle of wine somebody dropped. And behind all the other sounds there's always the sirens, bringing their bad news from far off and making you hold your breath until they pass so you know it ain't any of your people who's getting arrested or being taken to the hospital. *[p. 2]*

It isn't the amount of detail that counts, but how vivid it is. As Grant Wiggins (1992) reminds us, "too many essay scoring systems reward students for including merely more arguments or examples; quantity is not quality, and we teach a bad lesson by such scoring practices" (p. 30).

Paper 1: "Making Decisions" (Expository, Grade 8)

FIGURE 4.1
Paper 1:
"Making Decisions"

When making a decision, take your time and not rush into a hasty conclusion. Clarify the decision you are making. Be sure you understand all aspects of your decision, without confusion. Reason out the consequences your decision will effect. Question whether the concluding effects will be positive or negative.

Before proceeding ahead with any decision making process, devise other alternatives, if any, noticing who and what may be effected. Be sure to ask others for their opinion on the subject. Keep in mind, however, that their opinion may not be correct or even helpful. Quality decision making depends on facts, not opinions. Eventually, your decision will have an impact on other things. These impacts cannot always be foreseen. Take your time in determining which impacts are most effected, and be careful in the end.

■ *Suggested Scores for Focus Trait: Ideas*

Ideas: 1–2, 2 (a 1–2 split on the five-point scale, 2 on the six-point scale)

■ *Lessons Learned from Paper 1*

✔ Generalities weaken ideas.
✔ Specific examples (in this case, a decision with good or bad results) are a must.

■ *Comments*

This paper doesn't sound half bad when you skim it, does it? It seems to say something. The problem is, it's a compilation of generalizations and platitudes.

No people populate this paper. It is sterile. The strengths of the piece (compare the text of any inflated political speech) are fluency and conventions. While it says virtually nothing, it flows smoothly enough to come across as authoritative. The language is sophisticated but imprecise: "Take your time in determining which impacts are most effected." This probably means "Take time to figure out how your decision will affect your life." That revision is clear—but still general. Think how different this paper would be if the writer had chosen one difficult decision (say, leaving home or giving up drugs) and given us possible outcomes; then the writer might have gotten more involved, and so might we.

■ *Suggested Scores for Other Traits*

Organization: 1, 2
Voice: 2, 2
Word choice: 2, 2
Sentence fluency: 4, 4
Conventions: 4, 4

Paper 2: "Harder Than You Think" (Personal Essay, Grade 10)

FIGURE 4.2
Paper 2:
"Harder Than You Think"

I walk up the hill with my friends, turn into our cul-de-sac, go to the front door, put the key in the lock, turn, and step in. The house breathes a kind of spooky hello as I set my books down and go to the kitchen where the inevitable note is waiting: "Have a snack. Be home soon. I love you." As I'm munching cookies, I think how I'd like to go out and shoot a few hoops if I had someone to do it with. You can play Nintendo by yourself, but it isn't the same. So I forget that for now. I should be doing my Spanish homework anyway. Too bad I don't have an older brother or sister to help conjugate all those dumb verbs. I could call a friend, sure, but if I had a brother or sister, I'd have a built-in friend.

continued

While I'm feeling so sorry for myself, I hear my friends Kelly and Kyle across the street. She's screaming bloody murder because he is throwing leaves in her hair and threatening to put a beetle in her backpack. She has just stepped on his new Nikes. I do not have these squabbles. I guess the big advantage, if you call it that, to being an only child is my room is my own. Nobody "borrows" my CDs or my books or clothes. I also get a bigger allowance than I probably would if I had siblings. My parents take me everywhere, from the mall to the East Coast. Maybe they wouldn't if they had other kids. (On the other hand, it would be more fun going if I had someone my own age.)

All these great advantages are overshadowed by one big disadvantage, though, and it's the main reason I would change things if I could. When you are an only child, your parents depend on you to be the big success all the time. You are their big hope, so you cannot fail. You have to be good at sports, popular, and have good grades. You need a career goal. You have to have neat hair and clothes that look pressed. You have to have good grammar, clean socks, good breath, and table manners. If you've ever felt jealous of somebody who is an only child, don't. It's a lot of pressure. I often wish for a little screw-up brother my parents could worry about for a while.

So—while having a neat room with nothing disturbed is great, I'd take a brother or sister in a minute if I could. The big irony is, if I had that mythical brother or sister, I would probably be wishing myself an only child again the first time my baseball shirt didn't come back or my stereo got broken. Life is like that. What you don't have always seems to be the thing you want.

■ *Suggested Scores for Focus Trait: Ideas*

Ideas: 5, 5 (a 5 on the five-point scale, 5 on the six-point scale)

■ *Lessons Learned from Paper 2*

✔ Beginning with an anecdote or image sets the scene.
✔ Multiple examples make an argument convincing.

■ *Comments*

I like this paper. It's authentic. The writer uses two contrasting examples—the neighbor children squabbling and his own home life—to make some key points about how peaceful yet rather lonely it can be to go through life as an only child. The examples are realistic, and the writer seems to have thought through what he has to say. The opening paints a clear picture of life as an only child; some readers feel that it could be condensed. The ending is even stronger, and it makes an important point, too—without being redundant. The voice, a definite presence in paragraphs 1 and 2, springs to life in paragraph 3, bolstered by precise, original ideas. This is a fluent, well-edited, readable piece.

■ *Suggested Scores for Other Traits*

Organization: 5, 5

Voice: 5, 5

Word choice: 4, 5

Sentence fluency: 4, 5

Conventions: 5, 6

ORGANIZATION: SHOWCASING IT
Focus for Assessing and Teaching Organization

✔ Writing a crackerjack lead
✔ Staying *on the path* (not wandering from the message)
✔ Showcasing information with a pattern or structure that fits
✔ Using transitions to link ideas
✔ Pacing the piece, spending time where it matters
✔ Wrapping it up with a thoughtful conclusion

PRACTICE PAPERS
What To Do

✔ Follow the same directions given for *ideas*—this time making sure that you have the scoring guide for *organization* in front of you.

GETTING A MINDSET

How do ideas and organization differ? Imagine that you are designing a display window for a department store. What you put into the window represents your *ideas*. How you arrange it is your *organization*. Organization is an evolutionary trait. It wraps itself around the ideas as they grow and change, just as your skin wraps around you. Take something out of your window display, and you cannot just leave a hole there. You rearrange so that no one notices. Got a new item to display? You make space. Good organization is similarly quiet and unobtrusive. Without drawing attention to itself, it makes ideas shine. Notice that organization can take many forms depending on the message: small ideas to main points in an argument, step by step in a recipe, and chronological with flashbacks in a memoir or mystery.

Tips on Scoring Papers for the Trait of Organization

Organization should be solid but subtle. We don't want to be hit over the head ("*My first point. . . . Next I'll explain. . . . Now, for the third step. . . . Having considered all three reasons. . . .*"), but we want the comfort of knowing that the writer knows where he or she is headed. Look for a powerful lead that truly sets up the piece and tells you that this writer has a sense of direction. Look for an insightful conclusion that shows that the writer made some discoveries and is hoping that you did, too. In addition, good writing should follow a pattern—however flexible. Like a roadmap, that organizational pattern gives the reader a clear main path that makes the writing (even with surprise twists) easy to follow. Notice how author Jeffrey Eugenides (2003) guides the reader's eye in this description of the new family car from his Pulitzer Prize–winning novel *Middlesex:*

> Not a spaceship then, but close: a 1967 Cadillac Fleetwood, as intergalactic a car as Detroit ever produced. (The moon shot was only a year away.) It was as black as space itself and shaped like a rocket lying on its side. The long front end came to a point, like a nose cone, and from there the craft stretched back along the driveway in a long, beautiful, ominously perfect shape. There was a silver, multi-chambered grille, as though to filter stardust. Chrome piping, like the housing for circuitry, led from conical yellow turn signals along the rounded sides of the car, all the way to the rear, where the vehicle flared propulsively into jet fins and rocket boosters [p. 253].

Good writing is writing by design. Ask, "Can I follow this with ease? Is the writer lighting the path for me?"

Paper 3: "Some Cartoons Are Violent!" (Persuasive, Grade 3)

FIGURE 4.3

Paper 3: "Some Cartoons Are Violent!"

> Some cartoons are violent. And sometimes ther not! Some ar just funny like Tinny Tunes but some aren't. Take loony Tunes wich is violent but ther not all violent. They could be both. I wach cartoons alot and some are violent. Thers boms that get thrown down in som cartoons. and blows them up. But me I like cartoons some of the time. never will I stop waching but well more are violent than the loony toons. but if I were to mak a cartoon myself I would have well mabe just 1 mane violent thing and then just keep the rest funny OK?

■ Suggested Scores for Focus Trait: Organization

Organization: 1–2, 2 (a 1–2 split on the five-point scale, 2 on the six-point scale)

■ Lessons Learned from Paper 3

✔ Choose a side before trying to persuade others.
✔ Organization is very difficult when the main idea is unclear.

■ *Comments*

The questions of how much violence is too much and whether violence has redeeming social or artistic value continue to plague television and film executives, so we should not be too surprised that this question proved challenging to a third grader. Nevertheless, this young writer takes an exuberant stab at the prompt she is dealt. She sticks with the main theme—violence—but has a very hard time choosing sides. Her thinking goes something like this: A little violence in cartoons is entertaining; too much could be a bad thing (for reasons not fully explored)—but won't hurt me because I know it's phony! What this piece lacks in persuasive logic and organization (it's almost humorously random), it makes up for in voice. The writer is clearly speaking to an audience and invites us to share her to-and-fro thinking. By the end of the essay she is negotiating for position: How about just one violent episode per cartoon and keep the rest funny—what do you say? Had she begun here (the point to which her thinking led her), both ideas and organization would have been stronger.

■ *Suggested Scores for Other Traits*

Ideas: 2, 2
Voice: 4, 4–5
Word choice: 3, 3
Sentence fluency: 3–4, 4
Conventions: 2, 2

Paper 4: "The Baseball" (Narrative, Grade 5)

FIGURE 4.4
Paper 4:
"The Baseball"

I remember the day I got it well. It was an everyday type day until the doorbell rang. I got up to awnser it. But my sister beat me to it, as usual. It was dad's friend Tom. He got back from a New York yankes baseball fantasy camp a couple weeks ago. I said hi to him and he asked me if I knew who Micky Mantel was. I said of corse I do. At that point I was a little confused. Thenhe haded me a baseball. It wasen't the kind of baseball we use in little luege. It was nicer than that. Made of real leather. It even smelled like leather. Like the smell of a new leather jacket. And the seems were hand stitched too. I turned it around in my hand then I saw it. I saw a Micky Mantel aughtograph. I coulden't believe it. I had an aughtograph in ink of one of the greatest baseball players of all time. Wow. I teushered it ever since that everyday type day that changed at the ring of a doorbell.

■ *Suggested Scores for Focus Trait: Organization*

Organization: 5, 6 (a 5 on the five-point scale, 6 on the six-point scale)

> *"If in the first chapter you say that a gun hung on the wall," Chekhov said, "in the second or third chapter it must without fail be discharged."*
>
> **—Playwright Anton Chekhov, quoted in Ralph Fletcher**
> *What a Writer Needs, 1993, p.51*

■ Lessons Learned from Paper 4

✔ Readers pay attention to leads and conclusions.
✔ Only bring it up (e.g., Mickey Mantle) if it matters.

■ Comments

Small moments make the best stories, as this writer shows us so well in his tale of the "everyday type day that changed at the ring of a doorbell." Notice how the story comes full circle, beginning with the doorbell and returning to it at the end, when it's even more powerful because now we know its importance. Throughout, ideas drive the organization, which is why the piece works so well. You have to respect a writer who, even as a fifth grader, is so careful with his details. There is a reason behind everything. Consider the question about Mickey Mantle. It's not a throw-away detail; it matters. The writer does not understand why the question is important at first, and neither do we, but all becomes clear by the end of the story. Notice the moment of revelation: *"I turned it around in my hand then I saw it. I saw a Micky Mantel aughtograph."* Good organization thrives on high points.

■ Suggested Scores for Other Traits

Ideas: 5, 6
Voice: 5, 6
Word choice: 4, 4
Sentence fluency: 4, 4
Conventions: 2, 2

LOOKING AT ADDITIONAL PAPERS

In the remainder of this chapter we will consider 11 additional papers, this time focusing scoring practice on two traits, *ideas* and *organization*. (Scores for all traits are given, but the practice will focus on these two.) This will enable you to see how the two traits work together (and begin to think about how they interact with other writing traits as well). Follow the same format and procedures; but this time give each paper two scores. Check your responses against the recommended scores.

Paper 5: "Unscripted Television: Enjoy It While You Can" (Persuasive, Middle School)

FIGURE 4.5
Paper 5: "Unscripted Television: Enjoy It While You Can"

After several decades of sitcoms, news shows, detective and adventure shows, legal dramas and all the rest, most Americans feel they can predict the outcome of just about anything on television after five minutes. You can't always predict who gets voted off "Survivor" or who the American Idol will be, though. Sometimes it's refreshing not to know the ending. Reality TV should really be called "unscripted" TV since this is the factor that makes it different and (for now, anyway) appealing. We love it right now, but will it have a lasting impact? I doubt it. Does anything on television? We remember it, sure. People remember Bob Hope and Milton Berle and "I Love Lucy," but can we honestly say we know people who try to be like them?

For now, I think the only thing we can say for sure is that unscripted television is a reflection of our culture. Reality TV shows tend to show a lot of gossip and intrigue. They show people scheming to outdo or outwit one another for money. This isn't very attractive, maybe, but it's a little naïve to say that reality TV is bad for us, when in fact, it only shows who we are. Reality shows often feature hosts that push people into dangerous or humiliating situations (which frankly, most of them seem to enjoy or else they enjoy whining about it), and sometimes people on the shows are very rude, too. Will this teach Americans to be rude? Get real. We're already rude. Have you driven on a freeway lately? It could help us actually to get this dose of "reality." Maybe it will make us think more about how we ARE in our real lives and how we should be.

Unscripted TV is mostly about entertainment, though, not about character building or enlightenment. When people watch a show like "Survivor," they don't necessarily think they are like the person on the show or that they should be like that person. What they do is wonder what they would do in the same situation. They like to compare themselves. Would I be that low? Would I betray my friend? Would I dare to do that stunt? This is no different from watching "Jeopardy" and asking yourself the questions the contestants have to answer. It's just more about personality and ethics on "Survivor" and not so much about knowledge. (By the way, people on "Jeopardy" are trying to bump each other off just like the contestants on "Survivor." They just use their knowledge to do it instead of winning challenges or telling lies. Does this really make them more noble? Their motives are just the same and they are just as money-hungry.)

Reality shows (unscripted shows) are entertaining because they let us ask ourselves what we would do in the same situation. This doesn't influence us to be a certain way, but it does let us look at ourselves to see who we are. Maybe people in the twenty-first century just find themselves more fascinating than they find made-up stories about predictable, boring characters' lives. When it comes to entertainment, however, Americans are very unpredictable, too. Nothing lasts forever, even "Seinfeld." So when it comes to reality TV, there might be one "survivor," and the rest will disappear, like most TV shows. Being the last survivor does not necessarily make you the best, however. Look at the cockroach.

■ *Suggested Scores for Focus Traits: Ideas and Organization*

Ideas: 5, 6
Organization: 4, 5

■ *Lessons Learned from Paper 5*

✔ It is possible to have more than one key point—if you can keep all the balls in the air.
✔ Connecting with the reader (Have you driven on a freeway lately?) is a useful strategy.

■ *Comments*

The main point of this paper is that reality television is unlikely to have any lasting impact on American culture. As part of this discussion, however, the writer makes some other intriguing points as well: Reality television is actually unscripted television; it's appealing because we do not know what will happen next; it's a reflection of our culture; and it isn't bad for us because we're already rude and wretched. I had no problem following this discussion, although some readers feel that it jumps from point to point. I simply felt that the writer had a lot of related points to make (it's a complex paper), but you may agree with the slightly lower organization scores. The point about contestants on "Jeopardy" being as ruthless as those on reality shows is well made and reinforces the idea that we watch television in part to see who we are. Virtually everyone likes the ending, and by the last paragraph, voice is in full swing.

■ *Suggested Scores for Other Traits*

Voice: 5, 6
Word choice: 4, 5
Sentence fluency: 5, 6
Conventions: 5, 6

Paper 6: "Einstein" (Expository, Grade 5)

FIGURE 4.6
Paper 6: "Einstein"

Who lived about 100 years ago? Who made great mathematical theories and ecuations? Albert Einstein, one of the greatest scientists who ever lived! Of course, all scientists are great, but Albert was special. He could look at the smallest thing, study it for hours, and see things others would just miss! He had an eye for detail, and he was never bored. Ever. Even when he was all alone!

What kind of family do you think a genius would have? Not much different from yours or mine, actually. Alberts' parents didn't even know for a long time that he had a great mind. They worried about him because he was alone so much. He liked staring at the stars for hours on end instead of playing with other kids. They didn't think this was normal. They worried that he didn't like to play war games. Instead he would just sit with his blocks and work them into different shapes for hours! What kind of kid was this? finally, when Albert's father realized he was a genius, he felt very proud.

You would think a genius like Albert einstein would love school. Wrong! he hated it! the only classes he liked were math and physics. Albert was so good at math he had to go to a special school to take classes. His math and physics teachers inspired him to become a great scientist.

Albert invented many math theories, but he is most famous for the theory of relativity, which people find fascinating even though they do not understand it. Albert also invented two bombs: the hydragen bomb and the adom bomb.

Einstein made a difference in the world because of his great math theories and his many ecuations. Even though Einstein is dead now, teachers are still teaching his theories. Who knows? People could still be teaching them right on years after you and I are dead, too.

Suggested Scores for Focus Traits: Ideas and Organization

Ideas: 3–4, 4
Organization: 4, 4

Lessons Learned from Paper 6

✔ Small details (Albert staring at the stars) add interest.
✔ Gather enough information before writing.

Comments

Although this piece is not a powerhouse, it has a kind of quirky appeal. The picture of Einstein as a child offers a fresh, interesting spin on a popular biography. Who knows? Maybe Albert's parents *did* fret over his less than social side. Of course, there must be more to the story, and that is the problem here: What's done is fairly good, but details are sketchy for a life story. The lead and conclusion work reasonably well; this writer needs only a good punch line—a significant moment, turning point, or spectacular surprise—to bring the organizational structure of the piece together. One other problem plagues the piece (as it does many assigned topics); namely, the writer seems to find Einstein mildly interesting but not quite fascinating. One moment of true joyful discovery could have boosted this piece from pleasantly engaging to riveting. All the same, voice ("What kind of kid was this?") is the strength. Given the right topic, this curious writer will fly.

■ *Suggested Scores for Other Traits*

Voice: 4–5, 5

Word choice: 3–4, 4

Sentence fluency: 3–4, 4

Conventions: 3, 3

Paper 7: "On Writing" (Memoir, Grade 12)

FIGURE 4.7

Paper 7: "On Writing"

I have been born with a soul that craves cascading ink over paper, and it is the nearly painful joy I feel with pen in hand that drives this desire that seems to have been with me before speech, before thought, before existence. Who I am is shaped by what I write; all that I pen down merely a reflection of my imagination, of those thoughts that run rampant through my mind hour after hour, day after day.

I have been writing since I was a child; small stories with hugely fantastical settings, epics, dramas, diaries, poems, songs. For years the clutter in my room has been growing with the addition of my hasty unfinished works of art, as precious to me as if from the mouths of those certified genius' of the writing world—my Roald Dahl, my Jane Austen, my Victor Hugo.

Writing is solace for my soul; words seem to enrich the otherwise dull monotony of everyday life and add depth to the world not discernible on the surface. From reading my first child's book while still learning to speak, words have always been my fascination, my weakness and my treasure. I spun my first yarn at age six, which evolved into a room filled with ideas scrawled on scratch paper and notebooks bulging at the seams with stories begun before I can remember. I wrote on napkins, I would read at the dinner table—still do. I rummage almost daily through my mom's purse in a vain search for a pen and Kleenex to scribble the lyrics to a song lest they fade and wither before they are recorded. Sudden bursts of inspiration always come at the worst possible times; Trig class, the car, two A.M. on a school night; but they always find their way into my hand, arms, notebook, or clothing. They are pieces of me, and as long as they are recorded, protected, I am still whole. But if I lose that napkin, that flyaway piece of fiction or song lyric, I feel as though part of me has been irrevocably lost, that the foundation of my life has one less stone, that the walls of my castle aren't burnished as brightly, or shining as vibrantly.

And yet what I wrote was never revealed. The world never knew the girl frantically writing stories in her free time, letting pieces of her soul slip into her words as she read and reread and laughed and lived. So many works went unfinished, not for lack of inspiration but for lack of dedication. Nobody but me saw, nobody but me cared.

I don't remember the exact day I discovered the Internet, when I sat stunned in my chair, realizing there was a place where people could read what I wrote, see what I saw. But I do remember how I worked, how the idea of opening my heart to the world changed me as I diligently collected my starving dimmed ideas from the recesses of my mind and dusted them off until gleaming and bright. And I remember how I wrote, and wished, and waited.

After several hours suffering in suspense, holding my breath in anticipation, I read my first review and found myself nearly crying. They liked it! People liked me! Though only one name among the thousands of authors whose dreams and eagerly beating hearts crave to edify the world, I cling to my reviews, to the knowledge that someone out there has taken hold of a piece of my soul and perhaps, just perhaps, waits breathlessly for more.

■ *Suggested Scores for Focus Traits: Ideas and Organization*

Ideas: 5, 6
Organization: 5, 6

■ *Lessons Learned from Paper 7*

✔ A strong sense of purpose drives organization.
✔ Take it easy—don't overwrite.

■ *Comments*

This piece is extremely clear and easy to follow. The organizational pattern is deeply embedded and goes something like this: I was born a writer; I loved words even as a child; I must write—even on Kleenex; for years, no one knew I was a writer; then came the Internet; I was discovered—and it was magic. Terrific. This writer is at her best when she allows her own natural language to take over: *"words have always been my fascination, my weakness, and my treasure"* or *"I wrote, and wished, and waited."* At times, she is pushing harder than she needs to (her natural voice is so strong that it doesn't need an energy boost), and the result is a little gushy and breathless: *"lest they fade and wither"* or *"my starving, dimmed ideas."* Once the cake is frosted, best to leave it alone. This writer, if we can get her to throttle back a bit, truly will burn up the Internet with her writer's voice. Outstanding conventions and fluency. A reader.

- ## Suggested Scores for Other Traits

Voice: 4, 5

Word choice: 4, 5

Sentence fluency: 5, 6

Conventions: 5, 6

Paper 8: "A Great Book" (Literary Analysis, Grade 8)

FIGURE 4.8
Paper 8:
"A Great Book"

There are many themes in To Kill a Mockingbird. Three of the themes that stand out are fairness, justice and courage. These themes are widely spread throughout the book. Harper Lee helps explain these themes through her characters and the way she writes about them.

Fairness is one of the many interesting themes in this great book. The main character Atticus shows the importance of fairness by the way he tries to treat others. Other characters demonstrate fairness as well.

Respect is another important theme of the book, though not as frequent as some of the other themes. Atticus shows respect for his community and for Tom Robinson, and they respect him as well. This is one of the main themes throughout the book.

Courage is a very important theme in this book. Jem shows courage in several parts of the book. Atticus shows courage by defending Tom in the trial.

These three themes of courage, fairness and justice are important parts of this book just as they are important to our society.

- ## Suggested Scores for Focus Traits: Ideas and Organization

Ideas: 2, 2

Organization: 3, 3

- ## Lessons Learned from Paper 8

✔ Organization can be too predictable.
✔ Organization without content is hollow.
✔ Literary analysis demands quotations and/or characters "in action."

- ## Comments

Here's a cheery but lightweight analysis of Harper Lee's novel, *To Kill a Mockingbird*. The paper is fluent, pleasant, and noncontroversial. It says virtually nothing except that, apparently, there are some "themes in this great book." This is a handy approach because this report can now be used for other books, too—*Moby-Dick, The Great Gatsby,* or really, any book having themes.

Oddly enough, the organization is stronger than the content only because the writer presents points in an orderly fashion, skipping right along, never pondering, reflecting, or enlightening us for a moment. Where are the specifics, the examples, the quotations? We want to picture Atticus thundering away in the courtroom or see Scout reaching out to Boo Radley. The organization is not driven by the content, however; the opposite is true, and this is why the piece lacks punch. It's a fill-in-the-blank paper. The voice is not daring, revealing, or personal. It's distant, almost a dust-jacket voice, except that we're tempted to ask (Don't say you didn't think of it), "Did you actually *read* the book?" Language is generic and redundant: "Jem shows courage in several parts of the book." Which parts? How? Did you notice that the "great themes" started out as fairness, justice, and courage but shifted to fairness, *respect,* and courage?

■ Suggested Scores for Other Traits

Voice: 2, 2
Word choice: 2–3, 3
Sentence fluency: 3–4, 4
Conventions: 4, 4

Paper 9: "Writing Is Important" (Expository, Grade 11)

FIGURE 4.9
Paper 9:
"Writing Is Important"

Writing is important. It allows you to express your thoughts but also your feelings. through writing you provide entertainment and information which is useful to others. Writing is both useful and enjoyable. it helps you explore ideas and issues you might not think of otherwise. If you are going to write, you will need plenty of information.

Writing well means knowing what you are talking about. This takes research and information. If you do not know enough about your topic, your reader will not be convinced. It also means putting feelings into your paper. no one wants to read something where the writer sounds bored and like they wish they were doing something else. it can take courage to say what you really think and feel but it is worth it. You will get your audiences attention.

third, keep your writing simple if you want it to be affective. Trying to impress people with big long super complicated sentenes and five dollar words does not work. They might just decide reading your writing is not worth the time and trouble it takes. So keep it simple if you want to have an audience.

the most important advice of all is to write about what you know about the best. If you are a good auto mechanic for instence maybe you should write about cars or if you have a summer job at the veteranian's office,

continued

you could write stories about the animals you treat. If you try to write what you do not know it will be obvious to your audience and they will not believe in you. Use what you know and use your experiences from everyday life

writeing is important in all occupations. Today, it is more true than ever before. If you do not believe it just ask around. Everyone from doctors and dentists to garage mechanics and salesmen have to write as part of their job. But the most important reason is because writeing is a way of sharing the ideas that belong to you. If you work on your writeing skills, It just might help you in ways you have not even throught of.

■ Suggested Scores for Focus Traits: Ideas and Organization

Ideas: 4, 4
Organization: 2, 3

■ Lessons Learned from Paper 9

✔ Writing about two things at once makes a piece hard to follow.
✔ A good ending sometimes makes the best beginning.
✔ If you shift focus, toss the reader a transition.

■ Comments

Despite some banal truisms, this writer makes some insightful points, but they need to be ordered, expanded, and set up better. The writer is trying to tell us two things, really: Everyone writes, making it an important skill (see the final paragraph), and several things (knowing your topic, keeping it simple, having the courage to say what you think) are key in writing well. These ideas could easily be connected with thoughtful transitions, but that hasn't happened as yet. The lead is stiff (the writer is still warming up); the conclusion is far stronger and could be bumped right up front. It sets the stage for why writing well is important in the first place. The voice comes and goes, and word choice is fairly routine. There's nothing really wrong, but the writer does not snap us to attention either. Many sentences are short and choppy, which breaks the flow and creates the impression that the thinking is simplistic, too—which it is not. Careful reading could correct many small problems with conventions.

■ Suggested Scores for Other Traits

Voice: 3–4, 4
Word choice: 3, 4
Sentence fluency: 3–4, 4
Conventions: 2–3, 3

Paper 10: "Under the Knife" (Expository, Grade 12)

FIGURE 4.10
Paper 10: "Under the Knife"

Nip, tuck, trim, suck, lift, stitch, and peel. These words describe what we know as cosmetic surgery. Cosmetic or plastic surgery has over the years been tainted with the idea that it is purely vanity surgery for those of the rich and famous. But today it has evolved into much more.

Throughout the country people, in particularly women have been obsessed with the way they look. Women want to be more professional, young, and lively in order to compete with men in the work place, often times going to the extreme to get what they want.

Then there is the fashion media on TV, in books, magazines, stores and on the internet. Images of fake plastic smiles and Barbie figures are paraded in front of us, telling us in an unspoken language, this is what we should look like. This will make you happy. But is this really true? I tend to disagree.

No matter the motive the fact still remains that plastic surgery is an increasing trend in today's society that needs to be closely monitored. I don't know of one person that is completely satisfied with the way they look. Does your bust size really determine your amount of happiness and quality of life? No, it should not but does that mean cosmetic surgery is wrong? No.

Everyone is responsible to take care of their own body. So you exercise and diet correctly and everything should be under control. Some people may still not be satisfied and that's okay, as long as your health comes first. With any surgery you must look at the risks involved and weigh your choices wisely. Breast implants for example are dangerous and could cause severe problems such as poisoning or even death. This is not a wise decision. Obesity is dangerous to your health, therefore liposuction or stapling your stomach might be your best option when exercise and dieting fail.

I believe that improving the way we look is always a good thing. But as with everything moderation is the key. Cosmetic Surgery is not a cure all. You have to like who you are on the inside first, than look at the outside and see what you can improve. If you're not happy with yourself when you go under the knife, chances are you won't be happy with your self when you come to. Looking good on the outside may improve your self esteem but not your self worth.

So what makes you a happy person, how do you improve your quality of life? By a use of many different means. Be healthy; surround yourself with things that make you happy. Don't look to the knife to make you happy, rather look at it as a means of self improvement. Everyone is an individual work of art; make it reflect the you inside.

- ## Suggested Scores for Focus Traits: Ideas and Organization

    Ideas: 4, 4

    Organization: 4, 4

- ## Lessons Learned from Paper 10

✔ Trying to round up too many ideas—even if they're related—makes organization challenging.

✔ A clearly expressed thesis can help to keep your reader on track.

- ## Comments

This piece is about a draft away from achieving its potential. It has a strong title, lead, and conclusion. The voice is evolving and shows much promise. The problem is, it's hard to get a grip on what the writer thinks: Cosmetic surgery has a reputation as pure vanity surgery, women are obsessed with looks and so may take risks, the media are not helping, and surgery won't make you happy—yet "improving the way we look is always a good thing," and we should look at cosmetic surgery "as a means of self-improvement." We wind up feeling a bit confused. The writer *does* tell us that moderation is the key; perhaps this is a place to begin. She may be saying that surgery isn't a good recourse except when the need is extreme. I like the ending—"Everyone is an individual work of art." But if that's so, why do we need surgery? A better-defined thesis, clearly expressed, will give this "almost there" piece the strong sense of direction it needs—organization, voice, word choice, and fluency will all come along for the ride.

- ## Suggested Scores for Other Traits

    Voice: 4, 4

    Word choice: 3, 4

    Sentence fluency: 3, 4

    Conventions: 4, 5

Paper 11: "Reading Is Fun" (Personal Essay, Grade 7)

FIGURE 4.11

Paper 11: "Reading Is Fun."

My parents have tried many times before, but I just stunk at reading. It took me many tries, many weeks, many months to learn to read.

It was a challenge to learn to read, but now I can do it. I first had to learn my ABC's. But it just wasn't the ABC's, I had to learn the different sounds each letter made. This felt like it took me years to do. After I learned the ABC's, I learned how to say a couple letters together to make small words like is, up, on, go, and it. I was so happy I learned how to do this. The first word I ever learned to read was, "go." After I learned this word I finally knew I could read. I wouldn't really call it reading though, more like t-t-t ummmmm h-h-h, oh yah th, th-e oh yah the. Eventually I could read larger words, but it took some time.

I am now in the seventh grade. At the beginning of this year I didn't like reading at all. Now at the end of the year I like reading again. I think I like reading now because I only read books I'm interested in, and if I don't like a book I'm reading I just quit. My teacher Marie suggested this to me. This advice has really kept me interested in reading.

Reading is a great thing. In my situation my whole family, except my younger siblings, helped me learn to read. Reading is fun and can also bring your whole family together.

■ *Suggested Scores for Focus Traits: Ideas and Organization*

Ideas: 4, 4
Organization: 3, 4

■ *Lessons Learned from Paper 11*

✔ Don't end with a generality.
✔ Honesty makes for strong voice—every time.

■ *Comments*

The title is a fooler. This paper has real impact—and it comes right out of the writer's honest portrayal of his struggles learning to read. He dissects the journey very clearly from the ABC's to sounds, to combining letters, and to that deceptively simple word *the*. Notice how he takes it apart first from the nonreader's perspective; that gives us some insight. I love Marie. Many people never learn the joy of moving on to another book. The final paragraph falls back on generalities. This is too bad because we know that this writer is doing something interesting with reading or writing that could make a powerful finish. Reading *is* a great thing, but his piece has already told us that. A closing scenario or reference to a specific book or conversation would really stand this paper on edge. A different title might get our attention, too.

■ *Suggested Scores for Other Traits*

Voice: 4, 4
Word choice; 3, 3
Sentence fluency: 4, 5
Conventions: 4, 5

Paper 12: "Tobacco" (Persuasive, Grade 7)

FIGURE 4.12
Paper 12:
"Tobacco"

Tobacco. Jeez, it's just one simple word. You wouldn't think that it could harm lives like it does. People chew it, it's in cigarettes so they smoke it, and it can even kill them.

Pretend I had a friend named Jim, and Jim smoked cigarettes. Well being Jim's best friend, I feel that I should do something about it. My next stop would be to go talk to his parents. Now Jim has his parents on his back, and he knows it's because of his best friend. Jim becomes really upset and angry. Jim comes up and talks to me, and says he doesn't want to be my friend anymore; he has no idea I probably just saved his life in the future.

Time goes by, Jim and I grow up, and Jim is still puffing away at these cigarettes and chewing tobacco. All of a sudden Jim gets lung cancer, and dies a few weeks later. God, what kind of a choice was that? Instead of listening to his best friend, who was always there for him and always had advice for him, he decides to go smoke and use drugs and tobacco and cigarettes like this. Why? Why would you cut loose your best friend, the closest thing you've got, because you believe you're cool because you smoke, when you don't realize you're not cool, because smoking ruins lives, it takes away the future, and your lungs just give out. Now what's so cool about dying, it might be said to be the next great adventure, but you die anyway, so why now. Live life at the fullest, that's what's cool, the adventure can wait.

Don't ruin your life by drugs and crap like this. It's not a good decision. No one wants to die; you must be crazy if you do. Stay away from cigarettes, tobacco, drugs, and alcohol. You only have one life so make the right choice.

■ *Suggested Scores for Focus Traits: Ideas and Organization*

Ideas: 3, 4
Organization: 3, 4

■ *Lessons Learned from Paper 12*

✔ If you begin with a good example, follow through.
✔ Don't get in a rush—make sure each sentence stands alone.

■ *Comments*

This piece has strong voice—and some problems with fluency, notably in the third paragraph. The writer clearly believes in the message and is eager for us to believe it. The beginning and ending are fairly strong and command attention. In addition, the introduction of hypothetical Jim is a good touch, but we just get engaged in the story when Jim dies—"all of a sudden." Paragraph 3 then dissolves into generalities about smoking—it seems "cool," but it's "not cool"—we should "live life to the fullest" because "that's what's cool." The clauses pile up like cordwood here, and the writer seems in a hurry to finish. The introduction of Jim was a good device because it allowed the writer a simple and natural way to explore the conflict between the appeal of smoking and the potential danger. Once Jim leaves, the writer resorts to platitudes, and the argument loses force. The language communicates on a general level. Despite some missing punctuation, conventions are reasonably strong.

■ Suggested Scores for Other Traits

Voice: 4, 5
Word choice: 3, 4
Sentence fluency: 2, 3
Conventions: 4, 5

Paper 13: "The Funeral of My OREO" (Narrative, Grade 4)

FIGURE 4.13
Paper 13: "The Funeral of My OREO"

I look at my pray, drooling, like a tiger looking at an antelope in the wet forests of India. I pounce. "Natalie," my weird brother announces his presence "be nice." I look regretfully at the hurt OREO. I had snuck a poor OREO from the vet hospital while my dog had an appointment.

I am about to tell you of the steps with which I dissect my OREO. I let it suffer slowly. I do this by, so very carefully, lifting off the top cookie so the frosting is saved.

Then, I nibble on the chocolate cookie. I do this like a mouse until it's gone. I then clean the chocolate off my face.

After that, I start to eat the rest of the cookie. I start by taking tiny bites. After I chew about a millimeter away, I eat the cookie in bigger bites.

Finally, I finish. But there's only one problem . . . I now have a whole lot of chocolate crumbs spread all over the table! The tiger in me sweeps the remains of its prey out of the den with a broom and curls up on the couch until the time comes to devour yet another OREO!

■ Suggested Scores for Focus Traits: Ideas and Organization

Ideas: 4, 5
Organization: 5, 6

■ *Lessons Learned from Paper 13*

✔ One metaphor at a time.
✔ Let paragraphs reflect your organization.

■ *Comments*

Adopting the persona of the tiger hunting its prey is very effective—as is the interchange with the "weird" brother that snaps the writer (temporarily) back to reality. Unfortunately, the writer forgets herself briefly and turns into a mouse in paragraphs 3 and 4 (this is what lowered the ideas scores). She's back to her tiger self in the final paragraph, and a good thing too, or we'd miss the predatory sweeping of the crumbs. The tiger metaphor gives this piece plenty of voice, and the notion of a cookie as prey is irresistible. Word choice is very strong: *drooling, announces his presence, look regretfully, let it suffer, dissect, nibble, sweeps, devour.* Too many sentences begin with *I*, but this is a relatively simple thing to remedy. Conventions are strong.

■ *Suggested Scores for Other Traits*

Voice: 5, 6
Word choice: 5, 6
Sentence fluency: 3, 4
Conventions: 5, 6

Paper 14: "Computing Batting Averages" (Expository, Grade 6)

FIGURE 4.14
Paper 14: "Computing Batting Averages"

Math is all around us in almost everything we do. Math is involved in banking, shopping, the weather, the national economy and just about every thing we do. It is hard to think of even one thing that doesn't use math in one way or another.

You wouldn't think math would be such a big part of sports but it is. Take baseball for example. In baseball people use math for many things. One example is figuring out batting averages. This is important because when players see how well they are doing, they have a way to improve. How would players improve if they didn't know how well they are doing.

A batting average is really like a percentage. To find out your batting average, all you need are two numbers: how many times you are up and how many times you hit safely (meaning that you get at least to first base on a hit). Then you need to divide the number of times you hit safely by the total number of times you are up to bat.

Here is an example of a batting average. Lets say you are up 50 times and hit safely 25 of those times. Your batting average would look like this: 25/50. You would have a batting average of .500, which is pretty good. Suppose you hit safely every time you were up. Your batting average would then be 50/50, or 1.000—which is pronounced "one thousand". This were we get the famous saying "batting a thousand." Of course, nobody could ever bat this well in real life.

With the use of batting averages it is easy to set goals for yourself and see how well you are doing. A good batting average for a pro ball player is somewhere between .300 and .400. The all time record is held by Ted Williams, who batted .410.

My best batting average was in the summer of 1998, when I averaged .370. Maybe it was me, or maybe it was the pitching!

Think about your own life for a minute and you'll be surprised what a big role math plays.

■ Suggested Scores for Focus Traits: Ideas and Organization

Ideas: 4, 4
Organization: 3, 4

■ Lessons Learned from Paper 14

✔ Sometimes your paper starts with the second paragraph.
✔ You may not need that last line.

■ Comments

This paper is flanked by generalities that hurt the forcefulness of the whole piece. You don't always have to link your little point to a larger world view. Let it go. Readers will make their own connections. The explanation of how to compute batting averages is clear and easy to follow. The voice is pleasant and reasonably engaging, although the piece is not quite a read-aloud yet. Or is it? Cut the beginning and ending, and what's left has more voice. Excellent conventions. And I'm told that the true average for Ted Williams is .425. Details, details.

■ Suggested Scores for Other Traits

Voice: 3, 4
Word choice: 4, 4
Sentence fluency: 4, 4
Conventions: 5, 6

Paper 15: "Cats or Dogs" (Persuasive, Grade 6)

FIGURE 4.15

Paper 15: "Cats or Dogs"

Cats or dogs, that is the question. My opinion is I like both. Cats are one of the most groomed animals in the world. Dogs are one of the most loyal. There are just some problems about both.

I really like cats because they are so clean. They always like to clean there selve's a lot. Most cats are very well mannered and they love people. They are also very fast. I have a cat, kind of. They really like string.

I also like dogs. They can run real fast to. I really like dogs because they can jump real high and catch a Frisbee. They can also do a lot of tricks like swimming.

There are some problems with both. I wish I could have both but it can't happen. Dogs just like to chase cats. Cats cough up fur balls. Dogs bark and eat lots of weird stuff. Now you see the reasons I like both. I really like cats. Dogs I really like to but there are some problems. I just can't decide.

■ *Suggested Scores for Focus Traits: Ideas and Organization*

Ideas: 3, 4
Organization: 2, 2

■ *Lessons Learned from Paper 15*

✔ Comparison papers need to be set up carefully.
✔ "I just can't decide" makes an ineffective ending.

■ *Comments*

This paper has some good points to make: Cats are clean and well-groomed; they are well-mannered and love people. Dogs can run, jump, and catch things (so they are fun to play with), and they make loyal pets. Each has problems: Cats "cough up fur balls," whereas dogs "eat lots of weird stuff." Two things keep ideas and organization from working well. First, the writer refers to the problems in paragraph 1, raising our expectations, but does not get to them until much later. Second, both good qualities and problems are presented essentially as lists, with minimal development. The sentence "I have a cat, kind of" is bewildering: It isn't really mine? Or the identity is a mystery? Overall, the jump from dogs to cats and back again makes the discussion hard to follow; even the writer is baffled at the end. Questions could help: *What kind of person gets along best with cats (or dogs)? If you could only have one pet, what would you pick?* Smaller issues: The conventions are fairly clean (despite "thereselves" and "to" for "too"). The word choice, by contrast, is quite simple, and the sentences are short and sometimes choppy, disrupting the fluency.

■ *Suggested Scores for Other Traits*

Voice: 3, 3

Word choice: 2–3, 3

Sentence fluency: 2, 3

Conventions: 4, 4

See Chapters 8 and 9 for numerous instructional ideas relating to ideas and organization.

CHAPTER 4 IN A NUTSHELL

● Ideas form the foundation of any piece of writing.

● Strong organization showcases the ideas, so these two traits work in harmony.

● Focusing on one trait at a time is an effective way of introducing traits; gradually, we need to put them back together to create a "total package."

● Each piece of writing has specific lessons to teach about writing; choosing a paper for the lessons it teaches provides us with good models for instruction.

EXTENSIONS

1. Based on your experience scoring papers in this chapter, how would you rate your understanding of the traits of ideas and organization?

_____ Excellent. I feel that I could rate almost any piece of writing on either trait.

_____ Fair. I think that I still need more practice, but my understanding is growing.

_____ Not there yet. I feel confused about one or both traits.

2. Think of a teacher you have now or have had in the past—or a colleague with whom you work. Imagine yourself scoring papers with this person. Do you think most of your scores would agree—or not? Write a journal entry about this.

3. If you are teaching now, do you find it difficult to score papers at a grade level different from that at which you teach? What features differ most grade to grade? Which remain the most consistent? Discuss this with colleagues.

4. Did bias (see Chapter 3) influence your scoring on any of the papers in this chapter? If so, in what way? With colleagues, discuss steps teachers can take to minimize bias in assessment.

5. Rescore one of the papers from this chapter with a partner. As you do so, use a highlighter to mark specific words or phrases in *the rubric* (for ideas, organization, or both) that influence your scores. Also highlight those portions of *the paper* that influence your scores on a particular trait. Compare your markings. What specific *criteria* are influencing each of you most? What specific features of the *writing sample* are influencing each of you most? Talk about what you learn from this comparison.

6. Try the same activity with a student writer. Do you find that you and the student respond to different features—or different parts of the student's text? What do you learn from discussing these differences?

7. Select a paper from this chapter that you could use for a classroom lesson on revision. Consider scoring the paper, discussing strengths and problems, and asking students (individually or with a partner) to address any problem you see by revising the text to make it stronger.

WHY I WRITE

Writing to me is like drinking a cup of hot coffee. At the beginning, it's hard to drink because it's so hot. If you drink, you'll burn yourself. That is like writing. You can't rush your ideas.

—**Ellie Oligmueller,** student writer

Sometimes writing can be like a mosquito. Pesky and annoying. Buzzing around you, as if it will never leave. Finally it bites you, and makes you itch.

—**Chelsey Santino,** student writer

LOOKING AHEAD

You are now acquainted with the foundational traits: ideas and organization. In Chapter 5 we'll broaden our horizons, adding flavor to the mix with voice, word choice, and sentence fluency.

5 Adding Flavor
Voice, Word Choice, and Sentence Fluency

*V*oice is the imprint of the writer on the page. It is the heart, soul, and breath of the writing—the spirit and the flavor. Writing without voice is lifeless, dispassionate, remote. More than any other quality, it is voice that speaks to us from the page, that calls us to a favorite chair or hammock and says, "Come with me. Come into the world of the book." Word choice and fluency are first cousins of voice and indeed enhance voice tremendously. Voice comes, in part, from the words a writer chooses and the way he or she arranges them to create expressive and appealing rhythms. Here are two writers writing about feelings of loneliness—in very different ways. Listen to the voice of author Sandra Cisneros (1989) in this passage about "Four Skinny Trees." Notice the power of her verbs and modifiers and the way her fluency gains momentum until the last four words strike our ears like hammer blows.

The writer must learn how to stalk the inner voice.

—Ralph Fletcher
What a Writer Needs, 1993, p. 69

Voice allows the reader to hear an individual human being speak from the page.

—Donald M. Murray
A Writer Teaches Writing, 2004, p. 21

> Their strength is secret. They send ferocious roots beneath the ground. They grow up and they grow down and grab the earth between their hairy toes and bite the sky with violent teeth and never quit their anger [p. 74].

Now compare the voice of travel writer Bill Bryson (2001). Notice how his phrasing (. . . *melancholy . . . Obviously . . . whip away . . . facing a pillar* . . .) mixes loneliness with humor and how the bouncy rhythm of his prose helps us to hear and see the annoyingly cheerful waiter.

> Do you know what is the most melancholy part of dining alone in your hotel? It's when they come and take away all the other place settings and wineglasses, as if to say, "Obviously no one will be joining you tonight, so we'll just whip away all these things and seat you here facing a pillar, and in a minute we'll bring you a very large basket with just one roll in it. Enjoy!" [p. 89].

And now, if I shared two more samples, one Bryson and the other Cisneros, you'd have no trouble telling which was which. The language and the way the writer crafted sentences each would reflect the writer's unique voice.

As in Chapter 4, I will break each of these traits out for you first, giving you a chance to read, review, and score two papers just for that trait. Then we will put foundation and flavor together, scoring papers for five traits. And as before, your purpose is twofold:

1. To teach *yourself* the traits of *voice*, *word choice*, and *fluency* first by assessing, discussing, and reflecting on student work.
2. To discover papers you can share with your students as you teach them these same traits.

VOICE: FINGERPRINTS ON THE PAGE
Focus for Assessing and Teaching Voice

> *Enthusiasm is the force that keeps you going and keeps the reader in your grip.*
> **—William Zinsser**
> On Writing Well, 2001, p. 52

✔ Discovering personally important topics
✔ Writing with honesty and passion
✔ Knowing the topic so that confidence explodes from the page
✔ Thinking about audience: What do they already know? What will they find interesting?
✔ Bringing the topic to life through detail, language, and energy

PRACTICE PAPERS
What To Do

✔ Be sure that you have a copy of the rubric in front of you.
✔ Make a copy of the scoring grid (Figure 3.9) if you are working with a group.
✔ Make copies of papers if you wish to write on them.
✔ Make overheads of the papers if you wish to share them with a group.
✔ Read each paper aloud prior to scoring.
✔ Score each paper for the focus trait (and any additional traits you wish to practice on).

✔ Discuss your scores and the reasons for them with a partner or group.

✔ Check your scores against the suggested scores provided in this book.

✔ Consider and discuss the "lessons learned" for each paper.

GETTING A MINDSET

Voice is many things: personality, passion, engagement with the topic, energy and enthusiasm, and audience sensitivity. Because voice builds a bridge from writer to reader, it is much more than a fancy accoutrement; it is a tool for ensuring that the reader pays attention to the message. Voice connects us to the text as surely as the thread from Esmeralda's needle binds her gentle hands to the wounded face of Ruben Iglesias as she neatly stitches him up in *Bel Canto:* "It hurt, the little needle. He did not like to see it pass before his eye. He did not like the small tug at the end of every stitch that made him feel like a trout, caught" (Ann Patchett, 2001, p. 48). Voice comes in many guises and shifts with writer, audience, and purpose: "All writing has an intended audience, even the telephone book . . . " (O'Connor, 1999, p. 13). Most of us speak in different voices when we talk with a beloved soulmate on the phone or cheer the local football team on the field. Similarly, our writing voices can (and must) dress to suit the occasion.

Tips on Scoring Papers for the Trait of Voice

Voice is addictive. Once you've read text that is alive with voice, it is much harder to tolerate voiceless writing. One surefire way to measure this trait is to ask whether you feel an irresistible urge to share a piece aloud. Think of the books that you like reading to students in the classroom. I don't mean those you feel you *should* read but those you cannot wait to dive into. Here are just a few of the books and stories from which I like to take read-aloud moments:

Wild Thoughts from Wild Places, by David Quammen (1998)

Seabiscuit, by Laura Hillenbrand (2001)

A Christmas Memory, One Christmas, and The Thanksgiving Visitor, by Truman Capote (1996)

The House on Mango Street, by Sandra Cisneros (1989)

Iron Man, by Chris Crutcher (1995)

Boy: Tales of Childhood, by Roald Dahl (1984)

No More Dead Dogs, by Gordon Korman (2000)

The Pooh Story Book, by A. A. Milne (1996)

Harris and Me, by Gary Paulsen (1993)

Amos and Boris, by William Steig (1971)

Charlotte's Web, by E. B. White (1974)

Angela's Ashes, by Frank McCourt (1998)

Leaving Home, by Garrison Keillor (1987)

> *Voice is the quality, more than any other, that allows us to hear exceptional potential in a beginning writer; voice is the quality, more than any other, that allows us to recognize excellent writing.*
>
> **—Donald M. Murray**
> A Writer Teaches Writing, 1985, p. 21

These pieces resound with voice. They are easy to read with expression because the author's sheer joy in the writing comes through in every line. Similarly, if a student's writing has voice, you may feel like tugging someone's sleeve. "Listen to this," you hear yourself saying. You will not feel compelled to share "The Redwoods." This is how you'll know.

Paper 1: "Why You Need a Job" (Persuasive, Grade 9)

FIGURE 5.1

Paper 1:
"Why You Need a Job"

Young adults in our country need to learn more responsibility, and having a job while you are going to school is one way to get there.

Many times, young kids take their lives and theyre parents for granit. Parents have been around to care for them as long as they can remember. But it doesnt last forever. Sooner or later you will be out on your own without one clue of your life or responsibility. A job teaches kids to care for themselves without help from their parents. To buy things like clothes and insurance. Jobs are not just about money though. A job shows you how to get a long with people out side your family. A job is good for your future. It introduces you to new skills and new people. This paper gives solid reasons for getting a job while you are in school. Do it. You will not be sorry.

- ■ *Suggested Scores for Focus Trait: Voice*

  Voice: 3, 3

- ■ *Lessons Learned from Paper 1*

  ✔ Generalities weaken voice.
  ✔ To be convincing, persuasive writing needs examples.

- ■ *Comments*

Instead of crafting an argument, the writer simply states an opinion, and generalities squeeze the life right out of it: A job gives you experience, teaches you new skills, and is good for your future. The beginning is fairly forceful, and if the writer had sustained this level of voice, the paper could have become truly persuasive. Notice that voice emerges in spurts—*"you will be out on your own without one clue of your life"*—but quickly retreats. It picks up the tempo in the conclusion: *"Do it."* But by then we're tired. This is functional voice at best and does not seem directed to any specific audience. (*Note:* Reviewers for the third edition gave this piece a 4 in voice on the six-point scale; reviewers for this edition felt that it did not quite "leap the river.")

■ *Suggested Scores for Other Traits*

Ideas: 2, 3
Organization: 2, 2
Word choice: 3, 4
Sentence fluency: 3, 4
Conventions: 3, 3

Paper 2: "Zeena and the Marshmallows" (Persuasive/ Narrative, Grade 5)

FIGURE 5.2
Paper 2: "Zeena and the Marshmallows"

Zeena, I know just how you feel. I love chocolate covered marshmellows too! But let me tell you what happened to me.

My mom came home from the store one day and let me have a chocolate covered marshmellow. It was love at first bite. So lite, fluffy, chewy and slipped down my throat like a small piece of heaven. Just thinking about it makes me want to have another one until I recall what happened when I finished my last bag of those squishy delights.

My mom told me I can help myself to a few and before I knew it the whole bag was gone. My mom called me to dinner, and you know, the last thing I wanted or even cared about was dinner, but you know how mothers are, I had to sit down and take one bite of everything. And after that, I had diaria, diaria, diaria. But I was convinced it wasn't the marshmellows.

Last fall my mom bought me all of these cute clothes for my birthday, shorts, jeans, skirts, so when the weather got warm, and I went to put on my new clothes, they didn't fit to my amazement and not because I had grown too tall, just because I couldn't even zip them up. But it couldn't be the marshmellows, their too lite and fluffy; infact a whole bag of marshmellows doesn't weight as much as one orange.

One day, when I put the tight clothes out of my mind, I grabbed myself some chocolate covered marshmellows, when I was biting down on one, a sharp stabbing pain went up my tooth and the side of my head. And when ever I ate, my teeth hurt. So my mom took me to the dentist, and let me tell you it was not a pretty picture. I had seven expensive, painful cavities.

So Zeena, you can keep popping those marshmellows into your mouth, but before you do, remember not everything about chocolate covered marshmellows is sweet.

■ *Suggested Scores for Focus Trait: Voice*

Voice: 5, 6

■ *Lessons Learned from Paper 2*

✔ Anecdotes enhance voice and clarity.
✔ When we identify with the situation, we feel the writer reaching out to us.

■ *Comments*

"Zeena and the Marshmallows" is a knockout in voice. This young writer speaks right to her audience, and the main thing we want to say is, "Thank you for helping us understand why diets do not work." It's that dieter's logic: "A whole bag of marshmallows doesn't weigh as much as one orange." She leads us into the world of dieter's temptation and remorse without ever preaching or moralizing. Strong imagery enhances the voice—*"slipped down my throat like a small piece of heaven . . . I had to sit down and take one bite . . . couldn't even zip them up . . . a sharp, stabbing pain went up my tooth."* Readers love the way this writer pokes fun at herself, along with the dieting world. It's true comedy, with just the tiny dose of pain and suffering that comedy needs to work. Although basically persuasive, this paper (contrast Paper 1) uses three humorous anecdotes to make the point. It's a good technique. Many of us can identify with the bingeing, the tight clothes—even the trip to the dentist. A relevant story is nearly always more compelling than a bulleted list of reasons.

■ *Suggested Scores for Other Traits*

Ideas: 5, 6
Organization: 5, 5
Word choice: 4–5, 4
Sentence fluency: 4, 5
Conventions: 3–4, 4

WORD CHOICE: THE BRIDGE FROM MESSAGE TO VOICE
Focus for Assessment and Teaching Word Choice

✔ Painting a verbal picture
✔ Choosing words selectively—going for precision
✔ Embracing everyday language (not writing to impress)
✔ Finding a fresh, original way to say it
✔ Energizing writing with strong verbs
✔ Keeping it concise
✔ Avoiding jargon, inflated language, and modifier overload

Tips on Scoring Papers for the Trait of Word Choice

Pretend that you're holding a yellow marker in your hand, and imagine that you are going to highlight each word or phrase within a student's paper that strikes

GETTING A MINDSET

Word choice and voice are inextricably connected. A writer creates one voice with the words "I killed myself polishing off that blasted report" and another with "Everything I believe and feel is on these pages." Words make a bridge between message and tone, message and voice. Choose the *just right* word, and a simple image conveys a world of meaning—in Laurie Halse Anderson's classic *Speak,* the narrator drowns in the despair of her alienation: *"I dive into the stream of fourth-period lunch students and swim down the hall to the cafeteria"* (1999, p. 7). Everyday language, carefully chosen, has power to put us at the scene. We not only see the action, but also feel it in our joints and muscles, as in Jane Leavy's reverent description of pitcher Sandy Koufax: *"His front leg came up. The right knee, as it rose, seemed to touch his elbow. His toe extended like a dancer on point. For an instant he seemed in equipoise, his back leg a pedestal. It was his only point of contact with the earth. Every other part of his body was flying"* (2002, p. 12). David Quammen's haunting portrayal of the zoo tiger, its wilder self numbed by dependency on humans, leaves a distinct chill in the air: *"When a human looks deep into the eyes of a zoo animal . . . the human is alone"* (1998, p. 89).

> *Adjectives and adverbs are rich and good and fattening. The main thing is not to overindulge.*
>
> **—Ursula K. LeGuin**
> *Steering the Craft,* 1998, p. 61

you or captures your attention—words and phrases that seem right or noteworthy or commanding in some way. Perhaps you wish you'd written them, or you think, "That's original. I never heard it said quite like that." Your word-choice score is a function of how often the words and phrases grab your attention. Every line? That's a 6. Often? That's a 4 or 5. Now and then? Perhaps a 3. Rarely or never? That's a 2 or 1.

Paper 3: "Chad" (Descriptive, Grade 3)

FIGURE 5.3
Paper 3: "Chad"

My friend is great because likes the same things I do. His name is Chad.

If theres nothing to do around the house, we get together and do stuff. I phone him up or he phones me. He's a real neat person. He's fun to do stuff with because we mostly like the same games and TV shows. He comes to my house or I go to his house. He has brown hair and is tall, about five feet! It is cool having a friend who is alot like you and likes the stuff you like. Chad is my friend.

> *I haunt used-book stores, searching for books that contain unusual words. El-ementary Seamanship has a glossary of sea terms: scup-per, bulwark, winch, windlass, scuttles. The book is a cup of possibility for those days when I'm thirsty for words.*
>
> **—Georgia Heard**
> *Writing Toward Home*, 1995, p. 47

■ *Suggested Scores for Focus Trait: Word Choice*

Word choice: 2, 3

■ *Lessons Learned from Paper 3*

✔ Such words as *stuff* and *things* are too weak to carry meaning or feeling.

✔ We crave words that help us picture what the writer is talking about.

■ *Comments*

This paper has the beginnings of a character sketch (Chad is five feet tall, has brown hair, and likes the same games and TV shows as the writer), but Chad has not become a person yet. We know that he's "neat," "great," and "fun" to be with and that it's "cool" having him for a friend, but we need the clarity of a good close-up to help us see Chad and experience the "stuff" these friends do together. Tired words kill any message. Imagine this paper with just two strong verbs and specific replacements for *stuff*, *neat*, *cool*, and *great*. Tiny changes shoo the fog away.

■ *Suggested Scores for Other Traits*

Ideas: 2–3, 3
Organization: 2, 2
Voice: 3, 3
Sentence fluency: 3, 3
Conventions: 4, 4

Paper 4: "Pets Are Forever: An Investigative Report" (Expository, Grade 8)

FIGURE 5.4

Paper 4: "Pets Are Forever: An Investigative Report"

Many pet owners worry about that difficult day when they must say goodbye for the last time. A new method of preservation could make that day a whole lot easier. It's a sort of mummification of the 90s, minus the fuss of wrapping and the mess of embalming fluid. The new method, believe it or not, involves freeze drying your pet. It's clean, rela-tively affordable (compared to the cost of a live pet), produces authentic results, and enables you to keep Fluffy beside you on the couch forever, if you wish.

Freeze drying is really a simple procedure. First, highly trained techni-cians remove all the pet's internal organs. They do leave muscle tissue and bones intact, however, so there will be something to freeze dry. They replace the eyes with lifelike glass marbles in the color of choice. A spe-cial procedure temporarily reverses the effects of rigor mortis, allowing the owner to pose the pet as he or she wishes—sitting, lying down, curled by the fire, about to pounce, and so on. It is important to work quickly before the effects of rigor mortis resume. As a finishing touch, the technician uses special blow dryers with a fine nozzle to make the pet look more lifelike. One client posed her cat in the litterbox; apparently, that was her most striking memory of "Tiger."

Freeze drying costs from $500 to $1,000, depending on the size of the pet and the complexity of the final pose. "About to strike" is more expensive than, say, "napping by the woodstove." The entire procedure takes about six months, but satisfied clients claim the wait is worth it. After all, once the pet is returned, you have him or her forever—maintenance-free except for occasional re-fluffing of the fur. Technicians report that freeze-dried pets hold up best in a relatively low-humidity, dust-free environment.

Experts also offer one final piece of advice: It is NOT recommended that pet owners try freeze drying their own pets. Proper equipment and experience are essential if you wish your pet to bear a true resemblance to his or her old self.

■ Suggested Scores for Focus Trait: Word Choice

Word choice: 5, 5

■ Lessons Learned from Paper 4

✔ Simple, natural language has power.
✔ If you enjoy writing it, the reader will enjoy reading it.

■ Comments

One secret to putting voice into expository writing is to like the topic. Clearly, this writer does. We get the idea that she is mildly horrified by the idea of freeze-drying and stuffing a pet yet also intrigued. The humor in this piece is ironic, extremely understated, and highly controlled for a writer this age. Who can help recoiling but snickering at the image of Tiger posed in the litter box? Notice that her language is technically correct yet totally natural: *"mummification of the 90s," "A special procedure temporarily reverses the effects of rigor mortis," "'About to strike' is more expensive than, say, 'Napping by the woodstove.'"* Awareness of audience is very strong, adding to voice. Each word and phrase seems chosen for impact. The prose is direct, forceful, and crisp, appropriate for expository writing with flair. (I have no problem giving this a 6 in word choice. Some teacher-raters feel that it's shy of "quotable." I disagree—but 5 is still a worthy score.)

■ Suggested Scores for Other Traits

Ideas: 5, 6
Organization: 5, 6

Voice: 5, 6
Sentence fluency: 5, 6
Conventions: 5, 6

SENTENCE FLUENCY: VARIETY AND RHYTHM

Focus for Assessing and Teaching Sentence Fluency

✔ Varying sentence beginnings
✔ Varying sentence lengths
✔ Combining short, choppy sentences to smooth the flow
✔ Using transitional words (*after a while*, *nevertheless*) to keep the sentence-to-sentence rhythm going
✔ Writing dialogue that rings true
✔ Using repetition and fragments sparingly—and only for effect
✔ Reading aloud to see how it plays to the ear

Tips on Scoring Papers for the Trait of Sentence Fluency

Read the text aloud. You don't have to read the whole thing (although that's often helpful). Put expression in it. Don't be inhibited, or you'll wind up scoring your own inhibition and not what's in the text. Imagine that you are trying out for a highly competitive part in a stage play; you won't get the part unless you summon every bit of emotional fiber within you and project. *Now* read. Does the text help you to give a good performance? Is it easy to relay meaning, nuances, flavor, feelings? Can you awaken that sleepy guy in the back row? Do you feel as if you're floating from one sentence to the next almost effortlessly?

GETTING A MINDSET

Sentence fluency is all about how the text plays to the ear. Reading aloud is essential to understanding and scoring this trait. You must *hear* the writing—put it in motion. Where does the emphasis go? Where do the beats fall? Is repetition purposeful and dramatic, or does it strike the ear like a wrong note? In most instances variety is the soul of fluency. Variety in length. Variety in beginnings. Variety in structure. Sometimes, though, as in the example I have just created, repetition reinforces a key word or idea. Listen. Your ear will tell you the difference. Just as it will tell you whether a fragment is a quagmire impeding the flow or a natural diversion of the current. Like this. With fluency, the general pattern of development is from irregular and disjointed—to predictable—to smooth, balanced, and musical: *"It was the best of times, it was the worst of times, it was the age of wisdom, it was the age of foolishness, it was the epoch of disbelief, it was the epoch of incredulity, it was the season of light, it was the season of darkness, it was the spring of hope, it was the winter of despair . . ."* (Charles Dickens, *A Tale of Two Cities,* 1859, p. 1).

Then you know the fluency is strong. Score down a bit if you bump along, need to stop frequently and reread, or find yourself repeating patterns.

■ *Caution on Conventions!*

What if there's no punctuation? When addressing fluency, read for rhythm and flow, and do some light mental editing with punctuation as needed. If that light editing puts everything in order, the real problem is with conventions. Editing may not be sufficient, however. Capitals and periods alone will not wholly solve problems caused by choppy sentences, repetitive structure, or endless connectives. If restructuring is needed, the problem is with fluency—as well as (usually) conventions.

> *Writing is talk on paper. . . . And for centuries before humans wrote, they told stories and passed information along orally. Even when they began to write, the flavor of orality remained.*
>
> **—Tommy Thomason**
> *Write Aerobics: 40 Workshop Exercises to Improve Your Writing Teaching*, 2003, p. 21

Paper 5: "A Rescue" (Narrative, Grade 4)

FIGURE 5.5

Paper 5: "A Rescue"

Once a bunch of my frieneds and I went to this old hounted house and I'm not talking about some amusement park thing or something like that but but this was a for real hounted house, but we couldn't go in becuuse we were too scared and my friend Robert kept making these jokes that made us laugh so hard we couldn't walk so we just kept talking about should we do it or not?.

So the next day we went back and this time we followed Robert into the front door and I was right behind him and I could hear him breathing in this kind of panting way and I told him to keep quiet or he would wake up the gosts. So just then I saw something real creepy move in the corner of the kitchen, and robert said Shhhh its only a stray cat but I said ha I don't think so buddy in a million years so I took off like a rocket from the moon and waited outside in the fog that was nice and creepy and then I saw the thing again and this time I knew it was too big for a cat so I ran back into the house to save my freniends. I grabed Robert by his hair and he let out this inormous shreek but I had to get him out of the monster's claws and I pulled and pulled and finally got him out of the house and he said what in the name of holey moley are you doing?? I had yainked some of his hair clean out of his head and he didn't like it much. I gues he didn't apreschiate beging saved from the gost so I took off for home to have dinner. And then had dinner and went to bed and that is the last time we went to that house, but me and Robert still are best friends as long as I don't pull his hair.

■ *Suggested Scores for Focus Trait: Sentence Fluency*

Sentence fluency: 1–2, 2

> *If you ride, think of a horse's gaits: walk, trot, canter, gallop. If you're musical, use your toe or an imaginary baton to mark the tempo: adagio, andante, allegro, presto. Think of an oncoming train, the waves of the sea, wheels on a cobblestone street.*
>
> **—Patricia T. O'Connor**
> *Words Fail Me*, 1999, p. 79

■ Lessons Learned from Paper 5

✔ When the reader gets breathless, fluency is usually the problem.
✔ Endless connectives (*and, and so, so then*) not only impair fluency but also make ideas difficult to follow.

■ Comments

While this stream-of-consciousness style may echo the way some people speak, it can cause the reader to lose all sense of the message. Joining clauses like links in a chain creates the illusion that ideas are related, even though the writer has supplied no real transitions or thoughtful connections. It could be argued that this breathless flow reflects how people really feel when exploring a haunted house; I would be more persuaded that the writer were doing this deliberately if he shifted out of it at the end, but he does not. On the bright side, the piece has moments of voice and effective word choice—strengths on which to build. (Note that punctuation alone will not correct the problem.)

■ Suggested Scores for Other Traits

Ideas: 2, 3
Organization: 2, 2
Voice: 4, 4
Word choice: 3, 4
Conventions: 2, 3

Paper 6: "The Joke" (Narrative/Expository, Grade 7)

FIGURE 5.6
Paper 6: "The Joke"

My grandma is 81. She has had rheumatoid arthritis for twelve years. When it was first diagnosed, her chief problem was constant, relentless pain. Now she can no longer walk, take herself to the bathroom, brush her own teeth, or lift a fork to eat; forks and toothbrushes are too heavy for her to hold. To move from her bed to a chair she has to be lifted; sometimes, just the pressure of lifting under her arms causes her to shriek with pain. Despite her problems, though, she loves to sit up and talk with her family. "I'll start dinner in a minute," she tells us.

Unfortunately, pain and medication have dulled her memory, but they have never gotten the best of her imagination. She has many conversations with old friends and long-gone relatives. Sometimes she "goes shopping," then tells us of the bargains she found or the clerks who gave her a hard time. My grandma is feisty, and tolerates no backtalk, even in her imagined world.

Last month, she had two molars pulled. Although she had dreaded it, she really liked the orthodontist, which made her experience a little better. She liked him so much, she wanted everyone to benefit from his services. She told my brother and me—we're 12 and 14—that we should get our teeth pulled now because it would be so much harder if we waited till we were her age. "Just go now and get it over with," she said.

My brother nearly choked on his chicken. It was funny and sad at the same time. I remember my grandma's face. She was so happy to have made her grandson laugh, it made her laugh with us. It was her way of joining in the joke.

■ *Suggested Scores for Focus Trait: Sentence Fluency*

Sentence fluency: 5, 5

■ *Lessons Learned from Paper 6*

✔ Writers may ease into fluency following a bumpy start. Transitional words improve the sentence flow and help readers to connect ideas.

■ *Comments*

This is a heartfelt, understated piece that makes a good point (love overcomes many traumas of life)—and it is an excellent read-aloud for illustrating both voice and sentence fluency. This student's perception of her grandmother's world is very acute. Notice her quick read of grandmother's face at the end, where she senses both the joy of the moment and the sorrow at her grandmother's loss of memory. The beginning and ending are strong, although the first two sentences (very direct in style) do not quite match the grace of subsequent passages. Overall, though, the text is easy to read aloud and dances easily from line to line with strong transitions and minimal repetition (a little heavy on *she* in the next-to-last paragraph).

■ *Suggested Scores for Other Traits*

Ideas: 5, 6

Organization: 5, 5

Voice: 5, 6

Word choice: 4, 5

Conventions 5, 6

LOOKING AT ADDITIONAL PAPERS

In the remainder of this chapter we will consider nine additional papers, this time focusing scoring practice on five traits: *ideas, organization, voice, word choice,* and *sentence fluency.* (Scores for conventions are also given, but the practice will focus on these five.) You should review the rubrics for ideas and organization if you have not scored papers on these traits for two days or more. Follow the same general procedures:

✔ Make copies of rubrics and papers.
✔ Read each paper you score aloud.
✔ Discuss scores and lessons learned with a partner or group.

Paper 7: "A Sunflower Seed" (Expository/Reflective, Grade 5)

FIGURE 5.7
Paper 7:
"A Sunflower Seed"

Now most people I know would think something like a football is most important but this sunflower seed ment a lot to me. It helped me understand the struggles and needs to stay alive in this world. How the seed needed water to live, and that water to me represented the thirst to stay alive. How it needed the sun to grow, and that sun is like our need to be with others.

I thought the sunflower seed died because it had been more than week since I had planted it. The next morning, a clot of dirt was being held midair by the sunflower, so I choped up the dirt to make it softer so the sunflower could grow easyer. In life you have to eas up on other people so they can relax in growing up and don't have to push or force their way up. In life there will be people that will hold you back from what you want (just like the dirt) and you have to break free from them if you want to live your own life.

Just like the seed you must prosper or life will pass you by.

■ Suggested Scores

Ideas: 5, 6
Organization: 5, 6
Voice: 5, 6
Word choice: 5, 5
Sentence fluency: 5, 5
Conventions: 4, 4

■ Lessons Learned from Paper 7

✔ Go for the unique topic—the sunflower seed, not the football.
✔ Strong voice doesn't have to be emotional, just heartfelt.

■ Comments

The philosophical message and tone of this piece are very strong. The sunflower seed metaphor works well; it is like the hub of a wheel, to which all other ideas connect. Few papers are so well centered. Organization (along with voice) is a real strength here. We picture the writer "[chopping] up the dirt to make it softer" and thinking to himself, *"This is how life is for us all."* Here's a writer speaking from reflective experience. The paper makes us think and makes us want to "[ease] up on other people" and encourage them to do the same for us. Words are simple but carry weight. The writer uses fragments, but they work. Conventions need some attention.

Paper 8: "The Big Road" (Narrative, Grade 7)

FIGURE 5.8

Paper 8: "The Big Road"

From the moment my sister got her license, I knew there would be interesting and dangerous adventures ahead. Whenever there was anywhere to go, Jessica always volunteered for the job. She went here and there and everywhere. What a pro. She liked to go to the store and pick up dinner. She would do anything. She went to the gas station, the Cleaners, the Mall. Naturally, when it was time to go to my baseball game, Jessica volunteered for the job without hesitation. Obviously, after being driven everywhere by my parents my whole life, I was a little apprehensive about being driven to a big game by some one who was fairly inexperienced. I told my parents I wouldn't feel safe, but they didn't think anything of letting Jessica drive with me in the car. Was my life worth so little?

While I put my baseball uniform on, Jessica gathered all of the things that she likes to take with her whenever she drives: her coffee cup from Starbuck's, her sunglasses, and her favorite Beatles CD's. We both got into the car. I buckled up and pulled the thing snug, wondering if the airbags worked. Jessica started the car and jolted back out of the driveway. She seemed to drive well without speeding. As we pulled out of the neighborhood, Jessica popped in a CD and we headed toward the field. I began to relax. After a few minutes I noticed that Jessica had picked up the habit of yelling at drivers who tailgated or drove too slow. It was pretty funny to hear her ask the other drivers if that piece of #@#$!! had a gas peddle. We got to the field safely and I had a great game. I was a little nervous about the trip home even after being driven safely to the field. After all, it would be dark by the time the game was over. "What if she can't see in the dark?" I thought. "But what can I do? I don't want to walk home with all of my gear." The game ended and she pulled up to the walk and I hopped in the car. The stars were bright in the cloudless sky. Jessica turned on the signal to pull out of the field parking lot. She made the turn and pulled out. "Oh God!", I yelled. A car was tearing right for us. Jessica hit the gas and we lurched to safety. "That was close!" She said. "It sure was," I said back.

■ *Suggested Scores*

Ideas: 5, 5

Organization: 4, 5

Voice: 5, 6

Word choice: 5, 5

Sentence fluency: 4–5, 5

Conventions: 5, 6

■ *Lessons Learned from Paper 8*

✔ Humor can be subtle.

✔ Little details (the Beatles' CD, the glasses, the Starbucks cup) add texture and interest.

■ *Comments*

This is a greatly understated paper with a fine theme. So many students feel that they have nothing to write about; here's a perfect example of an everyday event turned into a revealing personal essay. It is easy to picture every part of this scenario. Can't you see Jessica gathering necessary paraphernalia for the big trip? Some readers wanted a stronger ending, though personally, I liked it. I read it as veiled sarcasm, and it works for me, but you may wish the writer's response to the near miss were more dramatic. I see him saying, "I'm hard to rattle—even with Jessica's wild driving." Strong voice. Easy on the ear fluency.

Paper 9: "Football and the 4.0s" (Persuasive, Grade 8)

FIGURE 5.9

Paper 9:
"Football and the 4.0s"

Something is crippling our educational system. Something that is the only reason some kids wish to attend school, rather than to learn. That something is somehow praised and respected by students, parents, and administrators alike. That something is sports and cheerleading. Yes, school sports and the cheerleading program seems to me to be taking a bite out of my education.

We are always hearing schools and teachers whine about how they need more money to teach. And they certainly have reason to, as our class sizes are already bursting in size. If they need more money, I say cut the sports programs. That would certainly solve some of the financial problems today's schools have.

The purpose of schools is not to put athletes and others up on pedestals because of their athletic achievements. They hold pep assemblies and give them trophies, while the 4.0 students are left to the end of the year where they receive a certificate and a small pin. The purpose of a school is to educate the students so they can become of use to society. Against what most boys my age think, they will most likely not make the NFL.

Sports and Cheerleading in schools are only ways some kids use to show off. They think that they are in a higher class than everyone else just because they made the football team or something else. Shouldn't we prize the qualities in our students that really matter?

Many people will say that Sports are a great way to give kids something to do. Keep them out of trouble and off drugs among many other things. And I agree. However, if we could spend more time, money, and effort on teaching them, maybe they would be more interested in their education. Wouldn't that give them something more productive to do? Sports are sort of the "Right thing in the wrong place." They just simply shouldn't be incorporated into schools.

Obviously, taking sporting programs out of our schools would solve many problems, financially and socially. I think we could certainly use the money. I hope that you will consider joining this fight against sports in schools.

■ Suggested Scores

Ideas: 4, 4

Organization: 5, 5

Voice: 4, 5

Word choice: 4, 5

Sentence fluency: 4, 5

Conventions: 5, 6

■ Lessons Learned from Paper 9

✔ Consider the other side when crafting an argument.

✔ Don't get personal ("They think that they are in a higher class . . . ").

■ Comments

This writer presents a clear, direct, and forceful argument and has reasons for his opinion: Sports cost too much money (money that could go for other things); sports draw attention to athletes and cause schools to overlook high-achieving students; and they distract us from the real problem of providing strong, motivating instruction. Clarity and focus are excellent. The problem lies with fair representation of the other side's position (which ultimately could strengthen the argument). It could be argued, for instance, that sports also help raise money for schools, that giving trophies to scholars too would alleviate the problem, and that success in sports helps students to perform successfully in other areas. Such issues need to be addressed. The language, like the paper itself, is direct and clear, although it is not marked by memorable phrasing. Sentence fluency is strong in most places, although some sentences in paragraph 1 are a bit wordy. Good conventions.

Paper 10: "Fishing" (Narrative/Expository, Grade 11)

FIGURE 5.10
Paper 10: "Fishing"

"I'm jumping out," I yelled frantically to my father. It was in response to the flopping northern Pike that was near my feet in our boat. I was six and on my first trip to Canada to fish. It was a totally different fishing experience than I was accustomed to in Pennsylvania. It was not like catching Bluegills in Leaser Lake. Surely I had a right to be scared. The Northern Pike is an extremely mean looking fish with sharp teeth which it uses to kill its prey. Being six, I thought I was on its list of prey. My father responded to my plea by saying, "Go ahead and jump, but there are a hundred more in that water. "

Most of my knowledge and love of fishing came from that same man who told me to "Go ahead and jump." Since I can remember, I have always fished. My father probably taught me to fish before I could walk. At first he taught me the basics: tying a swivel to a line, threading the line through the pole, removing hooks from any part of the body that they may enter, how to get a lure out of a tree, why to check the inside of hip boots that have been sitting in the garage all year before putting them on, if the sign says "No Fishing—Violators will be prosecuted," it usually means it, and probably most important, if you have to go to the bathroom while on the boat what to do. Occasionally, he also revealed a hot tip while fishing, such as, "See this lure, son? This one is going to catch the big one. It's only legal in two states and this isn't one of them. "

The key to fishing, I was taught, is patience. Obviously, my father has a little of that if he could teach me to fish. There were numerous occasions when I crossed my line with his and caused a "rat's nest," or the several times that I used a lure and forgot to close the tackle box, and when he picked it up, all the lures fell out. One time he really showed his patience when I reached back in the boat to cast, but accidentally hooked onto his hat and threw it into the water. My brother and I laughed hysterically while I reeled it in through the water. Eventually, my father joined in.

Since I was young, there was one aspect of fishing my father heavily emphasized. Fishing is not about the amount of fish you catch, but the amount of fun you have. There were times when we wouldn't catch one fish but would still have a great time. I learned fishing is a time to just be with nature and your thoughts, a time to relax and share good times with friends. Anyone who only cares about catching fish all the time is missing the true meaning. Fishing is like an education. It is a lifelong experience. After high school, you could go to college and get a Bachelor's degree. In fishing, if you graduate from regular fishing, you could go on to ice fishing or maybe deep sea fishing. Then, if you move on to get your Master's degree, maybe you could start fly fishing.

One day, I will be teaching my kids to fish and will probably hear them complain about not catching any fish. I will think for a minute what Pop would say: "The worst day of fishing is better than the best day of work. "

■ *Suggested Scores*

Ideas: 5, 6
Organization: 5, 6
Voice: 5, 6 (7 really)
Word choice: 4, 4
Sentence fluency: 5, 6
Conventions: 5, 6

■ *Lessons Learned from Paper 10*

✔ Begin right in the middle of things.
✔ Tell the truth because in the end we want Dad to be human—not perfect.

■ *Comments*

Fly fishing as a master's degree? That's ingenious. There is so much to love about this paper, from Dad giving the wonderful tip about the illegal lure to the son's recognition of a parent's patience when he spills the contents of the tackle box or uses Dad's hat for casting practice. The voice seems to echo the reverence this writer feels for his father and for the magic of fishing. The beginning and ending are trophy winners. Notice the value of small details, too. Nothing is really wrong with word choice; it just did not shine quite so much as other traits (but then, that's asking a lot).

Paper 11: "Should High School Graduation Requirements Be Raised?" (Persuasive, Grade 9)

FIGURE 5.11

Paper 11:
"Should High School Graduation Requirements Be Raised?"

Did you know that these graduates are our future? The high school students should need more credits because these teenagers need to learn hard work. I'm tired of our state not having a good name when it comes to education. I believe the High School students should step it up a notch and prove to adults what they can do!

The future of the older generations always lies upon the younger generation when they become too old. They will be the explorers for the

continued

next 50 years. Wouldn't you like to see that responsibility lie in the hands of the most highly educated man/woman? I know I would.

You would be shocked to know that 9 out of ten High School students spend 8 hrs. on a weekday watching TV. That includes going to school. These students must not be challenged. We owe them a good education! Some people may think they have enough time to handle all of the credits as it is. Don't you think if they are watching that much TV, some time could be spent on homework?

How many of our citizens hate it that we have low educational scores compared to other states? I know I do! This is our chance to become something bigger. It would definitely be worthwhile. Some students may think, "So? Who cares?!" Trust me, you will in the future.

In conclusion, I believe we can do it! We have the chance for a future! We should grab it by the handles. It may be hard, but it is definitely worth it! We will never know until we try. So let's all learn about the value of hard work and raise the requirements for high school graduation.

■ Suggested Scores

Ideas: 4, 4

Organization: 4, 5

Voice: 5, 5

Word choice: 4, 4

Sentence fluency: 5, 6

Conventions: 5, 5

■ Lessons Learned from Paper 11

✔ Rallying the troops is one way to end, but a powerful argument requires a striking fact.

✔ Cite sources for statistics.

✔ If your argument is truly powerful, you don't need exclamation points.

■ Comments

This paper is right on the cusp of providing a solid argument. I believe everything the writer says (but mostly because I agreed with her before reading the paper). I like the word *explorers* (paragraph 2) and even the notion of grabbing the future "by the handles" (last paragraph). If she had more factual evidence of the sort stated in paragraph 3, the argument would be bolstered immeasurably. We need to know how low the state's scores are, how much time students do spend on homework, how many credits the average student is taking now and which classes require the most homework, and how these various statistics play out for students who are successful. We also need sources for such information. Question: How can time spent watching TV "include going to school"? The "value of hard work" is a given in this paper. Should it be? Some people who have never gone to college or done much traditional homework enjoy great financial success. I can think of my own examples to show how educated men and women can better guide the future, but I want the writer to do that. Strong fluency, voice, and conventions (but easy on those exclamation points).

Paper 12: "Sixth Grade" (Descriptive/Expository, Grade 6)

FIGURE 5.12

Paper 12: "Sixth Grade."

Have you ever wondered what goes on in the sixth grade? Have you ever feared what goes on in the sixth grade? Well, let me tell ya, it sure isn't what you'd call ordinary. Scary? Maybe. Weird? Now that's a given.

Take language, for example. We're not like the other kids. Instead of memorizing the prepositions, we're obligated to learn pictures that go along for all forty of the little buggers. Those annoying parts of speech. At least the pictures help. Now, let me introduce you to Shakespeare.

Ah, Shakespeare, the part of school that allows you to yell inside. How delightful. I just love the feeling you get when you know that you're disrupting everyone else in the school. I just wish I had the chance to be one of those spectators. The voice that comes from deep in your throat echoes in the gym like a bowling ball colliding with the pins. Noise, how wonderful.

Do you know any odd teachers? I do. No wait a minute, stop. I wouldn't quite say Mrs. M is odd. Maybe peculiar—but my, she is brilliant. Even though she claims she has a score to settle with Mr. Webster. I guess I would, too. What was that guy thinking? Mrs. M says that he probably despised children. I agree.

Now I'm going to answer the question that you probably have had in mind. Does lunch improve? Definitely not! I'm pretty sure that the reason school lunch was put on this earth was to torture your taste buds. It's just a theory, but I can support it. How much grease is on the pizza? Five tons. How long has the orange juice been frozen? Nine hours. You get the picture. Luckily, I've come up with some fairly good advice. Bring your lunch! Then you can eat whatever you're in the mood for. Case closed.

So what is seventh grade? I'm still trying to figure that out, but one thing's for sure, whatever it turns out to be, I'll love it.

■ *Suggested Scores*

Ideas: 4, 4
Organization: 3, 4

Voice: 5, 5
Word choice: 4, 5
Sentence fluency: 4, 5
Conventions: 5, 6

■ Lessons Learned from Paper 12

✔ Connect the dots!
✔ Fragments, if well done, add to fluency.

■ Comments

Writing seems effortless for this writer. The voice just flows. Ditto fluency. The fragments work well: *"Those annoying parts of speech. Maybe. Noise, how wonderful. Definitely not! Five tons."* The piece has an easy, conversational style that fits like a glove. In addition, the writer provides interesting information: the prepositions, yelling in rehearsal, the wonderful Mrs. M, and of course, the infamous lunches. These bits and pieces are just that, though; they're not connected, except in the loose sense that sixth grade is "weird." Also, paragraph 3, the one about Shakespearean rehearsal, requires some inference. This is an enjoyable piece to read and share, just the same. Whimsical and funny.

Paper 13: "Cambiando Mundos: Changing Worlds" (Memoir/Narrative, Grade 9)

FIGURE 5.13
Paper 13
Cambiando Mundos:
Changing Words

I guess I should introduce myself. My name is Isidro. I am in the ninth grade and my English teacher has just assigned us to write a story on ourselves and a moment in our lives that we will never forget. Most kids are doing something irrelevant like a baseball game or piano recital, but I guess that a moment in my life I would never forget is more like a whole day . . .

I suppose that it all started in a far away place of Ameco, Jalisco. Ameca is a little *pueblito*, or village, on the outskirts of the big city of Guadalajara. I was born on January 1, 1987, to my father Ramon and mother Maria, with an older sister. My father was 20, my mother was 16, and my sister was only a year older than I. I was born in a little red brick house. It was more like a room, with a fireplace and stove.

When I was three, we moved to Tijuana, with one more member in our family, my baby sister Consuelo. In Tijuana, we had a little hut to live in. We did not know anyone there and had to fend for ourselves.

When I turned five, we moved to Nevada. My dad had already found a job as a farm worker, because he had a brother there. I had never met my *Tio* (Uncle) Miguel before, or his family, and was very nervous. We were treated very kindly. Our new home was part of the migrant housing, but was very welcome compared to our old hut in Tijuana. In the following few weeks, we got to know the other migrant workers, all with different stories and backgrounds, but all united in the same cause, to make a better life for themselves and their families, in such a promising country.

We had gotten there only a few days before school started, but were thrown right into the system. In the morning, I still remember having butterflies in my stomach. We went to school on a yellow bus, and were to go home the same way. The process in which my sister and I were enrolled is all a blur to me, but I do remember that I could not understand a thing anyone was saying. Because at that time, I only understood Spanish.

That first day of school was like a nightmare that wouldn't end. I sat in my desk completely clueless about what was going on around me. I could only guess at what they were saying, so in my mind I was no longer in class. I had drifted back to Tijuana, playing soccer in the field.

Back in the classroom, I came to the horrible reality that I had to go to the bathroom, and I had no idea how to communicate with these people that spoke a foreign language. I decided it was better to wait for a while and see if I was to stay much longer. A while came and passed, but nothing happened. Now the people around me had all gotten out toys and started to play with each other. I felt like I was going to burst, but bit my lip until I tasted blood. Then everyone was returning to their seats, and I knew I could hold it no longer.

I felt ashamed and embarrassed, but no one had directed any comments toward me. I peed my pants. There was no other option, so I then tried to imagine myself in my mother's arms. That always comforted me, the thought of my mama.

I was half dry, and it seemed like eternity had passed when all the children were running out of the door and screaming. The class was almost empty, so I decided it would be better for me if I would follow the others. When I was outside of the doors, a mass of children playing, yelling, and laughing surrounded me.

" Isidro, Isidro," Griselda yelled in Spanish.

I turned to see my sister in a pink faded flowered skirt rush towards me. Her dark face was very detectable amongst all of the light skinned people around me. She grabbed me and we held each other there, next to the swing set. She was not going to let me go, and I wouldn't let her either. "*Come te fue, Isidro?* (How did it go, Isidro?)" she asked in a very maternal way. I summed up the morning's events and started to cry.

" *No te precupes, hermanito. Estoy contigo, todo va ' star bien* (Don't worry, little brother. I'm with you now. Everything will be all right)." She always knew how to comfort me.

" *Pero, no entiendo nada, no quiero regresar* (But I don't understand anything. I don't want to come back)," I said amidst my sobs.

" *Ya se, ya se, pero tenemos que tratar* (I know, I know, but we have to try)," Griselda said, although I knew she felt the same as I did. By that time all the children had already gone into their classes. And there we

continued

stood, holding onto each other, without a chance of letting go. We cried in each other's arms, but were both so happy to know we had each other, and knew that we could not be parted anymore.

A yelling voice from the school building startled us both, and I recognized the face as my teacher from the morning. We wiped off each other's tears. We could not understand what this man was saying, but knew that he wanted to separate us. Then a lady appeared. " *Mi maestra* (My teacher)," my sister said with a hint of fear in her voice.

While we were still in each other's arms, our teachers escorted us back into the building. When we got to the hallway, each teacher grabbed one of our hands to lead us to class. Griselda and I burst into tears, for we knew we had to part but would not go without a fight. We held onto each other like a dying man holding on for breath. We squeezed so tight, for a moment there I felt as though I <u>couldn't</u> let go. But the moment came when our teachers took our hands and we knew it was time. I walked one way and Griselda the other. We watched each other until Griselda turned a corner up ahead.

"*Despues de clase, voy a ir por tigo para ir a casa. Te amo* (After class, I will come for you so we can go home. I love you)," Griselda yelled to me as we were parting, and I knew she would.

After class, Griselda fulfilled her promise and found me. Together, we got onto the bus and sat in the first available seat. We had caught a glimpse of our cousins and assured them that we were all right. Griselda held my hand all the way home. We got off the bus together, to be greeted by our mama, with Consuelo and Felis at her side. She picked us up in her arms and gave us a long hug.

I won't forget what she looked like that day. She was wearing a faded dress. It buttoned up all the way and had a collar. It had light purple and green flowers on it. It was stained on the sleeve, from what I assume was Felis's burping. Her long black hair was braided and went almost to the middle of her back. She wore no make-up, for we didn't have the money, but her beautiful big brown eyes made up for it.

My mama took us into the house where she made us a special surprise of my favorite meal, potatoes and eggs with home made tortillas. We ate hungrily and then told my mother of the eventful day we had had. That evening, my dad came home and we had to replay our day for him again, this time over dinner.

That night we went to bed very tired. We had pleaded with our parents all during dinner to never make us return to that horrible school, but to no avail. We were to go to school the next day and all the days after that. Of course, there were the usual playing sick tricks, but I was never a good liar. I got used to school, and the language, but I will never forget that first day.

■ *Suggested Scores*

Ideas: 5, 6
Organization: 5, 6
Voice: 5, 6
Word choice: 5, 6
Sentence fluency: 5, 6
Conventions: 5, 6

■ *Lessons Learned from Paper 13*

✔ When you make the reader feel it, that's voice.
✔ Simple images (Mama meeting the bus) can be stunning.

■ *Comments*

What a haunting piece of writing. This writer truly takes us inside the experience of a second-language speaker, a small child faced with adults who are not sensitive to his needs. We feel his fear. Following a slow introduction, the story moves at a good pace, experience to experience, right up to that brilliant frozen moment when Mama (symbol of comfort and home) meets the bus. The writer actually remembers what he ate for dinner on that day so long ago. The bilingual segments add tremendously to the voice, which is off the chart. Read this one more than once.

Paper 14: "Why I Read!" (Expository, Grade 7)

FIGURE 5.14
*Paper 14:
"Why I Read!"*

Reading. What can I say about reading? Reading is a flowing stream of letters that runs out of my faucet; drinking it is delectable, cool and refreshing. However at other times, it runs down the toilet, like what I hear goes in one ear and out the other. It is useless, annoying information poisoning my simple mind. It gives me brain cramps . . .

The words in a story always flow together, no matter in a circle, or a straight line. The words some how blend together. It reminds me of making a smoothie. Put bananas, raspberries, strawberries, blackberries, ice and orange juice in it; it sure tastes good. The orange juice would probably be the plot, and without it, it would be bad. I hope the writers are as good at smoothie making as they are at writing, because that sounds pretty good right now.

Reading is a big bunch of thoughts put together in a small, little book. Sort of like how they put all that tuna in one tiny can, or how many sardines they fit into the long, silver metal container. They are jam-packed! Those are good books! The bad books are like potato chip bags. They give you so little chips in a bag that it is worthless to get into it. Bad

continued

books are boring because their ideas are too broad and nondescriptive . . . can you see the relationship?

Mistake, I made not. *Stargirl* is an excellent book. Let me tell you why. *Stargirl* took me to her high school and made it feel like I was there in a real high school. I met her friends, and while I was doing that, it was like I was finding my own friends and what these friends would turn into eventually. The truth can come from these books, you know.

I read so one day I might endorse my own books, like Dr. Seuss, or Cynthia Voigt. The happiness it would bring me, just as much as being the winning pitcher in a World Series game. I shall learn like a sponge, absorbing what others write; what works and what doesn't.

I can't wait to open and close books every day. As I do the same with opening one door or another; what lies behind them; could there be a window of opportunity? Books and doors, both can be interesting . . . you never know what is hiding within!

Reading is a never-ending river; it will never stop, unless you choose it to. Don't let those letters run through your fingers like they're nothing. Grasp onto them before it's too late.

■ Suggested Scores

Ideas: 5, 6

Organization: 4, 5

Voice: 5, 6

Word choice: 4, 4

Sentence fluency: 4, 4

Conventions: 4, 5

■ Lessons Learned from Paper 14

✔ When you write, stuff a sardine can, not a potato chip bag.

✔ Never cave in to a cliché (*"window of opportunity"*) when you know you're capable of an original phrase (*It gives me brain cramps . . .*).

■ Comments

This is the perfect complement to "Why I Write" (Paper 15). This writer doesn't always go back to smooth a wrinkly sentence (*"Reading is a big, bunch of thoughts put together in a small, little book"*), but the piece overall is thoughtful and engaging. The metaphoric thinking gives this piece much of its voice—words as a river, books as tuna cans or potato chip bags, books as doors. It's always pleasurable to read the work of a thinker. *"Truth can come from books, you know."* Ah, yes.

Paper 15: "Why I Write" (Expository, Grade 7)

I write for no reason. If I'm forced to write, my pencil is my enemy, but if I'm bored in my room or a teacher won't stop talking and there's a piece of paper in front of me, a pencil is my best friend because in my opinion, writing passes the time better than any conversation.

I write to make people cry and talk to make people laugh because it's easier to make people laugh when you're in the moment than to write it in a story. Sadness is the greatest thing to write about because everybody has a different sense of humor, everybody has their opinion on who's interesting, but everybody knows what's sad: change and death.

I write because everyone thinks writing pieces will never be perfect, so they don't expect my stories to be. If you do sports everybody wants you to be the best, but with writing, they accept the fact that you don't have writing talent. They think that if you're not good at a sport, you can practice and be good. The same is true with writing, except no matter how many workshops you take, you may never have that certain edge it takes.

I write to make people use the dictionary. I think it's one of the greatest books ever written and if I use the dictionary it will create a chain of using it: I look up a few words in the dictionary and use them in my story, the person that reads it looks them up, then they will probably show off their improved vocabulary to their friends, and their friends will want to know what the word is. It's all a process of making the world less idiotic.

I write because writing is like a thousand piece puzzle. There are almost a million ways to arrange the giant thing, but you have to carefully arrange it piece-by-piece, step-by-step. It seems like a never-ending process, some people think it is, but once you have done all of your trial and errors, your mistakes, and slip ups, you find yourself looking at a masterpiece.

I write to teach someone ignorant a lesson. Whether it's something about my life, life in general, or that I'm not a moron, they will learn something. When you read my stories, you might love it, hate it, or just want to shoot me for trying, but when you see the story you will learn a thing or two about a thing or two.

■ *Suggested Scores*

Ideas: 5, 6

Organization: 4, 5

Voice: 5, 5

Word choice: 3, 4
Sentence fluency: 4, 4
Conventions: 4, 5

■ *Lessons Learned from Paper 15*

✔ A key phrase can connect otherwise disjointed thoughts in a personal reflection.

✔ Insight (*"Everybody knows what's sad: change and death"*) is one key to voice.

■ *Comments*

Disconnected thoughts? Well, not really. As in "Why I Read!" (Paper 14), these reflections together form a cohesive essay. Perhaps the writer thought of several at once or thought of them on different days. They are moments that define who this writer is. The voice in this piece shifts from funny to reflective to philosophical, serious, and even a little superior in the closing paragraph. It's always there, though, always present, a force driving the writing. Word choice is a bit erratic, sometimes strong (*"when you're in the moment," "that certain edge," "thousand-piece puzzle"*), sometimes more routine (*"it's one of the greatest books ever written"*). There are a few small errors in conventions— nothing serious. The trouble is, when you write this well, people start to expect it all the time.

See Chapters 8 and 9 for numerous instructional ideas relating to voice, word choice, and sentence fluency.

CHAPTER 5 IN A NUTSHELL

● Voice is the imprint of the writer on the page. It is more than personality, though; it springs from confidence, enthusiasm, passion for the topic, and sensitivity to the needs and interests of the audience. It is also a tool for getting—and holding—a reader's attention.

● Word choice is both creation of imagery through colorful language and strong verbs and precision in selecting the *just right* word or phrase to convey meaning. Word choice supports voice and builds a bridge connecting voice to message.

● Sentence fluency is a measure of how writing plays to the ear. Strong fluency is marked by variety in sentence length and structure and is both achieved and measured through continual reading aloud of the text. Sentence fluency also supports voice.

● Each piece of writing has specific lessons to teach us about writing; careful assessment helps reveal those lessons.

EXTENSIONS

1. Based on your experience scoring papers in Chapter 4, how would you rate your understanding of the traits of voice, word choice, and sentence fluency?

    _____ Excellent. I am developing my own personal definition for each of these traits.

    _____ Fair. I need more examples, but my understanding is growing.

    _____ Not there yet. I feel confused about _____.

2. Did you find yourself agreeing (within a point) on most of the suggested scores within this chapter? If you disagreed repeatedly, what do you think was the cause of the disagreement? Write about it.

3. If you are teaching now, which of the traits that we have covered so far seems strongest in your own students' writing? Why do you think this is so? Discuss your perceptions with colleagues.

4. Identify three or more favorite pieces of literature. By reading aloud to students or colleagues, identify selections ("moments" of 50 to 100 words or so) that you could use as models of voice, word choice, or fluency. Make a list.

5. In your own words, write a definition of each of the traits covered so far. Do not refer to the rubric as you do this. Later, check the rubric to see how your personal wording differs. At some point ask students to create their own personal definitions, too.

6. Pick a topic—any topic—about which you care deeply. Write a short piece on this topic—perhaps a paragraph or two or as much as a page or two. Tuck it away for three days or longer. Pull it out and read the piece aloud, making any changes that feel right. Then revise deliberately using these guidelines: (1) Tell the truth, (2) make the verbs strong and keep modifiers to a minimum, (3) vary the sentence beginnings and lengths, (4) add one quotation or bit of dialogue, and (5) give it a title after all other changes have been made. Now read it aloud again. What do you hear?

WHY I WRITE

I write so I can be in my own little world. . . . I love having my own little world because it's all me and most of the time I think the world revolves around me. A lot of people say to me, "Madison, the world doesn't surround you." But I think it does. . . .

—**Madison Sessums,** student writer

LOOKING AHEAD

You are now acquainted with the foundational traits ideas and organization, as well as with the three traits that add flavor to any written piece: voice, word choice, and sentence fluency. In Chapter 6 we'll frame the picture with conventions and presentation, putting all six traits together to create a performance profile.

6 Framing the Picture:
Conventions and Presentation

Conventions belong to all of us. In acquiring them we gain the power to say new things, extend our meaning, and discover new relationships between ideas. For too long, teachers and editors have stood guard over conventions, as if they were esoteric knowledge available only to the few.

—Donald H. Graves
A Fresh Look at Writing, 1994, p. 210

We are dealing with a complicated system, and every element of that system, down to the conventional signs for pauses and nuances, has had a long testing. Its function is to help reproduce in cold print what was a human voice speaking for human ears.

—Wallace Stegner
On Teaching and Writing Fiction, 2002, p. 63

With this chapter we add the sixth trait—conventions and presentation—to the mix, giving us a very complete profile for any piece of writing. This trait puts the spit and polish on a piece of writing and, in so doing, further clarifies the message. Attention to conventions is, as much as anything, a courtesy to the reader. When we invite guests into our homes, we tidy up, dust, vacuum, dim the lights, turn on the music, light the candles. In so doing, we say, in effect, "I want you to feel at home here." Tidying up text is a way of making readers feel at home within our writing. Editing and formatting also bring closure to writing—in much the same way that framing celebrates and brings closure to an artist's work.

CONVENTIONS AND PRESENTATION: EDITING AND FRAMING

Focus for Assessing and Teaching Conventions and Presentation

> In conversation you can use timing, a look, inflection, pauses. But on the page all you have is commas, dashes, the amount of syllables in a word. When I write I read everything out loud to get the right rhythm.
>
> **—Fran Lebowitz**
>
> *Writing With Style: Conversations on the Art of Writing*, 2000, p. 105

- ✔ Reading with an editor's eye
- ✔ Understanding the concept of conventions as what is currently acceptable or favored in print materials
- ✔ Understanding and applying current rules governing spelling, punctuation, grammar and usage, capitalization, and paragraphing
- ✔ Editing all text to ensure readability
- ✔ Knowing and using copy editor's symbols
- ✔ Giving sufficient attention to layout to make text presentable and readable for the intended audience

PRACTICE PAPERS

What To Do

- ✔ Have a copy of the rubric in front of you.
- ✔ Agree on a handbook that you will use as the *final authority*, if needed.

GETTING A MINDSET

Conventions fall into two categories: textual and visual. *Textual conventions* cover anything a copy editor would deal with: spelling, punctuation, grammar and usage, capitalization, and paragraphing (which supports organization but is scored here). Such conventions clearly change over time, and so to assess or teach them well, we need to rely on up-to-date handbooks and dictionaries and use them often. Textual conventions not only support meaning but also help readers to understand intended inflection and voice. In Roald Dahl's book *Matilda*, for example, five-year-old Matilda asks her television-addicted father to buy her a book, and conventions (italics, abbreviations) show us precisely how to read his response: "A *book*?" He said. "What d'you want a flaming book for?" (1988, p. 12).

Visual conventions (also known as *presentation*) are so called because they visually organize text, guiding the reader's eye and making certain points stand out. They include such things as graphics (maps, charts, photographs) that support text or expand meaning, use of bulleted or numbered lists, and use of titles and subheads. Visual conventions are more important in some kinds of text than in others (e.g., layout is of particular concern when drafting a business letter or printing a newspaper, poster, or menu), and you should respond to them accordingly. They need not be considered for every paper.

✔ Make a copy of the scoring grid (Figure 3.8) if you are working with a group.

✔ Make copies of papers you will score so that you can write on them.

✔ Make overheads of any papers that you wish to share with a group.

✔ Read each paper aloud prior to scoring.

✔ Score each paper for conventions and presentation (along with any additional traits you wish to practice on).

✔ Discuss your scores and the reasons for them with a partner or group.

✔ Check your scores against the suggested scores provided in this book.

✔ Discuss the "Lessons Learned" for each paper.

Tips on Scoring Papers for the Trait of Conventions and Presentation

This one should be easy, shouldn't it? Isn't it the most clear-cut? Not really. We do not all agree on what is conventionally correct, for one thing. How many commas go in a series? Which words should be capitalized? Which numbers should be spelled out? Is it ever all right to begin a sentence with *and*? Is *data* plural? What about *none*? Do you cringe at *firstly*? *Secondly*? Is second person sometimes *alright*? Do you use it *alot*? Little things get to us all, and we strike back: *Score of 1 for you!* Such things as failing to capitalize the pronoun *i* or writing *alot* as one word might be annoying, but they are not federal offenses and should not cause a drop in a student's score from, say, a 5 to a 1 or 2, but sometimes this is what happens.

Part of the problem lies in our tendency to define conventions strictly in terms of correctness. This is limiting. Conventions exist to serve the message and to make interpretation of the message easier. Thus conventions are clues that guide reading, both reading for meaning and reading for voice. The first time I recall thinking about this was when my sixth grade teacher asked us to consider the difference between these two sentences:

"Let's kick, John!" said the coach.
"Let's kick John!" said the coach.

Correctness is not the issue here; using conventions to help ensure that the reader's interpretation matches the writer's intended message is the issue. Picture George in your mind as you read these two sentences:

"Please. Close the door," said George, turning to face me.
"Please!! CLOSE THE *DOOR!!*" said George, turning to face me.

In the first sentence, George is concerned and has something of consequence (requiring privacy) to say. In the second sentence, George is red-faced and ferocious, and I wouldn't close that door on a bet.

Here are some keys to assessing conventions well:

1. *Look beyond spelling.* Spelling is important, yes, but it is not the whole of conventions. How is the punctuation? The paragraphing? The grammar? Some students who do not spell well have other things very much under control.

2. *Score conventions first.* Conventions, for better or worse, often influence how we see a piece as a whole. Therefore, to keep your scoring fair and accu-

rate, it may be helpful to score that trait first and get it out of the way, especially when conventions are noticeably weak or strong.

3. *Look for what is done well*, not just the mistakes. Balance the two.

4. *Do not overreact.* One mistake—or two or three—cannot spoil the whole performance. If we put three skilled editors in a room, it is highly doubtful that any of us could create text of any length or complexity that would pass the critical eye and pen of all three, nor would they likely agree on which texts were conventionally strongest. We make a mistake when we demand conventional perfection of students, for we cannot teach to such a standard or even meet it ourselves. So ask, "Overall, how well does the student control and use conventions to make meaning clear?"

5. *Do not consider neatness or handwriting in assigning a conventions score.* Such things may be important, but they are separate issues. Writing beautifully (or even legibly, for that matter) and editing text to make it conventionally correct and communicative are different skills altogether.

6. *Think of yourself as a copy editor.* Ask, "How much work would I need to do to prepare this text for publication? Heavy editing? That's a 1 or 2. Moderate? That's a 3 or 4. Very light—touch-ups only? That's a 5 or 6.

7. *Focus on control, not perfection.* How often have you found a typo in a newspaper or novel? Such copy has been rigorously scrutinized by professional editors, yet tiny irregularities often escape their eagle eyes. We should set high but realistic goals. Perfect text is not the ultimate goal anyway, is it? We want young writers/editors who are in control of conventions, who can spot errors given opportunity and time, and who know how to correct them (without our having to tell them what to do).

■ *What About Presentation?*

My recommendation is to consider presentation to the extent that it is critical to the success of the piece. If your students are creating newsletter copy, business letters, posters, brochures, or other forms of writing in which layout and graphics play an important role, then by all means take time to consider visual conventions. I would look specifically for the following things so far as each is applicable and relevant to the writing:

- ✔ Appropriate business letter format
- ✔ Use of a title or main heading to capture the essential message
- ✔ Use of subheads to mark sections
- ✔ Consistency in subheads (e.g., font size and style, placement, spacing)
- ✔ Use of graphics that support the text
- ✔ Consistent labeling of graphics
- ✔ Restraint in the use of fonts (no more than two or three per page)
- ✔ Font style and size that enhance readability
- ✔ Sufficient margins to make text width comfortable for reading
- ✔ Use of bulleted or numbered lists, as needed

These features are easy to recognize and check. I would comment on them and encourage them. I would give them very modest weight in assigning scores, however, and would consider them in assessment only when the purpose for writing made presentation critical. Visual conventions such as graphics and bulleted lists can be very helpful in guiding a reader's eye and certainly can give writing appeal. Most of us look carefully at book covers and front pages of newspapers before purchasing them. In the end, however, serious readers will choose a newspaper for thorough, intelligent journalism, not for splashy charts and photos. Writing is not about appearance. It's about *thinking on the page*. If we shift focus and begin to weigh how writing looks equally with what it says and how effectively it says it, we give students a mixed message about what writing is.

Keep in mind too that in the real world of publishing, layout is usually handled by persons who are gifted specialists in artistic presentation; we must be careful about connecting this skill to writing. What appeals to me may not appeal to you at all (perhaps you like a subdued look, whereas I prefer something more flamboyant and colorful; you swoon over Monét, whereas I revel in the whimsy of Jules Feiffer), and coming up with guidelines to govern assessment of layout introduces serious potential for bias and inconsistency.

For classroom purposes, if students keep the number of fonts per page to a reasonable minimum, respect margins and clearly identified rules of layout (for business letters or citations, say), print in a font size that is readable, and use graphics that support the main points of the text, that should (in most cases) be sufficient to meet our expectations.

Let's look at two pieces just for textual conventions: spelling, punctuation, paragraphing, grammar and usage, and capitalization. We'll then briefly consider presentation and put all traits together in a number of practice papers.

Paper 1: "Haircut from Hell" (Narrative/Imaginative, Grade 7)

FIGURE 6.1
Paper 1:
"Haircut from Hell"

I failed to tell the new worker at "Haircroppers" how I wanted my hair cut. He swung my chair away from the mirror. The noises that fallowed sounded like chainswas, hedge trimmers, and helocopters. Then he swung my chair back to face the mirror. . . .

From the time he swung my chair around, I knew that would be my last visit to "Haircroppers."

My hair, or what was left of it was tinted a brown olive green color. I felt my hair. A slimey sticky residue came off on my hand. I gave a quick smurk and vigorously rubbed the slime onto my pants.

Unbelievably enough, the quick smile I had given the nin-cum-poop barber was taken to be genuine and he quickly responded, "Glad you like it sir That's my best one yet!"

Disgusted, I turned back to my hair. Maybe a wig was the way to go. I felt some of the olive green goop dribbel down my neck.

I felt my hair again and was immediately stopped by a blur of barbers hands. With rage in his voice he yelled "What are you trying to do, ruin my masterpiece?!"

" Your masterpiece??!! More like your mess. What is this junk anyway? Some kind of axel greese?"

His voice was wavery, but refused to crack. "Its my own creation . . . face mud, hair spray, avacado dip . . . "

I let him get as far as turtle wax when I roared "Hold it!!"

My face was beginning to twist, my scalp to burn. "Hose this junk off, you incompitent moron. If my head doesn't just role to the floor, I'll have your hide!" I couldn't wait a moment longer. I grabed the hose and turned it on myself. Whew. The solution came out into a brown puddle on the floor, along with great chunks of my hair.

Fortunatly, I didn't have to pay for what I call today my hair's "mass suicide. "

■ *Suggested Scores for Focus Trait: Conventions*

Conventions: 2, 3

■ *Lessons Learned from Paper 1*

✔ Faulty conventions can distract the reader.
✔ Good dialogue adds voice.

■ *Comments*

Many of the conventional errors in this paper seem to be the result of hasty editing. Apostrophes are overlooked, and commas and capitals missed. There are too many paragraphs. A scrupulous editor will make corrections as he or she reads, but this should be the *writer's* job. The thing that saves this paper from lower scores in conventions is the writer's skillful use of some conventions, such as ellipses, question marks, and exclamation points to reinforce voice. By contrast, the imagery is vivid, and voice is *very* strong. Lead and conclusion are excellent, and dialogue is authentic. Notice the strong verbs. Read it aloud to appreciate the fluency. This is a highly imaginative piece.

■ *Suggested Scores for Other Traits*

Ideas: 5, 6

Organization: 5, 6

Voice: 5, 6

Word choice: 5, 6

Sentence fluency: 5, 6

Paper 2: "The Ritual of Rocks and Sticks" (Imaginative, Grade 6)

FIGURE 6.2

Paper 2: "The Ritual of Rocks and Sticks"

While visiting America I had the opportunity to attend a ritual called the baseball game. In this ritual, an enormous crowd of people gather around, sitting on multi-leveled seats, watching a crowd of people perform.

The performers of the ritual are dressed in striped clothes similar to a zebra. They have pieces of cowhide tied to one hand, and they beat the cowhide with their free hand and make loud grunting noises. Sometimes they spit, and everyone seems to enjoy this part. Their heads are covered in bright colored cloth, which they touch quite often, sometimes running their hands along the front part of the cloth, which hangs over their eyes. When one does this, other performers nod and slap the cowhide hard. Clearly, this is a significant part of the ritual.

The performer in the middle of the flat area is known as the pitcher. He stands on a small hill and throws a hard ball of string at another performer, who holds a long stick. The stick man, also known as a batter, tries to hit the ball of string. If he succeeds, he immediately drops his stick and runs in a huge circle, touching white squares as he passes. The people dressed in stripes run after the ball of string, and then go after the stick man, tossing the ball of string hard as they go. They rarely catch him, but if they do, he yanks the cloth from his head and whacks his leg with it, giving out a mighty yell. The crowd yells with him. This much I have figured out: Once the stick man hits the ball of string, he does not want it back. He is very unhappy if the other performers return it to him.

This hitting and running part of the ritual is performed many times until both the performers and the people in the multi-leveled seats grow tired. As they go, they make more grunting noises and hit one another on the back quite a lot. This means the ritual is over for that day. But they will hold it again. They always take their balls of string and their sticks with them to be ready for the next time.

■ *Suggested Scores for Focus Trait: Conventions*

Conventions: 5, 6

■ *Lessons Learned from Paper 2*

✔ Understatement can be effective.
✔ Let the reader figure it out—but be sure you provide good clues.

■ *Comments*

How might the game of baseball look to someone seeing it for the first time? This is the premise of this understated but strong piece. Fans will identify with various parts of the ritual—spitting, slapping the cowhide hard, and the wonderful line about the runner not wanting the hard ball of string back. The pacing is good; the writer provides good imagery but does not take us play by play through a whole game. We go smoothly from players to fans and back again. The language is perfectly functional and includes a few strong verbs—*nod, whack, slap*. The writer's word choice effectively emphasizes the physical side of the game. The rocks mutate into hard balls of string, but this is a minor point—it doesn't confuse us. Sentence fluency is also strong, although more transitions would smooth the flow. Conventions are excellent.

■ *Suggested Scores for Other Traits*

Ideas: 5, 6

Organization: 5, 6

Voice: 5, 6

Word choice: 4, 5

Sentence fluency: 4, 5

EXAMPLES OF PRESENTATION

Let's consider, briefly, two pieces for which presentation is important. I do not wish to put scores on them but only to use them for discussion purposes. The first is a poem (Figure 6.3) that is beautifully formatted to capture the rhythm and guide our reading. Format is important in poetry because it helps determine how we read and how we pick up specific images, e.g., "dark thundering thoughts" or "half-drenched ladybugs." Punctuation in poetry is important, too, but it does not follow the same rules as punctuation in prose. A writer who omits terminal punctuation, for example, creates the sense that thoughts are floating and continuous. In this poem, the short lines are punchlines, and they serve the function of periods.

For a second example, I have chosen several pages (Figure 6.4) from the work of a young published writer, Kelsea Larson (*Sunset Dream*, 1998). As you look through Kelsea's book, notice the font and artwork she chose for her cover, the way she set up her dedication and title pages, the way text complements art, and the author's page with which she finishes her piece. Inclusion of these key pieces is conventional, and students

---

FIGURE 6.3   *"Rain and Ivy," by Kira (poetry, grade 3)*

Rain and Ivy
By Kira

Green, delicate, smooth, light green
Clumps of ivy
Shadows rain down with
Dark thundering thoughts
Rain
Rustling leaves whisper in your ears
It's silent, then it whispers
Soft, soothing
Mind-reading words
Rain pours down
You reach for your umbrella
Still keeping your eyes on those ivy leaves
You notice that ladybugs shelter under those leaves
Trying to keep dry
Rain thunders down
And your mother is calling you
To come
So you don't get drenched
You go
Leaving the ivy alone in the rain
Sheltering those poor half-drenched ladybugs
The next morning
You go to check on the ivy
After that you always look
At that ivy
With loving eyes.

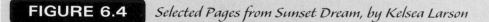

FIGURE 6.4 *Selected Pages from Sunset Dream, by Kelsea Larson*

Sunset Dream

written and illustrated

by

Kelsea Larson

One misty evening in early spring, a young girl and her dad went fishing. The fog was just beginning to settle over the lake as they cast their lines into the water. The girl felt a cool breeze rush across her face.

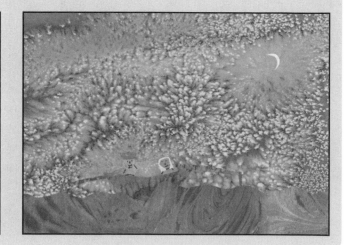

FIGURE 6.4 *continued*

The boat gently rocked back and forth in the quiet lake. Just as the sun was setting, the young girl fell asleep. She dreamed that she and her friend turned into two wiggly worms.

All of a sudden, the girl woke up. She found herself back in her boat staring up at the glistening stars. She sat up and leaned over the side of the boat. Sunset salmon were jumping all around! The young girl smiled to herself.

About the Author/Illustrator

My name is Kelsea Helena Larson. I am nine years old. I live in Newmarket, New Hampshire. I like to swim in my river, climb trees, eat fruits and vegetables, and do art.

I made my collage pictures from the beautiful papers I painted. I cut out shapes and pasted them on my background papers. My story idea just kept growing as I cut and pasted. I got the words for my story by looking at my pictures.

I think my pictures are lovely because I added lots of details. I hope to be an artist when I grow up.

who publish should be familiar with them. Clearly, this is a work for which presentation plays an integral role. Kelsea has kept her presentation very clean and clutter-free. It is easy to read. Most impressive, though, is the way text and illustrations blend to support meaning and mood. For a master lesson on layout, publication of a children's book is tough to beat.

PUTTING ALL TRAITS TOGETHER

It's time to look at all six traits together, creating a complete performance profile. In assessing the remaining papers, follow the usual procedures, making copies of rubrics and papers, reading pieces aloud, and discussing both scores and lessons learned.

Paper 3: "File Sharing Is Not the Spawn of Satan" (Persuasive/Expository, Grade 12)

FIGURE 6.5
Paper 3: "File Sharing Is Not the Spawn of Satan"

I'm in my car, driving to who knows where, doing who knows what. Sunroof open, windows down, and the radio playing. Life is good. One song ends and another begins. This new song catches my attention. It has a nice beat and rhythm and the lyrics aren't half bad. I think to myself, "Self, who is this song by? I have no idea." I then wait until the song ends for the radio DJ to enlighten me as to who it was. I realize that this is a group that I've never heard of before and I liked the song so much that I may actually consider purchasing their CD. Here presents a problem: What if this band is just a one-hit wonder and the rest of the music on that reflective circle is flat-out horrible? That would be thirteen dollars down the drain. Thirteen dollars for one song is a little pricey for my tastes. So what do I do instead? I start up my friendly file-sharing software and, slowly but surely, get the one song I want to listen to at a savings of roughly thirteen dollars. Who can argue with that? Apparently the Recording Industry Association of America (RIAA) can.

The RIAA claims that users (I am a former user, not because of the impending threats, but because I can only download one song a day in 56k-land and as they say, "Only a song a day keeps the RIAA away.") are illegally downloading copyrighted material and costing themselves and poor, starving artists such as Madonna and Eminem millions of dollars. Because of this, the RIAA is now suing the Al-Gore-invented-pants off of folks who are allowing such a heinous crime, royalty endangerment, to occur on their computer. How much are they saying they have been deprived of and are rightfully due? A mere $100,000 per song.

Songs cost that much these days, right? That's how much an artist receives in royalties for one use of one song, isn't it? Oh, wait, it's not. So how did the amount of this penalty originate? How is it justified as fair retribution? Why am I worried about fairness, you may ask? Oh, I don't know, I just thought that we, as Americans, were protected from unusual punishment or something like that in something I once heard referred to as the Bill of Rights. I could be wrong. Wait a minute, I get it! Madonna lives in England so we're exempt from the United States Constitution! That must be it!

Why is it that in the day of the information superhighway, the RIAA is trying to close it and send us on a detour? Have they just realized that bootlegging is a problem, that we can now, all of a sudden, just make copies of music onto cassettes (gasp!) and CDs? Oh, wait, we've been able to do that for years. Why has it taken them till now to act?

Does the RIAA not realize that trying to fix this problem will make it worse, will make people more determined to try and circumvent the threats of lawsuits? Who in their right mind would voluntarily stop getting something for free and start paying for it? Lawsuits will cause even more people to hate the RIAA and find more ways to get free music. This musical can of worms (which, when opened plays "I Can't Get No) Satisfaction" by the Rolling Stones and can be yours for (insert number of illegally downloaded songs here) easy payments of $100,000) that has been opened will cause many more problems along the way than the RIAA ever dreamed of on its starving-artist-saving stairway to heaven.

■ Suggested Scores

Ideas: 4, 5

Organization: 4, 5

Voice: 5, 6 (You may score it lower if you find the sarcasm inappropriate.)

Word choice: 4, 5

Sentence fluency: 5, 6

Conventions: 5, 6

■ Lessons Learned from Paper 3

✔ Sarcasm is risky—but it's a voice some readers will love.
✔ You need to give the other side equal time.

■ Comments

This one is good practice because your take on the writer's position—and on his voice—could influence your scores, possibly unfairly. First, let's acknowledge that the writer is highly skilled and (if you respond to the voice) very funny as well. The argument is well crafted in terms of its clarity and the specific examples. Slightly lower scores in ideas reflect the fact that the writer does not seriously consider the infringement of copyright issue—which affects many people less wealthy than Madonna. The point about the severity of the penalty is well taken and well argued. The logic breaks down a bit, though, with the suggestion that downloading music must be okay because we've gotten by with similar stunts for years—and besides, those RIAA people just aren't likable. Sorry, but this doesn't make the pirating of copyrighted materials okay. Nevertheless, despite the flippant tone, this one had me laughing, and I'd like to meet the writer. The language is simple but effective. Notice the masterful use of conventions to reinforce voice. Scathing, risky—well done.

Paper 4: "A Beautiful Dream" (Memoir, Grade 12)

FIGURE 6.6

Paper 4: "A Beautiful Dream"

I live in a small town with a low crime rate. The town I come from is so small, I doubt it is even on a map. Everyone knows everything about everybody. In my town, the vast majority of people are white. I, however, come from a mixed background and I am dark-skinned.

I will never forget my third grade year when our class briefly discussed the Civil War, thus leading to a conversation on slavery. Most third graders could care less about skin color, however, I met someone that day whom I bothered a lot because I was not white. After drinking from the water fountain, a boy in my class told me he would never drink from that fountain again because "my black slave lips" were near it. He said that because I looked black, I did not belong in the class. That night, I told my mother what had happened and cried for hours. It was my first taste of the 'real world' and I hated it.

Throughout the rest of the year, I dealt with hurtful remarks made by this boy who did not even know me, just knew I was not white. I dreaded talking about American History and slavery. I would sink down in my seat at the mention of the word "slave." There I was, an innocent eight year old girl who felt ashamed and angry at her parents for not "making her" white.

In my seventh grade year, I found myself sitting across from the very boy that made me resent my color for years. Just seeing him made me want to hide under my desk because I still was not white. That year, we learned about underwater creatures, human life and what made living things 'operate.' Though biology was not my major, I understood the material. He didn't. I could have made fun of him for not understanding the very thing he was—a living creature—but I chose not to. Instead, I offered to help him during class. At first, he was more than just a little skeptical, but I insisted I could help him pass the class. It was the hardest thing I ever had to do that year. I tutored him for a little over a month. Throughout that time, we became friends. When we would pass each other in the halls, we'd smile and say 'hi.' On Mondays, we would talk about our weekends. We were far from *best* friends, but we were friends. That's all that mattered.

We've grown apart since then, and sadly, he converted to his old behaviors. However, he played a crucial influential role in my life. He confirmed my decision to become a teacher. The fact that, despite his intense dislike for me, he was willing to learn and I was willing to teach proved to me that I am capable of being a teacher. I know I can look past students' attitudes and focus on their need to acquire knowledge. I am dependable, caring and unselfish—all traits needed to be an excellent teacher.

Eleanor Roosevelt once said, "The future belongs to those who believe in the beauty of their dreams." I believe my dreams will become a reality with the persistence for a college education. It is my dream to influence and affect students in a positive manner. Now, I think that is a beautiful dream.

■ Suggested Scores

Ideas: 5, 6

Organization: 5, 6

Voice: 5, 6

Word choice: 4, 5

Sentence fluency: 5, 6

Conventions: 5, 6

■ Lessons Learned from Paper 4

✔ Quiet voices can be powerful.

✔ Tell the truth and hold readers in your hand.

■ Comments

Voice is the stand-out trait in this heartfelt memoir. Don't overlook the excellent organization, though. The writer sets up the piece and then pulls from memory two distinct but clearly connected events that together lead to the resolution—her decision to teach. Particularly significant is the fact that there is not one formulaic thread in this piece. The closing quotation from Eleanor Roosevelt is a nice touch. There are excellent transitions and smooth sentences. Language is simple, but it works. Clean conventions.

Paper 5: "A Strange Visiter" (Narrative/Imaginative, Grade 5)

FIGURE 6.7
Paper 5:
"A Strange Visitor"

The doors flew open, the wind whipped around the room. The startled men looked up. Standing in the door was a man. His royal purple cloak rippled in the draft. The room was silent. There was a sudden noise as the men put down their wine goblets. Tink, tink, tink. The room grew hot and sweaty. Some men tried to speak but nothing came out. The gleam of the strange visiters eyes had frightened the knights who had slain many dragons, and fought bravley for the King. The errieness was unbearable. The visitor's gray beard sparkled in the candlelight giving it an errie glow. The windows let the dark seap in. The large room decorated with banners seemed to get smaller and smaller. The heavy aroma of wine hung in the air like fog on a dull morning. Their dinner bubbled in their stomachs. Their rough fingers grasped their sowrds stowed under their seats. The round table again fell silent. Then slowly the man spoke: " The King has come." The End

■ Suggested Scores

1Ideas: 5, 6
Organization: 5, 6
Voice: 5, 5
Word choice: 5, 6
Sentence fluency: 3, 4
Conventions: 3, 4

■ Lessons Learned from Paper 5

✔ Disturb the silence with the clink of wine glasses, and the reader will hear it.
✔ Tension heightens readers' interest.

■ Comments

Problems in this piece are minor compared with the strengths. The paper does need some work in conventions, although many things are done correctly (including spelling of difficult words). "The End" is an unfortunate conclusion—but again, I'm being picky. Sentences tend toward the short side. A little sentence combining and more variety (too many *the*'s and *their*'s) would raise these scores significantly. On the other hand, there is extraordinary attention to detail—mood, tension, colors, sounds. I feel that I'm right there in the castle. Who is the mysterious visitor in royal purple? Why, the very man you've risked your life for—the *king*. Why don't they know? Remember, this is medieval times, when you might not know what the king looked like unless you had met him. This is a great touch. The language has a simple elegance: "*The aroma of wine hung in the air like fog on a dull morning."* The writer uses mostly one-syllable words. This is why it's strong, not overdone.

Paper 6: "The Day My Grandfather Died" (Personal Narrative, Grade 4)

FIGURE 6.8
Paper 6:
"The Day My
Grandfather Died"

> The day was dark and gloomy. It was the day my grandfather died. I felt like a turtle who couldn't come out of its shell. All I did was cry and mope around the house. I was shocked by the horrifying news. There was so much yet to tell him. I was really hurt but I knew my grandfather wouldn't want me to feel that way. So I didn't let his death hold me back.
>
> I tried to deal with the fact that my grandfather was gone. All I had were memories, but they were good memories. Instead of playing, I wrote in my diary. It became my best friend. That helped me deal with the sorrowful truth. It was a bitter-sweet moment. When my grandfather died, we all knew that his suffering was over. Yet we were sorrowful because my grandfather was gone.
>
> My favorite memory of my grandfather was when we were walking through the park, and he told me of his childhood. It gives me peaceful thoughts just to think of that memory. It seems like just yesterday, but it's a good memory. My grandfather will never leave that special place in my heart.

■ Suggested Scores

Ideas: 4, 5

Organization: 4, 5

Voice: 5, 6

Word choice: 4, 5

Sentence fluency: 4, 5

Conventions: 5, 6

■ Lessons Learned from Paper 6

✔ Images make the difference in ideas and voice.

✔ Some papers touch us in a way that makes scoring very hard.

■ Comments

Scoring this paper feels almost disrespectful, so you may find it very difficult to respond in that way. I do. This is a touching and emotional piece. The voice is very strong. Ideas are clear to be sure—the turtle inside its shell, so much left to say (Doesn't that touch a chord?), the best-friend diary, the bittersweet truth. These moments, so strong, so telling, make up for the fact that we do not get to hear the grandfather speak in the last paragraph, the favorite-memory stroll through the park. Sentences are consistently short (with a couple exceptions). This is a minor problem in a paper that is very moving.

Paper 7: "Should People Be Allowed to Go Barefoot?" (Persuasive, Grade 6)

FIGURE 6.9

Paper 7: "Should People Be Allowed to Go Barefoot?"

I think people should not be able to go barefoot because it stinks. It's okay if people don't were shoes in their own houses. I refuse to not were shoes in public places. If there going to go barefoot at least wash your feet first. People don't want to smell your sweaty feet!

One time when I was at my house, my brother ask a friend if he could come over and watch a movie. His friend came and he took off his shoes. And it stunk so bad that we had to make him go wash his feet. Not pointing any fingers (Sean!). It was so nasty.

I think people should not were barefeet because you can see there toenails and they are useually dirty if you see someones barefeet. Some people paint there toenails, that looks cute, But you can still smell it.

Sandels. Sandels are okay as long as there not sweaty because you can still smell them if they are sweaty. If your going to were sandles. I ask you to not let us smell the sweat!

My conclusion is that Sandels are okay as long as you don't let us smell the swet. Toe nails need to be clean, and Sean isnt coming over anymore unless his feet are clean.

- ## Suggested Scores

    Ideas: 4, 4
    Organization: 3, 3
    Voice: 5, 5
    Word choice: 3, 4
    Sentence fluency: 4, 4
    Conventions: 3, 3

- ## Lessons Learned from Paper 7

    ✔ Even if you make a point three ways, it's still the same point.
    ✔ Real-world examples (Sean) are stronger than hypothetic examples ("Some people paint their toenails. . . .").

✔ Watch out for shifts from third person to first person—"If *they're* going to go barefoot at least wash *your* feet first."

■ *Comments*

The writer is enthusiastic and committed to her topic; this enthusiasm puts power into her voice. Her main point is clear: Feet smell, so people should not go barefoot. She remains focused on this point and does not change her position halfway through the piece, as many young writers will do in persuasive mode. This focus and clarity earn her a fairly strong score on ideas, despite some repetition. Painting toenails and wearing sandals are ways of disguising bare feet, but these cosmetic changes, she argues, do not hide that odor. She could make her argument stronger by providing more real-world examples and exploring other issues, e.g., the discomfort of going barefoot or the hazards of not wearing shoes. The piece is playful and lively (so much so that readers may overlook many small conventional errors); this is a writer on her way.

Paper 8: "Computer Blues" (Narrative, Grade 12)

FIGURE 6.10
Paper 8:
"Computer Blues"

So there I was, my face aglow with the reflection of my computer screen, trying to conclude my essay. Writing it was akin to Chinese water torture. It dragged on and on, a never-ending babble about legumes, nutrients and soil degradation. I was tranquilizing myself with my own writing.

Suddenly, unexpectedly—I felt an ending coming on. Four or five punchy sentences would bring this baby to a close, and I'd be free of this dreadful assignment forever! Yes!

I had not saved yet, and decided I would do so now. I scooted the white mouse over the pad toward the "File" menu—and had almost reached home when it happened. By accident, I clicked the mouse button just to the left of paragraph 66. The screen flashed briefly, and the next thing I knew, I was back to square one. Black. I stared at the blank screen for a moment in disbelief. Where was my essay? My ten-billion-page masterpiece? Gone?! No—that couldn't be! Not after all the work I had done! Would a computer be that unforgiving? That *unfeeling?* Didn't it care about me at all?

I decided not to give up hope just yet. The secret was to remain calm. After all, my file had to be somewhere—right? That's what all the manuals say—" It's in there *somewhere.*" I went back to the "File" menu, much more carefully this time. First, I tried a friendly sounding category called "Find File." No luck there; I hadn't given my file a name.

Ah, then I had a brainstorm. I could simply go up to *Undo.* Yes, *Undo* would be my savior! A simple click of a button and my problem would be solved! *Undo,* however, looked a bit fuzzy. Not a good sign. "Fuzzy" means there is nothing to undo. *Don't panic . . . don't panic . . .*

continued

I decided to try exiting the program, not really knowing what I would accomplish by this, but now feeling more than a little desperate. Next, I clicked on the icon that would allow me back in to word processing. A small sign appeared, telling me that my program was being used by "another user." Another user? What's it talking about? I'm the only user, you idiot! Or at least I'm trying to be a user! Give my paper back! Right now!

I clicked on the icon again and again—to no avail. Click . . . click . . . clickclickclickclickCLICKCLICKCLICKCLICK!!!!! Without warning, a thin trickle of smoke began emanating from the back of the computer. I didn't know whether to laugh or cry. Sighing, I opened my desk drawer, and pulled out a tablet and pen. This was going to be a long day.

Student's Comments

In this essay, I tried to capture the feelings of frustration that occur when human and machine do not communicate. The voice in this piece comes, I think, from the feeling that "We've all been there." Everyone who works with computers has had this experience—or something close to it. I also try to give the writer—me—some real personality so the sense of building tension comes through. A tiny writer's problem (not being able to find a good ending) turns into a major problem (losing a whole document). This makes the ideas clear, and also gives this little story some structure. I think the reader can picture this poor, frustrated writer at her computer, wanting, trying to communicate in a human way—but finding that in its own mechanical way, the computer is just as frustrated with her!

■ Suggested Scores

Ideas: 5, 6

Organization: 5, 6

Voice: 5, 6

Word choice: 5, 6

Sentence fluency: 5, 6

Conventions: 5, 6

■ Lessons Learned from Paper 8

✔ Good conventions emphasize voice.
✔ Fragments are working when they sound natural.

■ Comments

This piece flows well and echoes real speech. Anyone who has worked with an uncooperative computer will sympathize with the writer's attitude—and it's that attitude that produces the voice, together with the very effective strategy of having a "conversation" with a machine. Notice the wide range of conventions used effectively to enhance the writing. For an excellent lesson in how conventions work, compare this piece with "The Redwoods" (Figure 3.3)—also conventionally clean but lacking the nimble conventional manipulations of this writing. The lead and ending are outstanding—very subtle. Does her reflection match your respone?

Paper 9: "The Frog Pond" (Narrative, Grade 6)

FIGURE 6.11

Paper 9: "The Frog Pond"

Up in the mountains by my old house is a quiet little frog pond where my friend Carley and I used to catch frogs. We'd tell our parents that we were going out to play. Then we'd walk down the gravel road until we reached the field.

Next we would start on the worn path that was hidden in the trees. It would wind around for what seemed like forever. Eventually we reached the pond the water was shallow and really dirty. We would stand around the edge of the aqua and descend into the thick gooey mud.

Waiting patiently until we saw a ripple in the water, indicating the presence of a frog, I'd lunge forward and try to grab the slimy critter. Finally, after some difficult performance, we'd catch a frog. It was really tough to grasp because of the slippery skin. I'd cup it in my hand and run home as swiftly as my legs could go. When we got home our moms would be so mad we had brought a reptile into the house they didn't even notice how muddy and wet we were. After a long, fun day we were exhausted, but thrilled.

Don't you want to go to this quiet little frog pond in the mountains? Well, here's your invitation.

- **Suggested Scores**

    Ideas: 4, 5

    Organization: 4, 5

    Voice: 4, 5

    Word choice: 4, 5

    Sentence fluency: 4, 5

    Conventions: 5, 6

- **Lessons Learned from Paper 9**

    ✔ Remember that frogs are amphibians.
    ✔ Don't run out of steam at the end.

- **Comments**

This paper just needs one more round. The opening is very strong. It sets the stage and provides just the right amount of detail—the worn path winding around forever, the gooey mud, descending into the aqua—to put us right at the scene. The details of frog hunting are nicely staged and easy to picture, although some readers do find the "reptile" reference a distraction. At the end, the writer seems to tire, becoming "exhausted, but thrilled." One pithy comment from mom would effectively replace this generality. Conventions are excellent, and word choice is strong, especially in the beginning. The ending works well.

Paper 10: "The Woman a.k.a. the P.B. and J." (Persuasive/Expository, Grade 12)

FIGURE 6.12
Paper 10: "The Woman a.k.a. the P.B. and J."

In your lifetime, you may meet some interesting people, but none as interesting as me. You may come across persons who astonish you with their intellect, but none will compare with me. You might encounter those with a sense of humor that will have your stomach in knots, and your face muscles cramping from laughing so hard, but no one will make you crack a smile like me. You might think Elle MacPherson is God's gift to men, but once you get one look at me, your mind will instantly change. I am perfect in every way, there's only one problem, I don't exist.

I am the woman every other American female despises. I am the Barbie, the super model, the Julia Roberts, the Meg Ryan, the perfect woman. If you wanted to cook me up and serve me, I'd be the smoked Alaskan salmon dipped in lemon-dill sauce and served on a silver platter at your favorite five-star restaurant.

Yet, for all my beauty, intelligence, and all around excellence, I bring nothing but hurt. In my short lifetime, I've brought about bulimia, anorexia, the sudden popularity in "shrinks" across America, not to mention the dreaded need for tweezers. My presence, while adored by testosterone-driven men, brings nothing but jealousy and "the sore loser" syndrome to ladies. You may ask where plastic surgery came from. Don't worry, you can thank me later.

I'm in every make-up set in America. I lurk in the background of every woman's full length mirror. True, I don't exist . . . in physical form. No, for I live only in the back of every woman's mind, thriving on the superficial and self conscious. I am of a greater evil, one which will live forever. As long as womankind allows me to dessimate her self-esteem, I will never die.

The truth of the matter is, with all of women's achievements, political progress and obstacles overcome, it amazes me that I continue to penetrate their vulnerable side. You would think that so much knowledge gained would bless them with the wisdom, that they're more beautiful, and stronger than me in every way. Yet, with every swig of Slim-Fast, every face-lift, every diet pill, they continue to take a step back on a path which they've fought so hard to change.

Perhaps they'll soon come to realize that Alaskan salmon in a five-star restaurant will never compare to that P.B. and J. for a midnight snack.

■ *Suggested Scores*

Ideas: 5, 6

Organization: 5, 6

Voice: 5, 6

Word choice: 4, 5

Sentence fluency: 5, 6

Conventions: 4, 5

■ *Lessons Learned from Paper 10*

✔ Perspective helps define voice.

✔ Metaphor enhances meaning if done well.

■ *Comments*

This paper is a no-holds-barred indictment of the shallowness of American society and our worshipful attitude toward appearance for its own sake. The writer's voice is spunky, self-assured, and insightful. It's edgy but more humorous than bitter. Taking the perspective of the "perfect woman" allows the writer a bit of irony, too—*"it amazes me that I continue to penetrate their vulnerable side."* Here and there, commas link independent clauses: *You may ask where plastic surgery came from. Don't worry, you can thank me later.* Overall, though, conventions are strong. The Alaskan salmon metaphor allows for a nice ending—the reference to the P.B. and J. snack—the woman of real quality, presumably.

Paper 11: "Gun Control" (Persuasive, Grade 8)

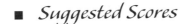

FIGURE 6.13
Paper 11: "Gun Control"

I am writing about guns because they are in the news. They are out of control. We have too many accidents and shootings. Kids do not feel safe in the schools. Parents do not feel safe sending their kids to school, which is ridiculous. School should be one of the safest places.

I know people need guns to hunt, though not as much as in the old days. Not that many people eat moose and elk that I know of, but if you

continued

do, it is ok to have a gun. It is not ok to use automatic weapons for hunting though. Give me a major break! What would be left of a moose or deer after you killed it with an automatic weapon. This is not hunting to eat. This is hunting to kill plane and simple.

The other reason is we should have stricter laws governing who gets to buy guns and when. Just a wating period doesn't do that much. Alot of criminals do not have guns registered because they buy them on the black market.

If you do own a gun, you need to take care of it. You should be sure the safety is on when you store it and it is not loaded when it is in the house. Keep it in a locked cabinet when you are not using it for a good purpose. Make sure children cannot get at it. Also, do not forget to clean your gun.

■ *Suggested Scores*

Ideas: 2, 2
Organization: 2, 2
Voice: 3, 3
Word choice: 3, 3
Sentence fluency: 2, 3
Conventions: 4, 4

■ *Lessons Learned from Paper 11*

✔ One controlling thesis is essential to strong ideas and organization.
✔ Good persuasive writing demands backup, not just opinions.
✔ An abrupt ending weakens writing.

■ *Comments*

The writer is passionate, but the piece needs focus, development, and support. Voice in persuasive writing must come from knowing the topic thoroughly; persuasive writing minus evidence is not convincing. While the opening paragraph leads us to believe that more discussion of safety will follow, a host of other issues are introduced, although none is fully developed. Guns are "out of control"—and so is the thesis. The writer slaps down concepts, notably school safety, automatic weapons, and black market sales, almost as if dealing cards, leaving us to pick them up and put the hand together. The pop-up ending is unexpected and abrupt to say the least: *"Do not forget to clean your gun."* Sentences are choppy. Despite distracting spelling errors, conventions emerge as a relative strength.

Paper 12: "Verona Tribune: Early Edition" (Imaginative/Literary Analysis, Grade 9)

FIGURE 6.14

Paper 12: "Verona Tribune: Early Edition"

Late last night, there was a party at the Capulet's house. All of the beautiful girls in Verona were there. Many guests came and danced. There were also very interesting events that took place.

The party was going rather peacefully until, to the horrifying discovery of Capulet's nephew, Tybalt, a Montague and a few of his friends showed up to crash the party. Tybalt says that he was furious that a Montague would show up to his enemy's party and try to ruin it. Blood may have been spilt at a perfectly peaceful party if it were not for Capulet, who knew the Montague as Romeo, a well-behaved gentleman.

When Romeo was asked why he showed up at the party, he replied that he only wanted to see his only true love, Rosaline. The love-stricken Romeo had no intention of causing any trouble. He didn't know how much trouble he was really going to cause.

As he was standing and watching everyone dance, he caught a glimpse of what he said was "a jewel too rich for me." As he continued to gaze at the beauty of Juliet, he soon forgot his love for Rosaline. Soon, Romeo and Juliet were found in the center of all the dancers. They didn't know each other's names, yet they were talking. Suddenly, they kissed, then kissed again. Juliet's mother, seeing Juliet with a young man she didn't know, quickly called her over as the guests began to leave.

Not knowing who his new love is, he inquires at the door, only to be shocked to discover that she is a Capulet, whom he is supposed to hate. He is heard to exclaim as he wanders out the door, "Oh dear account! My life is my foe's debt."

Juliet, who is also wondering who this young man was that she fell in love with, sneakily stood by the exit, watching people as they left the party. She inquired about people she didn't know, and when it was the young man's turn, she asked about him, saying, "If he be married, My grave is like to be my wedding bed." She felt that she was very unlucky to have "my only love, sprung from my only hate."

Count Paris, who is an important figure in Verona, witnessed the whole scene. He was at the party to try to win the favor of Juliet, whom he had asked for a hand in marriage that very day. He said that he didn't want to mention it to anyone, because he thinks that Juliet has made a terrible mistake. He thinks he still has a chance to win Juliet's favor.

■ *Suggested Scores*

Ideas: 4, 5
Organization: 4, 5
Voice: 4, 4
Word choice; 4, 5
Sentence fluency: 4, 5
Conventions: 5, 6

■ *Lessons Learned from Paper 12*

✔ There's more than one way to do literary analysis.
✔ Readers need visual detail to get grounded.

■ *Comments*

What a clever approach—reporting on the doings of the Montagues and Capulets from the perspective of a society column. This writer is stretching to find her reporter's voice, and is very close. She has teased from the original text enough detail to give us a solid account and weave in some apropos quotations. She may feel inhibited about inventing detail, but knowing what the guests wore (How did Juliet do her hair? Was she radiant in gold velvet?) or ate (Did Romeo nibble delicately at fresh mushrooms or down whole venison steaks?) would help readers searching for something sensory to cling to. As a reader, I need a few more props on my visual stage. The beginning and ending are strong and newslike. The writer occasionally switches tenses, which disrupts the otherwise strong fluency. Conventions are outstanding.

THE NEXT STEP

Assessing and discussing papers are good ways to teach ourselves what makes writing work. If you have worked through many of the papers in the preceding three chapters, you should know the traits well—even if you did not agree on all the scores. Use these papers to spark discussions of writing with your students, too. Share hard copies they can mark up, if possible, and encourage them to keep a notebook of lessons learned, adding other pieces of writing you read and discuss together. The next five chapters all deal in some way with teaching writing using a trait-based approach. With assessment (looking within) as a foundation, we are ready to look at many other things you can do to strengthen your students' writing skills.

CHAPTER 6 IN A NUTSHELL

● Conventions are not just about correctness. They offer a reader interpretive clues about meaning and voice.

● Conventions by nature define what is acceptable at the moment and are continually changing.

● Presentation, or layout on the page, is critical in some forms of writing (e.g., a children's picture book, a poster advertising a play), less so in others.

● For classroom purposes, attention to presentation can focus on such features as sizes and types of fonts, use of headings or subheadings, bulleted or numbered lists, and consistency both in citations within or at the end of text and labeling of graphics.

⬤ Putting all six traits together gives us a thorough and complete profile for a piece of writing.

EXTENSIONS

1. How much emphasis do you place on conventions in your own teaching?

   _____ A great deal. I consider them essential.

   _____ Some. I consider them important but do not let them overshadow other traits.

   _____ Very little. I consider other features of writing more important.

   Why do you think you feel as you do?

2. How much emphasis do you place on presentation?

   _____ A great deal. Presentation is a critical element of writing in my curriculum.

   _____ Some. I consider presentation important for selected pieces.

   _____ Very little. I prefer to focus on other features of writing.

   Why do you think you feel as you do?

3. When conventions are particularly strong—or not strong—do you find that factor influencing your scoring of other traits? Discuss this with colleagues.

4. Choose a writing sample from a journal, newspaper, or any publication and assess it for conventions. What issues other than correct versus incorrect arise from your assessment? What does this teach you about what you personally find conventionally important?

5. Make a list (individually or with a group of colleagues/students) of the ways in which you have observed conventions changing in modern American writing. Which changes do you applaud? Which bother you? Write a journal entry about this.

6. Choose any piece of writing (not necessarily in this book) for which presentation is important. Assess it for this feature, talking about how effective you find it. What issues arise out of your discussion?

7. Make a list of writings for which presentation would be important. If possible, assemble a collection. Talk about how you might use such examples in your instruction.

8. Imagine that one of the students from the preceding three chapters is in your class. Write a brief personal response to that writer based on his or her work. What can you say that goes outside the bounds of the rubrics?

WHY I WRITE

I write because it is a way to create a thunderstorm when the weather is too dry. With my imagination, I create rain which turns to thunder, which turns to lightning, which makes the dry land (my paper) wet and beautiful. It is a way to give others a gift without having to take out my wallet.

—**Katie Miller,** student writer

LOOKING AHEAD

In Chapter 7 we'll look at how the six traits fit with writing process and begin considering ways (in addition to sharing writing samples) of teaching the traits to students in the classroom.

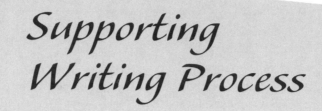

7 Supporting Writing Process

Assessment is not the private property of teachers. Kids can learn to evaluate their own writing. They must take part in this . . . it is central to the growth of writing. Even before they write, they need to know about what makes writing strong or effective. And they need to know the criteria by which their own writing will be judged.

—Marjorie Frank

If You're Trying to Teach Kids How to Write . . . You've Gotta Have This Book, 1995, p. 175

At the beginning of the composing process there is only blank paper. At the end of the composing process there is a piece of writing which has detached itself from the writer and found its own meaning, a meaning the writer probably did not intend.

—Donald M. Murray

Learning by Teaching, 1982, p. 17

*T*he teaching of writing begins with process: finding and rehearsing ideas, drafting to get something on paper, sharing what we have written, shaping it through revision and editing, (possibly) publishing in some way, then assessing or reflecting on what we have done. Trait-based instruction *never* replaces this process but rather supports it at every step—most notably during revision. Let's see how this works.

"FOR MONDAY . . ."

When I first became a teacher, I did not teach writing at all. I assigned it. That's because the assigning of writing, followed by the collecting and correcting of writing, is what had been modeled for me. My teachers focused so heavily on the final *product* (along with due dates, minimum lengths, and conventions) that they scarcely concerned themselves at all with the *how* of writing, nor did they teach anything like a step-by-step writing process, much less model it. Few were writers themselves, and those who were looked on writing as a private act. They did not write with or in front of us and so, of course, did not revise as we looked on. What we knew of revision as student writers we invented for ourselves.

A good bit of the time we felt stumped and bewildered. We did not know exactly what the teacher wanted, but we were pretty sure we were not leading the kinds of lives writers need to lead if they hope to write something worthwhile—a Jack London kind of life out of which rollicking adventures spew like lava. In *'Tis* (1999), author Frank McCourt talks about the fear that gripped him when he was asked to write about a favorite object from his childhood. In McCourt's impoverished experience, treasured objects did not exist. His family had a tiny allotment of space in which to live—a little food on good days:

> I can't think of anything like the things other students talk about, the family car, Dad's old baseball mitt, the sled they had so much fun with, the old icebox, the kitchen table where they did their homework. All I can think of is the bed I shared with my three brothers and even though I'm ashamed of it, I have to write about it *[p. 172]*.

Like McCourt, we often felt on the outside looking in, feeling the stress of "putting on" someone else's topic that seemed to fit us as badly as hand-me-down shoes. A few of our papers were labored over from Friday right through Sunday—but many were written against the locker door just before the bell rang. We usually met the requirements of the assignment because over the years we'd learned some writers' survival tricks: Make it neat, type it if possible (a process that looks as primitive to today's students as chiseling on stone), use words from the weekly vocabulary list, spell everything right. We wrote to get by and to get done. We wrote for grades. Only occasionally and quite by accident did we produce something we cared about deeply.

WHAT REAL WRITERS DO

It is not, for me, any rigid set of rules. I don't write a rough draft, conference, reorder, conference, rewrite, conference, and then write out my final draft. Every time I write, my need to draft is different.

—**Mem Fox**

Radical Reflections, 1993, p. 39

In the early 1970s, Janet Emig, Donald Murray, and Donald Graves and then Lucy Calkins, Nancie Atwell, and others revolutionized the teaching of writing by looking at the things writers really *do* when they write. Because these people were writers themselves, they knew firsthand that, as Don Murray puts it, "meaning is not thought up and then written down" (2004, p. 3). They recognized the artificiality and constraint of trying to plan every line in advance or creating precisely 100 note cards for your report on Brazil.

> *I started searching for the writing process under the illusion I could find a way to make writing easy—the sword would come right out of the stone. I didn't realize then that the importance of writing lies in the fact that it is not easy, and should not be.*
>
> **—Donald M. Murray**
> *A Writer Teaches Writing,*
> 2004, p. 9

From their own experience and from years of research observing successful writers at work, these writers/teachers learned (and taught us) that drafting is not the whole of writing—nor even, many times, the most time-consuming part. Successful writers spend extensive upfront (prewriting) time defining a topic, collecting information, sorting and discarding, and rehearsing an idea in their minds until it has shape and substance. Later, when a draft has cooled, they spend a great deal of reflective (revision) time rereading what they've written and reworking it.

Further, they taught us that writing process charts a personal path that is slightly different for each writer—and is virtually never linear. One step is not completed before the next is begun. We're still rehearsing as we draft, still rehearsing and drafting as we revise, and still revising as we rehearse new bits to be added to the whole. In his masterpiece, *A Writer Teaches Writing* (2004), Donald Murray explains that "the writer passes through the process once, or many times, emphasizing different stages during each passage" (p. 4). Because various steps within the process are interdependent and overlapping, you move through them not like a train on a track but more like the way you bounce on a trampoline, coming back to earth again and again to pick up more momentum and with each rebound launching yourself a bit higher (see Figure 7.1).

"READ ALL ABOUT IT"

Many of us learned about the process approach to writing as teachers, not students, so it's hardly surprising that we're continuing to unravel its mysteries. Often what we learn we gain from workshops or conferences or from books that tell us about writing process. As Mem Fox says, we "tend not to *discover* the writing process—we only read about it and imagine that's good enough. It isn't" (1993, p. 35). Reading about process is helpful but doesn't take us where we need to be as teachers. We must *write* in order to appreciate the difficulties and joys of finding our own topics; or to appreciate how much revision depends on reading text over and over, hearing it, living with it in our heads even when we are not writing, and rehearsing new ideas as we revise; or to know the agony of having an editor say, "You're going to have to cut 40 pages."

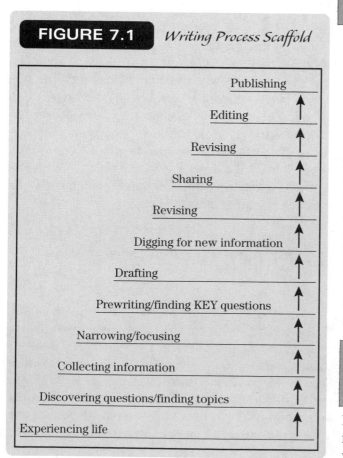

FIGURE 7.1 *Writing Process Scaffold*

Publishing
↑
Editing
↑
Revising
↑
Sharing
↑
Revising
↑
Digging for new information
↑
Drafting
↑
Prewriting/finding KEY questions
↑
Narrowing/focusing
↑
Collecting information
↑
Discovering questions/finding topics
↑
Experiencing life

WE NEED TO MODEL IT

Being writers ourselves teaches us writing process from the inside out. This is a big step toward making writing process successful within our classrooms.

> *Teachers should write so they understand the process of writing from within. They should know the territory intellectually and emotionally: how you have to think to write, how you feel when writing. Teachers of writing do not have to be great writers, but they should have frequent and recent experience in writing.*
>
> **—Donald M. Murray**
> *A Writer Teaches Writing,*
> 2004, p. 74

> *[Effective teachers] write and share their writing— especially the false starts, the writing that doesn't work—with their students.*
>
> **—Ralph Fletcher**
> *What a Writer Needs,*
> 1993, pp. 27–28

> *We are afraid to fail; our students are terrified by failure. They have been taught, by teachers and parents, the press, and their own instinct, that everything must be done perfectly the first time.*
>
> **—Donald M. Murray**
> *A Writer Teaches Writing,* 2004, p. 9

Still, you'll hear teachers say, "I use process, yet it doesn't seem to make a difference." It can—it *will*—if we show students how it looks as it is happening. When teachers say, "I *use* writing process," what they really mean, quite often, is "I *describe* writing process to my students." Describing achieves almost nothing. If we do not *model* the steps, students do not really understand what to do. You are modeling process for students if you are doing these things—or something like them:

✔ Sharing topics you are thinking of writing about—explaining how you bumped into them and how you will pick one over another.

✔ Showing students one or more prewriting strategies that work for you—e.g., drawing, talking, listing.

✔ Exploring possible leads—perhaps writing two, three, or more from which your students will help you choose the most effective.

✔ Drafting one paragraph (or more) so that your students can see how it looks when you generate copy.

✔ Reading a draft (or some portion) aloud to get students' responses.

✔ Working out a writer's question/problem—vague wording, awkward sentence structure, lack of voice, lack of detail—and asking for students' help as you do so.

✔ Ruthlessly chopping deadwood (what is not needed) as students watch.

✔ Using the reviser's friends—double spacing, big margins (elbow room to work), arrows, carets for inserted text, and so on.

✔ Making a mess. Students need to see cross-outs and rewritten passages. They need to see the thinking behind the writing much more than they need to see the finished, polished piece.

✔ Crafting a conclusion—for many writers, the toughest challenge.

✔ Thinking of a title that fits the piece well.

✔ Screwing up—and being very, *very* unhappy with what you have written, then talking through what you will do.

If you can say yes to these questions (or your own versions of them), and if your students see you do these things, then truly you *are* teaching process, making writing come alive for your students.

PROCESS FIRST, THEN TRAITS, THEN MODES

Because the six traits are so revision-focused, students make better use of trait language if they are well grounded in writing process. So teach process first, and let that be the bedrock of your writing program. Use traits to support process. *Then* explore modes or genres. Modes—or forms—of writing come last because the traits vary across modes.

Modes, such as descriptive, narrative, informational, business, or persuasive writing, are defined by purpose. We write to paint a picture, tell a story, entertain, inform, establish good public relations for a company, or defend a position. As purpose shifts, the traits shift just a bit, too. Consider how different the introduction to an Edgar Allan Poe mystery or a political speech is from the introduction to a business letter. Also think about how various modes or genres of writing differ in voice, word choice—and even conventions. See how much more sense it makes to talk about these variations once you know the traits? Do keep in mind, of course, that the best writing usually incorporates multiple forms: I may use a story to teach a concept about the behavior of bees or to present a case for letting students choose their own writing topics. The compulsion to separate modes artificially distorts this sense of purpose, and we need to get beyond it. As Barry Lane reminds us, "Editors never ask writers for five-paragraph themes or expository writing. . . . like toddlers exploring limits of their universe, strong writers will stretch the rules and expectations of any genre" (1996, p. 4).

Now let's consider how the various steps within the writing process connect to the traits. As we go along, you may wish to refer to Figure 7.2 to help you visualize the many ways in which traits support each part of the process.

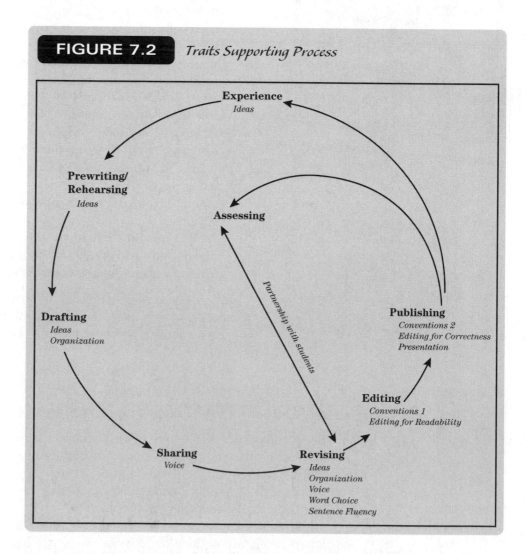

FIGURE 7.2 *Traits Supporting Process*

EXPERIENCE: THE WELL WE DRAW FROM

Writing does not really begin with prewriting, as many diagrams suggest. It begins with life. Out of our personal experience come ideas, our sense of what is important, what is worth sharing. In *Winterdance* (1994), Gary Paulsen writes of the Iditarod, the stillness of the Alaskan northlands, the beauty of the aurora borealis, and his near-death experiences from freezing and being attacked by an enraged moose. In *Travels* (1988), Michael Crichton writes of his personal challenges in completing medical school—how he nearly fainted drawing blood and had to hang his head out the window to keep from passing out in front of his patients, how his hands shook when he dissected his first cadaver.

Occasionally, we take the task of finding writing topics out of students' hands. This is all right sometimes. Part of writing is learning to deal effectively with writing tasks required by someone else, including employers. If we write ourselves, though, we also know how important it is for writers to identify the topics that are important in their own lives. "Children who are fed topics, story starters, lead sentences, even opening paragraphs as a steady diet for three or four years," says Donald Graves (1983), "rightfully panic when topics have to come from them. The anxiety is not unlike that of the child whose mother has just turned off the television set. 'Now what do I do?' bellows the child" (p. 21). Writers must learn to sense the moment when writing begins. Listen to Sue Monk Kidd as she describes the inspiration for her novel *The Secret Life of Bees*:

> The whole idea for the novel began one evening when my husband reminded me that the first time he'd visited my home to meet my parents, he'd awakened in amazement to find bees flying about the room. After he told that story, I began to imagine a girl lying in bed while bees poured through cracks in her bedroom walls and flew around the room. I couldn't get the image out of my head *[2002, p. 5]*.

Sometimes inspiration comes from visiting a place that makes an impression so strong that the characters grow out of the setting:

> When we hear Billie Letts say, "I walked in a Wal-Mart and looked around and I thought, 'You could live here. There's everything you need. You could exist in this place.'" This happening, this walking-into-Wal-Mart, was the beginning that led Letts to write the novel *Where the Heart Is* (1995). So we hear her say this and then we know: writers get ideas for writing when they are away from their desks. Writers can get ideas at Wal-Mart [Katie Wood Ray, *What You Know By Heart: How to Develop Curriculum for Your Writing Workshop*, 2002, p. 4].

It is not the job of the teacher to legislate the student's truth. It is the responsibility of the student to explore his own world with his own language, to discover his own meaning.

—Donald M. Murray
Learning by Teaching, 1982, p. 16

Identifying topics requires sifting through the sands of your experience, looking for what is writing worthy, and listening for moments that speak to you. In order to teach this, you must find the treasures buried in the sand of your own life and share what you find with your students.

Donald Murray (2004) tells of pulling topics from his childhood: "I came from a background that was filled with sin, guilt, and threats of Hell and damnation. I was brought up with a grandmother who was paralyzed when I was young, and it was my job when I woke up early in the morning to see if she was still alive" (p. 11).

My own writing comes largely from family memories and childhood experiences as well. Among my most vivid recollections is the sight of my mother, an air pistol tucked neatly beneath her apron, preparing to protect my friend Gail from an attacking dog. She shot the dog neatly, without a flinch or regret (he was stunned and frightened but not injured), and returned to her baking. More than 30 years later, I was wheeling my mother—who by then had lost her sense of time and place—through the corridors of a nursing facility, trying to hold back my tears, and she was asking me if I had lost my mind and, if not, why in God's name I had selected this particular hotel as the place to spend our holidays. Both scenes are chapters in an upcoming book. I also have written extensively of my grandmother, who taught a K-12 class in a single room in North Dakota and who could slice the head off a rattlesnake as cleanly and swiftly as Emeril dices celery. Her kitchen, with its uniquely rustic linoleum-covered table, smelling of vanilla, bread, chocolate, and coffee, was my place of refuge, where I listened to stories of my father, Jack, as a child and of her legendary feral cat, Snooky, who killed everything that dared to invade her territory, including smaller dogs. I remember my grandmother's fierce and sparkling eyes, the reassuring and surprising strength of her arthritic fingers, how her hamburgers (sautéed in butter) tasted a hundred times better than anyone else's, and how she hugged me as if I'd shown up to rescue her. She served me coffee when I was 13 because, she said, "It makes the stories better."

When you model topic selection, help your students to see how writing topics grow out of humble adventures—tasting your first cup of coffee, dealing with your neighbor's biting dog, watching your grandmother bake bread. The best topics, Donald Graves suggests, come from an "everyday reading of the world." If we don't teach children how to seek out what matters, they will think only trips to Disneyland or emergency appendectomies make good copy. They will feel compelled to "draw only on the experiences of others, which they do not necessarily understand" (1994, p. 58).

My everyday reading of the world leads me back to my family, my travel, and my work. These are the things I know best. This is where my writing comfort lies—and where my heart is. If I decide to write about Wall Street investment policy or auto racing, I will need to do considerable research to fill the well. In considering a topic, students must ask

✔ What do I know now in my own heart and mind?
✔ What could I reasonably invent?
✔ What will I need to look up?

Something we can teach our students as they scan the world for topics is the notion of developing a writing frame of mind. As Donald Murray reminds us, writers are *always* writing: "The most important writing takes place before there is writing—at least what we usually think of as writing: the production of a running draft. Writers write before they write" (2004, p. 17). Next time you are running through ideas in the shower or in the car while stalled in traffic, realize that you are in fact *writing* and that your thinking is just as important as moving pencil over paper or attacking the keyboard. Then share that insight with your students.

PREWRITING/REHEARSING: GIVING SHAPE TO THE INSTINCT

In prewriting or rehearsing, we give shape and focus to the ideas that come from experience. Rehearsal techniques are as varied as the writers who use them, so we do well to give our students a wide range of strategies. I like to talk. When my mother was confined to a nursing home, she had a friend named Grace, whom my husband and I visited regularly. Grace was very proud of her hair, which was a beautiful silver color and very curly. As we conversed one day, she confided, "I didn't always wear my hair this way, you know. It was different before the bank robbery." That's an interesting milestone, don't you think? I found myself telling friends about Grace's gravelly voice, her passion for red clothes, her way of punctuating each sentence with a wink—and how dangerous she could be playing wheelchair tag. That's when I knew I would write about her.

Many writers like webbing (see Figure 7.3), and although it does not work well for me, I think it's important to teach it and model it because it does work well for many writers. I love lists of potential readers' questions and often

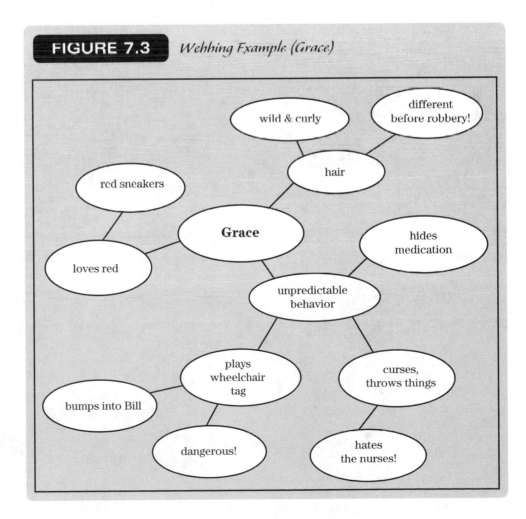

FIGURE 7.3 *Webbing Example (Grace)*

FIGURE 7.4   *Listeners' Questions*

- ✔ Why did she shoot the dog?
- ✔ Was it your dog?
- ✔ Did it die?
- ✔ How old were you?
- ✔ Was this the first time she did this?
- ✔ What set her off?
- ✔ What happened after she shot it?
- ✔ What sort of gun did she use?
- ✔ How did you feel when it happened?
- ✔ How was she feeling at the time?
- ✔ Were you frightened?
- ✔ Were you angry?
- ✔ Did anyone see her do it?
- ✔ Did you see her do it?
- ✔ Did she ever do it again?
- ✔ What sort of person was she?

will elicit these from a class of students (see Figure 7.4) by presenting them with a one-liner, e.g., *My mother shot a dog.* Then I simply ask, "What would you like to know?" This is my favorite prewriting technique because the draft flows right out of answering the questions. It's a way in for writers like me, to whom webbing does not come naturally. Some writers find drafting itself to be a good prewriting technique. "It gets the garbage out," one teacher told me. "You find your paper really begins on page 3, but you had to write through all that junk on pages 1 and 2 to get there."

Rehearsing could include drawing a picture or life map. See Figure 7.5 for an example, courtesy of my teacher friend and colleague Sally Shorr. This sketch captures main events in Sally's life from about 1970 to the present, any of which could provide fuel for a story, poem, or essay. In creating this life map, Sally must reflect very deeply on what memories are most vivid or what events have helped define who she is. Your life map, of course, would look very different. Create one and see.

FIGURE 7.5   *Sally's Life Map*

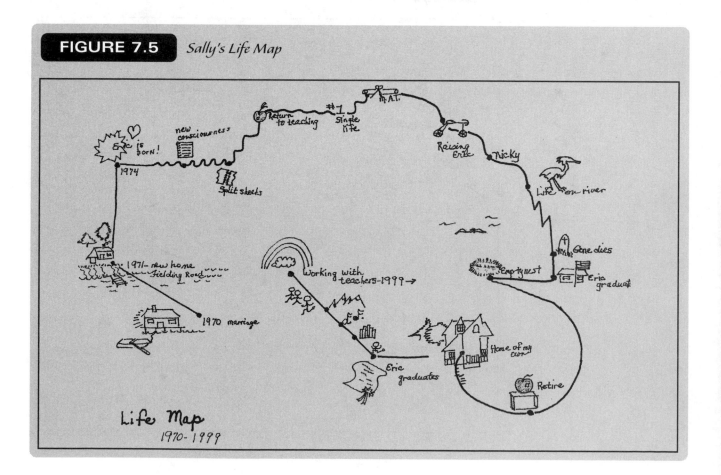

> *The more a writer writes, the more processes of choice and rehearsal occur, and at unpredictable moments. Facts restlessly push their way to the surface until the writer says, "I'll write about that."*
>
> **—Donald H. Graves**
> *A Fresh Look at Writing,* 1994, p. 75

> *Much of the bad writing we read from inexperienced writers is the direct result of writing before they are ready to write.*
>
> **—Donald M. Murray**
> *A Writer Teaches Writing,* 2004, p. 17

> *All writing begins life as a first draft, and first drafts are never (well almost never) any good. . . . Write a first draft as though you were thinking aloud, not carving a monument.*
>
> **—Patricia T. O'Connor**
> *Words Fail Me,* 1999, p. 38

> *There is no substitute for really knowing what you are talking about. The books with staying power are the ones that speak from large knowledge and add something to a reader's comprehension.*
>
> **—Wallace Stegner**
> *On Teaching and Writing Fiction,* 2002, p. 45

Additional prewriting techniques include interviewing, reading, viewing a film, browsing through the Internet, or just looking out the window. Many writers talk to themselves or role-play the part of a character. When I wrote about my grandmother, my prewriting activity was poking through old family albums to see what stories her clear gray eyes and deeply lined face would tell.

DRAFTING: CREATING SUBSTANCE

You cannot sculpt air; you need clay. Drafting provides writers some substance with which to work. The key to drafting, therefore, is to *keep writing* so that later there will be *something to revise.* Moreover, writing is generative. You discover what you want to say *not* so much during prewriting (as nonwriters often suppose) but during the act of writing itself. One idea leads to another, so writing itself helps you think—more than, say, staring at notes. During the process of drafting, ideas are both refined and expanded. These seemingly conflicting processes in fact work in harmony to shape what we wish to say.

As teachers, we often think drafting means stretching and extending ideas. True. But as writers, we soon learn that before we can expand, we must bring our ideas under control, draw them in close, hold them in our hands, and say, *"This.* I will write about *just this."* As Barry Lane says, "Write small." Don't write that the "Holocaust was inhuman"; describe a "mountain of children's shoes." Don't write about how messy your brother is; tell the reader how you hate finding hair on the soap (*Reviser's Toolbox,* 1999, pp. 52–53).

Drafting depends on information—a wealth of it—and can go nowhere without the fuel that information provides. When students write in generalities, we often say, "Be specific." This is not very helpful advice because we are treating the symptom, not the problem. The student's writing style is not at fault; it's the limited knowledge base—mental "shelves" low on inventory. "Read," we should say. "Investigate. Interview someone. Ask questions. Make notes. Don't write another line until you've collected a wealth of information on this topic." When Sebastian Junger wrote *The Perfect Storm* (1998), he didn't write, "Hurricanes are powerful storms. They do enormous damage and threaten people's lives every year." He waited until he had enough information to write this: "A typical hurricane encompasses a million cubic miles of atmosphere and could provide all the electric power needed by the United States for three or four years. During the Labor Day hurricane of 1935, winds surpassed 200 miles an hour and people caught outside were sandblasted to death. Rescue workers found nothing but their shoes and belt buckles" (p. 129). Writers, says Junger, do not need to start out knowing everything about a topic. They "just need to ask a lot of questions" (p. 299).

Research is foundational in informational writing, of course; everyone knows that. What many writers overlook is that it is equally important in fiction. Keeping one foot grounded in reality gives any writing authenticity. In writing about Brian's battle with north woods mosquitoes in *Hatchett* (1999), for instance, Gary Paulsen didn't just count on imagination. Instead, he drew on his own experience, which he recounts in *Guts* (2001), a nonfiction book on real-life research:

> I must have attracted every mosquito in the county. The cloud swarmed over me, filled my nostrils and my eyes, flooded my mouth when I breathed. They blinded me, choked me and, worst of all, tore into me like eight or nine thousand starving vampires. I don't know how much blood I lost but I do know that when I regained the house—after a wild, blind run through two hundred yards of dark woods—there wasn't a square inch on my body that hadn't been bitten *[p. 60]*.

Organization is critical to drafting, too, for a writer must think how to begin, where to go next, how and when to end. The hardest line to write is the first one. Begin with the most startling thing you know: *"Pearl did not see the sleek, fast-moving coyote that stalked her through the tall summer grass."* Beginning makes the next line easier: *"She was too busy taking in the smells of the wetlands: frog-thick waters, Canada geese with their young, reeds housing blackbird nests, and track-covered mud flats where hours before deer, raccoon, and a scavenging black bear had all stopped to drink."* And this line makes the next one and the next come to me: *"For a spoiled toy poodle who had seldom known anything beneath her feet but city pavement, the wetlands were a wide, expansive carnival of sounds and smells, stocked with everything necessary to enchant a poodle brain. I watched the coyote—as he watched Pearl. Only one thing stood between him and gourmet lunch. It was Pearl's owner Roberta, who now turned her face to the spring sun, soaking up its warmth, closing her eyes and tilting her chin to let the soft glow spread over her face and upturned throat."*

Drafting is more than keeping on keeping on, though. It needs to be free. It is important, for instance, not to get too locked into an outline. Remember how quickly we learned in grade school to write first, *then* outline so that we would seem to follow our outlines precisely, as the teacher had told us we must? Rarely—except perhaps when doing a technical manual, recipe, or other step-by-step sort of writing—does a writer know where the trail will lead when he or she begins. It is important to have the mental freedom to follow an unexpected impulse. Outlines are useful for establishing an initial plan, rather like a grocery list you make out so that you won't forget anything important for the big birthday dinner. Once you get to the store, however, you may decide that the fresh fish looks a whole lot better than the chicken. Unless you feel compelled to sabotage your own dinner party, you'll give yourself some shopping flexibility. You need the same freedom with the writing outline. When I made notes for "Crack Shot," the story of my mother shooting the dog, I planned to begin with Cinder attacking Gail and end with him running home over the snow. The story got much bigger as I wrote, virtually telling itself (see Figure 7.6 for an excerpt from the rough draft).

A critical part of drafting is getting everything down beginning to end so that we have a sense of the "whole" and can see where the informational gaps are. Then we can write questions about what is missing—questions that can be dealt with later.

Equally critical is reading aloud, a vital habit to teach our students. Only through reading aloud do we discover whether the message makes sense,

| **FIGURE 7.6** | *Excerpt From a Rough Draft of "Crack Shot"* |

"Crack Shot"

Cinder was a black lab known for his mean disposition. I know — labs are usually friendly and gentle, but not this one. He liked to bite, and he was sneaky about it. He would circle around the victim, come up fast, and go for the left leg. ~~Always the left leg.~~

[margin note: no growling, no barking first.]

[margin note: reverse these ¶s]

When he moved, my mother shot him. Bang. From one foot away. No chance to miss. And Cinder let go of poor little Gail's mitten and took off howling.

[margin note: Of course, that wasn't how it started.]

---

whether the sentences are fluent as written on the page, and whether the voice is true. Author and teacher Mem Fox talks of reading aloud everything she writes: "As I write this chapter, I hear every cadence, listen to every pause, and check every beat. I'm hoping that if you enjoy the rhythm of my words, you might be inclined to like my content as well" (1993, p. 114).

Time is critical in drafting. Donald Graves notes that although the time provided for writing within our classrooms has increased substantially in recent years, it is far short of what we need to promote successful writers. Writing is complex and requires substantial time to develop. But that is only part of the problem. The larger issue is that writing requires continuity. It is easier for me to carry my writing over day to day to day without a break than to leave it for a week. Recapturing my train of thought will be as difficult for me then as finding my car in a huge and crowded parking lot after a seven-day absence. As Graves tells us, "Professional writers experience near panic at the thought of missing one day of writing. They know that if they miss a day, it will take enormous effort to get their minds back on the trail of productive thought." As I write this book, I find myself continually snagging another quotation and rehearsing what I will say, running the text through my head. It is never quiet. I have entered into what

The ear hears the voice— and hears when that voice fades or is lost. The ear is aware of the rhythm and melody.

—Donald M. Murray
A Writer Teaches Writing,
2004, p. 55

> *I have an audience for this book—my editor, at least, if no one else. Although I care deeply about it, I wouldn't have dreamed of writing it had I thought that no one would read it and find it interesting, irritating, useful, old hat, provocative, or something.*
>
> **—Mem Fox**
> *Radical Reflections, 1993, p. 38*

> *When [my students] saw me, the vulnerable, egotistical writer, offering up my work to their questions, it gave them an incentive to do the same.*
>
> **—Roy Peter Clark**
> *Free to Write, 1987, p. 41*

> *I know some very great writers, writers you love who write beautifully and have made a great deal of money, and not one of them sits down routinely feeling wildly enthusiastic and confident. Not one of them writes elegant first drafts. All right, one of them does, but we do not like her very much.*
>
> **—Anne Lamott**
> *Bird by Bird, 1995, p. 22*

Graves calls "a constant state of composition" (1994, p. 104). When children enter this state, they truly become writers, for they are seeing the world through a writer's eyes.

SHARING: PLAYING TO AN AUDIENCE

For many writers, sharing is the most difficult part of the whole process. Most of us probably felt this way in middle and high school, when we were writing not for an audience but for a grade. We did not always love what we wrote. We mumbled, looked down at our shoes, spoke too softly to be heard, rushed, and never used any inflection because that might have implied that we felt our own writing was worth sharing. The result? No voice.

Over time, however, a writer's need for an audience grows. Sharing becomes meaningful then because it's linked to revision. When we begin to write for an audience and not just for a grade, our writing begins to seriously improve—and voice begins to emerge. Your students will learn to share by watching you model it. Read your writing aloud, with confidence, but with an open mind. Invite suggestions for revision. Show the next draft so that your students can see how or whether you used any of their suggestions. This thinking and coaching are as important to their becoming writers as actual writing practice.

REVISING: REMODELING THE HOUSE

Ask any teacher what is the most difficult part of the writing process to teach, and 999 out of 1000 will say "revision" without hesitation. Why is this? Simple. Students do not know what to *do* once they finish a draft. We do not always know what to suggest either. We need a stronger sense of how writing grows, a sense that comes from being writers ourselves. And we need a stronger sense of what good writing looks like, a sense that comes from assessing not to score or grade but to understand.

To an experienced writer, revising feels good—and scary. The framework of the house is up, and you can picture it. Here's your best chance to make *big* changes before the sheetrock goes on the walls. Revising involves expanding or clarifying ideas, discovering new connections, deleting trivial or irrelevant information, reordering sections, condensing, ending things in a whole new way, gaining a clearer sense of audience, changing your voice—and more. It is big, bold, and sweeping. It could involve hacking out whole paragraphs or even starting over. Like knocking out a wall to join two rooms, it changes the look and feel of everything. When I teach this to students, I tell them, "Revision is restructuring, adding a fireplace, vaulting the ceiling, putting in a new bank of windows. Editing, on the other hand, is cleaning and neatening to show off the existing structure at its very best—making sure the light is just right, turning on music to set the mood, lighting the fire." Editing is extremely important, make no mistake; it simply does not take the place of reworking the thinking underlying the writing. If revising and editing are connected but distinct in their minds, students are less likely to kid themselves that they have revised when they have only corrected the spelling.

Five questions underlie *most* revision:

✔ Is my purpose (e.g., to tell a story, to teach, to persuade) clear?

✔ Is the underlying message clear, interesting, and focused? Is it what I wanted to say?

✔ Is the information organized in a way that makes reading simple and engaging—or difficult and stressful?

✔ Does my personal voice drive the ideas, organization, and word choice? Or to put it another way, does this writing reflect the truth as I see it?

✔ Does the writing flow—and if not, what's getting in the way?

Beyond these five basic questions, look at your rubrics for the first five traits, particularly the levels of strong performance (scores of 5 or 6). Every descriptor, every bullet suggests a possibility for revision. In addition to these specifics, here are a few general strategies that make revision powerful:

✔ Ensure that meaning is carried by nouns and verbs—go easy on the modifiers.

✔ If it can be cut, cut it. Filler adds length, not depth.

✔ Even in persuasive or informational writing, people the draft with characters who move, act, and speak in engaging, sometimes unexpected ways.

✔ Keep it small, and keep it focused, meandering only if a sidebar makes a point.

✔ Keep 20-word+ sentences to a minimum.

✔ Save the best for last.

✔ Put the next best first.

✔ Go for clarity. If you must show off vocabulary skills, attach a glossary.

✔ Tell the truth.

Timing is critical. While drafting calls for total immersion in the text, revision demands a mental break. Ideally, a writer should step back for a few days—for some writers (I am one), a longer period works better. This pause gives the writer mental distance and allows him or her to view the writing more the way an objective reader would.

Approach is vital, too. Younger children may revise by reading a whole draft through once and making any changes that occur to them. This is adequate for a beginner but should not be our goal in teaching more experienced writers. True revision requires multiple readings of a draft (changing a word or phrase one time, a whole paragraph or chapter the next) and requires reading aloud, too, unless you are very, *very* good at hearing text in your head. In addition, a skilled writer will not always go methodically through a text beginning to end but will enter the text at different points—through different

---

Because the best part of all, the absolutely most delicious part, is finishing it and then doing it over. That's the thrill of a lifetime for me.

—Toni Morrison
In Donald M. Murray, *Shoptalk*, 1990, p. 186

Few of us express ourselves well in a first draft. When we revise that early confusion into something clearer, we understand our ideas better. And when we understand our ideas better, we express them more clearly, and when we express them more clearly, we understand them better. . . . and so it goes until we run out of energy, interest, or time.

—Joseph M. Williams
Style: Ten Lessons in Clarity and Grace (7th ed), 2002, p. 9

When I see a paragraph shrinking under my eyes like a strip of bacon in a skillet, I know I'm on the right track.

—Peter de Vries
In Donald M. Murray, *Shoptalk*, 1990, p. 187

doors, if you will—perhaps coming in on the lead one time but slipping into the middle another or jumping right in at the conclusion yet another time.

Author Louis Sachar (*Holes*, 2000, reprinted edition) says that he rarely revises any piece fewer than five or six times and that along about draft number 3 he can begin to really sense and feel where he wants to take the writing (Florida Reading Association Conference, Orlando, FL, October 16, 1999). Even as he completes each draft, he is already revising it in his head (maybe on paper, too)—and still prewriting as well, for he is continuing to gather new information. Sharing, for this author, does not occur until after draft number 6; that's the first time, according to Sachar, that his editor, or *anyone* other than himself and his dogs ("who cannot read, anyway"), sees what he has written.

> *I learned the need to disre-spect the typewritten page, even to take satisfaction in plowing up those neat rows of words with a pencil if they didn't seem to serve my porpose..*
>
> **—Bruce Ballenger**
> In Barry Lane,
> *After THE END*, 1993, p. 119

EDITING: MAKING THE READER "AT HOME" IN YOUR TEXT

Editing is a way of helping readers feel at home within our text. It's a courtesy really, a way of saying, "Here, let me make the reading as easy as possible for you so that you can relax and enjoy the message."

Most editing occurs after a draft is finished—or finished for now. Certainly, I will correct *exacerbate* if I see clearly I have misspelled it, but why get in a frenzy over punctuation if I think I may wind up tossing the whole paragraph?

Editing involves correcting spelling, punctuation, and grammar; deciding issues of formality (contractions or not?); considering usage and idioms; and ensuring that sentences are complete and grammatical, that parentheses come in pairs, that colons do not follow verbs, and that paragraphs begin where they should. Editing also means ensuring that conventions support meaning. The best editors

✔ Use excellent handbooks and check what is currently correct, for conventional correctness is forever in flux
✔ Use every tool available, including personal dictionaries and spell check programs
✔ Ask for help if a qualified editor is available
✔ Read text both silently and aloud to check for errors
✔ Leave text alone for a time prior to editing in order to gain mental distance
✔ Double space and allow wide margins so that there is room for corrections *or* (if editing on a word processor) so that reading/proofing is easier

Editing can occur at two levels, as I have indicated in Figure 7.2. On one level, we edit text for readability so that we can process it with ease. At this point we want students, as much as possible, to take responsibility for their own editing, doing the best they can. We should ask for attention to detail but not demand perfection. A misspelled word, for example, should not keep us from posting a piece on the wall or celebrating other qualities (e.g., ideas, voice) within the writing.

If we publish something formally, whether through a school publishing house or a professional publishing house, editing at another level is required.

For that purpose, it is important to make the copy as clean as possible; this means that it needs to be seen by another pair of eyes. This is also the time to attend to layout and appearance in addition to correctness.

PUBLISHING: HONORING AND PRESERVING WRITING

> *You just can't force romance. If an assignment is dying . . . bury it!*
>
> **—Marjorie Frank**
>
> *If You're Trying to Teach Kids How to Write . . . You've Gotta Have This Book*, 1998, p. 106

> *In fact, the student, who is closest to the work in progress, whether in reading, writing, math, or science, ought to be and is the most important evaluator. . . . [The teacher's] primary role is to teach the students how to evaluate, how to read their work, and how to ask critical questions.*
>
> **—Donald H. Graves**
>
> *Testing Is Not Teaching*, 2002, p. 28

Publishing can take many forms. Sometimes it involves making a book or even submitting work to a publishing house. Other times it may be more informal—reading from an author's chair or posting work on a wall. Such informal publishing does not, in my view, demand the attention to conventions that more formal publishing requires.

Although publication honors the writer's work, it should not be mandatory. Some classrooms are in a veritable publication frenzy these days. Why? To what end? I doubt that our writing process gurus *ever* meant for this to happen, but we are inexplicably guilt ridden if we leave a single step out of the process. Stop. Stop right now and think. Would you wish to begin today a regimen of having to publish *everything* you write for the next year? How stressful! I sympathize fully when Mem Fox (1993) declares, "It depresses me utterly to see children being forced to finish a piece of writing when they're sick of it, lacking in inspiration, and getting negative feedback in writing conferences. No one forces me to finish my writing, and I'm a published writer, so why should any writer be ruled in such a manner by someone who doesn't own the writing anyway?" (p. 39). Do not ask students to revise everything. Do not publish or assess everything. Toss this burden away like a big rock you just discovered sitting on your left shoulder. You will feel freer, and so will your students.

Remember that in the real world of publishing writers do not work alone. This book is the work of numerous people, including photographers, layout specialists, and editors of various kinds, whose work is acknowledged in the introductory materials. Sometimes in the world of the classroom a single writer wears all these hats, but when others are involved, they should receive credit. A simple introductory page will take care of it (see Figure 7.7).

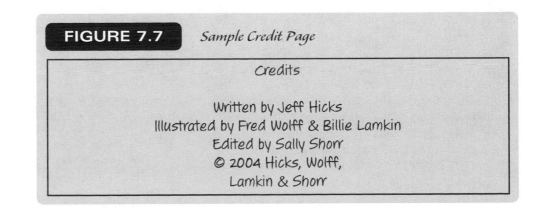

FIGURE 7.7 *Sample Credit Page*

Credits

Written by Jeff Hicks
Illustrated by Fred Wolff & Billie Lamkin
Edited by Sally Shorr
© 2004 Hicks, Wolff,
Lamkin & Shorr

ASSESSING: A PARTNERSHIP

Assessment typically comes at the end of the writing process, is typically teacher-directed, and is usually associated with grades. In Figure 7.2 I suggest making assessment a partnership in which both teacher and student play an important role. Without minimizing the importance of *teacher-based* classroom assessment, let me suggest that the most important evaluator needs to be the student and that the student's assessment of his or her work needs to occur prior to and during revision, not after handing the paper in.

Students who not only can assess their work but also can use that assessment to revise and edit have gained personal control of their own writing process. The student assesses to revise; the teacher, to evaluate. And in so doing, they become partners in the process of learning about writing.

ENDNOTE

Twenty-first-century writing process will, I believe, emphasize student independence. Students will direct every step, from selection of topics to determining what and how to publish. They will assess their work in the way professional writers do, for the purpose of revising or editing, and will seek an audience for the joy of knowing their writing has reached a reader's heart, and not just for the validation of a formal grade.

CHAPTER 7 IN A NUTSHELL

● Process-based writing should be the foundation for writing instruction. The six traits do not replace process but support it by giving students a vocabulary for talking and thinking about writing and by strengthening students' understanding of how to revise.

● In planning your instruction, think process first, then traits, then modes (genres of writing).

● The reason for teaching genres last is that traits change slightly from one genre to another. Voice in a business letter, for example, is slightly different from the voice in a personal narrative.

● Each step within the writing process connects in an important way to the traits:
  ✔ *Experience:* living life, finding/discovering ideas.
  ✔ *Prewriting:* Refining thinking about ideas.
  ✔ *Drafting:* Getting ideas down on paper; shaping, expanding, and fine-tuning ideas; beginning to or-

ganize information—thinking how to begin, where to go next, and how to end.
  ✔ *Sharing:* Connecting with an audience through voice.
  ✔ *Revising:* Reshaping text to clarify and extend thinking.
  ✔ *Editing:* Polishing finished text to ensure readability and to help readers interpret meaning correctly and hear the writer's intended voice.
  ✔ *Publishing:* Sharing writing informally (posting, reading) or formally (book making).
  ✔ *Assessing:* As students assess to revise and teachers assess to evaluate, they become partners in learning about writing.

● Twenty-first-century writing process will emphasize independence, with students in charge of each step.

EXTENSIONS

1. If you are currently teaching, do you use a process-based approach to teaching writing? If so, do the connections presented in this chapter match those you would make to the traits? Explain any differences.

2. On which part of the writing process do you spend the most or least time?
   ✔ As a writer?
   ✔ As a teacher?
   Why do you think this is? Write a journal entry about this.

3. As a writer, what specific strategies do you find most successful for prewriting/rehearsing? Share these with a study group or with your class. Model one of them.

4. As a writer, what specific strategies do you personally find most successful for revising your writ-

ing? Share these with a study group or with your class.

5. Have you ever felt yourself in what Donald Graves calls "a constant state of composition"? Describe the experience in a story or a poem.

6. Create an original piece of text, going through all the steps of the writing process as you normally would. Ask your students to do the same. Then, in writing or through a picture, describe your own writing process. Share the results. Is it true, based on your findings, that process is individual and differs for each person? Why would this be so?

7. Create a list of three or more topics you could write on right now. Discuss your list with colleagues or students, comparing topics and talking about where writers get ideas. What do you learn from this experience?

WHY I WRITE

I write because I know that every bone in my body will appreciate my work, the long hours I put into it, and all the gears in my head working to their full capacity.

—**Ryan Sterner,** student writer

LOOKING AHEAD

In Chapter 8 we will look at specific strategies for using traits to unlock the door to revision, whether you use writer's workshop or another process-based approach to instruction.

8 *Unlocking the Door to Revision*

Children are seldom shown how to read their work using actual texts. Rather, they are cajoled into "writing better" without knowing how good writing unfolds or how a writer thinks. Worse, they aren't made aware of strong writing within their own text. Even in my poorest piece, I need to know the best section, the strongest line, or the best use of language.

—Donald H. Graves
A Fresh Look at Writing, 1994, p. 222

We need to think hard about how we talk about writing—to our colleagues, to our students, to ourselves. Language, as the linguists tell us, is also the language of thought. In the end, the words we use to explain such concepts to our students will be the words they use to explain them to themselves.

—Ralph Fletcher
What a Writer Needs, 1993, p. 6

*L*et's suppose that you have an in-depth understanding of writing process and that you begin your year by teaching (or reinforcing) that process with your students, giving them opportunities to identify personally important topics, rehearse, draft, share, revise, edit—and occasionally publish. Your students are writing frequently and for multiple purposes—and you are modeling each step of the process yourself. Let's also suppose that although your instruction is process-based, you do not require students to take every piece clear through the process to publication. Some pieces are drafts, kept in a folder for another day. Everything is in place for you to say, "Choose a draft you'd like to take to the next level—something you like enough to spend some time on. I want to show you some things you can do to make your writing and revision more powerful than it's ever been." You're about to unlock the door.

FOUR STEPS TO TEACHING TRAITS

Given writing process as a base, teaching traits to students involves four key steps, each of which we will explore in this chapter:

Step 1: Surround students with writers' language, i.e., trait language.

Step 2: Teach students to be assessors of their own and others' work and to use their self-assessment in revising and setting goals.

Step 3: Use written works (including your own writing) to illustrate strengths and problems in writing.

Step 4: Use focused lessons (including practice revision) to help students develop skills in each trait.

All these things can occur within a writing process-based classroom or as an integral part of writers' workshop. For example, you might open your workshop by modeling a strategy that will be helpful to many of your student writers, given where they are in process right now: adding detail or using voice to reach an audience. Perhaps you follow this focused lesson by reading a passage from Roald Dahl, Sandra Cisneros, or Walter Dean Myers that reinforces the point of your modeling lesson. Then you turn your students loose to write, revise, and share their writing.

As you go through this chapter, you'll likely make the happy discovery that you are already teaching the traits. You cannot help it, really, for it's virtually impossible to discuss or model writing without addressing details, main ideas, leads, wording, or the crafting of sentences. As one teacher told me, "I never knew what that something was that I was responding to so strongly in students' writing. Now I have a name for it—*voice*. It's so much easier to teach something when you know what to call it."

Let's look at these four steps in more detail.

Step 1: Surrounding Students with Writers' Language

Students need their own copies of the scoring guide. In Figure 8.1 you'll find a student version of the five-point scoring guide to use with students. Figure 8.2 provides a six-point scoring guide for students.

Provide a copy of the scoring guide you select to parents too, if possible. When you do this, you ensure that everyone with a stake in creating strong writers is using the same language. You will notice several features in the student guide:

✔ Simpler language (in comparison with the teacher version)
✔ A first-person perspective
✔ A positive approach to help students see scores of 1 or 2 as beginning points, not points of failure

FIGURE 8.1

STUDENT 5-POINT WRITING GUIDE

IDEAS & DEVELOPMENT

5 *My writing is clear, focused, and filled with important, interesting details.*
- I have a clear main message or a story to tell.
- My paper is focused. It sticks to the main topic or story.
- I chose unusual details—things not everyone knows.
- I know this topic well, and it shows.
- I cover the topic, but I don't bury readers alive in details no one needs.

3 *I have made a good beginning. You can see where I'm headed.*
- I have a main message or story.
- *Most of the time,* I stick to that message or story.
- I chose some interesting details. Some information you have heard before.
- I know *a little* about this topic. I wish I knew more.
- I think I wrote too BIG and tried to tell too much. Or else, I left out important details.

1 *I wrote something, but I really don't have a message or story in mind—yet.*
- I am not sure what it is I'm trying to say.
- Mostly, I tried to fill space. I did not stick to any main topic.
- I threw in everything I could; I'll pick out what's important later.
- The truth is, I don't know enough about this topic to write about it.
- I'm not sure if I said too much or not enough.

ORGANIZATION

5 *This is so easy to follow it's like I drew you a road map.*
- I know right where I'm going, beginning to end.
- My lead gets you hooked; my conclusion brings things to a close.
- Everything comes at the right spot.
- Ideas are connected—to each other, and to my main idea.
- I spent time explaining where it was needed. Otherwise, I kept things moving.

3 *You can follow this if you pay attention.*
- I go down a few side roads, but you won't get lost. Sometimes, I followed a formula: *My first point, My second point,* and so on.
- I have a lead and conclusion. I'm not totally happy with them yet.
- When I read this over, I feel like I could move some things around.
- Some ideas are connected. Sometimes, you have to build the bridge yourself.
- I did not always stop to explain things. Or, I spent too much time on trivia.

1 *Reading this is like taking a bumpy path through the dark woods. Good luck!*
- My writing wanders. Even *I* don't know where I'm going.
- Lead? Conclusion? Hey, I just started in, and then stopped.
- This writing is like a messy closet. It's just a collection of thoughts.
- I don't see the connections between ideas—so it was hard to help a reader see them.
- I couldn't tell what to spend time on.

FIGURE 8.1 *continued*

STUDENT 5-POINT WRITING GUIDE

VOICE

5 *I love this topic, and I want you to find it fascinating, too.*
- My tone and voice are just right for this topic and audience.
- This sounds like me and no one else. I hear my voice in every line.
- I thought about my audience all the way through. It's like I'm having a conversation with them.
- My writing is honest; it's how I see things. It's also lively. I worked to make this topic interesting for a reader.
- I think someone would want to share this aloud.

3 *This is an OK topic, and I think I sound interested—maybe not excited, though.*
- The tone and flavor seem all right to me.
- At times it sounds like me. At times, it's an anybody paper (*Blah, blah*) or an encyclopedia voice (*Fact, fact, fact . . .*).
- Sometimes, I put my heart into it and tried to reach the audience. But sometimes, I was just trying to get through it.
- I think it has moments of real honesty or liveliness.
- I can see someone reading a line or two out loud. Maybe not the whole piece.

1 *I could not get into this topic. I just wanted to get the writing done.*
- I don't know if this voice goes with my topic or audience. Does it matter?
- I am not sure if this sounds like me. It's just words on paper.
- I really wasn't "talking" to an audience. I wrote what came into my head.
- Honest? Lively? I don't know. I felt bored when I wrote it.
- I wouldn't share this out loud. I'm not sure anyone would read it who didn't have to.

WORD CHOICE

5 *I chose every word or phrase to make the message clear—or create an image in the reader's mind.*
- My meaning is crystal clear from beginning to end.
- My words and phrases are fresh, accurate, and memorable—sometimes quotable.
- Lively verbs give my writing power.
- I went easy on the modifiers. I left out clichés and tired words, and I did NOT write to show off.
- I avoided repetition.
- Find any favorite words or phrases? I did.

3 *My words communicate. They get the job done.*
- You will get the general message. Can you picture it? Maybe not . . .
- My words aren't always original, but they usually make sense.
- I have a strong verb or two—guess I could use more.
- Some parts are too flowery—or too flat. Sometimes, I tried to impress the reader, even if I had to pull out the old thesaurus.
- I repeated a few words. Oh, well!
- If you hunt, you'll find a striking word or phrase.

1 *I couldn't seem to find the right words to say what I wanted to say.*
- I don't know the meaning of some words I used. I'm not sure my message makes sense.
- Sometimes I used the first word or phrase that came into my mind: *fun, nice, awesome, bad, cool, dude, real, too much*—you know, the usual words.
- I used too many modifiers, not enough verbs.
- I overdid it in spots—*The chili was superlative.*
- Or, I used words too many times: *The wonderful speech was wonderful.*
- I don't spot any quotable moments—yet!

FIGURE 8.1 *continued*

STUDENT 5-POINT WRITING GUIDE

SENTENCE FLUENCY

5 *My writing has rhythm, like music or poetry. It's easy to read aloud.*

- You can read this with expression and voice. Try it and see.
- My sentences begin many different ways. Some are long—some short.
- Connecting phrases—*After a while, On the other hand*—show how one idea links to another.
- You can almost hear the beat when you read this out loud.
- If I used fragments, they work. If I used dialogue, it sounds like real people talking.

3 *This writing hums along with a steady beat. Not musical maybe, but you can read it.*

- It's pretty easy to read aloud if you practice.
- My sentences aren't *all* the same length—and they do not *all* begin the same way, either.
- Connecting phrases? Now that you mention it, I could use a few more.
- It's a little stiff in spots, but it has some good moments.
- My fragments do not all work. My dialogue is a little forced. It needs to sound more like real speech.

1 *This is a challenge to read aloud, even for me!*

- It's hard to tell where my sentences begin and end. You'll have to work hard to read this aloud.
- I need to combine some sentences and shorten others. Too many begin exactly the same way.
- I used words like *and then, so then, and because* to connect phrases and make one BIG "sentence" that will leave you breathless!
- This does not sound right. It's just not smooth.
- Did I write sentences or fragments? I'm not sure. Dialogue? How is *that* supposed to sound?

CONVENTIONS

5 *I know my conventions and it shows. I can use them to bring out meaning—and voice.*

- An editor would get bored looking for mistakes in my copy.
- Spelling, punctuation, grammar, caps, and paragraphing are correct.
- I did my best editing to make reading easy.
- It might need a few touch-ups, but no more.
- I used layout to draw your eye to key points.

3 *I know my conventions pretty well. You might catch a few errors.*

- I see mistakes when I read this over. I did some things well, though.
- I read this too quickly. You'll need to do some mental editing as you read.
- I need to read this aloud, use a ruler to read line by line, and use a dictionary or spell checker.
- The mistakes do not get in the way of the message—but they don't help!
- My layout isn't dazzling, but it's OK.

1 *My conventions are out of control. Help!*

- I have *many* mistakes. You may need to read once just to de-code.
- I haven't edited this yet. I have errors in spelling, punctuation, capitals—maybe other things, too.
- I need to read this aloud word-by-word with a partner to help me.
- The mistakes get in the way of the message.
- Layout? Oops. Never got to it.

FIGURE 8.2 *Student Six–Point Writing Guide*

STUDENT 6-POINT WRITING GUIDE

IDEAS

6
- ☐ My writing is clear and focused. It will hold your attention.
- ☐ I know this topic inside and out.
- ☐ I help readers learn, think, and gain insight.
- ☐ The details I chose will surprise and delight you.

5
- ☐ My writing is clear and focused.
- ☐ I know a lot about this topic.
- ☐ I consistently share important information.
- ☐ I use many details/examples to support main ideas.

4
- ☐ This paper is clear and focused—*most* of the time!
- ☐ I have *some* knowledge of this topic.
- ☐ My paper offers readers *some* new information.
- ☐ I came up with a few details and examples.

3
- ☐ Some of my writing rambles—I ran out of meaningful things to say.
- ☐ I wish I knew more about this topic.
- ☐ It was hard to think of new information all the time.
- ☐ I scrambled to come up with details!

2
- ☐ My writing rambles—not all of it makes sense.
- ☐ I did NOT know this topic well enough to write about it.
- ☐ I said some things I could not prove or support.
- ☐ I couldn't come up with many details.

1
- ☐ This is not clear. I could not figure out what I wanted to say.
- ☐ I did not have ANY information on this topic.
- ☐ These are just notes and thoughts—whatever came into my head.
- ☐ I have all these bits of information—but do they *go* with anything?

ORGANIZATION

6
- ☐ My organization will guide you through the text like a light in the dark.
- ☐ My lead will hook you—the conclusion will leave you thinking.
- ☐ I link ideas in a way that highlights important connections.
- ☐ The structure takes you from point to point with a real sense of purpose.

5
- ☐ My organization will help you zero in on key ideas.
- ☐ I have a strong lead—and my conclusion wraps up the discussion.
- ☐ My transitions show how ideas connect.
- ☐ The paper's structure helps you keep track of ideas.

4
- ☐ My organization works with the ideas.
- ☐ I have a lead and conclusion. They seem OK.
- ☐ My transitions are helpful, I think.
- ☐ You can follow it, but sometimes you know what is coming next.

3
- ☐ When I read this over, I feel like moving some parts around.
- ☐ My lead and/or conclusion could use work.
- ☐ I forgot some transitions. OR, I followed a pattern (*My first reason, second reason*).
- ☐ This is hard to follow at times—OR, you *always* know what's coming!

2
- ☐ I feel like re-organizing *everything*—beginning to end.
- ☐ I have no lead or conclusion, OR, it's the same thing you always hear.
- ☐ My transitions are missing—OR they don't make sense.
- ☐ This is hard to follow, even when you pay attention.

1
- ☐ This is like stumbling through the woods, without a flashlight.
- ☐ It just starts and stops. There's no real lead or conclusion.
- ☐ I can't link ideas—I'm not even sure they go together.
- ☐ No one can follow this. I can't follow it myself.

FIGURE 8.2 *continued*

STUDENT 6-POINT WRITING GUIDE

VOICE

6
- ☐ This writing is as individual as my fingerprints.
- ☐ Trust me—you will need to share this aloud.
- ☐ I use voice to make the message resonate in your head.
- ☐ Hear the passion in my voice? I want you to love this topic.

5
- ☐ This is original and distinctive. It's definitely *me*.
- ☐ I think you will want to read this aloud.
- ☐ This voice goes with the topic, and reaches out to the audience.
- ☐ The paper is lively and expressive. It has energy.

4
- ☐ This writing strikes a spark or two. You *might* recognize me.
- ☐ You might share a line or two aloud.
- ☐ My voice might fade here and there—*usually* I reach out to the audience.
- ☐ This paper is sincere. It sounds like I mean what I say.

3
- ☐ My voice comes out here and there. I'm not sure you can tell it's *me*.
- ☐ There could be a "share-aloud" moment in there somewhere.
- ☐ I wasn't *always* thinking of the audience.
- ☐ My voice is pretty quiet in this paper. It's a careful, reserved voice.

2
- ☐ I'm hiding behind the words. It's not *me* yet.
- ☐ This has a *hint* of voice, but it's not ready to share.
- ☐ My voice is very faint. It's hard to hear even when you listen closely.
- ☐ I sound bored—or maybe like an encyclopedia. It's not the *right* voice.

1
- ☐ I'm not "at home" in this paper. I can't hear myself. Not an echo.
- ☐ I don't think anyone will share this aloud.
- ☐ I couldn't get excited about the topic. I didn't think about my audience.
- ☐ My voice . . . is just . . . missing . . .

WORD CHOICE

6
- ☐ I found original, creative ways to use everyday words.
- ☐ You'll want to read this more than once—you might quote a phrase.
- ☐ Every word carries its own weight.
- ☐ I used the power of verbs—not too many adjectives.
- ☐ My words make pictures in your mind—or touch your senses (sight, sound, etc.).

5
- ☐ I write to make meaning clear, not to impress you.
- ☐ Once you start reading this, you won't want to stop.
- ☐ I chose words to make the message clear. I kept it concise.
- ☐ I used strong verbs—and found new ways to say things.
- ☐ My words make pictures in your mind—or touch your senses.

4
- ☐ My writing is clear. I used words correctly.
- ☐ You'll spot some strong words or phrases.
- ☐ I have a few vague words (*fun, nice*) and parts are wordy, but it makes sense.
- ☐ I need *more* strong verbs.
- ☐ *Sometimes* my writing makes a picture in your mind.

3
- ☐ I wrote the first words I thought of. You'll get the general idea.
- ☐ Here and there is a word or phrase I like.
- ☐ Vague or wordy passages make my message unclear at times.
- ☐ Not enough verbs—and too many modifiers clutter up the message.
- ☐ You might need to re-read to "see" it in your head.

2
- ☐ Watch out for tired words, vague words, thesaurus words.
- ☐ You have to look hard to find strong moments.
- ☐ Wordiness and flat language make the message fuzzy.
- ☐ *Way* too many adjectives—and verbs rode into the sunset.
- ☐ These words paint no clear pictures.

1
- ☐ I wrote *anything* just to fill space.
- ☐ It was a struggle to get words—*any* words—on the page.
- ☐ The message got lost in here somewhere . . .
- ☐ I need more words, stronger words—*different* words! Help!
- ☐ What was I trying to say or describe?

FIGURE 8.2 *continued*

SENTENCE FLUENCY

6
- ☐ This is easy to read with voice.
- ☐ It flows just like a good movie script.
- ☐ You won't believe how much variety I have in sentence style and length.
- ☐ If I used fragments, they add punch. My dialogue is like listening in on a conversation.

5
- ☐ You can read this with expression.
- ☐ It has an easy rhythm and flow.
- ☐ My writing has quite a lot of variety in sentence style and length.
- ☐ If I used fragments, they are effective. My dialogue echoes real speech.

4
- ☐ My writing sounds natural. It's easy to read.
- ☐ It's pretty smooth—with an awkward moment or two, maybe.
- ☐ There is some variety in sentence style and length.
- ☐ If I used fragments, they work. If I used dialogue, it sounds fairly authentic.

3
- ☐ It's a *little* bumpy, a rocky ride, but you can get through it.
- ☐ There are awkward, choppy moments. It's smooth here and there.
- ☐ Too many sentences start the same way. Too many are the same length.
- ☐ Fragments do not work. This dialogue isn't real.

2
- ☐ You can read this *if* you are patient—and *if* you rehearse.
- ☐ I have many run-ons, choppy sentences. Are these all sentences?
- ☐ If I found a good sentence pattern, I stuck with it.
- ☐ If I used fragments, they were an accident. I'm not sure if I wrote any dialogue.

1
- ☐ This is very hard to read, even for me.
- ☐ Even if you practice, you will need to re-read and fill in some blanks.
- ☐ These sentences don't sound right, but I'm not sure why.
- ☐ I'm not sure where sentences start and stop.

CONVENTIONS

6
- ☐ Only the pickiest editors will spot errors.
- ☐ This is carefully edited. Conventions bring out the meaning and voice.
- ☐ My paper shows off a wide range of conventions.
- ☐ My layout (*optional*) is appealing and leads the reader to main ideas.
- ☐ This is virtually ready to publish.

5
- ☐ I have some minor errors, but they are easy to overlook.
- ☐ I edited the paper. The conventions support meaning and voice.
- ☐ This paper shows that I know many different conventions.
- ☐ My layout (*optional*) enhances the presentation of ideas.
- ☐ This is ready to publish with light touch-ups.

4
- ☐ There are noticeable, minor errors. My message is still clear.
- ☐ I edited this paper, and it's fairly easy to read.
- ☐ This paper shows control over basic conventions, like capitals.
- ☐ My layout (*optional*) seems fine. It draws attention to main ideas.
- ☐ This piece needs a good once-over before it's published.

3
- ☐ This many errors could slow a reader down.
- ☐ I edited too quickly—I missed a lot of things.
- ☐ My paper shows problems even with basic conventions (easy spelling).
- ☐ I should give more attention to layout (*optional*).
- ☐ This piece needs thorough, careful editing before it's published.

2
- ☐ The errors are getting in the way of my message.
- ☐ It's hard to see I even edited this.
- ☐ I made numerous errors even on basic conventions.
- ☐ I did not think about layout much yet (*optional*).
- ☐ This piece needs line-by-line editing before it's published.

1
- ☐ There are so many errors it's almost impossible to read this.
- ☐ Even patient readers will struggle! This needs work.
- ☐ Errors on basic conventions put up reading road blocks.
- ☐ I need to re-work the layout (*optional*).
- ☐ This piece needs word-by-word editing before it's published.

In providing student scoring guides, you've already taken an important step, but there's more you can do to bring writers' language into your classroom.

■ *Know the Traits Well Yourself*

If *you* know the traits well, you'll find yourself referring to leads, conclusions, and transitions as easily as a surgeon refers to sutures and tracheotomies. So this is one way to surround your students with trait (i.e., writers') language. You can and should use your own version of trait language (don't feel compelled to quote a rubric) in the comments you make on students' writing: "Your conclusion surprised me," "The paragraphing in this essay was dead on," "This paper rings with voice—I could hear you in every line."

■ *Make Posters*

You can also put up posters highlighting the key components of each trait. Make your own, or see the chart on the inside back cover for copy you can use if you wish.

Step 2: Teach Students to Be Assessors

If you do not do one other thing differently in your teaching because of the six traits, try this: Once a week (or more often, if time permits), ask students to assess and discuss writing by anonymous student writers or work by any writer who is not a member of the class. Through your sharing of examples, student writers learn more about what to do—or not do—than they could learn through almost any other means. In fact, research by George Hillocks, Jr., explicitly points to use of criteria and student samples—what he calls "environmental" instruction—as being among the most effective of all strategies for teaching writing (1986, p. 247).

The sample papers from Chapters 4, 5, and 6 (as well as from Chapter 11 if you wish to work with informational pieces exclusively) provide many samples from which to draw. Form a team of colleagues, and you can add to this collection by together saving your own students' samples (with their permission, of course) for use in years to come. Here are some things to keep in mind as you make your choices and share examples with students.

1. *Use samples in pairs to create contrast.* If I were structuring a lesson on ideas, I might begin with "My Bike" (Figure 8.3), a good paper to use because it clearly lacks detail. Many students write in this general, floaty way, but they have a much easier time seeing the problem in someone else's work. Then contrast it with "Fishing Lessons" (Figure 8.4). As you read this piece, can you picture these two fishermen together, with the sun "just creeping over the horizon"? The detail in this story is striking, and you might begin with just asking students to list im-

| FIGURE 8.3 | *"My Bike" (Descriptive/Narrative, Grade 3)* |

The neatest gift I ever got was a bike I got for my birthday. It was really cool. It was red and kind of silver but mostly red. I had been wanting a bike for a long time, and when I finally got one, I just could not believe it was mine. It was the best gift I got for my birthday. It was very shiny with red paint and lots of chrome on the wheels. I was only eight when I got it, so I could not ride it right away. But soon after I got it I could ride it and then I rode it all the time. I had that bike for a long time, and it really meant alot to me.

> **FIGURE 8.4** *"Fishing Lessons" (Narrative, Grade 7)*
>
> It was a cool, crisp morning, about the time when the dew begins to form on the grassy banks of the stream. I had been anticipating this moment for some time and now it was here. Grandpa and I were going fishing at an ideal spot swarming with fish. We had left at about 4, but by the time we got there and unpacked, the sun was just creeping over the horizon.
>
> Grandpa pulled the rod back and let it fly, right down stream, farther than I could see. Then, I lowered my toy fishing line down until it was just under the surfcace. Right away, Grandpa got a tug on his line, but it wasn't a fish, it was a baby alligator. The alligator was semi-small, but it still put up a fight. Grandpa would gently reel it in, give it some line, then reel it some more. Just then, I realized he had gotten the scissors and was trying to cut the jumping line. Before I could blink, he cut the line and the alligator swam into a drain pipe. That really surprised me because that was his favorite hook.
>
> I pondered over this while I doodled around with my plastic hook in the water. About when the sun got all the way over the horizon, and it slowly was starting to get hot, we headed home with a puny guppy I caught in my plastic net. On the way to the house, I asked Grandpa why he hadn't just caught the alligator or at least reeled it in. He replied with a question—"Why cause the little fella any more pain than what life dishes out?" I learned that day that all things have a right to life and that life has a reason to be had.

ages that come to mind—or even connections to personal experiences. Sensory details are vivid. But best of all, I think, is the strong sense of friendship between grandfather and grandson, which is never stated outright. Embedded within each of these features is an important lesson to learn about writing.

2. *Start with papers that are clearly strong or problematic.* Mid-level papers are the most difficult to score, so save these for when your students know a trait well.

3. *Do not worry about the grade level of the writer.* You can use third grade papers with high school students and vice versa. Select papers that clearly make a point; for example, "Detail creates voice" Or "Varied sentence beginnings add interest."

4. *Read the papers aloud.* All writing plays differently to the eye and ear. If conventions are weak or the piece looks a little sloppy on the page, students may have a hard time getting beyond cosmetics to the heart and soul beneath.

5. *Encourage students to work in pairs or teams.* It is critical that all students talk, and many will not do so in a large-group setting. They need to share their thinking, the reasons behind the

> *Terms like "coherent" and even "specific" are notoriously hard for students to grasp because they do not read stacks of student writing.*
>
> **—Peter Elbow**
> *Embracing Contraries*, 1986, p. 154

score. Don't let students get by with saying, "It's a five," or, "It sounds like a one or a two." *Anyone* can score writing. It's having to defend your score that teaches you to think like an evaluator, a reader—and a writer.

6. *Do not limit your practice to student papers.* Once you've warmed up a little, apply your skills to scoring other forms of writing: a job application letter, a sample of technical writing, a brochure from the local aquarium, or a test. One of my favorite stories about the student-as-assessor comes from Donald Graves. He tells of a student taking a standardized test ("No talking") who insistently interrupted his teacher, despite her protests, to whisper, "Who wrote this anyway? This stuff doesn't have any voice" (1994, p. 122).

Step 3: Use Written Works to Illustrate Strengths and Problems in Writing

When I began teaching the traits to students, I gathered some of my favorite literature and scanned it for samples that would show the traits in action. Passages from *To Kill a Mockingbird* helped to illustrate strong ideas (not to mention one of the all-time great leads), whereas passages from *Lonesome Dove* seemed just the ticket for voice. The lyrical writing of Dylan Thomas (1954/1962) was truly stunning in its fluency and its creative, unconventional word choice:

> I was born in a large Welsh town at the beginning of the Great War—an ugly, lovely town (or so it was and is to me), crawling, sprawling by a long and splendid curving shore where truant boys and sandfield boys . . . watched the dock-bound ships or the ships steaming away into wonder and India, magic and China, countries bright with oranges and loud with lions *[p. 5]*.

You don't need a thesaurus to write "bright with oranges" or "loud with lions." You only have to love language.

You *do not need to read a whole book* to illustrate a trait. Short passages work beautifully. I emphasize this because so often teachers tell me, "I don't have time to read three or four books aloud per trait." I realize then how unclear I have been on this point. So let me clarify now: Collect *brief* passages—*moments* I call them—to illustrate each trait. In that way you'll always have time for a read-aloud (or two or three), and you'll be able to share multiple samples to show the many ways a trait can reveal itself. Here, for example, are five favorite moments you could use for the trait of voice, and notice that because they're so short, you can use them with writers of many ages (even those who are too young to appreciate the text in its entirety):

> It's a funny thing about mothers and fathers. Even when their own child is the most disgusting little blister you could ever imagine, they still think that he or she is wonderful [Roald Dahl, *Matilda,* 1988, p. 7].

> Calves come early in the spring.
> It was how we knew the winter would die, would end.
> In the dark of the barn night when it was still cold enough outside to make things break, in the warm dark night of the closed barn they came, and when we would open the door in the morning to start chores we could smell them, the new calves [Gary Paulsen, *Clabbered Dirt, Sweet Grass,* 1992, p. 3].

In English my name means hope. In Spanish it means too many letters. It means sadness, it means waiting. It is like the number nine. A muddy color. It is the Mexican records my father plays on Sunday mornings when he is shaving, songs like sobbing. . . . At school they say my name funny as if the syllables were made out of tin and hurt the roof of your mouth. But in Spanish my name is made out of a softer something, like silver [Sandra Cisneros, *The House on Mango Street,* 1989, p. 11].

Warts are wonderful structures. They can appear overnight on any part of the skin, like mushrooms on a damp lawn, full grown and splendid in the complexity of their architecture [Lewis Thomas, *The Medusa and the Snail,* 1979, p. 76].

In Lake Wobegon, we grew up with bad news. Since I was a little kid I heard it wafting up through the heat duct from the kitchen below. Our relatives came to visit on Saturday evenings and after we kids were packed off to bed, the grownups sat up late until ten-thirty or eleven and talked about sickness, unhappiness, divorce, violence, and all the sorrows they felt obliged to shelter children from, and I lay on the bedroom floor and listened in, soaking up information. [Garrison Keillor, *We Are Still Married,* 1989, p. xix].

Hearing many voices enriches our understanding of this complex trait. Roald Dahl is a master of satire, but even more than this, we admire the way he never shrinks from stating outright just how he feels. *"Disgusting little blister"* is not polite phrasing, but it's unflinchingly honest. Honesty is a crucial ingredient in voice.

Gary Paulsen's voice is powerful but quiet. In *Clabbered Dirt, Sweet Grass,* his tribute to farm life, he creates humble but beautiful phrases—*"the dark of the barn night"* and *"cold enough outside to make things break"*—that transport us into a Minnesota winter.

Few writers go so deeply and daringly inside the human spirit as Sandra Cisneros, whose profound insight captures the way the world looks and feels to a child. *The House on Mango Street* presents many faces of human experience, from humor, joy, and whimsy to melancholy, jealousy, heartache, and love.

Lewis Thomas can be enthusiastic and eloquent on almost any topic, from cloning to punctuation and, yes, warts. Who knew warts had architecture?

Then there's Garrison Keillor, who slips his humor in on you as subtly as a second piece of chocolate cake during a Saturday soiree.

Don't overlook the bad writing. When I purchased a computer several years ago, I quickly discovered that I could use the manufacturer's instructions as a sample of perfectly wretched word choice. Here is the opening line in my *Concise User's Guide,* which runs 400 pages (think if they'd printed the *Not-So-Concise Guide*):

Most computers are sold with an operating system pre-installed. However, if your computer doesn't have this version of the MS-DOS operating system installed, you must run the Setup Program. You cannot run the MS-DOS directly from the Setup disks because the files on those disks are compressed [Microsoft Corporation, 1994, p. 1].

Veteran computer buffs will scorn my inability to enjoy this kind of "technospeak," but when I read this, not only do I find it strenuous to follow, but (what is worse) I also feel as welcome inside this book as surprise in-laws who pop in for the weekend. Compare that with this introduction from one of my son's college textbooks:

In most college courses students spend more time with their textbooks than with their professors. Given this reality, it helps if you

Every book you pick up has its own lesson or lessons, and quite often the bad books have more to teach than the good ones.

—Stephen King
On Writing, 2000, p. 145

> *A good writer is one you can read without breaking a sweat. If you want a workout, you don't lift a book—you lift weights.*
>
> **—Patricia T. O'Connor**
> *Woe Is I*, 1996, p. 195

like your textbook. Making textbooks likable, however, is a tricky proposition. . . . [We] have tried to make [this] book lively, informal, engaging, well organized, easy to read, practical, and occasionally humorous [Weiten and Lloyd, *Psychology Applied to Modern Life*, 2003, p. xxix].

I confess that I *do* like this textbook (if I were teaching the course, I'd order it), and equally important, I like the authors. It is comforting to take instruction from someone who sounds human, someone who will have a conversation with us.

■ *Tip 1: Be a Collector—and Get Color Coded*

Start today collecting pieces of writing from everywhere: Collect annual reports, sports stories, book and film reviews, voters' pamphlet inserts, catalogs, editorials, advertisements, manuals, menus, brochures, theater programs, greeting cards, résumés, song lyrics—anything. Keep 12 folders, two for each trait, one for the good writing and one for the not-so-good writing. (*Hint:* Color code them to simplify your life so that each trait is a different color—ideas red, organization white, and so on.) From your collection, you can always pull a read-aloud (perfect for a minilesson on any trait) and, if you like, turn it into an overhead so that you and your students can score it or discuss it in detail or use it as a practice piece for revision. When your collection grows, begin keeping just one item in each folder, well labeled.

■ *Tip 2: Don't Overlook Your Own Writing*

> *. . . in the case of struggling writers, explicit instruction should be added to the largely intuitive development of writing abilities at the heart of workshop methods.*
>
> **—James L. Collins**
> *Strategies for Teaching Struggling Writers*, 1998, p. 7

Share pieces you are working on as well. I sometimes share several drafts with students and ask them to tell me which was written first, second, and third. See Appendix 3 for an example of this lesson using a piece entitled "The Pitcher."

Step 4: Use Focused Lessons

Focused lessons allow students to tackle writing one small bite at a time. For writers who thrive on a little more direct instruction, focused lessons can be just the thing. A focused lesson may be as short as three or four minutes (Some people call these *minilessons*) or may run 20 minutes or more. Here, trait by trait, are some I find useful.

FOCUSED LESSONS FOR IDEAS

- ✔ Main idea
- ✔ Detail
- ✔ Clarity
- ✔ Focus
- ✔ Interest

When you're teaching ideas, picture students looking at the world through a magnifying glass. You're trying to teach them to write with detail, with a sharp eye, with clarity, and with focus. Here are a few suggestions:

1. *Encourage student writers to choose their own topics*, at least part of the time. There will be those special times when you're studying the laws of physics or the Holocaust that you wish students to focus their writing on a specified topic, but even then they often can personalize or narrow topics within prescribed bounds. How to find topics? Keep lists, borrow from one another, read extensively—and *talk*. Model for students by creating a list of topics *you* are currently thinking of writing on, and talk about where you get your ideas. I am forever losing things (my glasses, my hair dryer, books, papers), so losing or forgetting are recurrent themes in my writing. Like anyone who flies frequently, I miss sleep, get separated from my luggage, or get grounded in unexpected places; a life on the road is nowhere near as exotic as people think, and the little realities (cockroaches in the overhead, toilets that back up at 2 A.M., hotel rooms without lights or door locks) give me a continual source of writing topics. Still, everyone comes up dry now and then.

In *Shoptalk* (1990), Donald M. Murray describes himself as a great observer of life but confesses that sometimes even he does not "feel the muse" perched on his shoulder, and so uses questions such as these to uncover possible topics (pp. 79–80):

- ✔ What surprised me recently?
- ✔ What's bugging me?
- ✔ What is changing?
- ✔ What did I expect to happen that didn't?
- ✔ Why did something make me so mad?
- ✔ What do I keep remembering?
- ✔ What have I learned?

Your students can ask themselves similar questions to get ideas flowing.

2. *Seize the main idea.* Writing flows more clearly when the writer has his/her main message clearly in mind. The writer should be able to complete this sentence: *My main message is _____.* Further, recognize that a *single word* is only a topic; a thesis requires a *statement*. *Cats* is a topic. *Cat are highly intelligent* is a thesis—a main message, if you will. *Traffic* (one word) is a topic. This is a thesis: *Traffic now moves so slowly that the average commute has lengthened to an hour in our city.* A one-word topic leads to sprawly writing; a thesis gives writing direction and focus. Ensure that students can express a main message in sentence form.

3. *Dig for the potatoes.* Significant details that go beyond common knowledge strengthen writing. Barry Lane (*Reviser's Toolbox*, 1999) calls the good details the "potatoes"—because they're hidden, or at least less than obvious, and you have to dig for them. Try this with your students. Make a list of details on any topic (for the purposes of illustration, I have chosen *sharks*)—you should have at least 20 in all. Of the 20, about 5 should be "potatoes" (*"sharks are revered as ancestors in Hawaii; sharks cannot blink or cry"*). The rest should be general information (*"sharks live in the ocean; sharks can be dangerous"*). Ask students, in pairs, to go through the list (see Figure 8.5) and pick out the "potatoes." Discuss their findings as a class. Do they agree on what's significant? If you wish to extend this lesson, use the results (the "potatoes") to create a how-to poem that focuses on the topic at hand. See Figure 8.6 for "How to Be a Shark." How-to poems, which are written in a recipe format (*Do this, don't do that*), can be used to explore any concept, term, or person (How to be

---

FIGURE 8.5	*Details About Sharks*

1. Sharks live in the ocean.
2. Sharks cannot swim backwards.
3. There are many types of sharks.
4. Sharks cannot blink.
5. Sharks sometimes eat unusual things, such as tires or wood—even metal.
6. In Hawaii, sharks are revered as reincarnated ancestors.
7. Sometimes you see sharks in the movies.
8. Many people fear sharks.
9. The word "shark" comes from the German "shurke," meaning *villain*.
10. Sharks lose their teeth—sometimes tens of thousands of them— throughout their lives.
11. Many books have been written about sharks.
12. Newborn sharks are often eaten alive by their parents shortly after birth.
13. Some sharks are much larger than others.
14. Sharks have few natural enemies.
15. A shark's skin is extremely thick and tough.

---

a democracy, the color blue, Ground Zero, a triangle, cubism, right field, Ghandi) and so work with any content area. They are excellent for literary analysis, too (How to be Atticus Finch, Hestor Prynne, Professor Dumbledore, Moby-Dick, Mr. Twit, Stanley Yelnats, Nurse Ratchett).

4. *Put your senses to work.* What sights, sounds, smells, tastes, and feelings (tactile or of the heart) come to mind when you recall a time, place, person, or incident? Make a list, and use it to construct a sketch full of detail (see Figure 8.7 for an example of how to organize sensory information). It also helps to see how a professional writer does it. In his classic autobiography, *Boy: Tales of Childhood* (1984), author Roald Dahl takes us into a combined world of revulsion and wondrous enticement: the sweet shop in Llandaff, run by Mrs. Pratchett. We learn that she was a *"small skinny old hag with a moustache on her upper lip and a mouth as sour as a green gooseberry."* We can certainly picture her now, but that's not enough for Dahl. He forces us right up close, where the details are most revoltingly vivid: *"Her blouse had bits of breakfast all over it, toast-crumbs and tea stains*

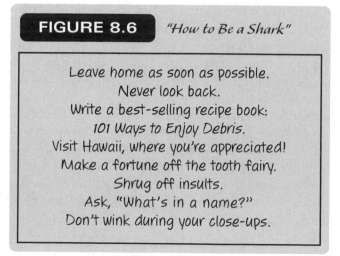

FIGURE 8.6	*"How to Be a Shark"*

Leave home as soon as possible.
Never look back.
Write a best-selling recipe book:
101 Ways to Enjoy Debris.
Visit Hawaii, where you're appreciated!
Make a fortune off the tooth fairy.
Shrug off insults.
Ask, "What's in a name?"
Don't wink during your close-ups.

FIGURE 8.7	*Sensory Details Chart for Future Paper on My Grandmother's Kitchen*

Sights	Sounds	Tastes & Smells	Feelings
• Old furniture	• Screen door banging	• Coffee perking	• Scratchy upholstery
• Linoleum floor	• Kids laughing	• Butter melting	• Bread dough—thick and moist
• Old wood table	• Sprinkler hissing	• Cinnamon	• Sweat running down my back
• Fading wallpaper	• Dog howling at the cat	• Vanilla	• Tired, achy feet
• Cat sleeping	• Grandmother's voice—laughing	• Damp wood	• Breeze coming through the screen
	• Tick of old clock	• Old rubber boots	• Contentment
		• Fresh mown grass	• Peace

and splotches of dried egg-yolk" (p. 33). We see her, we smell the candy shop—filth and chocolate, toast and eggs, swirling. And now we hear her shrill, piercing voice, too: *"I'm watchin' you so keep yer thievin' fingers off them chocolates!"* Eleven tiny words that teach us as much about Mrs. Pratchett as we need to know—for now.

5. *Let one detail tell all.* Head-to-toe description does not necessarily make for the best character sketch. Good writers look for that single detail that tells all. In *Speak* (Laurie Halse Anderson, 2001), high schooler Melinda describes one of her English teachers, focusing on the feature that commands attention most:

> My English teacher has no face. She has uncombed stringy hair that droops on her shoulders. The hair is black from her part to her ears and then neon orange to the frizzy ends. I can't decide if she had pissed off her hairdresser or is morphing into a monarch butterfly. I call her Hairwoman [p. 6].

Your students can try this, too. Think of a memorable person, and then ask, "What one feature comes immediately to mind? Hair, hands, voice, or walk?" Create a character sketch in which that one feature reveals something important about the person.

6. *Find a lesson waiting to happen.* Here's an idea that's not just for the *ideas* trait. Start with a writing sample that's problematic—"The Redwoods" is an ideal choice for detail because it is written in generalities. Ask students to practice revision using this sample, giving them editorial freedom to invent and weave in any details they like, and the results will surprise you. Here are two revisions of "The Redwoods," one middle school and one high school (see page 42 for the original):

The Redwoods, Revised (Grade 8)

Last summer, my family and I went on a vacation to see the California Redwoods. Most of the time was great, though not everything turned out the way we expected. We spent most of our time basking in the sun and hiking. We basked so much I got a sunburn from head to toe, and had to spend the next several days peeling my outer layer of skin.

One day we hiked the Sunrise Trail. The cool morning air was easy to hike in so we ended up doing the whole thing. The giant ferns were like something out of a pre-historic movie. Three of us linking arms could not reach around the trunks. It was amazing to think how old they were and to try imagining what they had lived through. It made us feel tiny and transient.

Like sun bathing, hiking had its drawbacks. The main one being my brother. We saw a gorgeous sunrise and several deer. I had never been close to a deer before and I was very excited, but I knew better than to yell. Not Tom! He came crashing out of the brush yelling, "A deer! A deer! Look you guys!" We just glared at him. That was the last time we took the Sunrise Trail.

My parents aren't big hikers, so they spent their time visiting friends, mostly people I wasn't too fond of, but my parents loved. They took what seemed like thousands of pictures. Practically every rock was photographed. Every tree was in a picture. It got quite nerve-wracking having a camera pointed in my direction constantly, so I took off for the woods, secretly hoping to get lost.

Maybe we'll come back next year, or go someplace different. It doesn't really matter as long as I am with my family. Next time, though, I think our camera may experience an unfortunate accident.

This is a vast improvement, full of telling details about the sunburn, the enormous ferns and trees, the boisterous Tom, and the omnipresent camera. Here's how a high school writer handled the same paper:

The Redwoods, Revised (Grade 12)

I'll be the first to admit I've pretty much outgrown the family vacation. So when my father announced that we were going to spend a week down in California seeing a bunch of trees, you can imagine how thrilled I was. Until the day of the trip, I kept hoping for some ailment to afflict and rescue me from this world of family fun. Nothing struck. No compassionate neighbors volunteered to take me in. No desperate local business people called with an urgent job to be filled. I was free, capable of packing, and unemployed. It looked more and more as if I'd have to go.

The day we set out (or as I like to think of it, "Hell: Day One") arrived. I packed in five minutes flat, yanking items at random out of my drawer (Who cares what you wear in the woods? It's dark in there, isn't it?), stuffed my bag in the trunk of the car and plunked onto my side of the backseat (already polluted with my brother's gum wrappers, inane video game magazines, and empty remains of old gummy bears bags). Mom turned and smiled gamely at me, and I tried to respond, but the corners of my mouth seemed frozen as if shot through with Novocain.

Dad swung back out of the driveway and headed out with a cheery "Here we go!" Mom's shoulders took on a kind of jaunty look, and knowing better than to sigh out loud, I slumped down low into my backseat prison. One whole day of my life, stuck next to my un-shampooed little brother. Luckily, I had brought a book, and immersed myself in it as soon as we hit the freeway. "Don't touch my book," I hissed at him, knowing his fingers were sticky with gummy bear remnants. "I don't want your dumb old book," he retorted. "Play a game with me." Dear God, I thought, this is going to be a long trip. Cooped up with a non-reading Video-Maniac.

Finally, we arrived at the Redwoods. I didn't look up from my book at first, even though my parents were pleading with me to "Look! Oh, look!" At length, I raised my eyes, and for just a moment, I couldn't breathe. I hadn't thought that a sophisticated, worldly high school student like me would be in awe over a few big trees. Yet, I was. They towered over our car like huge pre-historic creatures, breathing gently, allowing us to pass.

I dropped my book, forgetting about the world of courtroom trials, corrupt judges and the unsolved mysteries of dead wives and lovers. I felt compelled to touch one of those trees, the way you always want to touch amazing things like orchid petals or the inside of an oyster shell.

My reflective thoughts were interrupted as Jimmy the Gooey blurted out in his squeaky eighth grade voice, "Stand in front of the tree, Dodo-Head, so I can take your picture." I stood in front of the tree, looked deep into his camera and smiled— not at Jimmy, of course, but at the whole feeling of being alive. That photo is still in on of our albums at home. I will leave it to you to imagine what the Video-Maniac wrote as a caption, but I'll give you this hint: He didn't come close to capturing what I felt.

A focused revision lesson like this one requires that students know the traits well and have rubrics to which they can refer as they work. It also helps to have them work in teams. *Any paper* from this book that has a problem of any sort (however small) is a lesson waiting to happen. Look at the "Lessons Learned" following each paper (Chapters 4, 5, 6, and 11) to help you choose those that will work best with your students.

7. *Put it to the test.* Good informational writing teaches. The outstanding nonfiction book, *Jellies: The Life of Jellyfish* (2000), by Twig C. George, for example, begins this way: *"If you were a jellyfish you would have two choices—to go up or to go down. That's it. Two. You would not have a brain, so you could not decide what to have for breakfast or where to go for lunch."*

You can tell in a heartbeat whether an informational piece is satisfyingly rich in detail by asking, "Could I write a *good* multiple-choice test based on this piece?" In the case of *Jellies*, it would be a snap, for George gives us clear, expansive information to work with. For example, I could write

Jellies are not capable of worrying because

  a. They live in the ocean, a tranquil environment.
  b. They have no brains.*
  c. Vertical motion suppresses stress.
  d. They are too preoccupied searching for food.

Writing your own multiple-choice items, by the way, is not only an effective method for checking out detail, but it's also a good strategy for remembering what you have read and guessing (often quite accurately) what likely will be on someone else's test.

8. *Demystify detail.* The concept of *detail* is not always an easy one for students to grasp. I have had exceptional success teaching this concept using Harriet Ziefert's book, *Lunchtime for a Purple Snake* (2003). In this book, the young artist Jessica learns from her grandfather to be thoughtful about her art, not to overpaint (much like overwriting), to trust, and to turn mistakes into something good (under Grandpa's guidance, a spilled drop turns into meatballs and spaghetti). Jessica and Grandpa begin their painting with a central "message" (the purple snake) and together add details (flowers, rock, bug, sun) until the painting feels finished. As you share this timeless story, students from 4 to 84 will watch details transform the canvass.

FOCUSED LESSONS FOR ORGANIZATION

✔ Lead
✔ Pattern/structure
✔ Transitions
✔ Pacing
✔ Conclusion

Organization is about packaging information so that readers can process it. Here are some things to emphasize:

1. *Nail the lead.* If you are writing a brief essay or story, model three or four leads you *might* use, and ask students to help you choose the most effective one. Here are a few possibilities for my story about a teacher who terrorized our class:

✔ She stood six feet tall and ate whole apples, core and stem included.
✔ Her voice was a weapon, capable of paralyzing anything that moved.
✔ We could feel her coming before we heard her.

Which would you choose? Discuss differences, and then ask students to try two, three, or four leads for pieces *they* are working on and to share them in response groups.

You can extend this instruction by sharing leads from a number of sources and asking students to rate them plus (+), meaning I would definitely keep reading; check (√), meaning I *might* keep reading; or minus (−), meaning I would stop right there. How would you rate these?

Lead 1 ___ (Plus, Check, or Minus?)

People who create computer Web sites to attract attention to catch new customers are borrowing an idea millions of years old. Even before there were dinosaurs, spiders were luring insects to their web sites [Margery Facklam, *Spiders and Their Websites*, 2001].

Lead 2 ___

Cole Matthews knelt defiantly in the bow of the aluminum skiff as he faced forward into a cold September wind. Worn steel handcuffs bit at his wrists each time the small craft slapped onto another wave. Overhead, a gray-matted sky hung like a bad omen [Ben Mikaelson, *Touching Spirit Bear*, 2002].

Lead 3 __

My name is India Opal Buloni, and last summer my daddy, the preacher, sent me to the store for a box of macaroni and cheese, some white rice, and two tomatoes and I came back with a dog [Kate DiCamillo, *Because of Winn-Dixie*, 2000].

Lead 4 __

The title of this book alludes to a scarce resource. Wild places, in the ordinary sense of that phrase, are in precious short supply on planet Earth at the end of the twentieth century [David Quammen, *Wild Thoughts from Wild Places*, 1998].

I confess that these are all pluses for me, but you may respond quite differently. That's fine. It gives us a reason to talk about why. And when you do this with students, you are provoking them to think about why some leads speak to them—and some do not.

2. *Play the scramble game.* Begin with a sample of text that is well organized: good sequencing, clear transitions. It should not be too long—perhaps three lines for younger students, up to nine or ten lines for older students, but not much more. (As an alternative, use whole paragraphs, rather than sentences, as the basic "chunks" of text.) If the piece has a clear beginning and ending, so much the better. Copy it, line by line (or paragraph by paragraph). Cut the copy into strips so that students can play with it like a puzzle. If you're ambitious and can afford it, laminate the strips so that you can use them over and over. Give them to students out of order, and ask them, working in groups of three or four, to order the strips so that they make sense. Try this one (see Figure 8.8) from Sneed Collard's extraordinary book, *The Deep-Sea Floor* (2003). I chose this text because informational writing is slightly more challenging than narrative; yet Collard's writing is always characterized by clear organization and thoughtfully embedded transitions. (*Hint:* There are two paragraphs. The answer is at the end of this chapter.)

Students' final version may or may not match the author's original, and that is okay *if* they have a good reason for ordering things as they did. It is important to this lesson to ask students to identify specific clues within the text that helped them to organize the information in a way that made sense. What line begins the piece? How do they know? What line ends it? How do they know?

Stories work well for beginners because they usually have a clear event-to-event flow. Informational writing (like the Collard example) is a little harder; you have to connect each supporting detail to a main idea. Persuasive writing is harder yet: thesis, support, counterargument(s), closing argument, and conclusion. Consider, though: If you do one of each, you can talk about how organization shifts with mode.

3. *Choose an ending.* Give students three possible conclusions for a book you're reading from (any kind, fiction or nonfiction, any grade level), and see if they can tell which is the author's actual conclusion. For example, Pamela Duncan Edwards' picture book *Barefoot* (1997) tells the story of how slaves escaped using the "underground railroad." In her authentic yet fanciful tale, sympathetic animals befriend the slaves, aiding their escape. Which do you think is her ending?

✔ So it all worked out, and the barefoot found refuge in the cabin. Later, other slaves would escape along the same route, and the animals would help them,

| FIGURE 8.8 | *Out-Of-Order Lines from Sneed B. Collard's The Deep-Sea Floor* |

The Deep-Sea Floor
Sneed B. Collard III • *Illustrated by Gregory Wenzel*

The sonar made loud noises that bounced off the sea bottom.

As recently as the mid-nineteenth century, many people believed that the ocean was bottomless or that no life existed in the deep.

During World War I, they began mapping the ocean bottom with a new invention called **sonar**.

In the 1870s, though, scientists began a serious search for deep-sea animals by lowering nets and other collection devices far below the surface.

Photosynthesis, the production of food using light energy from the sun, cannot take place on the deep-sea floor.

The echoes from these noises gave people a detailed outline of what the deep-sea floor looked like.

Others felt sure that the deep sea was filled with terrifying sea serpents or animals that had disappeared from shallower waters millions of years before.

For most of history, the geography and animal life of the deep-sea floor have remained a total mystery.

too. The Underground Railroad made an important contribution to U.S. history.

✔ The barefoot escaped and that is the end of my story. I hope you liked it.

✔ Silence fell along the pathway, and the animals slept. But through their dreams the heron's cry once again screamed a warning.
  Another barefoot was approaching.

You probably have little difficulty determining that the third conclusion is how Edwards ended her story. Students usually can tell, too, but the interesting question is, How do you know? Why is the third one different?

4. *Collect conclusions.* Talk about why they work. Here are some possibilities:

- ✔ Conclusion to *The Deep-Sea Floor:*
  Our challenge will be to explore and use the deep sea while keeping it healthy for future generations [Sneed B. Collard, 2003, p. 28].
- ✔ Conclusion to *Zero: the Biography of a Dangerous Idea:*
  All that scientists know is the cosmos was spawned from nothing, and will return to the nothing from whence it came. . . . The universe begins and ends with zero [Charles Seife, 2000, p. 215].
- ✔ Conclusion to *Charlotte's Web:*
  Wilbur never forgot Charlotte. Although he loved her children and grandchildren dearly, none of the new spiders ever quite took her place in his heart. She was in a class by herself. It is not often that someone comes along who is a true friend and a good writer. Charlotte was both [E. B. White, 1974, p. 184].
- ✔ Conclusion to *The Life of Pi:*
  Very few castaways can claim to have survived so long at sea as Mr. Patel, and none in the company of a Bengal tiger [Yann Martel, 2002, p. 319].

5. *Consider the concept.* Sometimes we have difficulty teaching organization because we focus so much on organization of *writing* and so little on what organization itself is. You might begin by asking students what things we organize in our daily lives: our time, our furniture, closets, hair, clothing, curriculum, an anniversary party, a trip—the list is endless. Now ask them to organize one thing, such as coins. Put students in groups of three or four and give them 12 to 15 coins of various denominations. Now, as a group, have them organize the coins as many ways as possible and record their methods, e.g., by year, by value, by size, by color. Continue until they can no longer come up with a new way to organize (There are dozens, so don't let them quit too soon). Use the experience to talk about how many ways there are to organize information and why a person chooses one way over another. Under what circumstances, for instance, would you organize coins by value? By size? By year? By condition? What *is* good organization? Presenting information in a way that underscores or clarifies the message.

FOCUSED LESSONS FOR VOICE

- ✔ Individuality, perspective
- ✔ Passion for the topic
- ✔ Connection to audience
- ✔ Honesty, expression
- ✔ Confidence

Some elements of voice—such as connecting with an audience—can be taught as strategy. Others, such as honesty, must be invited, applauded, valued, and nurtured. Here are some suggestions:

1. *Provide a safe environment for sharing.* Putting voice into writing is an act of courage. It only occurs in an environment where students feel safe

> *The best writing classes I visit are taught by teachers who work hard at creating an environment where children can put themselves on the line when they write.*
>
> **—Ralph Fletcher**
> *What a Writer Needs*, 1993, p. 26

> *Composition teachers all know the thrill of hearing— with a student—that student's voice for the first time.*
>
> **—Donald M. Murray**
> *A Writer Teaches Writing*,
> 2004, p. 2

> *We speak differently at home and on the street corner, in class and in the locker room, at the Saturday night party and the Sunday morning church service.*
>
> **—Donald M. Murray**
> *A Writer Teaches Writing*,
> 2004, p. 22

> *You have to give and give and give, or there's no reason for you to be writing. You have to give from the deepest part of yourself, and you are going to have to go on giving, and the giving is going to have to be its own reward. There is no cosmic importance to your getting something published, but there is in learning to be a giver.*
>
> **—Anne Lamott**
> *Bird By Bird* 1995, p. 203

writing the truth and sharing it aloud. When you share your own writing and when you ensure that all writing is received respectfully, you set the stage for this.

2. *Have a good time.* Forcing students to share of themselves is like teaching them to swim by throwing them into the water. If you wade in first and let students see you having a good time, you invite them to join you. So when you read your writing aloud, have fun. Laugh at yourself. Accept comments gracefully. When you read a book you love, bring it to class—even if it's not something you plan to read to students. Just let them know what joy reading brings you.

As Donald Murray reminds us, "You can command writing but you can't command good writing." Such writing comes "only by invitation" (2004, p. 83).

3. *Respond to students' work with unabashed enthusiasm.* Of all the gifts we can give our young writers, none is so sweet as full-out appreciation: "Your piece moved me," "Your writing had me laughing aloud," "You seemed so caught up in this story, and you know? So was I." Nothing in all the world of writing is so seductive as the image of an excited reader waiting just to receive your work.

4. *Read aloud.* Read from the books you love, and as you do, encourage students to listen for the voice within. Ask them to describe the voice they hear. Is it timid, bold, funny, irreverent, brazen, accusatory—what? Each voice is different, and voices have names, character, and personality. Read the three voices in Figure 8.9. One is by Jerry Seinfeld, one is by Dr. Phil McGraw, and one is by Ernest Hemingway. Can you identify each? What word(s) would you use to describe each voice?

You can vary this voices game by identifying the people differently (other than by name, that is); your list might include an irate teacher, an upset parent, or an exasperated fourth grader. How might those voices differ?

Or try this. Ask students to say one line: *Shut the door.* Say it the way a friend might speak to a confidante in whom she's about to confide a secret, or the way a tour guide might address a group in an art gallery, or the way a frustrated older brother might speak to a younger sibling who kept going in and out of his room. Hear the difference? The tone, the attitude—that's *voice*.

5. *Go for contrast.* I often read a passage from Carolyn Lesser's *Great Crystal Bear* (1996) and one from an encyclopedia entry on polar bears—and then ask students which is which and how they know. (They always know.) You could make the same contrast using a sports page account of a basketball game and an encyclopedic summary of basketball. Topic does not matter. You just need one piece that is full of voice and one that is drier.

6. *Ask students to read aloud.* Reading with inflection and writing with inflection are mirror images of the same skill. For this reason, reading aloud is critical in developing voice. Ask students to bring passages from favorite writers to class, to read them aloud with feeling, and to see if other students can identify the voice or at least describe it. Then encourage them to read *their own work*

FIGURE 8.9   *Three Voices*

Seinfeld, Dr. Phil, Hemingway
Which is Which?

Voice 1

I have no plants in my house. They won't live for me. Some of them don't even wait to die, they commit suicide. I once came home and found one hanging from a macramé noose, the pot kicked out from underneath. The note said, "I hate you and your albums."

Voice 2

Then he began to pity the great fish that he had hooked. He is wonderful and strange and who knows how old he is, he thought. Never have I had such a strong fish or one who acted so strangely. Perhaps he is too wise to jump.

Voice 3

You are sold "self-improvement" the same way you're sold everything else: it's easy; five simple steps; you can't help succeeding, because you're so wonderful; your results will be fast, fast, fast. But we're paying dearly—in more ways than one—for this polluting flood of psychobabble.

> **Voice 1**: Jerry Seinfeld. 1993. *SeinLanguage*. New York: Bantam Books. 143.
> **Voice 2**: Ernest Hemingway. 1980. *The Old Man and the Sea*. New York: Scribner. 48.
> **Voice 3**: Phillip C. McGraw, PhD. 1999. *Strategies*. New York: Hyperion. 23.

with the same passion and intensity; if they do not bring out the inflection with oral reading, it will be hard for them to "hear" the voice as they write (and also difficult to punctuate properly). Remind students that reading one's own text aloud is essential to revision. (There is *no* substitute for this.) Here are two passages that speak to me. Try reading them aloud with all the intensity you think the author intended. Then find two or three of your own.

Passage 1

Something about the ruffled grouse reminds me of an onstage Elvis Presley, especially in his later years. The plumpness, the strutting, the black neck ruff extending like an upturned collar. . . . If only Elvis had been a drummer, the picture would be complete [Patricia K. Lichen, 2001, p. 26].

Passage 2

When the ship veered into the Cape of Good Hope, Mum caught the spicy, woody scent of Africa on the changing wind. She smelled the people: raw onions and salt, the smell of people who are not afraid to eat meat, and who smoke fish over open fires on the beach and who pound maize into meal and who work out-of-doors. She held me up to face the earthy air, so that the fingers of warmth pushed back my black curls of hair, and her pale green eyes went clear-glassy. . . . "Smell that," she whispered. "That's home" [Alexandra Fuller, 2003, pp. 38–39].

7. *Do a quick-write on voice.* Build on what you learn from these read-alouds (as well as personal reflective reading). By doing a quick-write in which you and your students create one-liner definitions of voice. Post them on a bulletin board, along with professional writers' definitions and perhaps some sample passages. Here are some of my favorite one-liners on voice:

✔ Voice is hearing the exclamation point, even when it's not there.
✔ Music, making harmony between writer and reader.
✔ A bond that says, "I want to let you in."
✔ It's the passion that makes words dance.
✔ The need to be heard.
✔ Intense curiosity about life, about the world.
✔ The writer reaching out to the reader.
✔ The careful use of words to create that just right sound.
✔ Lighting a fire.
✔ Attitude—and from attitude comes meaning.
✔ The writer's gift to the reader.

8. *Write letters.* One biology teacher tells his students, "Don't just write about photosynthesis. Explain it the way you would explain it to Miss Piggy." Letters elicit voice because the audience is built in. Students might write to local companies (complaints, inquiries, or commendations), political figures, sports figures, celebrities, or favorite authors. Figure 8.10 shows a fourth grader's letter to author Roald Dahl.

Nikki's letter rings with voice because she is speaking right to the person whose writing has touched her. As Mem Fox tells us, "Clarity, voice, power and control are much more easily developed through letter writing [than through writing stories] because, perhaps, the audience is so clearly defined and will, if all goes well, respond" (1993, p. 28).

9. *Remind students to tell the truth.* Take to heart the words of Anne Lamott (1995): "The very first thing I tell my new students on the first day of a workshop is that good writing is about telling the truth" (p. 3). Don't flinch. Don't retreat. Above all, do not qualify: "*In some circumstances, often, it could be a good approach to come close to telling what some would view as the truth.*" Jump in. Dare. Let your vulnerability show.

Truth, of course, is not just literal facts. Truth is the world as you see it and encompasses your response to that world—what horrifies or amuses you, intrigues or enchants you, or makes you cry deep inside, where no one but you can see the tears. In his moving book, *A Dog Year* (2003), author Jon Katz opens with the story of his first dog, an animal his parents clearly did not want. When Lucky gets distemper, the parents seize the opportunity to have him "transported to the countryside," where, Jon's dad tells him, Lucky will have to stay for some time. What do you read between these lines?

> Then he took me to Rigney's Ice Cream Parlor on Hope Street and bought me a black raspberry cone. Excursions with my father were a rare thing, reserved for the most extraordinary occasions. My father never said a word as we slurped our cones, and neither did I. . . . I was

> *You see Pudge Rodriguez step into the batter's box and settle in to prepare for pitch. Even if Pudge was traded and is now wearing a different uniform, you know from watching his unique mannerisms just who's at the plate. . . . poets and musicians—and even athletes—have an individuality in their approach. They leave their fingerprints on what they do and what they create. In writing, we call it voice.*
>
> **—Tommy Thomason**
> WriteAerobics: 40 Workshop Exercises to Improve Your Writing Teaching, 2003, p. 42

> *When I write, it feels like I'm carving bone. It feels like I'm creating my own face, my own heart—a Nahuatl concept.*
>
> **—Gloria Anzaldua,**
> Poet and critic
> In Deborah Brodie, 1997, p. 139

FIGURE 8.10   *Nikki's Letter to Roald Dahl*

Roald Dahl
c/o Bantam Books
666 Fifth Avenue
New York, New York 10103

Dear Roald Dahl:

I'm nine years old. My purpose of writing is to tell you I know all of your books by heart.

I think you should write more books, and make them come out all around the globe. I'm talking about books with voice, like Matilda. Maybe even some sequels. Like Matilda II or Twits II and III. Maybe more Revolting Rhymes.

I've always wondered how you get such creative ideas, and I am hoping if you send back a letter, you will send some tips for putting in just the right amount of information.

When you do send your letter, I would like it hand written and signed in pen. I hope you can come to our school.

I better sign off now. My time is limited.

Your truly grateful, super wonderful fan,
Nikki

young but not stupid. It would be years before I loved a dog that much again [pp. xi–xii].

FOCUSED LESSONS FOR WORD CHOICE

✔ Accuracy
✔ Strong verbs
✔ Fresh, lively words and phrases
✔ Word pictures
✔ Freedom from redundancy, wordiness, vague phrasing, jargon

Good word choice comes from love of language. People who are writers to the bone love the sound of words, love playing with various ways to phrase a thought, and collect snippets of language the way other people collect rare coins or fishing flies. How do we urge our children toward this passion?

1. *Read, read, read!* The books of William Steig, Gary Paulsen, Roald Dahl, and Mem Fox are all renowned for excellent word choice for younger readers/writers—although I would not overlook them for older writers either. Any high schooler who has not read *Matilda* (which is really more a book for adults than for children, no matter how much kids love it) has missed the best of reading times. Don't forget to check out the nonfiction. I wish my history textbooks had contained more passages like Alistair Cooke's description of Eli Whitney's cotton gin:

> Whitney . . . came up with a simple box, the cotton gin. Inside was a suspended wooden cylinder that revolved at the cranking of a handle. The cylinder was encircled with evenly spaced metal spikes that clawed at the deposited raw cotton, shed the seeds behind the cylinder, and let the pure lint come foaming up in front. . . Like so many fundamental discoveries, like the propositions of Euclid, it was so simple that it seemed incredible nobody had thought of it. Once demonstrated, it was indeed so simple that any wheelwright could make it, and it was Whitney's misfortune that most of them did [Cook, 1976, p. 193].

2. *Harness the power of verbs.* Verbs give writing energy. No passage in recent memory brings this concept home more clearly than Laura Hillenbrand's description of the stirring race between underdog Seabiscuit and legendary thoroughbred War Admiral:

> They ripped out of the backstretch and leaned together into the final turn, their strides still rising and falling together. The crowds by the rails thickened, their faces a pointillism of colors, the dappling sound of distinct voices now blending into a sustained shout. The horses strained onward. Kurtsinger began shouting at his horse, his voice whipped away behind him. He pushed on War Admiral's neck and drove with all his strength, sweeping over his mount's right side. War Admiral was slashing at the air, reaching deeper and deeper into himself. . . . Woolf saw Seabiscuit's ears flatten to his head and knew that the moment Fitzsimmons had spoken of was near: One horse was going to crack [Hillenbrand, 2001, pp. 272–273.]

Powerhouse writing (of the sort needed to capture heroic sports events) pulls its power from verbs, not modifiers. To reinforce students' awareness of *verb power*, try an idea I learned from my friend and colleague Lynne Shapiro. Read a strong passage such as Hillenbrand's aloud, only *deflate* the verbs, letting students know that you are playing with the author's original. Then ask them to help you brainstorm some. Imagine, for example, that the last two lines read, "War Admiral was *touching* the air, *going* deeper and deeper into himself. . . . Woolf saw Seabiscuit's ears *move closer* to his head and knew that the moment Fitzsimmons had spoken of was near: One horse was going to *give up*." Hear the difference? What happened to War Admiral's desperation or Seabiscuit's cunning? As students brainstorm alternatives for your weaker verbs, they learn how little nuances of change create different images and moods. After brainstorming possibilities, read the writer's original and compare. Then invite students to look at their own writing and to identify one or two words for which they could, within response groups, brainstorm alternatives.

3. *WOW your students.* If you've ever felt discouraged by the number of students who forget all or most of the weekly vocabulary list within seconds of completing the quiz, this idea is for you. *Word of the Week posters* (WOWs) are an idea borrowed from middle school teacher Susan Doyle. In creating WOWs, students each celebrate one word (chosen by luck of the draw from a basket) by defining it; giving pronunciation, part of speech, and etymology; using it in a sentence; and illustrating it (see Figure 8.11).

4. *Create vocabulary-building tapes.* We have all seen (and some of us have used) tapes designed to "build a strong vocabulary in 30 days or less." But who's really getting smarter? Why, the people making the tapes, of course.

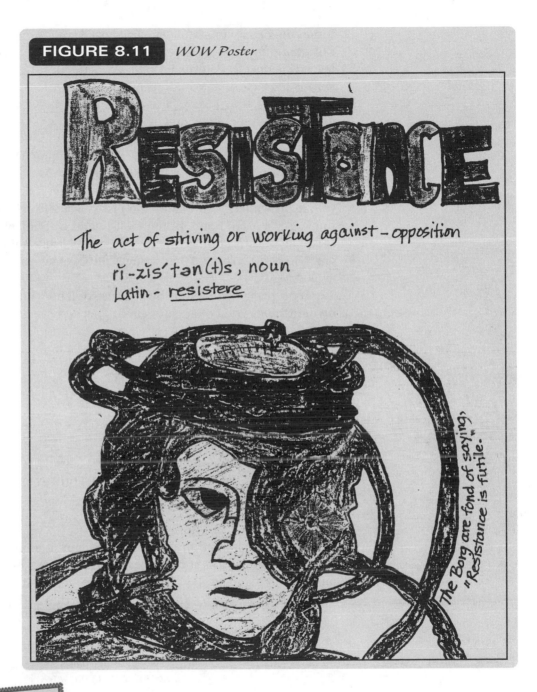

FIGURE 8.11 *WOW Poster*

What if students created these tapes (or CDs) themselves? You may wish to listen (as a class) to excerpts from existing tapes and to provide some suggested sources from which students can draw information; then let them write their own scripts and produce the results. For older students, the book *100 Words Every High School Student Should Know* (2003) is an excellent starting point. For younger students, start with Debra Frasier's book, *Miss Alaineus: A Vocabulary Disaster* (2000). You also can pull words from current literature you are reading, from textbooks, from newspapers—anywhere. Think creatively.

   5. *Advertise.* Sometimes, we get so caught up in building vocabulary (through reading, use of tapes or lists, whatever) that we forget the beauty of simple language used well. Advertisers are experts at this. For some time, the J. Peterman Company has advertised its "reckless, wide-legged" pants ("J. Peterman Dog-Days Manual," August 2003, p. 18) as that dangerous garment that could make you seem "too noticeably lanky, too tallish, too feminine, too elegant." I've always loved the word *lanky* (and wish it really *did* describe me), and I cannot help but think what a masterful choice of words *reckless* is. How many of us, deep down, would like to see ourselves as reckless (lanky, too)—and so wouldn't mind spending $40 or $50 on a pair of pants that might make us so? In the 2001 holiday "Owner's Manual No. 4" (which I saved purely for the pleasure of reading the ads) I find the "Nantucket Sweater" (p. 7): "In winter, you breathe the lost sea smell. Winter is the time to come, I think. Try a small hotel. Bring books, good walking shoes. Give the fire in the fireplace the attention it deserves. Read . . . drink a little wine, eat thick chowder." Book me a room. I'll pack my Nantucket sweater—*and* my reckless wide-legged pants.

Try writing ads of your own; your students can create ads for things they own or things you collect as a class. This activity gives voice and word choice a workout.

FOCUSED LESSONS FOR SENTENCE FLUENCY

- ✔ Smooth flow
- ✔ Variation in sentence beginnings
- ✔ Variation in sentence lengths
- ✔ Transitional words and phrases to build bridges
- ✔ Fragments for effect
- ✔ Authentic dialogue

Fluency is about rhythm and grace, not just grammar. It's the difference between placing your feet in the appropriate marks on the floor and gracefully moving to the music. Try these ideas for teaching it:

1. *Do it as poetry.* Where do we see rhythm and grace in real life? Here are some things students have mentioned. Put them together, and the result is a poem—a kind of tribute to fluency:

Wheat in the fields
Grass blowing in the wind
Flags waving in the breeze
A mountain creek
Waves pounding on the shore
Geese in formation
Falling stars
Rising sun
Drifting clouds
Gravy pouring
Chocolate melting
A ballet dancer, conductor
Bull fighter, glass blower
A comic working the audience
Water
Falling, flowing, pounding, trickling

Tears . . .
. . . and smiles
A trapeze swinging
Horses running
Salmon leaping
Penguins toddling
A hand writing
Feet skating
Eyes darting
A heart pumping
Your very soul in flight—
That's fluency.

> Mention *rhythm and most people think of music: hip-hop, polka, fugue, march, waltz, rockabilly. But almost everything in life has everything in life has rhythm, from your heart-beat to the clickety-clack of your keyboard, from a jack-hammer in the street to rain drumming on the roof. And your writing has it, too.*
>
> **—Patricia T. O'Connor**
> *Words Fail Me,* 1999, p. 171

2. *Hear it.* Developing a sense of fluency is an aural skill. You need to *hear* it. Read aloud yourself, focusing on poetry, where the rhythm's built in. Throw yourself into it, bringing out every drumbeat. Don't be shy, or your students will be shy in their reading, too, and they will never hear the voice that was waiting to be pulled out. Encourage students to read aloud, too. Build a simple "phone" of PVC pipe, allowing students to hear their voices in magnified and extraordinarily clear tones, literally shutting out the rest of the world. You'll find this simple little tool will help students tune in to both fluency and voice—and also will help them to snag those errors in conventions that escape the eye (e.g., missing words, missing punctuation).

3. *Perform it.* Whether it's a bit of drama from Shakespeare, a poem by T. S. Eliot, or any text that allows itself to be divided into sections, your students will benefit by presenting it orally. Seek out samples with dialogue, and you'll find yourself combining voice and fluency. Books for younger students that lend themselves to choral reading include

- ✔ *Water Dance,* by Thomas Locker (1997)
- ✔ *My Man Blue,* by Nikki Grimes (2002)
- ✔ *Dogteam,* by Gary Paulsen (1993
- ✔ *Insectlopedia,* by Douglas Florian (1998)
- ✔ *Joyful Noise: Poems for Two Voices,* by Paul Fleischman (1992)
- ✔ *The Big Box,* by Toni and Slade Morrison

For older students, try

- ✔ *Poems from Homeroom A Writer's Place To Start,* by Kathi Appelt (2002)

Students discover their own voices via PVC phones.

✔ *The House on Mango Street*, by Sandra Cisneros (1989)
✔ *Seedfolks*, by Paul Fleischman (1997)
✔ *You Hear Me? Poems and Writing by Teenage Boys*, edited by Betsy Franco (2000)

5. *Cut the clutter.* Good business writing and informational writing have a rhythm and style all their own. It's generally clean and crisp, a compact waltz versus an improvisational tango. Create an effective lesson by taking an ordinary business letter and making it grotesquely wordy (see Figure 8.12). See if your students can cut it back to sanity. Junk mail is full of inflated letters like this one, awaiting your students' slashing red pens. If you cannot find one, make up your own. If you work with older students, *let them* write (in groups) letters to each other for editorial critique. They'll learn from both the writing and the revising.

6. *Target specific fluency problems.* Problems with fluency often stem from one of several things:

✔ All sentences begin the same way.
✔ All sentences are the same length.
✔ Too many sentences are short and choppy.
✔ Sentences are hooked together with endless connectives.

You can readily create minilessons for any of these problems and model solutions on the overhead or chalkboard—or ask students to work on them first. Figures 8.13 through 8.16 present examples of the four problems just listed. How would you correct each one?

FIGURE 8.12 *Wordy Business Letter*

Acme Enterprises
400 South Main
Anywhere, USA

Dear Mr. Ford:

It is with great pleasure that I accept your very kind invitation to tour the facilities at Acme Enterprises. We are extremely interested in and intrigued by the efficient manner with which you manage your business, and the resulting high profit margin that your company has enjoyed during the past twelve months or so. It is our hope that an on-site visit will reveal some of the corporate strategies that have led you and your company to the exceptional financial results your annual report so proudly displays. Thank you for your cordial invitation to let us observe and learn from the methods you employ.

Sincerely,

Tom Gardner, Manager
Eastwood Company

FIGURE 8.13 *Sentences Begin the Same Way*

In Chicago, there are a million things to do. Chicago is a really interesting city. In Chicago they have museums and a wonderful aquarium, not to mention an art gallery. Chicago is one place you will never get bored.

FIGURE 8.14 *Sentences Are All the Same Length*

Calvin was thinking of running away. His life was so very dull. The same things happened every day. He could not take it much longer. Running away could be an answer. He needed a change of scene.

FIGURE 8.15 *Sentences Are Short and Choppy*

Samone looked up. The sun beat down. She felt hot. She felt tired. The race was long. It was too long. She would not make it. Her legs were cramping. Her face was flushed. Where was the finish?

FIGURE 8.16 *Endless Connectives*

So if I had to find a way to describe Ike, I would say he was this dog you wouldn't notice at first except for his personality which was extremely friendly but he wasn't the sort of dog to catch your eye, not that looks are everything, but he wasn't exactly gorgeous, but then looks are not as important in a dog as a good disposition, if you know what I mean.

7. *"Try dialogue," she said.* In *Bird by Bird* (1995), Anne Lamott notes the heady pleasures of encountering dialogue as we read: "Good dialogue is such a pleasure to come across while reading, a complete change of pace from description and exposition and all that writing. Suddenly people are talking, and we find ourselves clipping along" (p. 64). I agree. Dialogue is refreshing *if* it's well done. Sometimes dialogue reads like this:

"Let's watch TV," Bob said.

"OK," said Fran.

"What's on?" Bob said.

"I don't know," said Fran.

"Why don't you check?" Bob said.

"OK," said Fran.

This dialogue is going nowhere. The worst part is that when this scene ends (five pages from now), we will move to the porch for a similar dialogue on snacks. We need to help students see that dialogue is not filler. Good dialogue does one (or more) of these things: advances the action, reveals character, or creates mood.

Consider this excerpt from the *Secret Life of Bees* (2002) by Sue Monk Kidd:

"You don't scare me," I said, mostly under my breath.

He'd already turned to leave, but now he whirled back. "What did you say?"

"You don't scare me," I repeated, louder this time. A brazen feeling had broken loose in me, a daring *something* that had been locked up in my chest.

He stepped toward me, raising the back of his hand like he might bring it down across my face. "You better watch your mouth" [p. 38].

This dialogue bristles with tension. This child is courageous, maybe even reckless, her father menacing. Who's going to come out on top? This is dialogue you could perform—and you'd know how to read the part.

To practice writing dialogue, ask students to work in pairs, each partner coming up with a character. Define each character by age, sex, and general personality. Then give them only this direction: The two characters are in a conflict of some sort—could be serious, could be light (which film to see). Write the dialogue line by line, each character writing his or her part, responding to what the other says. Read the results aloud, like a miniplay. Students are usually surprised by the results. As a variation, try an idea from Valerie (a Texas teacher), who suggests asking students to listen—well, *spy*, actually—as real people speak (in grocery lines, theater lines, restaurants) and to write down the results. "You find out," she explains, "that people don't speak in neat sentences. Write that way, and it sounds fake."

8. *Break the rules*. This is what playwright Lynda Barry (in Feiffer and Feiffer, *Home*, 1995) does as she takes on the voice of a teenage boy defending his right to have his own room the way he wants it. Notice her use of conventions to guide the voice in your head as you read:

Keep Out. Keep OUT. THIS MEANS YOU. Keep! Out! But Mom always comes in with the bogus excuse of "Here are some clean socks and underwear, I'll put them in your drawer." As if I can't get my own socks and underwear from the laundry room, as if I need to get them at all, why can't I just keep them by the dryer but no, she just needs any excuse to come into my room and yell "This room looks like a tornado hit it!" As if she has ever seen anything hit by a tornado, and then she's coming back dragging the vacuum cleaner, as if she has the right to vacuum my room! [p. 153].

Notice how Barry achieves voice by letting the syntax roll on like a river, echoing the speaker's thinking. (Try rewriting this piece without fragments or run-ons, and listen to the difference when you read it aloud.) Students can play with structure, too, as in the excerpt from "The Advice of Coach" in Figure 8.17 that captures voice and fluency as the players hear it.

FOCUSED LESSONS FOR CONVENTIONS

✔ Editing for spelling, punctuation, grammar and usage, capitalization, and paragraphing
✔ Developing a proofreader's eye
✔ Learning to recognize, read, and use copy editor's symbols
✔ Checking layout and presentation, as needed

Conventions are receiving a great deal of attention these days—in classrooms, in the workplace, and on state examinations. The teaching of conventions is time-consuming—and challenging. It is tempting to take the shortcut and correct everything students write. Correcting, however, is not teaching. It does not take the place of modeling (showing students what to do) nor of editing practice (during which students hold the red pen). Here are some things that do work:

1. *Help students to understand the reasons behind conventions.* Giv thm some unedted copie lik this thet let's their sea what happens? When, convin-

---

FIGURE 8.17   *"The Advice of a Coach" (Advice Poem, Grade 10)*

Get in the game! Show up for practice. If you don't play, shut up. If you don't play, don't rake the field. Winning is more fun than losing. You guys are KILLIN' ME!! If you ever get the chance to play, then you had better show me something. If you have any questions, always come to me first. Don't try to go over my head. Warm up if you have time. Don't play catch on the apron. Stay warm in case I need to put you in. Always be ready to play. Don't sit on the bench. Don't spit when I'm talking to you. Keep your eye on the ball. Don't forget to warm up the pitcher. Remember to treat the equipment with respect. Try to remember all of the signs. If you are late, don't bother coming. Homework always comes before sports. If you don't show up, you will not play in the next game. You probably wouldn't have played anyway so you could have at least had good grades. Listen when I'm talking to you. You guys think you're good, but you're not. Don't stand directly behind me. Don't ask. Don't tell. At least look ready to play. Don't leave your hat at home. Keep the locker room clean. Don't come to practice without your cleats. And damn it, don't forget your sleeves. Don't talk back to the coach. I have no conscience. I can watch you run all day.

tions is use incorrect. Porlie riten Koppey helpsthem seee the valeu; of Strong convenshons in Klewing. The reader?

    2. *Teach copy editors' symbols* (see Figure 8.18). Make a poster. Demonstrate use of the symbols, one at a time, on the chalkboard or on an overhead.

FIGURE 8.18   *Copy Editors' Symbols*

Symbol	Meaning	Example
ℓ	Delete the material	There are ~~six~~ six traits.
(SP)	Spell it out.	I LOVE the 6 traits.
⌒	Close the gap.	Organi zation is critical.
⌒ (with delete)	Delete material and close the gap.	Barry Lane has a wirry sense of humor.
stet.	Return to the original.	Never ever write without voice.
∧	Insert a letter, word, or phrase.	Mem Fox has voice. *a powerful, original*
∧	Change a letter or letters.	He's a slack writer.
#	Make a space.	The lead must be a grabber.
∪	Transpose letters or words.	Gary Paulsen says, "Read a like wolf eats."
∧ (comma)	Insert a comma.	Write with voice, spirit and detail.
⊙	Add a period.	Say what you think. Tell the truth
∧;	Insert a semicolon.	Good conventions won't make up for lack of thought they cannot rescue voiceless writing.
∧:	Insert a colon.	Use these punctuation marks sparingly colons, parentheses and exclamation points.
∧ —m	Insert an em dash (like two hyphens).	Kate DiCamillo what a fine writer.
∧?	Add a question mark.	Who stole my scoring guide
∨	Insert an apostrophe.	Garrison Keillors essay on letter writing inspired me.
=	Insert a hyphen.	Novelist poet Maya Angelou rocks the room when she reads.
≡	Change lower case to capital.	Roald dahl never shrinks from reality—even if it's ugly.
/	Change capital to lower case.	The Truth lies in the Details.
¶	Start a new paragraph.	"What can one exclamation point tell us?" queried Watson. "You'd be surprised," retorted Holmes.
No ¶	Run lines together. No new paragraph.	*Lonesome Dove* is a long book. Of course, *Moby-Dick* is long, too, but not everyone finishes *Moby-Dick*.
∨" ∨"	Add quotation marks.	I try to leave out the parts people skip, said Elmore Leonard.
ital.	Italicize.	A Prayer for Owen Meany left me breathless—and laughing. *ital.*
‖	Align.	My favorite books are these: *Lonesome Dove* *Angela's Ashes* *Fried Green Tomatoes*
] [	Center.	The Origin of Six-Trait Assessment

FIGURE 8.19	*Copy Editors' Symbols for Young Writers*	

Symbol	It means	Use it like this
∧	Put something in.	loves Paul∧cats.
ℯ	Take this out.	Don is a ~~big~~ huge guy.
⩑#	Put in a space.	Amy loves⩑#apples.
⊙	Add a period.	The horse saw us⊙
≡	Make this letter a capital.	We live in o≡regon.
/	Make this letter Lower case.	Do you eat /bacon?
___	Italicize this title.	Our teacher read the book <u>Crickwing</u> to our class.

Encourage students to use them. Continue modeling daily to be sure that students understand. Gradually increase the difficulty of your samples, and always ask students to try spotting and correcting errors before you show them how it's done.

3. *Help even very young students to become independent editors* by sharing with them the copy editors' symbols they might be able to make use of (see Figure 8.19) and then gradually adding to the list. [See Spandel, *Creating Young Writers* (2004), for a more extended discussion of teaching editing skills to beginning writers.]

4. *Base editing lessons on the problems your students are encountering right now.* Next time you are going through your students' work, keep a blank sheet of paper at your elbow, and write down the conventions problems that come up repeatedly. Stop when you hit 20 (for older students) or 10 (for younger students). Let each thing you jotted down—e.g., use of apostrophes, capitalization of the pronoun *I*—be the basis for a minilesson on conventions. Now your instruction is relevant, not a series of isolated minilessons or drills, but instead a series of useful tips for struggling writers who need the information for their everyday work. No series of editing lessons out there can compete with what you create yourself because no one knows as well as you do what your students need *now*. No one out there has looked at their work. But you have—and you know. Our instruction in conventions has impact when, and *only* when, we teach it within the context of real writing. I like Tommy Thomason's analogy: "If you apprenticed yourself as a novice to a master carpenter, he would not begin by teaching you about the types and functions of nails. Instead, you would begin by learning to build things, and in the context of building, he would teach you about the different kinds of nails you would use" (2003, p. 85).

When you design a lesson, make the print *large*, put *plenty* of room between lines and words for corrections, and make sure you keep the practice *simple* at first. The rule is this: *If you have to do it for your students, it's too hard.* When it counts, you won't be there (unless you plan to follow them on to college and then to the job site).

Figures 8.20 and 8.21 show focused editing lessons (one on spelling, one on punctuation) based on "The Redwoods," a paper that is pretty clean in the original. I put this paper on the computer, make multiple copies, and then design editing lessons to meet a particular need. By keeping the task focused, I increase the chances that the student editor will be successful—and confident. If you wish, you can increase the odds of success even more by identifying for students the number of errors in the total piece or just within each given line. Also, encourage students to work with partners *as long as no grade hangs in the balance.*

FIGURE 8.20   *Focused Editing Lesson: Spelling*

The Redwoods

(Editing Practice: Spelling ONLY)

Last year, we went on a vaction and we had a wonderful time. The waether was sunny and warm and there was lots to do, so we where never boared.

My parents visted freinds and took pictures for their friends back home. My brother and I swam and also hiked in the woods. Wen we got tried of that, we just ate and had a wonderful time.

It was exiting and fun to be together as a family and to do things togeather. I love my family, and this is a time that I will rember for a long time. I hope we will go back agin next year for more fun and an even better time than we had this year.

(12 errors. How many does spell checker identify?)

FIGURE 8.21   *Focused Editing Lesson: Punctuation*

The Redwoods

(Editing Practice: Punctuation ONLY)

Last year, we went on a vacation and we had a wonderful time? The weather was sunny and warm and there was lots to do, so we where never bored

"My parents visited friends and took pictures; for their friends back home." My brother, and I, swam and also hiked in the woods. When we got tired of that, we just ate and had a wonderful time.

It was exiting and fun—to be together as a family and to do things together. I love my family: and this is a time, that I will remember, for a long time. I hope we will go back again next (year) for more fun and an even better time than we had this year.

(12 errors. How many did you find? _____ Unneeded punctuation? _____ Missing punctuation? _____ Wrong punctuation?)

5. *Take it one problem at a time.* We want to fix it all; the problem is, the shotgun approach overwhelms many students, who continue to feel that conventions are beyond their reach. In the best journalism classes, professional editors are taught to spot *one* sort of error before moving on to another, gradually adding more and more to their repertoire until nothing escapes their glance. We should follow their lead.

This one-thing-at-a-time approach is especially helpful for students who make numerous errors in their texts. Their own panic over their conventions is infectious. We panic, too, and our remedy is to mark every last problem. Relax. Ask yourself this: Will struggling editors be more successful if we send them into the world armed with corrected copy? We might like to think so, but the truth is that they are unlikely even to look at it, much less learn from it. Better to put one or two editing fundamentals into their arsenal (e.g., capital at the beginning of a sentence, period at the end) with each conference or practice—no more.

6. *Practice on the work of others.* H. G. Wells once said, "No passion in the world is equal to the passion to alter someone else's draft" (in Donald M. Murray, 1990, p. 187). We can take advantage of this very human tendency by letting students work first on *text that is not their own.* After they have practiced looking for spelling errors in a paper like my reworked "The Redwoods," they can check their own copy for the *very same kinds of conventional errors.*

Keep in mind that editing our own copy is perhaps the most difficult of all editing tasks. Why? Because we know what we meant to say. So we do not see what more objective eyes pick up readily. See Figure 8.22 for a summary of how students acquire conventional skills.

7. *Avoid worksheets.* Many of us (and many of our students' parents) grew up with worksheets, drills, sentence diagramming, and lots of correction. Research indicates, however, that such an approach is not helpful. In fact, as George Hillocks, Jr., points out in *Research on Written Composition: New*

FIGURE 8.22   *How Students Acquire Conventional Skills*

Step 1:	Recognize a convention on sight
Step 2:	Name the convention
Step 3:	Use conventions at random
Step 4:	Use conventions appropriately
Step 5:	Explain/teach conventions to others
Step 6:	Identify errors in others' text
Step 7:	Edit others' text
Step 8:	Identify errors in own text
Step 9:	Edit own text
Step 10:	Experiment with conventions to add nuances of voice and meaning
Step 11:	Invent their own conventions

Directions for Teaching (1986), an isolated skills emphasis combined with overcorrection actually may *restrict* students' growth as writers:

> The study of traditional school grammar (i.e., the definition of parts of speech, the parsing of sentences, etc.) has no effect on raising the quality of student writing. Every other focus of instruction in this review is stronger. . . . In some studies a heavy emphasis on mechanics and usage (e.g., marking every error) resulted in significant losses in overall quality. . . . [Those] who impose the systematic study of traditional school grammar on students over lengthy periods of time in the name of teaching writing do them a gross disservice which should not be tolerated by anyone concerned with the effectiveness of teaching good writing [p. 248].

In fact, students who are regularly subjected to worksheets become skilled in just that—completing worksheets. As an alternative, model use of conventions within the context of a real piece you are working on yourself; e.g., "I need a semicolon here because I want to link these two short sentences" *or* "Would this be a good place to use a comma or dash? What do you think?" Similarly, invite students to practice their editing skills on actual pieces of writing.

8. *Give the red pen to the student.* The teachers I have known to be most successful in teaching editing have required students to do the majority of their own editing (helping, of course, when the student is baffled or requests assistance). This is a hard stand to take. Colleagues and parents who do not understand that correcting is not teaching may look askance. In addition, you may feel guilty yourself—all those errors, slipping, slipping away.

When you are editing for students, it feels as if you are *doing* something. Actually, it feels as if you are doing a *lot*. You are. You are burning yourself up. Never mind that there is no research to indicate that students learn from these corrections. So when we know better, why do we edit students' writing anyway? Because we run out of time and patience. In the end, if we do not correct the copy, who will? *No one.* Some copy is *never going to get corrected,* and effective editing teachers learn early on to live with this. They explain. They define. They model appropriate use of conventions. They offer frequent guided practice in editing, with students working *first on the text of others,* then on their own text. They simply do not edit *for* students. To understand why this is so important, imagine yourself teaching multiplication of fractions. If one of your students got 10 of 20 problems wrong, would you provide additional instruction and practice—or would you simply do the problems *for* the student so that he could copy the correct answers?

9. *Remember the 72-hour rule.* Ever tuck a "perfect" piece of writing into the file—only to have it sprout errors before you looked at it again two weeks later? Time is the editor's friend. If you allow students to wait three days—or even more—between writing and editing, they'll edit much more efficiently. That mental break helps you see your writing more the way you'd see someone else's.

10. *Edit daily.* Students need to practice editing *every day,* not just now and then. Practice can be short (five to ten minutes),

> *Teachers and administrators feel pressure from a public that worries about handwriting, spelling and grammar. . . . Yet rarely do parents complain about the inability of their children to formulate and express ideas in a clear and logical fashion.*
>
> **—Donald H. Graves**
> *A Fresh Look at Writing,*
> 1994, p. 32

> *Traditions in the teaching of English hold that compositions must be marked and commented upon—the more thoroughly, the better. But research reported in this review suggests that such feedback has very little effect on enhancing the quality of student writing—regardless of frequency or thoroughness.*
>
> **—George Hillocks, Jr.**
> *Research on Written Composition: New Directions for Teaching,*
> 1986, p. 239

but it must be frequent if you wish to see results. Some students write only once in two or three weeks—or less. Suppose that they are editing only their own work—and only what gets published? How reasonable is it to expect that they will develop any editing proficiency when they are editing about as often as many of us get a haircut?

11. *Respond to content first.* Do you have a friend or relative who always seems to spot the cobweb on the lampshade before appreciating the music or noticing how great the new sofa looks? Then you may sympathize with seventh grader Christopher, who told me one day, "I hate it when the teacher *only* looks at my spelling. I want to spell things right, OK? But part of me also wants to scream, 'Did you even *read* this?'" Respond to content first; then offer *one or two* suggestions on improving conventions.

12. *Use Post-it dictionaries.* Eighth grader Bill made numerous spelling errors in recounting the heart-warming tale of his girl, Tammy, and a number of them involved the word *fiancée*, which Bill spelled "feonsay." A word such as this can go on a Post-it note in one corner of Bill's paper. Not having to wrestle with an intimidating dictionary makes the correction problem much simpler for a student who finds spelling a challenge.

13. *Encourage students to edit with their ears, not just their eyes.* Good editors read text more than once, and they read *aloud*. Oral reading also helps students punctuate, as well as notice missing or repeated words.

14. *Remind students to read from the bottom up.* Reading from the bottom up is a lifesaver for many students who struggle with spelling. You cannot skim (easily) when you read backwards.

15. *Become sleuths.* Ask students to join you in hunting for samples of conventional problems in textbooks, memos, letters, advertisements, newspaper articles, and elsewhere (A local grocery marquis recently advertised "brocoli," "onoins," and "pottatoes"—all on the same day. Time for "stoo"—or "soop," perhaps.). Give extra-credit points to students who can find a conventions problem in print—another point for leading the class in a lesson on correcting the problem.

16. *Support a coordinated editing program* at your school, where students edit (at least a little) in all subjects. Word-processing classes provide an obvious opportunity, of course. However, every content area—math, science, art, physical education—has its own conventions, symbols, and marks that help to convey meaning. Help students to identify these in textbooks and other subject-related writings. You may even wish to have students conduct some minilessons on "The Conventions of Algebra," or "Conventions in Sports Writing."

17. *Look for what's done right.* Many teachers find it useful to mark two or three conventions handled *well*, along with, perhaps, *one or two* suggestions for improvement. As writer and teacher Donald Murray (2004) assures us, "We learn to write primarily by building on our strengths, and it is important for the teacher to encourage the student to see what has potential, what has strength, and what can be developed" (p. 157).

18. *Use peer editing with caution.* Teaming for *practice* is an excellent instructional strategy because no grade hangs in the balance. When the editing is for real, though (the result is going to be graded), peer editing should be used with great caution. No one wants to edit herself into a lower grade than she

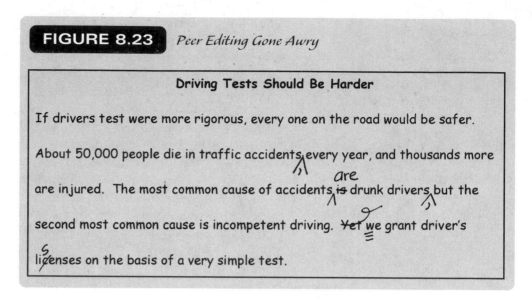

FIGURE 8.23 *Peer Editing Gone Awry*

would have received had she left the text alone! Figure 8.23 shows a sample of peer editing gone awry.

What about peer review? Let's be clear. Peer *review* does not call for students to look for errors or to make corrections but rather to respond to voice, clarity, organization, and meaning. It does not entail the same risks.

21. *Keep resources handy*—and model ways to use them. Here are some possibilities for any well-stocked serious editor's book shelf:

Ballenger, Bruce: *The Curious Researcher: A Guide to Writing Research Papers.* Boston: Allyn & Bacon, 2004. *Among the most detailed, thorough, and genuinely entertaining books ever written on the how-tos of sound research. Middle school and high school.*

Blake, Gary, and Robert Bly: *The Elements of Technical Writing.* New York: Macmillan, 1993. *A concise, superb guide to the basic elements of technical, informational, and business writing. Excellent examples. Middle school and high school.*

Grossman, John (ed.): *The Chicago Manual of Style,* 16th ed. Chicago: University of Chicago Press, 2004. *Complete and authoritative, this is the place to look it up when in doubt. High school through adult.*

O'Conner, Patricia T.: *Woe Is I.* New York: Grossett/Putnam, 1996. *Lessons on modern grammar taught with wit and knowledge—plus predictions on where we're headed. Upper elementary through high school.*

Sebranek, Patrick, Dave Kemper, and Verne Meyer: *The Write Source Handbooks for Students.* Burlington, WI: Write Source. *Highly readable, authoritative, and user friendly. Kindergarten through college.*

Strunk, William, Jr., and E. B. White: *The Elements of Style,* 4th ed. Needham Heights, MA: Allyn & Bacon, 2000. *Legendary. The essence of good writing in fewer than 100 pages.*

Trimble, John R.: *Writing with Style: Conversations on the Art of Writing,* 2d ed. Upper Saddle River, NJ: Prentice-Hall, 2000. *Written to be read, not shelved. Thorough, informative—the best book of its kind since* Elements of Style.

Truss, Lynne: *Eats, Shoots & Leaves: The Zero Tolerance Approach to Punctuation.* London: Gotham Books, 2004. *A witty enjoyable book filled with tips on putting punctuation to work for you.*

Walsh, Bill: *The Elephants of Style.* New York: McGraw-Hill, 2004. *The best book out there on contemporary usage.*

Zinsser, William: *On Writing Well: The Classic Guide to Writing Nonfiction,* 25th Anniversary Edition. New York: HarperCollins, 2001. *Witty, readable, and straight to the point. Clear-cut, no-nonsense advice on writing about science, art, travel, yourself—or any subject. One of a kind.*

WHAT TO TELL PARENTS ABOUT CONVENTIONS

Even parents who do not spell or punctuate well themselves often have high (sometimes unreasonable) expectations for the speed with which their children will develop conventional proficiency. They look to you to make it happen. You can assure them that it *will* happen, but (1) it will take time and patience because editing your own work is harder and takes longer than having the teacher do it for you, and (2) they (parents, that is) can help.

First, let parents know that their children will be taught to think and to work like editors, that they will practice first on text that is not their own, and that as their knowledge and skill improves, they will be responsible for editing their *own* text. It may not come home corrected at first because you will not be editing *for* students, and they may not (unless they're skilled high school editors) be up to editing every line they write—*yet.* They'll get there.

Invite parents in to observe editing lessons (even to participate) and to coach students in small groups or one on one (assuming that they're good editors themselves—*ask*). A note like the one in Figure 8.24 can help.

CHAPTER 8 IN A NUTSHELL

Given a process foundation with emphasis on frequent writing, four basic steps will help you teach traits:

1. Surround students with language (through comments, posters, student-friendly rubrics).
2. Teach students to assess writing, both their own and that of others.
3. Use writing samples of all kinds to illustrate strengths and problems related to each trait.
4. Use focused lessons to target specific skills related to each trait, e.g., for organization, *how to write a lead.*

Good literature (along with the not-so-good) provides a basis for numerous focused lessons on traits.

Each student paper or other piece of writing you share is a "lesson waiting to happen" because students can use it for revision practice.

Modeling is an integral part of focused lessons as well. Base your modeling on problems students are having, e.g., coming up with a good conclusion, getting rid of choppy sentences.

FIGURE 8.24 *Letter to Parents*

Dear Parents,

This year, your child will be gaining many skills essential to becoming an independent editor. Independent editors proof and correct their own text. To support the growth of these important skills, I will be doing these things:

- Sharing copy editor's symbols, the same marks used by professional copy editors in preparing text for publication (attached).
- Modeling for the class exactly how to use each of these symbols.
- Providing time in class for your child to practice using copy editor's symbols by proofing and correcting faulty text (a sample is attached).
- Encouraging your child to proof his/her own writing, making corrections just as a professional editor would.
- Encouraging your child to use the scoring guide for conventions (attached) to review and assess his/her skills.

I will demonstrate the appropriate steps to take in proofing/correcting text as often as necessary, and students will have *numerous opportunities* to practice their editing skills. I will also answer ANY editorial questions your child has. I will not correct text for him/her, however—because research shows such practice has minimal instructional value. It improves the teacher's editorial skills, but not the student's. This is not our goal.

As a parent, you can do several things to help:

- Ask your child to *teach* you the copy editor's symbols. Practice writing and using them together.
- Remind your child to skip every other line when writing a draft so that there is plenty of room later to make corrections.
- If possible, provide a dictionary and handbook that your child can refer to when a question arises. Ask your child to *teach* you how to use each one.
- Practice together hunting for errors on faulty text I will send home from time to time. Discuss what you learn. This practice will help student writers develop an eagle eye.
- Together, look for conventional errors throughout the world of print: in newspapers, magazines, advertisements, junk mail. Keep track of those you find, and encourage your child to bring samples to class to share as a way of improving everyone's editorial skills.
- When *you* write, ask your child for editorial help, proofing or correcting. Practice makes strong editors.

Finally, please do not ask for editorial perfection right away. Editors need time and practice to gain skill. With enough of each, you will see your child's editing skills grow week by week, month by month. Celebrate each error your child is able to find, and find all the ways you can to express confidence that your child will become an independent editor.

Sincerely,

EXTENSIONS

1. Assess your instructional approach. If you are teaching currently, which of the following things do you do? (Which, if any, might you add?)
   _____ Model writing for students
   _____ Write with students and/or share personal writing samples
   _____ Share rubrics and/or encourage students to assess others' writing
   _____ Encourage students to assess their own writing as a prelude to revision
   _____ Read aloud to illustrate strengths or problems in writing
   _____ Present focused lessons to emphasize specific skills

2. Imagine that you are going to begin a collection of writings to illustrate strengths or problems connected to the traits. What pieces would you plan to use right now? List them in your journal or share your list with colleagues.

3. Was your work (as a student writer) heavily corrected? How do you feel this helped or hindered your growth as a writer? Write about this in your journal.

4. If you are teaching now, do you encourage students to do their own editing, or do you do much of the correcting for them? Do you think this might change? Discuss your approach with a colleague.

5. If you are currently teaching, choose *one* trait and think of all the things you are currently doing to support that trait with your instruction. Make a list and compare it with suggestions in this book.

6. Ask colleagues to bring to your discussion group one book that is a favorite. See if you can find passages *from that one book* to illustrate strengths (or problems) within *each* of the six traits. If you can, what does this tell you?

7. Choose one of the lesson ideas in this chapter and model it for students or for teachers, putting your own personal spin on it. How did you adapt it?

8. Create a new lesson or series of lessons by doing the following things:
   ✔ Select a trait.
   ✔ Choose two sample papers that illustrate a contrast in that trait; papers may come from this book or from your own collection/search. (Read them aloud to yourself for practice and identify strengths/issues/problems that will prompt useful discussion.)
   ✔ Find two passages from literature to illustrate strengths in the trait. (Read them aloud to yourself for practice.)
   ✔ Select one focused lesson (from this book or from your own curriculum) that would support students' understanding of the trait.
   ✔ Design an expanded writing activity that would allow students to show skill in the trait.
   ✔ Present your lesson(s) to students or members of a study group. Do a critique based on how well the sample papers and literature illustrate points you wish to make about the trait and the extent to which your focused lesson and expanded writing activity build understanding of the trait and of writing in general.

9. Design an editing lesson that will improve students' editing skills without your making corrections for them. Use it with your students or present it to colleagues, asking for a critique on the lesson's effectiveness.

WHY I WRITE

I write because the day is over and the night is young and someone just had a baby and someone or something just died—and whatever it is, I must write about it.

—Kirsten Ray, student writer

LOOKING AHEAD

In Chapter 9 we'll continue our discussion of instruction by troubleshooting some of the writing problems connected with each trait.

FIGURE 8.25　*Answers to Sneed Collard Scramble Game Activity, Page 184*

Paragraph 1:

✔ For most of history, the geography and animal life of the deep-sea floor have remained a total mystery.

✔ As recently as the mid-nineteenth century, many people believed that the ocean was bottomless or that no life existed in the deep.

✔ Others felt sure that the deep sea was filled with terrifying sea serpents or animals that had disappeared from shallower waters millions of years before.

Paragraph 2:

✔ In the 1870s, though, scientists began a serious search for deep-sea animals by lowering nets and other collection devices far below the surface.

✔ During World War I, they began mapping the ocean bottom with a new invention called **sonar**.

✔ The sonar made loud noises that bounced off the sea bottom.

✔ The echoes from these noises gave people a detailed outline of what the deep-sea floor looked like.

Note:
The line—

Photosynthesis, the production of food using light energy from the sun, cannot take place on the deep-sea floor—

is not part of the original text! If you deleted it, that was a good instinct. Organization is partly about ensuring strong connections among ideas, and discarding what does not fit.

$\mathcal{9}$ Troubleshooting:
Dealing with Common Writing Problems

Being a writer is hard work, and perhaps this is the first thing we should share with students. I agree with Marjorie Frank when she says, "Students should be told about the energy it takes to write" (1995, p. 92). In the end, nothing takes the place of writing, writing, writing. Nevertheless, as writing coaches, we can help to diagnose various kinds of writing troubles and provide some direct help.

While Chapter 8 dealt with strategies for teaching traits in the context of a process-based curriculum, this chapter offers more of a "Dear Trait Person" approach—which is to say, things teachers have found helpful when specific problems arise. At the close of

> *I hate to tell ya, but there's no easy answer. If you want discipline you have to keep slowly adding, building, and staying with it until one day, doing it feels better than not doing it. It's like doing sit-ups.*
>
> **—Nancy Slonim Aronie**
> *Writing from the Heart,* 1998, p. 103

> *Writing is about hypnotizing yourself into believing yourself, getting some work done, then unhypnotizing yourself and going over the work coldly. There will be many mistakes, many things to take out, and others that need to be added.*
>
> **—Anne Lamott**
> *Bird by Bird,* 1995, p. 114

> *After fifty years of writing, I have pretty much gotten over my fear of writing. Not all, but most of it. I wouldn't want to get over all of it. A little terror is stimulating. Writing is important, and you can say something that is wrong, stupid, silly, clumsy. And you will.*
>
> **—Donald M. Murray**
> *Shoptalk,* 1990, p. 69

this chapter I also will suggest some strategies that are effective with challenged writers or with students who have been through trait-based instruction before.

IDEAS

Problem: The information is too skimpy! This paper doesn't say anything.

■ *Strategies*

1. *Share students' own voices.* Many students who start out believing that they have nothing to say feel differently when they encounter the voices of peers. Suddenly they are inspired to share thoughts about how it feels to be a young person today, the joys (and headaches) of driving, depression, tattoos, "instructions for life," loneliness and alienation, cultural awareness, parents and grandparents, music, work, envy, poverty, love and loss, friendship and betrayal, cosmic truth, violence, self-esteem, and memories. These topics are not mine. They are the selected topics of students assembled in a remarkable little book called, *You Hear Me? Poems and Writing by Teenage Boys* (2000), edited by Betsy Franco. Not many students will tune out when you share Nick's account of growing up with Tourette syndrome, which begins, "It all started in second grade. There was this kid and he would jump on my desk and chair. He also would call me inappropriate things. My teacher would say, Stay away from him. I said, *He* comes to *me*. She didn't care" (p. 20).

As third grader José discovered, poetry sometimes springs from mundane events. He said, "I have nothing to write about," but found that he did (see Figure 9.1).

2. *Go beyond stories.* Not all young writers feel comfortable as storytellers. We also need to read good nonfiction aloud, prompting them to try another genre, too. Here are some of my favorites to get you started; asterisks mark those well suited to younger reader-writers:

✔ Diane Ackerman, *A Natural History of the Senses* (1995)
✔ Jennifer Armstrong, *Shipwreck at the Bottom of the World* (1998)
✔ Bill Bryson, *In a Sunburned Country* (2001)
✔ Thomas Cahill, *How the Irish Saved Civilization* (1995)
✔ Sneed B. Collard III, *The Deep-Sea Floor** (2003)
✔ Margery Facklam, *Spiders and Their Web Sites** (2001)
✔ Twig C. George, *Jellies: the Life Jellyfish** (2000)
✔ Twig C. George, *Seahorses** (2003)
✔ Laura Hillenbrand, *Sea Biscuit* (2001)
✔ Stephen King, *On Writing* (2000)
✔ Julius Lester, *To Be a Slave* (1998)
✔ Bill Nye, *The Science Guy's Big Blast of Science** (1963)
✔ David M. Schwartz, *G Is for Googol** (1998)
✔ David M. Schwartz, *Q Is for Quark** (2001)
✔ Charles Seife, *Zero: The Biography of a Dangerous Idea* (2000)

3. *Make it fun.* For dozens of ideas on finding and reporting information with style and energy, I recommend Barry Lane's book, *51 Wacky We-Search Reports* (2003). Barry shows how to

> I loathe writing stories. The plot nearly kills me. *Possum Magic* took five years to perfect, and the book that followed, *Wilfrid Gordon McDonald Partridge*, was such torture to write that I thought I'd never write again. . . . being a writer has helped me understand that story writing is one of the most difficult of all the writing acts. I now tap into kids' concerns and their memories . . . instead of burdening them with a task that makes me quail.
>
> **—Mem Fox**
>
> *Radical Reflections*, 1993, p. 37

FIGURE 9.1　*"Problems," by José Garcia*

Problems
By Jose Garcia

Cars cost too much
My dad can't drive.
My mom, dad, sister and me
Walk on hot days, cold days
Windy days, and foggy days,
But
We have fun
When I go to summer school
We take the bus when we go to
Summer school
We go on the bridge
When we go home.
I can't stand the sun.
I take water,
We take a break
At the park.
When I get
Home, I rest a lot.

put life into the old research report by borrowing sales techniques, creating want ads or posters, writing parody, doing job interviews and talk shows, and otherwise making use of professional writers' proven skills. Personification and role playing can be effective ways for students to show off their knowledge. In "Freddy: A Day in the Life of a Neuron," for example, the student writes, "Freddy was especially fond of Nervana, the neuron nearest to him, whose dendrites were only a synapse away. Many a time he passed messages from his axon to her dendrites but she remained aloof" (p. 89).

4. *Take ten.* An inordinate amount of difficulty with writing comes from sheer procrastination. Here's a way to fight it. Gather around you all the notes (if any) from which you will draw your information. Write the very best lead

When I wrote reports in school I used a dump truck. I'd take my dump truck to the library, fill it up with facts, and then backload it onto the paper. . . . I didn't know that facts were fun, that facts were funny. Did you know, for example, that a hummingbird's heart is half the size of its body? That the Roman legions used urine as laundry detergent?

—**Barry Lane**

51 Wacky We-Search Reports, 2003, p. 13

you can. Then set a timer for ten minutes, and within that time, write the most complete report your knowledge of the topic allows. Beginning to end: you *must finish.* Here's the trick, though: Write on *every other line,* and once you've finished, go back and use questions to identify gaps where you will need to expand your thinking or add detail. You now have a barebones structure and (if your questions are good) a sense of direction for further writing. Best of all, you have silenced that insidious, accusatory voice: "Your masterpiece is due tomorrow and *you* haven't even written one pathetic line, oh time waster!"

5. *Leave some writing unfinished at the end of the day.* A little trick I have learned is to stop in the middle of a paragraph—or even the middle of a line. It allows me to plunge right in the next day, to get the wheels turning. That first line is always the toughest; finishing a line or paragraph I had begun is easier than starting from scratch. Like many writers, I also find it helpful to write at the same time and for a certain length of time.

6. *Draw.* Some writers start right in putting words on paper. For others, drawing works well because it documents detail and stimulates thinking. Notice Logan's sketch (see Figure 9.2) of Mrs. Pratchett [based on Roald Dahl's book, *Boy: Tales of Childhood* (1984)]. Logan has effectively captured Mrs. Pratchett's surly disposition, not to mention her promi-

FIGURE 9.2   *"Mrs Pratchett," by Logan*

nent mustache. Older writers may be reluctant to sketch, thinking that this is a habit they should have abandoned years prior. Not so. Ever get an idea while doodling on a napkin in a restaurant? Then you know. Pass it on.

Problem: There's too much information. Help! It's huge.

■ Strategies

1. *Cut the copy in half.* Ask wordy writers to imagine they're writing for a newspaper and can only fill so many inches on the page. Ask them to cut the copy they have by half *without losing content.* That's the trick.

2. *Whittle big topics down to size.* Wordy, rambling writing is often triggered by a topic that's just too big to get hold of. For instance, *baseball* is too big, so let's skinny it down:

✔ *How to pitch* (Better—but not there yet)
✔ *How to throw a fastball* (Focusing in)
✔ *How to pitch against the best hitter in the league* (Almost small enough)
✔ *How to pitch under pressure: a 3-2 count and a cramp in your back* (That's it!)

Now, instead of "Pitching can be a challenge," I can write, "The secret to good pitching is seeing the strike zone as the whole world. You have to tune out the pain, the numbness in your legs, the screams of the fans—even the piercing eyes of the league's champion batter, willing you to blow it."

ORGANIZATION

Problem: My students still have problems with leads.

■ Strategies

1. *Make multiple leads routine.* Students rarely write multiple leads for their own work. This is unfortunate because this practice needs to be a habit. Ask each student to write three to five potential leads for a given piece of his or her own writing. Share the leads in writing groups. Ask peers to identify the leads they like best and to say why.

2. *Offer options.* For some students, sample leads are enough. Others need a concrete list of "Ways to Begin." Here are a few:

✔ An anecdote that frames what the paper is about
✔ A startling fact that will wake your readers up

> If you give me an eight-page article and I tell you to cut it to four pages, you'll howl and say it can't be done. Then you'll go home and do it, and it will be much better. And after that comes the hard part: cutting it to three.
>
> **—William Zinsser**
> *On Writing Well,* 2001, p. 18

> I try to leave out the parts that people skip.
>
> **—Elmore Leonard**
> In James Charlton, *The Writer's Quotation Book,* 1992, p. 27

> Think small. The best things to write about are often the tiniest things—your brother's junk drawer, something weird your dog once did, your grandma's loose, wiggly neck, changing a dirty diaper, the moment you realized you were too old to take a bath with your older brother.
>
> **—Ralph Fletcher**
> *What a Writer Needs,* 1993, p. 162

> One thing that will make it easier to get started is to write three leads to your paper, instead of agonizing over one that must be perfect.
>
> **—Bruce Ballenger**
> *The Curious Researcher,* 1994, p. 168

✔ A question to readers (maybe the question that prompted your paper)
✔ An intriguing quotation from someone connected to the topic
✔ Action, action, action
✔ Dialogue that raises the issue you will explore
✔ A promise to readers; e.g., "You'll be a cook within one week!"
✔ A striking description that sets the scene
✔ A striking image that provides information or sets the tone
✔ A summary of a problem—to which the paper offers a solution
✔ A profile of someone key to the story or the research

3. *Go bad on purpose.* Shake out the cobwebs by writing bad leads for one or more of the books you are reading. For example:

✔ *Hi, I'm E. B. White, and I want to tell you the story of Charlotte the spider and her friend Wilbur. Ready? Here we go!*
✔ *Do you like chocolate? In this story you'll learn about a determined boy named Charlie and the way chocolate changed his life.*
✔ *It was a dark and stormy night. Ahab paced the deck, smoking his pipe. Somewhere out there lurked Moby. Moby-Dick. But where?*

Host a "Bad Leads" award ceremony, where you can have some fun reading these aloud and voting for the worst of the lot: "Lead Least Likely to Get a Reader's Attention," "Most Action-Free Lead," "Most Obnoxiously Perky Lead," and so on.

4. *Go for the kill.* Want a killer lead? You need killer detail. Weak leads are spawned by scant information. This activity yields striking results because of its immediacy. Students create information right on the spot and then sift through that information for a striking moment that will pull a reader in.

Ask students, in pairs, to *interview* each other for three minutes each. Encourage them to avoid dead-end questions (e.g., *When were you born? What is your middle name?*—Who cares?) and to ask the kinds of questions that will yield intriguing information:

> *Therefore your lead must capture the reader immediately and force him to keep reading. It must cajole him with freshness or novelty, or paradox, or humor, or surprise, or with an unusual idea, or an interesting fact, or a question. Anything will do, as long as it nudges his curiosity and tugs at his sleeve.*
>
> **—William Zinsser**
> *On Writing Well,* 2001, p. 56

✔ What bugs you?
✔ What did you fear most in your life that never actually happened?
✔ Where would you least (or most) like to be stranded for a week?
✔ If you were afraid, what would you be?
✔ If you could spend a day with one person, living or dead, who would it be?
✔ What is one thing most people would never guess when they first met you?
✔ What film or book comes closest to describing you?

Then ask them to pull out the most intriguing detail on which to base a lead. Read results aloud. Compare them to a few biographical leads you track down in your school library. Which are stronger?

Problem: Trying to follow this writing is like running through a giant maze.

■ *Strategies*

1. *Clean the attic.* The steps in organizing a piece of writing are very similar to those in organizing a closet or an attic: Get rid of what you don't need, group the rest (so that you could find something if you needed to), and figure out what's missing so that you can add it to your collection. For an expository piece, brainstorm a list of details, asking students to help, based on what they know. Print out your list, and cut it into strips. Then ask students, in groups of three, to "clean the attic"—delete what does not matter and group what is left into chunks (just the way you'd put the attic stuff on shelves). Then make a list of "What's Still Needed," things a writer would need to research later.

2. *Tell it orally first.* Talking is an excellent organizational strategy because it's fairly quick and because the speaker can see at once if listeners are puzzled or are following along with ease. This is harder, usually, with writing, where the audience may not see the writing for a time. Practice with a story first. You can model this yourself. Think of something unusual, frightening, funny, or otherwise significant that has happened to you in the past year. Tell the story to your students. Then list everything that happened on an overhead, including a few details you *don't* need (what time you got up, what TV show you were watching when the phone rang, what you had for lunch). List events in random order, and omit one or two important details. See Figure 9.3 for an example based on my overnight adventure in a strange city. As you can see, I have asked students to eliminate what is not needed, reorder what is left, and ask questions to fill in what is missing. This strategy works for any piece of writing, any genre.

3. *Plan it like a road trip.* Outlining isn't a bad idea if we use it well. Like a map that charts new territory, an outline can keep you from getting lost on your journey. But you do not want to be a slave to an outline—or a road map. Good writers understand that organization is organic. Each sentence, paragraph, or chapter flows out of what came before, just as road trip plans sometimes change based on experience. Teach students to outline in general terms that will allow flexibility. For example, if I am writing an informational piece (on any topic at all), my outline might look like this: (1) Opening that startles and informs the reader, (2) quick summary of the main question I mean to answer or the reason I think this topic is important, (3) two or three of the most intriguing things I learned from my research, (4) confirmation or rejection of one or two commonly held beliefs about this topic, (5) something to connect this topic to the reader's life so that he or she will care, (6) a closing surprise—intriguing fact, quotation, or discovery from my own research. This outline is specific enough to guide me (like a good map) without telling me exactly where I can or cannot go. We recognize the organic nature of organization when we routinely ask our students as part of writers' workshop, "Where did your writing take you today that you did not expect to go?"

4. *Use graphic organizers.* Students who are visual often find organizers in picture form infinitely helpful. See *Writer's Express* (Kemper, Nathan, Elsholz, and Sebranek, 2003) and *Write Source 2000* (Sebranek, Kemper, and

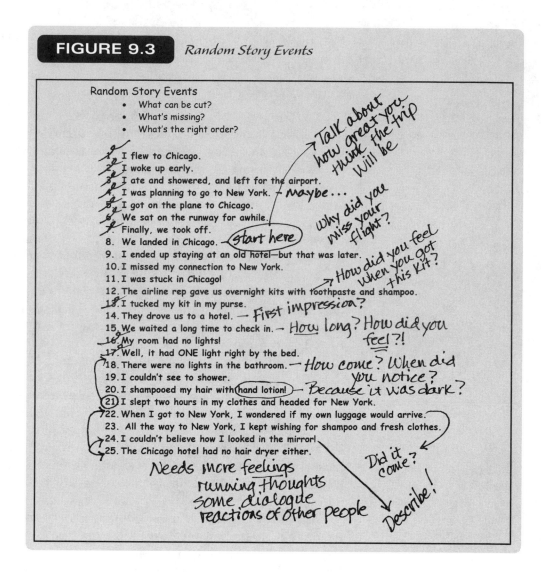

FIGURE 9.3 *Random Story Events*

Meyer, 2004) for several innovative and extraordinarily helpful examples that support various forms of organization, e.g., chronological, comparison-contrast, cause-effect.

5. *Look for clues.* As we write, we create expectations in the mind of the reader—we are planting seeds in the reader's mind. When Louis Sachar introduced the yellow-spotted lizard on page 4 of his novel *Holes* (2000), he knew very well what a crucial role this reptilian villain would play. And how disappointed we readers would have been not to have the lizard show his scaly face again.

Before you can learn to leave good clues yourself, you must learn to look for them as you read. So begin there. Ask your students to look for the clues good writers have left along the trail—clues a thoughtful reader tracks right up to the all but inevitable ending. A good ending may not be happy, but it always feels right and always grows out of what has come before. This is why Ahab couldn't just settle down in Nantucket and open a nautical supply store.

In *The Tale of Despereaux* (2003), a charming fairy tale featuring a princess, an arrogant king, a very courageous mouse, and a diabolically evil rat, author Kate DiCamillo deliberately explains how in any fine piece of writing, all things are connected, and no detail stands in isolation:

> The rat's soul was set afire, and because of this, he journeyed upstairs, seeking the light. Upstairs, in the banquet hall, the Princess Pea spotted him and called out the word "rat," and because of this Roscuro [the rat] fell into the queen's soup. And because the rat fell into the queen's soup, the queen died. You can see, can't you, how everything is related to everything else? [pp. 117–118].

6. *Give "beginning, middle, and end" a face lift.* We know what a *beginning* is: a lead, a hook, a way of getting the reader's attention. Similarly, an *ending* is a resolution of the problem—or sometimes a confession that resolution will be hard to achieve. But what the heck is a *middle?* It's the writer's way of answering questions or expanding ideas raised by the lead, and guiding the reader toward the intended resolution. My suggested face lift, then, is a vision of organizational structure adapted from Barry Lane (1999, p. 37):

Set-Up (*Beginning*), Exploration (*Middle*), Wrap-Up (*End*)

> ✔ **Set up** what follows, simultaneously drawing the reader in.
> ✔ **Explore** by expanding the main message—and pulling the reader in deeper. Present problems and proposed solutions, details the reader needs for
> understanding, explanations, complexities, the little details (zooming in), counter-arguments, or (in the case of narrative) the unraveling plot. Move forward through action, character development, information, or argument. Then, zap—
> ✔ **Wrap it up.** End with a revelation, resolution of the conflict or problem, discovery, moment of truth. Say goodbye.

> *Endings grow from beginnings and reveal themselves through clues within the story, characters, or ideas.*
>
> **—Barry Lane**
> *Reviser's Toolbox*, 1999, p. 39

Problem: Transitions Are Weak or (Help!) Missing Altogether.

■ Strategies

1. *Invent your own transitions.* Choose a published piece with strong transitions, and rewrite it with all transitional phrases missing. Ask students to fill in transitional words and phrases that make sense. This passage comes from *Jack's Black Book* (Jack Gantos, 1999). In this scene, Jack is taking an aptitude test and has broken his pencil. The rigid Mr. Ploof will not allow him to start over or use a sharpener because the rules say he "must keep going." See if you can fill in the blanks:

> I didn't have a pencil sharpener __ I began to gnaw at the wood around the lead, spitting out the pulp, ____ I exposed the blunt end. I felt even more like a white laboratory rat, ____ I pulled myself together and raced through the test. _____ it didn't seem too difficult or take very long _____ I got off to a rough start [p. 16].

The missing words and phrases, in order, are *so, until, but, For something so important,* and *even though.* You might not have chosen those very words (your students might not either), but could you come up with words that linked the ideas together logically? If so, you understand the importance of connecting ideas—that's the point of the lesson. (Read this piece aloud without the transitional words and phrases to appreciate their importance.)

2. *Brainstorm a list of good transitional words and phrases: However, In a while, Therefore, Next, Because of that, In fact, On the other hand, To tell* *the truth, For example, Nevertheless,* and so forth. Make a poster from which student writers can "borrow" when they need a way to link ideas. For a longer, more complete list, see *Write Source 2000* (Sebranek, Kemper, and Meyer, 2003, p. 106).

Problem: Conclusion? What conclusion? It just stops. Wait—no, not that! Not the dreaded dream ending!

■Strategies

> The perfect ending should take your readers slightly by surprise and yet seem exactly right.
>
> **—William Zinsser**
> *On Writing Well*, 2001, p. 65

1. *Imagine yourself saying goodbye.* A good ending feels so right because it gracefully says goodbye to the reader, much the way you might say goodbye at the door after visiting with a friend. You might comment on what you learned about serving a great Caesar salad or suggest something interesting that you might do the next time you get together. Probably you would *not* say, "So, in summary then, we ate, talked, played cards, played with the dog, and spoke of meeting next week."

2. *Talk about specific ways to end.* Use your own experience along with what you learn from professional writers. Make and post a list:

> Nice story, Aesop. I love the moral too. Very true, but did you ever wonder what happened the next day, the next year, the next decade?
>
> **—Barry Lane**
> *The Tortoise and The Hare Continued . . .*, 2002, Introduction

- ✔ Something the writer has learned
- ✔ Something the writer regrets
- ✔ A hint of what's to come
- ✔ The writer's emotional response or observation
- ✔ A comment on how things have changed
- ✔ A stirring image
- ✔ A telling conversation
- ✔ An unexpected twist or revelation
- ✔ An echo of the lead (coming full circle)
- ✔ The answer to a question the reader has likely been pondering

3. *Invent your own bad endings for books you or your students are reading.* There is much to be learned by reminding yourself how not to do it. Remember the "Bad Leads Contest"? Host a similar event for conclusions, creating, with your students, some like these:

The Tortoise and The Hare Continued . . .

- ✔ Then I woke up and it was all a dream. There was no scarlet letter, after all.
- ✔ I hope you liked my book and learned a lot about wizards. . . .
- ✔ So Stanley and all the Yelnatses lived happily ever after. . . .

4. *Use the power of the sequel.* In his book *The Tortoise and The Hare Continued . . .* (2002), author Barry Lane points out that the ending of one piece is merely the beginning of another. Read this book to your students. Then test the theory: Take the ending from one piece of writing and use it to craft the lead for a sequel. After practicing this strategy, your students can use it to test their own endings. If a conclusion is too dead to give life to a new piece, it probably needs work.

VOICE
Problem: There Is No Voice Here. I've Listened. . . .
■ Strategies

1. *Encourage students to* think *I.* Many teachers object to the use of the personal pronoun *I* in informational or persuasive pieces, and with reason. It's easy for writing to degenerate into a self-serving opportunity to vent: *"I feel that school uniforms are stupid because I hate them."* The problem is that writing can become *so* impersonal that it is difficult to sense anyone at home within the words: *"One wonders about the motivation underlying school uniforms."* Somewhere between these extremes lies a balance of supported thinking and personal investment: *"Many people were surprised when a recent survey of local middle schools showed attendance soars when students wear uniforms. But—does that mean the students like them? Apparently not."*

William Zinsser suggests that even when the pronoun *I* is not permitted, "it's still possible to convey a sense of I-ness." He recommends writing a first draft with *I* then taking it out, to "warm up your impersonal style" (2001, p. 22)—and *thinking I* even when you cannot use it.

2. *Make it dramatic.* Sneed Collard, a master of nonfiction writing, maintains that the best nonfiction boasts a sense of drama because readers cannot survive on facts alone. His book, *The Deep-Sea Floor* (2003), for example, opens not with a definition or list of facts but with a scene right from an underwater play (facts come on the following page):

> Far from land, a mile below the sea surface, a tripod *fish* rests on the bottom of the ocean. In total darkness, with water temperatures just above freezing, the fish silently waits for a meal. A shrimplike *copepod* (KO-peh-pod) drifts by. The tripod fish lunges and gulps it down . . . [p. 7].

3. *Get someone talking.* We can only plod so long through text in which no one lives, breathes, or speaks. In third-person writing, the writer is—theoretically, anyway—not speaking *right to* the reader. Fine. Quote someone else. This can help to satisfy a reader's natural longing for human contact. William Zinsser (2001) does this with stunning timing, inviting such worthy writers as H. L. Mencken, Garrison Keillor, and Loren Eisley into his conversation about good writing. He wraps up his discussion of the invaluable surprise ending by quoting Woody Allen: *"I'm obsessed,"* Woody says, *"by the fact that my mother genuinely resembles Groucho Marx"* (p. 67). This helps me to remember the point better than if Zinsser had just said, "End on a comic note." We need to teach our students the magic of inviting others into the conversation, too.

> Writing from the heart is not just about writing from the heart. It's also about writing from and for all the senses. Readers want to feel, they want to taste, they want to smell.
>
> **—Nancy Slonim Aronie**
> *Writing from the Heart: Tapping the Power of Your Inner Voice,* 1998, p. 143

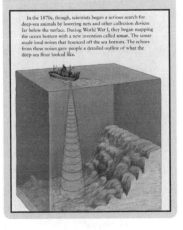

The Deep-Sea Floor

In the 1870s, though, scientists began a serious search for deep-sea animals by lowering nets and other collection devices far below the surface. During World War I, they began mapping the ocean bottom with a new invention called sonar. The sonar made loud noises that bounced off the sea bottom. The echoes from these noises gave people a detailed outline of what the deep-sea floor looked like.

4. *Have a good time.* Research writing can be dry, but it's not a requirement. Voice comes, as much as anything, from loving the writing you are doing and daring to be a little playful about it. One writer who seems to be having a really good time is Anne Lamott. I laugh aloud clear through Lamott's books, but the moment that unhinged me was her description of her mother (It could have been mine) reacting to her book: *". . . whenever I show her a copy of my latest book, she gets sort of quiet and teary, and you can tell that what she's feeling is 'Oh, honey, did you made that yourself?' like it's my handprint in clay—which I suppose in many ways it is"* (1995, p. 150).

5. *Lighten up.* Not everyone can be as funny as Anne Lamott. So it might not be fair to require humor. A respectable first cousin of outright humor is the light touch. Nonfiction writing can become very heavy-handed: *"The Stellar's jay is 11 inches long and makes its home in coniferous forests. Its Latin name is* Cyanocitta stelleri." Such text has a late afternoon in August kind of feel to it. Compare Patricia Lichen's lighter fare: *"I'm not sure who compared Stellar's jays to 'crows in blue suits,' but the description is apt. These birds are in the crow family, and like their basic-black-garbed relatives, they are raucous, bold, and intelligent"* (2001, p. 63). Lichen may not be a comic (at least in her writing), but she invariably sounds friendly, engaged, and bemused by the creatures she writes about. Her voice says, "Pull up a chair—I think you'll find this interesting."

6. *Bring the reader inside.* Our students need to identify the audience to be sure, but if the exercise ends there, we have not accomplished much. This is like noting who is at the front door, then slamming it shut. *Bring the reader in.* Find a way to make him or her at home in the text. Bill Nye has a genius for this. I can open *Big Blast of Science* (1993) to any page and feel as if I have been invited in for tea and physics. Bill helps me relate every topic to my own life: *"As you read these words, you and this book and whatever you're sitting on are being pulled down by gravity. If you're reading in an airplane [I was, actually], the plane is being pulled down by gravity. That's why planes need wings and engines"* (p. 35). I looked out, saw the wing, and felt I *was* defying gravity—Bill had said so. *Ha!*

7. *Listen for moments.* On partly cloudy days, the sun still shines. Now and then it's hidden behind a cloud, which makes us appreciate its warmth all the more when it returns. Voice comes and goes like that. We need to listen for just those moments and celebrate them by noticing and by commenting. Once you know that your voice has touched someone, it's hard not to want to do it again. This is why writers write, after all. We need to react. Laugh. Gasp. Applaud. Cheer. Then students know their writing and their risk taking have made a difference—if only for a line.

8. *Personalize the topic.* It is no secret why voice is so hard to wring from the writing we get in state assessments: Writers are responding to someone else's topic—and only those who have the luck to land a serviceable topic or the talent to personalize a poor one will succeed in investing their writing with voice. How do you take a topic and make it your own? You stretch it, bend it,

> Go with what comes up. Don't make time for your inner editor to happily announce, "They'll really think you're sick if you write that."
>
> **—Nancy Slonim Aronie**
> *Writing From the Heart*, 1998, p. 77

> Even in a bad piece of writing, the mentor reaches into the chaos, finds a place where the writing works, pulls it from the wreckage, names it, and makes the writer aware of this emerging skill with words.
>
> **—Ralph Fletcher**
> *What a Writer Needs*, 1993, p. 14

and coax it into a slightly different form. Once, in writing about a memorable place, a colleague chose "inside her grandson's eyes." Now that is taking the notion of place to a whole new dimension. When writing about "memorable person," students often think, "Who is my best friend right now?" or "Could I write about one of my parents?" There the thinking stops. But there are so many other possibilities: a dangerous driver you encounter on the freeway, a person whose writing you can't get out of your head, an annoying neighbor, the class bully from years ago, an actor whose performance moved you, the inventor of something you value, someone from history you wish you could have met, or a stranger who did a good deed. You've got to move the fenceline out . . . out. . . .

9. *Take voice out.* By taking the voice out of a strong piece, students often discover what made it strong in the first place. A student said one day, "What if the 'The Redwoods' writer had written 'Mouse Alert'?" What indeed? It might have sounded more like this:

> Last year we went to Yellowstone and we had a wonderful time. We stayed in a cabin by a lake and it was fun. The weather was beautiful and sunny so there was lots to do. We were never bored. My parents took pictures for their friends back home. My sister and I swam and hiked in the woods and even caught a mouse! Later we let it go. Then we just ate and had a wonderful time. I hope we go back again next year for an even better time and a chance to see even more creatures than we saw this time.

The student who wrote this needed to think about what created the voice in "Mouse Alert" and what kept voice suppressed in "The Redwoods." Is she more prepared now to put voice into her own writing? Absolutely.

10. *Write to your best listener.* My friend and colleague Sally Shorr, a veteran teacher, offers this excellent piece of advice—which has worked for me and for many students with whom I've shared writing ideas: Think of your *very* best listener, the person in whom you would confide your most important secrets. Write as if you were writing *just to that person.* Who are your own best listeners?

11. *Try role playing.* From Mary Ann Beggs, Melbourne, Florida, comes a knockout idea that combines writing, drama, a bit of historical research, and practice in developing story and character while writing letters. Her students take a given situation and set of characters—say, a pilot writing home during World War II, or a Japanese child in an internment camp writing to a non-Japanese friend during World War II, or students during the 1960s anti-Vietnam war protest marches writing to family members or politicians. Students explore the political realities of the time, research main characters and circumstances (right down to the cost of postage stamps), and develop their characters through letter writing. In Figures 9.4 and 9.5, tenth graders Kendall Irvin and Jessica Pauley create correspondence between William Windrich, a fictional marine in the Korean conflict, and Gloria White, his fictional girlfriend. Notice how their careful research adds to detail and voice in this tiny excerpt from a much larger (and most impressive) research piece. Research references appear parenthetically in each piece.

> The challenge is not to find a unique topic (save that for your doctoral dissertation) but to find an angle on a familiar topic that helps readers see what they probably haven't noticed before.
>
> —**Bruce Ballenger**
> *The Curious Researcher,*
> Fourth Edition, 2004, p. 50

> Whenever I write, whether I'm writing a picture book, an entry in my journal, a course handbook for students, or notes for the milkman, there's always someone on the other side, if you like, who sits invisibly watching me write, waiting to read what I've written. The watcher is always important.
>
> —**Mem Fox**
> *Radical Reflections,* 1993, p. 9

FIGURE 9.4	*William to Gloria*

September 7, 1950

Gloria,

You don't have to worry about me so much just yet. We aren't even in Korea yet. The officers say we won't reach it until about mid September, which is fine with me. Maybe by then, all them Koreans will have killed each other. Let God sort them out, us Marines say, not us.

I ain't anxious to get there at all. Back in the States before we got on this ship, I met a man returning from Korea. He was British and had been in Korea for weeks fighting for the U.N. (James) He was missing a leg.

I said, "Christ, man, what happened to ya?"

He said, Land mines." (Magerkurth)

"Landmines?" I asked.

He just laughed and it scared me. There was such coldness in his tones. "Hey, boy, I'm one of the lucky ones. You'll see. "

I just walked away then. He gave me the creeps.

You don't pay no mind to your old man. He don't know a thing about politics, or theology. The only reason he knows about this war is because he sits in front of the radio all day drinking. Even with a buzz that's lasted three years you're bound to learn something. You just be careful around him until I get back.

All right, sweet girl—looks like it's lights out here on the ship. Sleep tight, and remember we're under the same stars.

Love,
William

Problem: This voice doesn't work for the topic or the audience.

■ *Strategies*

1. *Switch audiences.* Students only gain a sense of audience by writing for more than one person or group. Ask students to imagine an uncomfortable situation, e.g., receiving a traffic ticket or getting caught in a lie. Then ask them to write about this incident to several different audiences, e.g., a parent, a good friend, a teacher, and a traffic court official. Does the voice change as the audience shifts? Why?

2. *Get an attitude.* Actors often approach a scene from a particular attitude: *"In this scene my friend is being completely unreasonable—so I need to seem increasingly angry."* It helps to do this in writing, too. What attitude are

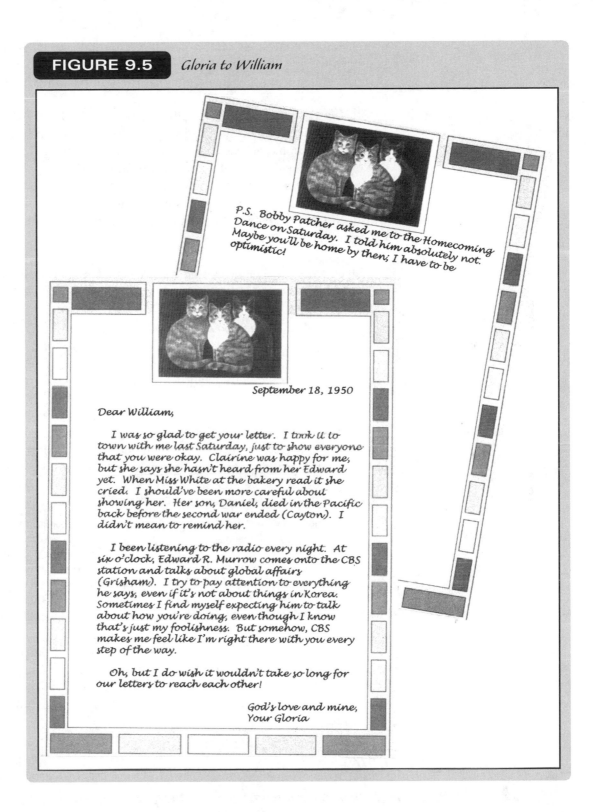

FIGURE 9.5   *Gloria to William*

P.S. Bobby Patcher asked me to the Homecoming Dance on Saturday. I told him absolutely not. Maybe you'll be home by then; I have to be optimistic!

September 18, 1950

Dear William,

I was so glad to get your letter. I took it to town with me last Saturday, just to show everyone that you were okay. Clairine was happy for me, but she says she hasn't heard from her Edward yet. When Miss White at the bakery read it she cried. I should've been more careful about showing her. Her son, Daniel, died in the Pacific back before the second war ended (Cayton). I didn't mean to remind her.

I been listening to the radio every night. At six o'clock, Edward R. Murrow comes onto the CBS station and talks about global affairs (Grisham). I try to pay attention to everything he says, even if it's not about things in Korea. Sometimes I find myself expecting him to talk about how you're doing, even though I know that's just my foolishness. But somehow, CBS makes me feel like I'm right there with you every step of the way.

Oh, but I do wish it wouldn't take so long for our letters to reach each other!

God's love and mine,
Your Gloria

you projecting? Helpful? Authoritative? Sorrowful? Joyous? Amazed? Get into the mood of your writing.

3. *Take time to vent.* Almost everyone has an issue with some local business group or other. Express your concerns in letters. The complaint letter is a challenge. You need to hit the right note: serious protest coupled with a professional, courteous undertone. If your students can hit that just-right blend, they have a leg up on achieving good business voice. Save letters (and responses, if you get them) and compile them into a class book entitled, *Effective Business Voices.*

4. *Interview businesspeople.* If possible, invite local businesspeople into your classroom to talk directly to your students. Find out how they want their employees to come across to the audiences they serve. Don't be surprised to discover that the *quality* of voice—warmth, friendliness, a personal touch—is more valued than ever by many business executives, who regard an ability to communicate with an audience as an essential survival skill in a competitive world. Notice, for instance, how the Xerox Corporation (Brown, 1991) ends its welcoming letter to new employees:

> If you come to work here, you will sacrifice the security of the safe approach in which you can count on arriving at a predictable goal. But you will have an opportunity to express your personal research "voice" and to help create a future that would not have existed without you [p. 105].

4. *Write for yourself, too.* Wait a minute, you're saying. Aren't we supposed to consider audience? Absolutely. But the writer needs to be part of that audience. We do our best writing when we write something we actually might want to read ourselves a month—or year—from now.

5. *Relax.* Tension is the mortal enemy of voice. If you can relax as you write, the *self* is more likely to emerge. Safety first yields "The Redwoods." No risk, no gain. In the introduction to *Essays That Worked for Business Schools* (1987), authors Boykin Curry and Brian Kasbar summarize the responses of admissions officers—and their observations are telling:

> The overwhelming complaint from undergraduate admissions officers was that reading 13,000 essays on the same few topics . . . is a mind-numbing experience. Most essays are dry and overwritten. They are often "corrected" by so many friends and relatives that the life gets sucked out. . . . Anxious applicants become so afraid of saying the wrong thing that they end up saying nothing. Such sterilization can mean unbearable monotony . . . so don't treat your essay like a psychological minefield. What seems "safe" to you is probably deadly boring to a weary admissions officer [p. 12].

Curry and Kasbar quote one admissions officer in particular who tries to liven up the essays by reading them on his boat for a change of scenery: *"You know what? Even that doesn't help,"* he claims (p. 12). The moral? Relax. Be yourself. Say what you think. Readers appreciate it—and it makes your writing stand out.

> *You are writing for yourself. Don't try to visualize the great mass audience. There is no such audience—every reader is a different person.*
> **—William Zinsser**
> *On Writing Well,* 2001, p. 25

WORD CHOICE

Problem: The vocabulary is too simple, too general, too vague.

■ *Strategies*

1. *Hunt for striking words.* like this passage from Margaret Atwood's *Alias Grace* (1996) because it makes a movie in my mind: *"Dora is stout and pudding-faced, with a small downturned mouth like that of a disappointed baby. Her large black eyebrows meet over her nose, giving her a permanent* *scowl that expresses a sense of disapproving outrage"* (p. 57). Words like *pudding-faced* and *disappointed baby* help me to see Dora and make me less likely to invite her to my birthday party. Reading Atwood reminds me that taking time to find the right word is worth it.

2. *Brainstorm a list of "tired" words.* Maybe these words need a permanent rest: *fun* (as an adjective), *awesome, great, nice, bad* (meaning good), *way cool, grand, great, special, super, downer, pushing the envelope,* and so on. For each tired word or expression, brainstorm as many different "ways to say it" as you can think of; *great,* for instance, can be *high-minded, noble, humane, beneficent, magnificent, kind-hearted, just, fair, lofty,* or *princely*—if we are referring to character. A *great party,* on the other hand, might be *marvelous, extraordinary, jim-dandy, wondrous, awe inspiring, astounding, smashing, unprecedented, first rate, tiptop,* or *stupendous.* Create word walls for younger students, and build your own dictionary of synonyms with older students' help. Student-created dictionaries for younger students work wonders for both groups.

3. *Read above* (well *above*) *grade level.* This is vital. I would not enjoy being cut off in the bookstore by a clerk who said, "Sorry—you're not ready for that book just yet." *That's* now the one I want. We want the whole world of books open to us. Don't our students deserve the same?

4. *Learn words in context, not in isolation.* Many young elementary students would be hard-pressed to define these words in isolation: *imprison, individual, invader, renew, elastic, cascade, canvas, harbor.* In context, though, the words reveal their identity in a way that no vocabulary list can duplicate:

> Our skin is what stands between us and the world. If you think about it, no other part of us makes contact with something not us but the skin. It imprisons us, but also gives us individual shape, protects us from invaders, cools us down or heats us up as need be, produces vitamin D, holds in our body fluids. Most amazing, perhaps, is that it can mend itself when necessary, and it is constantly renewing itself. . . . Skin can take a startling variety of shapes: claws, spines, hooves, feathers, scales, hair. It's waterproof, washable, and elastic. Although it may cascade or roam as we grow older, it lasts surprisingly well. For most cultures, it's the ideal canvas to decorate with paints, tattoos, and jewelry. But most of all, it harbors the sense of touch [Ackerman, 1995, p. 68].

This selection is from Diane Ackerman's *A Natural History of the Senses* (1995), a book most would classify as secondary or adult level. I am not suggesting reading this book in its entirety to younger students—or *any* students. I am suggesting harvesting passages with rich language from *many* sources to share with students of *any* age. Will they recall every word? Perhaps not. So what? They'll recall some, and they'll get a *sense* of the deeper meaning. Language in context is infinitely more powerful than language by list. We must teach it that way.

5. *Predict verbal lifespans.* The Usage Panel for the *American Heritage Dictionary,* which includes teachers, writers, editors, and journalists, meets regularly to discuss what ought or ought not to be considered "acceptable" English: *"Today's spoken garbage may be tomorrow's written gold"* (Zinsser, 2001, p. 42). Among those newer words that made the panel's *useful* list: *cyberspace, meltdown, skyjacker, wetlands, software, yuppie,* and *fax.* Not all

One group of researchers tried to sort out the factors that helped third and fourth graders remember what they had been reading. They found that how interested the students were in the passage was thirty times more important than how "readable" the passage was.

—Alfie Kohn

Punished by Rewards, 1993, p. 145

new words are long-lived, though: *"The 'happenings' of the late 1960s no longer happen, 'out of sight' is out of sight, and even 'awesome' has begun to chill out. The writer who cares about usage must always know the quick from the dead"* (p. 43). What words or phrases are popular with your students right now? Make a book. For each entry, use words in context, and write a short argument (good practice with persuasive writing) predicting whether the word will still be part of English usage in 50 years.

6. *Share your love of language.* What are your own favorite words? Share them with your students. I have a special affinity for *legendary*, *serendipity*, *cosmic*, *luminous*, *candle*, *mystery*, and *sleuth*. They have associations, yes, but beyond this, I just love their sound. Ralph Fletcher calls these "trapdoor" words: *"For some words, the conventional meaning hides a secret trapdoor that leads down to an unexpected or previously forgotten layer of memory underneath"* (1993, p. 39).

Problem: This student suffers from thesaurus-chained-to-the-desk syndrome. Everything's overdone.

■ *Strategies*

1. *Perform it.* Look up a simple word in the thesaurus (e.g., *slow*). Use the word in a sentence: "Jake moved at a *slow* pace." First, try substituting some alternatives offered by the thesaurus. Then eliminate the need for *adjectives* by making the *verb* stronger:

> Jake moved at a *tortoiselike* pace. (Jake *crept*.)
>
> Jake moved at a *leisurely* pace. (Jake *strolled*.)
>
> Jake moved at a *sluggish* pace. (Jake *inched* along.)

Ask students to *act these out.* Writing definitions is nowhere near as powerful as performing them when it comes to driving home subtle changes in meaning.

2. *Enter the Bulwer-Lytton Fiction Contest at San Jose State University.* You'll need to begin by reading excerpts from *It Was a Dark and Stormy Night*, or *Dark and Stormy Night: The Final Conflict*, or any of the zany, hilarious collections of what is considered to be some of the world's most overwritten writing. Here's just one example:

> Daphne ran swiftly across the windswept moor scarcely noticing its heather perfume, down to the rocky cliff where she paused momentarily atop the jagged precipice, looked down at the waves crashing far below, and wished that she had been born anything other than a lemming [Little, 1996, p. 83].

Give your thesaurus-happy students a chance to take a crack at this—you try, too. When you've had your fill of laughing at your overbaked results, send the best of them in to the contest:

Bulwer-Lytton Fiction Contest
Department of English
San Jose State University
San Jose, CA 95192-0090

Entries are generally only one sentence long and not more than 50 to 60 words.

3. *Keep it to one syllable.* This activity is harder than it sounds, but it definitely tames overwritten text. Ask students to write a paragraph on any topic (e.g., weather report, summary of a math lesson, letter to a friend) in one-syllable words only. No cheating. *"The fog crept through the fields. Sun strove to burst through. . . . "*

Problem: Too Many Modifiers!

■ Strategies

> I believe the road to hell is paved with adverbs, and I will shout it from the rooftops. To put it another way, they're like dandelions. If you have one on your lawn, it looks pretty and unique. If you fail to root it out, however, you find five the next day . . . fifty the day after that . . . and then . . . your lawn is totally, completely, *and* profligately covered with dandelions
>
> **—Stephen King**
> On Writing, 2000, p. 125

1. *Go on a modifier diet.* One of my students once wrote a piece about a sensory-overload deli where the pickles were *tart, juicy,* and *crisp;* the corned beef *succulent* and *delectable;* the mustard *tangy* and *refreshing;* and the bread *fluffy* and *fragrant.* Even the clerk was *gracious* and *accommodating.* I felt stuffed without taking a bite. Put yourself on a low-modifier diet, and the same passage might sound like this:

> The pickles snapped when you bit into them, and made your mouth pucker. The bread took you back to grandmother's kitchen. The corned beef required no chewing and the mustard opened even the most resistant sinuses. The clerk always greeted me as if I'd been gone for a month and he'd had nothing of interest to do in my absence.

2. *Spend adverbs frugally.* Adverbs can be useful, but we need to spend them like money. Notice the following examples:

> "He shut the door *forcefully*" versus "He *slammed* the door."
>
> *"She talked* loudly and *shrilly"* versus "She *screeched.* "
>
> "Her voice spoke to us *alluringly*" versus "Her voice *seduced* us."

Never let an adverb steal work that should go to a worthy verb.

SENTENCE FLUENCY

Problem: short, choppy sentences break the text up into bite-sized pieces.

■ Strategies

1. *Remember an old friend: sentence combining.* It still works magic. Make your own samples based on creative revisions of famous texts: *Macbeth,* the Constitution, *Winnie the Pooh*, essays by Ralph Waldo Emerson, Edgar Allan Poe's "The Cask of Amantillado," or "Desiderata":

> Go. Go placidly. Go amidst the noise. Go amidst the haste. Remember things. Remember peace. Peace may exist. Look for it in silence. Be on good terms with people. Feel this way toward all people. But only feel this way as much as possible. Do not surrender.

Alternatively, chop up some text from a cookbook, lawn mower warranty, legal contract, auto show advertisement, or headline news story. Don't forget to compare your students' revisions to the originals.

2. *Turn on the music.* Music illustrates rhythm and flow like nothing else. Make your own selection—rock, rap, jazz, or pop—so long as it has a definite beat and understandable lyrics. Musical lyrics, especially if written by someone gifted such as Randy Newman, Paul Simon, or Stephen Sondheim, can be irresistibly rhythmic. Some lyrics are repetitious, some not. Be careful. Repetition for effect can be stirring; repetition for its own sake is deadly.

Problem: All sentences begin the same way. I think I'm drifting off.

■ *Strategies*

1. *Ask students to list sentence beginnings*—just the first three or four words—on a separate sheet of paper. Do they all look alike? There's your problem.

2. *Practice variations.* Start with any sentence: *"You have to be clever to survive school."* Ask students to rewrite the sentence as many ways as they can in three minutes (or slightly longer, if you wish). If you like, give students sample sentence beginnings:

Being clever . . .
Surviving school . . .
Survivors . . .
School . . .
Cleverness . . .

Problem: It has variety—but it still sounds mechanical.
■ *Strategies*

1. *Hit the end note.* Where is the power of the sentence? At the end. In time, most experienced writers learn to embed the most important word or thought right there—like a punch. After awhile, this becomes automatic, but at first, you have to point it out. You have to nurture it, coax it. Which of these sentences has more power?

✔ Victor turned, slowly raised the gun, leveled it, and fired.
✔ Victor raised the gun, leveled it, and fired, even as he turned.

To a writer's ear, the second sentence simply sounds *wrong*, putting the emphasis on *turning*, not *firing*. Read any piece by Diane Ackerman, John F. Kennedy, Winston Churchill, or Carl Sagan (to name a few fluent writers), and you'll hear your voice automatically marking the rhythm of the sentence endings. It isn't just sentences that are guided by this organizational structure; it's writing itself. Sentences, paragraphs, and whole pieces all drive, relentlessly, toward the rhythm, the force, the power of the end note. This is where you want to embed the most significant words or messages (and it's the *real* reason not to end with a preposition, except when it's awkward not to).

2. *Master parallel structure.* Parallel structure, or *patterning*, in sentences adds the same kind of rhythm that percussion adds to music. Read the following passage aloud, and hear the rhythm build to a crescendo in the closing line, a masterpiece of parallel structure:

> Lobstermen seek lobsters wherever those creatures may roam, and this means lobstermen chase their prey all over the shallow sea and the cold-water coastline. This means lobstermen are constantly competing with one another for good fishing territory. They get in each other's way, tangle each other's trap lines, spy on each other's boats, and steal each other's information. Lobstermen fight over every cubic yard of the sea. Every lobster one man catches is a lobster another man has lost. It is a mean business, and it makes for mean men. As humans, after all, we become that which we seek. Dairy farming makes men steady and reliable and temperate; deer hunting makes men quiet and fast and sensitive; lobster fishing makes men suspicious and wily and ruthless [Gilbert, 2001, p. 5].

You can teach parallel structure through examples such as this one and through practice. Begin with a piece that is not parallel, and ask students to re work it. Try these yourself:

- ✔ She was tenacious. In addition, her manners weren't very good. What's more, she often scared the living daylights out of us.
- ✔ Some called the January weather in the mountains dangerous. One thing was certain: You couldn't predict it. Though it wasn't always deadly, it had the potential to be deadly at times.

Problem: Endless connectives turn the whole paper into one monstrous "sentence" that chokes to death any sense of meaning.

■ Strategies

> There is no minimum length for a sentence that's acceptable in the eyes of God. Among good writers, it is the short sentence that predominates. And don't tell me about Norman Mailer—he's a genius. If you want to write long sentences, be a genius.
> —**William Zinsser**
> *On Writing Well*, 2001, p. 72

1. *Encourage the short sentence.* I have often seen assessment rubrics that encourage long, complex sentences. What the writers of these rubrics are thinking I have no clue. Brevity is an invaluable tool. Short sentences are especially important when the content is complex or unfamiliar to the reader; like small steps on a slippery path, they allow the reader to feel in control. Suppose that I am writing about black widow spiders, for example, and I write this:

> Black widows don't really look around for people to bite and in fact they just hang upside down in their webs and so are seldom seen and that is part of their danger because they choose a web site where they will have a good supply of insects, which is where the people usually are, although years ago. . . .

See how tiring this is to read? Fortunately, author Margery Facklam, from whom I borrowed this information, writes much better than this, dividing her text into bite-sized chunks:

> Black widows don't go around looking for someone to bite. They hang upside down in their messy cobwebs, where they are seldom seen, and that is part of their danger. They choose a web site wherever there is a good supply of insects, which is usually where people are, too. Years ago, when most families had outhouses in the backyard instead of indoor bathrooms, black widow bites were more common because the spiders liked living where the fly supply never ran out [2001, p. 15].

We need to teach students the value of manageable sentences. They add clarity. And contrary to the rumors, they challenge the writer. It's hard to hide in a small sentence; you need to *say something.*

2. *No* ands *or* buts. Ask students to write three paragraphs with no *ands* or *buts* or *becauses* at all. This is challenging, perhaps, but quite possible.

3. Listen *for the punctuation.* Sometimes students omit punctuation because they simply do not *hear* it. Start with a punctuation-free piece of writing. Read it aloud, pausing clearly and fully for each comma, semicolon, period, or question mark and using plenty of inflection to accentuate the punctuation. Ask students to fill in the punctuation they hear *as you read:*

> Outside the rain was falling hard and fast it hit the roof like the thunder of an impassioned drummer we lay in our beds listening wondering when it would stop like small birds in a nest we looked up at the ceiling as if expecting the rain to come through it never did of course.

CONVENTIONS

Because problems with conventions are so numerous and varied (and because this issue is covered thoroughly in Chapter 8), I will simply add a few tips for making your teaching of conventions and editing easier.

1. *Create a style sheet.* Publishing houses give authors style sheets, which govern many issues of layout: size and format for headings and titles, models for handling citations, margin sizes, use of graphics or photographs, and other design issues. Your classroom is like your own publishing house. Design a style sheet (see Figure 9.6) that reflects your personal preferences—how you'd like graphics titled, where you want titles placed, how you want the writer's name (or yours) to appear, how many fonts you want to see per page, how you'd like references cited, how you'd like captions for graphics handled, and so on. You may wish to enlarge one copy and post it for students.

2. *Model, model, model.* Even though students do their own editing, you must show them what is correct, how to spot an error, and how to correct it using appropriate copy editor's symbols. Model often.

3. *Keep your own conventional skills current.* This is harder than it sounds because conventions are ever-changing. Rely on a good handbook and use it frequently. You can keep a whole shelf full of handbooks, but you should designate one as the class authority and refer to it often. Ask students to help you look up the answers to any questions of usage or correctness about which you feel uncertain.

4. *Encourage students to include samples of their editing practice in a portfolio* or writing folder so that they have a visual representation of how their editing skills are growing. This record also gives parents impressive physical evidence of what their students can do.

HELPING CHALLENGED/BEGINNING WRITERS

Many students dread writing. It may be difficult for them, or they think—rightly or wrongly—that they are not very good at it. A lifetime of negative comments only reinforces this internal assessment. The writing-process approach promises help to challenged writers by offering them more time for writing

FIGURE 9.6 *Sample Style Sheet*

1. Please use 12-point Times Roman for basic text.
2. Major headings should be set in 16-point and centered.
3. Sub-heads should be set in 14-point, flush left.
4. All major and sub-heads should be **boldfaced.**
5. All margins should be 1" wide.
6. Please use endnotes, not footnotes.
7. In citing sources, please refer to *Write Source 2000,* pages 231–232.
8. The first paragraph of any text may be block style (flush left). All other paragraphs should be indented 5 spaces.
9. Text should be double-spaced.
10. Bulleted or numbered lists are acceptable.
11. Any illustrations or other graphics should be clearly labeled as Figure 1, Figure 2, and so on, and referenced in the text.
12. At the top right, please put your name, my name, class period, and the date when you turn in the paper. Use the following this format:

> Charles Naka
> Marlin
> Period 3
> February 1, 2004

13. A title page is optional. If you prepare a title page (optional), please include the title of the piece, your name, and the date, all centered on the page.
14. Use *italics,* not underlining, to indicate emphasis.
15. Avoid **boldface** except for headings.
16. Avoid FULL CAP'S except when quoting fully capitalized material.
17. Keep exclamation points to a minimum.
18. Contractions are fine.
19. Set quotations of more than 25 words apart from text, single-spaced, and with an extra five spaces to right and left, e.g.,

> Always write with the reader in mind. Re-read your text, asking yourself whether it makes sense and whether you are having a good time going through the material. If your answer to either one is no, revise! (Marland, 2003, 47)

20. Number pages, after the first page, in the upper right corner.

than many of us used to be given. But time is only useful if you know what to do with it. Students who have no idea how to revise could have years to rework an assignment, and it wouldn't help. Traits can help writers understand what it is writers actually *do* when they revise, and even if they do only *one* thing to revise a given paper, it's a step, one for which they should receive credit. Here are

> *. . . we need to be gentle. Raymond Carver, writer and teacher, was revered by his students. The harshest criticism he would give to a student was: "I think it's good you got that story behind you."*
>
> **—Ralph Fletcher**
> *What a Writer Needs*, 1993, p. 18

> *Other instructors are obsessed with motivating writing. When they share their techniques I am reminded of cattle prods that "motivate" the steer up the ramp towards hamburger land. Good writing is rarely "motivated" from the outside but has to be drawn out of the student.*
>
> **—Donald M. Murray**
> *A Writer Teaches Writing*, 2004, p. 84

some ways to make traits work for writers who find writing difficult or just unappealing:

1. *Focus early conferences on the* writer, *not the writing.* Ask students to share their interests. What are their favorite activities, hobbies, dreams, hopes, worries? Get to know the person first because out of this well comes the writing. How do we motivate writers? The same way we motivate friends: by telling them that we're truly interested in what they have to say.

2. *Keep writing short.* If you're not much of a runner, you probably would rather not sign up for the 26-mile marathon. Fifty yards is plenty. So let students write a little at a time (a paragraph, say) and write *often.*

3. *Do lots of group writing.* Give reluctant or challenged writers partners, and let them write a story together. They will learn from each other as they talk and work. Brainstorming leads or conclusions or best phrasing lets everyone in on the thinking part of writing.

4. *As a class, critique and analyze* anonymous *writing.* Even people who do not like to write themselves or who fear writing enjoy evaluating and discussing the writing of others, and they will learn more from being assessors than you think.

5. *Model writing.* It is much easier to swim, drive a car, ride a horse, or write if you have seen someone do it. Let them see you. You don't have to razzle-dazzle them. Write simply. Write often. Solicit their help. How should you begin? What should you put in? Take out? Get them to problem solve with you as you go. Then you can tell them—honestly—"Look, you're doing it already as you're guiding me. The only difference is *you* need to be the one moving the pencil sometimes."

6. *Give serious time and thought to prewriting.* Many writers stumble because they are pushed into drafting before they are ready. Fear of failure makes them choke—and what we get is limited in length, scope, and feeling. Rehearsing is about exploring and loosening up. Many unsure writers discover that they know more than they thought if they are allowed to use two techniques: talking and drawing. Given time to chat, many students will discover that they are not alone in their apprehension. This is step one. They also discover the value of having a partner in planning how to begin and where to go from there. This is step two. Finally, they have a resource for endless questions, and from questions flows content. This is step three. For some students, sketching adds a whole new dimension; it awakens a creative side of the brain that feeds the writing process. In teacher Penny Clare's classroom (see Chapter 10), students use what they know to make notes, and then they draw. This extra little step in the writing process yields amazing results—and, according to Penny, vocabulary that just would not emerge without the art. See Figure 9.7 for an example.

7. *Encourage dictation.* Many students would write more and with greater confidence (and style) if they could dictate all or part of what they say. Talking feels more natural and more comfortable. Let them write on tape—or talk to you. Make notes on what they say so that you can show them that they had more ideas than they thought; they can then use your notes in their writing:

FIGURE 9.7   *Reilly's Paper*

Day slowly awakens. She lazily opens one eye, pushing royal purples high into the sky, leaving the teals and aquas to linger. A tree stands alone with no one to turn to on a barren landscape. Finally day reaches a warm hand to touch the hard frozen ground.

"Here you told me your hamster died, but then you went right into your shopping trip at K-Mart. How did you feel when your hamster died? Who buried it? Where did you bury it?" These probing questions from teacher Lois Burdett turned a brief sketch of a hamster's last moments into a touching story of loss, in which we see the second grade writer gently touch the body of her now-dead hamster, hoping for a sign of a heartbeat but finding none, and then trying to hold back the tears as Dad descends the stairs to the basement and she breaks the news. Later we see Dad digging a small grave, watch the writer softly place the body inside and say goodbye and then, after pulling up a soft earth blanket, mark the grave with her beloved Hamster's name—and e-mail address (a reminder of our times).

> *We should see our students as smart and capable. We should assume that they can learn what we teach—all of them. We should look through their mistakes or ignorance to the intelligence that lies behind [emphasis in original].*
>
> **—Peter Elbow**
> *Embracing Contraries*, 1986, p. 53

> *Your unconscious can't work while you are breathing down its neck. You'll sit there going, 'Are you done in there yet, are you done in there yet?' But it is trying to tell you nicely, 'Shut up and go away,' "*
>
> **—Anne Lamott**
> *Bird By Bird*, 1995, p. 182

8. *Allow a freebie.* Everyone needs a mental health day occasionally, writers included. Struggling students appreciate the notion that they can disregard one assignment of their choice. Most will do this anyway, so why not make a tradition of it?

9. *Build on the positive.* Sometimes it's hard. It may be buried or tough to spot. Look harder. Just one moment of voice or convention used correctly is cause for a small celebration. Think *little victories*. Let the student feel the success. Build confidence before you find fault. And when you comment, don't be gushy, but don't hold back either. No one wants to hear, "Well, your voice is starting to emerge." What is that? A compliment or a complaint? Be enthusiastic: "Your voice grabbed me by the lapels right at this point. I got the chills." The more voice you put in your comments, the more voice you're likely to see in the next paper.

10. *Love it yourself.* Tell your students that *you* love to write. Relish your own small victories. Read your writing aloud for them to hear and celebrate with you.

HELPING STUDENTS WHO KNOW THE TRAITS WELL

Maybe your students have worked with the six traits previously and know them well. The last thing you want to hear is, "Oh, no, not 'The Redwoods' again!" Often, I'm asked if there isn't something called *advanced traits*, a term I always find amusing because it sounds as though once we master these basic, simple traits, we can move on to the more sophisticated traits—wit, innuendo, subtlety, profundity, and so on.

Actually, working with the traits is like anything else; it can be as simple or as difficult as you make it. If you wanted to get better at bike riding, you'd ride faster or farther, strap weights to your back, or challenge yourself to take on tougher terrain. You get better at working with the traits pretty much the same way. It is not the *traits* that get more advanced after all, but the *writing, thinking, reading, and discussing*. It's the way in which we *apply* the traits. Here are some suggested strategies for challenging yourself—and your students.

1. *Ask students to score and comment on* your *writing.* Ask them to write essays defending their scores.

2. *Ask them to self-assess their own work* and, again, to write an essay defending that self-assessment. In Ellen's AP English class (see Chapter 10), students assess themselves and write essays defending their assessments. One example is provided by Lauren's writing (see Figure 9.8) and reflections (see Figures 9.9 and 9.10). Notice how self-reflection takes Lauren first inside the world of her own writing—and then into writing in general.

3. *Create your own rubrics.* Rubric development builds thinking skills. It's harder than it might seem, and will make you come face to face with what you think good writing is, regardless of what the six-trait model says. You can specialize: a rubric for persuasive writing, business or tech writing, drama, or poetry. Start with student samples. Read and rank them: high, developing, beginning. Record what you find, and use the results to create a rubric or checklist written in your own words. (See Appendix 3 for copies of rubrics

| FIGURE 9.8 | *Lauren's Paper, "What Confuses Me"* |

What Confuses Me
By Lauren Rothrock

Last night I watched a starving child cry.

I could see the sharp outline of his bones jutting out from beneath his taut skin—his rib cage heaving visibly as the sobs shook his poor, fragile body. I saw his swollen belly and the way his limbs hung limply at his sides, like broken twigs. But what stayed with me were his eyes. Sunken and shadowed in their sockets, his tears seeming to glitter from the depths of some profound emotion that I could not seem to grasp or understand. I watched as they carved shiny, silver traces through the dust on his cheeks, and for a brief moment I wondered whether he could really see me.

Seconds later he was gone—replaced by the image of a dancing Coca-Cola can as the news broadcast switched over to a commercial. And I sat there, mulling over his predicament while wondering whether or not to start my Calculus homework. To me, he was nothing more than a poster child, and I had homework to do.

You ask me what confuses me in life. I'll tell you. I'm confused by the fact that I sleep in a two-story, four-bedroom house while an African family of twelve huddles in a dilapidated old shack made of sticks and mud. I'm confused by the fact that I'm five pounds overweight whereas others haven't seen a bite of food in over a week. I'm confused by the fact that the bracelet I wear around my wrist could support a child for over a month. I'm confused by the fact that I watched that helpless little boy cry—and didn't shed a tear.

I wonder when I changed, when I became so devoid of human emotion that I could look misery in the eye and merely shrug my shoulders. Tough break, kid! Life's rough. When I think about it, I frighten myself. It seems as though there's a side of me that I didn't even know existed—one that has become so numb to the tragedies of this world that it no longer feels the tug of simple human kindness. I can rant and rave about the injustices of this world until I'm blue in the face . . . I can spout out Bible verses about love and charity until my voice turns hoarse . . . But the fact remains the same: I didn't cry. That confuses me.

That night as I lay in bed, the boy's image flashed before me again in my mind. And suddenly it occurred to me: he has a name. In that single, swift instant, something inside of me seemed to give way. He was a real person, flesh and blood—living under the same sky, sleeping under the same moon. It's hard to force yourself to see something you are so willing to ignore. It's easier to spare yourself the pain than embrace the truth. But at that moment I knew that I was helpless to change the reality before me. That boy had gone to bed hungry.

But he no longer cries alone.

---

based on the six-trait writing rubric. One is a rubric on public speaking developed by Millard Public Schools and the other a rubric for rating video production.)

4. *Compare traits across modes of writing.* As your students write for various purposes, talk about how voice changes (informational to descriptive

FIGURE 9.9	*Lauren's Reflections on "What Confuses Me"*

I have to admit, this essay was very difficult for me to write. At first, I was temped to choose another topic and spare myself the grief rather than dredge up emotions I didn't want to face. But because the subject is so personal to me, I felt that I was able to express myself effectively through my voice (score of 5 on 5-point scale).

By using the example of the African boy, I sought to draw the reader in and give the essay more impact. It is through this experience that I explain my confusion with the world and my apathy towards it. I thought the organization (4) was good—by returning to the boy in the concluding paragraph, I tried to leave the reader with something to think about.

The ideas and content (4) may be a little sketchy—when writing on a subject like "confusion," it's hard to convey your ideas without sounding confused yourself. I had a hard time expanding on my central theme; it was as if I got to a certain point and had nothing more to say. I felt that if I wrote any more, I would just be generating a lot of filler to take up more space, so I went ahead and ended it. This may actually have been to my advantage; sometimes, shorter is better.

I admit that my word choice (4) may have been less than exemplary, but I was trying to avoid a "scholarly" tone and keep it on a more personal level. I tried to make up for the basic word choice by constructing powerful imagery when describing the boy. Reading over it, I wonder whether I may have unintentionally used too many clichés. I guess that's for the reader to decide.

As for sentence fluency (4), I noticed that I like to use a lot of parallel structure. Though that may be good in some cases, there is something called "too much of a good thing." I think that in the future I should experiment a little more with how I construct my sentences. One thing I did like is the way I placed the opening and closing sentences by themselves. I think that some phrases belong alone, without the distraction of a surrounding paragraph.

Overall, I am satisfied with the essay, because I think I was able to get my point across in a powerful way. Besides just answering a question, it gave me the chance to learn something about myself. (Conventions, 5. Our scores were all 5s. Lauren is modest.)

> *I know no greater time-saver than helping students evaluate their own work . . . I need to help them acquire the skill to be able to reread their own work critically, but I do so with the certain knowledge that rereading will result in better work.*
>
> **—Donald H. Graves**
> *Testing Is Not Teaching,*
> 2002, p. 77

to narrative) or how even conventions differ in creative versus business or technical writing. When you bring modes (forms, purposes) of writing into the picture, you open up a whole new world of ways to apply and think about traits. They change in subtle but important ways as the purpose of the writing shifts. You can create checklists to define these shifts (see Chapter 11 for samples). As an alternative, create checklists for a children's picturebook, textbook, dictionary or other reference book, job application letter, film script, play, poem, résumé, or any type of writing that is important to your students.

5. *Invite students to keep portfolios.* Within those portfolios, they can show samples of writing that reflect quality performance on each of the six traits—plus growing editing skill to demonstrate proficiency in conventions.

FIGURE 9.10   *Lauren's Reflections on Herself as a Writer*

To me a piece of writing is like a photograph. Be it in color or black and white, it can capture a single moment and hold it forever. In my experiences as a writer, I have often found that I am not content until I have "frozen" such moments on paper, a need that leaves me scribbling notes on everything from gum wrappers to the back of a shopping receipt. As can be seen by the pile of wrappers on my desk, most of my writing never reaches an audience. But for some reason, that doesn't seem to matter. Writing is the only outlet through which I can express myself honestly and without inhibitions.

Whether or not my desire to become a novelist will pan out remains to be seen. I may never see my name grace the spine of a New York Times best seller—in fact, I may never even see my name in print. But that's only the frame on the photograph. I'll never stop taking pictures.

6. *Assess and discuss more challenging pieces using the traits.* Look at conventions or word choice in a legal document, résumé, or job application letter; voice or organization in a play, recipe, board game, a letter of resignation, or set of directions on a box of pancake mix; word choice in a travel brochure, weather forecast, or college manual; fluency in a film review or set of song lyrics; and ideas in a political speech or doctoral dissertation. Assess pieces from Poe, Chaucer, Shakespeare, Melville, Norman Mailer, Virginia Woolf, Emily Dickinson, Tim O'Brien, Maya Angelou, Pablo Picasso, Thomas Jefferson, Nelson Mandela, Abe Lincoln, John F. Kennedy, or Franklin Roosevelt. Hold a contest: Who can think up the most challenging assessment? The most unusual? The most riveting? Stretch. Grow. There is always a more difficult assessment task ahead.

7. *Ask students to design their own lessons for teaching traits.* You may wish to assign one trait to each of several groups in your class. Let them use student writing samples, other writing samples, pieces from literature, or activities to enrich the lesson. They should feel free to be inventive! Once they've designed lessons for their own classmates (this is just the warm-up), have them do lessons for

- ✔ Younger children
- ✔ Parents
- ✔ Members of the business community
- ✔ Content area teachers

8. *Conduct your own classroom research.* How do the six traits influence your students' performance—or that of students in another class? Set up an investigation using observation, interviews, and possibly a pre- and postwriting exercise. Document what you learn. Publish the results.

9. *Finally, personify the traits and portray them theatrically.* How does Voice dress and speak? Is Conventions really the stuffed shirt that everyone says he (or she) is? What if Fluency crashed the party? Would she (or he) be attracted to the debonair Word Choice—or find him hopelessly dull? You can ask students to select a part and act out a short play—or just a dialogue. Be prepared to let your real attitudes about the traits show! Read Figure 9.11 to see two writers' personifications of the traits.

And remember. . . . In the end, it isn't the *traits* that become advanced, but our understanding of what makes *writing* work.

FIGURE 9.11 *Personification of the Traits*

Twins

Siamese twins, Conventions and Voice found the search for individuality daunting. Though each had competitive characteristics, their personalities complemented each other as well. Voice's emotional, spontaneous charisma was balanced by Convention's practical, empowering authority. As much as Voice attempted to inspire enthusiasm, Convention's proper organization kept them in balance—and always had the final say. Over the years, the twins discovered what they had, in their hearts, known all along: They needed each other to survive.

Friends

Voice likes clothes that flow, clothes of natural fabric. She never combs her hair or shaves her legs or apologizes for drop-in appearances. Ideas considers Voice her best friend, and hates going anywhere without her. For some reason, Ideas cannot quite get up her courage when Voice isn't around, and shies away from daring stunts like bungee jumping or hang gliding. Conventions is secretly in love with Voice, and is forever giving her small gifts like dashes or whole bouquets of italics. Who knows whether she notices? Her infectious laugh keeps Conventions coming back, though!

CHAPTER 9 IN A NUTSHELL

● Even when you work with traits and give students time for writing, they may continue to experience some roadblocks to success. Be persistent—or just come at a trait from a slightly different perspective.

● To strengthen ideas, voice—and all traits—ensure that students sometimes have the option of writing on personally important topics.

● Use literature you love to provide models for all the traits "in action." When you read, use all the inflection and expression you can muster.

● Continue to encourage students to read everything they write aloud. It will help them to develop an ear for detail, fluency, and voice and also will help them to catch small problems with conventions that the eye can overlook.

● Encourage prewriting/rehearsing. This part of the writing process must not be rushed, for it prepares students to write with comfort and confidence.

● Consider the power of talking and drawing for students who find rehearsal strategies such as webbing, listing, or preliminary drafting too challenging.

● Model the solution of various writers' problems. Your students will learn from helping you.

● Encourage challenged writers to use strategies such as talking, working with a partner, asking (and answering) questions, and dictation to achieve success.

● Take students who know the traits very well to new levels by asking them to assess more difficult pieces, assess and write in various genres, create their own genre-specific rubrics, design their own lessons, or keep portfolios with selected pieces showing strengths in various traits.

● Remember that ultimately it is not the traits themselves that are *advanced* but our understanding of how writing and writing process work.

EXTENSIONS

1. Do you keep portfolios in your classroom? If so, how might students use their knowledge of the six traits in selecting pieces to include? Write down some thoughts and/or share ideas with colleagues.

2. What are some strategies you have found to be effective in working with students who are experienced writers and/or who know the six traits well? With colleagues' help, make a list.

3. What strategies have you found to be effective in helping challenged writers to find success? Again, make a list.

4. Find an unusual piece of writing to assess—something others might not think of in connection with writing assessment (e.g., song lyrics). Bring it in for your study group or class to assess. Talk about the traits that are most important.

5. Look at any single trait—ideas, organization, voice, whatever—across several modes of writing, say, business writing, narrative writing, and persuasive writing. Talk about the changes you see. How might this affect your assessment of your own students' writing?

6. Create a modeling lesson based on a problem you believe struggling writers often face. Present it to students or colleagues.

7. In your class or group, personify and create a dramatic encounter among the six traits. What do you learn from this experience about your attitude toward the various traits? Do you like some more than others? Find some more important than others? Perform your written pieces as a play.

WHY I WRITE

I write when the day is gloomy and boring. I grab a pencil and a pure white piece of paper. The light bulb is bright and going strong. I look outside and everything is clear. I can write. It's possible.

—**Jovana Stewart,** student writer

LOOKING AHEAD

In Chapter 10 we'll hear the voices of nine teachers who have successfully made six-trait writing part of their process-based curriculum.

10

Listening to Teachers' Voices

*I*n this chapter we'll visit the classrooms of nine teachers to see how they incorporate the six-trait model into their instruction. As you'll see, they have very different ways of dealing with the traits and teaching them to students. There is no right way, and you should take what is most useful from their examples and experience, finding an approach that suits your own classroom environment, curriculum, students, and teaching style.

IN ELAINE'S SELF-CONTAINED SIXTH GRADE CLASSROOM

Elaine is a veteran classroom teacher of nearly twenty years. She has taught mostly fourth and sixth grades and is an unabashed advocate of trait-based instruction. "It's so much easier

What happens in your classroom with writing has everything to do with you and the kids. When instruction focuses on the skills . . . the goals . . . the plans . . . the systems—it often becomes mechanical, detached from kids, lifeless. When it focuses on the persons—the writers, it's just the opposite—it has life!

—Marjorie Frank
If You're Trying to Teach Kids How to Write . . . You've Gotta Have This Book!
1995, p. 21

Writing begins with listening. Don't we all, as writers, want to be listened to?

—Arlene Moore, K–1 teacher

for me to think about writing this way, I sometimes wonder why I didn't think of it before. But the funny part is, my *teaching* isn't any different. For instance, we've always done vocab, right? That's word choice. We do a lot of letter writing—now I put that under voice. I've always emphasized good details. That's ideas. So this stuff is not new. My way of *organizing* my teaching is just a little different."

Elaine writes with her students, reads aloud to them daily, and sometimes allows students to come up with a creative writing assignment for her to follow. "Kids always seem to be interested in the things that really happen to me, so I base a lot of my writing on that. One day, I got my head stuck in the chimney. While I was busy getting myself unstuck, I thought, well, you know, I can *use* this in my writing. Only writers or writing teachers think like this. So the next day, we worked on details. I told my kids, 'I got my head stuck in the chimney. What do you want to know?' *Well*—they had a million questions! I wrote for half an hour, and they kept asking more and more questions: *Did it hurt? Did anyone help you?* All I had to do was fill in the details. They *loved* it. And the next day, they were asking questions of each other."

Elaine teaches the traits one at a time, spending one to two weeks on each trait and then reinforcing all traits throughout the remainder of the year with a variety of focused lessons. She teaches conventions as she goes, with *lots* of practice in editing. "My favorite editing lessons are the ones where students watch me write on the board and tell me when they spot a mistake. They watch like eagles! Right after this, I have them look at their own writing, sometimes with a partner.

"My goal is three hours of writing a week. My kids write in every subject area—social studies, science, math, art, music, and PE. We do reports, posters, letters, invitations to parents to visit our classroom, travel brochures on our community, recipes, directions, maps, and so forth. We write lots of poems—and news stories. We write to people in the community. Kids love to write letters that get answered. It's like magic. Suddenly, there's a reason for the writing."

Once a week (or so), the class will score and discuss an anonymous student paper. Since the paper belongs to no one in the class, they can be very frank in their comments. "The kids love being critics," Elaine claims. "and they learn the traits *faster* than we do. They don't come to it with all that baggage we have from years of evaluating student work. They're these fresh little slates, and they pick up on it right away."

Elaine also uses pre-post tests to gauge her students' progress. "Every class is different, so I use preassessment to tell me where to focus my instruction. One year a class will be strong on conventions; another time it will be ideas or voice." Elaine does her preassessment during late September or early October. "My postassessment usually comes in April. Those results tell me how far my students have come and how well I've taught certain things. This gives me information I can't get from the state assessment. Kids and parents look at those two samples—October and April—and they can see big differences. You'll hear kids go 'Wow! Is that *my writing?*' when they see the October piece, and the parents go 'Wow!' too. Their eyes light up. Nothing speaks as loudly as real samples."

Here is one student's April reflection:

> ### Spring Reflection (Grade 6)
>
> Writing was easier for me this year because I knew what I was doing! Having the traits and the Student Writers' Guide really helped. In the beginning of the year, my writing had no organization at all. It just bounced around from there to here to there and back. I did not know how to write an introduction. Now I know about six different things to try. I did not know how to write a conclusion and now I do. I did not even know about the trait called voice. I thought textbook writing was boring because it had too many facts. Now I know it is just the voice. It doesn't have any! I am trying to write like a writer and not a textbook.

Parents are brought into the process, too. "On back-to-school nights, I ask parents to write—just for three, four minutes, you know. That's all the time we have. But you should see the fear on their faces. They're terrified! They even ask me if I'm going to collect the writing or if I'm going to read it. I tell them no, it's just for them. But I do ask them to think about how writing was assessed when they were kids. They remember this sea of red marks—so that's what a lot of them expect from me. I also ask them if they know what they're really good at as writers. A lot of them don't have a clue. Then I pass out copies of the *Six-Trait Scoring Guide for Students*—and it's like a whole world opens up. One dad asked me, 'Where was *this* when I was going to school?'"

Parents who are interested can attend a short two-hour training session on the six traits that Elaine does twice a year. Then they're encouraged to volunteer as *writing coaches*, which means that they can participate in student writing groups, confer with students who are revising their work or getting ready to publish, help students with editing, or—if they write—share samples of their own work. Elaine gives them a writing coach checklist (Figure 10.1)—reminding them to focus on *one trait* at a time—not the whole list!

Elaine's is a classroom in which the love of writing and reading shines from both teacher and students—and where parents feel welcome to join the party.

IN JIM'S HIGH SCHOOL CLASSROOM

Jim has been teaching high school for more than fifteen years. Each year, he introduces the traits a little differently, depending on the class and their experience. "This year I will introduce it in the second week as a means of discussing their summer reading essay. They write the essay the first week, and when I return it to them, I will introduce the traits by having them do a somewhat cursory, introductory assessment of their writing. For example, they will have to think about voice and wonder if their writing has any—and this provides an initial frame for us to discuss and work on those things throughout the rest of the year."

FIGURE 10.1 *Writing Coach Checklist*

(Please focus on *ONE* trait—student's choice)

Ideas and Development

1. Do you have a topic? (If not, ask questions/brainstorm possibilities.)

2. What do you see as your *main* idea or message?

3. What *one thing* do you want your reader to learn from your writing?

4. Does your message make sense all the way through?

5. Does your paper say what you want it so say?

6. *(If needed)* I have a question: _____

Organization

1. Does the lead hook your reader? Does it set up what's coming?

2. *For expository/persuasive* writing: Does your *most important point* stand out?

3. For *narrrative* writing: Does your story have a *turning point*?

4. Does your conclusion wrap up your story/discussion?

5. *(Only if needed)* As a reader, I felt confused when _____.

Voice

1. Will readers hear YOU in this piece?

2. Does this writing show what YOU think and feel?

3. What do you like best about your piece?

4. Do you think the writing speaks to your readers?

5. What would you like a reader or listener to *feel*?

6. Here's where your voice seemed strongest to me: _____.

Word Choice

1. Do you have favorite words or phrases?

2. These are the words or expressions that caught my attention: _____.

3. Are there any words you used for the first time?

4. Are there any words you weren't sure of?

5. Is there anything you wish you could say differently?

Sentence Fluency

1. Did you read the piece aloud?

2. Is it easy to read?

3. Do you hear some variety in your sentences?

4. Did you use any dialogue? *(If so)* Are you happy with how that sounds?

5. Are there any spots that could use some smoothing out?

Conventions/Editing

1. Have you edited your paper yet?

2. Have you tried any of these editing strategies: Reading aloud?_____ Reading silently? _____ Reading from the bottom up (for spelling) _____ ?

3. Any questions I could help with?

4. Do you use a handbook or dictionary? Is there anything we need to look up?

Working with the traits, Jim feels, gives his instruction focus and direction. "Students like it because it's very responsive to their needs as writers. It lends a structure, a good one, to the course. We'll work with, say, voice or sentence fluency for a time (keeping in mind other traits we've studied) and link our discussion of other writers to this as well. The traits create and sustain a culture of writing, give us a language for discussing their own writing and that of others. The traits also give their work a purpose. They like me to bring their work before the class on the overhead and work through the assignments we do each week. They read for a purpose, too—to examine and improve upon word choice, for instance. This sense of purpose gives them a compass to steer by and makes them more effective as readers."

Jim is careful to keep his instruction very focused, working on one trait at a time until students have gone through them all. "We are focusing on ideas and development at this point, for example. We'll work through their papers on that one trait using the overhead, handouts, and examples. The feedback they get is very targeted and concrete. They *feel* the difference because their writing visibly improves."

Because Jim's class is integrated with history, students have a wide range of reading samples to draw from in discussing traits, including nonfiction books as well as literature of all kinds.

What is most challenging for Jim's students? "The kids I work with need to work hard in two areas: generation [of ideas] and organization. They have ideas, but need to learn how to access them, then organize them. Logic seems increasingly important to me because many students seem to lack a strong sense of reasoning, and this results in muddled writing at best. To me the traits suggest not only a vocabulary of terms, but *habits of mind* when it comes to writing and thinking. I use the traits along with graphic organizers to help struggling students figure out what they have to say—and then make the text say what they want it to. Once they have generated and organized, we can begin to think about voice and fluency to give those ideas some polish, some kick."

The students in Jim's class enjoy comparing their responses to his. One way Jim does this is by marking text together. "They read through their papers and used a highlighter to mark the words or phrases they thought really worked. Then I read with a different color and marked the ones *I* thought worked. It was surprising to see how rarely they matched! This discrepancy initiated a useful series of activities and discussion about what makes language powerful or distinctive. It was remarkably instructive just to ask them why they thought a particular passage worked—and then explain why I responded to something else altogether."

The real strength of a trait-based approach to teaching writing lies, Jim feels, in its flexibility—the fact that you can do with it pretty much what you want. "An approach or strategy sometimes seems a good solution, but after a while you realize it can only take students so far. Because there's no built-in end point, six traits offers the flexibility and room for growth that you seek as a teacher—or as a department that wants to create a long-term program."

IN BILLIE'S SEVENTH GRADE CLASSROOM

Billie teaches middle school in a district where classes tend to be large—usually over 40 students. Her seventh graders use rubrics and posters and are used to assessing writing samples and discussing literature using trait language. For a number of students in Billie's class, English is a second language, and Billie uses a number of creative strategies to help them gain comfort with the writing process.

"We take brain breaks during class," she explains. "This consists of standing next to our desks and participating in the six traits calisthenics (Lamkin,

2004). It's a total physical response (TPR) activity, which is one way of teaching English language or second language learners, as well as all students who are kinesthetic learners. They work like this. For ideas, we stand with our hands made into fists just above our heads, then reach upward, one hand at a time. As each hand moves up, it opens up just like our ideas spring out of our minds and open themselves up to the world. I ask students to think about a topic they could write about, and I call on a few to share their ideas.

"Then I ask 'What do we need to do with our ideas as we write?' They call out, 'Organize.' Then we move to the motion for organization, which is stacking our hands (with a little space between) right in front of our bodies—put the left hand near your stomach, right hand about six inches above, then continue this pattern till we can't reach anymore—and reverse the process. As we do this, I ask students to call out organizational techniques . . . 'a catchy lead . . . pattern of ideas . . . good transitions . . . smooth ending.'

"Next I ask, 'What do we need to do to make sure the reader believes us?' and they respond, 'Tell the truth.' I add that in telling the truth, we reveal confidence in our organized ideas, and these must come from our heart—which is where the voice lies. I show the motion for voice by having my hands spring forth from just above my heart. Then I call on a few students to share a comment about something they are confident about in their writing.

"On to word choice. I ask 'If I am going to confidently organize my ideas, what do I need to choose to get my message out?' They respond, 'Words!' I tell them that yes, we need to choose our words wisely. For this trait, we reach and grab at the air in all directions. I bend and stretch as I'm reaching, to show students I want them to reach for the best way to say something. I then ask a few students to share favorite words, maybe one they heard when I read aloud to them today or one they found in their silent reading.

"As they are still reaching, I ask, 'What do we call it when we put a bunch of words together to convey one meaning?' They respond, 'A sentence!' I explain that to get our organized ideas out to the reader we need to choose words wisely and create rhythm with our sentences. Waves of the ocean are different lengths and crash against the shore with different force. We imitate this wave motion by intertwining the fingers of both hands and making a wave with our arms, right to left, then left to right, swaying as we move. As we're imitating fluency, I ask how we create fluency with writing. 'Begin with different words . . . have different sentence lengths,' they say.

"Finally we come to the last trait. I ask, 'What do we do to hold our organized ideas together so our chosen words create sentences that flow in a confident, truthful manner?' And they respond, 'We use periods, commas, and other punctuation!' I say yes, as I untangle my fingers, wrap both arms around my body, and give myself a big squeeze. I explain that conventions hold our thoughts together just the way a good hug holds us together.

"We then have silent peer conferences where the students read each other's writing pieces and are *only* allowed to use hand signals to point out positive trait usage. They will give a 'thumbs up' and then act out the trait that was very strong in the paper."

Billie also uses color coding to help students focus in on various traits within a piece of writing: "I color code the traits; then when we review student writing, I have the students color over the parts that help to convey the main idea in blue, organization in orange, voice in red, etc."

Teachers introduce traits in a variety of ways: through a student rubric, scoring practice—or sometimes literature. Billie has devised her own approach, which combines several strategies: "I put a very basic guideline for each of the traits on the overhead and talk with the students about each one. Then I share another outline of what I call RTC—reading, traits, and connections (see Figure 10.2 for a student example). I read Dr. Suess's *Hooray for Diffendoofer Day* aloud to the students [and] then we discuss each of the strategies and how the traits were represented for each. We then complete an RTC with the story. The students use the RTC method as a daily reflection of what they read in class. So we get a daily dose of six traits in a variety of literature as well as an understanding of how the students connect with reading."

What does Billie consider the most powerful type of lesson? "Reading aloud to my students. I want them to hear passages from literature that are strong in one trait or another; then I use these as a spring board or segue into a minilesson in which students revise their 'working writing piece' for that trait."

FIGURE 10.2 *Reading, Traits, & Connections*

Reading, Traits & Connections
By Hannah

Title of Book: *The Sign of the Twisted Candles*
Author: Carolyn Keene

Today I read the part where Carol fainted because Asa Sydney left a whole lot of stuff to her name. He also said that if she wants a new foster family that it should be looked into. The Semitts were not too happy about it. When everyone left from the will reading, Nancy noticed that Frank Sermitt went out in the old barn with two boxes. Nancy and Caro followed and inside the barn, it was a mess. They hid behind a pile of hay so they didn't see what was going on. Frank left—then the girls found a trapdoor. Later, they heard someone coming up the ladder and hid.

The strongest trait in this passage was ideas, I think. I could really picture the whole room in the barn. This part helped me picture it: " The second floor was merely an <u>unplastered attic.</u> A rusted iron bed stood under the eaves, and an <u>antique wardrobe,</u> its <u>doors awry</u> and its once fine <u>mahogany surface green with mildew,</u> leaned against the chimney." The author did a really good job with word choice. I felt like I was there with words like *awry, examined, gasped, moldering, betrayed, trembling.* Also, there is a cool, mysterious tone (voice) to the writing.

Billie's favorite book to use in writing instruction is Anne Lamott's *Bird By Bird* (1995). "I read aloud and discuss the chapter called 'Lunchroom.' I'll read a few paragraphs, then stop and ask students to reflect and write about any connections they had with that excerpt. I share with them what I have written, then call on a few volunteers to share what they have written. I continue reading and holding writing/discussion sessions until the end of the chapter. The discussions that evolve from this just tumble out of the student's memories of their experiences in the lunchroom. We then write a piece based on our memories. This is a favorite activity for most of my students."

In addition to her extensive use of literature, Billie views modeling as the most important of her instructional strategies. "Modeling my own writing with students is very effective. They look at, critique, and score my writing—then use the same strategies in their writing.

"My students are asked to have three writing pieces of their choice completed per quarter. When a writing piece is assigned, they are also given a blank calendar that shows only a three-week time period. They are also given a list of possible writing stages they may choose to use (brainstorming, drafting, self conference, revision, peer conference, editing, proofreading, publishing, reflection, scoring, etc.). They decide what date they are going to complete the writing piece first and then work backwards through the writing stages, allowing a few days for revision or just letting the paper sit and marinate for a few days to give it a fresh perspective until they reach the day that it was assigned. Backwards planning is used widely in the business world and works well in my classroom. The student chooses all of his or her dates and can make appointments for a conference with me based on those choices. It not only teaches students goal setting but also the responsibility of following a plan."

What if another teacher feels reluctant about using the traits in his or her classroom? "I tell that person, 'You are *already* using the traits—you just don't realize it.' I ask them to find their favorite lesson, show me a teacher model of the lesson and a student example; then I sit and point out how the traits are used in that lesson. Once they understand that connection, they are willing to adopt trait-based instruction in their classroom without feeling anxious about it."

What's the secret to good writing instruction? "Modeling, modeling, modeling and humor, humor, humor. Every assignment I ask students to do is presented to them with *my* writing example for that assignment. I share with them a variety of writing pieces that I take to writing workshops and ask for their opinion about one trait or another. They are ready and willing to tell me what works and doesn't work. They are more receptive to tackling their writing pieces when they have seen my modeling of the assignment, have discussed it using the terminology of the rubrics, and have scored it with a reflection piece to support their scoring.

"It's important to use a variety of literature, too. I can't think of a better way to start my day than to share a children's picture book with my students one moment, then a paragraph from a novel the next. The discussions that pop up from our reading aloud sessions are the best part of my days.

"And laughter . . . laugh a lot, at yourself and with your students. I tell my students that I have the best job in the world because I get paid to act like a 13-year-old all over again. There isn't a job out there that is as rewarding as hanging around middle school students for six hours a day."

IN ELLEN'S AP ENGLISH CLASSROOM

Ellen has been teaching advanced placement high school students for many years, and though the traits are an important focus for her curriculum, she is also a firm believer in teaching to the *writer* and in knowing who your students are before you begin advising them on matters of syntax and conventions.

"My first step is to help my students envision the world they want to live in, and to imagine how their personal, individual voices will contribute to that world. So I begin with the writers, not the writing; then I shape the writing tasks to what they say and what they see. I like to think I allow my writers to find meaning in contemporary culture—to recognize what's shallow, and even perhaps shoot a few holes in the hypocrisy they see in our society.

"When I teach ideas, I emphasize the importance of a writer opening up people's minds. Your ideas are what you teach your readers, I tell my students. I don't always expect closure, but I do expect them to think: to raise the right questions. 'Who are you? I ask them. Where do you stand on this issue or that? What is your philosophical approach to the world?' I use the traits to build thinking skills."

Ellen shares numerous samples of writing from many sources. "I always read everything aloud. It makes such a difference when the ear is trained. I'm afraid of how little they get to hear. Listen to television for even a short time and see how we are becoming conditioned to sound bites of language. It isn't just the meaning that's lost. So much of our modern language has no real rhythm. I want them to hear language at its best. I want them to slow down long enough to read good poetry, not just process it, to hear the rhythm of the lines rising and falling like the tides.

"To me all the traits are important, but in the end, the final question is, 'How does each trait bring out the writer's *voice?*' It's voice, to my mind, that most influences meaning. We start with an idea, but if our writing is good, we end up speaking person to person. 'When you sign a paper,' I tell my students, 'and you expect me to read it, you've made a commitment to me. I want to hear *your* ideas, *your* voice.' So much of this is missing from today's research writing. There's no passion for the topic, no concern for the audience. That's why it winds up piled in a corner somewhere. Many of our students do not have the patience it takes to sift through volumes of information—our world is so information-laden; we need to show them how. Otherwise, we get informational writing that's just plagiarism, a shortcut. Their eyes glaze over at the thought of doing research, and I think a lot of this is because they wind up writing in someone else's voice, a phony voice, an encyclopedia voice.

"I think it's a breakthrough moment when students are relieved of the burden of having to be someone else. I expect honesty and straightforwardness. I tell them, 'I don't want writing to impress. Write from deep inside you.'"

> *Becoming a writer is about becoming conscious. When you're conscious and writing from a place of insight and simplicity and real caring about the truth, you have the ability to throw the lights on for your reader.*
>
> **—Anne Lamott**
> *Bird By Bird*, 1995, p. 225

> *But feeling isn't a luxury; it's a necessity. It's your survival. It's your soul life. It's your truth. And without it, your art, your life, your writing will be generic—anybody's voice. With it, work will be authentic, powerful—your voice.*
>
> **—Nancy Slonim Aronie**
> *Writing from the Heart*, 1998, p. 79

> *I write from my life, from what I see and hear and smell and feel, from personal inspection at zero altitude and I write because it is, simply, all that I am, because in the end I do not want to do any other thing as much as I want to write.*
>
> **—Garl Paulsen**
> *Shelf Life*, 2003, P. 6

Ellen also sees writing as potentially therapeutic and empowering for many students. "When I first began teaching twenty-some years ago, students did every assignment. They didn't question anything. For kids today, it's different. So many are emotionally unsure. So many come from broken families and are struggling just to find themselves; school is an additional burden. But it *can* be a place of safety and emotional support, too, if we let it. I don't want this to sound presumptuous; I know my class is one small part of their lives. But I feel strongly that my job as a teacher is to tell students when they write, 'Your writing moved me. You have the power to change the world with these ideas.' Without that, we—and they—have no real reason to write."

> *You don't teach writing. You teach WRITERS. And believe me, there IS a world of difference between the two.*
>
> **—Marjorie Frank**
>
> *If You're Trying to Teach Kids How to Write . . . You've Gotta Have This Book,* 1995, p. 18

IN JUDY'S THIRD GRADE CLASSROOM

Judy is a veteran third grade teacher who has been working for some time to make her writer's workshop approach as effective and comfortable as her considerable expertise can make it. Her year opens with an opportunity for students to look at and listen to writing and to say what they notice—what makes writing work. This results in their own version of the traits, which they can then compare with those in a student rubric. Judy likes working with the traits because "they give us a common language to discuss and assess our writing." The importance of that common language is evident in every part of her writer's workshop.

Judy's workshop runs for one hour four times a week. She opens each hour with a minilesson, drawing on both writing process and the six traits for her organizational structure. Content might be as simple as one convention or something more complex—an explanation of what a paragraph is, modeling of how to write a strong lead, or sharing of a picture book with focus on a particular trait. Students then write for 30 to 35 minutes on personally selected topics while Judy holds individual conferences of about 5 minutes each. "I listen carefully to what the child is saying," Judy says, "and consider his work with respect. I usually ask the student two questions (inspired by Donald H. Graves):

1. What do you like about your piece?
2. What do you think needs improvement?"

Conferences are sometimes highly focused: line spacing, writing dialogue, speaking right to an audience, writing a lead or conclusion, and so forth. "I always end the conference by asking, 'What are you going to do now?'" This gives the child a chance to reflect on what he or she has learned and provides a transition into the act of writing.

Judy saves 15 minutes of the writer's workshop for sharing, a process that, she says, "never ceases to amaze me." Writers do not just read their work aloud but also explain why they are sharing, e.g., to get help finding a title or adding details. "You will be amazed by the quality of student comments and suggestions and how quickly the kids pick up writerly talk," Judy comments. Although some writers may be reluctant to share, within a few weeks, she says, "You will have more sharers than you have time."

Writing is noisy business, Judy has discovered: "My workshop is not a silent place. . . . I want us to be a community of learners who are (as James Britton described it) 'floating on a sea of talk.'" The talk pays off. Judy was delighted one day when one of her third graders echoed a lesson from earlier in the year during a sharing session: "Remember when we said we don't want to get to the end of the piece and then say, 'Huh?'" These third graders are thinking and working like writers.

Following are two short conferences between Judy and her students K.J. and Margaret—along with the samples of writing to which they refer in their comments.

FIGURE 10.3 *The Middle Ages*

The Middle Ages
By KJ Davis

A boy runs off the drawbridge
And spies the blacksmith.
He sees four woodcutters' huts,
One is his father's.
Lord Hickins walks by,
He drops to his knees.
The moat's water sparkles
In the very bright light.
He hears laughter from an inn.
He hears knights swords clack as they practice.
Suddenly, he hears the horn,
It blows a faint sound.
He runs to his house.
He thinks,
Why does it have to be this way?
The enemy catapult flings the heavy stones.
They hit the stone wall
Causing massive damage.
But the enemy falls back.
Later,
That calm smooth swift night,
They have dinner.
They have what they want,
They have meat, cheese, and apples.
The dad says,
" I got five pieces of gold."
The dad says,
" Taxes, taxes, taxes. "
The mother is proud,
But the boy is scared
That his dad might lose his job.
For this is the Middle Ages.

Conference 1, with K.J.

Judy: What is your author's purpose in this poem (See Figure 10.3)?

K.J.: Well, I really like the Middle Ages. It was a peaceful time and a hard time. Not a lot of people had money. So it seemed fun to write a poem about something I like.

Judy: Tell me about some of the beautiful word choice in your poem, like "swords clack" and "that calm smooth swift night"?

K.J.: Well, since I knew this was going to be shared on Poetry Night, I knew I needed good word choice. I just think of them in my head, and I think, "Well, that's just a really great word," and I put it on the paper.

Judy: Do you think about the way the words sound?

K.J.: Yeah, the word has to sound really perfect for a poem like this.

Judy: How do you decide?

K.J.: I've been reading for a long time. I get these words out of books.

Judy: How do you know what the right word is?

K.J.: The topic—it has to go with the Middle Ages.

Conference 2, with Margaret

Judy: Tell me about your poem "Sunset" (See Figure 10.4).

Margaret: I know what I was thinking. I was thinking about when I went to Pismo Beach and we saw the sunset.

Judy: How did you get some of these beautiful images from that day onto your paper?

Margaret: I just thought about what I saw and I described it.

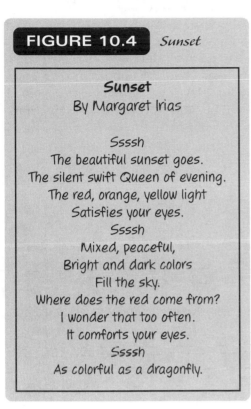

FIGURE 10.4   *Sunset*

Sunset

By Margaret Irias

Ssssh
The beautiful sunset goes.
The silent swift Queen of evening.
The red, orange, yellow light
Satisfies your eyes.
Ssssh
Mixed, peaceful,
Bright and dark colors
Fill the sky.
Where does the red come from?
I wonder that too often.
It comforts your eyes.
Ssssh
As colorful as a dragonfly.

Judy: Did you think about word choice?

Margaret: Yeah, I thought about *evening* instead of *night. Evening* sounds better.

Judy: What about when you talk about the colors "soothing" us?

Margaret: I said that because if it was black or blue, that wouldn't really relax you. The colors I saw were calm colors.

IN PENNY'S SECOND GRADE CLASSROOM

Penny teaches grade 2 and also works as an ESL consultant for multiple grade levels. She relies on the traits in both contexts—and also relies heavily on the use of art. "I believe strongly in art as a way of generating ideas, sequencing thoughts, incorporating detail, and coming up with language that helps you express ideas and feelings. Young writers may express themselves through art first, then write what they see, or what their art has made them think of."

In Penny's class, not all ideas have to come out of students' heads. Writing begins with the exploration of information. "If you want to draw from the well," Penny explains, "you must put something in. For instance, when we were studying Egypt, I began by talking about the history and time frame and showing pictures of the pyramids. Then students made a collage—using paper that gives a picture lots of texture and color. We did a 'whole class share' talking about the details in their pictures, and I did a lesson on personification: If the pyramid had human characteristics—hands, eyes, arms, movement—what would he (or she) say and think? To help them express their ideas, we brainstorm words. We start with nouns—like *mummy, pharaoh, jewels, sand, wind, desert*—then add adjectives and verbs to go with them, and the children draw on these in their writing. I ask them to write in first person, and most write poems. (See Chapter 12, Figures 12.12a, b, and c for an example.) They share them with partners and receive compliments and comments—then do a final draft to go with their pictures." Much of the writing Penny's students do has a nonfiction—science, social studies—base, even though poetry is often the form it takes.

If they are studying the ocean, for example, Penny will share pictures, books—possibly a film. They have class discussions to generate new information and validate what they are learning. When they are ready to write, they make lists of details—sometimes using the senses to categorize—as a prewriting strategy. They also talk to each other, and they draw or paint. Penny explains, "I see art as a way for children to do their planning and thinking, adding details first in the art and then in their writing. In the case of a story, art helps a child think of details and sequence.

"After hearing a lot of strong leads in literature, a child can more easily draw a picture to represent a story beginning. They discuss their pictures and what comes next. For a story, I have them do setting, character, problem, solution, and resolution, each with a picture first—*then* text. We brainstorm words to go with each part, so when they do write, the words just tumble out of them with enthusiasm and accuracy because they are describing a picture they have already drawn. Doing pictures first gives children a chance to think and rethink their descriptions as they fill in the colors and other details. Oral rehearsing—which goes with the sharing of pictures—gives us an opportunity for mini-lessons on simile, personification, metaphor, strong adjectives or verbs, mood, and many things. Whatever fits. Art offers students a way to expand their thinking and plan their writing" (see Figures 10.5 and 10.6).

FIGURE 10.5 *Art and Text Working Together*

The white snow lays on the ground and the blue sky stays over the trees. The trees dance to the wind because the wind is blowing and makes them move. The wind whistles. The baby birds cheep for their mom with a mouthful of food. A row of trees stay together like a family.

FIGURE 10.6 *Art and Text Working Together*

I am an egg. I had just hatched. I look down and I see snow that looks like crystals and then I see buds. They look like little green things sticking up from the snow. Then I look up and I see branches and leaves and I also see a hole in the tree. The colorful sky becomes a little dark. I am a bird.

We want to avoid dismissing the art of children as mere cuteness and learn to appreciate its authentic content and form.

—Bob Steele

Draw Me a Story, 1998, p. 11

Like most primary teachers, Penny relies heavily on literature to provide examples of how good writing looks and sounds. "I like to use the work of William Steig, the poetry of Thomas Locker. Almost every time I read aloud I find a great passage I can mark to use later." Penny keeps files of strong leads, conclusions, samples of character development, and so on so that she can easily find exactly what she wants to share with her students. She also models what she hopes students will do in their own writing, often rewriting a piece as they watch and offer suggestions.

Even the youngest students, Penny feels, can develop a remarkable writer's vocabulary. "That vocabulary comes out in their literature analysis and in their writing. It is not uncommon for one student to comment to another, 'You really made that character interesting. Your writing has voice.'"

IN ARLENE'S K–1 CLASSROOM

Arlene teaches a K–1 split that includes numerous children with late birthdays and others for whom the "school experience" is still too new or just plain bewildering. As Arlene cheerily puts it, "My job is to grow them up." It's a combination of providing strategies for learning and providing success that builds confidence. In Arlene's classroom, children find a world crafted especially for them, filled with colors, plants, mobiles, and light, with real or paper cut-out frogs, fish, beetles, snowmen, bats, cats, and rabbits, hundreds of words, and dozens of books—not to mention cozy corners to sit, ponder, think, read, and write.

"'Kid writing is magic.' That's the very first thing I tell my students. Most of them believe they *can* write—though it doesn't look like traditional writing yet—but a few will say, 'Oh, I can't write.' So I tell them, you can do *this*, can't you, like a bird flying? (See Figure 10.7.) And I model it on the board for them. Sure, they tell me, they can do that. So that's our first writing venture. Then I ask, 'Do you know *any* letters at all? Put them down, and when I come around, you can read your writing to me—and you can also do a picture to go with your writing.' This is where we begin—with the belief that all children can write. The secret, at this young age, is to accept *all forms* of writing as writing. When we accept where children are, they accept where they are—and feel good about themselves.

"The traits give me a structure for teaching; they help keep me organized and focused. I like to start with details—that's the word I use for what the scoring guide calls ideas. We start with pictures. I'm no artist, but I'll draw the outline of a face on the board. 'Now help me with details,' I tell the students. 'Does he need eyes? How do they look? A nose? How big? A mouth? What shape?' And so on. Then, when we're reading, we take time to look at the pictures, and I ask them to point out details to me. We also play the mind movies game, where every sentence adds a detail. I'll tell them, 'Today I saw *something*. I saw a *dog*. It was a *big dog*. It was *big and black with white paws and a curly tail*. I saw a big, black dog with white paws and a curly tail leap right onto the school bus—and eat someone's cheese sandwich!' I just keep adding detail, and they love it, and

> And in our haste to tell young writers how to do things, we forget that merely telling of new concepts doesn't usually lead to learning, and that students best learn what they're ready to learn, itching to learn.
>
> **—Tom Romano**
> *Clearing the Way: Working with Teenage Writers,* 1987, p. 100

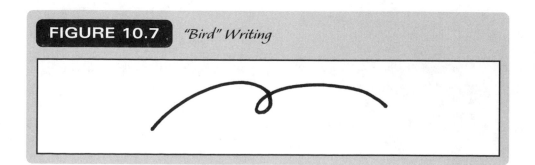

FIGURE 10.7   *"Bird" Writing*

often they help me. If I don't go fast enough, they start asking me questions. We're writing in our minds; we're not always putting it on paper, but we *are* writing.

"Organization, I think, should be taught as a concept. I start with one child's desk. I pull everything out—with the child's permission, of course!—and lay it on a table. Then the kids help me organize it. Then they organize their own desks. When we line up for the bus, I point out to them that we're getting 'organized.' When they come in from recess, I ask them to line up alphabetically—that's organization, too. It soon becomes a very familiar word to them.

"Of course, voice is my favorite trait. I use the word a lot, and not just about writing. When someone comes in with bright colors on, I'll say, 'Wow! That outfit has *voice!*' Soon they're saying it to me. I tell them voice is pizzazz, personality, being *you*. We talk about different voices—how sometimes you talk in a whisper, sometimes you shout or sigh or cry or laugh or scream. And of course, we also listen for voice in all the books we share. One of the moms told me they were driving down the street one day when her daughter said, 'None of those houses have voice, Mom—they're all the same color.' I love it when they teach traits to their parents!

"With word choice, I use my own writing a lot. I ask the children to help me find a better way to say it. '*Cute*,' I'll say, 'boy—I'm tired of that word, aren't you? You hear it *so* much.' I haul the trash can over and rip the word up in front of them and toss it into the can. Then I ask them to help me think of some alternatives and we list them in *big* letters. I use them in my writing and let me tell you, they listen for their words—the ones they suggested.

"For fluency, I read lots of poetry and, of course, we play songs. I encourage the children to snap their fingers or clap to the rhythm—or get up and move. When you feel the rhythm, then you know it's fluent. Of course, many of my children are not yet writing sentences, but they can dictate sentences—then hear them back. That's a kind of writing, too. And we do family journaling, where the parents write, if they're willing. They take down the child's thoughts and send it back to me. I tell them, 'Tonight your parents have homework.' The kids love that. I'll ask the parents to write with the child. For example, sometimes they write about 'George's Adventures'—he's our gorilla mascot, and he goes home over the weekend. Then George and the journal come back on Monday. (See Figure 10.8 for a sample parent-child journal entry.)

"At this age, you need to keep conventions simple. I teach it mainly through modeling. Every day we do a newsletter, which I write in front of them, and I ask lots of questions. The kids decide what's 'news' and they make up all the content—I don't do that part—but I'll say, 'OK, this is the beginning of a new sentence, so what kind of letter do we need? Here's the end of a sentence—should we put a period or exclamation point? That was a question—how do we show that? You use the moment to make a point instead of announcing, 'Today, children, we'll have a lesson on exclamation points.' Yuck. I wouldn't be able to stay awake myself."

Arlene has had her share of nonwriters and reluctant writers. "I had a little girl just last year who announced on the first day, 'I don't write.' I got down on her level, looked her in the eye, and said very simply, 'You know, in this class, we *all* write. Me, too.' She looked right back at me and said, 'OK, then.' And from that day on, she wrote—every single day. And as she could see for herself, we *were*

> *Aim for the stars, not the mud.*
> **—Mem Fox**
> *Radical Reflections*, 1993, p. 58

FIGURE 10.8 *Parent-Child Journal*

March 18

Dear Journal—

George rode home in my backpack, and he was glad to get out and play. We watched "American Gladiators" together, and you could tell it was George's kind of show. I got excited and tossed George in the air, but he said, "Hey, don't be so rough!" so I stopped.

Mom made chicken, baked potatoes, and green salad for dinner. George loved the salad and asked for seconds. After dinner, my friend Kevin tried to feed George some Red-Hots, but George said he'd prefer a banana.

Later, we went to the park to play. George liked the jungle gym best. We went down the slide, but since it was raining, we both got pretty wet. George didn't seem to mind. Later, Mom dried him off with the hair dryer, and gave him a great fluffy look. She offered him a bath, but George said he would rather just watch me.

Buttons our cat loved George and offered to play all night. George said no. I think he got too tired at the park. We slept like rocks. George doesn't snore too loud. Mom fed us both breakfast and a ton of vitamins. Thanks for coming, George!

Troy (and Mom, too)

all writers. A lot of it is expectations. We're afraid to expect too much, and when children sense our fear, it robs them of confidence. If we don't believe they can do brave and wonderful things, why should they believe it?"

IN ANDREA'S MULTIAGE SECOND-LANGUAGE CLASSROOM

Andrea is a specialist in working with second-language students, and her secret is a magical combination of deep respect for students' skills and creative adaptation of the six traits to fit the learning style of someone who is just learning to speak English. Keep it simple is rule one. "My way of adapting the rubrics for non-English or beginning English speakers is to identify the 'key words.' For example, I identify *details* and *main idea* for ideas and development. Students look at those two concepts *only*. We read sample papers and look at the quality of detail and assess if the story/essay sticks to the main point. As the language becomes more familiar, other components of the rubric or trait come in to play."

Andrea is also sensitive to the kinesthetic learning style of many students. "I use many, *many* physical activities. We go on 'digs' around campus, meaning we walk around, collecting words, phrases, and mental pictures of what we see. We put them on index cards, and these cards are later incorporated into dialogue or descriptions or made into found poetry. We listen to music and discuss fluency. We take pictures with disposable cameras and talk about details and 'focus.' We cook a lot to learn new words and to discuss following directions as a kind of organization. Just about any snack that can be made in the microwave or on a burner has been made in my classroom. We organize the classroom in many different configurations, looking for the right way to put it together. Any time there is a physical class or group activity that I can use to introduce or reinforce a trait, I do it."

In addition, Andrea is a whole-hearted believer in the maxim that to become a proficient writer, you must write. "My ESL students write. And write. And write. They write from the first day they arrive. If they have no English skills, they copy a paragraph I have typed out that introduces me and my classroom. If they have some English skills, they practice the act of writing during our writing time. They practice writing their vocabulary words, they practice writing their names in English, if they are not familiar with the alphabet. They never have an excuse not to write. I don't grade it the same, of course, but it is written and turned in and commented on. My philosophy is: If they can write letters, they can learn how to write words. If they can write words, they can learn how to write sentences, and if they can write sentences, they can write *anything*. ESL students can produce written work. They just need some support to get there. Not speaking English is a reason they struggle, but it isn't an excuse not to provide opportunities to stretch them as learners and writers. I provide opportunities to write every day."

To introduce the traits, Andrea doesn't rely on words so much as the concept of categories. "My very first thing is to have students categorize pieces of candy I have given them into six categories, six being their most favorite. This introduces the concept of a rubric and the fact that a six isn't an 'A.'"

Once they have the vocabulary, Andrea comments, second-language students feel that the traits are "easy" to work with. "They don't have to learn a new set of vocabulary for each class. For EL kids, that is a great thing." She also likes the fact that the traits break instruction into manageable bites: "I like the pacing of the six traits; I know that eventually we will focus on transitions, for example, so I don't need to race to get there. Without the traits, I think that I would feel pressure to teach everything about writing every time we wrote, because I would be afraid I'd forget something later. Students are often overwhelmed when they are writing for school . . . and a lot of that comes from the pressure to learn too many complex things at once."

Like many teachers who work with the six traits, Andrea relies heavily on literature to reinforce learning. "I have so many favorites. I use *Esperanza Rising* by Pam Muñoz Ryan to teach symbolism and sentence fluency. It's a great book for every trait.

"I also used the book to help students understand character. I make a journal for each student. On each page was an outline of a girl. I drew lines in her head, next to her feet, and in her body by her heart. For each chapter, the students found quotations that explain the character. In her head, the students wrote the something that she said or thought and the page number. In her heart, students wrote a quotation that showed something she felt, and next to her feet, students wrote something that showed an action, both again with page numbers. At the bottom of the page, the students wrote an assertion about the character, e.g., "Esperanza is very lonely." At the end of the book, students had collected enough quotations to write a response-to-literature essay, and we didn't have to flip through the book looking for quotations to support their thesis." (See Figure 10.9 for a reproduction of Andrea's outline for this literature response lesson.)

One of the things Andrea likes best about using the traits in her instruction is the feeling that it's very natural—that she is not really adding anything new but only organizing what she would be teaching anyway. "One of the most valuable parts of the six traits is the organization component. I don't have to teach everything I know every time I teach writing. I'm able to relax and really focus

FIGURE 10.9   *Thoughts, Feelings, Actions*

Thoughts . . .

Feelings . .

Actions . . .

on each component until I'm sure my students have an understanding of the current trait. Since the traits are so connected, once they understand ideas, they are really on the road to understanding all six traits. Students don't feel overwhelmed and neither do I."

IN SAMMIE'S "TIGER LEARNING CENTER"

Sammie works in an *enrichment room*—a special learning center devoted half to technology (with a computer lab) and half to personalized instruction in reading and writing. The center is well named. Sammie's students *are* tigers— ready to leap on new ideas and devour everything she has to give. Her main problem is time. She has but half an hour with each group (they spend the other half hour in the computer lab), and with a K–5 rotation, she sees each child only once every six days. Therefore, continuity is difficult, and extended lessons do not work well. Everything has to be tied up, package and bow, within 30 minutes. Sammie has found ways to make it work—and to make the six traits flourish. Her children do numerous poems and books, often class books, to which each child can contribute a page. They write paragraphs (they're short), and they tend to focus on known topics (no research required): themselves, their families, their experiences. Sammie regularly uses brief books or portions of books as models.

Pattern books (e.g., Margery Cuyler's *That's Good, That's Bad* and John Burningham's *Mr. Gumpy's Outing*) have been her main-stay. "When it's a pattern the children can see, they can mimic it, and it helps them feel they're doing it. They're writing. Many times they feel they do a better job than the original author, and sometimes, I agree! We do a lot of sharing. The atmosphere is very celebrational. When an author has finished a piece, that's reason to celebrate, to gather around and hear another person's work. We all take pride in what any one of us does.

"I also do a lot of reading. For many of my students it's a totally new experience—being read to. No one has done this with them before. We have a high mobility rate in our area. Many of our students do not regularly converse with their parents—or with *anyone* outside of school. Just talking is hard at first. They haven't had much practice at it. I have many fifth graders—kids practically shaving—who have not heard nursery rhymes before, and *love* them. They love the rhythm and the humor. If we don't attach grade levels to things, we give students the freedom to make choices, and why not? Wouldn't it annoy you if someone pulled a book out of your hands and said to you, 'Oh, you won't like *that*—it's only for 35 and under'?

"I talk traits all the time, right from day one. Fluency is a big trait for us because we use lots of pattern books and lots of poetry— "There Was An Old Woman Who Swallowed a Fly'—that's a favorite with students of all ages. We talk about word choice, too, and keep personal dictionaries. I put lots of words on the walls. And we talk about ideas—what do you picture in your mind? And voice—how does this piece make you feel? I comment on the voice, word choice, and so on in *their* work, too. At first it's just me. But by about the end of the second quarter or the start of the third, they're

> We need to water the desert so that writing will bloom. By watering the desert I mean providing children with the most wonderful lit-erature available: the clas-sics, the new, the beautiful, the revolting, the hysterical, the puzzling, the amazing, the riveting.
>
> **—Mem Fox**
> *Radical Reflections*, 1993, p. 67

> Worksheets do not develop writers who can think for themselves, who can create extended texts, who can be logical, who can use voice or tone, or who can write with power. It is perfectly possible to be able to fill in endless worksheets correctly yet not be able to write a single coherent paragraph, let alone a longer piece of connected prose.
>
> **—Mem Fox**
> *Radical Reflections*, 1993, p. 69

talking traits, too. This is very exciting because at this point they have some built-in, personal way to measure how their writing is changing.

"We do no skill and drill, no worksheets. We write and we read. I want them to love it, and they do. They *want* to come here, that's my goal, and it shows in the work we do together. We're moving all the time. We're moving to the rhythm of what we write. We yell, we beat on the tables. One of the teachers said to me, 'Sammie, I would swear I saw that portable move right up off its block.' Well, that's what teachers are *for*, isn't it? To rock the walls? The most important thing to me is how the kids feel when they leave here. In this room, I want every child to experience success."

CHAPTER 10 IN A NUTSHELL

- Every writing teacher who uses the six traits in his or her instruction finds a personal way of making it work.
- Despite differences, commonalities exist among teachers' instructional approaches, e.g., sharing literature to model examples of strong voice, word choice, or other traits; modeling writing or revision strategies; finding many ways to share and use trait language; keeping individual lessons simple and brief; respecting and expanding students' skills as evaluators; and encouraging students to self-assess.
- Teachers who incorporate the six traits into their instruction need not give up any of the personal instructional strategies they value—such as use of art, focus on literary analysis, or use of kinesthetic activities.

EXTENSIONS

1. How do you see yourself adapting the traits to your own classroom? Would your approach be similar to those discussed in this chapter—or something quite different? Write a journal entry about this.
2. Imagine that you are doing a teacher evaluation for any one of the teachers who speaks in this chapter. Without the advantage of seeing that teacher in action, write a short paragraph summarizing what you believe that teacher does well.
3. Talk or write about ways you could adopt one or more strategies from this chapter to suit your students and your own teaching style.

4. Some of the teachers in this chapter have adapted traits for kinesthetic learners or second-language learners. If you work with such students, what strategies have been successful for you? Share them with colleagues.
5. Do a written analysis of your own teaching style. Who are you as a teacher? What is it like to be in your classroom? What are your teaching strengths? (If you do not yet have a classroom of your own, use your imagination to envision the classroom as you would *like it to be*.)

WHY I WRITE

Writing is like painting a picture for me. Every color is a different letter. In your mind you have to picture what your masterpiece is going to look like. Then you put all those colors together. . . . Most of the time your inspirations come when you least expect it, like in a dream or when you are actually listening in math class. When you get your story in your mind and onto your paper, it can be a work of art, worth sharing with the whole world—or at least your parents.

—Stephanie Harris, student

WHY I TEACH THE SIX TRAITS

Each year I am amazed at how empowered my students become in working with the traits. They not only have a clear understanding of what makes effective writing, they become much more able to self-evaluate and be reflective of their own work. Through use of the traits, my students have been able to make meaningful revisions that greatly enhance the quality of their own work—and all this without ME as their primary guide! There is no question in my mind that the six traits of writing help to create independent, self-directed writers.

—Jennifer Wallace
Grade 4 Teacher, Bellevue, Washington

The writing traits are just the right tools. They just make sense—to teachers and to students. They provide that common language that moves the writer through brainstorming to assessment with such continuity. I think the reason the traits are so successful in my classroom is that they're concrete and practical—and they can easily be found beyond the classroom. If I am talking about voice, my students don't just write with voice . . . they wear clothes that have voice, they demonstrate voice with their hair. They even find voice in the cafeteria lunch!

—Peggy Fox
High School Teacher, Lee, New Hampshire

LOOKING AHEAD

In Chapter 11 we will consider ways of adapting the traits to fit your curriculum.

11 Adapting the Traits to Fit You

*W*hat if the scoring guide does not cover all the things you wish to emphasize in teaching writing? Say you are a biology or history teacher or you wish to focus primarily on literary analysis. Can you adapt the scoring guide to meet those needs? Absolutely. Countless adaptations are possible, and you should modify this or any scoring guide so that it will serve you and your students well. Lucy McCormick Calkins (1994), in fact, suggests that published rubrics are often most useful as "starting points from which we make our own rubrics" (p. 325).

THE SIMPLEST ADAPTATION: BEING SELECTIVE
- *From Biology . . .*

Just because there are six traits in the model, this does *not* mean that you have to give every paper six scores every time. For a particular writing assignment on how species adapt to environmental factors, you might wish to emphasize clear ideas, good organization, appropriate use of correct scientific terminology—and, perhaps, conventional correctness.

■ *To Geometry . . .*

Or suppose that you are asking students to determine how many different ways rectangular shapes can be combined to create a design for a one-story building. You want them to write an explanation of each step in their thinking process. For this assignment, you might choose to focus primarily on ideas (clarity), organization (steps in order), word choice (correct mathematical terminology), and conventions (including mathematical symbols).

■ *Or Global Studies . . .*

Suppose that you are asking students to write an editorial piece reflecting conditions in South Africa from the 1990s through the early twenty-first century. You might wish to emphasize ideas (understanding of the context and important issues) and voice (ability to reach and influence an audience).

Weighting

If you do not feel comfortable letting go of any trait altogether, try what many teachers have done: Weight the traits according to emphasis. For instance, suppose that students are involved in a group project designing a newspaper that might have been sold in London in the 1800s. What is important here? Knowledge of life in that time, certainly, but also an ear for language, including sentence fluency and vocabulary. In addition, some knowledge of nineteenth-century English writing conventions and newspaper layout. For this assignment (let's say that it's worth 100 points total), perhaps the traits would be weighted this way:

Ideas: 25

Organization: 10

Voice: 10

Word choice: 20

Sentence fluency: 10

Conventions and presentation: 25

You might weight them differently. That's fine. Just be sure your weightings give students a clear picture of what you consider critical.

SIMPLICITY ITSELF: THE CHECKLIST

Because it does not define performance level by level, a checklist is not as useful for *assessment* as a scoring guide (rubric)—but it's highly useful in guiding revision. See Figures 11.1 and 11.2 for copies of student informational writing checklists (one for older students, one for younger writers).

FIGURE 11.1   *Checklist for Informational Writing*

_____ At the center of the writing is a problem to be solved or a question to be answered.

_____ The writer uses various kinds of details (examples, anecdotes, facts, quotations) to provide elaborate and varied support for key points.

_____ Information seems thorough, relevant, and authentic/accurate, leading the reader to trust the writer.

_____ The text teaches the reader; it provides new or important information.

_____ The writer does not try to tell everything about the topic but keeps the writing focused on a key issue or question.

_____ Terminology is used with care and accuracy; technical terms are explained.

_____ Sources are cited as necessary.

Other Specialized Checklists

What about other genres? Let's say that you want your students to include certain key elements in narrative or persuasive writing. Could a checklist communicate that? Absolutely. The following three checklists are not set up trait by trait; rather, they capture, in a holistic way, some key elements of three genres: narrative writing (Figures 11.3 and 11.4), persuasive writing (Figures 11.5 and 11.6), and literary analysis (Figures 11.7 and 11.8). As I noted previously, a checklist does *not* take the place of rubrics for *assessment* purposes, but it makes a very useful reminder for students as they are creating or revising a piece, especially for students who know the basic six traits.

No matter what scoring guide or checklist you use, the important thing is to make sure that it gives students an exact picture—a vision—of what you are looking for.

FIGURE 11.2   *Simple Informational Checklist*

_____ Based on a key question or problem

_____ Filled with details: examples, anecdotes, facts, or quotations

_____ Correct information

_____ Teaches the reader something

_____ Tells what is most important

_____ Explains difficult terms/words

_____ Lists sources

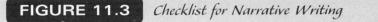

FIGURE 11.3   *Checklist for Narrative Writing*

____ This piece is a story, not a list of events. It has purpose and direction; there is a reason for the telling.

____ At the center of the writing is a problem to be solved, a conflict to be resolved, or a burning question to answer.

____ The main character in this piece (who might be the writer) grows, changes, or learns something as the story unfolds.

____ There is a turning point: a point of change, discovery, or maximum conflict.

____ A strong lead sets up the story and gets the reader engaged.

____ Events unfold in a natural, but not always predictable, way.

____ Characters are real, not cardboard cutouts. They have feelings, emotions, and motivations. They do things for a reason.

____ Dialogue, if used, sounds authentic, like real people talking. It has a purpose: to reveal character, advance the action, or influence the mood of the story.

____ The ending (resolution) ties up the story in a satisfying way. It may offer a surprise and may look ahead to what's coming next— or tell something a character has learned.

FIGURE 11.4   *Simple Narrative Checklist*

____ A *story*, not just a list of "things that happened"

____ Solves a problem, answers a question

____ Main character grows, changes, or learns something

____ A turning point: change, discovery, conflict

____ Characters seem real

____ Dialogue sounds real

____ Strong lead sets it up

____ One thing leads to another

____ Ending wraps things up

FIGURE 11.5 *Checklist for Persuasive Writing*

____ The writing takes the reader on a journey of understanding through an issue or set of issues.

____ The writer makes his or her position clear from the outset and sticks with that position.

____ The writer's main position (argument) is supported by evidence: facts, statistics, studies, quotations from experts, personal observations and conclusions.

____ The writer does not rely on opinion as <u>evidence</u> (e.g., *This is true because I think so.*).

____ The writer cites multiple reliable sources to make an argument convincing.

____ The paper summarizes clearly, fairly, and thoroughly any opposing points of view and addresses these in a clear and convincing manner.

____ The writer's voice is strong, confident, and compelling—but not angry, hysterical, overbearing, or sarcastic.

____ Usually, the writer saves the strongest argument (or piece of evidence) for last, where it has maximum impact.

____ The writer leads the reader to a conclusion that seems all but inevitable given the evidence presented and lays that conclusion out clearly.

____ At the end, if the paper has been successful, the reader understands the issues thoroughly and feels prepared to take his or her own position.

FIGURE 11.6 *Simple Persuasive Checklist*

____ Helps reader think through issues

____ Writer's position clear

____ Not *just* opinion

____ Offers *evidence:* facts, quotations, observations

____ Cites believable sources

____ Explains why others might not agree

____ Voice is confident, not angry

____ Saves strongest argument for last

____ Helps reader to make up his or her mind

FIGURE 11.7 *Checklist for Literary Analysis*

____ The paper is more than a summary of the plot.

____ The writing makes a key point (or points) relating to a work's theme, language, character development, style, or significance in light of important values or social issues.

____ Each major point is supported by direct references to the work itself and/or by quotations from that work.

____ In addition, the writer may quote professional writings that include commentary on this same work.

____ The writer may also connect this work to his or her personal experience, or research, agreeing or disagreeing with the author's major themes or points of view.

____ As appropriate, the writer shares personal responses to the work, but these *do not take the place of* commentary on theme, character, style, language, or social significance.

____ The writer may enrich the analysis by comparing this work to another by the same author or to a similar work by a different author.

____ The analysis may also be enriched through comments on the author's effectiveness *as a writer:* e.g., providing examples of the author's voice, word choice, sentence fluency, use of detail, or organizational approach.

FIGURE 11.8 *Simple Literary Analysis Checklist*

____ More than a plot summary

____ Makes a point about theme, language, character development, style, or importance of the work

____ Quotations from the work support key points

____ Writer connects this work to personal experience

____ Writer may share personal response to the work

____ Writer may compare this work to another, similar piece of writing

____ Writer may comment on the author's voice, word choice, sentence fluency, detail, or organization

SCORING GUIDES

Before the Internet, the secret to good research writing was getting our hands on *The Book* (there was always one main book that held all the critical information, remember?). Because they only seemed to order one copy per library, someone else nearly always got to it first. Then the librarian would patiently explain that *The Book* was checked out for two weeks—or some period that matched *exactly* the time available to complete the research.

These days, *finding* information is not the problem. The challenge lies in sorting through the warehouses of data we have collected to discover what is significant and then synthesizing and presenting it in a way that will engage and enlighten an audience. Teachers need an analytical scoring guide to match what they'd like to see in good informational writing. Here it is in six- and five-point versions, with student rubrics to accompany each (see Figures 11.9 through 11.12). These scoring guides will work well with informational, technical, persuasive, analytical, or business writing.

FIGURE 11.9 *Teacher Six-Point Informational Writing Guide*

TEACHER 6-POINT INFORMATIONAL WRITING GUIDE

IDEAS

6
- ☐ Clear, focused, explicit thesis. Expansively answers well-defined question.
- ☐ Takes reader on a journey of understanding.
- ☐ Writer pulls info from multiple sources.
- ☐ Accurate, relevant, helpful support gives weight to main idea.

5
- ☐ Clear, focused, explicit thesis.
- ☐ Gives reader important, useful information.
- ☐ Writer pulls info from more than one source.
- ☐ Strong support lends credibility to main idea.

4
- ☐ Identifiable thesis.
- ☐ Mixes new information with general knowledge.
- ☐ Research combined with personal beliefs.
- ☐ Gaps in support leave reader with questions.

3
- ☐ Thesis can be inferred with careful reading.
- ☐ Writer knows enough to write in broad terms.
- ☐ Limited research. Writer relies heavily on personal knowledge.
- ☐ Sketchy evidence/support hurts credibility.

2
- ☐ Reader can mentally construct an emerging thesis.
- ☐ Writer not at home with topic, scrambling for things to say.
- ☐ Random thoughts combined with popular beliefs.
- ☐ Evidence/support not helpful to someone who does not know the topic.

1
- ☐ No thesis yet. Topic/question undefined.
- ☐ Writer has no information from which to write.
- ☐ No research to provide a knowledge base.
- ☐ Minimal or unrelated details. Reader can't tell what the message is.

ORGANIZATION

6
- ☐ Design guides reader through the text, shadows writer's thinking.
- ☐ Lead gives reader mindset for discussion, conclusion feels just right.
- ☐ Structure directs and supports reader's growing understanding.
- ☐ Transitions clarify significant connections, give the piece cohesiveness.

5
- ☐ Design supports development of thesis/argument.
- ☐ Lead introduces topic, conclusion provides closure.
- ☐ Structure makes text easy to follow.
- ☐ Transitions provide important connections.

4
- ☐ Design fits harmoniously with purpose and content.
- ☐ Lead alludes to main topic, conclusion signals end of discussion.
- ☐ Structure helps reader keep track of main points.
- ☐ Transitions hint at connections—reader must help build bridges.

3
- ☐ Design not always a smooth fit with discussion/argument.
- ☐ Recognizable lead/conclusion.
- ☐ Structure present, but reader must pause, or re-read.
- ☐ Transitions more formulaic than reflective of underlying connections.

2
- ☐ Design seems at odds with writer's presentation.
- ☐ Lead/conclusion missing, formulaic, or not closely aligned with text.
- ☐ Structure too formulaic **or** hard to follow—reader works around it.
- ☐ Transitions missing, puzzling, or not helpful.

1
- ☐ No recognizable design or pattern. Writing is random.
- ☐ No real lead or conclusion—writing just starts, then stops abruptly.
- ☐ Structure is loose, disjointed, unrelated to the ideas.
- ☐ Nothing seems connected to anything else.

FIGURE 11.9 *continued*

TEACHER 6-POINT INFORMATIONAL WRITING GUIDE

WORD CHOICE

6 ☐☐☐☐
- Explicit, memorable words make message clear, sometimes quotable.
- Writer knows the language of the content area—uses it with ease and skill.
- Powerful verbs give writing energy, well chosen phrases add precision.
- Text free of wordiness, jargon, tired phrases, vague language.

5 ☐☐☐☐
- Carefully chosen words make message clear, interesting.
- The writer knows the language of the content area—uses it correctly.
- Strong verbs give writing energy, well chosen phrases lend clarity.
- Minimal wordiness, jargon, tired phrases, vague language.

4 ☐☐☐☐
- Functional language makes message reasonably clear.
- Writer familiar with language of content area, uses most terms correctly.
- Occasional strong verbs or "just right" phrases.
- Wordiness, jargon, and vague language not problematic.

3 ☐☐☐☐
- Imprecise, vague language begins to cloud message.
- Some important terminology used incorrectly or omitted when needed.
- Strong verbs, "just right" words or phrases infrequent.
- Problems with wordiness, jargon, vague language—message gets through.

2 ☐☐☐☐
- Generalities, vague words, or misused words create confusion.
- Writer lacks language to make message clear/effective.
- Word choice ambiguous, puzzling, or *so* general it lacks meaning.
- Wordiness, jargon, or vague language impair meaning.

1 ☐☐☐☐
- Words create no clear message.
- Words are misused or not meaningful—what is the writer trying to say?
- Writer consistently chooses words or phrases that do not speak to readers.
- Reader struggles but cannot break the code.

VOICE

6 ☐☐☐☐
- Professional, enthusiastic voice, well-suited to audience/purpose.
- Voice welcomes readers into the discussion.
- Confident tone reflects knowledge, inspires the reader's trust.
- Writer's clear enthusiasm for the topic grabs readers by the lapels.

5 ☐☐☐☐
- Professional, sincere voice, well-suited to audience/purpose.
- Voice reaches out to readers. You can hear the writer in the piece.
- Confident tone makes readers open to the message.
- Writer seems engaged by the topic.

4 ☐☐☐☐
- Sincere and appropriate, but inconsistent voice.
- Writer speaks to readers, then retreats behind lists or facts.
- Confidence appears in spurts, reflects variable knowledge of subject.
- Enthusiastic moments encourage readers to hang in.

3 ☐☐☐☐
- Voice out of balance—too little or too much of the wrong voice.
- Writer rarely speaks to readers.
- Writer projects limited confidence in his/her knowledge of the topic.
- Lack of engagement encourages readers to mentally "drift."

2 ☐☐☐☐
- Voice sounds distant, encyclopedic—or too chatty for purpose/audience.
- Writer makes little effort to engage readers—and often loses them.
- Serious lack of confidence suppresses voice.
- Readers must work to pay attention.

1 ☐☐☐☐
- Voice decidedly inappropriate or just a faint whisper.
- No one is at home in this writing.
- Writer does not know or like topic—writing to get it done.
- Lack of voice leaves readers feeling shut out.

FIGURE 11.9 *continued*

TEACHER 6-POINT INFORMATIONAL WRITING GUIDE

SENTENCE FLUENCY

6 ☐☐☐
- Sentences consistently clear, direct, and to the point.
- Text graceful, yet designed for rapid, easy reading.
- Purposeful beginnings (*Another point . . .*) provide natural, effective connections.
☐
- Varied length and structure enhance readability.

5 ☐☐☐☐
- Sentences clear and direct.
- Smooth phrasing enhances readability.
- Purposeful beginnings often connect sentences.
☐
- Varied length and structure add interest.

4 ☐☐☐☐
- Sentences generally clear and readable.
- Smooth phrasing outweighs awkward moments.
- Occasional transitional phrases—some repeated beginnings.
☐
- Writer avoids extremes of long or short.

3 ☐☐☐☐
- Sentences come clear with careful reading.
- Awkward moments outweigh smooth phrasing.
- Few helpful transitions, many repetitious beginnings.
☐
- Some never-ending or choppy sentences.

2 ☐☐☐☐
- Confusing structure demands re-reading.
- Awkward moments slow reader significantly.
- Beginnings repetitious or hard to spot.
☐
- Long, tangly sentences, awkward moments, or choppy sentences typical.

1 ☐☐☐☐
- Confusing structure obscures meaning.
- Can be read aloud only by mentally editing, filling in.
- Very hard to tell where sentences begin and end.
☐
- Irregular word patterns, extreme choppiness, or endlessly connected clauses, phrases.

CONVENTIONS & PRESENTATION

6 ☐☐☐
- Only the pickiest editors will spot errors.
- Thoroughly edited—conventions enhance meaning, voice.
- Sources correctly cited.
☐
- *Optional:* Enticing layout highlights key points.
- Virtually ready to publish.

5 ☐☐☐☐
- Minor errors—that are easily overlooked.
- Edited—conventions support meaning, voice.
- Sources correctly cited.
☐
- *Optional:* Pleasing layout guides reader's eye to main points.
- Ready to publish with light touch-ups.

4 ☐☐☐☐
- Noticeable errors—they do not affect message.
- Edited for general readability.
- Sources cited—light corrections needed.
☐
- *Optional:* Layout adequate for purpose.
- Good once-over needed prior to publication.

3 ☐☐☐☐
- Noticeable, distracting errors may slow reading, affect message.
- Erratic editing—many things missed.
- Citations need re-checking.
☐
- *Optional:* Problems with layout (e.g., print too small).
- Thorough, careful editing needed prior to publication.

2 ☐☐☐☐
- Frequent, distracting errors impair clarity, slow reader.
- Minimal editing—reader must do most of the work.
- Citations missing or faulty.
☐
- *Optional:* Serious problems with layout (e.g., hard-to-read fonts).
- Line-by-line editing needed prior to publication.

1 ☐☐☐☐
- Message hidden under serious, frequent errors.
- Even patient readers must struggle to "get it."
- Sources not cited.
☐
- *Optional:* No apparent attention to layout.
- Word-by-word editing needed prior to publication.

FIGURE 11.10   *Student Six-Point Informational Writing Guide*

STUDENT 6-POINT INFORMATIONAL WRITING GUIDE

IDEAS

6
- ☐ I keep my thesis or key question focused and state it clearly.
- ☐ I have an insider's thorough understanding of this topic.
- ☐ I pulled information from several sources.
- ☐ Complete, reliable support makes my main points credible.

5
- ☐ I state my thesis or key question clearly.
- ☐ I know this topic and offer the reader important information.
- ☐ I pulled information from more than one source.
- ☐ Evidence makes my main points believable.

4
- ☐ You can tell what my thesis is, even if I do not state it.
- ☐ My writing is a mix of new information and things I knew before.
- ☐ I did *some* research—but also wrote what I thought.
- ☐ I have *some* support for my ideas—you might have questions.

3
- ☐ If you read carefully, you will figure out my thesis (I think).
- ☐ I wasn't really comfortable with this topic.
- ☐ I didn't do much research. I relied on things I had heard.
- ☐ I only have a little support for my main points.

2
- ☐ My thesis is still coming together.
- ☐ I don't know much about this topic at all—help!
- ☐ This is mostly a collection of random thoughts—no research.
- ☐ My evidence will only convince you if you agree with me.

1
- ☐ You can't tell what my main point is—and I do not know either.
- ☐ My paper doesn't say much—I didn't have any information.
- ☐ I couldn't do research without a topic!
- ☐ This writing is detail-free.

ORGANIZATION

6
- ☐ My organization will guide you like a light in the dark.
- ☐ My lead invites you in, my conclusion leaves you thinking.
- ☐ The more you read, the more you'll understand.
- ☐ I show very clearly how each idea connects to others.

5
- ☐ My organization will help you make sense of the ideas.
- ☐ My lead invites you in, my conclusion wraps things up.
- ☐ The organization makes my thoughts easy to follow.
- ☐ I connect ideas to each other—or to a big picture.

4
- ☐ The organization works fine for this kind of writing.
- ☐ My lead gets the discussion started, my ending shows it's over.
- ☐ The organization keeps you from getting lost or off-track.
- ☐ I show some connections between ideas.

3
- ☐ I'm not sure the organization fits my discussion.
- ☐ My lead and conclusion could be stronger.
- ☐ You may need to re-read to figure out what's most important.
- ☐ I just followed a formula to connect ideas: e.g., *My first point . . . .*

2
- ☐ This organization is not working—*is there a pattern?*
- ☐ I forgot a lead/conclusion—OR it's one everybody uses.
- ☐ It's often hard to follow what I'm saying.
- ☐ I did not try to connect ideas—I'm not sure how.

1
- ☐ My writing is random. It has no pattern. Lights are out.
- ☐ I don't have a lead or conclusion. I just start in—then I stop.
- ☐ It roams from point to point—like a list or notes.
- ☐ Nothing is connected to anything else.

FIGURE 11.10 *continued*

STUDENT 6-POINT INFORMATIONAL WRITING GUIDE

VOICE

6
- My voice is professional and enthusiastic—just right.
- My voice speaks to my readers, pulling them into the conversation.
- I feel confident that my message is important and interesting.
- I like this topic—and want you to like it, too.

5
- My voice is professional and sincere—it suits my audience/purpose.
- I reach out to the reader. You can hear me in the writing.
- Knowing my topic helps me sound confident.
- I like this topic—you probably will, too.

4
- My voice is sincere—and appropriate for my audience/purpose.
- I reach out to the reader sometimes—sometimes not.
- I sound confident in those parts I'm sure about.
- I like this topic all right—most of the time.

3
- I can't seem to hit the right balance—too little voice, or the wrong voice.
- My voice either fades away—or takes over.
- I don't feel very confident about this topic—can you tell?
- I have to work hard at sounding enthusiastic.

2
- My voice sounds cold or bored—or way too chatty.
- Readers? I didn't really think about readers.
- I don't hear much confidence, either.
- I don't like this topic much. Good luck paying attention!

1
- I don't hear any voice, OR the voice is just wrong for this paper.
- This doesn't speak to readers.
- I don't have *any* confidence about this message. I just wrote to get done.
- I really don't care if anyone reads this.

WORD CHOICE

6
- My words are vivid and memorable. Every word enhances the message.
- I felt very comfortable with technical terms and used them well.
- I chose strong verbs and words/phrases you might underline, even quote.
- You will not find ANY wordiness, jargon, or vague language.

5
- My word choice makes the message clear.
- I know the language that goes with this topic and used it correctly.
- Look for lively verbs and words/phrases you might underline.
- No serious problems with wordiness, jargon, or vague language.

4
- My words are clear and functional. They get the job done.
- If I used any technical terms, I'm pretty sure they are correct.
- I put in some strong verbs. You might underline a word or two.
- Problems with wordiness, jargon, or vague language are not serious.

3
- Some vague words are clouding up my message. You'll still get the general idea.
- I tried to use terms correctly—I didn't always know the right word.
- Those "just right" words and strong verbs? I don't have enough.
- You might notice some problems with wordiness or jargon.

2
- Many words are unclear.
- I couldn't seem to come up with the right words to say what I meant.
- You'd have to hunt for strong verbs—or a phrase you might remember.
- My writing is wordy. Or I used too many vague words.

1
- These words do not make sense to me.
- I think readers will be *very* confused.
- I just put words down—whether they created a message or not.
- My writing is wordy or vague. *I* can't even tell what I meant.

FIGURE 11.10 *continued*

STUDENT 6-POINT INFORMATIONAL WRITING GUIDE

SENTENCE FLUENCY

6
- ☐ My sentences are clear, direct, and to the point. You get the meaning at once.
- ☐ I made sure you could read it quickly—*and* easily.
- ☐ My sentence beginnings are varied and show how ideas connect.
- ☐ I varied sentence length, but avoided extremes of long or short.

5
- ☐ My sentences are clear and direct.
- ☐ Smooth phrasing makes it readable.
- ☐ My sentence beginnings often show how ideas connect.
- ☐ I avoided sentences that were overly long or uncomfortably short.

4
- ☐ My sentences are generally clear and readable.
- ☐ Most are smooth—with just an awkward moment or two.
- ☐ Some beginnings are repetitious. I used connecting phrases, though.
- ☐ I avoided extremes of long or short, but sentence length does not vary.

3
- ☐ Most of my sentences come clear when you read carefully.
- ☐ Unfortunately, the awkward moments outweigh the smooth ones.
- ☐ Many beginnings are repetitious. I forgot connecting phrases.
- ☐ I have some long, gangly sentences or choppy sentences.

2
- ☐ When I read this aloud, it is a bumpy ride!
- ☐ There are enough awkward moments to slow a reader down.
- ☐ I can't always tell where sentences begin.
- ☐ I'm overrun by gangly, awkward, or choppy sentences.

1
- ☐ I'm not sure these are sentences. This writing hides the meaning.
- ☐ You can only read this aloud if you fill in words and make changes.
- ☐ It's very hard to tell where my sentences begin and end.
- ☐ My sentences are confusing, choppy, or tough to get through.

CONVENTIONS & PRESENTATION

6
- ☐ Only the pickiest editors will spot errors.
- ☐ My conventions bring out meaning and voice.
- ☐ I cited all sources correctly.
- ☐ *Optional:* I used layout creatively to guide the reader's eye to key points.
- ☐ This is ready to publish—no "mental editing" needed.

5
- ☐ I have some minor errors—they're hardly noticeable.
- ☐ My conventions support meaning and voice.
- ☐ I cited sources as needed.
- ☐ *Optional:* Pleasing layout guides the reader's eye to main points.
- ☐ This is ready to publish with light touch-ups.

4
- ☐ You might find some errors, but the message is clear.
- ☐ I have proofed this text; I should look again, though.
- ☐ I might need to correct some citations.
- ☐ *Optional:* The layout is OK for the purpose.
- ☐ Some light editing is all that's needed.

3
- ☐ You will notice errors—and they *might* slow you down.
- ☐ I did not proof carefully—I missed too many things.
- ☐ I need to re-check my citations.
- ☐ *Optional:* I have some problems with layout (e.g., print too small).
- ☐ This needs thorough editing before I publish it.

2
- ☐ The errors jump out at you. They get in the way of the message.
- ☐ This does not look edited—I left all the work to the reader.
- ☐ I'm not sure I cited all sources—or did it right.
- ☐ *Optional:* I have serious problems with layout (e.g., no margins).
- ☐ I need to edit this line by line before publishing.

1
- ☐ Too many serious errors make my message hard to decode.
- ☐ Even patient readers probably won't "get it."
- ☐ I forgot citations completely.
- ☐ *Optional:* Layout? I didn't worry about that.
- ☐ I need to edit word by word before publishing.

FIGURE 11.11   *Teacher Five-Point Informational Writing Guide*

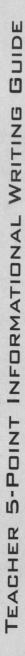

TEACHER 5-POINT INFORMATIONAL WRITING GUIDE

IDEAS & DEVELOPMENT

5 *The paper is clear, focused, and purposeful. It answers a well-defined key question in understandable, convincing, expansive terms.*

- The main idea, thesis, or research question is clearly defined. The paper is not simply a list of thoughts.
- The writer pulls information from multiple sources (experience, research, reading, interviews) to enrich detail and provide credibility.
- The writer continuously anticipates and responds to readers' informational needs.
- Supporting details (examples, facts, anecdotes, quotations) are accurate, relevant, and helpful.

3 *The paper addresses an identifiable key question by offering the reader general, basic information.*

- The reader can infer the main thesis or research question.
- Some information seems grounded in solid research or experience.
- Some seems based on common knowledge or best guesses.
- The writer sometimes responds to readers' informational needs. Yet, some important questions are left hanging.
- More knowledge, stronger support, and greater attention to detail would strengthen this paper.

1 *The writer has not yet clarified an important issue or research question. One or more of these problems is evident:*

- The writer has not yet defined a thesis or research question.
- Information is sketchy, limited, vague, or questionable.
- The reader is left with numerous questions.
- This paper would not be helpful to someone who did not already know the topic well.

ORGANIZATION

5 *A strong internal structure showcases main ideas, leading readers right to key points or important conclusions.*

- The lead engages readers and offers clues about what is coming.
- The order of details promotes readers' understanding/interest.
- Purposeful transitions help a reader see the big picture.
- The closing reinforces earlier concepts or resolves questions.

3 *Readers can follow most of what the writer says, but they may need to make some leaps or connections.*

- The introduction may be formulaic (*In this paper I will explain . . .*) or just slow in coming to the point.
- The order of information is sometimes helpful to the reader's understanding, and sometimes confusing.
- Ideas are not always clearly connected; the reader may wonder why a detail is included.
- The conclusion is recognizable, but may not provide a sense of resolution.

1 *Lack of organizational structure leaves readers confused. One or more of these problems is evident:*

- There is no real lead; the paper just begins.
- The reader struggles to see a pattern that is not there. The random order makes it is hard to keep track of the information.
- Missing connections make it hard to follow the writer's thinking.
- There is no real conclusion; the paper just stops.

FIGURE 11.11 *continued*

TEACHER 5-POINT INFORMATIONAL WRITING GUIDE

VOICE

5 *The writer uses a voice appropriate for topic, purpose, and audience.*
- The writer's confidence, authority, and enthusiasm for the topic are evident throughout the piece.
- The writer consistently draws the audience into the discussion, showing concern for their understanding.
- The reader finds him/herself caught up in the topic, regardless of previous interest or knowledge.
- In business or technical pieces, voice is professional and controlled, never overshadowing the message.

3 *The writer projects a voice that is sincere and generally appropriate for topic and audience.*
- The writer's confidence and enthusiasm intermingle with a more prosaic, encyclopedic voice.
- The writer sometimes—not always—reaches out to the audience.
- When voice fades, the reader must work to remain engaged.
- In business or technical pieces, voice may sometimes be too informal or personal, though it is not a serious distraction.

1 *The voice is missing or inappropriate for the topic, audience, or both. One or more of the following problems is evident:*
- The writer seems indifferent to the topic—or just anxious to be done with it. The enthusiasm needed to bring the topic to life is missing.
- The writer does not reach out to the audience—and may even write more to show off specialized knowledge than to engage or inform readers.
- The reader must work hard to stay engaged with the text.
- In business or technical pieces, an inappropriately informal voice becomes distracting.

WORD CHOICE & TERMINOLOGY

5 *Well-chosen words convey the writer's message in a clear, precise way, taking readers to a new level of understanding.*
- Consistently, the writer chooses words and phrases that will help a reader make sense of and remember important concepts.
- The writer uses the language of the territory with skill and ease.
- Language is thoughtfully chosen to suit subject and audience.
- Technical or little-known words are clarified or defined.
- The writing is clear and concise.

3 *Words are reasonably clear but not sufficiently precise to convey more than a general message.*
- Most language is functional; it is not always enlightening enough to take readers beyond the "big picture" level.
- The writer occasionally seems uncomfortable with the language of the content area.
- Vocabulary is sometimes well-matched to subject and audience, sometimes not.
- An occasional technical term goes undefined.
- Some deadwood could be cut.

1 *The language does not speak to the audience or enhance their understanding of the topic. One or more of the following problems is evident:*
- The writing is impenetrable and speaks *only* to insiders—OR, it is too vague to carry the writer's message.
- A limited vocabulary makes it hard for the writer to explore the subject in depth.
- Overall, the language does not suit the topic or audience.
- Undefined technical terms or jargon leave the reader on the outside looking in.
- Wordiness slows the reader down or smothers the message.

FIGURE 11.11 *continued*

TEACHER 5-POINT INFORMATIONAL WRITING GUIDE

SENTENCE FLUENCY

5 *Sentences are strong, clear, and skillfully structured to make reading fast and simple.*
- Meaningful sentence beginnings (*Then, Therefore, In contrast, To summarize*) lend variety and clarity to text.
- While sentences vary in length, most are compact.
- Meaning is clear with the first reading.
- The direct style makes text easy to interpret.

3 *Sentences are reasonably clear and complete.*
- Meaningful sentence beginnings sometimes help readers connect ideas.
- Some sentence variety is evident. A few sentences may be overly long and complex.
- Meaning is not always clear with a single reading: e.g., *The legislature is voting to re-enact road construction in the spring.* Text can be interpreted with careful attention.

1 *Sentences tend to be unclear or awkward. One or more of these problems is evident:*
- The writer rarely uses meaningful sentence beginnings to link ideas.
- Some sentences are so long and tangled the reader loses the thought—or so short and choppy the reader feels bumped along.
- Meaning is not always clear even with careful re-reading.
- Text is difficult to read and interpret.

CONVENTIONS & PRESENTATION

5 *The writer demonstrates a good grasp of standard writing conventions and uses them to enhance readability.*
- Basic conventions are virtually error-free.
- Conventions enhance meaning and voice.
- Informational sources are correctly, thoroughly cited.
- The layout of the text is appealing, given audience and purpose.
- Titles, subtitles, bullets, or other visual conventions guide the reader's eye to key points.
- Charts, graphs, or illustrations (if used) are helpful and relevant.

3 *The writer demonstrates a basic understanding of many writing conventions.*
- Errors in basic conventions are noticeable but do not seriously impair readability.
- Conventions often support the message and voice.
- Sources are cited, though citations may need work.
- The basic layout of the text is acceptable for audience and purpose.
- Visual conventions sometimes help readers locate information.
- Charts, graphs, or other illustrations may or may not be helpful.

1 *The writer demonstrates limited understanding of many writing conventions. One or more of these problems is evident.*
- Errors in basic conventions impair readability.
- Conventions make it hard to interpret the message and voice.
- Citations are missing, incomplete, or incorrectly formatted.
- The general layout does not work in harmony with the message.
- Visual conventions are needed to make "print-dense" copy more inviting or clear.
- Charts, graphs, or other illustrations are not clearly connected to text.

FIGURE 11.12   *Student Five-Point Informational Writing Guide*

STUDENT 5-POINT INFORMATIONAL WRITING GUIDE

IDEAS & DEVELOPMENT

5 *My paper is clear, focused, and purposeful. It answers a key question in an understandable, convincing way.*

- I make my main idea, thesis, or research question very clear.
- I pulled information from several sources, such as personal experience, research, reading, or interviews.
- I thought about my readers all the way through, and tried to answer their questions.
- You can tell by my examples, facts, anecdotes, or quotations that I have thought about this topic and know it thoroughly.

3 *My paper addresses a key question and gives the reader general, basic information.*

- A reader can easily figure out my main thesis or research question.
- Some of my information comes from research or experience. Some comes from common knowledge or my best guess.
- I tried to think about questions readers might have. I probably left some things unanswered.
- If I knew more about this topic or had done more research, the paper would be stronger.

1 *I don't really have a thesis or research question yet. My paper has problems:*

- It's a list of my first thoughts.
- My information is sketchy, limited, and vague—or not backed by research.
- A reader would be left with numerous questions.
- I doubt this paper would be helpful to someone who did not know the topic well.

ORGANIZATION

5 *My organization is strong and showcases ideas the way a display window showcases merchandise.*

- My lead hooks readers and gives them clues about what's coming.
- I arranged my discussion so it would be interesting and easy to follow.
- Ideas are clearly connected. You can see how they relate to each other or to a larger idea.
- My closing answers a reader's questions and points to logical conclusions.

3 *I think most readers can follow what I am saying most of the time.*

- My lead is an old standard, like *In this paper I will explain* . . . Or, it takes me a while to come to the point.
- My organization is sometimes helpful, sometimes confusing. I tend to repeat information. Or wander down a few side trails!
- My ideas are not always connected. Sometimes, you need to make the connection yourself.
- I have a conclusion. It won't tie up all the loose ends, though!

1 *My organization is confusing, even to me. My paper has one or more of these problems:*

- I don't have a real lead; the paper just begins in the middle of things.
- No matter how hard you try, you can't make this information fit any pattern.
- Because ideas are not connected, it's hard to follow my thinking.
- There is no real conclusion; the paper just stops.

FIGURE 11.12 *continued*

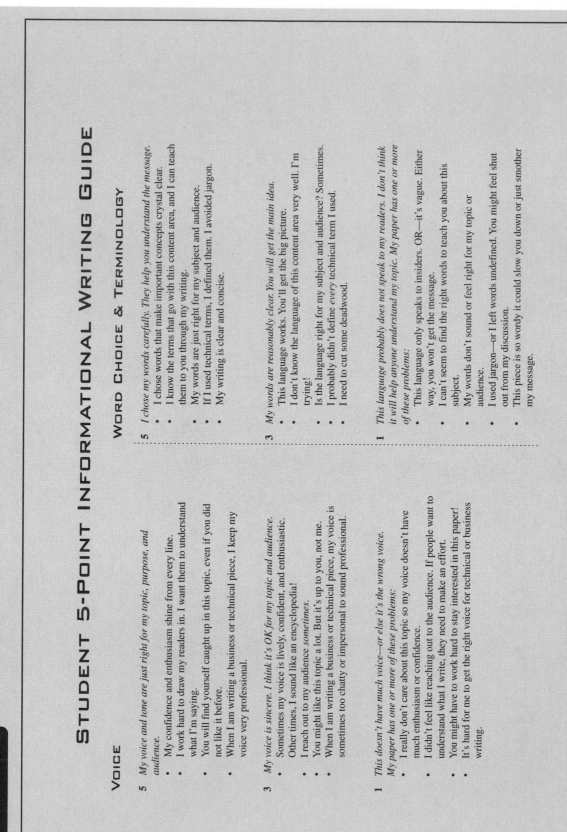

STUDENT 5-POINT INFORMATIONAL WRITING GUIDE

VOICE

5 *My voice and tone are just right for my topic, purpose, and audience.*
- My confidence and enthusiasm shine from every line.
- I work hard to draw my readers in. I want them to understand what I'm saying.
- You will find yourself caught up in this topic, even if you did not like it before.
- When I am writing a business or technical piece, I keep my voice very professional.

3 *My voice is sincere. I think it's OK for my topic and audience.*
- Sometimes my voice is lively, confident, and enthusiastic. Other times, I sound like an encyclopedia!
- I reach out to my audience *sometimes*.
- You might like this topic a lot. But it's up to you, not me.
- When I am writing a business or technical piece, my voice is sometimes too chatty or impersonal to sound professional.

1 *This doesn't have much voice—or else it's the wrong voice. My paper has one or more of these problems:*
- I really don't care about this topic so my voice doesn't have much enthusiasm or confidence.
- I didn't feel like reaching out to the audience. If people want to understand what I write, they need to make an effort.
- You might have to work hard to stay interested in this paper!
- It's hard for me to get the right voice for technical or business writing.

WORD CHOICE & TERMINOLOGY

5 *I chose my words carefully. They help you understand the message.*
- I chose words that make important concepts crystal clear.
- I know the terms that go with this content area, and I can teach them to you through my writing.
- My words are just right for my subject and audience.
- If I used technical terms, I defined them. I avoided jargon.
- My writing is clear and concise.

3 *My words are reasonably clear. You will get the main idea.*
- This language works. You'll get the big picture.
- I don't know the language of this content area very well. I'm trying!
- Is the language right for my subject and audience? Sometimes.
- I probably didn't define *every* technical term I used.
- I need to cut some deadwood.

1 *This language probably does not speak to my readers. I don't think it will help anyone understand my topic. My paper has one or more of these problems:*
- This language only speaks to insiders. OR—it's vague. Either way, you won't get the message.
- I can't seem to find the right words to teach you about this subject.
- My words don't sound or feel right for my topic or audience.
- I used jargon—or I left words undefined. You might feel shut out from my discussion.
- This piece is so wordy it could slow you down or just smother my message.

STUDENT 5-POINT INFORMATIONAL WRITING GUIDE

SENTENCE FLUENCY

5 *My sentences are strong and clear:*

- I used sentence beginnings (*Then, Therefore, in contrast*) to give my sentences variety and show connections.
- Sentences are different lengths, but most are fairly short.
- I come right to the point so you get the meaning the first time through.
- This text is easy to read. You can speed through it and still understand everything.

3 *Most of my sentences are fairly clear:*

- I used a few sentence beginnings (*By the following year, To illustrate further*) to help readers connect ideas.
- Sentences are different lengths. However, some are so long it could be hard to follow the thought.
- You might need to read some sentences two times.
- You'll get the meaning if you pay attention and take your time.

1 *Many of these sentences are unclear. My paper has one or more of these problems:*

- I did not try to vary my sentence beginnings or use words that would link ideas. Readers need to make their own connections.
- Some of my sentences are so long and tangled I can't even follow them—or so short and choppy they bump you along.
- Some sentences are hard to understand even if you're re-read.
- I cannot always tell where they begin and end.
- Even if you read slowly, you could miss the message.

CONVENTIONS & PRESENTATION

5 *I know conventions well, and I edited my paper to make it readable and appealing.*

- You will not find errors. I went through it carefully.
- My conventions bring out meaning and voice.
- If I used outside sources, I cited them correctly.
- If layout was important for this piece, I spent time on it.
- I used titles, subtitles, bullets, etc., to help the reader find important information quickly and easily.
- My charts, graphs, or illustrations are helpful.

3 *I know conventions pretty well, and I did some editing. It's fairly readable.*

- You might spot some errors. I need to go over it again.
- Conventions do not *get in the way* of the message—but they don't really bring out the voice.
- I need to check over my citations.
- I think the layout is OK.
- Titles, subtitles, bullets, etc. could have helped readers find information.
- If I used charts, graphs, or other illustrations, you might find them helpful.

1 *I know I have many errors in conventions. I didn't think about layout.*

- My paper has enough errors to slow a reader down.
- The errors hurt both the message and the voice.
- I didn't cite any sources. Maybe I should have.
- Layout? I didn't worry about it.
- I didn't think about titles, subtitles, or bulleted lists.
- I didn't use charts or graphs—OR they don't connect to the text.

SAMPLE PAPERS: AN INVITATION

No scoring guide is worth its salt unless it's helpful in getting inside a piece of writing (or, of course, creating or revising your own writing). I invite you to put the informational scoring guide in this chapter to the test with some student samples, just to see whether your scores match those of our teacher-raters. These papers were selected to represent a variety of topics, grade levels, writing approaches, and skills. Suggested scores and rationales follow each paper, but I suggest committing your own scores to paper first, before checking those in the book. To make your task easier, make a copy of the five- or six-point informational writing guide so that you can have it right in your hand as you look at each paper. You also may wish to try out one or more of the checklists—just to see if they cover those elements you feel are important to a specific genre. Keep in mind that checklists *do not result in a score.*

Suggested Scores and Comments for Informational Papers

As always, feel free to disagree with these scores *if you have a good reason.* Papers are scored on both five- and six-point scales, with scores for the *five-point scale listed first.*

Paper 1: "Bears in the Wild" (Informational, Grade 4)

FIGURE 11.13
Paper 1:
"Bears in the Wild"

Have you ever watched a black bear before? Once when we were driving I saw a black bear across the river. she was ambling along the river bank, with her two cubs.

Black bears are usually black but they can be brown or white. A black bear has four legs and five claws on each paw. The weight of a grown black bear is about 300 pounds or about 136 kilograms. Black bears are less than five feet long. the black bear has lots of thick fur and it has big teeth, long, sharp claws, and a huge head.

Some bears live in a hole under a tree or in a dug out cave. Bears eat different kinds of berries and some kinds of inseckts they dig out of rotton logs. They normally live in the woods where they are safe from people there main enemy. Bears also eat honey from bee hives. there thick black fur protects them from the bees they also eat many kinds of fish espeshially salmon. when you think about it, they like alot of the same foods we humans like eccept for the inseckts.

Most bears hibernate in the winter, but before they do they need to collect lots of food and stuff themselves to get fat and store food for the winter.

Lots of people think bears will attack you. But the truth is they wont. Bears are mostly gentle. They usually mind there own busness unless you pester them. In the woods in Canada once we got to track a bear but he never would let us get too close because he was just too shy. Its easy to find where bears have been from their tracks and droppings. They rub themselves on tree trunks and leave big tufts of there fur behind.

People are bears only enemies but we could be there freinds if we understood them. we should not kill bears just for bear rugs. there are not enough bears left and if we just keep building houses and shopping malls we will distroy their homes.

■ *Suggested Scores*

Ideas: 4, 5
Organization: 3, 4
Voice: 4, 5
Word choice: 4, 4
Fluency: 4, 4
Conventions: 3, 3

■ *Comments*

This paper needs a main message, but has good details. Bears are shy, they are threatened by people encroaching on their territory, they eat a variety of food (including insects), and they won't hurt you unless provoked. Although it gets off to a shaky start (the lead does not seem to make a point), the general organizational flow is easy enough to follow. The ending is strong, although a little abrupt. Two personal stories—seeing the mother bear and cubs by the river and tracking the bear through the woods—are begun, but the writer (frustratingly) never follows through. On the positive side, this writer seems to like the topic, and his enthusiasm results in quite a lot of voice. Fluency is by turns mechanical and *very* strong, making some parts highly readable. Conventions need work, and a bibliography would be helpful.

■ *Lessons Learned*

✔ Even fairly good organization seems weaker if the lead is not powerful.
✔ Conventional errors are distracting, even if not serious.

Paper 2: "Driving Tests Should Be Harder" (Persuasive, Grade 7)

FIGURE 11.14

Paper 2: "Driving Tests Should Be Harder"

If driver's tests were more rigorous, everyone on the road would be safer. About 50,000 people die in traffic accidents each year, and thousands more are injured. Most of these fatal accidents involve 16-year-old drivers. Although one of the problems is driving under the influence of liquor, an even bigger problem is incompetent driving. We

continued

could do something about this, but we grant driver's licenses on the basis of a very simple test.

Did you know that the part of the test in which you actually get out in a car and drive is only about 20 minutes long? What's more, the test givers are not demanding at all. They only ask drivers to perform a few tasks, such as turning left, turning right, parking and stopping. It has only been in the last few years that they have added entering a freeway to the test requirements. How often does anyone have to parallel park compared to entering a freeway? Yet it took all this time to update this test.

Tests are not conducted on the busiest streets or during heavy traffic hours. Anyone can pass this simple test in light traffic on a quiet street. It does not mean that driver is competent.

The true test is real-life driving. I mean things like driving in bad weather, such as on icy streets or in fog. Or coping with bad drivers, such as people who tailgate or honk for no good reason. Or learning to handle mechanical problems such as getting a flat tire. The current driver's test does not measure whether a person can handle any of these difficult but common situations.

Of course, a driver's test that had to cover all of these situations would be difficult to set up. It isn't easy to arrange for people to drive on icy roads, for instance. Plus it could be dangerous. Imagine if people got killed while taking their driver's test! Besides, a complicated test might cost more and there could be a long waiting line. Imagine if you were 16 and needed to drive to work and you could not get a license because the wait was so long. There is one solution. They could do part of the test as a computer simulation. That way, you would still need the skills, but you would not need to risk your life to show you were a competent driver.

There are several ways to make the current test better. First, make it longer, so people need to drive more. Second, use computer simulation to test skills under dangerous conditions. Third, make sure people really have to do the things they will do in everyday driving, like changing lanes on the freeway. Then, require a score of 90 to pass, not 70, which is too low. Right now, you can do a lot of things wrong and still pass.

Sure, it will cost a little to make the tests more rigorous. But lives are more important than keeping tests cheap. When was the last time you felt in danger because of an incompetent driver? Remember, almost every person in this country will have a driver's license at some time in his or her life. If even half of these people are not qualified, we are risking our lives every time we go out on the road. We need better driver's tests now!

Source: Oregon Department of Motor Vehicles.

■ Suggested Scores

Ideas: 4, 5

Organization: 5, 5

Voice: 5, 5

Word choice: 4, 5

Fluency: 5, 5

Conventions: 5, 6

■ Comments

The pluses in this paper are many: The voice is strong and sustained, the writer is very aware of his audience, the language is clear and crisp and appropriate for the topic, sentences are varied and readable, and the writer makes many good points. Had the writer further explored that intriguing idea of computerized driving tests, the ideas score would have gone up; the problem of how to make the test more rigorous without increasing costs remains only partially resolved. Still, this writer accomplishes a lot in a short space and expresses himself clearly.

■ Lessons Learned

✔ Don't run out of steam in the second half; keep the energy flowing!

✔ Simple, straightforward sentence structure makes an informational or persuasive piece easy to understand.

Paper 3: "Interesting Facts About Smoking" (Informational, Grade 10)

FIGURE 11.15

Paper 3: "Interesting Facts About Smoking"

Many teen-agers from 12 to 18 smoke every week if not every day. In 1987 along, lung cancer surpassed breast cancer as the leading cancer killer of women.

Cigarettes are one of the most dangerous drugs that is legal in the U.S. Almost 3 million packs of cigarettes are sold illegally to minors every year. People who began smoking as minors have a really hard time stopping.

Numerous cancers, heart disease and a lot of other ailments are blamed on smoking. Infact, 90 percent of all lung cancer is attributed to smoking. If people know all this why don't they stop? Though many wish they could but it is not that simple. Cigarettes are very addictive, though. You can become addicted in about four to five weeks even if you only smoke tow or three cigarettes per day.

People usually start smoking because they think it is cool and it is just a temporary thing. But, studies show that, almost everybody who starts cannot stop Most of the people who start are young women. Although more young women are smoking some studies show the number of blacks who smoke is declining. Who smokes depends a lot on who the advertisers are appealing to in their ads. If you smoke, just remember you may not be able to stop.

■ Suggested Scores

Ideas: 2, 2

Organization: 2, 2

Voice: 3, 4

Word choice: 3, 4

Fluency: 3, 4

Conventions: 2, 2

■ Comments

The title tells it all. This writer has a lot of points to make but has not focused or organized them to create a coherent argument. Platitudes (*"Smoking is dangerous," "Smoking is addictive"*) usurp attention that could be given to more complex issues (*"Advertising is primarily aimed at young people," "Tobacco is one of the few drugs that remains legal"*). There is no clear introduction; we have the feeling of having turned on the TV in the middle of the news report. Further, the paper meanders mercilessly, barraging us with facts and forcing us to make our own sense of it. The writer needs a strong theme—e.g., *"People who begin smoking as teenagers cannot stop."* The conclusion suggests—perhaps—what she wanted to say most. Despite the lack of focus, this writer speaks with some conviction, giving the piece more voice than it otherwise might have. It's also more fluent than it looks; if you do some mental editing and fix the punctuation (the real problem), most sentences are sharp and to the point. A bibliography is needed.

■ Lessons Learned

✔ Have a thesis. Individual points need integration and focus.

✔ Support claims or data by citing relevant sources.

Paper 4: "Electric Eels" (Informational, Grade 6)

FIGURE 11.16

Paper 4: "Electric Eels"

Eels are a type of fish. They live in the ocean, and many diferent lakes. They are long and slender. They have fins that help them swim. The coloring of eels is blackish brown and their bodies are covered with slimy coating, which makes them difficult to hold. Eels are usually not shorter than three feet long, and they can be as long as nine feet long, and can weigh up to 22 kg. It can be as thick as 12 to 18 inches.

The electric shock from the eels comes from muscles in their bodies, which have lost their ability to work like normal muscles do. These muscles are mainly in the long tail of the eel. The shock coming from their bodies works somewhat like jumper cables for car batteries. The tail of the eel is negatively charged. When an eel touches its tail and head to different parts of an animal, it sends electric shocks through that animal's body. Electric eels mainly shock other fish of different kinds, to stun them so they can eat them. They also shock other animals to keep the animal away from them. If we are in their living area, we scare them, and then they might shock us. However, their shock is only strong enough to knock us down, not kill us. The Electric Eel puts out as much as 500 volts, and can have up to 650 volts. The electricity can discharge at will. This is enough electricity to knock down a mule or light a small electric sign. The Eel's generating organs have the same structure as those of the electric ray, but the shocking strength of the Eel is much stronger, and greater. The Eel produces low energy pulses that flow outward in all directions. Anything nearby fixed or in motion, affects the flow pattern since it conducts electricity differently from water. The electric organs provide the fish with additional sensory, defensive and offensive mechanisms. The electric eel produces from 1-5 pulses per second when resting, and about 20 impulses per second when excited. The electric discharges surround the fish with an electric field, which is able to detect through highly sensory cells in its skin. If a field is distorted by some object of different electrical conductivity from that of the water, the electrosensory organs of the skin are stimulated and the fish is alerted.

The electric organ is made up of cells known as electroplaques. These cells have lost the elongate form of muscle cells and are flattened plates closely stacked in columns. The are as many as 700,00 electroplaques in the 3 pairs of electric organs of an electric eel.

Despite its name, the fish is not a true Eel but is related to characins in the order Cypriniformes. It is a sluggish creature.

The Electric Eel's scientific name is Electrophorus. It belongs to the family Gynotidae, all though it is often wrongly classified as Electrophoridae. The Electric Eel is related to the minnows and catfishes. It is found in South America fresh waters or the Amazon and Orinoco rivers. The electric organs, which are modified muscles, are columnar structures located on each side of the tail.

Electric eels do not shock each other because they don't want to eat other eels, and they don't usually get attacked by other eels. That is the main reason they shock other animals.

When an Eel swims, its body makes S-shaped curves. The outer edge of each curve presses against the water. The water is relatively less movable then the fish so the fish moves forward more, then the water is pushed backward.

Eels don't see very well, but they have a good sense of smell.

Eels usually eat whole shrimp, clams, and other kinds of fish.

■ *Suggested Scores*

Ideas: 2, 3

Organization: 2, 2

Voice: 2, 2

Word choice: 3, 3

Fluency: 4, 4

Conventions: 4, 5

■ *Comments*

This is not an easy paper to score. The writer presents an abundance of information, which would seem initially to be a strength. However, it is not information she knows well, so she is not fully in control. Chief problems are with ideas (unclear or repetitious), organization (circuitous, abrupt ending), and voice (encyclopedic). The description of how an eel shocks its victims seems endlessly circular; we get the same information over and over. Intriguing details (Eels shock us because we frighten them) are intermingled with confusing information about *electroplaques* (a term not explained) and conflicting statements. For instance, we are told that eels shock their prey but dine mostly on shrimp and clams; do these creatures need to be subdued? Eels move through the water by making S curves with their muscular bodies, yet they're "sluggish." They don't sound sluggish. Some text is flat out bewildering: *"Anything nearby fixed or in motion, affects the flow pattern since it conducts electricity differently from water."* Come again? We do learn that an eel has enough electricity to knock down a mule (so surely enough for a shrimp) or to light a small sign—that's good stuff, and we need more of it. When the writer lets her own voice shine through, the writing improves. She's better than the encyclopedia(s) she's using; if only she knew it.

> If you're bored by your research topic, your paper will almost certainly be boring as well, and you'll end up hating writing research papers as much as ever.
>
> **—Bruce Ballenger**
> *The Curious Researcher,*
> Fourth Edition, 2004, p. 25

■ *Lessons Learned*

✔ Know your topic—well. Knowledge drives ideas, organization, and voice.

✔ Don't be afraid of a conversational style; encyclopedias are useful resources, but people read them only out of necessity.

Paper 5: "Humboldt Penguins" (Informational, Grade 9)

FIGURE 11.17
Paper 5:
"Humboldt Penguins"

Probably the most startling fact about the gentle Humboldt Penguin is that it is the most endangered penguin in the world. They have been hunted for years. Moreover, their main staple food, krill, are dwindling in numbers with the warming of the oceans, and the range of the Humboldt Penguin is not very big—and is not getting any bigger. Their habitat is unique, and they do not seem able to adapt. The only place it can be duplicated is in the zoo. Odds are, we have only a few decades left—maybe less—to enjoy these remarkable and friendly animals.

Environment

Humboldt Penguins live along the rocky coastline of South America, from Peru to Northern Chile. The warm currents of El Niño bring in plenty of fish and krill—for now—so the penguins do not migrate. They nest right in the rocks, making themselves comfortable along hard, unforgiving rock walls that most creatures would find less than inviting. The rocks and ocean are all they know their whole lives. Because they do not migrate, they know nothing of forests or sandy beaches or even pebbled coves.

Physical Description

Male and female Humboldts are similar in appearance. Both are about 26 inches tall and weigh about ten pounds. They have a black mask with touches of pink around a sharp, heavy beak, well suited to fishing. A black stripe runs like an inverted "U" up and around their sides and down their back. Their belly is mostly white, with scattered black speckles. Penguins have very short legs, perhaps only two inches long, but can nevertheless jump amazingly high, for the leg muscles are very powerful. Their webbed feet are black with pink spots, and they have three toes, with sharp, scaly claws at the end. A penguin's feet work like paddles, propelling the penguin through the water, and are very powerful.

Penguins are normally fairly clumsy on land, and waddle along at a slow pace—though they have been known to "launch" themselves at an enemy if attacked or provoked. They are built for underwater speed, however, and move like tiny torpedoes in the water. Their smooth, oval shape is reminiscent of a dolphin or trout, and they swim with the same ease.

Everyone knows that penguins do not fly. However, scientists believe that once they did. They are almost certainly descended from a flying bird, but so far, nobody has located the "missing link" that would prove this theory.

Food

The diet of the penguin is healthy, if a little monotonous. They dine primarily on fish and crustaceans, plus an occasional squid. They are especially fond of fish like anchovies which swim in large schools. Penguins have a lot of body fat to maintain in order to insulate themselves from the cold water, so they must eat a great deal and eat often to maintain their oval shapes.

The bill of the penguin is equipped with small spines which help hook and hold a fish. Once a penguin gets a grip on its meal, the fish rarely escapes.

Predators

Penguins are hunted by seals, killer whales and sharks. For this reason, they like to hunt close to shore and near the surface. If a penguin ventures too far out to sea, it may not have the endurance to outrun a hungry seal.

Land predators include gulls, jaegers, skuas and other large birds. These birds will not take on an adult penguin, which is a fierce fighter, but will prey on young chicks and eggs.

Behavior

A surprising fact about penguins is that they are quite territorial. They will attack others that come too close to their nesting site. Like humans, they sometimes resent neighbors who invade their privacy or become too nosy. If a penguin must walk through a crowded area, he will keep his head high and feathers sleeked down, as if trying to look invisible. Generally,

continued

though, penguins are very social. They swim together and hunt in groups for protection. They watch out for one another and are very affectionate with their young. Humboldts have not learned to fear humans, and will often allow people to come quite close.

Conclusion
The Humboldt Penguin is among the most intriguing of all penguin species. It is more social than most penguins, and remarkably like ourselves. With luck, it may survive long enough for us to study its curious ways further.

Sources: Johnson, Russell. "Humboldt Penguins: An Endangered Species." In *Penguin World*. Vol. 4. No. 6. Spring 1992.
Seattle Public Zoo. Site visit. May 20, 1994.

■ *Suggested Scores*

Ideas: 5, 6

Organization: 4, 5

Voice: 5, 6

Word choice: 5, 6

Fluency: 5, 6

Conventions: 5, 6

■ *Comments*

This paper is a fine sample of expository writing at its best: informative, readable, well paced, and organized to help a reader understand and appreciate the subject. It does not attempt to tell all there is to know about penguins but selects some significant and intriguing information. It's interesting to learn, for instance, that penguins do not mind nesting in rocks, that they are affectionate with their young, that they bristle (like humans) when nosy neighbors come too close, that they can launch themselves ferociously at a rude intruder, and that they turn into feathered torpedoes in the water. At the end we want to say, "Thanks for sharing so many intriguing tidbits—I learned a lot." Our only complaint (and it's minor) is that sections seem a little out of balance, with a lot of time spent on appearance. The paper has fine conventions and a bibliography, too.

■ *Lessons Learned*

✔ Dig for the unusual details. They will make your paper stand out.
✔ Subheads are extremely useful, for both the writer and reader.

Paper 6: "The Middle Ages" (Informational, Grade 7)

FIGURE 11.18
Paper 6:
"The Middle Ages"

In the time of the Middle Ages many children drempt of being a knight. First they had to become a page. The next step to becoming a squire. Hard training and patience were required. A brave young squire could hardly wait to receive the accolade. During the period of being a squire you had to learn chivalry. Chivalry consisted of loyalty and devotion to the king or lord. Politeness and courtesy towards women was a very big part of being a knight. One also had to be brave and protect the defenseless.

A knight had to be wealthy in order to pay for the equipment. The equipment consists of a suit of armor, a shield, a sword, and of course a horse. The armor consists of many parts we won't name them all because it would take forever. However, we will name the helmet because it is the most important part of armor a knight could have because it protects the head from injury which could be fatal.

Tournaments took up what little free time a knight had. If a knight wasn't out on the battlefield he would be out jousting or sword fighting against another knight. The purpose of a tournament is to test one's strength. The object was not to kill a knight but to capture him.

Manors were the main ways of life during the middle age. They had farms, hunting grounds, people and castles. Castles were the main points of life in the middle ages. Castles were not built for comfort but for defense.

Well, after all that, there isn't much more to discuss, so for now, orevwa.

Source: Caselli, Giovanni. *The middle Ages.* New York, 1988, Peter Bedrick Books, pages 12–17.

■ *Suggested Scores*

Ideas: 2, 3

Organization: 2, 2

Voice: 3, 3

Word choice: 3, 3

Fluency: 3, 3

Conventions: 3, 3

■ *Comments*

If you already know a lot about the Middle Ages, you might sail right on through this essay, but if you are coming to the topic for the first time, you are likely to find the information skimpy at best: *"Next you would become a squire."* So? Tell us more. *"A brave young squire could not wait to receive the acolade."* What's an "acolade"? Why could he not wait? *"The armour consists of many parts we won't name them all because it would take forever."* Name a few— we'll wait. There are many unanswered questions: Why did children dream of becoming knights? How old were knights? Did many survive? Could anyone become a knight? Why did they have so little free time? *(So Lancelot, what do you do in your free time?)* Were the knights always at war? The writer seems to assume that the audience is right there in the social studies class and therefore can fill in the blanks. Moreover, the paper is dominated by knights and chivalry. Is that about all there was to the Middle Ages then—or should the title be changed? We need a better balance of details to give us a sense of history and some little-known information to spark the imagination. The bibliography is short, but at least there is one. That's it, so "Orevwa."

■ *Lessons Learned*

✔ Write your title last.
✔ A good ending should say goodbye metaphorically but not literally.

Paper 7: "Life in the Middle Ages" (Informational, Grade 7)

FIGURE 11.19
Paper 7:
"Life in the Middle Ages"

Imagine yourself living in a time when the average man grew to a height of about 5'2", the average woman to about 4'10". And almost no one lived to be more than 45 years old. At 20 you would be middle aged, and probably would have lost many, if not most, of your teeth. Your skin would be pock marked from chicken pox or acne. At 13, you would either be married or (if you were a male), thinking about becoming a priest or knight. They were about the only people who were educated enough to read, write, or do simple math. This is just a small glimpse of what life was like in the Middle Ages in the part of the world we now call Great Britain. As we will see, life was very different then—in almost every possible way.

Society during the Middle Ages was organized in a somewhat military fashion. At the head of everything was the King, who had life and death control over all his subjects. He could conscript people for service in his "army," or confiscate their goods for use by the state. Not that there was much to confiscate. People during those times owned very little-a few clothes and dishes, some crude tools, some pigs or chickens, and perhaps a small shelter that passed for a house. Only the wealthy had dogs or horses, elaborate clothing, good leather shoes, weapons, jewelry or, in the cases of kings and lords, castles in which to live.

Of course, wealth is a relative thing. Today, we think little of owning things like automobiles, microwave ovens, computers, cameras and televisions, all of which would have seemed like magic to people of the 1300s. On the other hand, they dreamed of living in stone castles, for that was the height of elegance at the time. If we could go back in time and recapture the sights, sounds and smells of the Middle Ages, though, most of us would be horrified. Imagine no indoor sanitation, only crude buckets to dump human waste down the rock walls. Picture hogs, dogs, sheep, chickens and rats all sharing the larger space surrounding the inner castle where the King lived; the noise was deafening, the smell overpowering. Yet people looked on these surroundings as luxurious, for they knew nothing else.

Probably the worst thing to happen to anyone was to become ill or to be wounded. You might be bled into a bowl, or be given an herbal potion to drink, or a so-called doctor might stitch up your wounds with a filthy needle and some cat gut. Strangely enough, people then believed that washing actually pushed germs into your body, so no one washed if they could help it, not even the "doctors." Not only did they smell, but it was dangerous to be treated by one. Few people survived "surgery," which was more of a mutilation.

Entertainment in the Middle Ages was lively, to say the least. Knights practiced their jousting, trying to knock each other from horseback with a lance, in open tournaments. Some engaged in sword fights. They were not usually to the death, but sometimes accidents did occur. Executions were almost always public and were treated kind as a kind of entertainment. Many people would come to see someone hanged or beheaded. And of course there was almost always a wedding or funeral to attend if nothing else interesting was going on.

All in all, life was hard for people born in 1300. Maybe it's lucky they did only live to 45. Probably for them, that seemed like a long time!

■ *Suggested Scores*

Ideas: 5, 6

Organization: 5, 5

Voice: 5, 6

Word choice: 5, 6

Sentence fluency: 5, 6

Conventions: 5, 5

■ *Comments*

Compare this piece with Paper 6, "The Middle Ages." This writer has definitely done some research, and the result is an interesting, eye-opening walk through life in the 1300s. We learn how tall people were, how early they married, what they ate, where they lived, what medical treatment was like, what they did for entertainment, and much more. The details are specific, filled with imagery. In addition, this writer sounds truly intrigued by the subject, so the voice is strong. Did you think that the language was pretty simple? Look again. Imagine that you have that highlighter pen in your hand, and ask yourself how many words and phrases you might mark (remember, this is a middle school student). Despite the length, this is an easy one to read aloud. Excellent conventions, but no sources cited.

■ *Lessons Learned*

✔ Tell what *you* find interesting—and you'll interest your reader, too.

✔ Know the topic well. That way, you can be choosey about details.

Paper 8: "Beautiful People" (Persuasive, Grade 12)

I can't tell you how many times, while aimlessly channel surfing, I have come across TV specials on plastic surgery. I have unwillingly glued my eyes to the train wrecks of liposuction, breast implants, calf implants, tummy tucks, face lifts, and numerous other mind-boggling mutilations of the human body. I have been awestruck by the amounts of money spent on these operations, winced at the painful recoveries, and I am constantly saddened by the fact that in our quest for "beauty," we have become a people who are incapable of being comfortable in our own skin.

Aren't we all taught to not judge a book by its cover? Can we all agree that a person's physical appearance has nothing to do with who they really are? Unfortunately we are often judged on our appearance. But who is perpetuating that standard of judgment? Is it just Hollywood, the music industry, and the fashion world? In reality, we are the ones holding ourselves down with the most brutal, relentless criticisms. We are taught to not judge people on the basis of their physical attributes, whether it be skin color, or any other feature. So why do we judge ourselves that way?

People, especially Americans, are always trying to fix things on an external level. This is a hopeless endeavor. Real beauty, real truth, real change of any kind has to come from the inside out. There is the saying, "If you look good, you feel good." Why not turn it around and say, "If we feel good, we look good"? We spend so much time focusing on our physical selves, that we so often forget to take care of ourselves spiritually and mentally. It's so much easier to create a flawless, picture perfect, external form than to really examine our minds and emotions, and figure out why we are so desperately needy and insecure.

Cosmetic surgery is simply the extreme of our debilitating insecurities. I am so often amazed at girls who think they can't leave the house without putting makeup on, or who don't eat because they want to be a size zero. I am surprised at some women, and men for that matter, who spend mass amounts of time and energy on maintaining a wardrobe of all designer clothing, always trying to be immaculately free of physical imperfection. Not to say that these behaviors necessarily equate with plastic surgery, but seriously, why are we all so hung up on ourselves? Truthfully, I bet most people really couldn't care less about what someone else looks like. Our criticisms of others are most often driven by our own fear of not being accepted. We are all too busy worrying about ourselves to pay any attention to someone else.

Why can't we be grateful for what we have? Why can't we appreciate our health and energy? Why can't we use our God-given bodies, as they are, to do something for someone else? Wouldn't it be nice to forget about ourselves for a while and use our energy to help other people?

No matter how hard we try, we can't fix all of our problems superficially without taking into account the internal aspect that drives our actions. What's the point in spending thousands upon thousands of dollars on a body that will eventually cease to exist? Our time would be better spent focusing on the part of us that is inescapable and eternal. What we really need to do is figure out how to be beautiful people, not just beautiful bodies.

■ Suggested Scores

Ideas: 4, 5
Organization: 5, 5
Voice: 5, 6
Word choice: 5, 6
Sentence fluency: 5, 6
Conventions: 5, 6

■ Comments

Exceptional fluency and word choice are the hallmark traits of this piece. This writer has such fluency, such grace in her style, that even complex thoughts are grasped readily. Voice is strong as well. She is passionate and holds our attention, inviting us into her conversation. Ideas are strong in that they are expressed clearly and backed by numerous examples; however, specific data on numbers of plastic surgeries performed or the money spent on designer clothing would have given her arguments a little extra edge. The lead is good, but it's the "train wrecks" of sentence two that mark the true beginning. This is a strong writer with a good ear.

■ Lessons Learned

✔ Even passionate arguments can be strengthened with some well-placed statistics—or a timely quotation. Let another voice in.
✔ Fluent writing carries meaning. Take time to read it aloud.

Paper 9: "How to Be a Good Driver" (Expository, Grade 12)

FIGURE 11.21
Paper 9:
"How to be a Good Driver"

Being a good driver is not a big fat secret. I have been driving for just over two years and I know what it takes: caution, the alertness of a cat on the hunt, and knowledge of your car. It takes a little luck, too—but that part will always be beyond your control.

If you want a clean driving record like mine—no tickets, no pull-overs—you must be cautious. That's number one. I don't tailgate, and I don't barrel

continued

into intersections without looking. I don't back up till I'm sure there's no one behind me, either. Also—fussy people will appreciate this one—I don't park so close to the car next to me you need a can opener to separate us. I know banging a car door into the next guy isn't like a head-on collision—but it still causes damage, both to your car and to your mental health. Courtesy and common sense are important components of caution, you see.

Right up there with caution is a sense of alertness. I don't mean gripping the wheel with everything you've got (like I see some drivers do) and staring straight ahead like your neck won't move. Alertness means being aware of all the other vehicles around you at all times, and that includes those way, <u>way</u> out there in the distance (as well as those behind and to the sides). There could be an accident or stalled vehicle a half mile out, so anticipate. Assume the guy next to you will cut you off, pull right in front of you barely missing your front fender, and then slow down—for reasons known only to him and his therapist. This kind of irritating maneuver is all too common. That guy behind you? The one following too close? He doesn't know you're going to need to stop for some kid or dog that's about to run into the road. If you didn't know he was even there, that means you're not looking in your rear-view mirror enough. You should also assume that people approaching a yellow light at an intersection will storm on through. Heck—at least one guy is going to sneak through on the red. Be ready. That's what it means to be alert. It could save your life.

Finally, you need to know something about how your car works. Could you change a tire if you had to? If not, stay out of remote areas and at least have a cell phone. (Or drive with a buddy who <u>can</u> change tires!) Watch that gas gauge; boy, nothing ruins a good time like hiking down the road for gas. Also, don't allow people to make a lot of noise in the car. Make them wear seat belts. Keep the radio to a level where you might hear a police or fire siren a block away. Occasionally, turn the radio off so you can see if your car is making unusual noises, like the sound of a muffler scraping on pavement.

See how much of this is common sense? Yet, how much of it is included in the typical driver's test? That's <u>right!</u> Almost none! Know what that means? See those people out there on the highway? That's right! They're not ready to drive—but they're driving anyway! So, be defensive. Be alert, cautious, and knowledgeable, and with some luck thrown in, you'll have a chance.

■ *Suggested Scores*

Ideas: 4, 5

Organization: 5, 6

Voice: 5, 6

Word choice: 4, 4

Sentence fluency: 5, 6

Conventions: 5, 6

■ **Comments**

This paper is fun to read, easy to follow, and filled with good, practical information. As with Paper 8, the already convincing arguments could be further strengthened by statistical support, e.g., the number of traffic accidents triggered by tailgating, running stoplights, or operating a car with faulty equipment. Still, the writer is direct and confident and states his points clearly. He is not afraid to weave in humor, but he does not rely on it, as many beginning writers do; he offers examples to back his points. The three key elements—caution, alertness, and knowledge of the car—are deftly separated into paragraphs, making this a classic five-paragraph essay. Yet this potentially formulaic structure works this time because the transitions are graceful and natural, not mechanical. Further, the structure *enhances* the message rather than fighting it. Notice the thoughtful ending, which summarizes the paper without being redundant. The language (*some kid, one guy*) is sometimes a little casual—hence the lower score in word choice. If you liked it, though, you are not alone; it can be argued that conversational language adds to the voice.

■ **Lessons Learned**

✔ The five-paragraph organizational structure can work *if* the content fits (as in this case) and the transitions are smooth.

✔ Similarly, the summary ending can work if you take a fresh perspective and avoid a word-for-word restatement.

Paper 10: "Expanded Definition: Resonance" (Technical/Informational, College Freshman)

FIGURE 11.22

Paper 10: "Expanded Definition: Resonance"

Resonance is the vibration of an object caused by a relatively small periodic **stimulus** of the same or nearly the same period as the **natural vibration** of that object. To understand the idea of resonance better, let's first look at some of the terms used in the definition above and then explore some examples to make the idea concrete in your mind.

The first term that needs defining is **stimulus**. A stimulus is something that acts on an object to create a response. For example, a stimulus may be wind, sound, friction, or many other things.

When speaking of **natural vibration**, we must explore an object at its molecular level. All substances are made up of millions of atoms, all either moving around freely, as in a liquid or gas, or attempting to move around, as in a solid. In a solid object, the atoms are packed tightly together, causing the object to hold its particular shape. Because the atoms are packed together, they cannot move freely. This causes the atoms to vibrate against one another, creating that object's natural vibration.

To better understand the definition of **resonance**, the first example we will be exploring is that of an old party favorite, the whining wineglass. When a person has a wineglass and rubs the rim with his/her wine-dipped fingers, a sound can be produced. Finding the glass's natural vibration creates that sound. When you first start rubbing your fingers against the glass rim, no sound is created. Why? Well, the natural vibration wasn't found. Continue to rub the rim and eventually the natural vibration can be found. Once the natural vibration is found and matched, the glass experiences **resonance**, producing the whining sound.

Another example is the Tacoma Narrows Bridge, also referred to as "Galloping Gertie." A suspension bridge has a natural vibration to it, the same as any other solid object. For this reason, it will resonate, given the right conditions. The Tacoma Narrows Bridge was faced with large amounts of wind from the Puget Sound area. This wind blew at the bridge and created a resonance. Much like the wineglass in the example above, the bridge vibrated and twisted because of its flexible structure and lightweight design.

Using what we know about resonance, many new developments have been made to prevent it. Though it is an interesting topic, it can be devastating for the structures that engineers create.

Works Cited

Hill, John W. and Ralph H. Petrucci. *General Chemistry*. Upper Saddle River, NJ: Prentice Hall, 1996.

"Resonance." *Encyclopedia Americana*. 1996 ed.

"Resonance." *Webster's Dictionary*. 1992 ed.

■ *Suggested Scores*

Ideas: 4, 5

Organization: 4, 5

Voice: 5, 6

Word choice: 5, 6

Sentence fluency: 5, 6

Conventions: 5, 6

■ *Comments*

This piece is useful in illustrating what technical writing should be: a way of making concepts clear. Perhaps the act of writing this definition helped clarify the concepts of natural vibration and resonance in the writer's mind, too. The text is very reader-friendly, with crisp, short sentences, definitions of terms, and useful examples a reader can picture and understand. We do wish the writer had defined the term *period*. Also, it is not totally clear how resonance (which seems related to sound, but clearly means more) damaged the Tacoma Narrows Bridge; we need a fuller picture. The voice is professional, appropriately engaging, and controlled—just right for a technical piece, and hence the high scores, even though the writer does not crack jokes or appeal to our feelings. This restrained (but helpful) voice is right for this kind of writing. This is a good example of "thinking 'I,'" as William Zinsser (2001) reminds us to do. What's missing (from my perspective) is a reason to care about resonance. We get to it in the final paragraph, with the comment that it is "devastating" for some structures. How so? Perhaps this would be a place to begin. Highlighted words are very helpful.

> *As you search for the right voice in doing your revision, look for a balance between flat, wooden prose, which sounds as if it were manufactured by a machine, and forced, flowery prose, which distracts the reader from what's most important: what you're trying to say.*
>
> **—Bruce Ballenger**
> *The Curious Researcher*, Fourth Edition, 2004, p. 233

■ *Lessons Learned*

✔ A dignified, professional tone can still be reader-friendly, even if it is not emotional; this voice works in technical pieces.

✔ Sometimes the concluding paragraph provides a good place to begin.

Paper 11: "A Simple Phone Call" (Persuasive/Expository, Grade 12)

FIGURE 11.23
Paper 11: "A Simple Phone Call"

One hundred and fifty years ago, holding a conversation with my boyfriend would have taken days (maybe even weeks), a book of stamps, and the U.S. Postal Service.

Luckily, it is 2003. To talk to him at the University of Delaware, I need only pick up my cell phone in Pennsylvania. I flip it open, push a button, say his name, and in two or three rings we are talking. Voice-dialing and nationwide long distance are hardly the alienation that some say technology has caused.

Ten years ago, debate team members had few sources from which to gather evidence. They were limited to the high school library, or any other library within driving distance, and the media. To get quotes, they needed to make phone calls. The chances that great sources—the White House, leading researchers, the president of the NAACP—answered their phone calls must have been slim to none.

Those research tactics are mere ghost stories today. The Internet was born and changed the way research is conducted. The information that is accessible by everyone via computer is staggering in its (potential) accuracy, currency, and availability. The Internet has done anything but alienate us. Never before could knowledge and opinions be shared in such an expedient and user-friendly fashion.

continued

Still, critics maintain that technology makes us cold and unfeeling; that everyone should simply put down their cell phones and **really** talk to one another. However, it is very unlikely that these same people get on a plane whenever they wish to have a conversation with a far-away relative. Such actions are just not realistic, and that's where technological advances have come to the rescue.

Technology has undoubtedly improved our lives. It allows us to talk frequently, travel quickly, and live more comfortably. At some point or another, while on the Pennsylvania Turnpike, drivers without EZ-PASS wish they had it. It is also extraordinarily convenient that no matter where you are, almost anywhere in the world, there is an ATM that will give you money.

Without technological advancements, we would not have many of the opportunities or conveniences we enjoy. Nations would be relatively isolated from one another. Technology is now vital to our lives because it makes us better informed and highly connected to the world around us.

■ Suggested Scores

Ideas: 5, 5

Organization: 4, 5

Voice: 4, 5

Word choice: 4, 4

Sentence fluency: 5, 6

Conventions: 5, 6

■ Comments

The very first paragraph gets this piece off to a strong start. The closing lacks this specificity but still works. The writer does an outstanding job of linking arguments to real everyday situations, such as making a phone call, conducting research without grief, or getting money from the ATM. The theme of the paper is clear and forceful: Technology might seem cold, but in truth it's the very fiber of human connection. Some moments of word choice are stellar: *"Those research tactics are mere ghost stories today."* At times, though, the writer lets a generality slip in: *"Technology has undoubtedly improved our lives."* Unfortunately, the piece ends on a fairly general note, so a bit of voice is lost. If the fresh originality of the opening paragraphs were sustained throughout, this piece (already strong) would be even better. Excellent conventions.

■ Lessons Learned

✔ Help the reader relate issues to his or her own life..
✔ Expose the weakness in the critics' argument.

Paper 12: "Ecto vs. Endo" (Informational, Grade 7)

FIGURE 11.24

Paper 12: "Ecto vs. Endo"

What are you? Of course you are a human, but you are also endothermic. Endothermic is an animal such as a dog, bird, or human capable of maintaining a stable body temperature regardless of surroundings. If you were a snake you would be ectothermic. Ectothermic is an animal such as a reptile or fish whose body temperature varies according to the external temperature. Ectothermic animals are also called cold-blooded animals.

The endothermic dog gets around like any other animal but a little lizard has a whole different style. When lizards walk, they're close to the ground and do "push-ups." Dogs stride off the ground. Dogs and lizards transport the same when they are walking, but dogs get around various ways. Sometimes they ride in cars to get places, or get carried around if they are small. On the other hand, lizards have to walk everywhere they go.

Every species has its own distinctiveness. For example a worm snake (ectothermic) has its own uniqueness. Other animals have different things to look for like the endothermic Pronghorn. The pronghorn is different than the worm snake because it can jump and skip but the worm snake digs underground. You look for different things when you look for these animals. For the pronghorn you would look for tan fur, a white belly and bottom, two white stripes on the breast and horns slightly curved with a prong pointing forward. What you would look for in the worm snake would be a round body, shiny back, black-brown with a reddish pink belly and a tail with sharp pointed end.

Another way you can tell endo. Or ecto. is by the senses. One of the five senses is smelling. Most animals breathe with their nose but some don't. For example, mud snakes use their tongue to smell for their prey. Would you believe that one mammal does not smell with its nose, it smells with its twenty-two pinky sensitive feelers around its nose? There is some evidence that the feelers can realize, in the low-level electrical fields, that there are earthworms. These creatures' feelers also substitute for its eyes because it doesn't have good vision. I bet you are wondering what this animals name is. It is endothermic (drum roll please . . .) and its name is a . . . star-nosed mole!

You know, you never know when you might run into an ectotherm or an endotherm. You probably didn't even know about endothermic or ectothermic, so let this be a learning experience for you.

■ *Suggested Scores*

Ideas: 2, 3

Organization: 2, 2

Voice: 4, 5

Word choice: 3, 4

Sentence fluency: 4, 5

Conventions: 4, 5

■ Comments

Here's a paper that gets off to a good clear start but loses readers a bit as the discussion continues. We have good definitions of *ectothermic* and *endothermic* but are then left to wonder why it matters how dogs and lizards get around (We can guess, but are we right?) or why we are looking at the pronghorn versus the worm snake. By establishing connections, this writer could make the examples helpful and meaningful. The ending is intriguing but abrupt. We never return to the broader discussion. Voice is strong; the writer has energy and curiosity. Sentences are well crafted and conventions are good. What is missing are clear answers to the many questions this piece raises; e.g., how do senses help us differentiate between endo- and ectothermic? Needs a source list.

■ Lessons Learned

✔ Anticipate the readers' questions and answer them.
✔ Connect examples clearly to the main idea. Guide the reader.

Paper 13: "Pablo Picasso" (Informational, Grade 7)

FIGURE 11.25
Paper 13:
"Pablo Picasso"

He was a short man of five foot two inches with dark, piercing eyes, and a bald head. Picasso is his name. Being born in 1881 in Spain, he loved to watch bull fights once he dubbed himself, "The Eye of the Bull."

Struggling with dyslexia he was a poor student that hated authority, he was a leader and hated to be pushed around. When he was 18 he moved to Paris because he thought he could create better art there.

Early in his life he went through two different periods where he produced different kinds of art, the Blue Period was 1901-1904. During that time he created sad pictures using cool colors. One of the pictures created in this period is *The Old Guitarist*. The other period of time was called the Rose Period. That was from 1904–1906, during that short period of time he produced warmer pictures with pinks, reds, and yellows. Those influenced his art work in many ways.

Inspired by many thing like lovely women and naked people. What inspired his famous cubism was sculptures done by Iberian and African people. Cubism is where he uses squares and geometric figures to create a familiar object in his art work.

Women were attracted to him including a ballerina, and other artists. Having four children and being married twice. Entertaining his children was a priority he would, do magic tricks, throw parties were everything is chocolate. As time went on he focused more on his art then his children.

Mr. Picasso taught himself, and wasn't really involved with major art movements. When his flat was robbed the thieves took every thing but his paintings, I bet they sure wish they did though. Pablo Picasso died in 1973 he had created hundreds of pieces of art, he had become quite famous. His estate was valued at $100,000,000 when he passed away. I don't know about you but I think that's a lot of painting to do.

Now he has died, but his soul remains; in his artwork.

■ Suggested Scores

Ideas: 4, 4

Organization: 4, 4

Voice: 3, 4

Word choice: 3, 4

Sentence fluency: 2, 2

Conventions: 3, 4

■ Comments

This piece has great potential. We learn that Picasso was dyslexic, influenced by African geometric sculpture, had four children and two wives, knew magic, loved chocolate, and was robbed—though not of his paintings. How ironic! In short, there is enough information here to create a very full, satisfying piece. There are two problems. First, the voice is erratic. At times, it is forceful: "*. . . he was a leader and hated to be pushed around.*" Then it retreats to encyclopedic mode: "*Those influenced his art work in many ways.*" Some sentences are run-ons; some are incomplete: "*Inspired by many thing like lovely women and naked people.*" We can put most of the pieces into the puzzle, but *we* shouldn't have to. Be careful not to score down for this skeletal sentence problem in *both* fluency and conventions. I put this one under fluency. The ending would work better if we had more sense of Picasso's soul throughout the piece. The next-to-last line feels interruptive. Still—it's just a draft away: Build on the voice, smooth out the sentences, cite your sources.

■ Lessons Learned

✔ Incomplete sentences and run-ons make your reader work too hard.
✔ Strong details provide the framework for a potentially strong paper.
✔ Interrupting your piece with a personal comment may diminish voice.

Paper 14: "Desert Tortoise" (Informational, Grade 7)

FIGURE 11.26
*Paper 14:
"Desert Tortoise"*

Guess what? I am doing a report on the Desert Tortoise and the Desert Tortoise also known as *Gopherus agassizii*. The tortoise is classified into the kingdom animalia, and its phylum is chordata, because it has a backbone. Its class is reptilia because, of course, it's a reptile. The desert tortoise is placed in the order testudines, and its family is testudinidae. A Desert Tortoises genus is gopherus, because it is a burrowing organism. Last, but not least, a Desert Tortoises species is agassizii.

The Desert Tortoises scientific name is *Gopherus agassizii*. Pretty strange, huh? Well this very weird scientific name does have a meaning. The meaning for this scientific name is burrowing, terrestrial tortoise. This means a turtle the burrows and does not swim, and basically stays on land. In this case, the desert.

All of the Desert Tortoises relatives are turtles and tortoises. Some examples of those would be the Berlandier Tortoise, the Gopher Tortoise, and the Gopherus flavomarginatus.

Some people in the world probably don't even know what a Desert Tortoise looks like, well I am about to tell you. The upper shell, also know as the carapace, ranges in length from 15 to 36 centimeters, and its color varies from dull brown to a dull yellow. Males are mainly bigger than females. An adult male averages around 20 kilograms in weight, and an adult female averages 13 kilograms. The desert tortoise has two shells, an upper shell, and a lower shell. The upper shell is called the carapace, as I have already noted, and the lower shell is called the plastron. They also have retractable legs and a retractable head. These are retractable because if an enemy or predator came near, the tortoise would pull in its arms and legs, so the predator wouldn't get them, since the tortoise isn't fast enough to run away. The head of a Desert Tortoise is scaly, and the body has thick skin. Desert tortoises also have extremely long nails, which are used in digging through the desert and to find a shelter.

The tortoise ranges from the Mojave and Sonoran deserts of southeastern California, southern Nevada, south through Arizona into Mexico. Desert tortoises inhabit semi-grasslands, desert washes with gravel, canyon bottoms and rocky hillsides, all below 3,530 ft. The tortoises north and west of the Colorado River live in valleys and on alluvial fans. In the Sonoran Desert of Arizona, however, the tortoises happen to live on steep, rocky type hillside slopes in the Palo Verde and Saguaro Cactus communities. As you can tell, the tortoise has only one biome and that is the Desert biome.

One really special adaptation that the Desert Tortoise has is the fact that they can live without water for many years. They do that by ingesting most of their water from plants and then storing it in their bladders. Pretty cool, huh?

The Desert Tortoise is primarily herbivorous, surviving on low-growing plants, such as grasses, herbs, and a wide variety of desert plants. But their primary nutritional source is fresh green grass and spring wildflowers.

Where does the tortoise fit in the food chain, you may ask? Well the Desert Tortoise is the primary consumer because they eat grass, wildflowers, and cacti. All those things are producers, so the tortoise would be the primary consumer. The ravens are the secondary consumer because they are the tortoises' main predator.

The female Desert Tortoises lay their eggs around May, June, and July. A mature female lays 4 to 8 white, hard-shelled eggs in a clutch and produces 2, sometimes 3 clutches in a season. Only a few hatchlings out of 100 actually make it to adulthood. One really interesting fact is that all males are born at temperatures, 79–87 degrees F; females are born at warmer temperatures such as 88–91 degrees F. Pretty interesting, huh? The nests are often dug near the tortoises burrow, but sometimes the nests are dug farther away from the burrow, usually under a shrub. After laying, the female leaves the nest and the soil temperatures support growth of the embryos.

Did you know that the Desert Tortoise is able to live where ground temperatures may exceed 140 degrees F. Also, 95% of the tortoises' life is spent in under ground burrows. How boring is that? Desert tortoise populations have declined 90% since the 1980s, all because people have kept them as pets, or used them for target practice. But the ravens haven't helped because they have caused more than 50% of juvenile desert tortoise deaths, because they have eaten a ton of Desert Tortoises, in some areas of the Mojave Desert. Because of all that the Desert Tortoise is now endangered and it is unlawful to touch, harm, harass, or collect a wild Desert Tortoise.

■ Suggested Scores

Ideas: 4, 4

Organization: 3, 4

Voice: 4, 5

Word choice: 4, 5

Fluency: 3, 4

Conventions: 4, 4

■ Comments

This writer seems to have done good research. She presents numerous intriguing details but also leaves questions unanswered. For example, if a mature desert tortoise produces, at most, 24 eggs in a season and only a few out of 100 make it to maturity, why is this poor creature not extinct? Also, why is the raven a threat to any but the very young tortoises? Surely a raven cannot take on a mature tortoise—so do they have any enemies but humans after a certain point? Why are they such favorites as pets? What's the penalty if you are caught taking one for your garden? The information is well organized, although a little predictable: how they look, where they live, what they eat, etc. What's missing organizationally are a strong lead and conclusion and a way of linking sections together. The writer projects a genuine sense of engagement and curiosity; this is a plus. She does not need the "Can you believe it?" questions that intrude periodically and clash with her more authoritative voice. The whole could be condensed significantly; *many* sentences could be combined. Conventions need another look (inconsistency in capitals; Fahrenheit needs to be spelled out), although nothing blocks readability. This piece is well on its way. Again—a source list would help.

■ *Lessons Learned*

✔ Open with an image or startling discovery; save the technical information for after the reader is hooked.

✔ *Think* "Pretty strange, huh?" to give the piece voice; then you do not need to actually ask the question.

ADAPTING THE GUIDE FOR NATIVE SPANISH SPEAKERS

In using this guide (Figure 11.27), please recognize that even though it is translated into Spanish, it continues to reflect many of the nuances of idea development, organization, expression of voice, choice of words, fluent speech, and conventions particular to American culture. What is valued by native speakers of other languages or by other cultures is likely to look a little different. For instance, Americans tend to favor economical organization and direct, systematic presentation of ideas. In another culture, a less direct presentation might be considered more appropriate—perhaps more entertaining or even more sensitive or polite. In short, this translation is not meant to reflect cross-cultural values about language use or construction but only to provide a bridge into the six traits for Spanish speakers. The scoring guide is followed by a Spanish checklist (Figure 11.28).

FIGURE 11.27   *Guía de Calificación para los Estudiantes Escritores*

Guía De Calificación Para Los Estudiantes Escritores

Ideas y contenido

5. Mi trabajo está claro, con enfoque y abunda en detalles importantes.

- Puedes ver que sé mucho sobre este tema.
- El texto está lleno de detalles interesantes que llaman la atención.
- Puedo resumir el tema de mi trabajo en una oración clara y simple:___
- Cuando empieces a leer no querrás parar.
- Puedes imaginarte sobre lo que estoy hablando. No cuento las cosas que suceden, las muestro.

3. Aunque mi texto atrae tu atención, aquí y allá podría utilizar algunos detalles picantes.

- Sé lo suficiente para escribir sobre este tema, pero más información me ayudaría a hacerlo más interesante.
- Algunos "detalles" son cosas que la mayoría de la gente probablemente ya sabe.
- Mi tema es demasiado amplio. Quiero decir demasiado. O quizás sea superficial.
- En algunas partes podría resultar difícil imaginar de lo que estoy hablando.
- Me temo que mis lectores puedan aburrirse e irse a invadir la nevera.

1. Simplemente estoy pensando en lo que quiero decir.

- Necesito mucha más información antes de que esté realmente listo para escribir.
- Todavía estoy pensando en el trabajo, buscando una idea.
- No estoy seguro de que alguien que lea esto pueda imaginarse algo.
- ¡No estoy siquiera seguro de que esté listo para que lo lea alguien más! Aún no
- ¿Podría resumirlo en una oración clara? ¡De ninguna manera! Aún no estoy listo para eso.

Organización

5. Mi trabajo es tan claro como un buen mapa de carreteras. Toma a los lectores de la mano y los guía en todo momento.

- El inicio da una pista de lo que sigue y hace que se quiera seguir leyendo.
- Cada detalle está justo en el lugar donde le corresponde.
- Nada parece estar fuera de lugar.
- Nunca te sientes perdido o confuso; sin embargo, podría haber una o dos sorpresas.
- Todo conduce a mi idea más importante o al suceso principal de mi historia.
- Mi trabajo termina en el punto justo y te deja pensando.

3. Puedes empezar a ver hacia dónde voy. Si prestas atención, no tendrás ningún problema en seguir.

- Ya tengo un inicio. Pero, ¿atraerá por completo a mi lector?
- La mayoría de las cosas están bien donde las he puesto. Aunque tal vez podría cambiar de lugar algunas.
- Por lo general puedes ver que una idea se enlaza con otra.
- Supongo que todo debería llevar a la parte más importante. Veamos dónde sería eso.
- Mi trabajo tiene un final. ¿Pero, resulta coherente para el lector?

1. ¿A dónde vamos? Yo mismo estoy perdido.

- ¿Un principio? Bueno, podría simplemente haber repetido la tarea.
- Nunca supe qué decir luego, por eso escribí lo primero que me vino a la mente.
- No estoy realmente seguro qué incluir, o en qué orden ponerlo.
- Todo está apilado—¡casi como si se fuera un viejo ropero!
- ¿Un final? Simplemente terminé cuando no tenía más qué decir.

FIGURE 11.27 continued

Voz

5. He puesto en este trabajo mi sello personal e inconfundible.

- Puedes oír retumbar mi voz por todas partes. Se sabe que éste soy yo.
- Me interesa el tema—y lo muestro.
- Me dirijo directamente a mi audiencia, siempre pensando en las preguntas que pudieran tener.
- La confianza reluce en el texto.
- Escribí para satisfacerme a mí mismo.

3. Lo que realmente pienso y siento a veces aparece.

- Tal vez no rías ni llores cuando leas esto, pero tampoco dejarás de leer.
- Estoy a punto de encontrar mi propia voz.
- Mi personalidad asoma aquí y allá. Podrías adivinar que éste es mi escrito.
- No pensé en mi audiencia todo el tiempo. ¡A veces escribía para terminar como fuera!

1. No puse demasiada energía o personalidad en este escrito.

- Podría resultar difícil saber quién escribió esto. No creo que mucha gente reconozca que es mío.
- Controlé mis sentimientos.
- Sí, este tema me gustara o si supiera más sobre él, podría darle mayor vida.
- ¿La audiencia? ¿Qué audiencia?

Elegir las palabras

5. Elegí las palabras correctas para expresar mis ideas y sentimientos.

- Las palabras y frases que he usado parecen estar correctas.
- Mis frases son vivas y alegres, sin exagerar.
- Usé de manera orginal algunas de las palabras mas usuales. Espera algunas sorpresas.
- ¿Tienes una o dos frases favoritas aquí? Yo sí.
- Cada palabra es precisa. No tendrás que preguntarte qué quiero decir.
- Los verbos llevan el significado. No cargo a mi lector con demasiados adjetivos.

3. Puede que no encienda la chispa de tu imaginación, pero mira, ¡transmite el significado básico!

- Es funcional y logra el objetivo, pero sinceramente no puedo decir que fui lejos.
- OK, así que hay algunos clichés escondidos en los rincones.
- Tengo una frase favorita que aparece por aquí en alguna parte.
- ¿Verbos? ¿Qué tienen de malo los viejos *es, son, era, eran . . .*?
- Tal vez he utilizado demasiado la funcionalidad de mi *thesaurus*.
- Pero, ¿puedes entenderlo, verdad? En realidad no hay nada *incorrecto*.

1. Es probable que mi lector pregunte, "¿cómo?"

- ¡Ve! Soy víctima de un vocabulario impreciso y de frases poco claras.
- Es muy difícil entender de lo que estoy hablando. Ni yo mismo sé qué quise decir, y yo mismo lo escribí.
- Tal vez usé mal una o dos palabras.
- Algunas frases redundantes podrían ser redundantes.
- Necesito la fuerza del verbo.

FIGURE 11.27 *continued*

La Fluidez de las oraciones

5. Mis oraciones son claras y variadas—es un placer leerlas en voz alta.

- ¡Vamos!, léelo con sentimiento. No necesitarás ensayar.
- Por el uso de oraciones variadas me distinga.
- ¿Oyes el ritmo?
- Se ha quitado todo lo que no era necesario. Cada palabra cuenta.

3. Mis oraciones son claras y legibles.

- Mi escrito fluye de forma natural, puedes leerlo sin problema.
- Algunas oraciones deberían unirse. Otras deberían separarse en dos.
- Hay algunas cosas que sobran, seguro, pero no cubren con verborrea las buenas ideas . . . , aunque debo admitir que no vendría mal suprimir algunas palabras innecesarias aquí y allá y recortar algunas cosas.
- Creo que en el inicio de las oraciones incurrí en una rutina. Supongo que podría usar más variedad. Algunas veces inicio las oraciones de forma diferente.

1. Debo admitir que leer en voz alta es un reto (incluso para mí).

- Tal vez tengas que detenerte de vez en cuando y releer; da la sensación de que una oración está correcta y en el medio de otra empieza una oración nueva y, caramba, estoy perdido . . . No puedo sacarle el sentido a esto.
- ¡Ojalá hubiera suprimido algunas partes por completo!
- Tantas oraciones que empiezan de la misma forma. Mis oraciones son similares. Necesitan variedad y más pulido.
- Algunas oraciones están cortas. Demasiado cortas. Realmente están muy cortas. Cortas. C-o-r-t-a-s. ¿Entiendes? Muy bien.
- Es como intentar patinar sobre cartón. ¡Que difícil!

Convenciones

5. Cometí tan pocos errores, que un editor se aburriría buscándoles.

- Todas las mayúsculas están en el lugar que les corresponde.
- Los párrafos empiezan en los lugares adecuados.
- La puntuación es genial—la gramática también.
- Mi ortografía le asombrará (incluso la de palabras complicadas y abstrusas).
- Un editor no tendrá mucho que hacer en este trabajo.

3. Algunos errores molestos aparecen cuando leo con cuidado.

- La ortografía de las palabras sencillas está correcta.
- La mayoría de las mayúsculas están correctas. aunque tal vez debería volverlo a revisor.
- Puede ser que la gramática sea un poco informal, pero es válida para lo mas cotidiano de cada día.
- Algunos pronombres no coinciden con el nombre al que sustituyen.
- Podrías tropezar con mi puntuación! innovadora.
- Se lee como si realmente editara un poco antes de tenerlo listo para publicar.
- Definitivamente necesito editarlo un poco antes de tenerlo listo para publicar.

1. Es mejor leerlo primero para descifrarlo y luego otra vez para entenderlo.

- Muchos errares acen difícil la letura.
- he olvidado poner algunas MAYÚSCULAS—otraS no son Necesarias.
- Buscar con cuydado los herrores de otografía.
- A decir verdad, no pasé mucho tiempo editándolo.
- Creo que tendré que apurarme si quiero que esté listo para publicarlo.

FIGURE 11.28 *Student Checklist in Spanish*

6-Rasgos de Composicion
Lista de revisión estudiantil

Ideas

___ Tengo un mensaje principal (cuento, punto de vista, problema).

___ Detalles intrigantes o inusuales apoyan y expanden mi mensaje principal.

___ Sé mucho de este tema—y se ve.

___ Mi composición tiene un tono de autenticidad—que viene de mis experiencias/percepciones.

___ Mi composición no contiene información innecesaria.

Organización

___ Una entrada fuerte alenta al lector a continuar leyendo mi composición.

___ La información se organiza pensativamente para realzar el mensaje.

___ Palabras de transición (como además o después) conectan ideas.

___ La composición tiene balance; se destacan las ideas principales.

___ La conclusión es gratificante (como despedirte de un amigo).

Voz

___ Este texto parece mío. Tiene mi sello.

___ Mi composición está llena de energía y entusiasmo.

___ Me gusta el tema y se nota en mi voz.

___ Este es un cuento que uno disfrutaría compartiéndolo en voz alta.

___ Pensé en mi audiencia: *¿De qué saben de este tema ahora? ¿De qué quisieran enterarse?*

Selección de palabras

___ Escogí mis palabras cuidadosamente para hacer que el mensaje estuviera más claro.

___ Verbos fuertes y vivos le dan a mi cuento energía e impacto.

___ Mis palabras le pintan al lector imágines claras en la mente.

___ Evité palabras aburridas y vagas como agradable, bueno, o divertido.

___ Usé unas de mis palabras y frases emocionantes y favoritas—palabras de que te acordarás.

___ La escritura es natural. Suena como si yo estuviera hablando, no como un tesauro.

La fluidez de las oraciones

___ Esto tiene un ritmo sauve y fluye bien cuando se lee en voz alta.

___ La composición invita la lectura oral expresiva. La fluidez la voz subraya.

___ Mis oraciones empiezan en maneras diferentes; la composición tiene una variedad.

___ Algunas oraciones son cortas e impactantes mientras que otras son largas y fluidas.

___ Si yo uso de diálogo, es como si las personas hablaran. Es natural.

Convenciones y distribución

___ Leí esto cuidadosamente y busqué los errores.

___ Esta copia está lista para publicar— con nada más que unos retoques pequeños.

___ No hay errores que detengan al lector o que cambien el significado del mensaje.

___ Revisé la ortografía, la puntuación, la gramática, el uso de mayúsculas y el uso de los párrafos.

___ La distribución de párrafos es agradable. El ojo del lector será atraído a las ideas principales y la presentación es atractiva en la página.

(With special thanks to Stephen Pollard for help in translation.)

CHAPTER 11 IN A NUTSHELL

The six-trait model exists to serve you as a teacher—and to serve your students. You should feel free to modify or adapt it as necessary to make your instruction easier or more effective.

Many kinds of adaptations exist, including being selective about which traits to assess, developing related scoring guides (such as that for informational writing), or creating checklists to compress information.

Scoring guides (rubrics) and checklists serve slightly different purposes. Checklists are handy guides to revision; scoring guides (rubrics), that define performance at multiple levels, are useful for assessment *or* revision.

The informational scoring guide presented in this chapter may be used to assess a wide variety of writing, including informational, persuasive, business writing, and technical writing—in short, any writing involving research or intended for a business or professional audience.

A second-language scoring guide, such as the one presented in this chapter, may not capture nuances of what is valued in writing by another culture; it does, however, provide a bridge to the traits for those who find the English rubric difficult to interpret or apply.

EXTENSIONS

1. What are the particular advantages or disadvantages of using a checklist versus a scoring guide? Which would you be more likely to use in your classroom? For what purpose(s) would you use it? Discuss this with colleagues.
2. With your colleagues or your students, develop a checklist for technical or business writing. How will you decide what elements to include?
3. Test your checklist by trying it out on at least three samples. What modifications does your document need to be truly useful? What does it teach you about writing in the genre you selected?
4. Rubrics and scoring guides are never perfect. They always need revision and adaptation. What, in your mind, are the chief characteristics of a good scoring guide, and why is it so hard to capture on paper what's in our hearts and minds? Write a journal entry about this.

WHY I WRITE

I write because I love to write. The words flow from my hand as if I am in the story, as if I am the writing. . . . I write because I am addicted to writing. I get one idea flowing out of my head and my imagination goes crazy like a maniac in a lab. . . . I write because I feel free, like an eagle stretching its wings across the canyon.

—Becca Zoller, student writer

LOOKING AHEAD

In Chapter 12 we examine the world of primary writing and provide some simplified scoring continuums that you can use with very young writers. Please note that a much more extensive discussion of primary writing can be found in the companion book, *Creating Young Writers* (Allyn and Bacon, 2004).

12 Exploring the World of Beginning Writers

*A*t the primary level, writing is wondrous and magical. It comes in many forms: sketches, scribbles, dictated stories, recordings, word play, "tadpole people" (mostly head, tiny arms and legs), pictographs—and conventional text as well. Sometimes text goes left to right on the page as we have been conditioned to expect, but primary writers, not yet bound by convention, find their own inventive ways to fill the page: right to left, bottom to top, around in a spiral—or clean off the page and on to adventure.

The writing of the very young reflects both their creative individuality and an uncanny ability to observe, recall, and use the conventions from the print that fills their world. At this age, there are no "errors" in the true sense, any more than beginning walkers make errors in foot placement. Rather, there are hundreds, thousands, of experiments by beginning writers finding their own paths to learning.

Children can write sooner than we ever dreamed possible. Most children come to school knowing a handful of letters, and with these they can write labels and calendars, letters and stories, poem and songs. They will learn to write by writing and by living with a sense of "I am one who writes."

—Lucy McCormick Calkins
The Art of Teaching Writing, 1994, p. 83

You do not need to be writing fluent sentences yourself to know what fluency is. Your ears will tell you. You do not need to write stories filled with voice to know voice when you hear it. The smile on your face, the tears in your eyes, or the chill up your back will tell you.

—Vicki Spandel
Creating Young Writers, 2004, p. 7

310

TEACHING OURSELVES WHAT TO LOOK FOR

We know that primary writing looks very different from that of older writers. But like impatient parents imagining our children at that first book signing, we watch for paragraphs to emerge, for the first use of quotation marks, for complete sentences and correct spelling. These things excite us and make us feel successful as teachers. We forget sometimes that there is much to get excited over long before these milestones of sophisticated writing ever appear.

Consider the very early piece of writing shown in Figure 12.1 in picture form by 4-year-old Nikki. What we see here may not be conventional writing, but it is remarkably expressive. Notice the expression on the face of the bat: humorous, mischievous—that's *voice*. How many writer-artists of this age have noticed that spiders have eight legs and multiple eyes? Notice the toes of the bat, too, and the hollow ears. This is a young writer-artist who takes more than a passing glance at the world around her. As a result, her work is brimming with detail—that's *ideas*.

Another sample of writing—by a slightly older writer, Mike, is shown in Figure 12.2. This piece is significant because it shows that wonderful moment of stand-alone writer-to-reader communication. We can say, "Mike—I read this without help, and it made perfect sense to me. You are an independent writer." Notice that Mike has created a complete sentence: "Mom, remind me to read my book." He signs his important message "Dear Mike" because when Mom writes to him, that's how she begins, so he now thinks of "Dear Mike" as his complete name.

Consider conventions in this piece, too. Remember for a moment that all conventions, even the simplest and most taken-for-granted things, must be learned. What do you see? Left-to-right orientation on the page and the beginning of spaces between words. Even a period at the end that seems to say, "Stop. This sen-

> *Many times children don't realize they can write. An effective writing teacher leads kids to an understanding of the four structures needed for early-childhood writing. . . . Are dictation, scribbling, drawing, and temporary spelling necessary to early writing development? Yes.*
>
> **—Bea Johnson**
> *Never Too Early to Write,*
> 1999, p. 42

> *Stressing neatness instead of content is an ever-present danger. Many of us were carefully taught the opposite during our school days. But especially in early childhood, all attempts at writing should be celebrated rather than corrected!*
>
> **—Bea Johnson**
> *Never Too Early to Write,*
> 1999, p. 33

FIGURE 12.1   *Bat and Spider, by Nikki, Age 4*

FIGURE 12.2   *Mike's Note*

tence is finished." These things seem so basic, but they are not automatic, nor are they necessarily simple to learn. This writer is also beginning to distinguish between capital and lowercase letters, although he does not yet use them correctly. Remember, though, discovery is worthy of celebration in its own right. Correct placement is a more sophisticated skill.

HELPING WRITERS SEE THEIR STRENGTHS

How do we help our young writers see what is strong within their work so that they can build on those strengths? First, we must teach *ourselves* to see what each writer is doing correctly across all dimensions of writing—not the gaps, not what's missing, but what is *there*. Then we must point it out: "Mike, I see you've discovered periods. Great! Can you tell me what they mean?"

Gentle, gradual encouragement is among the most effective of all teaching strategies. We have more or less abandoned this approach in much of our formal instruction, but most of us, if we think about it, instinctively know the power of a teacher who believes absolutely in our capability. Picture a father cheering on his 11-month-old daughter as she learns to walk. "That's it! Come on! One more step. You can do it! Yes! Good! Move your feet—that's it. Come on—I'll catch you. You're doing it! You're *walking!*" We need this image in our heads as we teach writing. We need to notice the little things (not just the big milestones) and put them to work to encourage our young writers, who are often doing much more than they get credit for.

The father in our scenario knows that correctness is a goal for later; exploration is the right goal for now. How surprised we would be to hear him say, "*No*, Martha, not *toe* first—*heel* first, remember? Do it the way I showed you. No, I really can't call that walking, not *real* walking. It's just kind of stumbling along. I'm afraid I can't give you credit for that. Oops, you fell— well, five points off." Sound ridiculous? How much more ridiculous is it than setting our expectations for young writers too high too soon?

> It's been a good thing that babies don't understand the concept of "clumsiness" or else they'd never learn to walk.
>
> **—Alan Ziegler**
> *The Writing Workshop*, 1981, p. 37

HOW TRAITS LOOK EARLY ON

Such things as voice, vocabulary growth, fluency, and expression of ideas show up in oral storytelling and in picture writing long before students begin to produce conventional text. So we must learn to *listen* for ideas, voice, and other important qualities even before we see them printed on a page. Next, we must learn to look for hints of these traits in even the earliest text, including pictures—then in letter play, letter strings, word strings, and finally—oh, joy—that first full sentence. Here are just a few things you might look and listen for in young writers' work—and in their responses to literature, too:

> When children can sit down and put their thoughts on paper quickly and easily, they are fluent writers even if they make errors. If the teacher is always correcting the students' spelling and punctuation errors, the children will stop guessing and trying. This will lead to dull writing with students afraid to use words they can't spell.
>
> **—Bea Johnson**
> *Never Too Early to Write*, 1999, p. 33

■ *Ideas*

✔ Little close-up details: veins in leaves, wings and legs on insects, expressive faces
✔ Signs of movement (e.g., a person or animal running)
✔ Multiple pictures that tell a more complex story

✔ Any message—no matter how delivered—that makes sense to you, the reader (i.e., if you can make meaning from it, the ideas are clear)
✔ Ability to retell a story (here, the child is making the meaning)
✔ Ability to recognize another writer's point or message

■ *Organization*

✔ Balance on the page—good use of white space
✔ Balance within pictures: proportion, sizing, coordination among parts
  ✔ Use of a title (an early beginning)
  ✔ Coordination of text with illustrations
  ✔ Layout that works and that's pleasing to the eye
  ✔ More than one detail or events put in order (e.g., through multiple pictures)
✔ Ability to predict events in a story (grasping the concept of organization)
✔ Ability to see how a picture and text go together (e.g., What extra information does the picture give you?)
✔ Ability to choose one beginning or ending over another
✔ Ability to group "like" things (by shape, color, size, etc.)
✔ Use of "The End," often the earliest form of a conclusion

■ *Voice*

✔ Originality and expressiveness—in color, shape, style, choice of images, choice of labels, choice of topics
✔ Expressiveness and emotion (What do you see on characters' faces?)
✔ Individuality, ownership (you can tell it belongs to *this* child and no other)
✔ An image, a moment, an idea that makes you *feel* something
✔ Love of life, love of writing/drawing
✔ Enthusiasm, exuberance
✔ Playfulness
✔ Pleasure in hearing strong voice in the writing of others

■ *Word Choice*

✔ Use of *words!* (They might be single letters, letter combinations, or letter strings at first, but in the young writer's mind, these are words.)
✔ Words that show action, energy, or movement (expressed orally or in writing)
✔ Words that describe
✔ Words that convey feelings
✔ A passion, a love, for new, unusual, or fun-to-say words
✔ Words that stretch *beyond* the child's spelling capabilities
✔ Words that help you see, feel, and understand
✔ Expressed curiosity about new words

■ *Sentence Fluency*

✔ Letter strings that translate into sentences
✔ Word grouping that imitates sentence patterns
✔ Sentence sense (an ear for what a sentence is)
✔ That first whole, complete sentence

> As a society, we allow children to learn to speak by trial and error. But when it comes to reading and writing, we expect them to be right the first time.
>
> **—Donald H. Graves and Virginia Stuart**
>
> *Write from the Start: Tapping Your Child's Natural Writing Ability,* 1987, p. 21

✔ Use of multiple sentences
✔ Patterns that reinforce meaning: "Cats sleep all day. Dogs sleep at night."
✔ A willingness to try new sentence forms—breaking out of patterns into variety (Compare *"I like my dog. I like my cat. I like school"* with *"I like cats and dogs. But I love my cat the most. Do you like school? Me too."*)

■ Conventions

✔ Left-to-right orientation
✔ Top-to-bottom orientation
✔ Spaces between words or lines
✔ Association of letters with sounds
✔ Letters that face the right direction
✔ *Readable* spelling
✔ Use of punctuation (whether placed correctly or not)
✔ Distinction between capital and lowercase letters (whether used correctly or not)
✔ Use of end punctuation
✔ Use of a title
✔ Awareness of margins
✔ Use of *I* (capitalized)
✔ Ability to spell own name
✔ Interest in environmental print

FIGURE 12.3   *"Clouds," by Nicole (Grade 2)*

Clouds

Clouds are big puffy things but what a cloud rely is a big bunch of water. You can find difrint shaps in them, they are some tims fun to look at, Clouds are veryvery big. In other words clouds are eanormos.

Any of these lists can—and should—be expanded as you notice other features of young children's writing. Keep track. Reward each step by noticing how far young writers have come.

IDEAS FOR TEACHING TRAITS TO BEGINNERS

Here are nine general ideas for teaching traits to beginning writers.

Idea 1: Don't Worry About Numbers—Yet

The key to good assessment that communicates *to young students* is observing signs of growth and change—not putting numbers on their performances. (Plenty of time for that beginning in third or fourth grade.) For younger writers, describe what you see, as clearly as you can, using language that makes sense to them, but do not worry about whether it's a 2, 3, or 4—or for that matter an A, B, or C. Numbers are used most effectively with students who can begin to understand the meaning *behind* those numbers. If we

*"Sam is My Friend,"
by Kean (Grade 1)*

> me   sam
>
> Sam is my friend we we're friends. Sins we were babys. I relly like Sam. And I ustu bit his finggers.

say to a primary writer, "Well, Bill, this piece of writing is about a 3 in ideas, but we're going to work on getting you up to a 4 or 5," we can't expect this to be anything but gibberish to Bill. It makes much more sense to say, "Bill, a while ago I had trouble sometimes reading your work without your help, but now I am recognizing some letters and even some words. I can understand your writing even when you're not there to read it to me. This is *so* exciting."

Consider Nicole's paper (Figure 12.3) on clouds. It has descriptive detail (*"big puffy things"*) as well as good information: *"What a cloud really is [is] a big bunch of water."* There's also a stretch for a new word—*"Clouds are very, very big. In other words, clouds are eanormos."* We also see the beginnings of real variety in sentences, something we do not always see at grade 2.

Kean's piece (Figure 12.4) is highly audience-oriented. It has a sincere, heartfelt tone (*"I relly like Sam"*). Words like *very* and *really* are early ways of injecting voice. But even better is Kean's willingness to share a secret. Psst—come closer: *"I ustu bit his finggers."* Direct connection to an audience is the very foundation of voice.

Lincoln, also a first grader, writes very lovingly of his brother Nick (Figure 12.5). *"He plays a lot if hes not bisey."* We have to be delighted with this line, imagining Nick making time for Lincoln and noting how much Lincoln appreciates it. He generously refers to him as the "faveist" (favorite). But the last line is best of all: *"His kindnis gits biger avre day."* Wouldn't you love to have a friend say that about you? We need to tell Lincoln just that.

Let's talk spelling for a moment because I know that some teachers get itchy when they see a line like that last one. They want to write little red corrections right above Lincoln's writing. I wouldn't do that, personally. Why? Because it puts the focus in the wrong place. Instead, I might say to the whole class, "Writers come across great words when they write. One of the words Lincoln discovered for us today is *kindness*. What a terrific word. If we learn to spell it together, we can all use it in our writing when we want to. This word has eight letters, so let me write eight blanks: _ _ _ _ _ _ _ _. Now, let's see if we can fill them in. Who wants to try the first letter?" I want Lincoln to know that his discovery of this wondrous word is more important to me than whether he spelled it right the first time. I also want him to know that by using a word that was new to him, he created a learning opportunity for everyone. That's a gift. The word *kindness* now goes on the wall for everyone to see and use. By the way, no need to attend to *every* misspelled word on each child's paper.

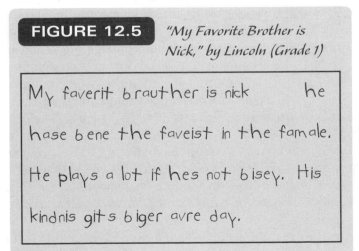

*"My Favorite Brother is
Nick," by Lincoln (Grade 1)*

> My faverit brauther is nick   he
>
> hase bene the faveist in the famale.
>
> He plays a lot if hes not bisey. His
>
> kindnis gits biger avre day.

| FIGURE 12.6 | *"I Like My Library," by Nicholas (Grade 1)* |

I like my library because I like to learn about everything!

and books can Take me anywhere like to the tomb of King Tut, and to the home of the Arctic Wolf. Books have also taken me to a den of lions with Daniel and to the Site of the first dinosaur discovery.

When I go to the library it's like talking to the Smartest person in the whole world— my Dad! First Im Greeted by my librarian, who always helps me pick out the right book. Then, It's up to me to explore Luckily, she is patient When I forget to return it.

the library is my Favorite place to be!

Pick two or three from the class. That's enough. Take it easy.

Nicholas is a confident first grade writer, and his confidence fills his writing (Figure 12.6) with voice. He uses his experience masterfully to fill his paper about the library with rich and personal details. This is not on-the-surface writing. We get right inside Nicholas' head. What a treat it is when a young writer shares so much of himself.

To appreciate the sophisticated sentence fluency of this piece, read it aloud. How many different ways does this writer find to begin? *"When I go . . . , First I'm greeted . . . , Then, it's up to me . . . , Luckily, she is patient."* This is beautiful writing—and quite remarkable from a first grader. We cannot expect that all first graders will attain this level of skill and grace. Nicholas writes with some ease and has begun experimenting with a wide range of conventions, including paragraphing, hyphens, dashes, commas, apostrophes, and exclamation points. Not all first graders yet have this repertoire of skills from which to draw, but we can enrich their worlds with samples of good writing, and we can read to them often with care and expression. We might surprise ourselves with how far we can take them. (To see this same writer's work 11 years after "I like my library," check out Figure 12.31, "If Men Were Angels . . ." at the end of this chapter.)

Jocelyn shows wonderful fluency for a young writer in an expanded story about a cat and dog on a shopping trip. Look for the moments of voice in Figure 12.7. It may remind you of some of your own shopping adventures. In addition, this particular piece shows remarkable control of many conventions and excellent experimenting with inventive (*temporary*) spelling. Notice the ellipses ("*ate them in the store . . . then called a taxi*"), as well as the quotation marks and exclamation points ('*this is disgusting!!!*'). The inventive spelling shows a sharp ear for sound: *seriel, grocry* (this is how most of us actually pronounce it), *cupbord,* and *somthing.* In addition, many words are spelled with conventional accuracy: *taxi, disgusting, opened, melted, jokes, uncles,* and *shopping*—not to mention *ice cream sandwiches* (Did she look at the label?). The ending shows the cat and dog doing what most of us do at the end of a long shopping day—swapping stories until they grow punchy.

FIGURE 12.7   *"Catdog Shopping," by Jocelyn (Grade 1)*

One day my cat and my dog were hungrey so they went to the cupbord to get somthing to eat but there was no cat or dog food in the cupbord and so they wint to the catdog shopping mall. They went to the grocry store and first they went to ial 8 and they looked at all the catfood and dogfood and they said 'this is disgusting!!!' so they went to ial 4 to get some sereil but all of the boxes of seriel were opened so they could not buy any seriel, and so they went to ial number 1 for ice cream sandwiches. they put the ice cream sandwiches in ther cart but the ice cream sandwiches melted and so they went back to ial 1 and got more ice cream sandwiches and they ate them in the store . . . then they called a taxi and on the way home they told jokes about ther mothrs and uncles and the dog laffed so hard he fell off the seat and then they were home and they went in the house.

Figure 12.8 shows Mason's first book, produced in kindergarten. Notice his organization. He has a cover page, plus two chapters. In Chapter 1 he's a good boy, but then, as so often happens as the plot unfolds, things go downhill in Chapter 2. I was struck by the fact that that he could spell *naughty* correctly, but as his teacher explained, when Mason is acting up, his mom sometimes

FIGURE 12.8   *"Mason's First Book" (Kindergarten)*

says, "Oh, Mason is being *n-a-u-g-h-t-y* again," and of course, Mason picked up that spelling at once. Perhaps we should work to keep the spelling of more words a secret.

What *does* it mean to be old—in the eyes of a young child? Perspective is everything. Years ago, when my 6-year-old best friend's brother turned 20, we thought it was all over; he was no longer one of "us." By comparison, Megan (Figure 12.9) is quite mature in her thinking, but notice the power of numbers; as soon as she puts a figure with her definition, she is afraid she's offended someone. Suppose that her reader meets her definition of *old*? And

---

FIGURE 12.9   *"Old," by Megan (Grade 3)*

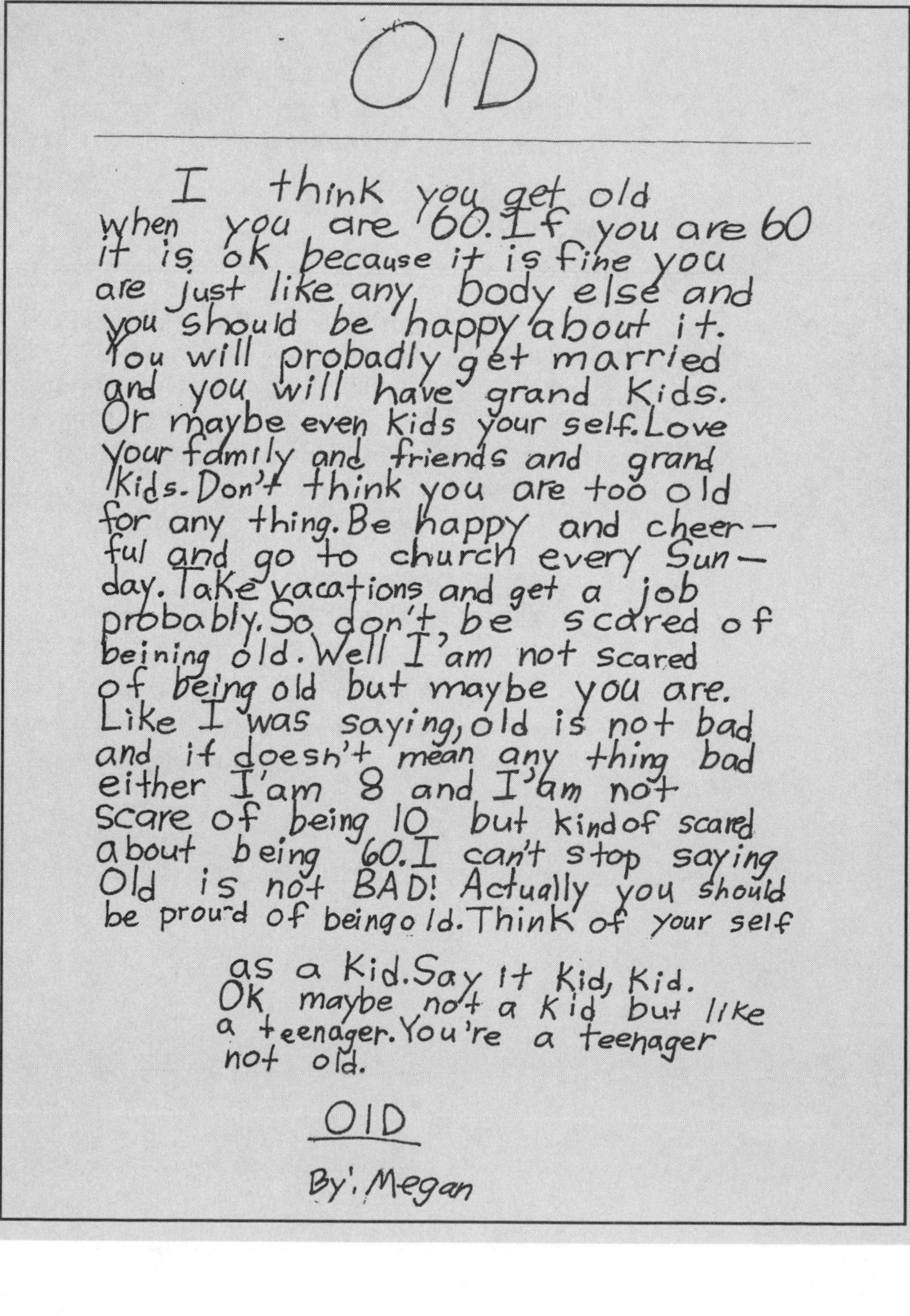

OID

I think you get old when you are 60. If you are 60 it is ok because it is fine you are just like any body else and you should be happy about it. You will probadly get married and you will have grand kids. Or maybe even kids your self. Love your family and friends and grand kids. Don't think you are too old for any thing. Be happy and cheerful and go to church every Sunday. Take vacations and get a job probably. So don't be scared of beining old. Well I'am not scared of being old but maybe you are. Like I was saying, old is not bad and if doesh't mean any thing bad either I'am 8 and I'am not scare of being 10 but kind of scared about being 60. I can't stop saying Old is not BAD! Actually you should be proud of being old. Think of your self

as a kid. Say it kid, kid. Ok maybe not a kid but like a teenager. You're a teenager not old.

OID

By: Megan

| **FIGURE 12.10** | *"Dear Tooth Fairy," by Leah (Grade 2)* |

Dear Tooth Fairy,

I don't have a tooth right now
because my dog ate my tooth.

So my point is, I lost my
tooth, my dog ate it, so do I
still get money?

Your still beliver,

Leah

P.S. I don't know if my dog
really ate it but I really lost it.

the remainder of the paper is spent comforting, reassuring the audience that it is okay, it is all right, you're a kid: *"Say it kid, kid. OK maybe not a kid but like a teenager."* Whew. That's a relief.

Letters, as noted earlier, are a powerful means for developing voice—as Leah's note to the tooth fairy (Figure 12.10) clearly illustrates. Like any good business letter, it comes right to the point. Notice in particular the postscript; Leah seems to reflect when writing to the tooth fairy that it may be best to come clean with the whole story.

Perspective is the foundation for "Jamey The Cat" (Figure 12.11). Second grader Veronica has had some help with her editing but also has done much of it herself, via computer, and it is work to be proud of. Even more impressive, though, is her take on point of view. Her teacher, an artist, has told the class how different the world can look, depending on who you are and where you are. Veronica's understanding of this concept is quite profound, as is evident in how she adopts the role of a cat who is loving yet a little resentful that her friend Sarah gets all the fun; revenge is afoot—a most sophisticated and subtle ending.

Brad (grade 2) combines art and text to create an impressive reflection on a pyramid, from the pyramid's point of view. Figure 12.12*a* shows his collage art depiction of pyramids against an Egyptian sky. In his rough draft (Figure

FIGURE 12.11 *"Jamey The Cat," by Veronica (Grade 2)*

"Jamey The Cat"

My name is Jamey. I am a cat. I like this window sill. I can see a lot from here. Sarah is outside. She is having a picnic with a friend. I love Sarah. I love outside. But I can't go outside now. I've been fixed. That means I can't have kittens anymore. I didn't want kittens anyway. They are a lot of hard work. My nails were pulled out too. If I go outside I will get clawed till I die. So I don't go outside. I'd like to, but I don't. I love Sarah, but I want to picnic too. When Sarah comes home I'm not letting her pet me!

by Veronica
Grade 2
St. Wilfrid

no nails →

12.12*b*), he does not allow spelling to interfere with his stretch for new, meaningful words (*protect, crumbling, officially, responsibility*). Compare his draft with the final (Figure 12.12*c*) to see how editing and formatting work together to create meaning for the reader.

In Figure 12.13, Andrew (a kindergartner) tries his hand at a full sentence: "Mr. Bear is loving." He gets just the first consonant of the last word and shows us a handy way for beginning writers to indicate a longer word they cannot quite spell yet. He'll be filling in the blanks in no time. He gets in some good practice with detail and spelling, first with his grocery list (Figure 12.14)—*peanut butter, bread,* and *honey*—and then with his "To Do" list (Figure 12.15)—*eat, play, [watch] TV, [go to the] park, [ride my] bike, read,* and *draw.* He is bursting with ideas; a list gives him a simple, coordinated format for expressing them.

Notice how much information second grader Connor packs into his piece "My Winter Vacation" (Figure 12.16). The voice is strong yet very controlled and sophisticated for so young a writer: "*I had to have an IV; it was very an-*

FIGURE 12.12 *Brad's "Pyramid" (Grade 2): (a) Collage Art: The Pyramids; (b) Rough Draft; (c) Final Draft, Revised and Edited in Poetry Format*

b

I can pirteot very preslsh
thing like the mumy and the
jewles but soon I will not
be a belle to pirtect
any thing for I am
crumbling before my eyes.
the heat wind and sand are
beating awae at me my
age is growing today
i'm ofishaly fourt howsin
years old. But at night when
I gaze over all the stars
I reamember wen I was
being bilt geting a new
reasponsebilite to portect
a mumy. I am a pyramid.

c

I can protect very precious things
Like the mummy and the jewels.
But soon I will not be able to protect anything
For I am
Crumbling before my eyes.
The heat, wind, and sand are beating away at me.
My age is growing.
Today I am officially four thousand years old.
But at night
When I gaze over all the stars,
I remember when I was being built
And getting a new responsibility
To protect a mummy.
I am a pyramid.

FIGURE 12.13	*"Mr. Bear Is Loving!" by Andrew (Kindergarten)*

Mr br is I Loving

FIGURE 12.14	*"My Grocery List," by Andrew (Kindergarten)*

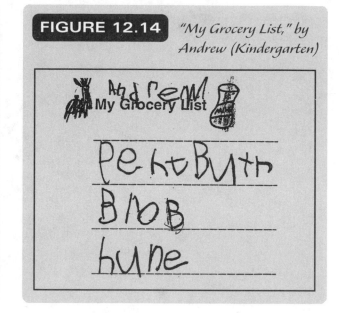

FIGURE 12.15	*"My To Do List," by Andrew (Kindergarten)*

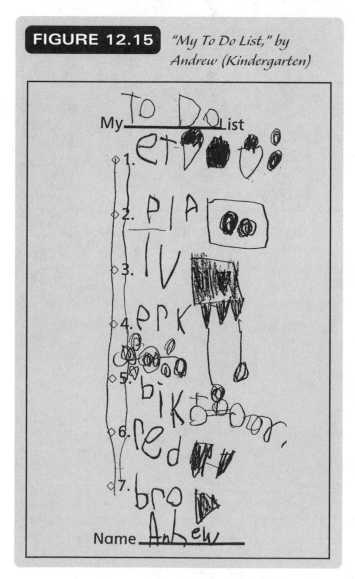

noying." *Annoying!* The perfect word. Then there's good old Aunt Helen, who provides Connor with an exceptionally thorough history book. Like many teachers, I was concerned about organization, thinking Aunt Helen had arrived right on the heels of the paramedics. But then, I was thinking *chronological order*, you see, and as Conner explained to me, "Uh, no—see, I was trying to explain the parts I *didn't* like so much and then the parts that were pretty good." That makes sense, and I love it that Aunt Helen provides the transition.

In second grade, Connor showed so much blossoming talent that I was thrilled to receive a comparison piece, "The Appendix Days" (Figure 12.17), written when he was in the sixth grade—coincidentally *on the same topic*. Voice and detail are striking. We sometimes worry that writers return to a topic again and again. We shouldn't, though. An impressive adventure provides a rich collection of detail from which to draw. How much do you learn about this writer's growing skill by comparing these two pieces? What has he learned (and what does his writing teach us) about voice, dialogue, imagery, and the value of small details?

Idea 2: Building Awareness with Language

How do we create criteria that primary or beginning writers can use? Simple. No elaborate rubrics—instead, we begin with writers' questions,

FIGURE 12.16 *"My Winter Vacation," by Connor (Grade 2)*

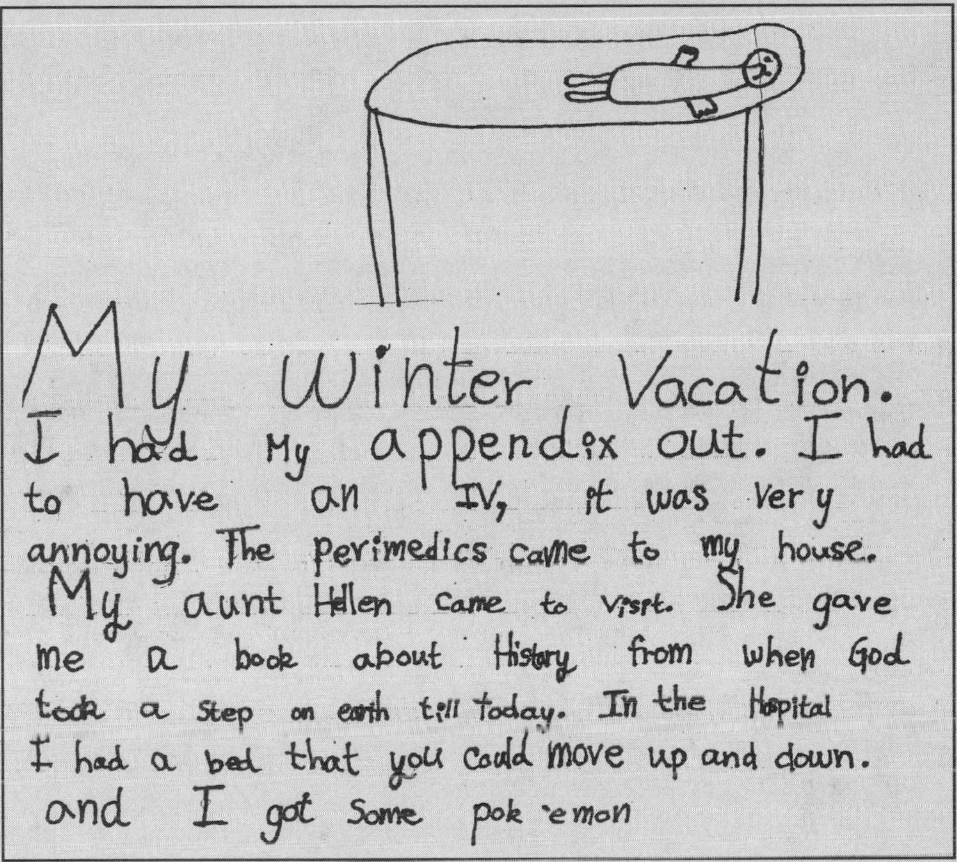
My Winter Vacation.
I had My appendix out. I had to have an IV, it was very annoying. The perimedics came to my house. My aunt Hellen came to visit. She gave me a book about History from when God took a step on earth till today. In the Hospital I had a bed that you could move up and down. and I got Some pok 'emon

> *Evaluation is embedded in all we do. Every time we make a choice—cereal or toast for breakfast, the black skirt or the black pants . . . each decision involves evaluation. We're all pros at it.*
>
> **—Jane Fraser and Donna Skolnick**
>
> *On Their Way: Celebrating Second Graders as They Read and Write,* 1994, p. 7

a list I call "Thinking Like a Writer" (see Figure 12.18). These questions show young writers, in a simple but clear way, how to begin thinking about their writing without the pressure of formal evaluation. Turn these into posters if you like.

This is a long list, but remember: You can introduce *one trait at a time* and *one question at a time.* Make individual trait posters. Don't rush. Use your own writing as a model, and ask yourself these same questions as you go. Then, as you read aloud from favorite literature, ask the questions with your students about books or other things you read. Let students know from the first that you value their opinions as evaluators. In this way you teach students to ask these questions of themselves as they write. And that is the goal.

Idea 3: Help Students Think Like Writers

Use writers' vocabulary routinely to talk about students' writing. *Never* miss an opportunity to point out a moment of voice or a small indication of detail, however tiny. Remember Nikki's picture in Figure 12.1? When you get a piece like that, it's a great opportunity to sneak in some trait language (*think writers' language*) that helps shape your student's thinking: "Nikki, you have really taken a

FIGURE 12.17 *"The Appendix Days," by Connor (Grade 6)*

Ouch! I awoke with a pain in the lower right part of my stomach. I touched my belly gingerly, and through my bed clothes, I could feel the cold. All I could see was bottomless blackness and my clock read 2:00 am. It was Christmas day.

I stumbled into my mom's room and said, "Mom, my stomach really hurts." Before I keeled over in a lifeless heap, I think I said, "Huh," and the sounded faded away like I turned off the TV. Everything went ink black and from the middle of my vision I saw a white streak. I saw bubbles rise and swirl away, and then, I heard a buzz in my ears and felt a cold weight bear down on my chest. My vision became clear and I saw a Christmas tree in the corner of the family room, and then . . . I saw paramedics all over the room. I looked up, and a paramedic took the stethoscope off my chest and said, "His appendix is infected. He needs to go to the hospital." My mom almost fell over. Her face turned green and then white, and finally turned bright red. Once she caught herself, the paramedic spoke again, "Ma'am, we can take him or you can." Although every kid drams of riding in an ambulance, my boring mom said, "Oh no, I'll take him."

When we got to Capital Medical Center, I was shocked when they rushed me right back to an examining room. I was used to waiting for hours and hours in the waiting room. The doctor poked me and asked me where it hurt. It didn't hurt terribly until Dr. Vasek asked me to roll over and sit up. I pulled myself up, and the pain shot through me, and I screamed out. (My mom later told me I then fainted.)

Finally, I was given my room. I looked around, and there was my bed. I began pushing the buttons on the remote control. It went up, down, and side to side. It warmed me and massaged my back. After that I probably went to sleep.

Later when I awoke, I realized I was still in my room. I found out later I was supposed to go into surgery at 3:00 am but there was this huge lady in front of me, and the doctor couldn't find her gall bladder. Her surgery took four and a half hours. Finally it was my turn. I cried and wanted my dog. Then, with no mercy, they said "It's your turn."

To get to the operating room, I was wheeled down long, dark halls. We passed open doorway where I could see other sick people lying in their beds. We finally arrived at the operating room. It was a room with light blue paint and knives lined up nicely by size on the blue countertops. The doctor was tall, had brown hair, and a big nose. He said, "We are going to put you in a sleep." He pulled out a mask and positioned it up over my nose. It was rubber, and it smelled like an old tire. The doctor said, "Connor, count backwards from 100." I began quickly, "100, 99, 98. . . , " It was the last number I remember.

I awoke with a lot more pain some time in the next afternoon, and I saw my grandpa. I didn't know it, but he had been with me the entire time. He said, "Nice popcorn seed." Then I laughed. And that hurt a lot.

After that day in the hospital, I had lost a lot of weight. So I decided to eat. The food was okay but not the best. After they ran me through my check up I was free to go.

When I got home, it was hard to move. Missy, my dog, helped a lost. She was a great dog. She lay next to me the whole time and kept me warm. She even helped me in and out of bed.

In conclusion, beware of getting popcorn seeds caught in your appendix and get a dog to help you when you do.

FIGURE 12.18   *Thinking Like a Writer*

Ideas

- What is my *message?*
- Is my *message* clear?
- Do I have enough *information?*
- Do I have *details?*

Organization

- How does my paper *begin?*
- Did I *organize* my details?
- How does my paper *end?*

Voice

- Do I really *like* this paper?
- Does this writing sound like *me?*
- How do I want my reader to *feel?*
- My favorite part is _____

Word Choice

- Have I used words I *love?*
- Can my reader tell what my words *mean?*
- Did I use any *new* words?

- My *favorite* word in this paper is _____

Sentence Fluency

- Did I use *sentences?*
- How *many sentences* did I write?
- How many ways did I *begin* my sentences?
- Did I use some *long* sentences?
- Did I use some *short* sentences?

Conventions

- Did I have *spaces* between words?
- Does my writing go *left to right?*
- Did I use a *title?*
- Did I leave *margins?*
- Did I use *capitals* to begin sentences and for the word I?
- Did I use *periods* or *question marks?*
- Did I use my *best* spelling?
- Could another person read this?

close look at spiders! You noticed they have eight legs and multiple eyes. That's detail! And this bat—I love his toes and the hollow ears. Look at this smile on his face. That's what I call voice!" Then perhaps Nikki will think, "I'm a person who takes a close look at things. My writing has detail. My writing has *voice.*"

With your comments, you plant a seed from which will blossom an amazing flower—*if* you nurture it. Talk about details, organization, voice, leads and endings, word choice, and fluency. Make these words and phrases part of your students' writing vocabulary. In this way you give them a tool for thinking about writing—and understanding their own potential.

Idea 4: Read and Celebrate Literature

If you love to read aloud (and what teacher of writing doesn't?), you already have at your command the most powerful means available for teaching the

From my own experience I realize that the literature I heard, rather than read, as a child resonates again and again in my memory whenever I sit down to write ... vocabulary and a sense of rhythm are almost impossible to "teach" in the narrow sense of the word. So how are children expected to develop a sense of rhythm or a wide vocabulary? By being read to, alive, a lot!

—Mem Fox
Radical Reflections, 1993, p. 68

traits to beginning writers. Think of the books that you love most. Chances are, many are strong in details and imagery (ideas), feelings (voice), word choice, or fluency. Many likely have catchy beginnings or surprise endings—both good for teaching organization. Or maybe they're full of surprises, so you can invite your students to make predictions that may or may not come true—also good for teaching organization. In *Creating Young Writers* (Spandel, 2004), a text that focuses on primary writing exclusively, I suggest many books to use in teaching traits to K–3 students and discuss writing activities to accompany each one. Here are just a few examples from books that are some of my favorites.

Who can surpass William Steig (1971) when it comes to word choice? In *Amos and Boris* we can savor every luscious syllable in his description of friendship between the intrepid, seafaring mouse, Amos, and his benevolent and courageous friend, Boris, a whale:

> Boris admired the delicacy, the quivering daintiness, the light touch, the small voice, the gemlike radiance of the mouse. Amos admired the bulk, the grandeur, the power, the purpose, the rich voice, and the abounding friendliness of the whale.

Listening to someone who relishes language as Steig does, students will find meaning in words they didn't know they knew. That's the power of a master who can make meaning clear from context.

To combine ideas with word choice, try a word picture from Faith Ringgold's (1991) magical tribute to a child's imagination, *Tar Beach:*

> I will always remember when the stars fell down around me and lifted me up above the George Washington Bridge.

We literally see and hear the hushed whisper of falling stars when those words are read aloud. We feel ourselves float. You might ask students to sketch a picture. It's one way to sense the power of ideas.

Do you want to teach the power of a strong lead? Share these opening lines from Petra Mathers's (1991) enchanting tale, *Sophie and Lou:*

> Sophie was shy—so shy she did her shopping during the lull hours, so she wouldn't have to talk to anyone. Every Wednesday the Book-Mobile parked in front of the supermarket, and every Wednesday Sophie almost went in. But the librarian was so tall!

What will become of someone so shy that she is afraid of tall people? Make a prediction. Predicting as you go is an important organizational skill, too.

As you read, ask students to tell you what they picture (ideas), what they feel (voice), and what expressions they notice (word choice). Ask them to listen for the rhythm or, sometimes, to say the words back and hear the beat, the fluency, as in this passage from Deborah Hopkinson's *Under the Quilt of Night* (2001):

> I run so fast, I lead the way; the ones I love race right behind. Pounding dirt and grass, jumping rocks and roots, my feet make drumbeats on the path.

In *Dear Mrs. LaRue: Letters from Obedience School* (2002), author/illustrator Mark Teague shows how perspective (writing from the dog's point of view) can add voice and humor—as in this letter home from Ike, who's been carted off to Brotweiler Canine Academy to learn manners:

> How could you do this to me? This is a PRISON, not a school! You should see the other dogs. They are BAD DOGS, Mrs. LaRue! I do not fit in.

In using books with primary writers, you can follow up by asking them to draw pictures, write letters to the author, pretend to be a character, ask questions, talk in groups about the book, write a similar story using the book as a model—or any of a dozen other things. But it's also important to realize that just reading aloud is often enough. When you share a book, you say, "I love books. I love to read." And when you ask students, "Listen for the voice in this piece," "See if you can pick out one favorite word," or "Tell me what you picture [ideas] as you listen to this story," you are enriching their listening by helping them to see what gives each book its special power.

■ *Favorite Books for Primary*

Here is a summary list of some of my favorite read-aloud books to use with primary/beginning writers (adult readers love these, too):

Animal Dads, by Sneed B. Collard III   ideas, word choice, organization

Beaks! by Sneed B. Collard III—ideas, word choice

Beast Feast, by Douglas Florian   word choice, fluency

The Big Box, by Toni Morrison—ideas, voice, fluency

Come On, Rain! by Karen Hesse—word choice, fluency

Courage, by Bernard Waber—ideas

Crickwing, by Janell Cannon—word choice, fluency

Days with Frog and Toad, by Arnold Lobel—ideas, voice, fluency

Dear Mr. Blueberry, by Simon James—ideas, organization

Dear Mrs. LaRue, by Mark Teague—voice, organization

Diary of a Worm, by Doreen Cronin—voice

Everybody Needs a Rock, by Byrd Baylor—ideas, fluency

Fables, by Arnold Lobel—ideas, word choice, voice

From Head to Toe, by Eric Carle—organization

Great Crystal Bear, by Carolyn Lesser—fluency, ideas

Growing Frogs, by Vivian French—organization

Hey, Little Ant, by Phillip and Hannah Hoose—ideas, voice

Hooway for Wodney Wat, by Helen Lester—ideas, voice

I, Crocodile, by Fred Marcellino—voice, word choice, fluency

I Will Never Not Ever Eat a Tomato, by Lauren Child—word choice, voice

In the Swim, by Douglas Florian—word choice, fluency

Insectlopedia, by Douglas Florian—word choice, fluency

Jellies, by Twig C. George—ideas, voice

Julius, the Baby of the World, by Kevin Henkes—voice

Lunchtime for a Purple Snake, by Harriet Ziefert—ideas

My Beak, Your Beak, by Melanie Walsh—organization

No, David! and *David Goes to School*, by David Shannon—ideas, voice, conventions

Old Black Fly, by Jim Aylesworth—fluency, word choice

Olivia Saves the Circus, by Ian Falconer—voice, word choice

A Pocketful of Poems, by Nikki Grimes—fluency, word choice, ideas

Roberto the Insect Architect, by Nina Laden—voice, word choice, conventions

Shades of Black, by Sandra L. Pinkney—ideas, voice

Something Beautiful, by Sharon Dennis Wyeth—ideas, voice

Stellaluna, by Janell Cannon—word choice, fluency, ideas

A Story for Bear, by Dennis Haseley—voice

Things That Are Most in the World, by Judi Barrett—organization

Think of an Eel, by Karen Wallace—organization, word choice

The Tiny Seed, by Eric Carle—organization

Twilight Comes Twice, by Ralph Fletcher—ideas, word choice

The Twits, by Roald Dahl—voice, word choice

Verdi, by Janell Cannon—ideas, organization, word choice, fluency

What Do You Do When Something Wants to Eat You? by Steve Jenkins— organization

Where the Wild Things Are, by Maurice Sendak—ideas, voice

Whoever You Are, by Mem Fox—ideas, voice, fluency

Wilfred Gordon McDonald Partridge, by Mem Fox—ideas, organization, voice

■ *Choosing Books*

I'm often asked how I know which trait to use a book for. Honestly, after so many years of working with students on traits, it seems to me that I start leafing through a book and it just shrieks, "Fluency! Use me for fluency!" or whatever. But here, as closely as I can identify them, are the qualities I look for:

Books for ideas: Is it very clear? Does it have one central idea or an easy-to-follow story? Interesting details? Glorious images? Does it make "movies" flow through your mind?

Books for organization: Does it have a powerful beginning? A strong or surprising conclusion? Is everything clearly linked to one main idea: bears, insects, whales, oceans, etc.? Does the book follow a pattern that student writers could imitate in their own writing?

Books for voice: Will I *love* reading this book aloud? Will I enjoy reading it more than once? Can I hardly *wait* to share it? Would I give it as a gift? Does it make me laugh or cry?

Books for word choice: As I skim through, do I notice words or phrases that I'd like students to know? Words I love myself? Are the words challenging without being *too* technical or difficult? Is meaning clear from context? Does it contain some words likely to be new to students? Are everyday words used in creative ways?

Books for fluency: Does it read like poetry? Are sentences highly varied in length and structure? Does it have a rhythmic flow when read aloud? Is there interesting dialogue? Does it have repeated choruses where kids could chime in?

Conventions: Does the book use a wide range of conventions that I could point out to students? Does it make unusual use of any conventions—capitals, exclamation points, quotation marks, etc.? Is the layout (how it's presented on the page) unusual or striking?

■ *Go for Strength—and Be Sure You Love It*

Writers do not sit down, of course, and say, "Well, last week I focused on *ideas*, so today I think I'll write a book that's got *voice.*" Nevertheless, all books have *relative* strengths, so when you're choosing books, go for the strength. Read what you like because you'll enjoy it more and you'll read better. If you don't read with expression and passion, you might as well forget the whole thing, and reading with passion is hard if you find the book tedious. So don't take anything from my list or anyone else's that you don't love right down to your toes.

Idea 5: Reward an Adventurous Spirit and View "Mistakes" as Experiments

> *Children who write before they read become better writers than those who don't.*
>
> **—Bea Johnson**
> *Never Too Early to Write,* 1999, p. 1

A professional diver will practice for months or years, entering the water tens of thousands of times. We do not look on all these early dives as "diving errors"; we look on them as *practice.* Primary students are practicing all the time, trying things out, testing new ideas.

Today or next week or the week after they may not copy all the print in their environment perfectly, but they will come ever closer. Meanwhile, we can continue to read from the best and most exciting literature we can dig up, and we can fill their world with a wealth of wonderful words that are fun to say and to think with— and therefore are worthy of copying and using: *festival, dilapidated, ego, quake, reverie, fortuitous, serendipity, ludicrous, legend, cauldron, stellar, flick, bedevil, malevolent, skitter, flummoxed, linger.* These words are more interesting and, ironically, are perhaps therefore *easier* to learn than *"The fat cat sat by the rat."* We can help children to see, hear, and feel (yes, some words do feel different on the tongue) the magic within words—a magic that comes to life in Tina McElroy Ansa's (1994) story of her early fascination with language:

> I asked [my mother] as a little girl why we didn't eat oatmeal, because people at my school, on cold mornings, would have a bowl of oatmeal. My mother made an ugly face and said, "I can't stand oatmeal. It multiplies in my mouth." And I recognized how wonderful her use of that word was, because I immediately started feeling this oatmeal multiplying in my mouth *[p. 18].*

As students write, we can stretch our vision to look beyond "mistakes" to find the hidden power within a growing repertoire of skills. A new discovery in conventions? Quotation marks? Apostrophes? Terrific. Notice, applaud, celebrate. Fret over meticulous placement later. The same curiosity that drove the child to copy these mysterious marks in the first place will drive him or her to decipher their meaning. Too often we trust our own didacticism more than we trust that curiosity.

Voice is individuality, so every time a writer allows herself to be lost in the crowd, a little bit of individuality is lost. To stand out, to stand alone, takes courage. We must reward students who dare to speak with strong voices. Re-

> *Writing with real honesty takes tremendous courage. Such writing should never be taken for granted. Writers of all ages often find they lack the nerve to write honestly.*
>
> **—Ralph Fletcher**
> *What a Writer Needs,* 1993, p. 25

> *We want to help children learn how to reread or "resee" their work. Above all, we want them to have a growing sense of options available to them during composing. . . . What we demonstrate [through our own revision] is not so much how to revise as a certain stance toward the world, a sense of our intentions, and how we listen to ourselves when we write.*
>
> **—Donald H. Graves**
> *A Fresh Look at Writing,* 1994, p. 239

ward them with recognition and appreciation. When your students have completed an assignment, you can say, "Do you know what I loved most about your essays on marine life? Each one was different. No paper was exactly like any of the others. It was as if I could hear every single writer's voice speaking right to me."

Idea 6: Write—and Talk About It

Model everything: A list of ideas for writing from which you'll pick one. A first sentence. A list of possible titles. A first draft. A picture to go with a story. Let your students see it happening. Model revision, too—*even if you do not ask it of your young writers.* And probably you will not ask it, for experiencing the joy of writing should be our primary goal for beginners. Many primary teachers feel uncomfortable with the whole notion of revision, and who can blame them? At this level, getting the first draft on the page is often an enormous effort. Now we're supposed to ask students to redo it? Are we insane? Indeed we are if we make revision too big. Copying over or correcting all errors is often a recipe for murdering the child's love of writing—right there on the page. But revision for beginners can be *tiny*—sometimes just adding one small detail (a bird in the tree, a smile on the frog's face) or changing one word (*went* to *skipped*). The size of the revision should not concern us, nor should we expect (or require) revision of every piece; what we need to celebrate is the child's discovery that he or she has control over the writing, not the reverse. Remember too that at primary level it's a huge step for young writers to know what revision looks like. You can show them.

■ Model More Than You Expect

Just because you *model* revision, that's no sign that you expect students to do everything you do. Particularly at K–1 level, revision should never be allowed to dampen writing spirits or to take precedence over achieving fluency in writing—the joy of generating ideas. Still, some children may surprise you by attempting more than you thought they could take on. The nice thing about modeling is that you and your students can work together, and they do much of the *thinking* even if you're the one doing the recording. This thinking and planning lay the groundwork for revisions to come. Here's a simple lesson based on an anonymous student paper entitled, "My Dog" (Figure 12.19).

For this lesson, choose a paper that does not belong to anyone in your class. In that way students will feel free to make suggestions without fear of hurting anyone's feelings. The purpose of the lesson is to show how writers play with writing—when they feel like it. And to see, of course, how different it sometimes sounds when they are done. To begin, I share the piece in large print, on an overhead or

FIGURE 12.19 *"My Dog"*

My dog is my friend and he plays with me when I come home from school. We do fun stuff. When my mom says to stop we stop. Then we go outside.

chart pack. I leave *lots* of space in between for writing, and I draw students' attention to this: "Sometimes after I write, I might want to add a sentence or even just a word, so I need to leave space." Now it's time to get serious about details. I will set the lesson up this way: "I want to add some details to my paper. Will you help me?"

From this point on, although I do the actual writing and reading aloud, I engage in a conversation with students the whole time, asking them to do a great deal of the thinking. What I say:

> *This paper is called "My Dog." Do you think we should give this dog a name?* Max? *OK, good . . .* Max is my friend—*but how good a friend? . . .Wow—yes, my* very best friend in the whole world. *Terrific. So he plays with me when I come home from school. How soon after I get home do we play? The* very second! *Excellent—I like that. It's specific. So,* The very second I get home, he plays with me. *What does he actually do, though? Can you see him? He* leaps for me? *Great—I can see that in my mind. OK, so—We do fun stuff. What kinds of things do we actually do, do you suppose? Play tag?* Race around the living room? *Can you see this? I can, too—much better than "fun stuff." When my mom says to stop—wait a second. What do you think Mom actually says? Let's hear her voice—right, good—*Mom yells, "It's too noisy in here!" *Then we stop—but what do you think Max and I actually do? Try to picture it—OK, we* fall in a heap on the floor. *And we laugh, right? Should I say that? OK—so* I laugh and Max barks. *All right, and then we go outside—what do you think we do?* Play catch—with my old tennis ball. *For how long?* Till it's dark. *Terrific. Now let's read the whole thing and see how it sounds . . .*

> Adding on is a very natural part of young children's writing. It can be regarded as an early form of revision or as part of drafting, for there is no clear division between the two.
>
> **—Lucy McCormick Calkins**
> *The Art of Teaching Writing,*
> 1994, p. 99

Figure 12.20 shows how it looks.

I read the finished piece aloud with all revisions in place, and I ask the students to help me illustrate it. Then I recopy it in its final form, and we give it a

FIGURE 12.20   *Revision of "My Dog"*

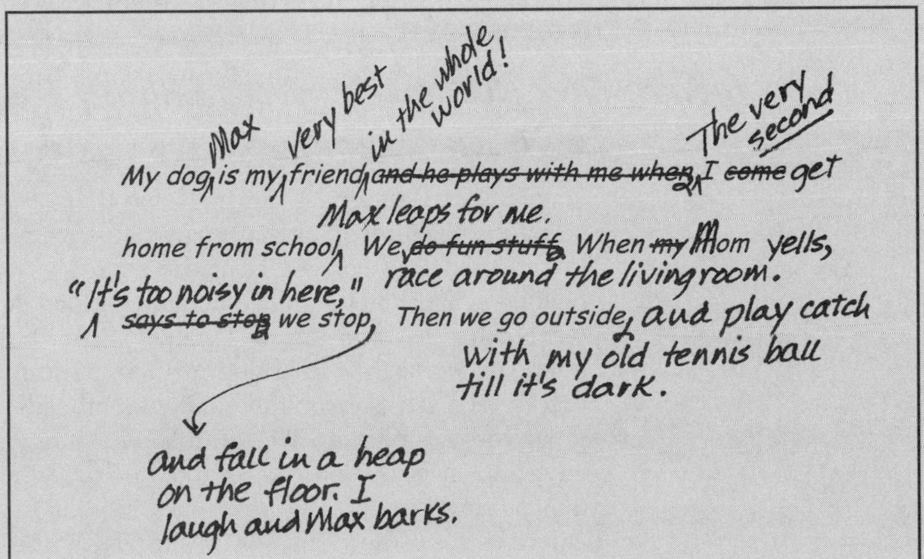

title (which we brainstorm together) and post the results. We may read it once more the next day and look at the pictures. After that, we'll move on to another piece. And though I have not requested it, it's likely that I'll see some playfulness with revision in students' own work.

The preceding lesson emphasizes

✔ Reading what you write aloud to hear how it sounds
✔ Adding little details that give your story life and help to paint a clear picture
✔ Asking yourself questions as you go to prompt those details
✔ Using art to reflect detail

Possible illustrations for "Wild and Wonderful Max" (previously "My Dog") include

✔ Max
✔ Max leaping for the writer
✔ Mom yelling, "It's too noisy in here!"
✔ The writer and Max racing through the living room
✔ The writer and Max falling in a heap on the floor
✔ Max and the writer playing catch

Idea 7: Respect the Many Forms That Writing Can Take

Primary students in particular need a variety of ways in which to express themselves, including pictures, dictation, oral storytelling, labeling, and planning. Pictures, as we've seen, reflect the beginnings of ideas (details), voice (emotion, playfulness, individuality, and humor), and organization (format and balance). Further, children who are not quite ready to create extended text (they may not yet have the concentration, ability to form words, or fine motor skills to make writing relatively simple) can dictate stories or simply tell them to others. In their telling, we hear the vocabulary, voice, sequencing, and development of ideas that they have no means yet to project through standard text. These things are part of their thinking and imagination, though, so why not encourage a "writing" form that lets them show that thinking in action?

Idea 8: Give Primary Writers Editing Tasks They Can Handle
■ Teach Conventions

Teaching conventions is not the same thing as *correcting* conventions—or assessing conventions, for that matter. Just because we wait a bit before expecting conventional correctness is no sign that we must wait *even a minute* to begin teaching and talking about conventions. Anyone who works with primary writers for just one day will be struck by how much they notice and how quickly they begin to include in their writing exclamation points, quotation marks, ellipses, semicolons, and parentheses—not always placed correctly, mind you, but present. We can take advantage of this curiosity by filling their environment with plenty of print to borrow from and by continually asking students, "Have you noticed this mark in your reading? Can you find one somewhere in this room? Why do you suppose writers use this? What does it show?"

Start with a treasure hunt. You can use any text at all for this, or you can post bits of text around the room for a true treasure hunt format. Choose pieces that show a variety of conventions; it is *not* essential that students be able to read every word from these passages. Then invite them, with partners if you like, to find (and put their finger right on) each convention as you name it. Here are some I've used, but you could make your own list:

- ✔ Capital letter
- ✔ Period, question mark, comma, semicolon, exclamation point
- ✔ Any proper name
- ✔ The word *I*
- ✔ Any simple word
- ✔ Italics
- ✔ Ellipses
- ✔ Parentheses
- ✔ Quotation marks
- ✔ Margins (How many fingers fit in the margin?)
- ✔ A title (Is the print in the title bigger? How much bigger?)

I played this conventions treasure hunt game with first graders not long ago, and because they were so exceptionally good at finding everything I could name, I told them I'd give them my conventions "challenge"—*ellipses.* One girl in the front row put her finger immediately on the ellipses and raised her hand. When I asked if she could explain how ellipses are used, she said sure. She stood up before the group. "Ellipses," she explained, "are when you . . . [and her voice drifted off for a time, then resumed] pause in your thinking—like that." Not bad.

You can also ask students to do very simple editing tasks, as shown in the "Simple Editing Checklist" shown in Figure 12.21. Even very beginning writers can do these things, and they will feel like independent editors if you call it editing. Later, as skills grow, you can add new skills to create a more advanced editing checklist (see Figure 12.22). You may wish to make posters of these checklists or make individual copies that you can attach to papers.

When students begin writing simple sentences, create simple editing practice that invites them to "track down" errors (see Figure 12.23). Notice that in this practice students are given the correct sentence first in big print. In this way you are not modeling errors—but rather helping them to find errors by matching other sentences against the correct one. Each practice sentence (1) is short and complete and (2) contains *only one* error. Put a copy on the overhead, and read sentences aloud, one by one, as you work together. You can do just one sen-

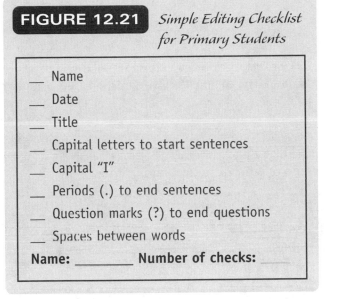

FIGURE 12.21   *Simple Editing Checklist for Primary Students*

___ Name
___ Date
___ Title
___ Capital letters to start sentences
___ Capital "I"
___ Periods (.) to end sentences
___ Question marks (?) to end questions
___ Spaces between words

Name: _____   **Number of checks:** _____

FIGURE 12.22   *Advanced Editing Checklist for Primary Students*

___ My name is on the paper.
___ The date is on the paper.
___ My title goes with the paper.
___ I used capital letters to start sentences.
___ I used capital "I."
___ I used periods (.) to end statements.
___ I used question marks (?) to end questions.
___ I used apostrophes (') to show ownership.
___ I used quotation marks ("Hello!") to show talking.
___ I have one-inch margins all around.
___ I did my very <u>best</u> spelling.
___ You can read everything.

Name: _____   **Number of checks:** _____

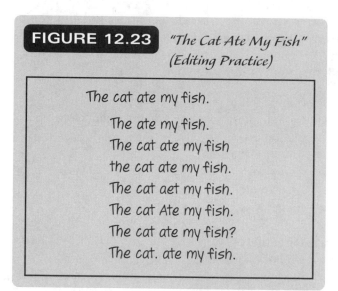

FIGURE 12.23 *"The Cat Ate My Fish" (Editing Practice)*

The cat ate my fish.

The ate my fish.

The cat ate my fish

the cat ate my fish.

The cat aet my fish.

The cat Ate my fish.

The cat ate my fish?

The cat. ate my fish.

tence or more than one depending on attention spans. Each time, though, you are looking for *one* mistake.

When you do a lesson like this one, make copies for your students. (You can run three or four on a single page and then cut them.) In this way, you can let them correct the text *first*, using the copy editor's symbols for beginning writers (see Figure 12.24).

Don't worry if they cannot do all the editing yet; let them try. When they've finished, ask them to check their text with a friend. Then have them tell *you* how to fix the text so that you can do it on the overhead for everyone to see. The process should be fast, lively, and interactive. No worksheets. Just a group of editors, talking and editing.

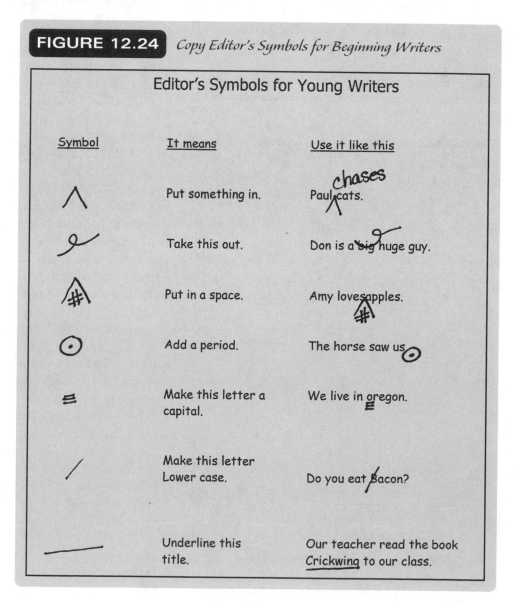

FIGURE 12.24 *Copy Editor's Symbols for Beginning Writers*

Editor's Symbols for Young Writers

Symbol	It means	Use it like this
∧	Put something in.	Paul∧cats. (chases)
ℓ	Take this out.	Don is a ~~big~~ huge guy.
⧎	Put in a space.	Amy loves⧎apples.
⊙	Add a period.	The horse saw us⊙
≡	Make this letter a capital.	We live in o̱regon.
/	Make this letter Lower case.	Do you eat Ɓacon?
___	Underline this title.	Our teacher read the book <u>Crickwing</u> to our class.

Idea 9: Keep It Simple
■ You Do Not Always Need to Host a "Writing Event"

For beginners, it's a comfort to know that brief, manageable assignments are sometimes acceptable. Beginners also enjoy interesting shapes on which to write. My friend Arlene Moore, who teaches a K–1 combination, gave her young writers 3 by 5 inch paper suitcases on which to write me short messages: "What I should be sure to pack as I travel around the country talking with teachers and students." Their *very short* recommendations included these—most of which I've followed:

✔ A snake so no one will steal your stuff
✔ A book to read
✔ Earrings to make you beautiful
✔ Roses for all the teachers you meet
✔ A charge card
✔ Plenty of chocolate so you won't get hungry
✔ Pictures of your children so you won't get lonely
✔ Clothes so you won't need to run around in your underwear

CONTINUUMS FOR CHARTING GROWTH

This section includes the continuums (see Figures 12.25 through 12.30) that form the basis for the book that complements this one, *Creating Young Writers* (Spandel, 2004). That text, written especially for K–3 teachers, includes many additional primary student samples and instructional ideas besides those covered in this chapter. As I discuss at some length in *Creating Young Writers*, the continuums reproduced here are not intended for large scale assessment but for use in the classroom. You might use them as checklists, marking things that your students do well. Or you can highlight skills with a colored marker, attach continuums to four or five writing samples collected throughout the year, and create a portfolio that will show striking growth.

You will notice that the continuums have no numbers. They are intended for use as performance records. To that end, the language is designed to reflect what students *can* do. When a child reaches the "Experienced Writer" stage consistently, across traits and across multiple samples of writing, that child is ready for assessment on the rubrics from Chapter 3 of this book. If you are a primary teacher, I invite you to try these continuums with your own students and to use what you find as a basis for celebrating writing proficiency with students and parents alike.

GIVE IT TIME

Some children pick up a pencil and begin creating meaning through text at a remarkably early age because for them writing is totally natural. Similarly, some children almost from the first day will write much the way they speak, gracing

FIGURE 12.25 Ideas Continuum

Ideas

Beginner	Borrower	Experimenter	Meaning Maker	Experienced Writer
☐ Makes marks on paper.	☐ Uses "words" and pictures to express ideas.	☐ Uses text/art to create interpretable messages.	☐ Creates clear message via text or text plus art.	☐ Creates a clear, detailed message through text/art.
☐ "Reads" own writing, invents meaning.	☐ Uses imitative/borrowed print to create signs, lists, rules, notes, etc. (not always interpretable without help).	☐ Has clear main message/idea expressed in one or more sentences.	☐ Expresses complex, extended thoughts.	☐ Uses multiple sentences to enrich ideas or extend story.
☐ Dictates a clear message/story.	☐ Likes to come up with personal ideas for writing.	☐ Can "reread" text shortly after writing.	☐ Uses multiple sentences to add detail.	☐ Incorporates significant detail to enhance meaning.
☐ Uses art to convey message/story.	☐ Notices detail in read-aloud text and in pictures.	☐ Creates decodable lists, labels, notes, statements, short summaries, "all about" or "how-to" pieces and/or poems.	☐ Connects images/text to main idea.	☐ Creates writing that explains, gives directions, tells a story, expresses an opinion, describes.
☐ Recognizes that print has meaning/significance.		☐ Can talk about main ideas and details.	☐ Creates images that show detail: eyes, expressive faces, fingers and toes, leaves and grass, etc.	☐ Creates informational and narrative text; may write persuasive paragraphs or poems.
☐ Hears detail in stories read aloud.			☐ Creates writing that is fully decodable by independent reader.	☐ Can summarize own text.
			☐ Can "reread" text after several days.	☐ Can recognize and comment on detail in text of others.
			☐ Adds stories to repertoire.	☐ Chooses personally important topics.
			☐ Can think about and choose personal writing topic from several choices.	☐ May revise by adding a detail.

FIGURE 12.26 *Organization Continuum*

Organization

Beginner	Borrower	Experimenter	MeaningMaker	Experienced Writer
☐ Fills space randomly.	☐ Can create picture and text that go together.	☐ Creates text/art with balanced look.	☐ Creates balanced, pleasing layout.	☐ Connects all text/art to main message.
☐ Can dictate sequential story or how-to piece.	☐ Creates layout with more purpose/balance.	☐ Consistently creates image and text that complement each other.	☐ Writes multiple sentences or images that suggest development/sequencing.	☐ Uses thoughtful titles.
☐ Can point to illustrations that go with text.	☐ May use two or more pictures to express story or message.	☐ May use title or THE END to signify beginning/ ending.	☐ Sometimes uses art to express sequence of events.	☐ Writes a true lead (usually, the opening sentence).
☐ Can "hear" beginnings/ endings in stories read aloud.		☐ Stays focused on message.	☐ Uses connecting words: *first, next, then, once, after, and, but, or, so, because.*	☐ Provides closure (usually, with final sentence).
		☐ Often creates labels/lists.	☐ Uses identifiable beginning and ending.	☐ Follows logical order/sequence.
		☐ Can organize recipes, all about and how-to-pieces, directions, and simple stories.	☐ Stays focused on message.	☐ Creates easy-to-follow text.
			☐ Creates organized summaries, stories, descriptions, short essays.	☐ Uses elaborate transitions: *After a while, The next day, Because of this, The first thing, Finally.*
				☐ Can structure stories, how-to pieces, short essays, and other forms.
				☐ Can use variety of organizational patterns: e.g., step by step, chronological, comparison, problem-solution, main idea + detail.

FIGURE 12.27 *Voice Continuum*

Voice

Beginner	Borrower	Experimenter	Meaning Maker	Experienced Writer
☐ Creates bold lines.	☐ Incorporates voice into art through color, images, facial features, etc.	☐ Uses expressive language.	☐ Creates some text recognizable as "this child's piece."	☐ Creates lively, engaging, personal text/art.
☐ Uses colors.	☐ Uses exclamation points/underlining to show emphasis.	☐ Often incorporates definite tone/flavor.	☐ Writes/draws with personal style.	☐ Creates writing that is FUN to read aloud.
☐ Expresses voice in dictation.	☐ Uses BIG LETTERS to show importance, strong feelings.	☐ Creates expressive pictures.	☐ Creates individual text, art.	☐ Is able to sustain voice.
☐ Responds to voice in text read aloud.	☐ Shows preference for text/art with voice.	☐ Creates tone that reflects feelings.	☐ Elicits emotional response in reader.	☐ Provokes strong reader response.
		☐ Puts moments of voice throughout most text.	☐ May use conventional devices (exclamation points, underlining) to enhance voice.	☐ Uses voice to influence meaning.
		☐ Recognizes voice in text of others, and can describe personal response: e.g., "I liked it," "It was very funny."	☐ Shows beginning awareness of audience: use of *you*, conversational tone, direct questions: *Do you like cats?*	☐ "Speaks" to audience.
			☐ Shows preference for certain types of voice in read-aloud pieces.	☐ Creates voice that is easy to describe: *Joyful* *Funny* *Moody* *Sarcastic* *Fearful* *Angry* *Wistful*
			☐ Often comments on voice in others' text/art: e.g., "That has voice," or "I want to hear that again."	☐ Shows growing awareness of own voice and is beginning to control quality and strength of voice.
				☐ Can rate extent of voice in others' text/art.

FIGURE 12.28 Word Choice Continuum

Word Choice

Beginner	Borrower	Experimenter	Meaning Maker	Experienced Writer
☐ Scribbles. ☐ Creates letter "shapes." ☐ Uses favorite words in dictation.	☐ Borrows recognizable letter shapes from environment. ☐ Labels pictures. ☐ Uses titles on text. ☐ Creates letter strings that contain one- or two-letter words: **lk** (like), **dg** (dog), **hs** (house), **m** (my). ☐ Chooses favorite words from read-aloud text. ☐ Repeats "comfort" (familiar) words in own text.	☐ Writes easy-to-read letters/numbers. ☐ Writes words with consonant sounds and some vowels. ☐ Writes decodable words/sentences. ☐ Uses many simple, familiar words. ☐ Uses sight words frequently. ☐ Has personal bank of favorite words. ☐ Enjoys adding new words to text. ☐ Adds new words to personal dictionary. ☐ Repeats some words.	☐ Writes easy-to-read words. ☐ Writes with variety—dares to try new, less familiar words. ☐ Loves descriptive words and phrases. ☐ Uses some strong verbs. ☐ Uses words to create images or add clarity, detail. ☐ Keeps growing personal dictionary of meaningful words. ☐ Selects some "just right" words to express meaning. ☐ Usually avoids repetition.	☐ Uses vivid, expressive language. ☐ Writes with vocabulary that may extend well beyond spelling ability. ☐ Sometimes uses striking, unexpected phrases: *"I felt like a once contented and proud swan who lost its feathers."* ☐ Uses many strong verbs. ☐ Keeps extensive personal dictionary. ☐ Repeats words only for emphasis/effect. ☐ Occasionally changes (revises) words to reflect preference.

FIGURE 12.29   Sentence Fluency Continuum

Sentence Fluency

Beginner	Borrower	Experimenter	Meaning Maker	Experienced Writer
☐ Dictates sentences. ☐ Enjoys poetry, rhythmic language.	☐ Creates letter strings that suggest sentences: **nohtipdin.** ☐ Writes text with a "sentence look" that may not be translatable. ☐ Dictates multiple sentences. ☐ Can hear rhythm, rhyme, and variety in read-aloud text. ☐ Can hear patterns—and may try imitating them.	☐ Writes letter strings that form readable sentences: **I lik skl.** (I like school.) **I HA DOG.** (I have a dog.) ☐ Writes more than one sentence. ☐ Usually writes sentences that complete a thought. ☐ Dictates a whole story or essay. ☐ Favors patterns: **I can pla. I can rid my bik. I can red.** (I can play. I can ride my bike. I can read.) ☐ Likes to repeat text read aloud with inflection.	☐ Consistently writes multiple sentences. ☐ Writes complete sentences. ☐ Creates easy-to-read text. ☐ Begins to show variety in sentence lengths, patterns, beginnings. ☐ May experiment with poetry—rhyming or free verse. ☐ May experiment with dialogue. ☐ Reads aloud with inflection.	☐ Can write two paragraphs or more. ☐ Consistently writes complete sentences. ☐ Creates text that sounds fluent read aloud. ☐ May use fragments for effect. **Wow! Crunch!** ☐ Creates text that is easy to read with expression. ☐ Often experiments with poetry/dialogue. ☐ Can read own/others' text aloud with inflection. ☐ Can combine sentences. ☐ May revise by changing word order or sentence length.

FIGURE 12.30 *Conventions Continuum*

Conventions

Beginner	Borrower	Experimenter	Meaning Maker	Experienced Writer
☐ Does not use recognizable conventions in own text.	☐ Imitates print: letters, "cursive flow (eee)," punctuation marks.	☐ Uses capitals and lower case—not ALWAYS correctly.	☐ Uses capitals and lower case with fair consistency.	☐ Uses wide range of conventions skillfully and accurately.
☐ Can point to conventions in print.	☐ Writes own name.	☐ Uses periods, question marks, commas, and exclamation points (often correctly).	☐ Uses periods, commas, exclamation points, question marks correctly.	☐ Creates easy-to-read text with few errors.
☐ Plays with letter or number shapes.	☐ Writes one to several sight words.	☐ Puts spaces between words.	☐ Correctly spells ever-growing range of sight words and some challenging words.	☐ Uses paragraphs, often in the right places.
	☐ Loves to copy environmental print.	☐ Spells many sight words.	☐ Uses some difficult conventions correctly: e.g., quotation marks, ellipses, dashes, parentheses.	☐ Spells most sight words and many challenging words correctly.
	☐ Creates letters that face the right way.	☐ Creates readable. phonetic versions of harder words.	☐ Gives some attention to correct format.	☐ Uses conventions to reinforce voice/meaning.
	☐ Can name/describe many conventions: e.g., period, capital, comma, question mark.	☐ "Plays" with more difficult conventions: dashes, ellipses, quotation marks.	☐ Sometimes uses paragraphs.	☐ Is careful with layout and formatting.
	☐ Asks about conventions.	☐ Can name/describe numerous conventions.	☐ Makes corrections in own text.	☐ Consistently checks/edits own text for many conventions.
	☐ Often writes left to right.	☐ Shows concern for correctness in own text.	☐ Writes left to right, notices margins.	☐ Writes left to right and respects margins.
		☐ Writes left to right.		

every line with that truest of voices that flows like water when the writing is an extension of self. As Gloria Wade-Gayles (1994) declares, "In the same way that being alive is about breathing, being alive for me is about writing. . . . Writing simply is. It is an expression of my 'who-ness'" (p. 103).

We must allow primary writers to express their "who-ness" while their belief in the power of writing is strong. It stands to reason they will not all reach milestones of achieving readable spelling, correct spelling, knowledge of terminal punctuation, skill with capital letters, ability to form complete sentences, and so on at the same time. We know this intuitively, yet (as parents and as teachers) we often become anxious when a child seems to fall behind others. "What's wrong?" we ask.

In most cases, not only is nothing wrong, but something is very *right.* That something is that the child is adventuring, playing with language in his or her own way, and finding a personal path to learning. A reading specialist once told me about the importance of filling the classroom with books and other printed materials because young readers were hungry for print. "So this is a way to encourage them?" I asked. She shook her head. "It isn't a matter of encouraging them," she explained patiently. "You can't *stop* them. I'm just providing the tools and getting out of the way."

 ## POSTSCRIPT

As a first grader, Nicholas told us that the library was his "favorite place to be" (see Figure 12.6). Eleven years later this student writer has new thoughts to share in a paper called "If Men Were Angels . . . ." How much we might all learn if assessment more frequently granted us this before-and-after picture (see Figure 12.31).

FIGURE 12.31 *"If Men Were Angels . . . ," by Nicholas (Grade 12)*

Tears swelled in every eye, and the heart of every American ached as the second plane crashed into the World Trade Center. This was no accident. There would be no innocent explanation for such utter destruction. Whoever lay behind it attacked not only America's sovereignty and economy, but its innocent citizens. Days later, President George W. Bush blew the horn to war at "Ground Zero," and stood before Congress, uttering some of the most famous words of our generation: "We will not tire, we will not falter, and we will not fail." It is no wonder why Congress then authorized the President to use any method necessary to seek out the perpetrators of this tragedy and to bring them to justice.

To prevent such events from happening again, they hastily passed the now infamous, "Patriot Act", giving our government great power in seeking out terrorists. However, we are forced to confront the same questions which have arisen in the past: what is truly the role of government, and how do we draw the line between protection and intrusion into our civil and God-given liberties?

What many may not know is that the Patriot Act does not vastly depart from previous United States policy, but it does reinforce the government's power to ascertain information for defense of the country. The most controversial portion, Section 215, gives the government the power to subpoena any third party records to help combat enemies of the United States. Such sources of information could include bank accounts, emails, library records, and even the permanent school records of children. It is continually reaffirmed, however, that such provisions are meant to be used only against terrorists, and FBI agents are still accountable to the law to acquire search warrants. In defense of the Patriot Act's intent, the FBI claimed that if such provisions existed years ago, Ted Kaczynski could have been apprehended much sooner, by matching his obscure literary references to his library records.

But what is truly the definition of terrorism? As common citizens we hardly think of ourselves as menaces to society. However, who among us hasn't disagreed with our government at one time or another? Should borrowing a book from the library be red-flagged for FBI agents? Should our government have the power to examine our bank statements, read our personal emails, tap our phones, and look deep into the records of our youth as true representations of who we are today? If I participate in an anti-war demonstration, does this make me a terrorist? This is not a world in which I would like to live.

Alexander Hamilton, and other found fathers, of our country believed that, "If men were angels, no government would be necessary." It is true that not angels, but demons walk among us, claiming to be honorable citizens. Such individuals have committed horrid atrocities against our country, whose effects are just being realized. We have fled to our leaders for protection after the unfathomable loss of life and resources. But in our moment of vulnerability, we may have lost some of the freedoms upon which this country was built and survives day to day. As conscientious citizens, we must be vigilant, we must be willing to voice our concerns in government, we must protect both our security and our liberties, searching for the day when we will become angels ourselves.

CHAPTER 12 IN A NUTSHELL

- At primary level, writing has its own look and may include scribbles, pictures, labeled pictures, letter strings—or sophisticated text of one or more paragraphs.
- Primary writers are not making "errors" in the conventional sense but exploring the world of writing, experimenting, daring, borrowing, and growing.
- Because primary writing looks different from more traditional writing, we must work hard to teach ourselves what to look for.
- We get further faster with primary writers by helping them to see their strengths than by pointing out endless things they must/should do differently.
- Young writers "hear" details, voice, fluency, and other significant qualities long before such features show up in their own writing, so reading aloud forms an important bridge into the world of print.
- We can and should use writers' language (details, voice, lead, ending) right from the very first. Primary writers pick it up faster than almost anyone else.
- At primary level, the four most important things that we can do to teach writing are to provide numerous opportunities for children to write; respond positively to students' work, having a conversation with them about it; model writing frequently; and read

aloud—with expression—from the very best literature that we can get our hands on.
- Primary writers can handle both revision and editing
if we keep the tasks very small and manageable and
if we use strategies to help them: providing checklists, working through problem solving as a group,

and modeling both revision and editing so that they
can see them in action.
- Children learn at very different rates, and we do our
primary writers a great service when we believe in
them—and do not become overly anxious about correct conventions or other hallmarks of good writing.

EXTENSIONS

1. It is important for teachers of all grades to write with
their students, but why might this be especially important at primary level? If you are teaching right now,
how much modeling do you do with your students?
   - _____ A great deal
   - _____ A little
   - _____ None

   Write a journal entry about your perspective on modeling—first as a student writer and then through the
eyes of a teacher.
2. What favorite books might you add to the list of read-
alouds in this chapter? Make a list and share it with
colleagues.
3. Without referring to the text, see if you can describe
in your own words just how each trait might look at
primary level. If you are currently teaching at primary level, see if you can find one sample from your
own students' work to illustrate performance in each
of the traits.

4. Choose a book that is appropriate for use with
primary writers. Share it aloud with a group of primary students, using it as the basis for a lesson
in one of the traits. If you like, expand your discussion of the book to include a writing/drawing/
role-playing activity. Discuss the lesson with colleagues.
5. Collect four or five samples of primary writing—or
use samples from this chapter. Assess them using
one or more of the writing continuums in Figures
12.25 through 12.30. Discuss what you see. Is there
any feature of writing that you feel should be added
to the continuums?
6. Model for your colleagues or your class a lesson on
writing, revision, or editing that you might use with
primary writers.
7. Read all or part of *Creating Young Writers* with a
study group, discussing the book's instructional
strategies and philosophy about assessment.

WHY I WRITE

*Who knows? I just might make millions of dollars writing books. I might
be the next J. R. R. Tolkien. Would that be sweet or what?*

—Carl Matthes, student writer

LOOKING AHEAD

In Chapter 13 we examine the importance of good communication through
comments, conferences, response groups, grades, and conversations with
parents.

13 Communicating with Students
Comments, Conferences, Peer Review, Grades, and Bringing Parents In

I tell people all the things I like about their piece—how wonderful the atmosphere is, for instance, and the language—and also point out where they got all tangled up in their own process. We—the other students and I—can be like a doctor to whom you take your work for a general checkup.

—Anne Lamott
Bird By Bird, 1995, p. 153

We must speak to our students with an honesty tempered by compassion: Our words will literally define the ways they perceive themselves as writers.

—Ralph Fletcher
What a Writer Needs, 1993, p. 19

A few years ago I was both amused and distressed to hear Grant Wiggins tell a large group of conference attendees about a new teacher who was saying farewell to her students after what had seemed a highly successful term. One of the students, Wiggins explained, paused to whisper a question she'd been too timid to ask earlier: "You've written this on so many of my papers, but I don't understand. What is 'va-goo'?" "Va-goo" (*vague*) all too often describes *us* as we try to clarify our expectations for students.

In this chapter I will talk about four important ways of communicating with student writers: through comments, conferences, peer review, and grades. I'll also talk about bringing parents into the conversation. Let's begin with comments, both spoken and written.

COMMENTS

Can you recall the most positive thing anyone ever said to you about your own writing? It might have come from a teacher or perhaps a friend, colleague, parent, child, editor, or anyone—a comment that inspired you and gave you confidence. Now turn the tables. Try to remember the most negative comment you ever received on your work—one that momentarily bumped you off the path or perhaps even stunned you, stopped you short.

Here are two examples from my personal experience. In a class on using writing to think, I had written a poem about moving to Oregon to get married. I'd left my mother distraught and in tears and my father sullen and angry (he thought I was too young to marry or to move so far from home), and we hauled our pathetic cache of belongings, my love and I, in a U-Haul truck that didn't do hills. The Rockies were a challenge. My poem was personal and profoundly emotional, and I felt nervous sharing it aloud. Later, I felt happy that I had shared it when the teacher wrote, "The way words move through you, through your pen. I envy that, *love* that." I saved her words and today have them taped inside a drawer because they gave me both encouragement and courage itself. (Thank you, Elaine!)

In eleventh grade I spent five days writing an essay on *The Great Gatsby*. I didn't know nearly enough about life to appreciate the book at that time, but like many 16-year-olds, I thought classics were supposed to be dull, and anyway, I'd worked hard on my essay, particularly the symbolism involving light. I received only one comment, written at the end: "Your most irritating habit is your relentless, *persistent* misuse of the semicolon. Please revise!" Relentless? Persistent? What an angry man to envision me plotting the strategic placement of semicolons to create maximum annoyance (I wasn't that clever)—not to mention the startling phrase "*most* irritating habit." Apparently, out of my vast array of annoying habits, this was the one—this semicolon thing—that provoked him most. He ended with "Please revise!" but I think what he really meant was "Please revise your*self*. Write differently. Write something else, for some*one* else, or at least, write some*where* else."

I have often asked other teachers to recall positive or negative comments and am startled to learn how long some comments have stayed in their minds.

■ *Teachers Recall the Good Times . . .*

✔ Good clear thinking. You always develop your ideas completely and show remarkable insight.
✔ You have a special way with words!
✔ You have a creative soul!
✔ You made me want to keep reading—even at 11 P.M.
✔ This sounds so much like you that I had to keep looking over my shoulder to see if you were in the room.

✔ I like the way you wrote this sentence. It makes me feel that I'm right there with you.

✔ I like your use of the word *flamboyant.* I can picture Irene perfectly.

✔ I like the way you write. You say what you have to say and then quit.

✔ Very convincing. I began this paper believing one thing, and though you haven't totally turned me around, you have really made me think.

✔ Beautiful sentence rhythm. I could use this to *teach* fluency. It's that good.

✔ You told me you couldn't write. You can. This proves it.

✔ Thank you for sharing your poem. It spoke to me.

✔ You took a technical, hard-to-penetrate idea and made it reader-friendly. I felt like an insider. Thanks!

■ *And the Not So Good Times . . .*

✔ I can't believe what I see here. There is nothing of worth, except that the documentation is perfect. It is only the documentation that boosts this paper to a D−. [*Boosts?*]

✔ Ugh!

✔ I think you may have it in you to write competently, but not brilliantly.

✔ Don't get cute.

✔ In looking at this paper again, I believe it is even worse than I originally thought.

✔ Reading this has depressed me more than I can say.

✔ I do not have time to read this much. Please be more concise.

✔ You simply don't know how to write.

✔ This is basically verbal vomit.

✔ No one would read this who was not paid to read it.

✔ Lay off the exclamation points. This isn't that exciting.

✔ What in the *world* are you trying to say? Just spit it out.

✔ You will never, ever be an author.

✔ You missed the point completely. F.

　✔ This could not possibly be your best effort.

　✔ Do the world a favor. Don't write.

　✔ I do not believe you wrote this. This is not your work.

　✔ Dialogue doesn't work. It sounds stilted, phony. *No one* talks this way.

　✔ Your writing reminds me of a porcupine—many points leading in meaningless directions.

　　One teacher's comment came in the form of a gesture: Her teacher shredded her paper and returned it to her in a paper bag. It takes only seconds to create a lifetime memory. We must think before we comment.

Is Anybody Listening, Though? Actually, Yes . . .

While some of the preceding comments seem bitter and rancorous, *most* teacher comments are, from teachers' perspectives at least, well intentioned. Sometimes, though, good intentions are

> I learned an important idea about teaching writing while preparing for the birth of my son. In our childbirth class, our teacher had this suggestion for husbands (and writing teachers) who are nervous about doing and saying the right thing at the critical moment. Relax, she told us. Try to remember that tenderness is more important than technique.
>
> **—Ralph Fletcher**
> *What a Writer Needs*, 1993, p. 18

not enough to bridge the communications gap. As the weeks tick by and we note no major changes in writing skill, we may wind up wondering whether anyone is even listening. As the samples that follow show clearly, student writers usually *are* responding to our comments but often not in the way we had imagined or hoped.

■ *When the teacher wrote "Needs work," students responded this way*

✔ Kind of rude. Work on what?
✔ I learn nothing from this comment.
✔ This is so harsh. It makes me feel hopeless.
✔ I have to ignore this or I'll wind up hating the teacher.

■ *When the teacher wrote, "Use examples to illustrate your point," students responded this way*

✔ If I have to give examples on every little detail, I'll never get the point across.
✔ I did use examples. You mean more examples?
✔ I don't have any other examples.

■ *When the teacher wrote, "You need to be more concise," students responded this way*

✔ I'm confused. What do you mean by "concise"?
✔ I'm not Einstein. I can't do everything right.
✔ I thought you wanted details and support. Now you want concise.

■ *When the teacher wrote, "Be more specific," students responded this way*

✔ You be specific. What exactly do you want?
✔ It's going to be too long then. What happened to concise?
✔ Maybe you need to read more closely. Maybe it's you not paying attention.

■ *When the teacher wrote, "You need stronger verbs," students responded this way*

✔ I lack verby power.
✔ I knew it. I should have used the thesaurus.
✔ I don't know any other verbs. Give me some examples.

■ *When the teacher wrote, "Weak ending," students responded this way*

✔ Weak? No way! That's a great ending. Read it again.
✔ I know I need a better conclusion, but I have no idea how to write one.
✔ Teach me about endings! *Teach* me!

Research by Maxine Hairston (1986) confirms that these responses are not isolated examples but are, in fact, typical of students who become defensive or overwhelmed by comments they do not understand. It might seem on the face of it that one of the best ways to help a budding writer is to point out what he or she is doing wrong. Yet the truth is that this usually *doesn't* help; it causes the writer to retreat and sometimes to avoid writing altogether.

Positive Comment + Modeling = Path to Success

What *does* help is to (1) point out what is going well and help the writer build on that and then (2) to follow up by modeling ways of dealing with problems. Let's begin with the comments.

This seems like the easy part, doesn't it? It's not. Good comments must be truthful and very specific. It's one thing to say, "Good job, Alex." That's not going to crush anyone's spirit, but you should know that it can, and often does, sound phony. Think of a 4-year-old showing off his new bike-riding skills to a father who's engrossed in the stock market report. "Look at me, Dad! Look at me!" the 4-year-old shouts. Dad maintains a running commentary—"Great, son, just great!" No one appreciates mindless approval. Showing that you actually read the paper calls for comments like these:

> As writers, what we all need more than anything else in the world is listeners, listeners who will respond with silent empathy, with sighs of recognition, with laughter and tears and questions and stories of their own. Writers need to be heard.
>
> **—Lucy McCormick Calkins**
> *The Art of Teaching Writing,*
> 1994, pp. 14–15

✔ Your examples convinced me that chocolate-covered marshmallows are not a good idea. I'm giving them up!

✔ Voice! I think you were horrified at the idea of freeze-drying a cat, but you were chuckling, too—weren't you? You really know how to connect with an audience.

✔ You really edited this essay, didn't you? Spelling, punctuation—all the conventions—made it so readable. Thank you!

As author/teacher Tommy Thomason (1998) tells us, "Praise works when it tells writers specifically what they did well. This motivates writers to keep on writing, to take chances, and to work even harder on areas where they have demonstrated their success" (p. 29).

What If You Don't Like the Paper?

> I genuinely believe it is possible to find something good in each piece of writing, and I think you'll find it becomes an acquired skill that is central to being a constructive critic.
>
> **—Barry Lane**
> *After THE END,* 1993, p. 126

Sometimes it's tough. Maybe you don't like the paper much, or there isn't that much there. Don't give up. Look within. *Listen.* Take time to comment. Make sure that the student knows you noticed because in all likelihood that student doesn't know the moment is there either unless you point it out. Find a word or phrase you enjoyed—just one; a detail that enriched the whole; an opening that shows improvement over others or an ending that surprised you; one transition that helped connect ideas; one sentence beginning that made the reading smooth; one line that needs no editing at all. If you look hard, you will find *something*. Make a very big deal of it. Next time there will be another something and then another after that. Remember that what you're responding to is not just the success of the text but the courage of the writer in sharing it.

Modeling Problem Solving

We tell our writers to "write small." Sometimes we need to "teach small." Don't model *"How to be a great writer."* Pick one manageable speed bump that you and the student can tackle together. Then, instead of simply tossing out advice—"Be specific"—you might say, "Notice what happens in your mind when I change 'dog' to 'old black Lab with a white muzzle and one inside-out ear, nursing a limp in his left front leg.' Do you see the difference? That's what I mean by specific detail. I need you to make pictures in my mind as I read. I depend on you, you see. Help me, as a reader, to *see* your meaning. Help me see the fishing boat you and Dad rode in that morning."

In his excellent and thorough book, *The English Teacher's Companion* (2000), teacher Jim Burke (whose voice we hear in Chapter 10) likens good teaching to his experience learning to play tennis (p. 80). For several years, he explains, he just mindlessly batted the ball around the court, and though he spent hours a day doing this, no serious improvement occurred—until his parents hired a coach. Now he had an "expert" who could observe, offer suggestions at appropriate times—and offer encouragement, too. Follow the lead of Jim's coach. Pace yourself. As students write, stop by for a moment to work on manageable writing problems like these:

✔ Coming up with a title that connects to the writing
✔ Starting sentences with words other than *There is* or *There are*
✔ Coming up with alternatives to the word *special*
✔ Writing dialogue that's authentic and meaningful

Step by step, little victories build writers. Barry Lane (1993) suggests dividing constructive criticism into three categories:

Questions—things the writer did not answer or just things you're curious about

Comments—including praise

Concerns—passages that confused you or potential problems the author may wish to pay attention to *[p. 126]*

Sometimes a comment expands into a conversation, and that's when it becomes a conference.

CONFERENCES

The very word *conference* can be horrifying to teachers who are already pressed for time. This is often so because they think that

1. They must control everything that happens during the conference (much like a conductor).
2. They must use the conference as an opportunity to "fix" the writing (sometimes a big task).
3. They must listen as the student reads the entire paper all the way through—regardless of length.

Think of a conference as a chat. That's all. I like Tommy Thomason's analogy [in *Writer to Writer: How to Conference Young Authors* (1998, pp. 62–64)] to the two neighbors talking about gardening. One is a veteran gardener, and one is a novice. The veteran might answer a question one day about when to plant lettuce. Another day he offers a suggestion on how to keep the flowers from falling off the tomato plants. But never does he take over the garden himself, examine every plant in the garden—or give a lecture on "All About Gardening." And if he did, then the next time he appeared at the fence, the novice gardener might feel a sudden need to have his teeth drilled. Like the veteran, we conference best when we stop by to "talk writing" for a moment.

Successful conferences are

✔ Short and focused (They do not try to "cover" everything.)
✔ Student-oriented so that the writer does most of the talking
✔ An opportunity to work on *one* writer's problem—not the world of writing

Our students know a lot about what makes writing work, and if we listen to them, we find out that this is so. Those who know the traits well are often more comfortable in a conference, though, because they also have a language for expressing their concerns or questions in writerly terms:

✔ I need help with my lead.
✔ I can't tell if I have one main idea—or two.
✔ I think this is too wordy, but I don't know how to cut it.
✔ This has no voice. What do I do about that?
✔ How should I end it? I don't want to just say, "The End."

> The important thing to realize is that students can be our teachers.
> **—Lucy McCormick Calkins**
> *The Art of Teaching Writing,*
> 1994, p. 54

The student who comes to a conference with a question in mind is prepared to take control of that conference—as the writer should. We must also look carefully at how students approach a conference, whether with trepidation or confidence. As Donald M. Murray (2004) reminds us, "the way the student walks into the conference, the way in which the student handles the paper—as if it were a golden gift on a platter or a stinking three-day-old fish—can be revealing" (p. 163). Reading our students is as important as reading their work. Equally important is coming to a conference with our whole selves, ready to listen. Such uncompromising attention is a gift we give to any writer.

Shorter Is Better

> Students walking away from a writing conference are frequently overwhelmed with information. It's important to teach them to learn how to listen to their own internal critics . . .
> **—Barry Lane**
> *After THE END,* 1993, p. 109

In *Free to Write*, Roy Peter Clark (1987) talks about the value of a short conference that focuses simply on where the writer is in the process and the most important problem or obstacle that writer faces—and that's it. This don't-drag-it-out approach comes from his experience as a journalist watching city editors deal with dozens of reporters in 30- to 60-second intervals: "City editors learn these techniques or die" (pp. 36–37).

A student should come away from a conference *not* with a polished, ready-to-go draft but simply with an idea of where to go next or, at the very least, a clear sense of one useful writing question to answer: *Does this make sense? Will this touch a reader? Should I begin (or end) differently?*

A Chance to Be Heard

> *If children don't speak about their writing, both teachers and children lose. Until the child speaks, nothing significant has happened in the writing conference.*
>
> **—Donald H. Graves**
> *Writing: Teachers and Children at Work*, 1983, p. 97

So often students feel that no one listens—really *listens* to them. One minute of good listening can be worth twenty minutes of canned writing advice, however conceptually sound. So, while you listen, really tune in; do not spend time thinking of the next strategic question you will ask. Take in the writer's thoughts, and take your cue from there. Also, let students know ahead of time that the conference will be an opportunity for them to ask questions; get them to write their questions on a small piece of paper or note card, if you wish. You may want to practice this with the whole class first, asking everyone to write one question and then quickly responding to a few. This modeling can get them into the questioning spirit—and encourage them to zero in on a pending question or two. A conference is not meant to hold you for life. It's meant to form a bond of trust between writer and writing coach—and sometimes to help the writer work through a current, pressing, real writing problem, and that's a lot.

■ The Amazing Two-Minute Conference

> *Two minutes—amazingly possible. For years I have been running workshops in which I have teachers write and respond to each other's drafts, cutting the conferences at two minutes. After two or three rounds of two-minute conferences, I will hear the teachers' voices fall before the two minutes are up. They have achieved a conversation about a piece of writing.*
>
> **—Donald M. Murray**
> 2004, p. 173

What can you do in two minutes? A lot, actually, if your whole attention is focused on the writer—*and* if you allow the student and his or her needs to direct the conference. Provide help with one kind of problem—no more. And for some students, hands-on help may be invaluable. Following are some useful things that you can *do* with students (especially those needing direct help) in less than two minutes (Do just *one* per conference):

- ✔ Together, brainstorm three possible leads (or endings).
- ✔ List 10 transitional words.
- ✔ Point out a moment when voice shifts, and talk about how/why the shift occurs.
- ✔ Brainstorm five possible titles.
- ✔ Identify the main idea of the piece.
- ✔ Point out a detail that really works because no one else might think of it.
- ✔ Ask a question that will lead the writer to a new detail or image.
- ✔ Weave in sensory detail: sounds, feelings, or smells.
- ✔ Replace two flat verbs with more powerful alternatives.
- ✔ Get rid of one "There is" sentence beginning.
- ✔ Add one line of dialogue to bring a character to life.
- ✔ Connect two choppy sentences to form one smooth sentence.
- ✔ Skim the page to see how many sentences begin in different ways.
- ✔ Brainstorm six alternatives to a tired word or phrase.
- ✔ Rewrite a sentence in three different ways—and choose the best one.
- ✔ Show how a semicolon works.
- ✔ Show how commas come inside quotation marks.
- ✔ Brainstorm six alternatives to *said*.
- ✔ Use brackets to mark unneeded words—and show students how powerful concise writing can be.
- ✔ Take *one sentence* closer to the truth—and watch voice soar.

What If the Writer Has Nothing to Say?

> Teach one thing, no more. . . . Overteaching means the child leaves the conference more confused than when he entered.
>
> **—Donald H. Graves**
>
> *Writing: Teachers and Children at Work,* 1983, p. 146

Often we *think* this is happening because we're in a hurry, and the student is reflecting. Be patient. Listen. Then, if the student simply can't think of *anything* to ask, here are a few prompting questions that may encourage a student to think about his or her writing in a useful way:

✔ What do you like about your piece?

✔ What do you think is your main message? Can you say it to me in a few words? Will that be clear to a reader? Why do you think so?

✔ Did you read the piece aloud? What did you learn by doing that?

✔ What is giving you trouble right now?

✔ What would you like a reader to see or feel as he or she listens?

✔ Do you think your lead will get readers hooked right away? Why?

✔ What does your conclusion leave me thinking about?

✔ Is this the paper you started to write—or did it change? If so, tell me what happened.

✔ What is the next thing you plan to do?

> Soup is no good when it's been sitting around coagulating. Potatoes get too mushy when they're old . . . If you tamper too much with your story, you'll lose the immediacy, the edge. Overworking your work is a form of fear.
>
> **Nancy Slonim Aronie**
>
> *Writing From the Heart,* 1998, p. 17

I want to add one more question to this list: "Have you thought about abandoning this piece and starting another?" I'm not saying that writers should do this as a habit. Writing is always a struggle, and you learn a lot by not giving up. Sometimes, though, the topic just goes dead, and you find yourself trying to make a succulent dish out of four-day-old leftovers. In that case, fixing a lead is like plunking parsley on last week's gefilte fish. Time to start fresh—without guilt. This is what I do, and it's sometimes (if not abused) a good strategy for students who are topic-weary.

What we want students *never to abandon* is writing itself. The writing habit. We want them to tuck a troublesome manuscript into the "in process" file for a time and let the subconscious work on it—which it will—while they turn their writing energies to something new. Writers must write, every day if possible. But there is no law stating that every *piece* of writing that's begun must be finished—tomorrow, next week, or ever. Let go.

PEER RESPONSE GROUPS

A few years ago, watching ABC's *Good Morning America,* I heard Charlie Gibson interview actor John Lithgow and ask him what he considered to be the most satisfying part of his career. Smiling, Lithgow replied that it was his years on Broadway. Why? Charlie wanted to know. Why not television or films? Because, Lithgow explained, on Broadway, you play right to an audience. That's when you find out if you can act. Response groups are like that—a chance to play to an audience. Writers—all writers—need this. Peer review can be a waste of time, though, if it's little more than a social hour, and often it disintegrates into this if students do not know what to do during the time they meet and share their writing. Here are 11 things you can do to make response groups more successful (and enjoyable) for everyone:

1. *Help students develop good listening skills.* Writers learn to be listeners first by having someone listen *to them*. In conferences, we must model what we hope to see. In addition, when students have a directed task—such as paraphrasing, giving their impression of the main point, telling what they see or feel, or noting words or phrases that spoke to them in particular—they learn to listen actively, to truly take in the reader's text, to respond to it, and to think about it. Someone must provide this direction, and it should be the *writer*, not you, who says what kind of response will be most useful.

2. *Teach students to use writers' language.* If students have no language for thinking about voice, leads, transitions, details, fluency, and phrasing, then "I liked your paper, Jim" may be the only comment that occurs to them. We must give them the tools (language + modeling) they need to make comments such as, "The conclusion, where your grandmother elopes with the taxidermist, was a total surprise—what a character!"

3. *Show students what* not *to do.* Ask a volunteer to read aloud a short piece of writing: the writer's own or one you provide (e.g., "The Redwoods"). Then illustrate the kinds of responses that do not work: staring at the ceiling, laughing inappropriately, making a negative remark ("How could anyone write with such a flat voice?"), or taking over the revision yourself: "You need to tell what the Redwoods looked like, where you hiked, what you saw, and the things you did." Ask your volunteer to let you know how each kind of response makes him or her feel. Then talk about it as a group.

4. *Distinguish between peer editing and peer review.* In peer *review*, listeners seldom see a writer's text. There is no need. They are not *correcting* the text. They're asking, "How does the writing play to the ear and to the imagination?" In peer *editing*, writers work together to proofread a text and correct faulty punctuation, spelling, grammar, paragraphing, capitalization, and so on. This is a completely different experience and should not become the purpose of a response group unless that is your explicit intention. (See Chapter 8 for more ideas on this.)

5. *Define roles clearly.* We often assume, because it may seem obvious to us, that students know precisely what to do in a peer response group. Often this is far from the case. No one is sure who should read first or whether writers must read the whole piece. Should the writer *show* the piece to the group or only read it aloud? What kinds of responses should listeners give? Are they responsible for the quality of the writer's revision?

The writer's role. Students frequently believe that the role of the writer is first to subject listeners to a rapid, low-volume, monotone reading of the text and then to sit passively as responders give any sort of feedback that suits them. The writer needs to take control of the group.

First, he or she should give the text the best interpretive reading possible, keeping in mind that it is fine to select just a portion if that's what listeners need to focus on. Second, the writer should tell listeners exactly what to listen for:

✔ Tell me if this makes sense.
✔ Tell me what you picture.
✔ Tell me what you feel as you listen.

> *Suggestions for how to fix something may be valuable, but should be offered respectfully. Even if you're sure you see just how it ought to be changed, this story belongs to the author, not you.*
>
> **—Ursula K. LeGuin**
> *Steering the Craft,* 1998, p. 154

✔ Do you have questions at the end, or is this enough information?

✔ Is my voice too conversational (sarcastic, formal)—or does it work?

✔ What's a good title for this?

> *Even very young children can listen and look for one colorful word or the most exciting sentence or a line that has interesting sounds or the scariest phrase.*
>
> **—Marjorie Frank**
>
> *If You're Trying to Teach Kids How to Write . . . You've Gotta Have This Book!* 1995, p. 140

The responder's role. We sometimes think that the writer is the only one in a tough poisition. After all, it's risky to share your writing aloud. We forget that responders are on the spot, too. They may feel a tremendous sense of responsibility, wondering whether the ultimate fate of the paper rests in their hands.

Help responders understand that they are not responsible for choreographing the revision of the piece; that is the writer's job. As responders, their job involves listening attentively, with every sense in tune—and then to offer supportive but honest feedback. What do they see, hear, smell, or feel as the writer shares a piece? How do they react emotionally? What makes sense, and what questions remain? These questions should be going through their minds as they listen, even if they do not share *all* this information with the writer.

6. *Encourage students to* write *one comment to the reader/author.* This tip comes from a very fine and creative teacher, Rosey Comfort, who taught both my own children. Rosey suggests that writers brave enough to share their writing should receive something for their efforts, so she encourages each listener to write a brief comment on a 3 by 5 inch note card, all of which then go to the writer. In a group, writers can hold their cards until everyone has shared; then they all read responses together. Writers of all ages treasure written feedback and quickly learn what kinds of notes are most helpful and most appreciated (see Figure 13.1 for samples).

7. *Begin with* I. We can teach students to frame negative responses in positive terms so as to make them less painful for writers. When you start with *I*, you shift the focus from the writing to you and your response, a much less accusatory position:

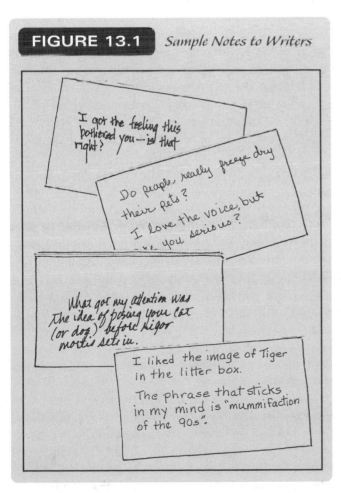

FIGURE 13.1   *Sample Notes to Writers*

✔ *Your title doesn't go with your paper* **becomes** *I had a hard time connecting the title to the rest of your paper. I kept listening for something about the Redwoods.*

✔ *You are writing about two topics* **becomes** *I wasn't sure if you were trying to tell me why writing was important—or how to be a good writer.*

✔ *You shifted from fairness, justice, and courage to fairness, respect, and courage* **becomes** *I felt confused when the three themes you talked about in the beginning of your paper changed.*

✔ *You didn't back any of your points with quotations* **becomes** *I was listening for a quotation that would show how Atticus felt about* **justice.**

✔ *Your argument about using computerized driving tests doesn't seem finished* **becomes** *I wondered if anyone was actually using computers in driving tests. Do you know?*

✔ *Your paper on eels is totally disorganized* **becomes** *I kept trying to figure out the two or three most important things to know about eels. Could you help me out?*

8. *Participate.* Join one of the class response groups yourself. Not every time—but now and then. Read your own work. Ask for the kinds of responses you'd like; give the kinds you'd like your students to give you.

9. *Remind students not to apologize.* So often we feel compelled to apologize for weaknesses, real or perceived, in our performance. Nowhere do we do this more often or more vocally than in preface to our own writing. "Remember," we say, "this is just a rough draft. I wrote this when I was recovering from knee surgery, and the computer was down. I had a sprained thumb, I had to use a crayon on butcher paper, and the neighbor's dog was howling." See what this does to an audience? It says to them, "Never mind the text; pay attention to *me.* I am very needy here." Most audiences will leap to the rescue, eager to make the writer feel better. Is that the kind of response we want, though?

When you share your own writing aloud, just plunge in. Later (if students do not notice), you can point out your raw courage and tell them, "You do this, too. Be brave. Dive in and read your text with confidence so that the feedback you get will be more about your writing and less about you."

10. *Make it real.* Many teachers feel more comfortable with a rule that says, "Each responder will make one positive comment prior to offering other kinds of feedback." This *can* work, provided that the comments are heartfelt and the writer does get his or her most important questions answered. In some ways, however, it seems a little formulaic. First, we'll say something nice to get the writer's guard down; then we'll slam her with the necessary criticism to ensure improvement.

Our responses to writing do not have to be couched in positives and negatives unless we choose to structure them in those terms. And why would we? Our first impression is more likely to occur in terms of asking ourselves, What do I *see* (if anything)? What do I *feel* (if anything)? A student said one day in response to a piece I'd written on a very tense, confrontational family Thanksgiving, "Your family seems very argumentative. *Very.* When you talked about staring into the candlelight reflecting off your mother's blue glass plates, I thought you were trying to escape. I used to do that." I had never before thought of myself as "escaping," but of course that is precisely what I was doing. This response was much more revealing to me than if the student had said, "I enjoyed your description of the candlelight reflecting on the plates." A compliment makes us feel good for a moment; an insight keeps us thinking for hours—sometimes forever.

11. *Don't drag it out.* Peer review is, by nature, a reflective activity, and we must respect that. On the other hand, allowing too much time can make students feel pressured to say more than they have to say, and soon the conversation drifts to unrelated topics. Try this (adjusting if the timing does not work for you): Put students into groups of three. Let students know that while they will have ample time to listen and respond, peer review will not go on forever. They need to stay focused and make comments that are to the point. Ask stu-

> *Why is it so difficult to give a simple human response? I think it is because we try so hard to be helpful we forget to be real.*
>
> **—Lucy McCormick Calkins**
> *The Art of Teaching Writing,*
> 1994, p. 232

dents to take a minute or so to decide who will go first, second, and third. Then give each student three to four minutes to read his or her work. Allow responders about two minutes to give a focused, clear, concise response to the reader's piece, either orally or on note cards. The whole process will take under 20 minutes.

Debriefing

At the end of the peer review session, take five minutes to debrief the process. Ask writers, "Who got a response that was really helpful today? What was it? How many of you have a strong sense right now of how you will go about revising your work? Did you get the feedback you need?" Effective response groups require learning (as a responder) to be a good listener and learning (as a writer) to take charge.

GRADING

To some educators, grades seem old-fashioned, cumbersome, and hopelessly out of synch with new approaches to assessment. Even educators who still advocate the use of grades will admit that, for many purposes, there are better, more thorough methods of measuring and recording student achievement. A well-designed portfolio provides a richer and more complete picture of what a student can do than reams of test scores. Similarly, a teacher's narrative record of student performance, if sufficiently detailed, provides a wealth of information no report card can match.

As Barry Lane (1993) tells us, "For a writing teacher who believes in encouraging revision, graded papers are nothing less than a curse. Low grades discourage and high grades imply that a piece is done. Even worse, students begin writing to improve their grade instead of finding out what they have to say" (p. 129). Donald M. Murray (2004) calls grades the "terminal response," meaning that once a grade is assigned to a piece of writing, it virtually dies, for the student will not look at it again.

In his book, *Punished by Rewards*, Alfie Kohn (1993) talks openly about the naïveté of believing that we can motivate students to strive for excellence with a simplistic carrot-and-stick, A-to-F grading system. A student's inner world, he assures us, is far too complex for this. When grades dominate the classroom environment, Kohn argues, students tend to

1. Place minimal value on things learned and to care only about the grade earned.
2. Become dependent on the reward, allowing themselves to be controlled by the threat of the grade.
3. Become unwilling to take any risk, however promising, that might jeopardize their grade point average (GPA).

Kohn also cites the research findings of John Condry (1977), who concluded that people motivated only by the offer of immediate rewards "seem to work harder and produce more activity, but the activity is of a lower quality, contains more errors, and is more stereotyped and less creative than the work of comparable nonrewarded subjects working on the same problems" (pp. 471–472).

> *The cost runs high when we coerce students (through grades, praise, favoritism), however subtly, to shoehorn their emerging language into the narrow parameters we set for what constitutes "good writing" in our classrooms.*
>
> **—Ralph Fletcher**
> *What a Writer Needs*, 1993, p. 25

> *Where do children learn to be grade-grubbers? From this: "You'd better listen up, folks, because this is going to be on the test." And from this: "A B-minus? What happened, Deborah?" And from this: "I take pride in the fact that I'm a hard grader. You're going to have to work in here."*
>
> **—Alfie Kohn**
> *Punished by Rewards*, 1993, p. 205

> *When I first began to teach, I was a tough grader right from the first day. . . . My students didn't realize I was terrified they might rise up and attack me. I put them in their place with grades.*
>
> **—Donald M. Murray**
> *A Writer Teaches Writing*, 2004, p. 142

Kohn suggests that comments are more meaningful and more motivational than grades and are far more likely to inspire excellent performance (p. 203).

What Do Grades Mean to Students?

Ask *students* what grades mean, and you're likely to get some startling answers. We may think of an A, for instance, as a sign of success. But many students will tell you that A's are mostly for parents (or for precollege records)—and sometimes translate into money, the right to drive the car, or other tangible rewards. They are not always intrinsically rewarding; they're simply the gateway to something else.

Do you think C means average and F means failure? Think again. Many students will tell you that the *worst* grade to receive is a C because while an F means that you didn't try or didn't care (This can even be a badge of honor), a C indicates that you did your best but *still* failed—and that's depressing.

What's more, though many of us hate admitting this, grades have no universal meaning beyond the most general level. The extremes of the grading scale are probably the most meaningful. To *most* teachers, an A signifies a job well done; an F, significant problems with performance. However, some teachers refuse ever to assign a D or an F because of the potential damage to self-esteem. One teacher I knew assigned grades of A, AA, AAA, and so on, to avoid any confidence-diminishing "lower grades." It didn't work, of course. Within a very short time, his students unraveled the code and were devastated to receive the low grade of "A." Go between the A-to-F extremes and you're likely to encounter an even wider range of responses. In a workshop one day I asked teachers to define what B– meant to them. Here are just some of their intriguing, diverse answers:

✔ You tried hard, but it needed work.
✔ Good job! Just needed that little something more.
✔ Close to what I expected—*almost!*
✔ Average work. It's what used to be a C.
✔ Between 80 and 82 percent—it's pure mathematics.
✔ I tried to like your paper, but I couldn't.

Clearly, grades are not consistent class to class. This is hardly news. On the one hand, we have the teachers who cannot crush students with low grades, and on the other, most of us have known (some of us have been) teachers who could hardly bear to hand out an A, as if suspecting that just down the road we would encounter a finer performance and then feel foolish for having been so easily impressed.

■ Being Consistent

Given these diverse responses, can we ever hope to achieve consistency, a clear definition of performance goals, and all-around fairness? We can. Indeed, we must. By connecting grades to criteria, we say to students, "We will define what we mean by various levels of performance, and we will apply those definitions as consistently as human nature will allow." It isn't a perfect system. How can it be when we are talking levels of quality and not rights or wrongs? But the more we read and write ourselves, and the more we practice assessment with our students, the more consistent our scoring becomes, and the more we draw students into our interpretive community.

Some ways of making grades work for us include these:

✔ Getting over our compulsion to assess *everything*
✔ Recognizing that working for the sake of completing the writing and taking satisfaction in it is (should be) a goal in itself
✔ Allowing mistakes—without lowering a grade (Perfectionism inhibits progress, especially in writing.)
✔ Offering extended comments in place of grades on some pieces
✔ Helping students to understand that positive audience response—not a grade—is an appropriate goal for a serious writer
✔ Grading a body of work rather than individual pieces of writing
✔ Connecting letter grades to explicit written criteria
✔ Avoiding grading on a curve, which artificially limits the number of students who can be successful and suggests that there is but one path to success
✔ Allowing students choices about topic and form so that grades, when assigned, will reflect performance on pieces that are personally meaningful to them
✔ Inviting students to be partners in the evaluation process by asking them to help define the criteria by which writing will be assessed
✔ Allowing students to challenge grades with which they do not agree and occasionally changing a grade based on reassessment of performance or additional work by the student

Finally, we ourselves can value knowledge and understanding more than we value grades, taking pride in what our students know and in what they can achieve, not in their tests scores or GPAs. They know the difference. They see what we care about. We cannot hide it.

How and What to Grade

Certainly student achievement (performance, that is) will be at the heart of most grading systems. But should other factors be considered as well? What about effort or attitude? Let's consider these factors one at a time.

■ Achievement

If we grade on achievement, we tell students, in effect, that those who attain a higher level of writing proficiency will receive higher grades. To many people, this seems a fair approach to grading, and I agree. After all, demand for high-level achievement is a reality of life, both in and out of the classroom. Writers whose work no one wants to read do not get published, nor do they get hired as journalists, technical writers, communications specialists, or editors. Performance

> We see that our evaluations are usually more trustworthy—and much more likely to enhance learning—when we find ways to describe the performance in question rather than measure or rank it.
>
> **—Peter Elbow**
> *Embracing Contraries,*
> 1986, p. 225

> Experienced teachers watch and listen closely for when students get things wrong. . . . Mistakes offer information about how a student thinks.
>
> **—Alfie Kohn**
> *Punished by Rewards,*
> 1993, pp. 212–213

> Perfectionism is the voice of the oppressor, the enemy of the people.
>
> **—Anne Lamott**
> *Bird by Bird,* 1995, p. 28

> If you grade a body of work, you will give students a better picture of their overall strengths and weaknesses.
>
> **—Barry Lane**
> *After THE END,* 1993, p. 128

counts everywhere, not just in school. Having said that, we must determine what kinds of achievement we wish to measure and how we will go about it.

Much of this book is devoted to defining and promoting a performance assessment approach that judges the quality of students' writing based essentially on final products. For many teachers, this is enough.

However, achievement also could include performance on foundational writing tasks, such as spelling tests, analytical scoring of someone else's work, or editing. In addition, creative assessors might look at such things as these:

✔ The student's ability to self-assess and defend that judgment
✔ The student's ability to assess the work of others and defend that judgment
✔ Full participation in the writing process
✔ Skill in coaching other writers

Many teachers prefer to focus more on process than product. They may ask questions such as these:

✔ Do students find their own ways in?
✔ Do they find prewriting strategies that work for them?
✔ Do they participate actively and purposefully in conferences or peer writing groups?
✔ Do they revise their work routinely and thoughtfully, without excessive prompting?
✔ Do they know how and when to edit?

Such questions can form the basis for assessing not only a student's understanding of the process of writing itself but also his or her ability to become an independent writer. One caution, though: Good process skills do not guarantee fine writing. For this reason, I prefer an assessment method that combines process with product.

■ *Effort*

Effort is an intangible commodity that is hard to measure and even harder to recognize. One teacher may define *effort* as "completing and turning in all homework on time," whereas to another it may mean "making a positive contribution to the classroom." The first definition is not so nebulous as the second, but still, such differences lead to inconsistency in grading. Furthermore, haven't we all known people whose specialty was making the next to impossible look easy? And haven't we, honestly, valued and sometimes even envied this capability? Imagine the difference in Fred Astaire's career had he lurched across the stage, huffing and puffing. Would anyone then have said, "Boy, that Fred Astaire is some dancer! What an *effort* the guy makes!" We don't want huffing, really; we want good dancing that looks effortless even when we know that it's not.

Keep in mind, too, that assertiveness can look a lot like effort. The student who is forever asking a clarifying question or seeking additional writing advice is often judged to be highly motivated. This may be a correct perception, but what of the quiet or shy writers who would love to have a fraction more of our attention but are too withdrawn to ask for it? Who knows how much effort it takes for those writers just to share their writing in a group or to compose pieces they know other eyes will see.

Suppose, then, that we do not grade on effort. It's only fair to ask, "What about the student who really *is* making an effort but simply cannot succeed? What, other than effort, will rescue this student from failure?"

Instead of rewarding the effort, which provides a hollow, unsatisfying kind of victory, why not reshape the task to better fit the student's skill? Change the assignment; let the student choose another topic or approach this topic in another way. Allow the student to dictate part of the piece or to flesh out a story with illustrations. If editing is involved, simplify the task by asking the student to search out fewer errors or fewer kinds of errors. Lengthen the time allowed to complete the assignment. In other words, let's find a way to help writers succeed with the business of writing. Then we won't hear ourselves saying to students, via artificially inflated grades (which fool no one), "I see that you cannot make it as a writer, but you seem like such a good person, here are some points for trying." It is, I believe, condescending and disrespectful to inflate performance scores. Students know when they have done a good job and when they need to work harder. Let's not demean them by pretending we see things differently.

■ *Attitude*

Do you have a good attitude toward writing? I do—mostly. Perhaps, like me, you actually get a good feeling picturing yourself sitting down at the keyboard with a little music playing and the scent of herbal tea drifting your way. When it's going well, almost nothing feels as good as writing.

I write virtually every day, but I do not feel positive and open about it every day. Once when I was working on a piece on economics (far from my favorite topic), the computer "ate" a large chunk of the chapter I had been struggling with for two weeks. On that day I wanted to be Mad Max—just for an hour—but of course computers are not yet sufficiently advanced to experience pain, so all this energy was wasted. I certainly would not have been happy to be visited just then by someone with a clipboard and checklist, assessing my attitude.

Keeping at it when you don't feel like it is my definition of good attitude. But then another teacher-assessor will look for a cheery disposition, a lengthy journal, or willingness to try a new form of writing. The point is, can we really define or recognize good attitude—any more than we can recognize effort? We probably can make some good educated guesses, but in the end we will all be left with our personal definitions. This means, bottom line, that we should reward effort with an appreciative smile and lavish praise, but we should *not* figure it into our grades.

Translating Analytical Scores into Grades

Begin with developing for yourself and for your students a "big picture." Spell out, in very specific terms, which tasks, assignments, or tests will affect students' grades and what percentage of the total grade will hinge on each. Be sure that students are familiar with the explicit criteria (e.g., the six-trait model or any other rubrics) that you will use to assess performance.

Following are a few suggestions for putting together that big picture for teachers who plan to use the six-trait scoring approach as part of their total assessment plan.

> *If you do a complete autopsy on every piece, your writers will perish from too much pruning.*
>
> —**Marjorie Frank**
> *If You're Trying to Teach Kids How to Write . . . You've Gotta Have This Book!* 1995, p. 104

1. *Do not assess everything.* We want to gather just enough information to make confident grading decisions and no more. We know that one or two samples are not enough. When we assess somewhere between four and six samples of writing, though, we see a *body* of work; then we are probably approaching a level at which we can feel confident that our assessment is meaningful.

Students, with your help, of course, can be selective about what is assessed. During a given grading period, if you are focusing on specific genres, you might ask students to select samples of each that they feel are worth taking clear through the writing process; others remain practice drafts—good for developing skills but never assessed. Normally, practice revision, free writing, journals, and beginning drafts would not be assessed either (except in the sense that the teacher may check to see that they are done).

2. *Score the traits that are most relevant.* You do not need to assess all six traits each time, although you can if this kind of "full picture" approach makes you more comfortable. Consider, though, that in a piece of technical writing, ideas, conventions, and word choice may be more important than, say, fluency. A student who is explaining how to tie a fishing fly must think about detail, organization, and word choice (terminology), whereas one who is telling the story of a narrow escape from a fire may focus most on imagery (another way of thinking about word choice) and voice.

3. *Do not* grade *individual pieces of writing.* If you are giving students scores, if they know the rubrics, and if you are offering your own personal comments in addition to scores alone, you are providing significant, meaningful feedback. A grade adds no new information. Students who know the traits know that if they're receiving 4s, 5s, or 6s, they're doing moderately to extremely well. Scores of 1, 2, or 3 mean that significant revision is needed. There's never any mystery.

> *Grades generate anxiety and hard feelings between students, between students and teachers, between students and their parents, and between parents and teachers. Common sense suggests they ought to be reduced to the smallest possible number necessary to find out how students are getting along toward the four or five main objectives of the program, but teachers keep piling them up like squirrels gathering nuts.*
>
> —**Paul Diederich**
> *Measuring Growth in English,* 1974, p. 2

4. *Remember: A 5 or 6 is not an A.* Remember that a letter grade is a holistic summary of how a piece of writing works overall: ideas, organization, conventions, voice—the works. A 5 in, say, *ideas* is an analytical response to one portion of the writing and does *not* equal an A (or any other holistic grade).

5. *Give students the option to revise.* In many classrooms, students who are unsatisfied with the formal assessment on any piece of writing have the option to revise and thereby raise their scores. This option not only reinforces the value of revision but also says to students, "Assessment is an impression, not an ultimate truth." For too long assessment has ruled (and often inhibited) students' academic behavior like the Wizard of Oz. When we step boldly forward like Dorothy and pull the curtain aside, we see that assessment is not infallible but is only a little display of fireworks sparked by human judgment.

6. *Keep written records of all scores earned.* Do not trust memory. Do not assume that you can recapture scores by looking through a work file or portfolio later. Record scores as soon as they are earned.

7. *Make students partners in the record-keeping process.* Let students know as they go along how they are doing in terms of total points earned and total points possible. This ensures that final grades will not be a surprise.

8. *Allow students time to self-assess during the revision process.* Early assessment, not for grading but to set up a plan for revision, is essential to making students partners in the overall evaluation process.

9. *Base grades on an average.* This is perhaps the simplest way to compute grades. Simply total the points earned and divide by the number of traits assessed. For example, let's say that I am using a six-point scale and that my students have completed three pieces of writing, each of which is scored on all six traits. One student—Pat—receives (for the sake of simplicity) all 5s (out of a possible 6) on two of the assignments and all 4s on the third. Pat's total points equal $5 \times 6 \times 2$ (or 60) plus 4×6 (or 24), for a total of 84. The average, then, is 84 divided by 18 (3 pieces of writing $\times$ 6 traits per piece). The resulting score is 4.67. What grade is this? Actually, that's entirely up to you. The way to figure it out is to make yourself a chart, like the one that follows, with grade cutoffs that suit you. Remember, the one in this book is *only a model;* please modify these numbers to suit yourself.

■ *Possible Grade Equivalents for a Six-Point Scale (The one used for Pat)*

5.5 A	4.5 B	3.5 C	2.5 D
5.2 A–	4.2 B–	3.2 C–	2.2 D–
4.8 B+	3.8 C+	2.8 D+	

■ *Possible Grade Equivalents for a Five-Point Scale*

4.5 A	3.8 B	3.0 C	2.2 D
4.2 A–	3.5 B–	2.8 C–	2.0 D–
4.0 B+	3.2 C+	2.5 D+	

10. *Or base the grade on a percentage.* Many teachers like percentages, and this is an easy way to compute grades, too. The grade is based on points earned as a percentage of total points possible, a percentage that is adjusted by reason of the fact that it does not represent a true total but an estimated position on a continuum.

In the third edition of this book, I provided a conversion table to simplify this adjustment, but since then, I have come up with a simpler way to get the same results—no conversion required. It simply requires adding 0.5 to each score assigned. Why? Well, picture that continuum for a moment, and you'll see that a score of, say, 4 is not really a 4.0 at all (in most cases) but exists somewhere along the path between 4.0 and 5.0. Sometimes it might be a 4.2 and sometimes a 4.7, and so on. On *average*, the 4 would hit right in the middle of that span between 4 and 5—it would be a 4.5, that is (see Figure 13.2 for an illustration). So that's the number I would add into a grade book. By the way, in case you're concerned, you are *not* giving the student extra points by adding in these percentages; you are not *giving* the student *anything.* You are simply making up for the fact that measurement on a continuum is by nature slightly imprecise, so we have to adjust it to make it fit

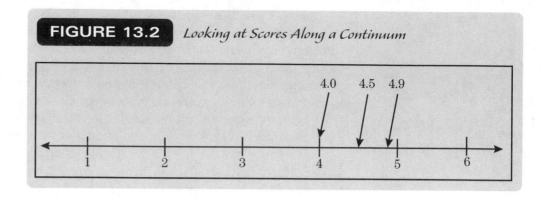

FIGURE 13.2 *Looking at Scores Along a Continuum*

our grading system. What about the points possible then? That number does *not* increase; it remains constant.

Let's go back to Pat for a minute. Pat's scores of 5 (if we're using a percentage system) become 5.5s, and the 4s become 4.5s. Thus Pat's *total points earned* translates into 5.5×12 plus 4.5×6, for a total of 93. We divide this by *points possible* (108) to get a percentage, and it's about 86 percent.

Again, that percentage can translate into any grade we wish. I likely would look on it as a B heading toward a B+ (the same grade Pat would receive if we averaged the scores), but you may decide that 86 percent is a B+ or a B–. It's whatever you want it to be.

If we did not add the 0.5 to Pat's scores but simply computed the percentage as is, it would come out to 77 percent. This would give Pat a high C at best (in most grading systems). Consider all those 4s and 5s, though, and you'll see at once that this grade is inappropriate. This is why adjustment (adding the 0.5) is necessary.

■ Differential Weighting

This system is precisely the same as the total points method except that certain traits are weighted for certain assignments. For instance, if you decided that the trait of ideas was especially important in an assignment on the Holocaust, you might weight that trait by a factor of 3, making it worth 3×5 (or 15) points total.

Communicating with Parents

Parents are used to letter grades. Now, suddenly, here you are with numerical scores, continuums, scoring guides, strengths and weaknesses, and the rest. How do you explain it all?

Perhaps the best way, if you have the luxury of a little time, is a mini–training session in which you summarize the six traits and even have parents attempt to score a paper or two. You might even, if you're very brave, ask them to write a short paragraph and assess their own writing. Nothing brings the traits so vividly into focus as looking at your own work!

■ Writing Goals

Explain that students will be learning the steps within the writing process together with the six traits as writing *goals* and that learning to be strong and independent writers will take time. Some papers that are sent home may be drafts in process and not ready for editing—*yet*. Explain that students will be learning editing skills and will apply these at the appropriate time during the writing process, after all (or most) revision has occurred. Parents are an important audience for their students' work—mostly because they show interest in that work—and it is helpful if they can be *listeners* rather than editors for a time, hearing their students' writing (*not* correcting it) and responding as if to a letter from a friend.

■ What Parents Can Do

Parents often want to know what they can do to help their children become stronger writers. *Many* things, actually. Here's a brief list of suggestions, to which you should add your own ideas based on your experience as a teacher, parent, or both:

■ For Parents of Student Writers

1. *Read to your child.* The reading-writing connection is powerful. When you read aloud to your child, you do many things: show that books are exciting and enjoyable to share, expand your child's vocabulary and "sentence sense," and help him or her to understand why writing matters—as a way of communicating to a reader. When you read, put all the passion you can into your reading. Have fun! Let go of inhibition, and let the text carry you. Don't be concerned if you do not know every word. You and your student writer can work your way through pictures and/or text together. What matters most is that your child sees and hears you enjoying reading.

2. *Encourage your child to read to you.* Students who read aloud learn to read for meaning. They also develop an ear for voice and fluency—two vital qualities of strong writing. When a child learns to read with expression, he or she becomes a confident reader and also learns to put that same kind of expression into his or her own writing. Really listen as your child reads. Sink into the world of the book. Let the text sweep you away.

3. *Be a listener.* Ask your child to share his or her writing—even if it is unfinished. Don't feel that you have to be a grammarian, teacher, or coach. Relax. The most important thing you can do is to listen with full attention and interest. Listen as you would to a cherished letter from a friend you have not seen in a long while. Respond to the content from your heart. Tell the student what you hear; what you love; what you picture in your mind; what you feel, think of, or remember; and what makes an impression on you.

4. *Talk about topics.* Many students have difficulty coming up with topics to write about. You can help. Talk with your child about experiences and interests you have shared. What do you like to do together? Have you overcome a frightening, sad, or challenging experience? Talk it through. Have you laughed together about something? Visited an interesting place? See if you can reconstruct it. Share family stories your child may have forgotten or may not know, including stories of his or her own childhood (and yours). Families make a great resource for writing topics. A family photo album or scrapbook (if you keep one) can be a good place to begin. Perhaps a sibling, aunt or

uncle, or grandparent has stories to share or can offer a geographic or historic perspective on life. Other general topic areas: places or people you remember, hobbies, sports, pets, school experiences, work, friends, interesting people, and favorite or least favorite foods.

5. *Write.* Let your child see you write—a note to a friend, a thank-you letter, an invitation, a letter of explanation, a letter of inquiry, a résumé or job application letter, an evaluation or report, a letter to the editor, a recipe, or a list. Each time you write, you show your child that writing is an important life skill and that it has many purposes.

6. *Ask your* child *to write.* Do you need to reserve a hotel room or a car? Do you need to correct an address or request something from an agency or company? Do you want to comment on a product or service? Are you planning a family get-together? Are you putting together an album or scrapbook? Are you sending a greeting card? Let your child write captions, letters, notes, explanations, or invitations. If he or she is very young, you can help, perhaps even doing some of the writing or keyboarding as your child comes up with ideas. When you do this, the child is still doing the *thinking* part of the writing—the most important part.

7. *Let your child be* your *teacher.* Writers and editors learn by teaching. So let your child be your teacher. Ask him or her to explain the meaning of a passage, interpret a piece of business correspondence, or help you to rewrite a sentence to make it shorter or more clear. Ask for help coming up with the right word, the best way to begin a letter, a correct spelling, or the just-right way to end a piece. You'll find that one of the best things you can do is to seek your child's help.

8. *See your child as a writer.* Virtually *nothing* you can do has more power and impact than believing in your child's ability to write. Take every opportunity you can to encourage him or her and to say to your child, in your own words, "You are a writer."

CHAPTER 13 IN A NUTSHELL

- The comments we make are a way of sharing our personal responses to students' writing, and the words we choose may have lasting impact.
- The most effective comments are honest and specific. We can (and should) help students to build on their strengths. We can (and should) offer feedback on problems, but in a positive way.
- Often, beginning with *I* is a good way to put a positive spin on a constructive comment.
- Conferences are most effective if they are brief and focus on one or two writing problems.
- To the extent possible, the student writer should guide the length and content of the conference.
- Peer response groups serve an important function in the classroom if they are managed carefully.
- Both writers and responders need to understand the roles they are to play.

- Grades are one form of communication, but students should not be encouraged to look on a grade as a substitute for personal satisfaction.
- Grades should be based on writing performance, not effort or attitude.
- Several factors can help make grading fair and consistent, including sharing the basis for grades with students; involving students in establishing criteria; not assessing everything; basing grades on a body of work; giving students choices about topics, forms of writing, and pieces selected for grading; and remaining flexible about changing grades if change is warranted.
- It is critical to involve parents by letting them know specific ways they can work with their student writers.

EXTENSIONS

1. What is the most positive or negative comment you have ever received in response to your writing? How did it influence you? Share comments with your study group or class if you feel comfortable doing so.

2. Write out the comments you would offer to any student writer whose work appears in this book. Compare your comments with those of colleagues.

3. If you are teaching now, do you involve your students in response groups? What strategies do you use to make that successful? List and share them.

4. For fun, act out a "bad response group" scenario, doing some role playing to illustrate the kinds of responses that you find least helpful.

5. Share a brief piece of your own writing with students or colleagues, asking them to be a response group for you. Invite them to make comments on note cards, and do the same with their writing. Discuss the most helpful responses you receive.

6. Are grades addictive? Write a journal entry about this.

7. This chapter makes an argument that grades should be based on performance, not attitude or effort. Do you agree? Why or why not? Discuss this with a group of colleagues.

8. Come up with a grading system that you think is fair that incorporates the six traits but may not be based solely on the six traits. Explain why you think your system is fair.

9. Compose an argument for maintaining or for doing away with grades. Defend your position. Hold a debate in your class or study group on this topic.

10. If you are the parent of a student writer, talk about ways your school has helped involve you in your students' learning. What (if anything) could have made your involvement more comfortable or productive? If you are currently teaching, what specific steps do you take to encourage parent involvement?

11. Compose a brief letter to parents explaining the six-trait model and suggesting specific things they can do to help their children become stronger writers.

WHY I WRITE

I write because it is a way to give someone the gift of love.

—Katie Miller, student writer

LOOKING AHEAD

In the closing chapter I'll reflect in the importance of believing in our student writers and in ourselves.

14 Believing

I believe the ultimate in education is reached when learners—both students and teachers at all levels—take charge of their own learning and use their education to lead rich and satisfying lives.

—Regie Routman
Literacy at the Crossroads, 1996, p. 147

What is needed is a culture of success, backed by a belief that all pupils can achieve.

—Paul Black and Dylan Wiliam
"Inside the Black Box: Raising Standards Through Classroom Assessment," 1998, p. 147

When my students and I discover uncharted territory to explore, when the pathway out of a thicket opens up before us, when our experience is illuminated by the lightning life of the mind—then teaching is the finest work I know.

—Parker J. Palmer
The Courage to Teach: Exploring the Inner Landscape of a Teacher's Life, 1998, p. 1

*M*any people these days are concerned that students cannot write and, further, that they are not receiving the instruction they need to turn that situation around. It is a time of skepticism and self-doubt in education, a time when we often hear only faint echoes of those strong and fearless voices—Donald Graves, Donald Murray, Lucy Calkins, Regie Routman, and others—whose eloquence once charted a path so sure we never questioned the truth at its core. We tend to tune out some voices these days because, after all, we are very busy—busy launching ourselves full sail from strategy to strategy, never weighing anchor long enough to know for sure whether we have reached safe harbor at last. Our fear makes us frenzied and impatient. Though we fly the flag of "writing process," an agonizing worry gnaws at us: What if teaching writing this way takes too long? The test, after all, is coming. It is *always* coming. So we blaze through articles and Internet sites, looking for a faster approach that will make writers of our students this year, this month, now. And of course, as we keep a lookout for the test that is looming, we simultaneously look back over our shoulders to check whether the education critics are closing in.

They are, of course. They are forever circling. For some people, criticism is a calling. But while it may be meager comfort to those they target, it is still worth remembering that almost nothing is as dark as some critics make it out to be. When we realize this, we make room in our hearts for the hope that perhaps we are, after all, in control of our own destiny, and there is much we can do to help student writers achieve their dreams. It all begins with what we believe. In the face of all the doubts, therefore, in that small, quiet place within you where you can for a time escape those nagging feelings of doubt that undermine teaching effectiveness, here are six beliefs I would ask you to cling to:

1. *Believe in the voices that once led us.* Process is the answer—the only answer. People learn to write by writing, by reading, and by living and working within a community of writers who can share their experience and their growing expertise. Writers do not learn to write overnight or through shortcuts. They can learn to fill pages this way, but only writing that touches readers is the real thing.

2. *Believe that the human spirit is too elusive, too vast, and too diverse to be defined by a single assessment.* Assessment gives us useful information (sometimes) and helps us to know where to put our teaching energy (sometimes). A single assessment cannot tell us whether a student can write or whether a teacher can teach. In his last years of public school, a young man received these comments on his writing: "This boy is an indolent and illiterate member of the class." "Ideas limited." "A persistent muddler." "I have never met a boy who so persistently writes the exact opposite of what he means." Some years later, in the early 1940s, this "persistent muddler" wrote an article about his military experiences, an article for which he received a then-amazing sum of $1000 from the *Saturday Evening Post*, and this encouraging comment from the novelist C. S. Forester: "You were meant to give me notes, not a finished story. I'm bowled over. Your piece is marvelous. It is the work of a gifted writer." The young man was Roald Dahl (2000, pp. 187–188, 198–199), and had he allowed those early assessments to define how he saw himself forever, think what we might have missed.

3. *Believe that change can be a good thing.* I have known teachers (likely, so have you) who would fight to the death to uphold treasured rules of diction or usage. It is good to value quality. Without change, though, we would never have acquired any treasured rules to uphold in the first place. Change, spurred by a need to clarify meaning or simply by a love of language, can be a very positive thing indeed.

Think how our language is enhanced by our passion for borrowing. We take on many words from other cultures just because we like their sound: *kangaroo*, *billabong*, *mate*, *jumbuck*, and *boomerang* from Australia and *voodoo*, *tote*, *juke*, *banana*, *bad-mouth*, *nitty-gritty*, *high five*, *banjo*, *okra*, and *jam session* from African cultures. Such diversity gives us not only a new collective voice but also a level of precision that we could not achieve without our ever-expanding word list: *cupola*, *balcony*, *piano*, *pizza*, *balloon*, and *volcano* from Italian; *paragraph*, *alphabet*, *school*, and *thermometer* from Greek; *canoe*, *toboggan*, *chipmunk*, *pecan*, and *kayak* from Native American; *shampoo*, *pepper*, *panther*, and *ketchup* from Asian cultures; *physician*, *milieu*, and *poetry* from French; *vista*, *mesa*, *barracuda*, *corral*, *fiesta*, *rodeo*, and *pronto* from

Spanish; *hamburger*, *pretzel*, and *kindergarten* from German; and *ski*, *knife*, *happy*, and *egg* from Scandinavian.

As we change culturally and technologically, we must create new words that let us talk about who we are and where we're going. No one needed to talk of *cyberspace*, *Web sites*, *computer hackers*, *computer viruses*, *modems*, or *virtual reality* 50 years ago, but these terms are part of our common language now.

Punctuation, a relatively new invention, has evolved to help us manage the ocean of language that now surrounds us. We didn't always have it. Not too many years ago, words wereruntogetherlikethis—making text much harder to process. Someone thought of putting spaces between words and then indenting paragraphs. And eventually, capital letters—then commas, semicolons, colons, and dashes became commonplace, joining the ranks of periods, exclamation points, and question marks to clarify stops and pauses. In the world of writing, though, no convention is forever. Some writers bristle at dashes or ellipses; others disdain formalities. In *Writing with Style*, John R. Trimble (2000) likens semicolons to the automatic coupling devices on railroad cars, handy for joining independent thoughts. Yet he confesses, "The average college student isn't ready for semicolons. She hasn't discerned any need for them, nor is she eager to. They look forbiddingly exotic—about as tempting as a plate of snails" (pp. 105–106). If Trimble's assessment is right, who knows whether semicolons will be around in 50 or 100 years?

Our usage is changing, too, and, like punctuation, often rides the tide of popularity polls, as Trimble points out: "*All right* is right; *alright* is wrong. So many people don't know alright is wrong, though, that eventually it will be accepted as Standard English" (p. 152). My spell checker accepts it now, so it looks as if Trimble called this one correctly.

Changes in language are not just about the addition of new words or shifts in usage or conventions, though. The whole rhythm of our speech fluctuates continually. Two hundred years ago, language we would now consider pompous and ornate was regarded as conversational. The *Boy's Own Book*, by William Clarke (1829), offers this advice in a chapter about swimming: "If one of your companions be in danger of drowning, be sure that, in endeavoring to save him, you make your approaches in such a manner, as will prevent him from grappling with you; if he once get a hold of your limbs, you both will almost inevitably be lost" (p. 94). This has an almost comic sound, reminiscent of Liza Doolittle in the transitional phase of her verbal transformation. These days we like our sentences to come to the point: "A drowning person has enough strength to pull you under. If you attempt a rescue, approach from behind." Some language, of course—like that of Milton, Shakespeare, Bacon, or Swift—has sufficiently strong architecture to withstand the erosions of time. A writer with much to say and an exceptional ear may hold readers' attention for decades—sometimes centuries. We all respect the power of the symphony, but down on the corner there's that little jazz band that makes you want to get up and dance, and it's itching to go mainstream. In 1919, H. L. Mencken wrote in *The American Language*, "A living language is like a man suffering incessantly from small hemorrhages, and what it needs above all else is constant transactions of new blood from other tongues. The day the gates go up, that day it begins to die" (McCrum, Cran, and MacNeil, 1986, p. 47).

4. *Believe in compassion.* In the David Mamet film *Heist*, Gene Hackman's character, Joe, explains how he manages to appear more intelligent and clever than he really is: "I try to imagine a fella smarter than myself, and then I try to imagine, 'What would *he* do?'" Let's adopt Joe's strategy. Let's imagine the world's best assessment, 50 years or 100 years from now, run by somebody smarter than we are. What would it look like? Would it be fast and slick, a model of stunning efficiency? Perhaps. I like to think though that today's "rush to judgment" approach might eventually be replaced by a more reflective style, tempered by a sense of compassion, which is to say, a genuine desire to help writers. We are so eager to discover what is wrong and who is to blame for it that we forget assessment's highest and best purposes: to identify strengths and to build understanding. That more compassionate assessment of the future would seek to uncover what students *can* do under the best of circumstances and would allow time to think, reflect, and revise.

Of those voices that have guided us in recent years, perhaps none has had more impact than that of Donald Graves—a man who is the very soul of compassion. Listen to this gentle man for a time, and you will be struck by the notable absence of lofty pronouncement-from-afar sentences beginning, "Today's fifth graders . . ." He speaks in soft tones, with an up-close, attentive style—about a writer whose sense of humor he cannot forget, another who couldn't seem to write more than a line or two, a student with such an ear for voice that he found test questions dull, a writer whose poetry gave him chills. At our best moments, we teach this way—to a single child. Graves teaches not as a speaker but as a listener, pulling the lesson out of the student instead of trying to drive it in. His attention to the writer, not the writing, and his unwavering belief that *the writer will find the solution to the problem* remind us that assessment of the very best kind always takes us forward and that it is our faith in our students and ourselves that gives it its momentum.

5. *Believe that students can write.* Although many student writers struggle, I personally encounter students every year whose writing both moves and teaches me. Some of their work, such as the poem by Corinne (Figure 14.1) appears in this book. Much of it is stunning. You will not see their talent or success lauded in the newspaper, probably because, as a reporter told me once, "Kids writing well? *That's* not news. People want to hear about the *problems*." Rubbish. The much-guarded secret that countless American students write somewhere between functionally and brilliantly is definitely newsworthy. Certainly it would be reassuring to parents desperate for their children to succeed in college or at the workplace. It would be emotionally lifesaving to teachers grading papers at 11 P.M. and wondering how else they can help their students "get it."

For the sake of argument, however, let's acknowledge that not all our student writers are achieving at a level that we can feel good about. Must we tolerate this? Not for moment. But let's also not kid ourselves that intolerance alone will be a powerful weapon. Intolerance breeds only disdain, not student improvement. So instead of joining the already overflowing ranks of critics or simply wringing our hands, let's do something to help. If you're an observer of today's educational scene, get involved. Volunteer. Coach. Read to kids. Be a writer and share your writing. If you have children in school, read to them and listen to their writing. Talk with your child's

FIGURE 14.1 *Family, by Corinne, Grade 4*

Without family you would be
a lone wolf
You'd be a stranger
to yourself
You would be the last leaf on the tree
Without family

teacher about the criteria he or she uses to score or grade work; suggest that those criteria be handed out in written form. If you're a teacher, don't give up, even if your students seem to dislike writing. Read to them. Write with them and share your writing. Show them how you revise or edit a piece of work. How you come up with an idea. Ask for their opinions. Six-trait criteria can help you. They speak to students in a language that makes sense—and suggest that they are capable and worthy critics, which they are.

While we're at it, let's not expect overnight miracles. Learning to write takes a lifetime, not a semester. It is *hard*. When our students do not master it quickly, it is not usually for lack of testing or lack of teaching or lack of effort. Most often it is the difficult and complex nature of the task itself. When we become writers, we learn not to mistake struggling for failure. All writers, including professionals, struggle. All writers, including professionals, have bad days and write drivel and despair of ever doing better. This does not mean that they are not being successful; this is how success looks en route to the finish line. They will reach that finish line faster knowing that we believe they can make it.

6. *Believe that you can teach.* It's what you were born to do, isn't it? Don't allow a test score or a whole battery of test scores to steal your rightful heritage from you. Remember, anyone can be a critic. Not everyone can teach. Only the brave teach.

Treasure that moment when you look out into a sea of faces and eyes look back at you with an unspoken message, "I understand." That moment is the most powerful assessment of a teacher's skill. So what if no one else sees or records it? Dare to value what cannot be measured.

Know that when you respond to the voice within the writing, you are responding to the writer, for voice is the truest extension of self and is a gift.

Don't give in to the temptation of formulaic writing, which provides the illusion of writing success without any of the satisfaction or flexibility needed for new writing challenges. Almost anyone can be taught to fill in blanks if we make the formula simple enough, just as almost anyone can paint by numbers. Formulaic writing lifts students to mediocrity, but the price is high, for it fosters formulaic thinking. Students who write to fill in blanks rather than to express what they passionately believe will never lead others to new levels of understanding, compel hungry readers to turn pages, knock down barricades of prejudice, or land Oscars for screenwriting. What a hefty toll to pay for a tiny formula that will be of use almost nowhere. Formula writers are followers of others' thinking, and we demean our students when we fear that this is all they are capable of. We demean ourselves when we make writing assessment so simple that we can do it at a glance.

Teach students to be strong editors—not by correcting conventions, as was done for us—but by modeling twenty-first century conventions as they are now used by the best editors of our time. Write to publishing houses; get copies of their editorial rules. Check current and reliable handbooks (see Chapter 8 for a list). Read from these sources routinely. Provide students with extensive, frequent practice in editing text of all kinds: poetry, fiction, informational text, technical pieces, journalistic reports—and your own writing. Don't edit for

> *Finally, we teachers know more than we think we know. It's just that our knowing cannot be measured and quantified, and we feel uncomfortable speaking out without hard data. Because we don't value our experiences and intuition enough, the public doesn't value it. We need to rethink how and what we know. . . .*
>
> **—Regie Routman**
> *Literacy at the Crossroads,*
> 1996, p. 165

them. No one learns to swim by clinging to the side of the pool. Encourage your students to let go. They can float.

Celebrate students' successes, however small, by noticing and sharing what you notice. When a student's writing moves you, don't tell a colleague or friend; tell the writer. Expect of yourself, because you *are* a teacher, that you can look deep within, that you can find even the smallest surprises that others would miss. In a tender and philosophical little book called *The Dot* (Reynolds, 2003), the young and blossoming author/artist Vashti can't bring herself to put more than a single dot on that huge white sheet of paper and is horrified by her own limitations, but she takes sudden pride in her work when her teacher asks if she will please *sign it*—and then posts it on the wall.

Finally, trust your heart. Believe that just round the bend is a new piece of writing to surprise and delight you. Never fear being too readily impressed. Never be ashamed of your unabashed joy at a student's success, however humble; it is the greatest gift you can give a new writer who longs for someone to love the words on the page. Believe that as a teacher you are doing the most important work anyone can do—opening doors to new thinking. As Parker J. Palmer reminds us, no innovation, no reform movement, no amount of restructuring, and no set of standards will "transform education if we fail to cherish—and challenge—the human heart that is the source of good teaching" (1998, p. 3). Believe that every time you listen thoughtfully to your students' work, share your own writing (good or bad), express your sense of joy in discovering a new, fine piece of literature, or help a student writer hear a moment of voice in his or her writing that just a second ago that writer did not know was there, you are making a difference   for you are.

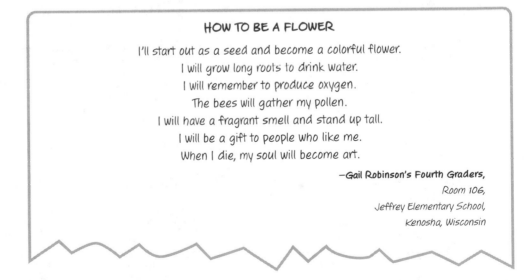

HOW TO BE A FLOWER

I'll start out as a seed and become a colorful flower.
I will grow long roots to drink water.
I will remember to produce oxygen.
The bees will gather my pollen.
I will have a fragrant smell and stand up tall.
I will be a gift to people who like me.
When I die, my soul will become art.

—Gail Robinson's Fourth Graders,
Room 106,
Jeffrey Elementary School,
Kenosha, Wisconsin

Thank you, Gail. Thank you, everyone.

Correlating the California Standards Test Scoring Rubric with the 6-Trait Model for Instruction & Assessment

GReaT SOuRCe
EDUCATION GROUP
A Division of Houghton Mifflin Company
www.greatsource.com
800-289-4490

California Standards	6-Traits Connection
The writing— • clearly addresses all parts of the writing task; • includes a clearly presented central idea with relevant facts, details, or explanations.	**IDEAS** • The writing is clear, well-supported or developed, and enhanced by the kind of detail that keeps readers reading. • The writer selectively chooses just the right information to make the paper understandable, enlightening and interesting. • The writer's knowledge, experience, insight or unique perspective lend the writing a satisfying ring of authenticity. **WORD CHOICE** • Precise, vivid, natural language paints a strong, clear, and complete picture in the reader's mind. • The writer's message is remarkably clear and easy to interpret. (Informational Rubric) **IDEAS** • The main idea, thesis, or research question is clearly defined. • The writer seems well-informed and draws from a variety of sources to amplify the main point. • Supporting details are accurate, relevant, and helpful in clarifying main ideas. **WORD CHOICE** • Well chosen words convey the writer's message in a clear, precise, and highly readable way, taking readers to a new level of understanding.
The writing— • maintains a consistent point of view, focus, and organizational structure, including the effective use of transitions.	**IDEAS** • Details work together to expand the main topic or develop a story, giving the whole piece a strong sense of focus. **ORGANIZATION** • The order, presentation or internal structure of the piece is compelling and guides the reader purposefully through the text. • An inviting lead draws the reader in; a satisfying conclusion ties up loose ends. • The entire piece has a strong sense of direction and balance. • Transitions are strong but natural. • Organization flows so smoothly the reader does not need to think about it. (Informational Rubric) **IDEAS** • The paper is clear, focused, and purposeful. **ORGANIZATION** • A strong internal structure highlights main ideas and leads readers right to key points and conclusions. • Purposeful transitions help the reader see how each point connects to a larger concept. • The closing effectively resolves important conclusions or assertions offered earlier. • The reader's understanding of the topic grows throughout the paper.

The writing— • demonstrates a clear understanding of purpose and audience.	IDEAS (Informational Rubric) • The paper is clear, focused and purposeful. It thoroughly answers a well-defined key question in understandable, convincing, and expansive terms. • The writer continuously anticipates and responds to reader's informational needs. VOICE (Informational Rubric) • As appropriate, the writer addresses the audience in a voice that is lively, engaging, and right for the topic and purpose. • The writer seems to know the audience well and to speak right to them. WORD CHOICE • The vocabulary suits the subject and audience. • Technical or little-known words are clarified or defined as needed. • Jargon and overly technical language are avoided.
The writing— • includes a variety of sentence types.	SENTENCE FLUENCY • Sentences are well-crafted, with a strong and varied structure. • Purposeful sentence beginnings show how each sentence relates to and builds on the one before. • Sentences vary in both structure and length, making the reading pleasant and natural.
The writing— • contains few, if any, errors in conventions of the English language.	CONVENTIONS • The writer shows excellent control over a wide range of standard writing conventions and uses them with accuracy and (when appropriate) creativity to enhance meaning. • Errors are so few and minor that a reader can easily overlook them unless searching for them specifically. • Only light touch-ups would be required to polish the text for publication. • Informational sources are correctly cited and would be easy for a reader to check or locate.
Specific Modes	

Fictional or Autobiographical Narrative—
• provides a thoroughly developed plot line;
• includes appropriate strategies.
	• See IDEAS
	• See FLUENCY
	  • original, natural phrasing
	• See ORGANIZATION
	  • compelling order
	  • natural pacing
	  • smooth flow

Response to Literature— • interpretation shows thoughtful, comprehensive grasp of text; • organizes interpretations around clear ideas or premises; • provides specific textual examples.	• See IDEAS • See ORGANIZATION • See CONVENTIONS
Persuasion— • authoritatively defends position with evidence; • convincingly addresses reader's concerns, biases, and expectations.	• See IDEAS and VOICE • See also WORD CHOICE

Summary—
• effectively paraphrases the main idea and significant details.
	• See IDEAS
	• See also
	  • FLUENCY
	  • WORD CHOICE
	  • VOICE

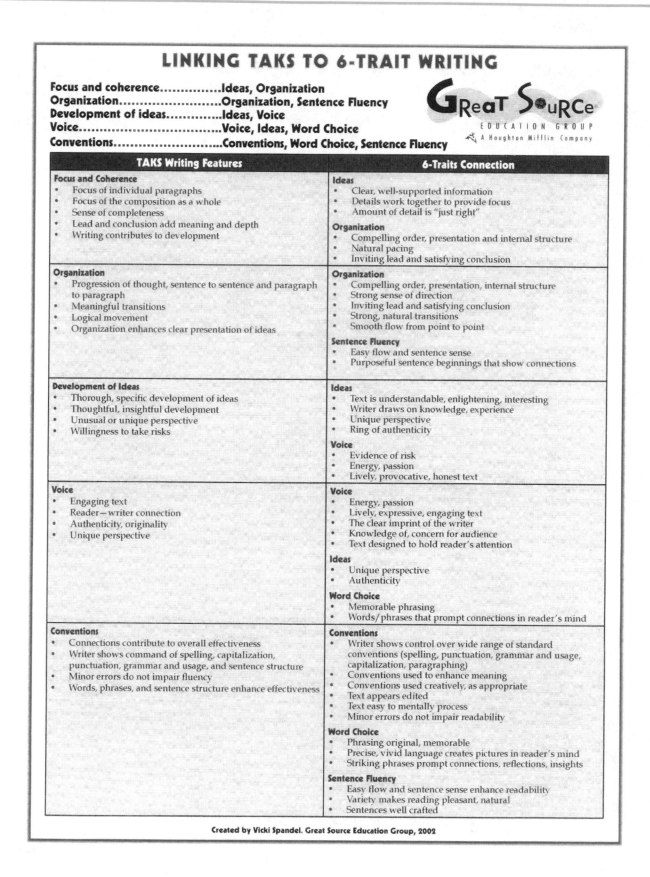

LINKING TAKS TO 6-TRAIT WRITING

Focus and coherence...............Ideas, Organization
Organization..........................Organization, Sentence Fluency
Development of ideas..............Ideas, Voice
Voice....................................Voice, Ideas, Word Choice
Conventions..........................Conventions, Word Choice, Sentence Fluency

GReaT SoURCe
EDUCATION GROUP
A Houghton Mifflin Company

TAKS Writing Features	6-Traits Connection
Focus and Coherence • Focus of individual paragraphs • Focus of the composition as a whole • Sense of completeness • Lead and conclusion add meaning and depth • Writing contributes to development	**Ideas** • Clear, well-supported information • Details work together to provide focus • Amount of detail is "just right" **Organization** • Compelling order, presentation and internal structure • Natural pacing • Inviting lead and satisfying conclusion
Organization • Progression of thought, sentence to sentence and paragraph to paragraph • Meaningful transitions • Logical movement • Organization enhances clear presentation of ideas	**Organization** • Compelling order, presentation, internal structure • Strong sense of direction • Inviting lead and satisfying conclusion • Strong, natural transitions • Smooth flow from point to point **Sentence Fluency** • Easy flow and sentence sense • Purposeful sentence beginnings that show connections
Development of Ideas • Thorough, specific development of ideas • Thoughtful, insightful development • Unusual or unique perspective • Willingness to take risks	**Ideas** • Text is understandable, enlightening, interesting • Writer draws on knowledge, experience • Unique perspective • Ring of authenticity **Voice** • Evidence of risk • Energy, passion • Lively, provocative, honest text
Voice • Engaging text • Reader—writer connection • Authenticity, originality • Unique perspective	**Voice** • Energy, passion • Lively, expressive, engaging text • The clear imprint of the writer • Knowledge of, concern for audience • Text designed to hold reader's attention **Ideas** • Unique perspective • Authenticity **Word Choice** • Memorable phrasing • Words/phrases that prompt connections in reader's mind
Conventions • Connections contribute to overall effectiveness • Writer shows command of spelling, capitalization, punctuation, grammar and usage, and sentence structure • Minor errors do not impair fluency • Words, phrases, and sentence structure enhance effectiveness	**Conventions** • Writer shows control over wide range of standard conventions (spelling, punctuation, grammar and usage, capitalization, paragraphing) • Conventions used to enhance meaning • Conventions used creatively, as appropriate • Text appears edited • Text easy to mentally process • Minor errors do not impair readability **Word Choice** • Phrasing original, memorable • Precise, vivid language creates pictures in reader's mind • Striking phrases prompt connections, reflections, insights **Sentence Fluency** • Easy flow and sentence sense enhance readability • Variety makes reading pleasant, natural • Sentences well crafted

Created by Vicki Spandel. Great Source Education Group, 2002

Appendix 2

Millard Public Schools—Rubrics for Six Traits of Oral Presentation

Student Name_____ Date_____ Type /Topic of Speech _____

	Excellent	Good	Satisfactory	Not Yet
Ideas and Content Presentation is insightful and focused. Presentation has • Clear purpose • Adequate content, supported details • Research/sources and citation when necessary	Speech has clear purpose and is focused. Content is excellent and supported by details. Research findings are presented.	Speech has clear purpose and is focused. Content is adequate and has some detail. There is some support from outside sources.	Purpose of the speech is understood but not fully developed. Content is acceptable; lacks detail. Speaker presents own opinions only.	Purpose of speech is not understood. Content is minimal. No supporting details are provided.
Organization Presentation is logical and on topic. Presentation has • Introduction and conclusion • Appropriate transitions • Appropriate pacing	Speech is organized logically for the topic. Excellent transitions are provided. Pacing is effective. Speech is easy to understand.	Introduction and conclusion are present. Transitions are used. Pacing is mostly effective.	It is possible to notice an introduction and conclusion. Some transitions are used. Pacing may be lacking.	Introduction and conclusion not easy to notice. No or few transitions used. Inappropriate pacing.
Voice Presentation is appropriate for audience and purpose of speech. Speaker uses: • Appropriate tone • Enthusiasm • Believable characterization of the character only when needed	Speaker uses excellent tone and is enthusiastic. Presentation is well designed for topic and audience. Characterization is good.	Speaker uses appropriate tone with enthusiasm. Presentation is appropriate for topic and audience. Characterization is good	Speaker uses fairly appropriate tone. Enthusiasm could be improved. Characterization needs improvement	Tone is not appropriate for purpose and/or audience. Speaker needs more vocal enthusiasm for topic.
Word Choice Speaker uses • Specific, precise and concrete words • Vivid images • Appropriate language with no slang • Appropriate vocabulary	Speaker chooses excellent vocabulary to provide vivid images and clear meaning.	Speaker uses appropriate vocabulary to convey purpose of speech.	Speaker uses some language that is appropriate. Images are not as clear as possible.	Speaker does not use appropriate, clear language. Some slang may be used.
Speaking Fluency Oral presentation has • Appropriate volume • Appropriate rate • Meaningful inflection • Smooth, graceful, natural delivery	Speaker uses excellent volume, rate, and inflection to provide smooth, graceful delivery.	Speaker uses appropriate volume and rate. Some inflection is used. Delivery is good.	Speaker can be heard. Rate of speech is appropriate. Delivery is acceptable.	Volume is too loud or soft; speech is too fast or slow. Fluency needs some work.
Conventions of Public Speaking Speaker uses • Eye contact with audience • Natural, meaningful gestures • Appropriate Dress • Visual aid when necessary • Memorization when appropriate Speaker: • Stands up straight • Appears relaxed and confident • Is organized and prepared	Speaker uses almost all the conventions of public speaking listed. Visual aids are excellent.	Speaker uses most of the conventions of public speaking listed. Visual aids are helpful.	Speaker uses some of the conventions of public speaking listed. Visual aids are acceptable, but could be improved.	Speaker does not use conventions of public speaking appropriately.
Time Requirement • Time requirement: _____ • Presentation is _____ minutes long.	Student meets time requirement.	Student meets time requirement.	Student meets time requirement.	Student does not meet time requirement.

Excerpt from CineLiterary
(The Video Traits) by Chris Hazeltine

IDEAS (RUBRIC)

The overall communication of the movie using relevant imagery, clear idea, and detailed plot.

6

The movie is exceptionally clear, focused, and interesting. It holds the viewer's attention throughout. Main ideas stand out and are developed by a strong plot and rich visual detail suitable to audience and purpose. The movie has:

- ✔ clarity, focus, and control.
- ✔ main idea(s) stand out.
- ✔ selected visual details that are relevant and carefully support the plot.
- ✔ a thoroughly detailed balance between image, dialogue, and subject matter.
- ✔ content and selected visual details that are well-suited to audience and purpose.

5

The movie is clear, focused and interesting. It holds the viewer's attention. Main ideas stand out and are developed by plot and visual details that fit the audience and purpose. The movie has:

- ✔ clarity, focus, and control.
- ✔ main idea(s) stand out.
- ✔ selected visual details that are relevant and carefully support the plot.
- ✔ a detailed balance between image, dialogue, and subject matter.
- ✔ content and selected visual details that are well-suited to audience and purpose.

4

The movie is clear and focused. The view can easily understand the main ideas. Plot and visual details are present, although they may be limited or rather general. The movie has:

- ✔ an easily identifiable purpose.
- ✔ clear main idea(s).
- ✔ visual details that are relevant but may be overly general or limiting to the plot.
- ✔ the balance between image, dialogue, and subject matter is clear, but occasionally disjointed.

- ✔ content and selected visual details that are relevant, but not always well-chosen for audience and purpose.

3

The viewer can understand the main ideas, but they may be overly broad or simplistic. Visual details are often limited, overly general, redundant, or sometimes stray off the main point. The movie has:

- ✔ an easily identifiable purpose and main idea(s)
- ✔ predictable or overly-obvious main ideas or plot; conclusions or main points seem to be the kind we've seen many times before.
- ✔ visual support of plot is attempted, but details are limited in scope or quantity, out of balance with too much or too little for particular points; somewhat predictable or overly general.
- ✔ the balance between image, dialogue, and subject matter is basic and serviceable.
- ✔ visual details are based on clichés, stereotypes, or questionable information.

2

Main ideas and purpose of movie are somewhat unclear or minimally developed. The movie has:

- ✔ an unclear purpose that require the viewer to guess the main ideas.
- ✔ minimal development; insufficient visual details.
- ✔ irrelevant plot points that are off topic and clutter the movie.
- ✔ the balance between image, dialogue, and subject matter is distracting and unclear.
- ✔ extensive repetition of detail.

1

The movie lacks a central idea or purpose. The movie has:

- ✔ ideas that are extremely limited or unclear.
- ✔ minimal or non-existent development; the movie is too short to demonstrate the development of an idea.
- ✔ the image, dialogue, and subject matter lack balance.
- ✔ visual details and plot are weak or lacking.

Appendix 3

The Pitcher: A Ranking Activity
(Put the Four Drafts in Order)

"THE PITCHER"—A

The bleachers are hard, splintery and unforgiving, as worn and raggedy as most of the district's out-dated PE equipment. They shake when you step aboard, and it's part of the fun—looking up to see if the guy at the top notices you're rocking the boat.

This coach isn't a screamer like some, but you can hear his voice above the wind all right. "Jesse! Kevin! Cody! Let's see some hustle!" They run for left field, grinning, pulling down red cap brims, dark blue legs pumping. Wind sweeps the grass and blows into our faces.

I'm not watching them. My eye is on one player. Normally shy, a kid with quiet eyes and a keep out of your way kind of walk, he strides up to the pitcher's mound like he owns it. Like it's his special place. One foot kicks the dirt, nudges, and shapes it, as if someone has messed it up in his absence and he has to tidy it all up. He turns a bit and stares, but you have to know him to know what he sees. It isn't the catcher nor the mitt the catcher holds up in anticipation. It isn't the plate. Or the fence. It's a spot. One spot in all the universe, special for no reason except it's there and it's all his. And when he hits it just right, the rest of the world goes away.

"THE PITCHER"—B

The bleachers are hard, splintery, and unforgiving. They shake badly as I step aboard and head for the top, where I can take in the whole field.

This coach isn't a screamer like some. He walks with the confidence of the 40-year-old former pitcher that he is, and when he speaks, the kids hop to it. "Jesse! Kevin! Cody! Let's see some hustle!" Eight kids run for left field, grinning, pulling down red cap brims, dark blue legs pumping.

I watch them go. Then my eye turns to the player who has stayed behind. Normally shy, a kid

with quiet eyes and a keep out of your way kind of walk, he strides up to the pitcher's mound like he owns it. Behind his back, he spins the ball in his hand till it feels right. His windup is so smooth, his delivery so long and sleek and swift that I barely see the ball fly *just* over the outside edge of home plate.. A smile curls the left corner of his mouth as he effortlessly snatches the catcher's slower return from the air. For a second, I think I see that same smile on the face of the coach, who turns now and heads for left field.

The kid stays. One foot kicks the dirt, nudges and shapes it. His right hand brushes the brim of his cap. He turns a bit and stares, but you have to know him to know what he sees. It isn't the catcher, nor the catcher's mitt. It isn't the plate. Or the fence. It's a spot. One spot in all the universe, special for no reason except it's his, and when he hits it just right, the rest of the world goes away. . . .

"THE PITCHER"—C

The bleachers are hard, splintery, and unforgiving, as worn and raggedy as most of the district's out-dated PE equipment. They shake badly as I step aboard and head for the top, but from my wobbly post I can see the whole field stretch out, from the fresh raked earth cushioning home plate to the far corner of center field. I settle in and feel the sun warm my back even as it warms the wood of the bleachers, and the satisfying thunk of balls smacking into mitts has an easy therapeutic rhythm.

This coach isn't a screamer like some. He walks with the confidence of the 40-year-old former pitcher that he is, and when he speaks, the kids hop to it. "Jesse! Kevin! Cody! Let's see some hustle!" Eight kids run for left field, grinning, pulling down red cap brims, dark blue legs pumping.

I watch them go. Then my eye turns to the player who has stayed behind. Normally shy, a kid with quiet eyes and a keep out of your way kind of walk, he strides up to the pitcher's mound like he owns it. One foot kicks the dirt, nudges and shapes it. He turns a bit and stares, but you have to know him to know what he sees. It isn't the catcher, nor the mitt the catcher holds up in anticipation. It isn't the plate. Or the fence. It's a spot. One spot in all the universe, special for no reason except it's there and it's all his, and when he hits it just right, the rest of the world goes away. . . .

His windup is so smooth that I am caught up in the grace of it, like watching a dance, and I never see the ball at all, never see it leave or curve ever so slightly left, then right, and only the slap of ball hitting leather tells me it is over. Just like that. A small smile curls the left corner of his mouth, and in his eyes, there is just a hint of light. For a second, I think I see that same smile on the face of the coach, who turns now and heads for left field.

"THE PITCHER"—D

The bleachers aren't too comfortable, but I like sitting here anyway. I like the feel of the wind in my face and the sounds of the ball field. I like watching the kids play ball. I'm glad this coach doesn't yell as much as some do.

The kids are warming up, and they head out across the field. I am watching the pitcher walk toward the mound to practice. He walks with a lot of confidence. You can see he's had a lot of practice. There is something about the way he stands that catches my eye. I love watching him throw, as if he can see right where the ball should go.

DISCUSSION AND ANSWERS

Which one was written first? Next? Last? Why do you think so?

The order in which they were actually written is

D   (A sketch.)

A   (More detail but still lean—a great ending. Many readers like this version best, mostly because of the ending. Some find the transitions a little rough.)

C   (Much more detail—lots of sensory detail. This is also a favorite with many readers, who like the interplay between coach and pitcher—and prefer the smile ending.)

B   (Here we see an effort to combine the best of A and C—richness of detail with that powerful ending from version A—trimming some excess along the way.)

Remember—the author's "final" may or not be your favorite. The main point of this exercise is to examine the kinds of things writers do as they revise. You can repeat this lesson with your students, using two or more drafts of any piece of writing. Use a student's sample or one you make up yourself, if you like. Be *sure* that you correct all conventions in advance so conventions alone do not provide a clue. Also, be careful that length alone does not provide the answer!

References Cited

Ackerman, Diane. 1995. *A Natural History of The Senses*. New York: Random House.

American Heritage Dictionary. 2003. *100 Words Every High School Graduate Should Know*. Boston: Houghton Mifflin.

Anderson, Laurie Halse. 2001. *Speak*. New York: Puffin Books.

Anderson, Richard C., Elfrieda H. Hiebert, Judith A Scott, and Ian A.G. Wilkinson. 1985. *Becoming a Nation of Readers*. Washington: U.S. Department of Education.

Angier, Natalie. 1995. *The Beauty of the Beastly*. New York: Houghton Mifflin.

Ansa, Tina McElroy. 1994. In "Tina McElroy Ansa." Rebecca Carroll, *I Know What the Red Clay Looks Like: The Voice and Vision of Black Women Writers*. New York: Crown.

Appelt, Kathi. 2002. *Poems from Homeroom: A Writer's Place to Start*. New York: Henry Holt and Company.

Armstrong, Jennifer. 1998. *Shipwreck at the Bottom of the World*. New York: Crown.

Aronie, Nancy Slonim. 1998. *Writing From the Heart: Tapping the Power of Your Inner Voice*. New York: Hyperion.

Atwell, Nancie. 1987. *In the Middle: Writing, Reading, and Learning With Adolescents*. Portsmouth, NH: Boynton/Cook.

Atwood, Margaret. 1996. *Alias Grace*. New York: Bantam Doubleday Dell.

Ballenger, Bruce. 2004. *The Curious Researcher*, 4th ed. Boston: Allyn and Bacon.

Ballenger, Bruce. 1998. *The Curious Researcher*. Boston: Allyn and Bacon.

Black, Paul and Dylan Wiliam. 1998. "Inside the Black Box: Raising Standards Through Classroom Assessment." *Phi Delta Kappan* (October), pp. 139–148.

Blake, Gary and Robert Bly. *The Elements of Technical Writing*. 1993. New York: MacMillan.

Bradbury, Ray. 1992. *Zen in the Art of Writing*. New York: Bantam Books.

Bragg, Rick. 1997. *All Over But the Shoutin'*. New York: Random House.

Bragg, Rick. 2001. *Ava's Man*. New York: Alfred A. Knopf.

Brandt, Ron. 1993. "On Teaching for Understanding: A Conversation With Howard Gardner." *Educational Leadership* 50 (September), pp. 4–7.

Brodie, Deborah. 1997. *Writing Changes Everything*. New York: St. Martin's Press.

Brown, John Seely. 1991. "Research That Reinvents the Corporation." *Harvard Business Review* (January-February), pp. 102–111.

Brown, Ruth. 1996. *Toad*. New York: Dutton Children's Books.

Bryson, Bill. 2001. *In A Sunburned Country*. New York: Random House.

Burke, Jim. 1999. *The English Teacher's Companion*. Portsmouth, NH: Heinemann.

Cahill, Thomas. 1995. *How the Irish Saved Civilization*. New York: Doubleday.

Calkins, Lucy McCormick. 1994. *The Art of Teaching Writing*, rev. ed. Portsmouth, NH: Heinemann.

Calkins, Lucy McCormick. 1986. *The Art of Teaching Writing*. Portsmouth, NH: Heinemann.

Cannon, Janell. 2000. *Crickwing*. New York: Harcourt Brace.

Capote, Truman. 1996. *A Christmas Memory, One Christmas, & The Thanksgiving Visitor*. New York: Random House.

Cappon, Rene J. 1991. *The Associated Press Guide to News Writing*. New York: Prentice-Hall.

Charlton, James, ed. 1992. *The Writer's Quotation Book*. New York: Penguin.

Chew, Charles. 1985. "Instruction Can Link Reading and Writing." In *Breaking Ground: Teachers Relate Reading and Writing in the Elementary School*. Jane Hansen, Thomas Newkirk, and Donald Graves, eds. Portsmouth, NH: Heinemann.

Cisneros, Sandra. 1989. *The House on Mango Street*. Toronto: Random House.

Claggett, Fran. 1996. *A Measure of Success*. Portsmouth, NH: Heinemann.

Clark, Roy Peter. 1987. *Free to Write: A Journalist Teaches Young Writers*. Portsmouth, NH: Heinemann.

Clarke, William. 1829. *The Boy's Own Book*. New York: Charles S. Francis.

Collard, Sneed B. III. 2003. *The Deep-Sea Floor*. Watertown, MA: Charlesbridge.

Collins, James L. 1998. *Strategies for Teaching Struggling Writers*. New York: The Guilford Press.

Condry, John. 1977. "Enemies of Exploration: Self-Initiated vs. Other-Initiated Learning." *Journal of Personality and Social Psychology* 35, pp. 459–477.

Conlan, Gertrude. 1986. "Objective Measures of Writing Ability." In *Writing Assessment: Issues and Strategies*. Karen L. Greenberg, Harvey S. Wiener, and Richard A. Donovan, eds. White Plains, NY: Longman.

Conroy, Pat. 1995. *Beach Music*. New York: Doubleday.

Cooke, Alistair. 1976. *Alistair Cooke's America*. New York: Alfred A. Knopf.

Cramer, Ronald L. 2001. *Creative Power: The Nature and Nurture of Children's Writing*. New York: Addison Wesley Longman.

Crichton, Michael. 1988. *Travels*. New York: Random House.

Crutcher, Chris. 1995. *Iron Man*. New York: Green Willow Books.

Curry, Boykin and Brian Kasbar. 1987. *Essays That Worked For Business Schools*. New York: Ballantine Books.

Curry, Boykin, ed. 1988. *Essays That Worked For Law Schools*. New York: Ballantine Books.

Dahl, Roald. 1984. *Boy: Tales of Childhood*. New York: Penguin Books.

Dahl, Roald. 1988. *Matilda*. New York: Viking Kestrel.

Dahl, Roald. 1980. *The Twits*. New York: Penguin Books.

Dahl, Roald. 2000. *The Wonderful Story of Henry Sugar*. New York: Penguin Books.

Diamond, Jared. 1997. *Guns, Germ, and Steel*. New York: W.W. Norton & Company, Inc.

DiCamillo, Kate. 2000. *Because of Winn-Dixie*. Cambridge, MA: Candlewick Press.

DiCamillo, Kate. 2003. *The Tale of Despereaux*. Cambridge MA: Candlewick Press.

Diederich, Paul B. 1974. *Measuring Growth in English*. Urbana, IL: NCTE.

Edwards, Pamela Duncan. 1997. *Barefoot: Escape on the Underground Railroad*. New York: HarperCollins Publishers.

Elbow, Peter. 1986. *Embracing Contraries*. New York: Oxford University Press.

Elbow, Peter. 1973. *Writing Without Teachers*. New York: Oxford University Press.

Enholm, Eric. 1963. *Basic Story Structure*. St. Petersburg, FL: Bayside Publishing Company.

Eugenides, Jeffrey. 2003. *Middlesex*. New York: Farrar, Straus and Giroux.

Facklam, Margry. 2001. *Spiders and Their Web Sites*. New York: Little, Brown and Company.

Feiffer, Sharon Sloan and Steve Fieffer, eds. 1995. *Home*. New York: Pantheon Books.

Fitch, Janet. 1999. *White Oleander*. New York: Little, Brown and Company.

Fleischman, Paul. 1992. *Joyful Noise: Poems for Two Voices*. New York: HarperCollins Juvenile Books.

Florian, Douglas. 1998. *Insectlopedia*. New York: Harcourt.

Fleischman, Paul. 1997. *SeedFolks*. New York: Harper-Collins.

Fletcher, Ralph. 1997. *Twilight Comes Twice*. Boston: Houghton Mifflin.

Fletcher, Ralph. 1993. *What a Writer Needs*. Portsmouth, NH: Heinemann.

Fox, Mem. 1989. *Night Noises*. New York: Harcourt Brace & Company.

Fox, Mem. 1993. *Radical Reflections*. New York: Harcourt Brace.

Franco, Betsy, ed. 2000. *You Hear Me?* Cambridge, MA: Candlewick Press.

Frank, Marjorie. 1995. *If You're Trying to Teach Kids How to Write . . . you've gotta have this book!* 2d ed. Nashville, TN: Incentive Publications, Inc.

Fraser, Jane and Donna Skolnick. 1994. *On Their Way: Celebrating Second Graders As They Read and Write*. Portsmouth, NH: Heinemann.

Frasier, Debra. 2000. *Miss Alaineus: A Vocabulary Disaster*. New York: Harcourt.

Fuller, Alexandra. 2003. *Don't Let's Go to the Dogs Tonight*. New York: Random House.

Gantos, Jack. 1999. *Jack's Back Book*. New York: Farrar Straus & Giroux.

Gardner, Howard. 1993. "Educating for Understanding." *The American School Board Journal* (July), pp. 20–24.

George, Twig C. 2000. *Jellies: The Life of Jellyfish*. Brookfield, CT: The Millbrook Press, Inc.

George, Twig C. *Seahorses*. Brookfield, CT: Millbrook Press.

Gerson, Sharon J. and Steven M. Gerson. 1997. *Technical Writing: Process and Product*. Upper Saddle River, NJ: Simon and Schuster.

Gilbert, Elizabeth. 2001. *Stern Men*. Boston: Houghton Mifflin.

Gordon, David George. 1996. *The Complete Cockroach*. Berkeley, CA: Ten Speed Press.

Graves, Donald H. 1999. *Bring Life Into Learning*. Portsmouth, NH: Heinemann.

Graves, Donald H. 1994. *A Fresh Look At Writing*. Portsmouth, NH: Heinemann.

Graves, Donald H. 2002. *Testing Is Not Teaching*. Portsmouth, NH: Heinemann.

Graves, Donald H. 1983. *Writing: Teachers and Children At Work*. Portsmouth, NH: Heinemann.

Graves, Donald H. and Virginia Stuart. 1987. *Write From the Start: Tapping Your Child's Natural Writing Ability*. New York: NAL Penguin.

Grimes, Nikki. 2002. *My Man Blue*. Reprint edition. New York: Puffin.

Hairston, Maxine. 1986. "On Not Being a Composition Slave." *Training the New Teacher of College Composition*. Charles W. Bridges, ed. Urbana, IL: NCTE.

Heard, Georgia. 2002. *The Revision Toolbox: Teaching Techniques That Work*. Portsmouth, NH: Heinemann.

Heard, Georgia. 1995. *Writing Toward Home*. Portsmouth, NH: Heinemann.

Hemingway, Ernest. 1995. *The Old Man and the Sea*. New York: Scribner.

Hegi, Ursula. 1994. *Stones From the River*. New York: Simon and Schuster.

Hillenbrand, Laura. 2001. *Seabiscuit*. New York: Ballantine Books.

Hillocks, George Jr. 1986. *Research on Written Composition: New Directions for Teaching*. Urbana, IL: ERIC Clearinghouse on Reading and Communication Skills.

Hillocks, George Jr. 2002. *The Testing Trap: How State Writing Assessments Control Learning*. New York: Teachers College Press.

Hoose, Phillip and Hannah Hoose. 1998. *Hey Little Ant*. Berkeley, CA: Tricycle Press.

Hopkinson, Deborah. 2001. *Under the Quilt of Night*. New York: Simon & Schuster.

Hout, Brian. 1990. "The Literature of Direct Writing Assessment: Major Concerns and Prevailing Trends." *Review of Educational Research* 60 (Summer). pp. 237–263.

Johnson, Bea. 1999. *Never Too Early to Write*. Gainesville, FL: Maupin House Publishing, Inc.

Junger, Sebastian. 2000. *The Perfect Storm*. New York: HarperCollins.

Katz, Jon. 2003. *A Dog Year*. New York: Random House.

Keillor, Garrison. 1987. *Leaving Home*. New York: Viking Penguin. Inc.

Keillor, Garrison. 1989. *We Are Still Married*. New York: Viking Penguin.

Kemper, David, Ruth Nathan, Patrick Sebrank, and Carol Elsholz. 2000. *Writers Express: A Handbook for Young Writers, Thinkers, and Learners*. Wilmington, MA: Great Source Education Group.

Kidd, Sue Monk. 2002. *The Secret Life of Bees*. New York: Penguin Books.

King, Janice M. 1995. *Writing High-Tech Copy That Sells*. New York: John Wiley & Sons.

King, Stephen. 2000. *On Writing*. New York: Scribner.

Kohn, Alfie. 1993. *Punished by Rewards*. Boston: Houghton Mifflin.

Kohn, Alfie. 2000. *The Case Against Standardized Testing*. Portsmouth, NH: Heinemann.

Korda, Michael. 1999. "Editing Explained." *Sky Magazine* (September), pp. 106–112.

Korman, Gordon. 2000. *No More Dead Dogs*. New York: Hyperion Books for Children.

Kuralt, Charles. 1990. *A Life on the Road*. New York: Putnam.

Lamott, Anne. 1995. *Bird By Bird*. New York: Bantam Doubleday Dell Publishing Group, Inc.

Lane, Barry. 1993. *after THE END*. Portsmouth, NH: Heinemann.

Lane, Barry. 2003. *51 Wacky We-Search Reports*. Shoreham, VT: Discover Writing Press.

Lane, Barry. 1996. "Quality in Writing." Writing Teacher 9 (3), pp. 3–8.

Lane, Barry. 1999. *Reviser's Toolbox*. Shoreham, VT: Discover Writing Press.

Lane, Barry. 2002. *The Tortoise and the Hare . . . Continued*. Shoreham, VT: Discover Writing Press.

Lane, Barry. 1997. *Writing As a Road to Self-Discovery*. Shoreham, VT: Discover Writing Press.

Lane, Barry and Gretchen Bernabei. 2001. *Why We Must Run With Scissors: Voice Lessons in Persuasive Writing*. Shoreham, VT: Discover Writing Press.

Larson, Kelsea. 1998. *Sunset Dream*. Durham, NH: Laboratory for Interactive Learning.

Leavy, Jane. 2002. *Sandy Koufax: A Lefty's Legacy*. New York: HarperCollins.

Lederer, Richard. 1994. *More Anguished English*. New York: Dell.

Lederer, Richard and Richard Dowis. 1995. *The Write Way*. New York: Simon and Shuster.

Ledermann, Marie Jean. 1986. "Why Test?" In *Writing Assessment: Issues and Strategies*. Karen L. Greenberg, Harvey S. Wiener, and Richard Donovan, eds. White Plains, NY: Longman.

LeGuin, Ursula K. 1998. *Steering the Craft*. Portland, OR: The Eighth Mountain Press.

Lesser, Carolyn. 1996. *Great Crystal Bear*. New York: Harcourt.

Leser, Julius. 1998. *To Be a Slave*. New York: Puffin Books.

Levy, Steven. 1995-1996. "The Year of the Internet." *Newsweek* (December 25, 1995–January 1, 1996), pp. 21–30.

Lichen, Patricia K. 2001. *River Walking Songbirds and Singing Coyotes*. Seattle: Sasquatch Books.

Locker, Thomas. 1997. *WaterDance*. New York: Harcourt.

Lunsford, Andrea A. 1986. "The Past—and Future—of Writing Assessment." In *Writing Assessment: Issues and Strategies*. Karen L. Greenberg, Harvey S. Wiener, and Richard A. Donovan, eds. White Plains, NY: Longman.

Mamet, David, writer/director. 2001. "Heist." A Warner Brothers film.

McCammon, Robert R. 1991. *Boy's Life*. New York: Pocket Star Books.

McCourt, Frank. 1998. *Angela's Ashes*. New York: Scribner.

McCourt, Frank. 1999. *'Tis*. New York: Scribner.

McCrum, Robert, William Cran, and Robert MacNeil. 1986. *The Story of English*. New York: Viking Penguin.

McGraw, Phillip C. 1999. *Strategies: Doing What Works, Doing What Matters*. New York: Hyperion.

McMurtry, Larry. 1985. *Lonesome Dove*. New York: Simon and Schuster.

Mailer, Norman. 1984. *Tough Guys Don't Dance*. New York: Random House.

Martel, Yann. 2002. *The Life of Pi*. New York: Harcourt.

Mathers, Petra. 1991. *Sophie and Lou*. New York: Harper.

Microsoft Corporation. 1994. *Concise User's Guide*. Redmond, WA: Microsoft Press.

Mikaelson, Ben. 2002. *Touching Spirit Bear*. New York: HarperCollins Publishers.

Milne, A.A. 1996. *The Pooh Story Book*. Reprint edition. New York: Puffin.

Mohr, Marian M. 1984. *Revision: The Rhythm of Meaning*. Upper Montclair, NJ: Boynton/Cook.

Morrison, Toni. In Donald M. Murray. 1990. *Shoptalk*. Portsmouth, NH: Heinemann.

Morrison, Toni and Slade Morrison. 1999. *The Big Box*. New York: Jump Sun.

Murray, Donald M. 1982. *Learning by Teaching*. Portsmouth, NH: Heinemann.

Murray, Donald M. 1990. *Shoptalk*. Portsmouth, NH: Bounton/Cook.

Murray, Donald M. 1984. *Write to Learn*. New York: Holt, Rinehart and Winston.

Murray, Donald M. 2004. *A Writer Teaches Writing*, 2d ed. Boston: Houghton Mifflin.

National Commission on Writing. 2003. *The Neglected "R"*. New York: College Entrance Examination Board.

Nye, Bill. 1993. *The Science Guy's Big Blast of Science*. Mercer Island, WA: TV Books.

O'Brien, Tim. 1990. *The Things They Carried*. Boston: Houghton Mifflin

O'Connor, Patricia T. 1996. *Woe Is I*. New York: G.P. Putnam's Sons.

O'Connor, Patricia T. 1999. *Words Fail Me*. New York: Harcourt Brace & Company.

Palmer, Parker J. 1998. *The Courage to Teach: Exploring the Inner Landscape of a Teacher's Life*. San Francisco: Jossey-Bass.

Patchett, Ann. 2001. *Bel Canto*. New York: HarperCollins.

Paulsen, Gary. 1992. *Clabbered Dirt, Sweet Grass*. New York: Harcourt Brace Jovanovich.

Paulsen, Gary. 1993. *Dogteam*. New York: Delacorte Press.

Paulsen, Gary. 2001. *Guts*. New York: Delacorte Press.

Paulsen, Gary. 1992. *Harris and Me*. New York: Bantam Doubleday.

Paulsen, Gary. 1999. *Hatchet*. New York: Bantam Doubleday.

Paulsen, Gary. 2003. *Shelf Life*. New York: Simon & Schuster.

Paulsen, Gary. 1994. *Winterdance*. Orlando: Harcourt Brace & Company.

Paulsen, Gary. 1989. *The Winter Room*. New York: Dell.

Proulx, Annie. 1999. *Close Range*. New York: Scribner.

Proulx, Annie. 1993. *The Shipping News*. New York: Simon and Schuster.

Purves, Alan C. 1992. "Reflections on Research and Assessment in Written Composition." *Research in the Teaching of English* 26 (February), pp. 108–122.

Quammen, David. 1996. *The Song of the Dodo*. New York: Scribner.

Quammen, David. 1998. *Wild Thoughts From Wild Places*. New York: Scribner.

r.w.t. Magazine for Writing Teachers K-8. San Antonio, TX: ECS Learning Systems, Inc.

Ray, Katie Wood. 2002. *What You Know By Heart: How to Develop Curriculum for Your Writing Workshop*. Portsmouth, NH: Heinemann.

Reynolds, Peter H. 2003. *The Dot*. Cambridge, MA: Candlewick Press.

Rice, Scott, ed. 1996. *Dark and Stormy Rides Again*. New York: Penguin Books.

Rice, Scott, ed. 1992. *It was a Dark and Stormy Night: The Final Conflict*. New York: Penguin Books.

Ringgold, Faith. 1991. *Tar Beach*. New York: Random House.

Robinson, Barbara. 1972. *The Best Christmas Pageant Ever*. New York: Harper & Row.

Romano, Tom. 1987. *Clearing the Way: Working With Teenage Writers*. Portsmouth, NH: Heinemann.

Romano, Tom. 1995. *Writing With Passion*. Portsmouth, NH: Boynton/Cook.

Routman, Regie. 1996. *Literacy At the Crossroads*. Portsmouth, NH: Heinemann.

Routman, Regie. 2000. *Conversations: Strategies for Teaching, Learning, and Evaluating.* Portsmouth, NH: Heinemann.

Ruef, Kerry. 2,000. *The Private Eye.* Seattle: The Private Eye Project.

Sachar, Louis. 1999 Keynote address: Author's Luncheon. Florida Reading Association. Orlando. October 16.

Sachar, Louis. 2000. *Holes.* New York: Yearling Books.

Schwartz, David M. 1998. *G Is for Googol: A Math Alphabet Book.* Berkeley, CA: Tricycle Press.

Seife, Charles. 2000. *Zero: The Biography of a Dangerous Idea.* New York: Penguin Books.

Seinfeld, Jerry. 1995. *SeinLanguage.* New York: Bantam Books.

Shaughnessy, Mina. 1977. *Errors and Expectations.* New York: Oxford University Press.

Smith, Frank. 1984. "Reading Like a Writer." In *Composing and Comprehending.* Julia M. Jensen, ed. Urbana, IL: ERIC Clearinghouse on Reading and Communication Skills.

Spandel, Vicki. 2004. *Creating Young Writers.* Boston: Allyn and Bacon.

Steele, Bob. 1998. *Draw Me a Story.* Winnipeg, Manitoba, Canada: Peguis Publishers.

Stegner, Wallace. 2002. *On Teaching and Writing Fiction.* New York: The Penguin Group.

Steig, William. 1971. *Amos and Boris.* New York: Puffin Books.

Steig, William. 1987. *Abel's Island.* Toronto: Collins.

Stiggins, Richard J. 2001. *Student-Involved Classroom Assessment.* 3rd ed. Upper Saddle River, NJ: Prentice-Hall.

Strickland, Kathleen and James Strickland. 1998. *Reflections on Assessment.* Portsmouth, NH: Boynton/Cook.

Strong, Richard, Harvey F. Silver, and Amy Robinson. 1995. "What Do Students Want?" *Educational Leadership 53* (September), pp. 8–12.

Strunk, William Jr. and E. B. White. 2000. *The Elements of Style,* 4th ed. Boston: Allyn and Bacon.

Teague, Mark. 2002. *Dear Mrs. LaRue: Letters from Obedience School.* New York: Scholastic Press.

Thomas, Dylan. (1954) 1962. Reminiscences of Childhood." In *Thought in Prose,* 2d ed. Richard S. Beal and Jacob Korg, eds. Englewood Cliffs, NJ: Prentice-Hall.

Thomas, Lewis. 1979. *The Medusa and the Snail.* New York: Penguin.

Thomason, Tommy. 1993. *More Than a Writing Teacher.* Commerce, TX: Bridge Press.

Thomason, Tommy. 2003. *WriteAerobics: 40 Workshop Exercises to Improve Your Writing Teaching.* Norwood, MA: Christopher Gordon Publishers.

Thomason, Tommy. 1998. *Writer to Writer: How to Conference Young Authors.* Norwood, MA: Christopher Gordon Publishers.

Thomason, Tommy and Carol York. 2000. *Write on Target: Preparing Young Writers to Succeed on State Writing Achievement Tests.* Norwood, MA: Christopher Gordon Publishers, Inc.

Tredway, Linda. 1995. "Socratic Seminars: Engaging Students in Intellectual Discourse." *Educational Leadership 53* (September), pp. 26–29.

Trimble, John R. 2000. *Writing With Style.* 2nd ed. Upper Saddle River, NJ: Prentice-Hall.

Twain, Mark. 1965. *Huckleberry Finn.* New York: Harper & Row.

Wade-Gayles, Gloria. 1994. In Rebecca Carroll, *I Know What the Red Clay Looks Like: The Voice and Vision of Black Women Writers.* New York: Crown.

Wasserstein, Paulette. 1995. "What Middle Schoolers Say About Their Schoolwork." *Educational Leadership 53* (September), pp 26–29.

Weiten, Wayne and Margaret A. Lloyd. 2003. *Psychology Applied to Modern Life,* 7th ed. New York: Wadsworth.

Welty, Eudora. 1983. *One Writer's Beginnings.* New York: Warner Books.

White, E. 1985. *Teaching and Assessing Writing.* San Francisco: Jossey-Bass.

White, E. B. 1936. *Farewell to Model T.* New York: G. P. Putnam's Sons.

White, E. B. 1974. *Charlotte's Web.* New York: Harper Trophy.

Wiggins, Grant. 1992. "Creating Tests Worth Taking." *Educational Leadership* (May), pp. 26–33.

Williams, Joseph M. 2002. *Style: Ten Lessons in Clarity and Grace,* 7th ed. New York: Pearson Longman.

Winokur, John. 1990. *W.O.W.: Writers on Writing.* Philadelphia: Running Press.

Wolcott, Willa, with Sue M. Legg. 1998. *An Overview of Writing Assessment: Theory, Research, and Practice.* Urbana, IL: NCTE.

Write Source Handbooks for Students. Wilmington, MA: Great Source Education Group.

Writing Spot. 2003. (Kindergarten). Elsholz, Carol, Patrick Sebranek, and David Kemper.

Write One. 2002 (Grade 1). Kemper, David, Carol Elsholz, and Patrick Sebranek.

Write Away. 2002 (Grade 2). Kemper, David, Ruth Nathan, Patrick Sebranek, and Carol Elsholz.

Write on Track. 2002. (Grade 3). Kemper, David, Ruth Nathan, Patrick Sebranek, and Carol Elsholz.

Writers Express. 2000 (Grades 4-5). Kemper, David, Ruth Nathan, Patrick Sebranek, and Carol Elsholz.

Write Source 2000. 1999. (Grades 6-8). Sebranek, Patrick, David Kemper, and Verne Meyer.

All Write. 2003. (Grades 6-8). Kemper, David, Patrick Sebranek, and Verne Meyer.

Write Ahead. 2004. (Grades 9-10). Kemper, David, Patrick Sebranek, and Verne Meyer.

Writers Inc. 2001. (Grades 9-12). Sebranek, Patrick, David Kemper, and Verne Meyer.

School to Work. 1996. (Grades 9-12). Sebranek, Patrick, David Kemper, and John Van Rys.

Write for College. 1997. (Grades 11-12). Sebranek,Patrick, David Kemper, and Verne Meyer.

Ziefert, Harriet. 2003. *Lunchtime for a Purple Snake.* Boston: Houghton Mifflin.

Ziegler, Alan. 1981. *The Writing Workshop.* Vol. 1. New York: Teachers and Writers Collaborative.

Zinsser, William. 2001. *On Writing Well.* New York: Harper-Collins.

Zorfass, Judith, and Harriet Copel. 1995. "The I-Search: Guiding Students Toward Relevant Research." *Educational Leadership* (September), pp. 48–51.

Index